Statistical Reasoning
in
Psychology and Education

Statistical Reasoning
in
Psychology and Education

EDWARD W. MINIUM
San Jose State College

John Wiley & Sons, Inc.
New York **London** **Sydney** **Toronto**

Library of Congress Catalog Card Number: 71-114009
SBN 471 60825 4

Printed in the United States of America

10 9 8 7 6 5 4 3 2 1

To Students Who Want to Learn
and
Instructors Who Like to Teach

Preface

Most of the students I teach are quite able to absorb the logic of statistics, but do not come to the subject well prepared in mathematics. This book is addressed first to them. It requires only an understanding of arithmetic and an elementary knowledge of equations, such as most acquire by the end of the ninth grade. To assist those who "once knew" but whose memory has now grown dim, there is an extended review of basic mathematical propositions in the Appendix. It is preceded by a pretest (with answers), and the questions are keyed to various sections of the review to facilitate further study. For those competent in ordinary algebra, mathematical notes are offered at the end of many chapters, but the text is designed to stand without them.

Although the book does not demand advanced mathematical competence, it is emphatically concerned with the student's conceptual growth. It develops statistical concepts, understanding of statistical logic, properties of statistical devices, assumptions underlying statistical tools, and considers what happens when theory meets reality. The development is accompanied by frequent summaries which stress these points.

Constant appeal is made to common experience and intuition. I have tried particularly to be clear on those points that tend to be stumbling blocks. For example, I have worked to obtain a treatment of statistical inference that is both accurate and understandable. At the same time, I have tried to avoid oversimplification. I have also tried to be clear on how-to-do-it aspects. If successful, instructors should have more time to devote to the difficult concepts.

Full treatment is given to descriptors. I believe that after inference is done, one must return to these measures to assess the meaning of the inquiry; they must be fully understood. Coded score methods of calculation are included. Those having access to calculators and computers may choose to omit them, but these methods often prove useful when one must work in terms of his own resources. Large sample procedures for inference about means receive the full treatment. Inference is hard enough to grasp without introducing the complicating characteristics of Student's distribution at the start; one step at a time.

Certain frequently neglected topics cried for treatment. Among them are: randomization as experimental control, determination of sample size required for inference about means, evaluation of the merits of the experiment versus the *in situ* study, the problem of regression in research, and the relative merits of hypothesis testing versus estimation. Topics such as these are introduced from time to time, but special consideration is given many of them in Chapter 19, *Some Aspects of Experimental Design.*

In many texts, the statistics of measurement is given lesser attention than the statistics of experimental analysis. I felt that both interests ought to receive adequate recognition. Accordingly, derived scores and interpretive aspects of correlation and regression are given substantial treatment.

Problems and exercises appear at the end of each chapter. Some give practice in how-to-do-it, and others require the exercise of critical judgment. Since easy availability of answers often negates the requirement of thoughtful analysis, answers appear in the instructor's manual but not in the book.

This book should serve very well for a one-semester text, and many will find it appropriate for two. It has been developed in a way to facilitate the selection which will be necessary for a one-semester course. First, a graded approach is used in several areas. For example, the elements of hypothesis testing are introduced in Chapter 14; Chapter 15 offers a detailed commentary on each of the steps. Similarly, there is a graded approach to correlation and regression: for each, the elements are presented in one chapter, and detailed interpretive analysis in another. The instructor of the one-semester course will often find it possible to develop a topic in basic form, and then, through appropriate selection, to supplement that development according to taste and time.

Second, topics which might be considered supplementary (e.g., the mean and standard deviation of a combined distribution) have been developed in a way such that their omission does not interrupt the continuity, and they are placed, wherever possible, at or near the end of the chapter.

To assist in making an appropriate selection, the Table of Contents lists section titles as well as chapter titles. In addition, a detailed analysis of the possibilities for selection is offered in a manual available to instructors.

These acknowledgments I make with pleasure. I am grateful to two former professors, Edwin E. Ghiselli and the late Edward C. Tolman, who taught me to say, "I don't know" when I don't, which is often, and that happiness in teaching comes from two sources: love of your subject and love of students.

The encouragement and understanding of my wife, Juanita, sustained me during the preparation of the manuscript. The enthusiastic and expert assistance of my former assistant, Mrs. Fonda Eyler, helped me finish it on time.

I am indebted to former students and present colleagues who read and criticised, and to those students who helped in some of the research.

I am indebted to Professor James B. Bartoo, of Pennsylvania State University, for his helpful comments. To Professor Robert B. Clarke, of San Jose State College, and to Professor William B. Michael of the University of Southern California, I owe a debt which can never be repaid. These gentlemen gave the manuscript the kind of detailed analysis that goes far beyond what a hopeful author has any right to expect. If the book appears to have merit, it may well be theirs, but if fault is found, it is mine.

Lastly, I am indebted to the several authors and publishers who granted permission to use tables and figures so necessary to this work. Among others, I am indebted to the Literary Executor of the late Sir Ronald A. Fisher, F.R.S., and to Oliver & Boyd Ltd, Edinburgh, for their permission to reprint Table V.A. from their book *Statistical Methods for Research Workers.*

EDWARD W. MINIUM

San Jose, California
April 1970

Contents

7
The Normal Curve

8
Derived Scores

12

Interpretive Aspects of Correlation and Regression 189

13

The Basis of Statistical Inference 208

17

Inference about Means: Small Sample Approach 293

Statistical Reasoning
in
Psychology and Education

1

Introduction

1.1 Descriptive Statistics

In a new school, a biology instructor contemplates the arrival of the first group of students. How much biological information will they already have? He wishes neither to bore them by underestimating their readiness, nor to lose them by assuming too much. Should he begin with a review of fundamentals? How extensive? In what areas? It would also be helpful to know if the students vary widely in background of biological knowledge. If so, he may make adjustments in his instructional method. Finally, he would like information about the students as individuals. Who needs special help during the initial weeks? Who is ready for special challenges?

Let us suppose that there is available to him a nationally developed test of biological knowledge subdivided into measures of botanical information and zoological information. He administers this test to his students at the first class meeting, and finds the number of correct answers for each student. After reading the test to get some idea of the kind and difficulty of the questions, he could compare each student's score with what he considers reasonable to expect. This approach would be useful, since he is an experienced teacher, but he could learn quite a bit more relative to his initial questions if he will "use statistics."

Let us assume that from the school research office, or from the test manual, he is able to learn how students in similar educational circumstances perform on this test. With this knowledge, he discovers, for example, that Mary Brown's score in zoology is better than that of 98% of students who are in the same grade, but that only 15% of students get lower scores than Martin Smith's.

Concerning the general level of knowledge of the students in his class,

1

he finds that there are too many scores to keep in mind at once. He needs a way to simplify consideration of the group, so he finds the class average on each subtest and for the complete test. Then he compares these figures with the performance data of other similar students. This comparison shows that, as a group, his students are approximately at the expected level in botany, and that their performance is superior in zoology. Pursuing the question of diversity within the class, he notes that the distance between the scores of the top student and the bottom student is not very great.

In each instance our instructor is making use of techniques which are part of the body of *descriptive statistics*. These tools help him to describe the level and homogeneity of performance of his students, and compare their knowledge with that of known groups in a way which will help him go about his teaching. This is an example of the primary function of descriptive statistics: to provide meaningful and convenient techniques for describing features of data which are of interest.

1.2 Inferential Statistics

What is the attitude of the voting public toward the elimination of capital punishment? Poll-takers find it impossible to put this question to all members of this group. Instead, they study the responses of a portion of it, and from that knowledge they estimate the attitudes of the whole. The outcome, like any estimate, is subject to error. But, if the voters selected for study have been chosen according to statistical principles, it is possible to know what margin of error is involved.

A second branch of statistical practice, known as *inferential statistics*, provides the basis for answering questions of this kind. The object of these procedures is to draw an inference about conditions which exist in a larger set of observations from study of a part of that set. This branch of statistics is also known as *inductive statistics*, or as *sampling statistics*.

Another application of inferential statistics is particularly suited to evaluation of the outcome of an experiment. Is it possible that a certain drug has an effect on speed of learning? Let us suppose that an investigator decides on the kind of subjects he wishes to study, selects at random two groups of 25 subjects each, and administers the drug to one of the groups. Both groups are given a learning task, and in all ways treated alike except for the drug. From the outcome of the study, he finds that the average learning score of the two groups differs by five points.

Now some difference between the groups would be expected even if they were treated alike, because of chance factors involved in the random selection of groups. The question faced by the experimenter is whether the observed difference is within the limits of expected variation. If certain preconditions have been met, statistical theory can provide the basis for an answer. If the experimenter finds that the obtained difference of five points is larger than can be accounted for by chance variation, he will infer that other factors must be at work. If examination of his experimental procedures reveals no reasonable cause for the difference other than the deliberate difference in experimental treatment, he may conclude that the drug is the responsible factor.

1.3 Relationship and Prediction

Experience tells us that there is some relationship between intelligence of parents and their offspring, and yet it is not perfect. We expect that the parents of the brightest boy in the class are also bright, but would not expect that they are necessarily the most intelligent among all parents of children in this group. Can we describe with greater exactness the extent of this relationship?

The personnel office of an industrial concern gives an aptitude test to its prospective clerical employees. Is there really any relationship between the score on this test and subsequent level of job proficiency? How much? If there is a relationship, what percent of applicants may be expected to succeed on the job if only those who score above a certain point on the test are accepted for employment? How does this compare with what would happen if the test were eliminated from their hiring procedures?

These are examples of the type of question which probes the existence and extent of *relationship* between two (or more) factors, and explores the potentiality of *prediction* of standing in one factor from knowledge of standing in the other. This kind of analysis is so frequently of interest that a considerable body of statistical techniques has been developed to deal with it. Because of the importance and distinctiveness of these two questions, they have been separately identified here. Nevertheless, both are problems in description and inference, the two major categories of statistical endeavor.

1.4 Kinds of Statisticians

Those who work with statistics might be divided into four classes: (1) those who need to know statistics in order to appreciate reports of findings in their professional field, (2) those who must select and apply statistical treatment in the course of their own inquiry, (3) professional statisticians, and (4) mathematical statisticians. The main interest of those in the first two classes is in their own subject matter; statistics is an aid to them in organizing and making meaningful the evidence which bears on questions which have been raised. Among their ranks are the biologist, educator, psychologist, engineer, census taker, medical researcher, geologist, agriculturist, physicist, personnel officer, counselor, businessman, and city manager; all these and many more regularly find that statistical procedures can be of assistance. We might think of them as amateur statisticians, and like amateurs in most areas, their statistical knowledge may range from novice to expert.

At the next level, we have the professional statistician. In earlier years, he may have received his training in a university mathematics department. If he is a recent graduate, he is probably a product of a department of statistics, and has undergone extensive training in statistical theory and relevant mathematics. The practicing statistician acts as a "middleman" in the process of research. He assists those with *substantive questions*† in finding and applying statistical models with which to examine evidence relative to their inquiry. The professional statistician's advantage is that he has expert knowledge of statistical theory and of its general applicability. His limitation is that he is not an expert in the field of application.

The three types of persons thus far discussed all have in common a primary interest in applied statistics, although the latter two may indeed have interest in and make contributions to statistical theory. The primary interest of a mathematical statistician is in pure statistics and probability theory. Professional statisticians have been heard to complain wryly that mathematical statisticians think them too practical, and those whom they serve as consultants think them too theoretical. In fairness, it should be pointed out that the latter view is less likely to emerge when those seeking advice have had some elementary education in statistics.

1.5 For Whom Is This Book Intended?

The reader has doubtless concluded correctly that this book is concerned with applied statistics, and that it is directed to the prospective amateur. It is intended to be of particular assistance to those who will encounter studies which incorporate statistical treatment, or who need to understand the properties of tools (e.g., mental tests) where important characteristics are stated in statistical language.

This book is equally directed to those who will have occasion to apply statistical procedures in their own inquiries. Knowledge of this kind will help to translate an initial question into a plan of inquiry more likely to bear directly on the issue, to think critically about evidence, and to conduct a meaningful study more economical of time and effort than might otherwise result.

Those who will be in a position to call on the services of a professional statistician will find that some statistical education will help them to know when such expert services are needed, to formulate a problem in a way amenable to treatment and interpretation, and to communicate with this specialist.

---

†A substantive question concerns the subject matter under study. For example: does reaction time depend on intensity of the stimulus? See Section 1.6 for further comment.

1.6 The Role of Applied Statistics

From the discussion so far, we can see that applied statistics is a tool, and neither a beginning nor an end by itself. An investigator poses a problem. He may turn to the body of statistical procedures to find a convenient and meaningful way of looking at the information he has collected which will help him answer his questions. *These procedures, per se, do not answer the question.* The best tools he can select only provide him with a certain kind of information. They will give him *one* view, a view characterized by certain properties. He will have to decide whether this particular view is adequate for his purpose, and he must keep in mind its known limitations.

We may compare this situation to that of a father whose son has become engaged to a young lady in a distant city. His son sends a black-and-white snapshot of his fiancée so dad can see what she is like. Father studies the picture. Fair of figure and erect in carriage? Apparently so. Beautiful features? He nods approval: eyes not set too close together, nose regular, high cheekbones, and an attractive mouth. Complexion? She is too distant to be sure. He continues his inspection. For some questions, the picture affords good information, and for others the evidence is incomplete. For another group of questions (musical voice? sunny disposition?) the snapshot is not relevant.

To return to our investigator, when he has completed his statistical examination of the data, he must evaluate the meaning of his statistical findings relative to the original question which he posed. *The use of statistical procedures is therefore always a middle step.* The typical steps of an investigation are:

1. A *substantive question* is formulated and refined, and a plan is developed to obtain relevant evidence. A substantive question is a question of fact in a subject-matter area; e.g., under such-and-such conditions, is retention better when learning takes place under spaced practice or massed practice? Some of the aspects of this step will include selection of the type of material to be learned, the kind of subjects to be studied, and the measure of retention to be used.

2. When appropriate, a statistical model is chosen to assist in organizing and analyzing the data to be collected. At this point, a *statistical question* may be developed, the answer to which may be expected to throw light on the substantive question. A statistical question differs from a substantive question in that it always concerns a *statistical* property of the data, such as the average of the set of measures. For example, if the problem above concerns verbal learning, we may ask whether the average number of words retained differs·so greatly under the two conditions of practice that chance variation cannot account for it. Often there are alternative statistical questions which are relevant to exploration of the substantive question. For instance, we might ask whether the *proportion* of subjects who retain three quarters or more of the words learned differs substantially under the two conditions of

practice. Part of the study of statistics is to learn how to choose among alternative statistical approaches.

3. Upon applying the statistical procedure, one arrives at a *statistical conclusion*. For example, a possible outcome of the verbal learning experiment is that the difference in average number of words retained under the two conditions is too great to be attributed to chance variation. Again, a statistical conclusion concerns a statistical property of the data: in this case, it is about averages.

4. Finally, a *substantive conclusion* is drawn. In the example above, the conclusion may be warranted that under the circumstances studied, retention is better when practice is spaced than when it is massed. Although the substantive conclusion derives partly from the statistical conclusion, other factors must be considered. If average performance under the two conditions is so different that chance variation among the groups cannot be considered the sole factor, it will not be clear that the difference in method of learning is the responsible factor unless the experiment has been so conducted as to rule out other factors. The investigator, therefore, must weigh both the statistical conclusion and the adequacy of the experimental design in arriving at his substantive conclusion.

When contemplating design of an investigation, the first and second steps ought to be considered together. It is often possible to include certain features in the plan of attack which will enable use of statistical techniques which are more relevant and economical than otherwise would be possible.

1.7 More about the Road Ahead

The preceding sections touch on some objectives for education in elementary statistics. For a clear view of the road ahead, a bit more needs to be said. One objective is to develop a better appreciation of the relation between questions which are asked and the role of a quantitative approach in answering them. Since statistical methods have a "point of view," it is necessary to understand their special characteristics in order to decide what analysis is appropriate to the problem.

Even when this seems satisfactorily settled, special characteristics of our data can affect alternative techniques in different ways. If properties of the techniques are understood, a basis exists for choosing from among them. Important assumptions often lie unseen behind a technique. We must know what they are and what happens when they are violated.

It is not enough to learn the properties of statistical techniques; we must also learn "how-to-do-it." This is essential not only for those who will themselves apply these procedures in their own work, but also for those who are simply attempting to become statistically literate. In addition to following the logic and comprehending the properties, a significant kind of understanding comes in the course of "making it work."

1.8 Dirty Words about Statistics

A number of complaints are issued about statistics: it is dry, it is depersonalizing because it considers the mass and not the individual, and it is misleading. Disraeli said: "There are three kinds of lies: lies, damned lies, and statistics." Other complaints heard are that statistical methodology dictates the nature of investigations, and that it is too mathematical for anyone but an expert to understand. Since there is some truth in each of these charges, we shall examine them.

A statistical result is simply a statement about the condition of data. This is bound to be dry unless the person is interested in the question to which the data relate, and understands the significance of those findings for the question. *It is the conclusion which may be drawn from the data rather than the state of the data which is of possible interest.* If an increase of 851 children is expected in the public schools of your city next fall, this information may not stir me greatly if your city is not mine. Even the average citizen of your city may feel that he has been told more than he wants to know. Mentally translating the figure into "quite an increase," he thinks it would be wise to vote to approve the school bond issue in the coming election. However, the detailed nature of the number is of vital interest to the school superintendent because it tells him how many new classrooms and teachers he must have ready and how much adjustment will be needed in the budget.

It is true that a statistical statement is usually one which is made about a group, rather than about an individual. Consideration of the individual is certainly possible, however. A batting average refers to the performance of a single person, and in the example at the opening of this chapter, our biology instructor used information about a group in order to get better knowledge about each individual. His aim was the antithesis of depersonalization.

In study of groups there may be much that is significant for the individual. Consider a study in educational technique, in which elementary statistics is taught by "standard" methods and also by an experimental method. Suppose that, at the conclusion of the study, average performance is substantially higher for the experimental group, and that average level of student anxiety during the course is substantially lower for the same group. This outcome does not mean that *every* student will profit in these ways from the new technique; for some students the possibility exists that the new method is worse. However, *in the absence of further information*, this experiment says that the odds are in favor of students who have the opportunity to study under the new method. Thus, the "group" approach can often be turned to the *probable* advantage of an individual.

In a given state college, it may be that 80% of the total number of credit units of instruction were taught by instructors holding the doctorate, that 75% of the courses were taught by instructors holding the same qualification, and that 65% of instructors in the institution hold the doctorate. If a journalist has taken the "rotten state of higher education" as his theme, we can guess which figure he is most likely to find enticing. On the other hand, if an economy-minded representative of the taxpayers association wishes to show that higher salaries are unnecessary to attract a fully qualified faculty, a different choice will be made. Unfortunately, if we are presented in a telling way with only one of these approaches, the possibility of others may never occur to us. We might remember the old saying: "figures never lie, but liars figure." Deception is not the only cause of trouble; many errors in thinking occur inadvertently. It is apparent that there can be value in knowing the properties of statistical procedures, and in remembering to inquire about the circumstances of their particular use. Misuse of statistics is an important topic, but limitations of space prevent detailed treatment here. Fortunately, works exist which give attention to these matters.†

One complaint has been that statistical procedures dictate the nature of investigations. It is true that some investigations lean more toward that which is objective and easily measurable than they do toward that which is meaningful. Statistics is not the culprit, since it is only a tool. The problem, rather, lies in the attitude of investigators. It is well to remember that it is the *question* which is of significance, and we ought to be sure we are asking an important one.

Is it true that statistics is mathematical, and that only experts can understand it? The realm of statistics extends to a considerable height, well beyond the domain of this book. A number of propositions in elementary statistics owe their existence to sophisticated mathematical derivations. Nevertheless, it is quite possible to acquire a good working understanding of the statistical procedures and logic included in this book with a knowledge of common arithmetic and elementary principles of high school algebra. A few matters will have to be taken on faith. If we know what assumptions were made, and what happens when they are not satisfied, our position will be sound.

1.9 Some Tips on Studying Statistics

Is statistics a hard subject? It is and it isn't. In general, learning how-to-do-it requires attention, care, and arithmetic accuracy, but is not particularly difficult. Learning the "why" of things varies over a somewhat wider range of difficulty.

What about the expected reading rate for a book about statistics? Rate of reading and comprehension differ from subject to subject, and a four-page assignment in mathematics may require the same time as forty in history. Certainly one should not expect to read a statistics text like a novel, nor even like the usual history text. Some parts, like this chapter, will go faster, but others

†D. Huff, *How to Lie with Statistics*, W. W. Norton and Co., New York, 1954; W. A. Wallis and H. V. Roberts, *The Nature of Statistics*, Collier Books, New York, 1962; W. A. Wallis and H. V. Roberts, *Statistics: A New Approach*, The Free Press, New York, 1956.

will require concentration and several readings. In short, the student is not called on to feel stupid when he finds he cannot race through a chapter, and that some "absorption time" is required. The logic of statistical inference, for example, is a new way of thinking for most people, and requires getting used to. Its newness can create difficulties for those who are not willing to slow down.

Another point where students often anticipate difficulty concerns mathematics. This has been partially clarified in the previous section. Ordinary arithmetic and some familiarity with the nature of equations is needed. Being able to see "what goes on" in an equation is at least necessary to perception of the kinds of things which affect the statistic being calculated, and in what way. For students who feel at home in elementary algebra, algebraic notes are included at the end of several chapters. They are intended to provide a supplementary "handle" by which the significance of statistical techniques can be grasped. Appendix A is especially addressed to those who feel that their mathematics lies in the too distant past to assure a sense of security. It contains a review of elementary mathematics of special relevance for study of this book, and discusses some other matters, such as interpolation and the use of tables, which will be needed but which may not have been encountered before. This appendix is preceded by a pretest, so the student may determine which elements, if any, could profitably stand review. Not all of these understandings are required at once, so there will be time to brush up in advance of need.

Questions and problems are included at the end of each chapter. Enough of these should be worked to feel comfortable. They have been designed to give practice in how-to do-it, in the exercise of critical evaluation, in development of the link between real problems and methodological approach, and in comprehending statistical relationships. There is merit in giving some consideration to all questions and problems, even though fewer may be formally assigned.

If you feel that a concept is not clear, do not hesitate to consult other texts written at a similar level. A little time in the library will reveal which ones will be helpful, or your instructor can provide suggestions. Although special effort has been directed toward clarity, often different words on the same subject will add to one's insight.

A word should be said about the ladder-like nature of the course in elementary statistics. What is learned in earlier stages becomes the foundation for what follows. Consequently, it is most important that the student "keep up." If he has difficulty at some point, he should immediately seek assistance from the library or from his instructor. Those who think matters may clear up if they wait may be right, but the risk is greater than in courses where the material is less interdependent. It can be like trying to climb a ladder with some rungs missing. Cramming, never very successful, is least so in statistics. Success in studying statistics depends on regular work, and if this is done, relatively little is needed in the way of review before examination time.

The final hope is that the student will exert special effort to perceive relationships in statistics. At one level, it is common to find that computational absurdities are accomplished without awareness. For example, when an average is computed, look at the data and see if it appears to make sense. At another level, a positive effort is needed to perceive relationships between techniques currently under consideration and those which have been examined earlier. One frequently finds that a given concept is applicable to several situations. Such relationships will be pointed out, but experience shows that effort is required to appreciate them. When adequate effort is made, statistics will be perceived less as a collection of disparate techniques and more as a sensible study, and easier to learn.

Finally, try always to relate the statistical tools to real problems. Imagine an inquiry of special interest to you, and consider which methods might be most suited to the hypothetical approach which you have designed in your mind. Statistics can be an exciting study, but only if you open your mind and reach out. It is a study with relevance to real problems.

PROBLEMS AND EXERCISES

Identify:

descriptive statistics

inferential statistics

inductive statistics

sampling statistics

amateur statistician

professional statistician

mathematical statistician

substantive question

statistical question

statistical conclusion

substantive conclusion

1. A candidate for school superintendent pointed out that reading test scores of 100 sixth grade students were lower this year than for similar groups in either of the two preceding years. Do you have any question which you might wish to raise before agreeing that the present administration is leading the schools to the dogs?

2. An experimenter may "wear two hats": that of subject-matter expert and that of statistician. Is he wearing primarily the first hat, primarily the second, or both about equally when he: (*a*) Thinks up the problem. (*b*) Translates it into a statistical question. (*c*) Draws a conclusion that average performance of experimental and control groups is really different. (*d*) Decides that the imposed difference in treatment was responsible for the difference in average performance. (*e*) Relates this finding to those of previous studies.

3. Are statistical statements always concerned with a group of observations? With more than one individual?

4. In what sense is a conclusion about individuals in general meaningful for a particular individual? Not meaningful for a particular individual?

5. In Section 1.8, three different percentages were given concerning teachers, the holding of the doctorate, and courses offered. Explain how these discrepancies could exist.

6. An advanced student was entranced by the capabilities of a particular statistical tool, and searched for a thesis problem which would allow him to use it. Is the student's enthusiasm misplaced?

2
Preliminary Concepts

2.1 Populations and Samples

In statistical work, the word population is often used in two ways. The meaning we consider first seems less in line with common usage, but is very important for statistical usage. Once understood, it clarifies much that can be confusing in statistical procedure. *Population* may refer to the complete set of observations (measures) about which we would like to draw conclusions. There are two interesting features about this definition. First, in this usage the word does not refer to people, but rather to some observed characteristics. Thus, if our interest is in the intelligence test scores of all currently enrolled pupils in Garfield Elementary School, it is the set of intelligence test scores which constitutes the population, and not, strictly speaking, the set of enrolled students. We shall call a single observation or measure an *element*. If our interest is in the number of rooms in homes in the city of Blakesburg, the number of rooms in a home is the observation we wish to take, the number of rooms in a particular home is an element of the population, and the complete set of figures, one for each home in the city, constitutes the population. It is possible for a population, statistically speaking, to exist even though we are talking about just one person. Suppose our interest is in determining reaction time under a given set of conditions for a particular person. The population would consist of the large number of possible reaction times which could be measured at various times for this person.

Second, this definition clearly indicates that the set of observations which constitutes the population is determined by the specific interest of the investigator. Defining the population is therefore not primarily a statistical question, but rather a precondition to the application of statistical procedure. Of course, *other things being equal*, the investigator will want to select his observations so that they will be amenable to the kind of statistical treatment which will shed maximum light on his question.

A *sample* is simply a part of a population. Numerically, a sample could be as small as a single element, or it could consist of all but one element of the population. Note that there is nothing inherent in the concept of a sample which specifies the way in which it is to be selected from the population. What constitutes a "good" sample will be left for later consideration.

Sometimes the word population is used to refer to a group of persons or objects for which some measure is of interest. Thus, the population of interest may be said to be the currently enrolled members of the freshman class, rather than the aptitude test scores of those same individuals. This definition is closer to the conventional use of the word. The first definition is often better for statistical work, because it avoids certain confusions. For example, we have seen that for some problems, the referent population may consist of a set of measures which characterize a single person. This follows logically from the first definition, but becomes awkward in terms of the second.

2.2 Random Samples

The notion of a *random sample* lies at the heart of inferential statistics, and is more sophisticated than it sounds. We shall examine it more closely in Chapter 13, as the study of inference is begun. At present, an approximate understanding of its nature is needed. For a sample to be random, it must have been selected in such a way that every element in the population had an equal opportunity of being included in the sample.

An example may be helpful. Suppose a deck of 52 cards is thoroughly shuffled, and four cards are drawn. The hand thus obtained may be considered to be a random sample of the population, because every card in the deck had an equal opportunity for inclusion in the hand, and every possible set of four cards had an equal opportunity of selection.

Three basic properties of random samples are worthy of our attention now. First, if several random samples are drawn (e.g., several four-card hands), the elements may well differ from sample to sample.† Second (and closely related to the first), the characteristics of the sample do not necessarily duplicate those in the population with exact proportionality. Although the deck contains an equal number of spades, hearts, diamonds, and clubs, it would be no surprise to find that the hand did not consist of one card from each suit. Third, characteristics of random samples tend to resemble those of the population more closely when samples are large than when they are small. Although it would not be too unusual to find our four-card hand composed of only two suits, it would be quite a

†Assume that after one hand is drawn, the four cards are returned to the deck and the deck reshuffled before the next hand is drawn.

surprise to find ten or more cards, selected in the same manner, to be so composed.

These three principles are general properties of random samples. They apply to data of all kinds, as well as to the card-drawing situation described above.

2.3 The Several Meanings of "Statistics"

So far, the term *statistics* has been encountered in several contexts. It can mean *applied statistics*, the science of organizing, describing, and analyzing bodies of quantitative data. It can also mean *statistical theory*. In this sense it is best regarded as a branch of mathematics, owing much to the theory of probability.

In a third meaning, statistics refers to a *set of indices*, such as averages, which are the outcome of application of statistical procedures. The general public often uses the word in this sense, as reflected in the request, "Give me the statistics."

A fourth meaning, similar to the third, is of significance later in this book. In this sense, a statistic is an *index descriptive of a sample*. The same index, if descriptive of a population, is called a *parameter*. Thus, the average of a sample is a statistic; the average of the population is a parameter.

2.4 Variables and Constants

A *variable* is a characteristic which may take on different values. Typical examples are: intelligence test score, height, number of errors on a spelling test, rank of a student in his class, position of a baseball team in the league standing, eye color, marital status, and sex. The concept of a variable does not imply that each observation must differ from all the others. All that is necessary is that the possibility of difference exists. Thus, if a school nurse interested in the height of seventh-grade students selects a sample of three for study and finds that they are all the same height, it is still proper to refer to height as a variable since the possibility of getting students of different height existed. On the other hand, her decision to study height only among the seventh-grade students means that grade level is not a variable in this inquiry.

When, in terms of the definition of the study, it is not possible for a characteristic to have other than a single value, that characteristic is referred to as a *constant*. In a particular study, there are often several variables and constants to which consideration must be given. Suppose we are interested in religious attitude among students in a college. Of prime concern is the variable of religious attitude. However, other variables such as age, sex, and parental religious affiliation may have to be taken into account in interpreting our findings. At the same time, membership in the specific college and the time when the data were collected are constants. Different results might be obtained in another college, or at the same college had the study been made ten years earlier.

2.5 Discrete and Continuous Variables

If we ask how many were present at a meeting, we might learn that 73 persons attended, or 74, but no value between these two figures is possible. Variables having this kind of property are called *discrete variables*. Values of such variables are stepwise in nature. Other examples of such variables are the number of books in a library, number of rooms in a school, kinds of occupations, prices of magazines, and steps in a salary scale which changes only by 5% increments. A discrete variable is therefore one which can take only certain values, and none in between.

The second kind is known as a *continuous variable*, despite the assertion of a student that it is called an "indiscreet" variable. Consider the question of length. It is possible for an object to be 3 ft 1 in. or 3 ft 2 in. in length, or any conceivable amount in between. The characteristic of a continuous variable is that, within whatever limits its values may range, any value at all is possible. The discrete variable has gaps in its scale; the continuous variable has none. Examples of common variables which are reasonably conceived as continuous include weight, age, temperature, intelligence, degree of approval of the current governmental administration, and musical talent.

The difference between the two types of variables has doubtless been noticed by everyone, although perhaps not completely analyzed. Although we accept as normal a statement that males of given age average 5.3 ft in height, we may find it a bit odd to be told that in the principality of Ruritania, 60-year-old males have had an average of 1.3 wives. The use of the average is, however, entirely appropriate in both instances. All that is required is to recognize what an average is, and that it does not necessarily characterize an individual.

Even though a variable is continuous in theory, the process of measurement always reduces it to a discrete one. Suppose we are measuring length, and decide to record our observations to the nearest ten-thousandth of an inch. A particular observation will then be recorded as 1.3024 in. if the object appears to be closer in length to that figure than to 1.3023 or 1.3025. As a result, our *recorded* measurement will form a discrete scale in steps of one ten-thousandth of an inch.

2.6 Accuracy in a Set of Observations

Numbers in a discrete series may be *exact numbers*. If we perform an experiment using 25 subjects, we may speak of 25 as an exact number, since there is *no* margin of error. Numbers lacking this kind of accuracy are known as *approximate numbers*. There are two ways in which we may be confronted with a set of approximate numbers. First, our method of collecting data may have degraded the potential accuracy in a set of discrete values.† This happens when we count

---

†Here and elsewhere in this book, *degraded* refers to a reduction in accuracy; often purposeful, it is not necessarily a bad thing.

the "house" at a theater by estimating how many seats are filled, or in reporting the national debt as \$182,000,000,000, rather than \$182,344,541,776.98. This may be appropriate when we are not interested in the detailed accuracy which could potentially be achieved.

Second, we have seen that recorded measures obtained from a scale that is essentially continuous constitute a discrete scale. However, such recorded values are approximate numbers. If we are measuring height to the nearest half inch, recorded height of 5 ft $4\frac{1}{2}$ in. means that the actual height lies somewhere within the range of 5 ft $4\frac{1}{4}$ in., and 5 ft $4\frac{3}{4}$ in. It should be clear that any measurement of a continuous variable must be treated as an approximate number.

In any event, it is up to the investigator to determine the degree of accuracy appropriate to his problem. A report of weight to the nearest pound will be adequate for determining your weight, but will not be satisfactory for buying candy, much less gold! Once the desired degree of accuracy is determined, it falls in the computational domain to adjust procedures so that in the process of numerical manipulation we do not arrive at an outcome which pretends to greater accuracy than is warranted, or which unnecessarily loses desired accuracy.

The matters discussed above bear on *permissible* accuracy in statistical computation. If our data are the number of pupils in each of a school's six first grade classes, we would be entitled to compute the average number of pupils per class to any degree of accuracy we wished. This follows, because both the total number of children involved and the number of classes are exact numbers. Consequently, when we divide the former number by the latter one, the result will also be an exact number. However, the average height of the same pupils, or their average reading test score would not be open to the same potential exactness, since both height and reading test score are best viewed as approximate numbers.

Rules governing accuracy of computation involving approximate numbers exist, but the problem is complicated by several factors. Of these, one of the more important is that of sampling variation.

Very often we are interested in studying the characteristics of a sample not just for its own sake, but because of the implication which the sample findings may have for the population from which the sample was drawn. In this case, we must deal not only with accuracy in the data at hand, but with the fluctuation attributable to sampling. Of course, the characteristics which we obtain in a particular sample will not be exactly duplicated in a second sample. Although the observations taken might be exact numbers, they are subject to inaccuracy from the standpoint of our primary interest in the characteristics of the population.

Several factors, then, govern the rounding back which we will want to accomplish at the end of a statistical computation. No simple set of rules is entirely convenient or adequate for maintainance of accuracy. Rather, we need to keep in mind the several aspects of the situation and do what is sensible.

In general, it is good to keep a little more accuracy in the course of a series of statistical computations than we think is the minimum to which we are entitled, since in a sequence of computations it is possible to compound inaccuracy. Once a statistical computation is completed, we should round back to a figure which seems sensible. In so far as the factor of sampling variation is concerned, remember that an outcome based on a large sample has, other things being equal, greater stability than one based on a small sample. The note at the end of this chapter further explores the question of computational accuracy.

2.7 Levels of Measurement

In measuring weight, we are accustomed to the idea that 40 pounds is twice as much as 20 pounds, and that the difference between 10 and 20 pounds is the same as that between 60 and 70 pounds. However, if we put baseball teams in in order of their standing in the league, we should not think that the number two team is twice as bad as the number one team, nor would we expect that the difference in merit between the first and second team is necessarily the same as that between the second and third team. It is apparent that numbers have a different significance in the two situations. The difference in usage of numbers has been clarified by the identification of four major kinds of scales of measurement.

Some variables are qualitative in their nature, rather than quantitative. For example, the two categories of sex are male and female. Eye color, types of cheese, and party of political affiliation are other examples of *qualitative*, or *categorical* variables. The several categories of such a variable are said to constitute a *nominal scale*. The fundamental principle of the nominal scale is that of equivalence; all observations placed in the same category are considered to be equivalent. In the pure form of this scale, there is no question about one category having more of the quality concerned; they are simply different. Numbers may be used to identify the categories of a given scale, e.g., Cheese No. 1, Cheese No. 2, etc. Numbers used in this way are simply a substitute for names and serve only for purposes of identification. If one football player bears the number 10 on his back while another bears the number 20, there is no implication that one player is "more than" the other in some dimension, let alone that he has "twice as much" of something.

At the next level of complexity is the *ordinal scale*. In this type of measurement, numbers are used to indicate the order of magnitude of the observations. Thus a supervisor may be required to express his view of the competence of seven workmen by arranging them in order of merit. The basic relation expressed in a series of numbers used in this way is that of "greater than." Among the persons ranked 1, 2, and 3, the first has a greater degree of merit than the man ranked second, and in turn, the second man has greater merit than the third. However, nothing is implied about the magnitude of difference in merit between adjacent steps on the scale. The difference in merit between the first and second workman may be small or large, and is not necessarily the same as that between the second and the third workman. Further, nothing is implied about the absolute level of merit; all seven workers could be excellent or they could be quite ordinary.

The next major level is the *interval scale*. This scale has all the properties of the ordinal scale, but with the further refinement that the distance between adjacent scores is meaningful. Examples of this type of scale are calendar years and degrees of temperature on the Fahrenheit or Centigrade scale. We can assume that as much time has elapsed between 1910 and 1920 as between 1940 and 1950. A given interval (e.g., 10 years) is considered to represent the same difference in the characteristic measured (e.g., time) irrespective of the location of that interval along the measurement scale.

When measurement is at this level, one may talk meaningfully about the ratio between intervals. For instance, one may say that twice as much time has elapsed between 1940 and 1960 as between 1900 and 1910. Nevertheless, it is not possible to speak meaningfully about a ratio between two measures. For example, it is not meaningful to assert that a temperature of 100° (Centigrade) is twice as hot as one of 50°, or that a rise from 90° to 99° is a 10% increase. The reason is that the zero point is arbitrarily determined, and does not imply an absence of heat. The point is illustrated in Figure 2.1. The first part of this illustration shows three temperatures in degrees Centigrade: 0°, 50°, and 100°. It is tempting to think of 100° as twice as great as 50°. However, the value of zero on this scale is simply an arbitrary reference point. The second part of the illustration shows the same three temperatures in degrees Kelvin. This scale uses the same unit for its intervals; e.g., 50 degrees of *change* in temperature is the same on both scales. However, the Kelvin scale has an absolute zero, indicative of an absence of heat. The values of 50° and 100° on the Centigrade scale are 323° and 373°, respectively, on the Kelvin scale. A little arithmetic shows that the rise of 50 degrees from 323° is an increase by a factor of 1.15, rather than by a factor of 2.

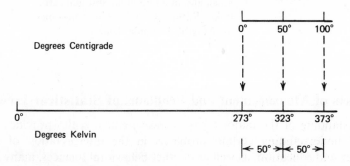

FIGURE 2.1 Three Temperatures Represented on the Centigrade and Kelvin Scales.

The *ratio scale* possesses all the properties of the interval scale, and in addition has the property of an absolute zero. Temperature measured on the Kelvin scale, length, weight, and measures of elapsed time, such as age, years of experience, and reaction time are examples of measures of this type. Not only is the difference between 40 in. and 41 in. considered to be the same as the difference between 80 and 81 in., but it is also true that 80 in. is twice as long as 40 in.

Characteristics of the four measurement scales are summarized in Table 2.1.

TABLE 2.1 Levels of Measurement and Their Characteristics.

Nominal scale:	Qualitative categories, only. Observations sorted into categories by principle of equivalence. Scale categories differ from one another only in a qualitative sense. Example: eye color.
Ordinal scale:	Observations are ranked in order of magnitude. Numerical ranks express a "greater than" relationship, but with no implication about how much greater. Example: workmen sorted according to order of merit.
Interval scale:	Numerical value assigned indicates order of merit *and* meaningfully reflects relative distances between points along the scale. A given interval between measures has the same meaning at any point in the scale. Example: temperature in degrees Centigrade.
Ratio scale:	Scale has all properties of an interval scale, and in addition an absolute zero point. Ratio between measures becomes meaningful. Example: length.

2.8 Levels of Measurement and Problems of Statistical Treatment

An understanding of the major types of measurement scales provides a framework for understanding certain problems in the interpretation of data. In psychology and education, as well as in other behavioral sciences, many common measurements can *not* be demonstrated to have the full properties of interval or ratio scales. An IQ of zero does not mean that the person had no intelligence, but simply that he could not answer the simplest question in the test. It may well be that questions could be found which would differentiate between still lower degrees of intelligence. Similarly, it is not certain that a difference of ten IQ points reflects the same difference in ability at different locations on the scale. Although some worthwhile attempts have been made, it remains that we have not been able to devise any thoroughly satisfactory set of operations to tell us when devices of mental measurement have been constructed so as unequivocally to have achieved the interval level of measurement.

To cite other examples, a test of spelling, or any of the ordinary achievement tests (including examinations prepared for college classes) almost certainly do not have an absolute zero. A score of zero in spelling means that the person could not answer the simplest question, but easier questions probably exist. At the same time, it is not clear that such tests have the property of measurement according to equal intervals.

We should, therefore, be alert to the necessity of resisting several erroneous but tempting propositions, such as the assertion that a person with an IQ of 150 is twice as bright as one with an IQ of 75, or that the difference between 15 and 25 points on a spelling test necessarily represents the same increment in spelling ability as the difference between a score of 30 and 40 points on the same test. In psychological measurement, this problem may be particularly critical when a test does not have enough "top" or "bottom" to make adequate differentiation among the group measured. For example, imagine a test of ability which has a maximum possible score of 50 points, and which is too easy for the group measured. Between two individuals who score 50 points, the score for one may indicate his maximum level of attainment, but the second person with the same score may be capable of a much higher level of performance: the measuring instrument is simply incapable of showing it.

"Scale problems" can sometimes cause headaches in interpretation of research outcomes. Consider, for example, the problem of evaluating a method of teaching spelling. We want to know whether the method is of differential effectiveness for bright and dull students. We select two such groups, measure their spelling performance before and after exposure to the teaching method, and consider comparing the average gain made by one group with that made by the other. But, if the two groups do not start at the same level (and they most likely will not in this study), we are in a poor position to compare the gains unless it is possible to assume that a given gain at one point in the measurement scale represents the same increase in ability as an equal amount of gain in another part of the scale. In short, we must be able to assume an interval scale to be certain that we can make an entirely sensible interpretation of the comparison of gains. We are well advised to be alert to possible scale problems. Fortunately, the weight of the evidence suggests that in most situations, interpretability of statistical outcomes is not seriously incapacitated by uncertainty of the level of measurement achieved.

NOTE

The discussion of accuracy in Section 2.6 has not specified exactly what consequences follow from computations involving approximate numbers. A few words are in order for those who wish to consider the matter in more detail. Consider these ten approximate numbers: 11, 34, 19, 27, 29, 23, 17, 22, 25, 24. Their sum is 231. However, the number 11 stands for a value which lies somewhere between 10.5 and 11.5, and in fact each number could be as much as half a point below or above its nominal value. If every number took a value as low as is possible, the series would read: 10.5, 33.5, etc., and its sum would be 226. Similarly, the highest possible value of the sum would be 236. In practice it would be unlikely that the "true" value of the sum would approach either extreme, since it is unlikely that every error would be as large as possible and that all errors would be in the same direction. Nevertheless, if we wish to know the maximum and minimum values which *could* result from a computational routine, they can be found by assigning all approximate numbers their maximum or minimum values and completing the calculations. Thus, the minimum value of $\sqrt{32}$ is $\sqrt{31.5}$, and the minimum value of the average of the ten scores given above is 22.6.

PROBLEMS AND EXERCISES

Identify:

population	degraded data
sample	exact number
element	approximate number
parameter	sampling variation
statistics	levels of measurement
variable	nominal scale
constant	ordinal scale
qualitative variable	interval scale
discrete variable	ratio scale
continuous variable	

    1. The example in Section 2.1 spoke of the population of intelligence test scores of all enrolled students in a particular school. If we were interested in the heights of these same students, should we speak of "the same population"? Explain.

    2. In the same school, suppose we are interested in the number of chairs in each room. (*a*) What is the observation to be recorded? (*b*) What is an element? (*c*) What is the population?

    3. If we are interested in ascertaining the existence of a TV set in the residences of Brownsville: (*a*) What is the observation to be recorded? (*b*) What is an element? (*c*) What is the population?

    4. You are going on a diet with the intention of losing weight. You decide to weigh yourself now, before entering the diet, and one month from now. In order to refine your "study," what variables would you find desirable to hold constant?

    5. We wish to set up an experiment to test the relative effectiveness of morning hours and afternoon hours as a time for study. Identify several variables which would be desirable to hold constant.

6. If the effect of the act of measurement is disregarded, which of the following variables are best regarded fundamentally as forming a discrete series, and which a continuous series? (a) temperature (b) time (c) sex (d) kinds of cigarettes (e) size of family (f) achievement score in mathematics (g) merit ratings of employees (h) score on an introversion–extraversion scale.

7. In a safety study, we might record the number of auto accidents incurred by each subject during a five-year period. This variable could be considered as discrete, or, from another point of view, as continuous. Explain.

8. Is number of errors in a learning experiment an exact number or an approximate one? Explain.

9. The weights of nine children were recorded to the nearest pound, and their average weight was found to be 118.555 lb. What do you think about reporting the average as: (a) 118.555? (b) 118.6? (c) 120 (rounded to the nearest 10 lb)?

10. In one state, voters register as Republican, Democrat, or Independent. Can we consider this variable as one of the four "scales of measurement"? If so, which one?

11. Instructor, assistant professor, associate professor, and professor form what kind of scale?

12. A student is asked whether he would rather have a grade of C for sure, or a 50-50 chance of getting a B or a D. He replies that he would prefer the certain C. It must be that for him the psychological distance between a B and a C is less than the distance between a C and a D. Therefore, the grades B, C, and D form a scale no higher in level of measurement than (which scale)?

13. If the student in the previous question had no preference, this would suggest that the three grades form for him a scale of what type?

14. Temperature in degrees Centigrade forms an interval scale. What kind of scale is formed by degrees Fahrenheit? Explain.

15. In an interval scale, is it proper to consider that an increase of 20 points is twice as much as an increase of 10 points? Explain.

16. Assume the following series of numbers form an interval scale: 0, 1, 2, 3, . . . , 19, 20. (a) Would it still be an interval scale if we added 10 points to each score? Explain. (b) Would it still be an interval scale if we multiplied each score by 10? Explain.

17. (a) If the numbers in Question 16 form a ratio scale, and 10 points is added to each, would we still have a ratio scale? Explain. (b) If we multiply each score by 10? Explain.

18. (*Based on Note*) What is the maximum true value of the sum of these approximate numbers: 42, 53, 55, 45, 48? What is the maximum true value of their average?

19. (*Based on Note*) What is the maximum true value of (a) 15×36, and (b) 15×14.3; when the first number in each pair is exact and the second is approximate?

20. (*Based on Note*) What is the minimum true value of (a) $\sqrt{9.5}$, and (b) $\sqrt{42}$, when both are approximate numbers (see Appendix, Table A, for square roots).

3

Frequency Distributions

3.1 The Nature of a Score

Consider three possible adjacent scores on a social science achievement test: 51, 52, 53. It is reasonable to think that the score of 52 represents a level of knowledge *closer* to 52 than that indicated by a score of 51 or 53. Consequently, the score of 52 may be treated as extending from 51.5 to 52.5. This interpretation of a score is illustrated in part A of Figure 3.1.

In general, the limits of a score are considered to extend from one-half of the smallest unit of measurement below the value of the score to one-half unit above. If we were measuring to the nearest 10th of an inch, the range represented by a score of 2.3 in. is 2.3 $\pm$ .05 in., or from 2.25 to 2.35 in. If we were weighing coal to the nearest 10 pounds, a weight of 780 lb represents 780 $\pm$ 5 lb, or from 775 to 785 lb.

On rare occasions, a score has a meaning different from that described above. Age is the only common example. When a person says that he is 52, he usually means that he has passed his 52nd birthday, but that he has not yet reached his 53rd birthday. In these terms, a score of 52 represents an interval from 52.0 to 53.0. This is pictured in part B of Figure 3.1.

Some sets of scores may have negative values, as in a record of temperatures. Negative scores could also occur in use of a test scored by subtracting the number of wrong answers from the number of right answers. In measuring judgment of distance, it may be convenient to record the score in terms of error of overestimation or underestimation, using positive and negative values to make this differentiation.

22

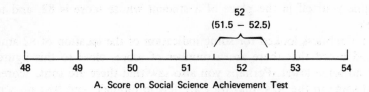

A. Score on Social Science Achievement Test

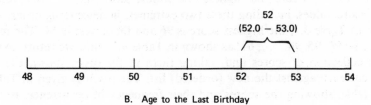

B. Age to the Last Birthday

FIGURE 3.1 Two Meanings of a Score.

3.2 A Question of Organizing Data

Suppose that a college history instructor has given a midterm examination, scored it, and returned the papers to his 50 students. Aside from the primary question about their grades, members of the class would like additional information. How do their scores compare with others in the class? What is the general level of performance of this class? One student asks, "Please tell us something about how the class did." In response, the professor writes the set of 50 scores on the blackboard. Since his gradebook is in alphabetical order, the result appears in the form shown by Table 3.1. Before reading further, you are invited

TABLE 3.1 Scores from Fifty Students on a History Class Midterm Examination.

84	82	72	70	72
80	62	96	86	68
68	87	89	85	82
87	85	84	88	89
86	86	78	70	81
70	86	88	79	69
79	61	68	75	77
90	86	78	89	81
67	91	82	73	77
80	78	76	86	83

to imagine yourself in the place of a student whose score is 82, and to study this table.

You doubtless looked for some indication of the location of 82 among the mass, and noted that there are a number of scores close to this figure, some higher and some lower. Perhaps you also saw that there are some scores in the 60's and some in the 90's, that they are few in number, and that no scores are lower or higher.

The simplest way to facilitate this kind of analysis is to put the scores in order. To do so, locate the highest and lowest score values. Then record all *possible* score values, including these two extremes, in descending order. Among the data of Table 3.1, the highest score is 96 and the lowest is 61. The recorded sequence is: 96, 95, 94, . . ., 61, as shown in Table 3.2. Now we return to the un-ordered collection of scores and, taking them in the order shown there, tally their occurrence against the new (ordered) list. The result is given in Table 3.2. Such a table, showing the scores and their frequency of occurrence, is called a *frequency distribution*.

TABLE 3.2 Scores from Table 3.1, Organized in Order of Magnitude.

Score	Freq	Score	Freq	Score	Freq	Score	Freq
96	1	86	6	76	1	66	0
95	0	85	2	75	1	65	0
94	0	84	2	74	0	64	0
93	0	83	1	73	1	63	0
92	0	82	3	72	2	62	1
91	1	81	2	71	0	61	1
90	1	80	2	70	3		
89	3	79	2	69	1		
88	2	78	3	68	3		
87	2	77	2	67	1		

Thus organized, many features of interest are easily perceived. We see that the score of 82 is a little above the middle of the distribution. Although scores range from 61 to 96, the bulk of the distribution lies between 67 and 91. There is one student whose competence stands above the rest, and two students who "aren't getting it." Eighty-two is not far from being quite a good performance in this class.

In this case, ordering the scores was sufficient for the purpose. When the spread of scores is large, it is often helpful to group the scores, in addition to ordering them.

3.3 Grouped Scores

Table 3.3 shows two ways in which the scores of Table 3.1 may be grouped into *class intervals*. There are several reasons why grouping may be desirable:

1. When the range of scores is widespread, the meaning may be easier to grasp when data are reduced to a small number of groups.
2. When further computation is to be done and a calculating machine is not available, grouping the scores makes computational work easier.
3. Grouping helps to smooth out irregularities in the distribution of frequencies. If the distribution tends toward a particular characteristic shape, it can be more easily seen when scores are grouped.
4. When the frequency distribution is to be represented graphically (see Chapter 4), the graph is usually less confusing when scores are grouped.

There are two potential disadvantages to grouping:

1. When scores are grouped, some information is lost. For example, if we observe that there are five scores in an interval labeled 120–129, one can not say for sure whether they are all at one end of the interval, all at the other, or spread throughout in some way.
2. A set of *raw scores* (the term for a set of scores in their original form) does not result in a unique set of *grouped scores*. Table 3.3 shows, for example, two different sets of grouped scores which may be formed from the raw scores of Table 3.1.

TABLE 3.3 Scores from Table 3.1, Converted to Grouped Data Distributions.

A		B	
Scores	Freq	Scores	Freq
94–96	1	95–99	1
91–93	1	90–94	2
88–90	6	85–89	15
85–87	10	80–84	10
82–84	6	75–79	9
79–81	6	70–74	6
76–78	6	65–69	5
73–75	2	60–64	2
70–72	5		
67–69	5		
64–66	0		
61–63	2		

3.4 Characteristics of Class Intervals

In converting raw scores to grouped data, there are several principles which should be kept in mind. As they are discussed, it will be helpful to refer to Table 3.3 from time to time.

1. *A set of class intervals should be mutually exclusive.* That is, intervals should be chosen so that one score cannot belong to more than one interval.

2. *All intervals should be of the same width.* Unequal intervals cause trouble when further statistical work is to be done.

3. *Intervals should be continuous throughout the distribution.* In part A of Table 3.3, there are no scores in the interval 64–66. To omit this interval and "close ranks" would create a misleading impression, and would make trouble when the distribution is used as a basis for further work.

4. *The interval containing the highest score value is placed at the top.* This convention saves the trouble of learning how to read each new table when we come to it.

5. For most work, *there should be not fewer than 10 class intervals, nor more than 20.* In Table 3.3, Distribution A meets this criterion; Distribution B does not. Few class intervals mean greater interval width, with consequent loss of accuracy. Many class intervals result in lesser convenience. This advice should be shaded according to circumstance. When the eventual product is to be a graphic representation, the number of class intervals should usually be closer to 10, in order to display such regularity as the data exhibit. When the eventual object is inference from the present sample to the population it represents, remember that large samples contain the potential for greater accuracy than do small samples. When data contain a greater potential for accuracy, they warrant use of more refined technique (in this case, more class intervals).

6. It should be noted that in Table 3.3 the limits of each class interval are recorded in *score limits.* For example, the lowest class interval for Distribution A is 61–63. The intent is to include scores of 61, 62, and 63. However, following principles outlined in Section 3.1, the score of 61 extends from 60.5 to 61.5, and the score of 63 from 62.5 to 63.5. Consequently, the score limits of 61–63 include all scores which might have values between 60.5 63.5. When the limits are actually written this way, they are called *exact limits.* Intervals are typically written in terms of score limits because they are less cumbersome, but we must remember the exact limits implicit in such notation. Both types of limits are shown in Table 3.4. (The data are those of Distribution A of Table 3.3.)

3.5 Constructing a Grouped Data Frequency Distribution

With these factors in mind, we are ready to translate a set of raw scores to a grouped data frequency distribution. We shall illustrate the procedure with the

TABLE 3.4 Data of Table 3.3A, Showing Exact Limits and Tally.

Score limits	Exact limits	Tally	f
94–96	93.5–96.5	/	1
91–93	90.5–93.5	/	1
88–90	87.5–90.5	⧄ /	6
85–87	84.5–87.5	⧄⧄	10
82–84	81.5–84.5	⧄ /	6
79–81	78.5–81.5	⧄ /	6
76–78	75.5–78.5	⧄ /	6
73–75	72.5–75.5	/	2
70–72	69.5–72.5	⧄	5
67–69	66.5–69.5	⧄	5
64–66	63.5–66.5		0
61–63	60.5–63.5	⌐	2

data of Table 3.1. The first step is to find the lowest score (61), and the highest score (96). The difference between these two figures, plus one unit, is the *range* of scores.† Therefore, the range is (96–61) + 1 = 36. Since there are to be from 10 to 20 class intervals, we must find an interval width satisfying this condition. Often this can be done by inspection. Alternatively, dividing the range by 10 gives the interval width necessary to cover all scores in 10 intervals. If 20 intervals were to be used, the width of the class interval will be exactly half of this amount. Consequently, we may choose an interval width equal to any convenient whole number between these two values. For our data, one-tenth of the range is 3.6, and half of this number is 1.8. It is apparent that an interval width of 2 or 3 will be satisfactory for the present data. Suppose we decide to use an interval width of 3. In statistical work, interval width is symbolized by the letter i; for this problem we have selected $i = 3$.

Next, we must determine the starting point of the bottom class interval. Since the lowest score is 61, the lowest interval (written in score limits) could be 59–61, 60–62, or 61–63. One may choose any convenient starting point; often it is convenient to start with the lowest score to be classified. In this instance we shall choose the score limits 61–63 (remember that in exact limits, this interval extends from 60.5 to 63.5, thus giving the required interval width of 3 points). Once this decision has been made, we record all class intervals necessary to classify the data. Remember that it is customary to place the intervals containing the highest score at the top. These intervals are shown in first column of Table 3.4.

Next, refer to the collection of raw scores in whatever order they may be,

---

†One unit is added to take account of the fact that a score of 61 extends *down* to 60.5, and the score of 96 extends *up* to 96.5.

and tally their occurrence, one by one, against the list of class intervals. Table 3.4 indicates the method of tally.† Then convert the tally to frequency (symbolized by f), as shown in the last column of Table 3.4. The total number of cases in the distribution is found by summing the several values of f, and is symbolized by n if the distribution is considered as a sample, or by N if it is a population.

Note that when it comes to the selection of width of the class interval, a choice is available between $i = 2$ and $i = 3$. Some class interval widths are more convenient than others. For example, because of the nature of our number system, an interval width of 5 or 10 (or multiples thereof) is particularly convenient in that it aids both classification and subsequent interpretation of the table. When such an interval is chosen its advantages will be fully realized if the starting point of the class interval is also in accord with the characteristics of our number system. For example, intervals of 10–19, 20–29, 30–39, etc. are preferable to those of 13–22, 23–32, 33–42, etc. The steps are summarized below:

1. Find the value of the lowest score and the highest score.
2. Find the range by subtracting the lowest score from the highest, and adding one (of the smallest units of measurement).
3. Determine width of the class interval (i) needed to yield 10 to 20 class intervals.
4. Determine the point at which the lowest interval should begin.
5. Record the limits of all class intervals, placing the interval containing the highest score value at the top. Intervals should be continuous and of the same width.
6. Using the tally system, enter the raw scores in the appropriate class intervals.
7. Convert the tally count to frequency (f).

3.6 Grouping Error

Once scores have been placed in class intervals, they lose their specific identity (see Section 3.3). Under the worst possible conditions, all scores might fall at one end of the interval. Of course, the more scores there are in the interval, the less the chance that this could happen. One factor related to potential inaccuracy is width of the class interval. Other things being equal, the narrower the class interval width, the less the potentiality for *grouping error*.

When further statistical work is to be done, it is frequently necessary to make an assumption about the location of scores within the intervals. For some purposes, one assumes that the *midpoint* of the interval (the point half way between the upper and lower limits) is the average of the scores therein. In any class interval picked at random, this assumption is not likely to be exactly correct. However, the way in which the assumption is false will differ from interval to

---

†The tally system shown in Table 3.4 (e.g., ⊿⊓) has all the advantages of the usual tally system (e.g., ✕✕✕///), and is less prone to error.

interval, and often good accuracy is maintained for the data as a whole through averaging out of positive and negative error over the entire set of class intervals.

For some purposes, the assumption that the scores are evenly divided throughout the interval is more relevant. If this assumption were true, then the other would necessarily also be true, but the former assumption could be correct when this one is not. They are not, then, quite the same.

3.7 The Relative Frequency Distribution

Often it is helpful to translate the obtained frequency for each class interval into proportionate frequency or percentage frequency, i.e., into a figure showing what proportion or percent of the total number of scores is located in that interval. Part A of Table 3.5 shows the data of Table 3.3 (Part A) expressed in this form.

The notion of percentage is simply a convenient way to establish a standard frame of reference for answering the question, "How much?", and is particularly useful when it is more important to know whether a number is *relatively large* rather than *absolutely large*. Should we think of 137 as a fairly large number? If this is the number of chemistry majors in a school of 2281 students, it may be more informative, depending on the question, to note that 137 is 6% of the students.

TABLE 3.5 Relative Frequency Distributions.

Score limits	A: Group 1 f	A: Group 1 Prop. f	A: Group 1 $\% f$	B: Group 2 f	B: Group 2 Prop. f	B: Group 2 $\% f$
97–99				1	.01	1
94–96	1	.02	2	1	.01	1
91–93	1	.02	2	3	.04	4
88–90	6	.12	12	3	.04	4
85–87	10	.20	20	4	.05	5
82–84	6	.12	12	7	.09	9
79–81	6	.12	12	8	.10	10
76–78	6	.12	12	9	.11	11
73–75	2	.04	4	12	.15	15
70–72	5	.10	10	6	.08	8
67–69	5	.10	10	11	.14	14
64–66	0	.00	0	7	.09	9
61–63	2	.04	4	2	.02	2
58–60				3	.04	4
55–57				3	.04	4
	50	1.00	100%	80	1.01	101%

Conversion of an absolute frequency to relative frequency is accomplished by dividing the frequency of the class interval by the total number of cases in the distribution (calculating f/n). This gives the proportion of cases in the interval, expressed as a decimal fraction, or parts relative to one. If percentage is preferable (parts relative to one hundred), this figure is multiplied by 100. Thus, the entry for the bottom class interval of Table 3.5 (Part A) is obtained by dividing the frequency of 2 by 50, which results in the decimal fraction .04, or 4%.

In some cases, it may be more convenient to compute the fraction $1/n$ and multiply the result by each f to obtain the proportional frequency. In the present situation, $1/n = .02$ exactly, and this method is therefore the quicker one.

In final presentation of the results of calculation of relative frequencies, there is little point in retaining more than hundredths in resulting decimal fractions, or units in the percents unless the scores number several hundred.

Use of relative frequency is particularly helpful when comparing two or more frequency distributions in which the n's are unequal. Table 3.5 shows two distributions. In one $n = 50$, and in the other $n = 80$; comparison of the two sets of frequencies is not easy. Conversion to relative frequency puts both distributions on the same basis, and meaningful comparison is easier.

Caution is in order when the distribution is comprised of a small number of cases. It can be misleading to say that 50% of a community's auto mechanics are alcoholics when what is meant is that one of the two of them is.

3.8 The Cumulative Frequency Distribution

Henry earned a score of 52 in an arithmetic achievement test; how many of his class scored less well? How many scored better? Mary earned a score of 143 on a college entrance test. Among college applicants, what percent obtains lower scores? On the same test, what score is so low that only 10% of applicants do less well? What score divides the upper 25% of the distribution from the lower 75%? These are examples of questions which are more easily answered when the distribution is cast in *cumulative* form.

A cumulative frequency distribution shows how many cases lie below the upper exact limit of the particular class interval. To construct such a distribution, we begin with the usual frequency distribution, as illustrated in the first two columns of Table 3.6. Starting at the bottom, we record for each class interval the total frequency of cases falling below its upper limit. These figures are shown in the third column, headed *cum f*. They are obtained by adding the frequency of the given class interval to the cumulative frequency recorded for the next lower class interval. As a check on computation, the cumulative frequency for the uppermost class interval should equal n.

If *relative frequency* is desired, the cumulative frequencies are converted by dividing each cumulative frequency by n. For example, in the interval 87.5–90.5, *cum f*$/n = 48/50 = .96$, the proportional cumulative frequency. These values are

TABLE 3.6 Data from Table 3.3A Presented in Cumulative Form.

Exact limits	f	*cum* f	Prop. *cum* f	*cum* $\% f$
93.5–96.5	1	50	1.00	100
90.5–93.5	1	49	.98	98
87.5–90.5	6	48	.96	96
84.5–87.5	10	42	.84	84
81.5–84.5	6	32	.64	64
78.5–81.5	6	26	.52	52
75.5–78.5	6	20	.40	40
72.5–75.5	2	14	.28	28
69.5–72.5	5	12	.24	24
66.5–69.5	5	7	.14	14
63.5–66.5	0	2	.04	4
60.5–63.5	2	2	.04	4
	$n = 50$			

shown in the fourth column of Table 3.6. If desired, they may be converted to percent frequency by multiplying each by 100, as shown in the last column. This kind of distribution is sometimes known as a "less than" distribution, because the meaning of a given cumulative entry is to specify how many (or what percent of) scores have values less than the upper limit of the corresponding class interval.

3.9 Centiles and Centile Ranks

The centile system is widely used in educational measurements to report the standing of an individual relative to the performance of a known group. It is based on the *cumulative percentage frequency distribution*. A *centile point* is a score point below which a specified percent of the scores in the distribution fall. It is often called a *centile*, or a *percentile*. The specified percent is the *centile rank* of the centile point. The two should not be confused: centile ranks may take values only between zero and 100, whereas a centile (point) may have any value that scores may have. It is perfectly possible to find that 576 is the value of a centile, for example. Suppose Mary earned a score of 143 on a college entrance test, and that this score is such that 75% of applicants score below it. Mary's centile is 143; her centile rank is 75.

We shall use the symbol C to represent a centile, and attach a subscript to indicate the centile rank. For Mary, we may write: $C_{75} = 143$. In Table 3.6, we find that C_{96} (the 96th centile point) is 90.5, the upper limit of the third-from-top class interval. Similarly, the same table shows that $C_{24} = 72.5$ and $C_{40} = 78.5$. In the next two sections, we will learn how to compute centiles and centile ranks from cumulative frequency distributions. Evaluation of the merits of this method of reporting scores will be postponed until Chapter 8, where comparison will be made with other systems.

3.10 Computation of Centiles from Grouped Data

In Table 3.7, the data of Table 3.5 (Part B) are presented in cumulative frequency form. This is the starting point for finding centiles. We shall suppose that our problem is to find the values of C_{25}, C_{50}, and C_{82}. What is C_{25}? It is the score point below which 25% of the cases fall. There are 80 cases, and since 25% of 80 is 20, C_{25} is the point below which 20 cases fall. Working up from the bottom of the distribution, we find that the 20th case will fall in the class interval 66.5–69.5 (we must be sure to think in terms of exact limits). At this point, it is not clear what score value should be assigned, since the point sought lies somewhere within the interval.

TABLE 3.7 Cumulative Percentage Frequency Distribution and Centile Calculation.

Score limits	f	cum f	cum % f	Centile calculations
97–99	1	80	100.0	
94–96	1	79	98.8	
91–93	3	78	97.5	
88–90	3	75	93.8	$C_{82} = 81.5 + \left(\dfrac{4.6}{7} \times 3\right)$
85–87	4	72	90.0	$= 83.5$
82–84	7	68	85.0	
79–81	8	61	76.2	
76–78	9	53	66.2	$C_{50} = 72.5 + \left(\dfrac{8}{12} \times 3\right)$
73–75	12	44	55.0	$= 74.5$
70–72	6	32	40.0	
67–69	11	26	32.5	
64–66	7	15	18.8	
61–63	2	8	10.0	$C_{25} = 66.5 + \left(\dfrac{5}{11} \times 3\right)$
58–60	3	6	7.5	$= 67.9$
55–57	3	3	3.8	
	$n = 80$			

There are 11 scores in this interval, and to proceed, *we will make the assumption that they are evenly divided throughout the interval.*† The results of this assumption are pictured in Figure 3.2. From this point on, grasping the

†This procedure is called *linear interpolation*. It is explained in Section A.10 of Appendix A.

procedure will be made easier by close study of Figure 3.2. The value of the 25th centile point will be located at a point 20 scores (cases) up from the bottom of the distribution. Since there are 15 cases below the lower limit of the class interval concerned, we must come up five more to reach this position. This means that we are to come up five out of the 11 equal parts in the interval, or 5/11ths of the interval's width. The width of the interval is three score points, and the calculation is as follows: $(5/11) \times 3 = 1.4$ points. This quantity is therefore added to the lower exact limit of the interval.

$$C_{25} = 66.5 + 1.4 = 67.9$$

A formula could be given for this calculation, but it is more important to follow the logic of the procedure. Once the logic is grasped, it is much easier to remember than any formula because it makes sense.

The steps in calculating a centile will be reviewed and summarized by determining C_{50}.

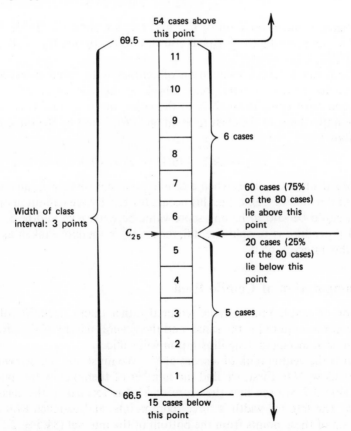

FIGURE 3.2 Location of the 25th Centile Point: Data from Table 3.7.

Problem: Find C_{50}.

1. First objective: find the class interval in which C_{50} falls.

   (a) C_{50} is the score point below which 50% of the cases fall.

   (b) 50% of $n = .50 \times 80 = 40$ scores.

   (c) The 40th score (from the bottom) falls in the class interval 72.5–75.5.

2. Determine the number of cases between the bottom of the distribution and the lower limit of the class interval containing the centile (in this case, 32).

3. Determine the additional number of cases required to make up the number of scores found in 1(c) (in this case, 8; $32 + 8 = 40$).

4. Assume the (12) scores in the class interval are evenly divided throughout the interval.

5. Find the additional distance into the interval needed to arrive at the score point (8/12ths of the interval width, or $(8/12) \times 3 = 2.0$).

6. Add this value to the lower limit of the class interval to obtain the centile:

$$C_{50} = 72.5 + 2.0 = 74.5$$

Elements of the calculation of C_{50} and C_{82} are shown in Table 3.7. To be certain that the procedure is grasped, you should verify that $C_5 = 58.5$ and that $C_{75} = 81.1$.

A good way to check calculation of centiles is to count *downward* in the distribution to the appropriate point. Checking the calculation of C_{25} by this method, one must come down 75% of the cases, or 60 scores. This is six cases below the upper limit of the class interval 66.5–69.5, and by the same reasoning applied above

$$C_{25} = 69.5 - (6/11 \times 3) = 67.9$$

A special situation arises when a centile point coincides with an empty class interval. In the data of Table 3.6, this occurs for C_4. By the definition of a centile point, C_4 could be said to be any score value between 63.5 and 66.5, inclusive. Preferred procedure is to split the difference; C_4 is therefore taken as the midpoint of this interval, 65.0.

3.11 Computation of Centile Rank

Calculation of centile rank may be required rather than calculation of centiles. The assumption required is the same, and the general nature of the procedure is parallel in both instances. One illustration will suffice.

What is the centile rank of a score of 87? We must find the percent of cases which lie below 87.0. First, we find the number of them below this point. Consulting Table 3.7, we see that the score of 87.0 is located in the class interval 84.5–87.5. The interval width is three score points, and to reach 87.0 one must come up 2.5 of these points from the bottom of the interval $(84.5 + 2.5 = 87.0)$. There are four cases in the interval, and we assume them to be evenly distributed.

We must come up $(2.5/3) \times 4$, or 3.3 cases from the bottom of the interval. Since there are 68 scores below this lower limit, the point in question is $68 + 3.3 = 71.3$ cases up from the bottom of the distribution. Finally, $71.3/80 = .89$, or 89%. The score of 87 is therefore at a point below which 89% of the cases fall, and therefore its centile rank is 89. The calculation may be summarized as follows:

$$\left. \begin{array}{l} \text{Centile rank of} \\ \text{a score of 87} \end{array} \right\} = 100 \left[\frac{68 + \left(\frac{2.5}{3} \times 4\right)}{80} \right] = 89$$

To be certain the procedure is understood, you should verify the following calculation of the centile rank of a score of 62:

$$\left. \begin{array}{l} \text{Centile rank of} \\ \text{a score of 62} \end{array} \right\} = 100 \left[\frac{6 + \left(\frac{1.5}{3} \times 2\right)}{80} \right] = 9$$

For further practice, verify that the centile rank of a score of 72 is 39, and that the centile rank of a score of 91 is 94.

PROBLEMS AND EXERCISES

Identify:

raw scores	grouping error
grouped scores	relative frequency
i	percentage frequency
f	cumulative frequency distribution
n	cumulative percentage frequency
N	distribution
score limits	"less than" distribution
exact limits	centile
midpoint	centile rank
class interval	C_{75}
range	linear interpolation

1. Write the exact limits for the following scores: (*a*) A score of 52; measurement is to the nearest digit. (*b*) 17 years; measurement is to the last birthday. (*c*) 800 yd; measurement is to the nearest 100 yd. (*d*) 460 lb; measurement is to the nearest 10 lb. (*e*) .6 in.; measurement is to the nearest .1 in. (*f*) .47 sec; measurement is to the nearest .01 sec.

2. "The notion that there ought to be between 10 and 20 class intervals is fundamentally an arbitrary convention." Evaluate the foregoing statement.

3. List the possibly objectionable features in the following set of class intervals:

50 and up	20–25
44–49	14–19
38–43	8–13
26–31	0– 7

4. The lowest and highest scores are given below for different distributions. Assume grouping is to be done as a preliminary to further statistical calculation. For each, state (a) the range, (b) your choice of class interval width, (c) the score limits and the exact limits for the lowest class interval, and (d) the midpoint of that interval: (1) 36, 75; (2) 54, 117; (3) 27, 171; (4) −22, +21; (5) 1.13, 3.47; (6) 287, 821.

5. Suppose we are recording weight in pounds, and one class interval has these score limits: 10–19. What are its exact limits? Its midpoint? The lowest class interval is 0–9. What is the best way to view its exact limits? Its midpoint? Would you view the interval, 0–9, differently if it represented performance on a test scored by subtracting wrong answers from right ones? Explain.

6. When $i = 1$, how do we write the exact limits for these scores: 47, 48, 49? The score limits?

7. The following scores were obtained by high school seniors on an achievement test in history:

Data 3A

44	35	20	40	38	52	29	36	38	38
38	38	41	35	42	50	31	43	30	41
32	47	43	41	47	32	38	29	23	48
41	51	48	49	37	26	34	48	35	41
38	47	41	33	39	48	38	20	32	37
29	44	29	33	35	50	41	38	26	29
32	26	24	38	38	56	56	48	34	35
26	26	38	37	44	24	44	47	29	41

(a) Construct a frequency distribution using $i = 3$, and 20–22 as the score limits for the lowest class interval. (b) Construct another frequency distribution from the same scores, using $i = 3$, but using 18–20 as the first class interval. Is the midpoint of the interval 27–29 representative of the scores which should be so classified in Data 3A? (c) Compare the appearance of the two distributions. Are they generally similar in appearance? One place where they appear to differ is in class intervals covering scores of 45 to 52. What explains this?

8. Construct a frequency distribution from Data 3A using $i = 5$, with the lowest interval at 20–24. Compare the result with the distribution obtained in Problem 7, writing your impressions.

9. Convert the frequency distribution requested in Problem 7a into a percentage frequency distribution.

10. Convert the frequency distribution requested in Problem 7b into a percentage frequency distribution.

11. Comparing group 1 and 2 in Table 3.5, (a) which group has proportionately more scores of 88 and above? (b) 66 and below? (c) between 70 and 81?

12. In Table 3.6, in which class interval is the score below which (a) 90% of the cases fall? (b) 30 cases fall? (c) 50% of the cases fall? (d) 10 cases fall?

Data 3B

76	72	77	65	70	69	60	68	72	69
68	73	67	73	63	80	68	74	75	71
65	75	64	81	77	76	64	72	73	67
71	74	78	66	78	63	68	76	71	72
70	75	69	67	71	68	72	75	73	74

13. For Data 3B, (a) construct a frequency distribution suitable for further statistical calculation, (b) obtain the cumulative frequencies, (c) obtain the cumulative percentage frequencies.

14. From the cumulative distribution of Problem 13, find: (a) C_{10} (b) C_{25} (c) C_{60} (d) C_{95}.

15. Verify the centile calculations in Problem 14 by counting down from the top of the distribution and interpolating downward from the top of the interval.

16. From the cumulative distribution of Problem 13, find the centile rank of scores of (a) 79.5 (b) 64.5 (c) 70 (d) 75.

17. Is it possible for a centile to have a value such as 432? Explain.

Data 3C

Retention Scores for Subjects Who Learned
Under Different Conditions of Practice

Score	Method A	Method B
155–159		1
150–154	2	2
145–149	4	7
140–144	7	12
135–139	12	10
130–134	14	7
125–129	25	4
120–124	23	3
115–119	18	0
110–114	20	2
105–109	12	1
100–104	8	0
95– 99	3	1
90– 94	2	
	$n = 150$	$n = 50$

18. Present the distributions of Data 3C as (a) percentage frequency distributions, (b) cumulative frequency distributions, and (c) as cumulative percentage distributions. Which method do you find makes comparison of the two easiest? Why?

19. From the cumulative distribution of the scores for Method A in Data 3C, find: (a) C_{20} (b) C_{60} (c) C_{75} (d) C_{95}.

20. Follow the procedure of Problem 15 to verify centile calculations made in Problem 19.

21. From the cumulative distribution of the scores for Method A in Data 3C, find the centile rank of (a) 139.5 (b) 126 (c) 100 (d) 97.

22. From the data for Method B in Data 3C, find: (a) C_8 (b) C_{22}.

23. Create a formula to express the process of finding a centile. Define the symbols you use.

24. In Table 3.5B, the percents add to 101, rather than 100. Why? In a table of ten class intervals, would it be possible for the total of the individual percents to be even farther from 100? Explain.

4
Graphic Representation

4.1 Introduction

Should a frequency distribution be presented as a table or a graph? A graph is based entirely on the tabled data, and therefore can tell no story which can not be learned by inspecting the table. However, graphic representation often makes it easier to see pertinent features of a set of data.

Graphic representation is one way of presenting all kinds of quantitative information, and there are many different kinds of graphs. Books are available which describe graphic procedures in variety and at length.† We shall limit consideration to the representation of frequency distributions. For this purpose, there are three main types of graphs: the *histogram* (and its variant, the *bar diagram*), the *frequency polygon*, and the *cumulative percentage frequency curve*. These graphs are illustrated in Figures 4.1, 4.2, 4.3, and 4.4, respectively.

4.2 The Histogram

Table 4.1 presents a frequency distribution of intelligence test scores for a sample of 100 adults selected at random. These data are graphed in the form of a *histogram* in Figure 4.1. The graph consists in a series of rectangles, each of which represents the frequency of scores in one of the class intervals of the tabled distribution. The rectangle is erected so that its two vertical boundaries coincide with the exact limits of the particular interval, and its height is specified by the frequency of scores for that interval. Either frequencies or proportionate frequencies may be represented by a histogram.

†One such is: H. Arkin and R. Colton, *Graphs: How to Make and Use Them* (2nd ed.), Harper and Brothers, New York, 1938.

39

TABLE 4.1 Army General Classification Test Scores:
100 Adults Selected at Random.

Score limits	Exact limits	Midpoint	f
	159.5–169.5	*164.5*	
150–159	149.5–159.5	154.5	1
140–149	139.5–149.5	144.5	1
130–139	129.5–139.5	134.5	3
120–129	119.5–129.5	124.5	10
110–119	109.5–119.5	114.5	14
100–109	99.5–109.5	104.5	20
90–99	89.5–99.5	94.5	21
80–89	79.5–89.5	84.5	11
70–79	69.5–79.5	74.5	11
60–69	59.5–69.5	64.5	6
50–59	49.5–59.5	54.5	2
	39.5–49 5	*44.5*	
			$n = 100$

There are some details of construction which apply to the histogram and to other graphs to be discussed in this chapter:

1. The graph has two axes: horizontal and vertical. The horizontal axis is often called the *abcissa*, or *X axis*, and the vertical axis the *ordinate*, or *Y axis*.

2. It is customary to represent scores along the horizontal axis, and frequency (or some function of frequency) along the vertical axis.

3. According to mathematical practice, the intersection of the two axes represents the zero point on both scales. If it does not, the reader should be warned. In Figure 4.1, for example, a break is introduced in the horizontal axis to indicate that a portion of the scale has been omitted.

4. A small graph is hard to construct with accuracy, and equally hard to read. If values are to be read from a graph, the larger the scale the better.

5. Convenient units should be chosen to identify position along the axes. Limits of class intervals or interval midpoints usually do not form the most convenient frame of reference for the horizontal axis. See Figures 4.1, 4.3, 4.4, and 4.5 for examples of convenient representation.

6. Whether the graph of a frequency distribution appears squat or slender depends on the choice of scale used to represent position along the two axes. Since it is desirable that similar distributions should appear similar when graphed, it is customary to choose a relative scale such that the height will be no less than .6 nor more than .8 of the width. Width and height are measured from the span of the graphed data, rather than from the borders of the graph. In Figure 4.1, for example, the width extends from scores

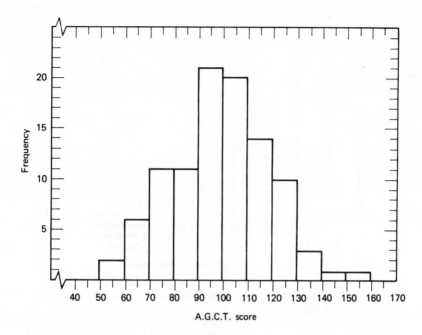

FIGURE 4.1 Histogram: Army General Classification Test Scores; 100 Adults Selected at Random.

of 49.5 to 159.5. First, decide on a suitable scale for the horizontal axis (scores). Then determine the number of squares (on the graph paper) required for the width of the graph. Multiply this number by .6 and .8, respectively, to find how many squares are to be used for the graph's height. Some trial-and-error may be necessary to create a graph suitable in size and convenient in scale.

7. The graph of any frequency distribution should have a title, as well as labels on both axes. The title should be both succinct and informative. Ideally, a graph should not need accompanying explanation.

By now you will have noted that some procedures are basically arbitrary and governed by conventions. These conventions are useful because they result in representations which we learn to expect. Then we do not have to approach each situation as a problem-solving exercise before absorbing its meaning. We could read a book just as well if the page order was reversed, but it would be a nuisance to find out which way a book was printed every time we picked up a new volume.

4.3 The Bar Diagram

If the problem is to graph categorical data, the histogram is a possibility, but the *bar diagram* is still better. The bar diagram is very similar to the histogram, except

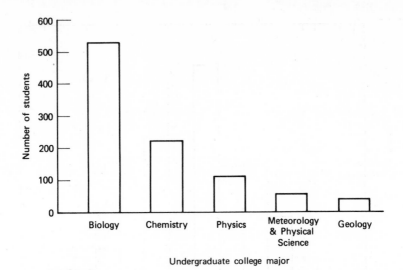

FIGURE 4.2 Bar Diagram: Comparative Frequency of Academic Majors in a School of Science.

that space is inserted between the rectangles, thus properly suggesting the essential discontinuity of the several categories. Figure 4.2 illustrates its use for nominal data. Since nominal categories have no necessary order, they may be arranged in order of magnitude of frequency, if desired. The bar diagram would also have merit in representing ordinal data or discrete data.

4.4 The Frequency Polygon

The same data plotted as a histogram in Figure 4.1 have been represented by a *frequency polygon* in Figure 4.3. In this type of graph, a point is plotted above the midpoint of each class interval at a height commensurate with the frequency of scores in that interval. These points are then connected with straight lines. If nothing further is done, the graph will not touch the horizontal axis. To rectify its otherwise peculiar appearance, we identify the two class intervals falling immediately outside those end class intervals containing scores. These are shown in italics in Table 4.1. The midpoints of these intervals are plotted at zero frequency, and these two points are connected to the graph. As with the histogram, either frequency or proportionate frequency may be represented in the frequency polygon.

4.5 The Cumulative Percentage Curve

Both the *cumulative frequency distribution* and the *cumulative percentage frequency distribution* may be cast in graphic form. We illustrate only the latter, since the

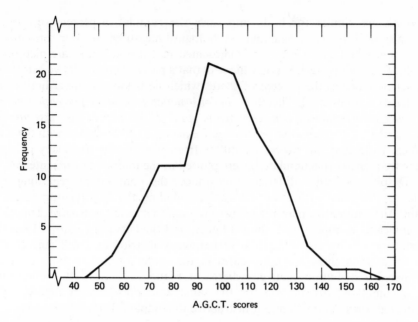

FIGURE 4.3 Frequency Polygon: Army General Classification Test Scores: 100 Adults Selected at Random.

TABLE 4.2 Cumulative Percentage Frequency Distribution

Score limits	f	cum f	cum % f
97–99	1	80	100.0
94–96	1	79	98.8
91–93	3	78	97.5
88–90	3	75	93.8
85–87	4	72	90.0
82–84	7	68	85.0
79–81	8	61	76.2
76–78	9	53	66.2
73–75	12	44	55.0
70–72	6	32	40.0
67–69	11	26	32.5
64–66	7	15	18.8
61–63	2	8	10.0
58–60	3	6	7.5
55–57	3	3	3.8
52–54		0	.0
	$n = 80$		

essentials are similar for both, and since the cumulative percentage curve is widely applied in educational and psychological measurement. For convenience, the contents of Table 3.7 are again presented in Table 4.2; they are pictured in graphic form in Figure 4.4. You will recall that a particular cumulative percentage frequency indicates the percent of scores which lie below the upper limit of the associated class interval. Therefore, *in constructing cumulative percentage curves, the cumulative frequency is plotted at the upper exact limit of the class interval.* For example, the cumulative percentage frequency of 10 is aligned with the score of 63.5. Note that this procedure differs from that for the frequency polygon, where frequencies (uncumulated) were plotted at the midpoint of the interval.

Despite its rather different appearance, the conventions regarding construction discussed in Section 4.2 apply, including the rule relating height to width. The cumulative percentage curve has another name: the *ogive*. This name is significant; it implies an S-shaped figure, and the curve in Figure 4.4 has this characteristic. Graphs of cumulative frequency distributions will tend toward this form when there are more cases in the center of the corresponding uncumulated distribution than elsewhere. In Figure 4.5, the dotted lines show the uncumulated distribution for the same data presented in Figure 4.4 in cumulated form. You will find it instructive to compare them.

4.6 Graphic Solution for Centiles and Centile Ranks

The cumulative percentage curve may be used to determine the centile rank of a score, or to find the centile corresponding to a particular centile rank. The

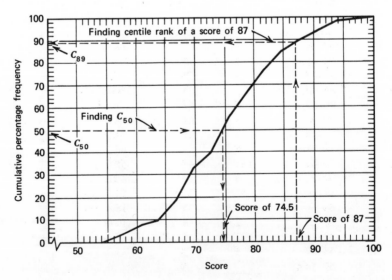

FIGURE 4.4 Cumulative Percentage Frequency Curve (Ogive): Data from Table 4.2.

dotted lines in Figure 4.4 illustrate this use. To find the centile rank of a score of 87, we locate it on the horizontal axis, and cast vertically upward until the curve is intersected. Then, reading horizontally to the vertical axis, we find the centile rank to be 89. The process may be reversed. If C_{50} is wanted, the graph shows it to be a score of 74.5; the second set of dotted lines illustrates this example.

Within limits of accuracy, graphic determination of centiles or centile ranks will yield the same result as that given by the computational procedures outlined in the previous chapter. Connecting the points on the cumulative curve with *straight* lines is the graphic equivalent of linear interpolation; both are the consequence of assuming that scores are evenly spread throughout the interval. The two points found by graphic solution above were found by direct computation in Sections 3.10 and 3.11. You may wish to refer to these sections for comparison.

4.7 Comparison of Different Distributions

Comparison of two or more frequency distributions is often made easier by application of graphic methods. *When distributions are based on unequal numbers of cases, comparison is facilitated when relative frequencies are shown.* Figure 4.5 shows the comparison of the two sets of data taken from Table 3.5. Looking at Figure 4.5, it is easy to see that the bulk of the scores for Distribution A appear higher on the scale, and the range of performance is a little less than for Distribution B.

Comparison of cumulative functions is also possible. Again, relative fre-

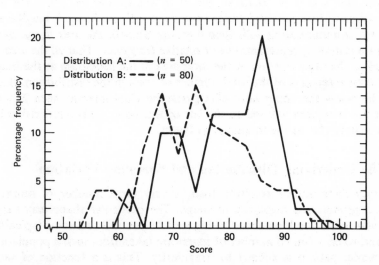

FIGURE 4.5 Relative Frequency Polygons: Comparison of Two Groups: Data from Table 3.5.

quency (proportional or percentage frequency) should be used when the number of scores differ in the distributions to be compared.

4.8 Histogram versus Frequency Polygon

Representing frequencies by rectangular bars suggests that the scores are evenly distributed throughout each class interval. It results in a stepwise picture of the distribution, and further suggests that the borders of the class intervals are points of decided change. If a definite trend exists over a span of several class intervals, such as an increase in frequency with increasing magnitude of score, the frequency polygon will reflect this with greater faithfulness, since the direction of each straight line in the polygon is determined by frequencies in two adjacent class intervals, whereas the horizontal top of each rectangle in a histogram is responsive only to what occurs in one class interval. In general, because of this feature and because of the greater suggestion of continuity, the frequency polygon often seems preferable when representing the distribution of a continuous variable.

This preference becomes even more definite when two or more distributions are to be compared, as in Figure 4.5. If the same comparison were attempted by forming two histograms, the confusion created by overlapping rectangles can readily be imagined. Simultaneous comparison of three or four histograms would be an absolute disaster, but that many frequency distributions may be satisfactorily compared by proportional frequency polygons if they are not too much alike. With data from an ordinal scale, or better yet a nominal scale, the bar diagram may be used with some success for comparisons. Figure 4.6 illustrates this possibility.

Two points may be made in behalf of the histogram. First, the general public seems to find it a little easier to understand, and hence it may be a good choice for communicating with such a group. Second, the area in the bars of a histogram is directly representative of relative frequency. That is, the area in any rectangle is the same fraction of the total area of the histogram as the frequency of that class interval is of the total number of cases in the distribution. If 25% of scores lie below the upper limit of a particular class interval, then 25% of the area of the histogram will fall to the left of this point. This relationship is only approximately true in the frequency polygon.

4.9 The Underlying Distribution and Sampling Variation

Frequency distributions resulting from a very large number of scores often exhibit a pronounced regularity of shape. The particular shape may vary with circumstances; if you look ahead to Figure 4.11 you will find some typical forms. However, when a limited number of scores are taken from such a population, the fundamental pattern is subject to irregularity. This is a function of sampling variation, or "luck of the draw." In general, the fewer the cases, the greater the

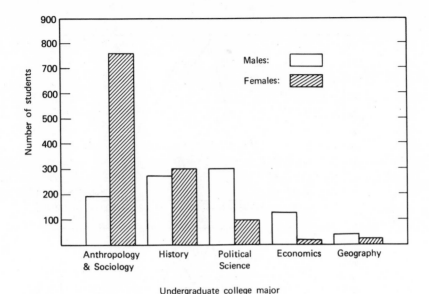

FIGURE 4.6 Area of Concentration for Male and Female Students in a School of Social Science.

irregularity. Figure 4.7 shows three samples drawn from a normal distribution (which has a regular, bell-shaped appearance; see Figure 4.11 (F)). Note the greater regularity and closer resemblance to the parent distribution as sample size increases.

If the purpose of graphic representation is to see what regularity exists, we may want to consider alternatives which tend to suppress irregularity. Since more scores reduce irregularity resulting from chance fluctuation, use of fewer class intervals tends to favor a graph of smoother appearance (see Section 3.4). Figure 4.8 shows three representations of the same raw scores; they differ only in width of interval used in grouping. It may also be noted that the graph of the cumulative function presents a smoother picture than that of the noncumulated function of the same data, since the line connecting two points may be horizontal or rising, but never descending.

Other methods of smoothing exist, such as the "running average," which bases the vertical position of a point not only on the frequency in the particular class interval, but also on the location of adjacent points. Such methods can easily be found elsewhere, but a warning is in order: smoothing is a "bootstrap" procedure. No clever amount of manipulation can make a relatively few cases tell the story of a large number. Figure 4.8 stands as an object lesson on this point. The data pictured were obtained by drawing a random sample from a symmetrical distribution like that shown in Figure 4.11 (F). Even the smoothing

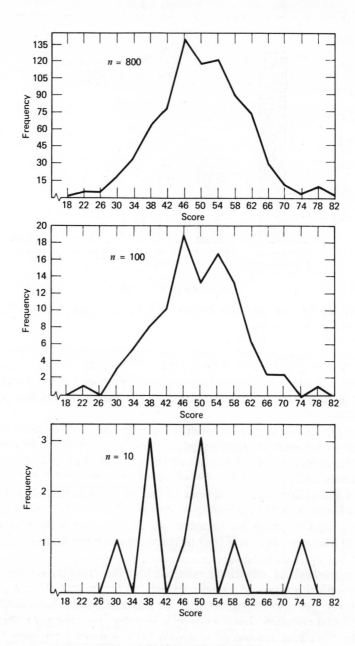

FIGURE 4.7 Effect of Sample Size on Regularity of the Distribution (Samples Drawn from a Normal Distribution).

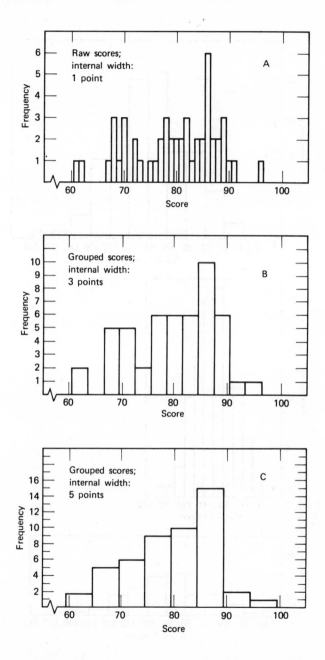

FIGURE 4.8 Effect of Varying Width of Interval in Grouped Scores (Data from Table 3.2 and 3.3).

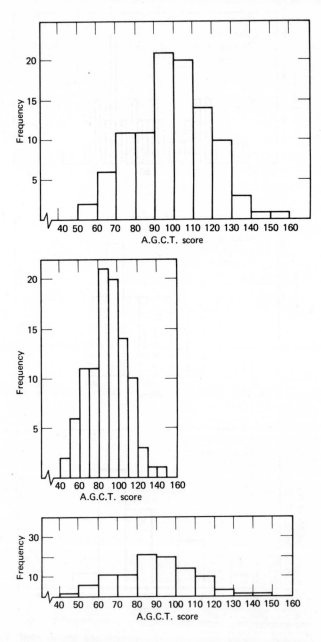

FIGURE 4.9 Effect of Change of Scale on Graphic Rendition: Data from Table 4.1.

induced by widening class intervals does not, in this particular case, tend to make the child resemble its parent very closely; in fact, Figure 4.8 (C) tends to resemble the distribution pictured in Figure 4.11 (C).

4.10 The Mythical Graph

There is no such thing as *the* graph of a given set of data. First, the same set of raw scores may be grouped in different ways (see Figure 4.8). Such variation will be reflected in the graph of the distribution.

Even more important is the matter of relative scale. Frequencies and scores are like apples and cows; no principle specifies what is an "equivalent" number of each. Consequently, the decision on relative scale is fundamentally arbitrary, and the resulting graph can be squat or slender depending on the choice made. Figure 4.9 illustrates three different renditions of the data from Table 4.1. One of these complies with the convention that height of the figure should be between .6 and .8 of the width; the others do not.

Special attention is called to the so-called *normal curve*, a distribution omnipresent in statistical work. It is typically represented as shown at A in Figure 4.10. It is so often pictured this way that it is easy to think that it is *the* picture of the normal curve. However, B and C are also possible representations of the same distribution.

4.11 Possible Shapes of Frequency Distributions

Certain shapes of frequency distributions occur with some regularity in statistical work. Figure 4.11 illustrates the general nature of several of these. The *J-shaped distribution* is pictured at A. Curves of this type have resulted from plotting the speed with which automobiles went through an intersection where an arterial stop sign was present. B and C show *asymmetrical (skewed) distributions*; B might result from a test which is too difficult for the group taking it, and C from the opposite situation. D is an example of a *rectangular distribution* which, among

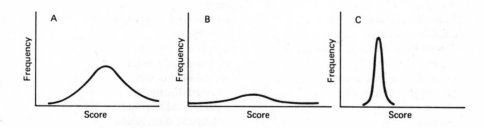

FIGURE 4.10 Three Graphs of the Same Normal Distribution.

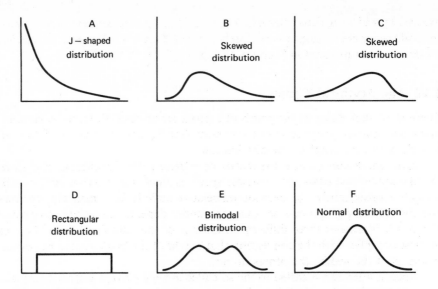

FIGURE 4.11 Shapes of Some Distributions Which Occur in Statistical Work.

other things, is the shape of the distribution of a set of ranks resulting from ordinal measurement. E shows a *bimodal distribution*; it could result from measuring strength of grip in a group consisting of both men and women. F shows the bell-shaped *normal distribution* which tends to characterize measurements of many different kinds and is of great importance in statistical inference. We will encounter this distribution many times, and the entirety of Chapter 7 is devoted to its properties.

PROBLEMS AND EXERCISES

Identify:

bar diagram
histogram
frequency polygon
cumulative frequency curve
cumulative percentage frequency
    curve
proportionate frequencies
percentage frequencies
abcissa
ordinate
X axis
Y axis
zero point on a graph

relative scale of a graph
ogive
graphic equivalent of linear
    interpolation
sampling variation
smoothing of a graph
normal distribution
J-shaped distribution
asymmetrical distribution
rectangular distribution
bimodal distribution
skewness

1. It has been held that a statistically knowledgeable person would rather inspect a frequency distribution than a graph. What supports this position? What is an argument against it?

2. When should a graph be large? When would a small graph be acceptable?

3. (*a*) Construct a histogram from the data of Table 3.5 (B). (*b*) Construct a percentage frequency histogram from the same data.

4. Repeat the tasks of Problem 3, but use the data of Method A in Data 3C.

5. (*a*) Construct a frequency polygon from the data of Table 3.5 (B). (*b*) Construct a percentage frequency polygon from the same data.

6. Repeat the tasks of Problem 5, but use the data of Method A in Data 3C.

7. In a university, male psychology majors are distributed as follows: 24 freshmen, 61 sophomores, 109 juniors, 104 seniors, and 92 graduate students. Comparable figures for females (in the same order of classification) are: 74, 58, 99, 53, and 67. Construct a bar diagram suitable for displaying the comparative relation between the sexes. What conclusions appear significant from inspection of these data?

8. Read the graph in Figure 4.4, and find the value of (*a*) C_{10} (*b*) C_{25} (*c*) C_{40} (*d*) C_{75}. Compare your answer to C_{25} with the direct calculation shown in Table 3.7.

9. Read the graph in Figure 4.4, and find the centile rank of scores of (*a*) 60 (*b*) 75 (*c*) 80 (*d*) 92.

Data 4A

Reaction Time in Milliseconds
to Simple and Complex Stimuli

Time	RT: simple stimulus f	RT: complex stimulus f
300–319	1	3
280–299	1	6
260–279	2	10
240–259	4	18
220–239	3	25
200–219	6	35
180–199	11	28
160–179	12	16
140–159	8	7
120–139	2	2
	$n = 50$	$n = 150$

10. (*a*) Plot the percentage frequency polygons for the two sets of data in Data 4A. Put them both on the same graph. Compare the two distributions and record your conclusions. (*b*) Repeat for the two distributions of Data 3C.

11. For the distribution of reaction time scores to complex stimuli in Data 4A, do the following: (*a*) Tabulate the cumulative frequencies. (*b*) Convert the cumulative frequencies to cumulative percentage frequencies and tabulate them. (*c*) Plot the cumulative percentage frequency curve. (d) Find graphically C_{20} and C_{60}. Show with dotted lines how you found C_{20}. (e) Find graphically the centile rank of scores of 195 and 245. Show with dotted lines how you found the centile rank of the score of 195.

12. (a) Plot the ogives for the two sets of data in Data 4A on one graph. (b) Compare these graphs of the cumulative function with those of the noncumulative function of the same data which you plotted in Problem 10a.

13. Repeat parts (a) through (d) of Problem 11, but for the data of Method A in Data 3C. Find the centile rank of scores of 108 and 137.

14. Repeat Problem 12, but as applied to Data 3C. The noncumulative functions for comparison are those requested in Problem 10b.

15. Figure 4.5 shows the frequency polygons for the two distributions given in Table 3.5. (a) Construct cumulative percentage curves for these same distributions, plotting them on the same graph for comparison. (b) How does the fact that the level of performance is higher in Distribution A show up in these curves? (c) How does the greater spread of scores in Distribution B show up in these curves? (d) Study your cumulative curves in comparison with the noncumulated ones in Figure 4.5. Which type of representation appears smoother? (e) For what kind of question is each type of curve best adapted to provide information?

16. Would there be any difference in the shape of a cumulative frequency curve and a cumulative percentage frequency curve if both were constructed from the same basic frequency distribution and if height and width were the same for both types of graphs? Explain.

17. The cumulative curve tends toward an S-shape when the noncumulated distribution has more scores in the center than elsewhere. Draw an approximation to the cumulative curve which would result if the noncumulated distribution had a shape like that pictured in (a) Figure 4.11 (B), (b) Figure 4.11 (C), (c) Figure 4.11 (D), and (d) Figure 4.11 (E).

18. For which distributions pictured in Figure 4.11 might the following be true? Explain. $C_{25} = 30$, $C_{50} = 40$, $C_{75} = 50$.

19. Only one of the distributions in Figure 4.11 could be characterized by each of the following sets of data. Identify which one. (a) $C_{20} = 60$, $C_{40} = 80$, $C_{60} = 90$, and $C_{80} = 110$. (b) $C_{20} = 130$, $C_{40} = 140$, $C_{60} = 150$, and $C_{80} = 160$.

20. For which distribution(s) might the following be true? $C_{10} = 70$, $C_{30} = 150$, $C_{50} = 200$, $C_{70} = 250$, and $C_{90} = 330$.

5
Central Tendency

5.1 Introduction

An investigator has constructed a test of manual dexterity, and has before him the scores of a group of men and a group of women. He wants to know whether one group scored better than the other, and if so, to what extent. He could set the two distributions of scores side by side, but this will give him only an approximate answer. Instead, he finds the *average* score of each group and compares them.

Measures of this type are called *measures of central tendency*. Their purpose is to provide a single summary figure which describes the level (high or low) of a set of observations. There are three situations in which use of a measure of central tendency is helpful. First, we may wish to compare level of performance of a group with that of a standard reference group. A principal may find that the average IQ of his students is 108. If so, he will be interested in the fact that this value is substantially above the expected value for the general population (100). Second, such a measure may indicate a standard of performance not previously known. Suppose an investigator of airplane pilots' behavior finds that the average time required to observe a dangerous situation and complete the appropriate response is three seconds. Some redesign of safety equipment or procedures may be in order, since an aircraft can travel over half a mile in that time. Third, it may be desired to compare the level of performance under two (or more) conditions or of two or more existing groups. Is the ability to see at night better if diet is supplemented by extra quantities of vitamin A? Is the grade point average of freshman women higher or lower than that of freshman men?

There are numerous measures of central tendency. We will consider only those in common use: *mode*, *median*, and *arithmetic mean*. In this

55

chapter we will take each in turn, define it, discuss computation, and then examine its properties. At the end of the chapter, a summary of the characteristics of each measure appears.

5.2 Some Statistical Symbolism

Some additional symbolism is needed to provide a convenient language. The capital letter X is used as a collective term to specify the particular set of scores concerned. A particular score in the set may be identified by a subscript, such as X_1 (the first score), X_8 (the eighth score), etc. For example, consider the set of three scores: 31, 21, 41. We may identify them as follows: $X_1 = 31$, $X_2 = 21$, $X_3 = 41$. Note that the subscript serves only as an identification number and carries no connotation about the relative size of the scores. A set of scores in a sample may be represented like this:

$$X: \quad X_1, X_2, X_3, \cdots, X_n$$

In the example above:

$$X: \quad 31, 21, 41$$

If there are 42 scores in a set, the last score will of course be X_{42}. To generalize, there will be n scores in a sample, and so the last score is X_n; in a population (see Section 3.5), the last score would be X_N.

When the scores in a set are to be summed, the capital Greek letter sigma, Σ, indicates that this operation is to be performed. It should be read "the sum of" (whatever follows). It is not called sigma because the lower case sigma (σ) has a different meaning in statistics (as we shall see), and confusion could result. Use of this symbol is illustrated below.

$$\sum X = X_1 + X_2 + X_3 + \cdots + X_n$$

For the set of three scores in the example above,

$$\sum X = 31 + 21 + 41 = 93$$

When two groups of scores are involved, the letter Y is often used to symbolize the second set. In general, capital letters near the end of the alphabet (W, X, Y, for example) are used to symbolize variables. Be sure to use capital letters; lower case letters are used in a different way (see Section 6.4). Constants are usually symbolized by letters from the front of the alphabet (A, B, C, and K are in common use). Constants may be represented either by capital letters or lower case letters.

5.3 The Mode

A common meaning of *mode* is "fashionable," and it has much the same implication in statistics. The mode is the score which occurs with the greatest frequency.

In grouped data, it is taken as the midpoint of the class interval which contains the greatest number of scores. Its symbol is *Mo*.

5.4 The Median

The median (symbol: *Mdn*) is the score point below which 50% of the scores fall. It is therefore another name for C_{50}, and for grouped data it is calculated by procedures given in Section 3.10. When the median is found directly from a small number of raw scores, the refinement of interpolation is often omitted. Thus, for the following scores:

$$5, 7, 8, 8, 8, 8$$

the median is taken as 8, rather than the interpolated value of $7.5 + (\frac{1}{4} \times 1) = 7.75$. For raw scores, then, the median may be thought of as the middle score. When there is an even number of scores, there is no middle score, so the median is taken as the point half way between the two scores which bracket the middle position. Note that this rule holds in the illustration above. Here are two more illustrations:

$$12, 14, 15, 16, 16, 22 \qquad Mdn = 15.5$$
$$37, 41, 45, 46 \qquad Mdn = 43.0$$

5.5 The Arithmetic Mean

If we sum all of the scores in a set and divide by the number of them we obtain the *arithmetic mean*. The arithmetic mean is the formal name for the measure of central tendency which most people think of as the "average." The latter name is not very satisfactory because the word average is sometimes used indiscriminately for any measure of central tendency. For brevity, the arithmetic mean is usually referred to as the *mean*, and we shall follow this practice.

The distinction between the mean of a sample and that of a population figures importantly in inferential statistics, so there are two symbols for the mean. The mean of a sample is represented by $\overline{X}$; read it as "X bar." The mean of a population is symbolized by μ_X (the Greek letter *mu*, pronounced "mew"). The fundamental formulas, and the ones which are directly applicable to calculation of the mean from raw scores are as follows:

Raw Score Formulas for the Mean
$$\mu_X = \frac{\sum X}{N} \quad \text{(mean of a population)} \qquad (5.1a)$$

$$\overline{X} = \frac{\sum X}{n} \quad \text{(mean of a sample)} \qquad (5.1b)$$

Remember that N stands for the number of cases in a population, and n for those in a sample. This distinction between sample and population is not crucial at a purely descriptive level, so to avoid unnecessary complication, symbolism appropriate to samples will be used whenever possible in these early chapters.

When the scores are grouped, we know only that scores in a given interval lie somewhere between the lower limit and the upper limit. To proceed, we assume that the *midpoint of the interval is the mean of the scores in that interval*, and use it to represent the scores in the interval. This assumption will probably be exactly correct in only a few intervals. If we have used at least ten class intervals, the width of any one class interval will be small enough to limit the magnitude of the possible error.

Under this assumption, we calculate the mean ($\overline{X}$) for the data shown in Table 5.1. The summation (starting from the bottom) might begin:

$$42 + 42 + 47 + 47 + 47 + 52 + \cdots$$

This process can be shortened by substituting multiplication for addition where appropriate. We multiply each midpoint (symbolized by X in the table) by the number of scores in the corresponding interval (f) and sum these products (fX) over all class intervals. For convenience, this process is expressed by a modification of Formula 5.1b:

Mean from Grouped Data $$\overline{X} = \frac{\sum fX}{n} \qquad (5.2)$$

where: $\sum fX = f_1 X_1 + f_2 X_2 + \cdots$, and the subscripts 1, 2, $\cdots$, identify the several class intervals. Use of this formula is demonstrated in the example shown in Table 5.1. This procedure is most useful for hand calculation when values of the

TABLE 5.1 Calculation of the Mean from Grouped Data.

Scores	X (midpoint)	f	fX	Calculation of the mean by Formula 5.2
90–94	92.0	2	184	
85–89	87.0	4	348	
80–84	82.0	9	738	
75–79	77.0	7	539	
70–74	72.0	10	720	$\overline{X} = \dfrac{\sum fX}{n}$
65–69	67.0	12	804	
60–64	62.0	9	558	
55–59	57.0	5	285	
50–54	52.0	3	156	$= \dfrac{4557}{66} = 69.0$
45–49	47.0	3	141	
40–44	42.0	2	84	
		$n = 66$	$\sum fX = 4557$	

midpoints and frequencies are small numbers. When they are not, a desk calculator will be helpful. Further simplification is possible, but we must lay some groundwork for it.

5.6 Coded Scores

Consider the following set of scores: 4, 5, 9. Their mean is 6. If we add 10 points to each score, they become 14, 15, 19, and their mean is now 16, 10 points higher. *If some constant amount is added to each score in a distribution*, the entire distribution is shifted up by the amount of the constant and *the mean will be increased by that same amount*. Similarly, *if a constant is subtracted from each score the mean will be reduced by that amount*. Other measures of central tendency discussed in this chapter are affected in the same way. This kind of transformation (adding or subtracting a constant) is a form of coding.

This property may be put to good use in simplifying the process of finding the mean. Suppose there are 40 raw scores ranging in value from 503 to 535. If 500 is subtracted from each, the resultant values range from 3 to 35. The mean of these altered scores is easier to compute, and adding 500 points to the mean of this altered series recovers the mean of the original scores.

Scores may also be coded by multiplying or dividing each score by a constant. If the scores 4, 5, and 9 are multiplied by 2, they become 8, 10, and 18; if multiplied by 10, they become 40, 50, and 90. Whereas the mean of the original set is 6, the mean of the second set is 12 (twice as large), and the mean of the third set is 60 (10 times as large). Evidently *multiplying each score by a constant also multiplies the mean by that amount*. Similarly, *dividing each score by a constant has the effect of dividing the mean by that amount*. If each score in the original set is divided by 10, the resultant scores are .4, .5, and .9, and their mean is .6, a value one-tenth of the original mean. The effect of multiplication or division by a constant holds true also for the mode and median.

Again, this property may be used to simplify calculation. If we have a series of scores such as:

$$3.42, \ 4.17, \ 5.56, \ \cdots$$

we may find it convenient to eliminate the decimal by multiplying each score by 100, find the mean of this set, and divide that value by 100 to obtain the mean of the original scores. Proof of the effect on the mean of these several ways of coding is given in Note 5.1 at the end of the chapter.

An interesting feature is that scores can be coded one way, then those coded scores can be coded again (not necessarily in the same way), and the mean can still readily be found. All that is needed is to "decode" the mean *in exactly the reverse order* of that used in coding. Taking the scores from our initial example (4, 5, 9), suppose each is multiplied by 2, and then 10 points is added to these values. The first step yields 8, 10, and 18, and the second 18, 20, and 28. The mean of this final set is 22. If from this value we *first* subtract 10 points, and then divide the result by 2, the original mean, 6, is obtained. This double coding process makes possible the convenience of the method of finding the mean discussed in the next section.

5.7 Calculation of the Mean: Coded Score Method

Calculation of the mean from grouped data can be simplified by substituting coded scores for midpoints, finding the mean of the coded scores, and then uncoding. To clarify the rationale of this method, we will show the coding process. In practical calculation, however, a shortcut makes the work much simpler than it sounds, as we shall see.

To illustrate, we turn to the data of Table 5.1, earlier employed to illustrate calculation of the mean by Formula 5.2. The class intervals and their midpoints are shown in the first two columns of Table 5.2. The midpoints are the "scores" with which we must deal. To simplify them, we select one (in this instance, 67), and subtract that value from each midpoint to arrive at a set of coded scores. The coded scores are shown in the third column. Although numerically simpler than the midpoints, they can be made still simpler by dividing each by i, the width of the class interval (in this instance, 5). The outcome of this second coding operation is shown in the last column. We symbolize these doubly coded scores by the letter x'.

Table 5.3 shows the class intervals, their frequencies, and the coded scores (rather than the interval midpoints). We now calculate the mean of the coded scores by Formula 5.2. Since these scores are labeled x', we may modify For-

TABLE 5.2 Converting Midpoints to Coded Scores.

Scores	X (midpoint)	1st code: subtract 67 from each X	2nd code: divide each coded score by i ($=5$)
90–94	92.0	$+25$	$+5$
85–89	87.0	$+20$	$+4$
80–84	82.0	$+15$	$+3$
75–79	77.0	$+10$	$+2$
70–74	72.0	$+5$	$+1$
65–69	67.0	0	0
60–64	62.0	-5	-1
55–59	57.0	-10	-2
50–54	52.0	-15	-3
45–49	47.0	-20	-4
40–44	42.0	-25	-5

TABLE 5.3 Calculation of the Mean by the Coded Score Method.

Scores	f	x'	fx'	
90–94	2	+5	+10	$\overline{X} = 67.0 + 5\left(\dfrac{+27}{66}\right)$
85–89	4	+4	+16	
80–84	9	+3	+27	$= 69.0$
75–79	7	+2	+14	
70–74	10	+1	+10	
65–69	12	0		$\Sigma(\text{positive})fx' = +77$
				$\Sigma(\text{negative})fx' = -50$
60–64	9	−1	−9	$\Sigma fx' =$
55–59	5	−2	−10	difference $= +27$
50–54	3	−3	−9	
45–49	3	−4	−12	
40–44	2	−5	−10	
	$n = 66$		$\Sigma fx' = +27$	

mula 5.2 as follows: $\overline{x}' = \Sigma fx'/n$. Following the procedure outlined in Section 5.5, a new column is prepared for the product of f and x'. We obtain the product, fx', for each class interval and record it in the next column, as shown in Table 5.3. $\Sigma fx'$ is obtained by summing the figures in this column; dividing this sum by n yields the mean of the doubly coded scores: $\Sigma fx'/n = 27/66 = +.4$. To find the mean of the original scores, we must "uncode." Since the *last* step in coding was to divide by 5, the mean of the coded scores must *first* be multiplied by 5. Then, 67, the amount subtracted in the first coding step, must be added to this quantity. The two steps of uncoding are given as follows: $\overline{X} = 67.0 + 5(+.4) = 69.0$. Note that this value is identical with that obtained by the grouped data method described in Section 5.5.

In practice, it is *not* necessary to go through the steps of the double coding process shown in Table 5.2. Instead, choose any convenient midpoint and assign to it the value $x' = 0$. We shall call this midpoint the *arbitrary origin*, or *A.O.* In successive class intervals above this point, assign successively x' values of $+1$, $+2$, etc., and below it, -1, -2, etc., as shown in Table 5.3. Find $\Sigma fx'$, and recover the true mean by Formula 5.3:

Coded Score Formula
for the Mean
$$\overline{X} = A.O. + i\left(\frac{\Sigma fx'}{n}\right) \tag{5.3}$$

where: $A.O.$ is the midpoint of the class interval to which the coded score of zero is assigned
  i is the width of the class interval
  $\Sigma fx'/n$ is the mean of the doubly coded scores

A summary of the procedure is contained in Table 5.4. Proof of the validity of the coded score method is given in Note 5.1, at the end of the chapter.

TABLE 5.4 Calculation of $\bar{X}$ by the Coded Score Method: Summary of Procedure.

1. Record the class limits and their associated frequencies. These are shown in the first two columns of the accompanying illustration.

2. Select an interval near the center of the distribution, and assign to it the value $x' = 0$.

3. Assign positive and negative values of x' to the remainder of the class intervals as shown in the illustration.

4. Multiply each f by its accompanying x', and record the product in the fx' column.

scores	f	x'	fx'
39–41	3	+3	+9
36–38	7	+2	+14
33–35	12	+1	+12
30–32	10	0	+35 −40
27–29	6	−1	−6
24–26	5	−2	−10
21–23	4	−3	−12
18–20	3	−4	−12
	$n = 50$		$\Sigma fx' = -5$

5. Sum the positive values of fx' and sum the negative values of fx'; $\Sigma fx'$ is the difference between these two sums.

6. Calculate $\bar{X}$ by Formula 5.3:

$$\bar{X} = A.O. + i\left(\frac{\Sigma fx'}{n}\right) = 31.0 + 3\left(\frac{-5}{50}\right) = 30.7$$

5.8 Properties of the Mean

The mean, unlike any of the other measures of central tendency, is responsive to the exact position of each score in the distribution.† Inspection of the basic formula, $\Sigma X/n$, shows that if a score is increased or decreased by any amount, the value of the mean will reflect that change.

    The mean may be thought of as the balance point of the distribution, to use a mechanical analogy. If we imagine a see-saw consisting of a fulcrum (balance point), a board (the weight of which shall be neglected), and the scores of a distribution spread along the board, the mean corresponds to the position of the

---

†In grouped score methods of calculation, the mean is not responsive to the exact position of a score within a class interval, however.

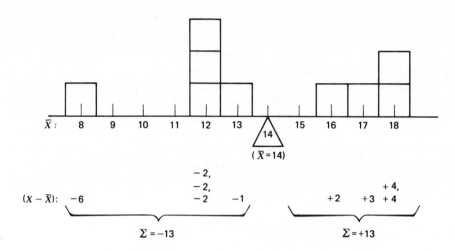

FIGURE 5.1 The Mean as the Balance Point of the Distribution.

fulcrum when the system is in balance. Figure 5.1 pictures this analogy. As with the ordinary see-saw, if one score is shifted, the balance point will also change.

There is an algebraic way of stating that the mean is a balance point for the distribution: $\Sigma(X - \bar{X}) = 0$.† This says that if the scores are expressed in terms of the amount by which they deviate from their mean, and due account is taken of negative and positive deviations (scores below the mean deviate negatively from the mean), their sum is zero. To put it another way, the sum of the negative deviations exactly equals the sum of the positive deviations. Figure 5.1 shows that $\Sigma(X - \bar{X}) = 0$ for the data given. A general proof of this proposition is given in Note 5.2.

The mean *is more sensitive to the presence (or absence) of scores at the extremes of the distribution* than are the median and (ordinarily) the mode. Further discussion of this property of the mean will be forthcoming when properties of the median are examined.

When a measure of central tendency should reflect the total of the scores, the mean is the choice, since it is the only measure based on this quantity. If a coach wanted to know whether his four best quartermile runners have, as a group, improved their performance, the total time for the four is a good criterion, and hence the mean running time would probably best reflect his interest. Insurance companies express life expectancy as a mean value, because it is most closely related to total dollars of income and expenditure, a primary concern.

The mean is amenable to arithmetic and algebraic manipulation in a way which the other measures are not. In consequence, it fits in with other important

---

†$\Sigma(X - \bar{X})$ means: $(X_1 - \bar{X}) + (X_2 - \bar{X}) + \cdots + (X_n - \bar{X})$. For example, for the three scores 3, 4, 5, $\Sigma(X - \bar{X}) = (3 - 4) + (4 - 4) + (5 - 4) = 0$

statistical formulas and procedures. At the moment, it is enough to remark that the mean is often incorporated implicitly or explicitly in other statistical procedures. *When further statistical computation is to be done, the mean is likely to be the most useful of the measures of central tendency.*

A characteristic of great significance concerns sampling stability. Suppose that, from a large population of scores, samples were repeatedly drawn at random.† Means of such samples would have similar, but not identical, values. This would also be true for the medians of the same samples, and for their modes. However, the means would vary least among themselves. *Thus, under ordinary circumstances, the mean resists most the influence of sampling fluctuation.* This is obviously a very desirable property if we propose to engage in statistical inference (see Section 1.2).

5.9 Properties of the Median

The median is the point which divides the upper half of the scores from the lower half. In doing so, *the median responds to how many scores lie below (or above) it, but not to how far away the scores may be.* A little below the median or a lot: both count the same in determining its value.

Since the median is sensitive to the number of scores below it, but not to how far they are below, *the median is less sensitive than the mean to the presence of a few extreme scores.* Consider this simple distribution:

$$X: 5, 6, 7, 8, 24$$

The median is 7; the mean is 10. The value of the top score, 24, is quite different from that of the remainder of scores. It strongly affects the total, and hence the mean, but it is just another score above the median. If the score had been 9 rather than 24, the median would be the same.

Sometimes one encounters a distribution which is reasonably regular except for several quite deviant scores at one end. If it is feared that these scores will carry undue weight in determining the mean, a possible solution is to calculate the median. The median will respond to their presence, but no more than to others which lie on that side of its position. Similarly, *in distributions which are strongly asymmetrical (skewed; see Figure 4.11), the median may be the better choice if it is desired to represent the bulk of the scores and not give undue weight to the relatively few deviant ones.* See Section 5.11 for further discussion of skewed distributions.

Of the measures of central tendency under consideration, *the median stands second to the mean in ability to resist the influence of sampling fluctuation* in ordinary circumstances. For large samples taken from a normal distribution, the median varies about one-quarter more from sample to sample than does the

---

†See Section 2.2 for an introduction to the notion of a random sample.

mean. For small samples, the median is relatively better, but still falls behind the mean.

The mean, as we learned in the last section, is frequently embodied in advanced statistical procedures. Not so the median. It has some use in inferential statistics, but much less than the mean.

Sometimes one encounters a distribution which is open-ended, such as the one shown below.

Scores	f
155–up	5
150–154	8
145–149	12
140–144	10
135–139	4
130–134	2

In this distribution the upper limit of the top class interval is not specified, and consequently the midpoint of the interval is unknown. *In open-ended distributions, the mean cannot be calculated, but calculation of the median remains possible.* Such distributions may therefore block the path to types of statistical analysis which would be very useful. The importance of thinking through the design of a study before gathering the data is apparent.

Finally, a word about ease of computation. Using grouped data, or raw scores when assisted by a calculating machine, the work involved in finding the mean and median is similar. However, from simple sets of ordered scores, the median is obtained with great ease by counting half-way up the distribution.

5.10 Properties of the Mode

The mode is easy to obtain, but it is not very stable. Further, when the data are grouped, the mode may be strongly affected by the width and location of class intervals. Another problem is that *there may be more than one mode for a particular set of scores.* In a rectangular distribution the ultimate is reached: every score shares the honor!

Sometimes the mode is just what we want. If a score is to be selected at random, the *modal score is the best bet if we must choose one "most likely" value.* It answers the question, "What is the *one* thing which happens the most frequently?" *It is the only measure which can be used for data which have the character of a nominal scale.* For example, no other measure of central tendency is appropriate for a distribution of eye color.

Some years ago, a national magazine made use of the mode in a way which capitalized ideally on its virtues. The magazine reported subscribers ratings, ranging from "excellent" to "poor," of motion pictures which they had seen. The large number of pictures so rated was arranged alphabetically, coupled with the percentage frequency distribution of ratings. A hypothetical illustration is shown below:

	E	G	F	P
Purple Passion	0	10	40	**50**
Puzzle Me Not	5	25	**55**	15

. . . .

As shown in the illustration, the modal percentage frequency was printed in boldface type. One could quickly examine the "excellent" and "good" columns, find the pictures having a modal value in these classifications, and, if desired, study further the characteristics of the distribution for that film. The mode was quite adequately functional in speeding the prospective theater-goer's task of sorting his possibilities.

5.11 Symmetry and Otherwise

In distributions which are perfectly symmetrical, i.e., in which the left half is a mirror image of the right half, mean, median, and (if the distribution is unimodal) mode will yield the same value. It is important to note that the widely occurring normal distribution falls in this category. Figure 5.2 shows what happens to mean, median, and mode in skewed distributions, as compared with the normal distribution. Equality of mean and median does not guarantee that the distribution *is* symmetrical, although it is not likely to depart very far from that condition. On the other hand, if the mean and median have different values, the distribution cannot be symmetrical. Furthermore, the more *skewed*, or lopsided, the distribution is, the greater the discrepancy between these two measures.

The distribution pictured at (A) in Figure 5.2 is said to be skewed to the left, or to be negatively skewed, and that at (B) is skewed to the right, or positively skewed. The nomenclature is easy to remember if you think of a closed fist with the thumb sticking out. If the fist represents the bulk of the scores and the thumb represents the tail of the distribution, the thumb points to the direction in which skewness is said to exist (see Figure 5.2).

In a smooth negatively skewed distribution (shown at A), the mode has the highest score value, and the median falls at a point about two-thirds of the distance between that and the mean. The mean, as might be expected, has been specially affected by the fewer but relatively extreme scores in the tail, and thus has the lowest value. In a positively skewed distribution (B), just the opposite situation obtains.† As a consequence, the relative position of the median and the mean may be used to determine the direction of skewness in the absence of a look at the entire distribution. At a rough descriptive level, the magnitude of the discrepancy between the two measures will afford a clue as to the degree of

---

†Remember that it is the position of the score along the horizontal axis which indicates the value of these measures of central tendency, and not the height of the ordinate erected at these points. The height is simply an indicator of relative frequency of scores at the particular location.

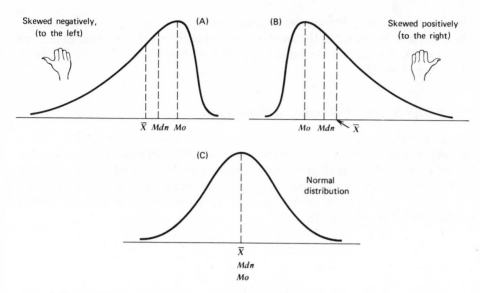

FIGURE 5.2 $\bar{X}$, *Mdn*, and *Mo* in the Normal Distribution and in Skewed Distributions.

departure from a state of symmetry. More sophisticated measures of skewness exist, but we shall forego them in this elementary text.

Information about symmetry may also be obtained from examination of the comparative location of C_{25}, C_{50} (the median), and C_{75}. These three centile points divide the area (and hence the frequency of scores) of the distribution into four equal parts. In the negatively skewed distribution, the distance between C_{25} and C_{50} is greater than that between C_{50} and C_{75}. In the positively skewed distribution, the opposite is true. Figure 5.3 shows these characteristics. In manuals accompanying mental tests, for example, these figures are often available, and a quick inspection will tell us quite a bit about the distribution of performance of the group on which the test was standardized.

We may wish to calculate more than one measure of central tendency for a particular distribution simply because each measure conveys a different kind of

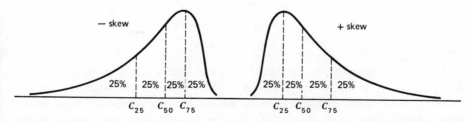

FIGURE 5.3 Relative Position of C_{25}, C_{50}, and C_{75} in Negatively and Positively Skewed Distributions.

information. With a distribution of family income for a particular year, it might be important to know that the income common to the greatest number of families was \$3,500, that half of the families earned less than \$5,500, and that the mean income was \$6,500.

5.12 The Mean of Combined Subgroups

It sometimes occurs that means are known for several subgroups, and it is desired to find the mean of all of the scores when the subgroups are pooled. We could begin anew, sum all of the scores, and divide by the total number of cases. However, the sum of the scores can be expressed as the sum of the subgroup totals, and the sum of all of the cases can be expressed as the sum of the cases in the several subgroups. Thus:

$$\bar{X}_c = \frac{\sum\limits_{\substack{\text{all}\\\text{cases}}} X}{n_{\substack{\text{all}\\\text{cases}}}} = \frac{\sum X + \sum Y + \cdots}{n_X + n_Y + \cdots}$$

where: $\bar{X}_c$ is the mean of the combined distribution

X and Y are the scores from the first and second subgroups

n_X and n_Y are the number of scores in the first and second subgroups

Now since $\bar{X} = \sum X / n_X$, it follows that $\sum X = n_X \bar{X}$. Similarly, $\sum Y = n_Y \bar{Y}$. Substituting these equivalent expressions for $\sum X$ and $\sum Y$ in the numerator of the formula above, we have:

Mean of Combined
Subgroups
$$\bar{X}_c = \frac{n_X \bar{X} + n_Y \bar{Y} + \cdots}{n_X + n_Y + \cdots} \tag{5.4}$$

To illustrate, suppose two groups have been given the same test, and the mean of each group is known:

Given: $\bar{X} = 40$ $\bar{Y} = 30$
               $n_X = 50$ $n_Y = 25$

$$\bar{X}_c = \frac{n_X \bar{X} + n_Y \bar{Y}}{n_X + n_Y}$$

$$= \frac{(50)(40) + (25)(30)}{50 + 25} = 36.7$$

Note that the mean of the combined group is nearer to the mean of the first group (X) than to that of the second (Y). This makes sense, because there are more scores in the first group than in the second. If all subgroups are based on the same number of cases, Formula 5.4 is not needed; the unweighted mean of the subgroup means will give the correct value.

5.13 Properties of the Measures of Central Tendency: Summary

The *mean* is:

1. Responsive to the exact position of each score in the distribution.
2. The balance point of the distribution.
3. The point about which the sum of negative deviations equals that of positive deviations.
4. More sensitive to extreme scores than the median and the mode.
5. An indicator of skewness when used in conjunction with the median.
6. The measure which best reflects the total of the scores.
7. Widely used, implicitly or explicitly, in advanced statistical procedures.
8. Least sensitive to sampling fluctuation under ordinary circumstances.

The *median* is:

1. The score point which divides the upper half of the scores from the lower half.
2. Responsive to the number of scores above or below its value, but not to their exact location.
3. Less affected by extreme scores than the mean.
4. Sometimes a better choice than the mean for strongly skewed distributions.
5. Not as useful as the mean for purposes beyond the level of description.
6. Easier to calculate than the mean in a simple set of ordered scores.
7. Somewhat more subject to sampling fluctuation than the mean.
8. The only relatively stable measure which can be found for open-ended distributions.

The *mode* is:

1. Determined by the most frequently occurring score, or the class interval containing the largest number of cases.
2. More affected by choice of class interval than other measures.
3. Sometimes not a unique point in the distribution.
4. Subject to substantial sampling fluctuation.
5. Useful for rough or preliminary work.
6. Easy to obtain.
7. Of little use beyond the descriptive level.
8. The only measure suited to data of a nominal (categorial) character.

NOTES

In this chapter, we begin a series of mathematical notes. From now on, many chapters will contain such notes. They are not intended to provide a rigorous derivation of the statistical procedures considered, nor does their coverage of the material in the chapter pretend to be complete. They are offered as a means of providing additional insight into statistical relationships to the student who wants to know more about the subject. No knowledge of college mathematics is presumed, but a feeling of reasonable comfort in mathematical expression is helpful. *The student whose path of learning does not follow into these "woods" should understand that the text is designed to stand on its own without these notes:* they are part of an "enriched curriculum."

To use these notes, first turn to Appendix B to learn the few but necessary algebraic relationships which exist when the summation sign appears in an equation. What follows is predicated on the assumption that these principles are understood.

NOTE 5.1 The Mean of Coded Scores (*Ref:* Sections 5.6 and 5.7)

A. Let $\overline{X + C}$ be the mean of a distribution which has been altered by adding a constant, C, to each score. Then:

$$\overline{X + C} = \frac{\sum(X + C)}{n} = \frac{\sum X + nc}{n} = \frac{\sum X}{n} + C = \overline{X} + C$$

If C may take negative values, we have without further proof:

$$\overline{X - C} = \overline{X} - C$$

B. Let $\overline{CX}$ be the mean of a distribution which has been altered by multiplying each score by a constant. Then:

$$\overline{CX} = \frac{\sum CX}{n} = C\frac{\sum X}{n} = C\overline{X}$$

If C may take fractional values, we have without further proof:

$$\overline{\left(\frac{X}{C}\right)} = \frac{\overline{X}}{C}, \text{ or } \frac{1}{C}\overline{X}$$

C. Let $\overline{[(X - C)/K]}$ be the mean of a distribution which has been altered *first* by subtracting a constant, C, from each score, and *then* by dividing these scores by a constant, K (this coding is used in the coded score method of finding a mean). Then:

$$\overline{\left(\frac{X - C}{K}\right)} = \frac{\sum \frac{1}{K}(X - C)}{n} = \frac{1}{K}\left[\frac{\sum(X - C)}{n}\right]$$

$$= \frac{1}{K}\left[\frac{\sum X}{n} - \frac{nC}{n}\right] = \frac{1}{K}[\overline{X} - C]$$

If $\overline{[(X - C)/K]}$ is known (this is $\sum fx'/n$ in Section 5.7), and it is desired to find $\overline{X}$, we must solve the above expression for $\overline{X}$:

$$\frac{1}{K}(\overline{X} - C) = \overline{\left(\frac{X - C}{K}\right)}$$

$$\overline{X} - C = K\overline{\left(\frac{X - C}{K}\right)}$$

$$\overline{X} = C + K\overline{\left(\frac{X - C}{K}\right)}$$

which compares with Formula 5.3 as follows:

$$\bar{X} = A.O. + i\left(\frac{\sum fx'}{n}\right)$$

NOTE 5.2 The Mean as a Balance Point (*Ref*: Section 5.8)

The algebraic way of saying that the mean is the balance point of the distribution is: $\Sigma(X - \bar{X}) = 0$. The proof is:

$$\Sigma(X - \bar{X}) = \Sigma X - n\bar{X}$$

$$= \Sigma X - n\frac{\Sigma X}{n}$$

$$= \Sigma X - \Sigma X$$

$$= 0$$

N.B.: $\bar{X}$ is a constant when summing over all values in the sample, so $\Sigma \bar{X} = n\bar{X}$

Note that no assumption has been made about the shape of the distribution.

PROBLEMS AND EXERCISES

Identify:

measures of central tendency	C_{50}
mode	$\bar{X}$
median	μ_X
arithmetic mean	x'
Y_7	arbitrary origin (*A.O.*)
Σ	i
K, C	positively skewed
Mo	negatively skewed
Mdn	

1. Using the data from Table 3.3A, find (*a*) the mode, (*b*) the median, and (*c*) the mean (use Formula 5.2 to find the mean).

2. Using the data of Table 3.3B, find the mode, the median, and the mean (use Formula 5.2 to find the mean). Compare these values to the answers you found in Problem 1. The two distributions were generated from the same set of raw scores. Are the several measures of central tendency the same for distribution A and distribution B? Explain.

3. Find the median and the mode for Data 3C, Method A.

4. Find the median and the mode for Data 3C, Method B.

5. The mean of a group of scores is 21. What would the mean be if the scores were first altered by each of the following procedures: (*a*) 20 points are added to each score? (*b*) 5 points are subtracted from each score? (*c*) each score is multiplied by 2? (*d*) each score is divided by 3? (*e*) 10 points is added to each score, and these scores are then multiplied by 2?

6. You are required to find the mean of a group of scores. The scores range from .600 to .658. These scores might be doubly coded, in order to simplify calculation. What do you suggest? After coding and finding the mean of the altered scores, what would you do to find the mean of the original scores?

7. Find the mean for Data 3C, Method A, by the coded score method.

8. Find the mean for Data 3C, Method B, by the coded score method.

9. A high school principal is interested in knowing whether the honor roll students, as a group, study more or fewer hours per day than the nonhonor students. What measure of central tendency would most likely reflect his interest? Explain.

10. A researcher finds that his collected data form a skewed distribution. He decides that he is interested in the bulk of the scores and does not want the few very deviant scores to alter extensively his measure of central tendency. Which measure will he use?

11. Which measure of central tendency would you use with the following distribution of scores:

Scores	f
32–up	3
29–31	5
26–28	6
23–25	2
20–22	3

Explain.

12. A social science researcher finds that the mean of his distribution of measures is 120 and the median is 130. What can you say about the shape of the distribution?

13. If $C_{25} = 30$, $C_{50} = 65$, and $C_{75} = 90$, what can you say about the shape of the distribution?

14. A personnel officer gave an aptitude test to three groups of job applicants. The group means were: $\bar{X}_1 = 52$, $\bar{X}_2 = 54$, and $\bar{X}_3 = 60$. The number of applicants in each group were: $n_1 = 10$, $n_2 = 20$, and $n_3 = 25$. What is the mean of all 55 applicants?

15. In finding the mean of combined subgroups, (a) Why must each subgroup mean be multiplied by the number of cases in the subgroup? (b) Under what condition is Formula 5.4 not necessary?

16. Some years ago, a newspaper editor claimed that more than half of American families earned a below-average income. Is there any sense in which his claim could be correct? Explain.

17. If the eventual purpose of the study involves statistical inference, which measure of central tendency is preferable, other things being equal? Explain.

18. The National Association of Manufacturers claims that the "average" wage for workers in the steel industry is a figure higher than that stated by the steel-workers union. Is it possible that both could be right? Explain.

19. (*Based on Notes*) By direct proof, show (a) that $\overline{X - C} = \bar{X} - C$, and (b) that $\overline{(X/C)} = \bar{X}/C$.

20. (*Based on Notes*) Show that $\overline{(KX + C)} = K\bar{X} + C$.

6
Variability

6.1 Introduction

Measures of variability express quantitatively the extent to which the scores in a set scatter about or cluster together. Whereas a measure of central tendency is a summary description of the level of performance of a group, a measure of variability is a summary description of the spread of performance.

Information about variability is often at least as important as that about level. We would not be happy with a weight scale which gives our weight correctly *on the average*, but on any given occasion might read five pounds lighter or heavier than it should. A manufacturer is interested in the consistency of the quality of his product as well as the level of quality. The satisfaction of his customers who occasionally receive a far better product than they expected will not balance the ire of those who find that it falls apart before they can get good use out of it. A poll-taker must not only estimate the percent of voters who favor a particular issue, but he must know the amount of variation attributable to sampling fluctuation, the "margin of error" inherent in such estimates.

When measures of central tendency were first discussed (Section 5.1), it was observed that there were three situations in which such measures were helpful:

1. comparison with a known standard
2. establishment of a standard previously unknown, and
3. comparison of two or more sets of scores obtained under different conditions.

The same is true for measures of variability. Comparison with a known standard may be illustrated by returning to the school principal who found the mean IQ of the students in his school to be 108, a figure substantially above average. Suppose that he also found that the variation in IQ of his students was only two-thirds of the amount that would characterize the general population. His students are not only bright, but they are substantially more homogeneous with regard to intelligence than might be expected. Since they will be more alike than usual in their readiness to take up certain aspects of study, some modification in teaching practice may be in order.

The second situation concerns the establishment of a standard. It is typical of mental tests that in their development there are no sound *a priori* grounds on which to conclude what the level and spread of performance should be. These characteristics depend heavily on such factors as the difficulty of the test items, the number of items, the time allotted for the test, and many other characteristics. Consequently, to develop a scale of measurement, it is necessary to give the test to a large number of persons to find out what performance will be. Measures of variability, as well as measures of central tendency, are needed to describe that performance.

The third situation is that of comparison of two groups. Consider an experiment designed to compare the effectiveness of two techniques of learning.

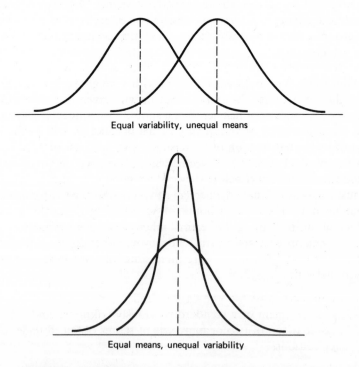

Equal variability, unequal means

Equal means, unequal variability

FIGURE 6.1 Different Conditions of Central Tendency and Variability.

Of course, we would want to know if the mean amount learned was different. In addition, it would be important to know if variability of performance was different under the two conditions. Even if the average amount learned was the same, it would be meaningful if it were found that the range of performance under one method was considerably greater than under the other method. The second picture in Figure 6.1 shows how the distributions might look if this situation existed.

Measures of variability are particularly important in statistical inference. In fact, measurement of variability is the keystone of this statistical structure. How much fluctuation will occur in random sampling? This question is fundamental to every problem in statistical inference; it is a question about variability.

We have said something about what measures of variability do; it is time to say what they do *not* do. A measure of variability does not specify how far a *particular* score diverges from the center of the group. It is a summary figure which describes the spread of the entire set of scores. A measure of variability does not provide information about the level of performance, nor does it give a clue as to the shape of the distribution. Figure 6.1 shows that it is possible to have two distributions which have equal means but unequal variability, or which have equal variability but unequal means.

We shall consider five measures of variability: *range, semiinterquartile range, average deviation, variance, and standard deviation.* Development will follow the same pattern used in the last chapter.

6.2 The Range

We met the *range* earlier, in constructing a frequency distribution. It is the minimum distance required to encompass all scores in the distribution. Its calculation from raw scores was discussed in Section 3.5, and will not be repeated here. Among grouped measurements, it is the distance between the lower exact limit of the bottom class interval and the upper exact limit of the top class interval. Like all other measures of variability, the range is a *distance*, and not, like measures of central tendency, a location. For example, all three of these simple distributions have the same range (21 score points):

$$3, 5, 5, 8, 13, 14, 18, 23$$
$$37, 42, 48, 53, 57$$
$$131, 140, 144, 147, 150, 151$$

All measures of variability *and* all measures of central tendency have one property in common: they are always expressed in a particular kind of measuring unit (e.g., feet, pounds, score points). As a consequence, it is not permissible to compare two distributions in terms of a measure of this type (e.g., the mean, or the range) unless it is certain that the same unit of measurement has been used in both. We would not be tempted to compare directly the means or ranges of two distributions when one set of measurements was in feet and the other in inches, but it is perhaps not so obvious that means (or ranges) of scores from two different mental tests may not be directly compared. The fact that both tests have the same title (e.g., "Verbal Aptitude," or "Spatial Visualization") does not make their scores comparable. The matter discussed in the fourth paragraph of Section 6.1 is pertinent to this understanding.

6.3 The Semiinterquartile Range

The *semiinterquartile range*, symbolized by the letter Q, is defined as one-half of the *distance* between the first and third quartile points, or,

Semiinterquartile Range $$Q = \frac{Q_3 - Q_1}{2} \qquad (6.1a)$$

The quartile points are the three score points which divide the distribution into four parts, each containing an equal number of cases. These points, symbolized by Q_1, Q_2, and Q_3, are therefore our old friends, C_{25}, C_{50}, and C_{75}, respectively. Formula 6.1a may therefore be rephrased in familiar terms:

$$Q = \frac{C_{75} - C_{25}}{2} \qquad (6.1b)$$

Because computation of centile points has been covered in Section 3.10 it will not be repeated here.

Another way of looking at the semiinterquartile range may help to clarify its meaning. It may be thought of as the mean distance between the median and the two outer quartile points. This relationship may be expressed in the following equation:

$$Q = \frac{(C_{75} - C_{50}) + (C_{50} - C_{25})}{2}$$

Inspection of this formula shows that it can be reduced to Formula 6.1b because the positive and negative C_{50}'s cancel. Although Q in no way *depends* on C_{50}, it can still be thought of as the average distance of Q_1 and Q_3 from this point. In Figure 6.2, we see an asymmetrical distribution. Q is one-half of the 10-point distance between Q_1 and Q_3, or 5 points. But note that the distance between Q_1 and Q_2 is 4 points, the distance between Q_3 and Q_2 is 6 points, and that the mean of these two distances is 5 points, the value of Q.

6.4 Deviational Measures: The Average Deviation

Another measure of variability is the *average deviation*, or mean deviation, as it is sometimes called. The average deviation is the mean of the distances between each score and the mean of the set of scores.

Symbolically, the deviation of a score from the mean is: $(X - \overline{X})$, or

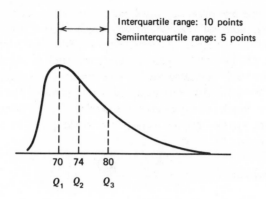

Interquartile range: 10 points
Semiinterquartile range: 5 points

70 74   80

Q_1 Q_2 Q_3

FIGURE 6.2 The Semiinterquartile Range.

$(X - \mu_X)$, depending on whether the setting is in a sample or in a population. Because the deviation score occurs frequently in statistical work, another symbol is commonly used for it: the lower case form of whatever letter is used to represent raw scores. Thus:

$$x = (X - \bar{X})$$
$$y = (Y - \bar{Y})$$

In any case, the meaning of x or y is that it specifies the location of a score by indicating how many score points it lies above or below the mean of the distribution. If the mean of a distribution is 100, then the raw scores of 85 and 110 can be expressed as deviation scores of -15 and $+10$, respectively. Translating the definition of the average deviation into symbolic form, we have:

$$Average\ Deviation \quad A.D. = \frac{\sum|X - \bar{X}|}{n} \quad or \quad A.D. = \frac{\sum|x|}{n} \tag{6.2}$$

where the parallel bars remind us to disregard the sign of the deviation scores in finding their sum.

On first acquaintance, the average deviation appears to be an attractive measure of variation. However, it has proved to have a mathematical intractability which severely limits its use. It is, for example, of no use in statistical inference. You may run across its use in older works, but it has seldom appeared in research literature in the past 30 years. It is mentioned here because it serves as an introduction to other, and superior, deviational measures, and because of its historical interest. We will not consider it further.

6.5 Deviational Measures: The Variance

The average deviation is a measure of the distance between each score and the mean. As a measure of distance, it is necessary to disregard the positive and negative signs which are normally attached to deviation scores. If they had not been ignored, the sum of the deviation scores would always be zero (see Section 5.8), and no measure of variability would result. Another strategem which eliminates positive and negative signs (and thus yields a measure of distance) is to square each deviation score. The *variance* is a measure which takes this tack. It can be defined as the mean of the squares of the deviation scores. σ^2 (the lower case Greek letter *sigma*) is the symbol for the variance of a population, and S^2 is the symbol for the variance of a sample. The defining formulas for the variance are as follows:

Variance of a Population $\qquad \sigma_X{}^2 = \dfrac{\sum(X - \mu_X)^2}{N} \quad$ or $\quad \dfrac{\sum x^2}{N}$ $\qquad\qquad$ (6.3a)

Variance of a Sample $\qquad S_X{}^2 = \dfrac{\sum(X - \bar{X})^2}{n} \quad$ or $\quad \dfrac{\sum x^2}{n}$ $\qquad\qquad$ (6.3b)†

The variance is a most important measure which finds its greatest use in inferential statistics. At the descriptive level, it has a fatal flaw: its calculated value is expressed in terms of *squared* units of measurement. Consequently, it is little used in descriptive statistics, and therefore examination of its properties will not engage us at present. This defect, however, is easily remedied. By taking the square root of the variance, we return to a measure expressed in the original units of measurement. This solution yields the measure next to be discussed.

6.6 Deviational Measures: The Standard Deviation

The most important and widely used measure of variability is the *standard deviation*.‡ It is the square root of the variance, and therefore the defining formulas are:

Standard Deviation of a Population $\qquad \sigma_X = \sqrt{\dfrac{\sum x^2}{N}}$ $\qquad\qquad$ (6.4a)

Standard Deviation of a Sample $\qquad S_X = \sqrt{\dfrac{\sum x^2}{n}}$ $\qquad\qquad$ (6.4b)

Calculation of the standard deviation by Formula 6.4b is illustrated in Table 6.1.

---

†Although there is uniformity in defining the variance of a population, some statisticians prefer to define the variance of a sample as $\sum x^2/(n - 1)$. Since some other texts follow this usage, you should know about it. This difference in view derives from the problem of estimating the variance of a population when we have at hand only the data from a sample. Under these circumstances, dividing the sum of the squares of the deviation scores by $(n - 1)$ gives a better estimate than that offered by Formula 6.3b. We shall treat this problem of estimation as a separate issue (see Sections 14.4 and 15.8).

‡Another name for the standard deviation is *root mean square deviation*. It is seldom used now, but may be encountered in the older literature.

TABLE 6.1 Calculation of the Standard Deviation: Deviation Score Method.

X	$(X - \overline{X})$	x	x^2	Steps
32	32–50.6	−18.6	345.96	1. Record each score
71	71–50.6	+20.4	416.16	2. Find $\overline{X}$
64	64–50.6	+13.4	179.56	3. Obtain x by sub-
50	50–50.6	−.6	.36	tracting $\overline{X}$ from each
48	48–50.6	−2.6	6.76	value of X
63	63–50.6	+12.4	153.76	4. Square each x
38	38–50.6	−12.6	158.76	5. Sum the values of x^2
41	41–50.6	−9.6	92.16	6. Enter Σx^2 and n in
47	47–50.6	−3.6	12.96	Formula 6.4b and
52	52–50.6	+1.4	1.96	simplify
$\Sigma X = 506$			$\Sigma x^2 = 1368.40$	

$$\overline{X} = \frac{506}{10} = 50.6 \qquad S_x = \sqrt{\frac{\Sigma x^2}{n}} = \sqrt{\frac{1368.40}{10}} = \sqrt{136.84} = 11.7$$

You are invited to follow the procedure carefully, because it gives important insight into what the standard deviation is up to. However, from the standpoint of ease of calculation, this method leaves much to be desired. In general, the raw score method (described in Section 6.7, and the coded score method described in Section 6.9) will be better choices for practical computation. When you have studied these methods, compare the several procedures and make your own judgment.

6.7 Calculation of the Standard Deviation: Raw Score Method

In calculating the standard deviation by the deviation score formula, the main remediable nuisance is that of calculating Σx^2 directly from deviation scores. Without the bother of changing raw scores to deviation scores, this quantity can be found by the equation:†

Raw Score Equivalent of Σx^2 $\qquad \sum x^2 = \sum X^2 - \frac{(\sum X)^2}{n}$ $\qquad\qquad$ (6.5)

Derivation of this formula is given in Note 6.1. The sum of the squares of the deviation scores may be calculated by Formula 6.5, and the resulting value substituted in Formula 6.4b. This method of calculation, which we shall call Method I, is illustrated for a set of ten scores in Table 6.2 (the data are from

†For the remainder of the chapter, only formulas appropriate to samples will be presented; modification appropriate to a population should be readily apparent.

Table 6.1). It is possible to combine Formula 6.4*b* and Formula 6.5 into a single formula:

Raw Score Formula for
the Standard Deviation $S_X = \dfrac{1}{n} \sqrt{n\sum X^2 - (\sum X)^2}$ (6.6)

The calculation using this formula, Method II, is illustrated in Table 6.2.
The following notes may be helpful:

1. The raw score method is practical for hand calculation only when scores are of modest size and there are relatively few of them. When these con-

TABLE 6.2 Calculation of the Standard Deviation: Raw Score Method.

X	X^2	Steps (for calculation by hand)
32	1,024	1. Record each score
71	5,041	2. Record the square of each
64	4,096	score
50	2,500	3. Obtain $\sum X$ and $\sum X^2$
48	2,304	4. Proceed according to Method I
63	3,969	or Method II
38	1,444	
41	1,681	
47	2,209	
52	2,704	
$\sum X = 506$	$\sum X^2 = 26{,}972$	

Calculation: Method I

$$\sum x^2 = \sum X^2 - \frac{(\sum X)^2}{n}$$

$$= 26972 - \frac{(506)^2}{10}$$

$$= 1368.4$$

$$S_X = \sqrt{\frac{\sum x^2}{n}}$$

$$= \sqrt{\frac{1368.4}{10}}$$

$$= \sqrt{136.84}$$

$$= 11.7$$

Calculation: Method II

$$S_X = \frac{1}{n}\sqrt{n\sum X^2 - (\sum X)^2}$$

$$= \frac{1}{10}\sqrt{(10)(26972) - (506)^2}$$

$$= \frac{1}{10}\sqrt{13684}$$

$$= 11.7$$

ditions are not met, use of a desk calculator makes the job very much easier. Other alternatives for easing calculation appear in Sections 6.8 and 6.9.

2. Squares and square roots of numbers are given in the appendix (Table A). Instructions for use of this table appear in Sections A.11 and A.12 of Appendix A.
3. Distinguish carefully between $(\Sigma X)^2$ and ΣX^2. To find the former, we must sum the scores and then square the sum. To find the latter, we must square the scores first, and then sum these squares. The result is *not* the same.
4. In using Method I, the value of Σx^2 *must* be a positive number, no matter what the raw score values are. A negative value for Σx^2 is a sure sign of an error in calculation. Similarly, in Method II, the quantity under the square root sign *must* reduce to a positive number.

6.8 Coded Scores and Measures of Variability

In Section 5.6, we found that coding of scores had a simple and predictable effect on measures of central tendency. What is the effect of coding on measures of variability?

Consider the following set of scores: 12, 13, 15. The distance between the first and second score is one point, and between the second and third scores, two points. If we add 10 points to each score, they become 22, 23, and 25. The inter-score distances, however, remain the same. If we had subtracted 5 points from each score, they would become 7, 8, and 10. Again, the interscore distances remain the same. Since measures of variability are indices of interscore distance, apparently these are not affected by either of these modifications. *Adding a constant to each score in the distribution, or subtracting a constant from each score does not affect any of the measures of variability described in this chapter.*

This property can be quite useful. If we have 40 raw scores which range in value from 503 to 535, the method of calculation of the standard deviation described in the previous section would be somewhat cumbersome. If we subtract 500 from each score, the resultant values range from 3 to 35. The standard deviation of these altered scores is easier to compute, and the value obtained will be exactly the same as though the calculation had been performed on the original scores.

Scores may also be coded by multiplying each score by a constant, or by dividing each score by a constant. If scores of 12, 13, and 15 are multiplied by 2, they become 24, 26, and 30. In their original form, the interscore distances are one and two points, respectively. In their altered form, they are doubled, becoming two and four points. If the original scores are multiplied by 10, the scores become 120, 130, and 150, and the interscore distances are now 10 points and 20 points. Apparently, when each of a set of scores is multiplied by a constant, the interscore distances become multiplied by the same constant. If the original set of scores were altered by dividing each score by 10, the scores would be 1.2, 1.3, and 1.5.

Interscore distances would now be .1 and .2, one-tenth of their original values. *When scores are multiplied or divided by a constant, the resultant measure of variability is also multiplied or divided by that same constant.* This also applies to all measures of variability discussed in this chapter except the variance.† Proof of the propositions concerning coding by adding, subtracting, multiplying, or dividing by a constant is given in Note 6.2 at the end of the chapter.

These properties may also be used to simplify calculation of measures of variability. If we have a series of scores such as:

$$3.42, \ 4.17, \ 5.56, \ \ldots$$

it is convenient to eliminate the decimal by multiplying each score by 100, find the standard deviation, and divide that value by 100 to obtain the standard deviation of the original scores.

Two-stage coding is also possible. Scores may be coded in one way, and then these altered scores may be coded again (not necessarily in the same way). As in the calculation of the mean, the standard deviation of doubly coded scores can be translated to the standard deviation of the original scores by reversing the process of coding. For example, suppose the original scores are coded by subtracting 100 points from each score, then each of these scores is divided by 10, and the standard deviation of the resulting scores is calculated. The standard deviation of the original scores may be found by multiplying the standard deviation of the altered scores by 10, since the process of division made the standard deviation one-tenth of its original size. Because subtracting 100 points had no effect on the standard deviation, no further correction is needed. This type of double coding is used in the method of calculation next to be described. Proof for the specific application of coding used in this method is given in Note 6.2.

6.9 Calculation of the Standard Deviation: Coded Score Method

If scores are sufficiently numerous and no desk calculator is available, the process of hand calculation may be considerably simplified first by grouping the scores and then by coding the midpoints of the class intervals thus obtained. The process is quite parallel to the coded score method for finding the mean. Indeed, *the initial stages are the same.* We shall first consider the mechanics of this method, and then return to examine the underpinnings.

The formula for finding the standard deviation by the coded score method is:

Coded Score Formula for $S_X = \dfrac{i}{n} \sqrt{n \sum fx'^2 - \left(\sum fx' \right)^2}$ (6.7)
the Standard Deviation

The process of computation is illustrated in Table 6.3. The first four columns are

---

†Variance is expressed in terms of squared units of measurement. Consequently, if each score is multiplied or divided by a constant, C, the variance is multiplied or divided by C^2.

TABLE 6.3 Calculation of the Mean and Standard Deviation by the Coded Score Method (Data from Table 5.2).

Scores	f	x'	fx'	fx'^2
90–94	2	+5	+10	50
85–89	4	+4	+16	64
80–84	9	+3	+27	81
75–79	7	+2	+14	28
70–74	10	+1	+10	10
65–69	12	0	+77 / −50	
60–64	9	−1	−9	9
55–59	5	−2	−10	20
50–54	3	−3	−9	27
45–49	3	−4	−12	48
40–44	2	−5	−10	50
	$n = 66$		$\Sigma fx' = +27$	$\Sigma fx'^2 = 387$

$$\bar{X} = A.O. + \left(\frac{\Sigma fx'}{n}\right)i \qquad S_X = \frac{i}{n}\sqrt{n\Sigma fx'^2 - (\Sigma fx')^2}$$

$$= 67.0 + \left(\frac{+27}{66}\right)5 \qquad = \frac{5}{66}\sqrt{(66)(387) - (27)^2} = \frac{5}{66}\sqrt{24813}$$

$$= 69.0 \qquad\qquad\qquad = 11.9$$

constructed in the same way as for coded score calculation of the mean, a process described in Section 5.7 (see especially Table 5.4). This enables us to find $\Sigma fx'$, needed for calculation of both the mean and the standard deviation. The fifth column, headed fx'^2, is new. Since fx'^2 can be thought of as the product of x' and fx', its value for a given row can be found by multiplying the values appearing in the two columns immediately preceding.† For the class interval 85–89, for example, $fx'^2 = 64$ may be obtained as the product of $+4$ and $+16$. Summing the entries in the fx'^2 column yields $\Sigma fx'^2$ and the appropriate values may then be entered in Formula 6.7, as illustrated. In practice, when we want the standard deviation, we almost always also want the mean, so its calculation has been included in Table 6.3 for convenient reference.

The nature of the coding process was discussed in Section 5.7. For the data of Table 6.3, the values of x' are obtained (in *principle*) by first subtracting 67, the midpoint of the interval 65–69, from each interval midpoint, and then dividing

†In the expression fx'^2, it is x' which is to be squared, *not the whole expression*. Thus, $fx'^2 = (x')(fx')$.

the resulting figures by 5, the width of the class interval. If the standard deviation of these doubly coded scores is then computed, coding must be reversed in order to recover the standard deviation of the original scores. Since the second coding was accomplished by dividing by i, the standard deviation of the doubly coded scores must be multiplied by that value. The initial coding involved subtraction of a constant from each midpoint, but this operation has no effect on the standard deviation. Consequently, no further correction is needed. If Formula 6.7 (for use with coded scores) is compared with Formula 6.6 (for use with raw scores), the only difference in *form* is that i appears in the former, but not in the latter.†
In short, Formula 6.7 asks us to find the standard deviation of the doubly coded scores (the x' values) and then to multiply that value by i to recover the standard deviation of the original scores.

6.10 Properties of the Standard Deviation

The range and semiinterquartile range are measures which yield easily to intuitive grasp. It is ironic that the standard deviation is more important in statistical work than the others and less easy to understand. Rather than laboring over the problem of grasping its nature intuitively, we shall try to develop a picture of its functional properties.

The standard deviation, like the mean, is responsive to the exact position of every score in the distribution. If a score is shifted to a position more deviant from the mean, the standard deviation will be larger than before. If the shift is to a position closer to the mean, the magnitude of the standard deviation is reduced. Consequently, we may expect that the standard deviation is more sensitive to the exact condition of the distribution than measures which do not share this property (the range and semiinterquartile range do not).

The standard deviation is more sensitive than the semiinterquartile range to the presence or absence of scores which lie at the extremes of the distribution (the range is, of course, defined by the two outlying scores). Consider the following seven scores: 2, 5, 7, 8, 9, 11, 14. Table 6.4 shows S, Q, and the range for this set of scores. Now a new (and extreme) score is incorporated in the set: 2, 5, 7, 8, 9, 11, 14, *24*. Table 6.4 shows the same measures of variability calculated after making this change. The figures showing the percent increase in magnitude of each measure of variability upon addition of the new score are the most important ones to study. Note that the standard deviation is affected more than the semiinterquartile range. The proportionate change would differ from distribution to distribution, but it is characteristic that the standard deviation is more profoundly affected by extreme scores than Q. Because of this characteristic sensitivity, *the standard deviation may not be the best choice among measures of variability when the distribution contains a few very extreme scores*

†The symbol f is present in Formula 6.7 but not in Formula 6.6. On comparing *form* of the two equations, however, it should be ignored; see discussion of Formula 5.2 in Section 5.5.

TABLE 6.4 Effect on Measures of Variability of Adding an Extreme Score to a Distribution.

	S_X	Q	Range
Original distribution ($n = 7$)	3.63	2.75	13.00
Distribution with extreme score added ($n = 8$)	6.29	3.25	23.00
Percent increase due to added score	73	18	77

or when the distribution is badly skewed. For example, if we wished to compare the variability of two distributions where one of them contained several extreme scores and the other did not, the difference in extreme scores would tend to exert an influence on the magnitude of the standard deviation which is disproportionate to their relative number. Of course, if n is quite large, and the extreme scores are very few in number, it will make little difference.

The sensitivity of the standard deviation to scores in extreme positions shows itself in another way. If a score which is far from the mean is changed by a few points, the standard deviation will respond somewhat more strongly than to a similar change imposed on a score closer to the mean. The fundamental reason is that the standard deviation is responsive to the square of a deviation, and squares of small deviations differ less from one another than squares of large ones. For example, if a deviation score is changed from $+2$ to $+4$, the difference in the *squares* of these numbers is 12, whereas if a deviation score is changed from $+10$ to $+12$, the difference in squares of these numbers is 44. This is not the whole story, since the change in location would also affect the mean slightly. Nevertheless, the influence under discussion is the predominant one.

When the deviations are calculated from the mean, the sum of squares of these values is *smaller* than if they had been taken about any other point. Putting it another way,

$$\Sigma(X - A)^2 \quad \textit{is a minimum when:} \quad A = \overline{X}$$

(or when: $A = \mu_X$ in the case of a population)

Proof of this proposition appears in Note 6.3. This property may seem to be an oddity which only a mathematician could love. In fact it is an extremely important notion, and one which reappears frequently in further study of statistics. For the moment, note that for a given number of scores, the magnitude of the standard deviation (and the variance) depends wholly on the magnitude of the sum of the squares of the deviation scores, or $\Sigma(X - \overline{X})^2$. Consequently, we may say that these measures, as defined, take on a minimum value. In other words, if we should attempt to compute the standard deviation, but take our deviations from some point which is *not* the mean, we would emerge with a value larger than the standard deviation. Incidentally, this gives us another way to define the mean.

It is the point about which the sum of squares of the deviation scores is a minimum.

Table 6.5 illustrates this property. On the left, the sum of the squares of the deviation scores has been calculated from deviations about the mean ($\overline{X} = 5$) of the four scores. On the right, deviations have been calculated about a score of 6. Note that the sum of the squares is smaller when taken about their mean.

TABLE 6.5 Comparison of Σx^2 when Deviations Are Taken from the Mean ($\overline{X} = 5$), and when They Are Taken from Another Point ($X = 6$).

Scores	x	x^2	Scores	x''	x''^2
8	$+3$	9	8	$+2$	4
6	$+1$	1	6	0	0
4	-1	1	4	-2	4
2	-3	9	2	-4	16
		$\Sigma x^2 = 20$			$\Sigma x''^2 = 24$
(deviations about $\overline{X} = 5$)			(deviations about $X = 6$)		

One of the most important points favoring the standard deviation is its resistance to sampling fluctuation. In repeated random samples drawn from the same population, the numerical value of the standard deviation tends to jump about less than would that of other measures computed on the same samples. If our concern is in any way associated with inferring variation in a population from knowledge of variation in a sample, this property is clearly of worth.

When we come to study further methods of statistical analysis, the surpassing importance of the standard deviation will be better understood. *The standard deviation appears explicitly or lies embedded in many procedures of both descriptive statistics and inferential statistics.* Indeed, in inferential statistics, the range and semiinterquartile range are of very little use.

In many ways, the properties of the standard deviation are related to those of the mean. In usefulness for further statistical work, stability in the face of sampling fluctuation, responsiveness to location of each score, and sensitivity to extreme scores, the position of the standard deviation relative to other measures of variability has much in common with that of the mean among measures of central tendency.

6.11 Properties of the Semiinterquartile Range

Like the average deviation, the semiinterquartile range has an approachable intuitive meaning. It is half the distance between C_{25} and C_{75}, or the mean distance between the median and C_{25} and C_{75}. To look at it another way, twice the semiinterquartile range is the distance which contains the central 50% of the scores.

The semiinterquartile range is closely related to the median, since both are defined in terms of centile points of the distribution. The median is responsive to the *number* of scores lying below it rather than to their exact position, and C_{25} and C_{75} are points defined in a similar way. We may therefore expect the median and the semiinterquartile range to have properties in common. For example, C_{75} is sensitive only to the number of scores which lie above it. Consequently, all scores above C_{75} are of equal importance in determination of the semiinterquartile range, and a very extreme score counts no more and no less than a moderately extreme one in its determination. *The semiinterquartile range will therefore be less sensitive to the presence of a few very extreme scores than the standard deviation.* If a distribution is badly skewed or if it contains a few very extreme scores, the semiinterquartile range will respond to the presence of such scores, but will not give them undue weight.

If the distribution is open-ended (see Section 5.9), it is not possible to calculate the standard deviation or the range without additional (and probably hazardous) assumptions. *With open-ended distributions, the semiinterquartile range may be the only measure which is reasonable to compute.* Unless more than a quarter of the scores lie in the indeterminate end category, the semiinterquartile range is computable in straightforward fashion.

Sampling stability of the semiinterquartile range is good, although not up to that of the standard deviation. Ease of computation is good if the scores are ordered or if they are grouped in class intervals. When either of these two conditions prevail, computation is likely to be faster than for the standard deviation.

The usefulness of the semiinterquartile range is essentially limited to the realm of descriptive statistics. It should be given particular consideration when its special properties can be put to good use and when the standard deviation would be adversely affected.

6.12 Properties of the Range

The range is a rough-and-ready measure of variability. In most situations, including those involving samples drawn from a normal distribution, the range *varies more with sampling fluctuation than other measures do.* Only the two outermost scores of a distribution affect its value; the remainder could lie anywhere between them. *It is thus not very sensitive to the total condition of the distribution.* In addition, *a single errant score is likely to have a more substantial effect on the range than on the standard deviation*, which we have seen is particularly sensitive to conditions at the extremes of a distribution. Like other measures, with the exception of the standard deviation, *it is of little use beyond the descriptive level.* In many types of distributions, including the important normal distribution, *the range is dependent on sample size, being greater when sample size is larger.*

On the other hand, *the range is easier to compute than the others and its meaning is direct. It is therefore ideal for preliminary work, or in other circumstances where precision is not an important requirement.* Sometimes, of course, it provides precisely the information we need. We have seen it in this role in the course of transferring raw scores into grouped data.

6.13 Measures of Variability and the Normal Distribution

Since the measures of variability considered in this chapter are defined in different ways, we would expect them to yield different values if all were calculated for the same distribution. Their relative magnitudes cannot be exactly specified in terms of a generalization true for all distributions, because special characteristics of some distributions (e.g., the relative frequency of extreme scores) have a different effect on the different measures. The normal distribution, however, is so frequently useful that properties of these measures in that distribution ought to be given attention.

In the ideal normal distribution, the interval:

$\mu \pm 1\sigma$ contains about 68% of the scores
$\mu \pm 2\sigma$ contains about 95% of the scores
$\mu \pm 3\sigma$ contains about 99.7% of the scores

These relationships are pictured in Figure 6.3. Of course, in any sample drawn from a normal distribution there will be a certain degree of irregularity and these statements will be only approximately true.

Figure 6.3 shows the interval $\mu \pm 1Q$ which contains 50% of the scores in the normal distribution. The illustration also shows that the numerical value of Q is smaller than that of σ. In the ideal normal distribution, $Q = .6745\sigma$.

Figure 6.3 also shows that the more extreme the score the greater the rarity of its occurrence in the normal distribution. Consequently, when a sample of limited size is drawn at random from a large number of scores which are normally distributed, very extreme scores may not be encountered. Roughly, the expected range of scores in a given sample approximates:

$3S$ when $n = 10$
$4S$ when $n = 30$
$5S$ when $n = 100$
$6S$ when $n = 500$

These relationships may be used as a rough check on the accuracy of computation of the standard deviation. Remember that they are only expectations, and that some departure due to sample variation is normal.

6.14 Variability of Combined Distributions

In the last chapter (Section 5.12), we considered the problem of finding the mean of a combined distribution when the means of the subgroups composing it are

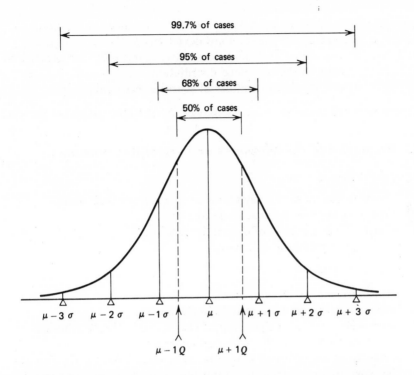

FIGURE 6.3 Relative Frequency of Cases Contained within Certain Limits in the Normal Distribution.

known. You will recall that the solution is to weight each of the several subgroup means by the number of cases in each subgroup, and to divide that weighted sum by the total number of cases. One might think that the standard deviation of a combined distribution could be obtained from the weighted mean of the subgroup standard deviations, but this will not work.

In concept, the standard deviation is computed in terms of the deviations of each score from the mean of those scores. For a combined distribution, the relevant mean is $\bar{X}_c$, the mean of the combined distribution. But the subgroup standard deviations have been computed (in effect) in terms of deviations from their own means. An approach is needed which takes into account the discrepancies between $\bar{X}_c$ and each of the subgroup means. The formula below is the appropriate one:

Standard Deviation of a Combined Distribution

$$S_c = \sqrt{\frac{(n_X S_X{}^2 + n_Y S_Y{}^2 + \cdots) + (n_X d_X{}^2 + n_Y d_Y{}^2 + \cdots)}{n_X + n_Y + \cdots}} \qquad (6.8)$$

where: S_c is the standard deviation of the combined distribution
S_X and S_Y are the standard deviations of the subgroups
d_X and d_Y are the differences between the subgroup means and the
mean of the combined distribution, e.g., $d_X = \overline{X} - \overline{X}_c$, etc.
n_X and n_Y are the number of scores in each subgroup

$\overline{X}_c$, required for calculation of the d's, may be found by the method of Section 5.12.

6.15 Properties of the Measures of Variability: Summary

The *variance* is:

1. The mean square of the deviations of scores from their mean.
2. A quantity expressed in squared score units.
3. Of little use at the level of descriptive statistics.
4. Important in statistical inference.

The *standard deviation* is:

1. The square root of the variance.
2. Defined in terms of deviations from the mean.
3. Responsive to the exact position of each score in the distribution.
4. Very good in its resistance to sampling variation.
5. Widely used, implicitly or explicitly, in advanced statistical procedures.
6. The most important measure at the descriptive level, and of great utility in inferential statistics.
7. More sensitive to extreme scores than the semiinterquartile range.
8. Smaller than if the same function were found, but with deviations taken about some point other than the mean.

The *semiinterquartile range* is:

1. The mean distance between the median and the first and third quartile points.
2. Related to the median in its constitution and properties.
3. Responsive to the number of scores lying above or below the outer quartile points, but not to their exact location.
4. Less sensitive to extreme scores than the standard deviation.
5. Particularly useful with open-ended distributions.
6. Of little use beyond the descriptive level.
7. Not as resistant to sampling fluctuation as the standard deviation, but substantially better than the range in most situations.
8. Easy to compute when scores are ordered or grouped.

The *range* is:

1. The distance spanned by the top and bottom scores of the distribution.
2. Unresponsive to the location of intermediate scores.

3. Dependent, in part, on sample size.
4. Generally poor in resistance to sampling fluctuation.
5. Of little use beyond the descriptive level.
6. Useful for rough or preliminary work.
7. Easy to obtain.

NOTES

NOTE 6.1 The Raw Score Equivalent of Σx^2 (*Ref:* Section 6.7)

$$\sum x^2 = \sum (X - \bar{X})^2$$
$$= \sum (X^2 - 2X\bar{X} + \bar{X}^2)$$
$$= \sum X^2 - 2\bar{X}\sum X + n\bar{X}^2$$
$$= \sum X^2 - 2\left(\frac{\sum X}{n}\right)(\sum X) + n\left(\frac{\sum X}{n}\right)^2$$
$$= \sum X^2 - 2\frac{(\sum X)^2}{n} + \frac{(\sum X)^2}{n}$$
$$= \sum X^2 - \frac{(\sum X)^2}{n}$$

NOTE 6.2 The Standard Deviation of Coded Scores (*Ref:* Sections 6.8 and 6.9)

A. Let $S_{(x+c)}$ be the standard deviation of a distribution which has been altered by adding a constant, C, to each score. Then:

$$S_{(x+c)}{}^2 = \frac{\sum [(X + C) - \overline{(X + C)}]^2}{n}$$

From Note 5.1A, $\overline{(X + C)} = \bar{X} + C$, and

$$S_{(x+c)}{}^2 = \frac{\sum [X + C - \bar{X} - C]^2}{n}$$
$$= \frac{\sum [X - \bar{X}]^2}{n}$$
$$= S_X{}^2 \therefore S_{(x+c)} = S_X†$$

If C may take negative values, we have without further proof:

$$S_{(x-c)}{}^2 = S_X{}^2 \quad \text{and} \quad S_{(x-c)} = S_X$$

B. Let S_{CX} be the standard deviation of a distribution which has been altered by multiplying each score by a constant. Then:

$$S_{CX}{}^2 = \frac{\sum (CX - \overline{CX})^2}{n}$$

$† \therefore$ = therefore.

From Note 5.1B, $\overline{CX} = C\overline{X}$, and

$$S_{CX}^2 = \frac{\sum(CX - C\overline{X})^2}{n}$$

$$= C^2 \frac{\sum(X - \overline{X})^2}{n}$$

$$= C^2 S_X^2 \therefore S_{CX} = CS_X$$

If C may take fractional values, we have without further proof:

$$S_{(X/C)}^2 = \frac{1}{C^2} S_X^2 \quad \text{and} \quad S_{(X/C)} = \frac{1}{C} S_X$$

C. Let $S_{[(X-C)/K]}$ be the standard deviation of a distribution in which scores have been coded first by subtracting a constant, C, from each, and then by dividing these values by a constant, K. Then:

$$S_{[(X-C)/K]}^2 = \frac{\sum\left[\frac{X - C}{K} - \left(\overline{\frac{X - C}{K}}\right)\right]^2}{n}$$

From Note 5.1C

$$\left(\overline{\frac{X - C}{K}}\right) = \frac{1}{K}(\overline{X} - C)$$

and

$$S_{[(X-C)/K]}^2 = \frac{\sum\left[\frac{1}{K}(X - C) - \frac{1}{K}(\overline{X} - C)\right]^2}{n}$$

$$= \frac{1}{K^2} \frac{\sum[X - \overline{X}]^2}{n}$$

$$= \frac{1}{K^2} S_X^2 \therefore S_{[(X-C)/K]} = \frac{1}{K} S_X$$

If we find the standard deviation by coding scores in this way, its value must be multiplied by K in order to recover the standard deviation of the original scores. With this idea in mind, compare Formula 6.6 with Formula 6.7.

NOTE 6.3 The Standard Deviation as a Minimum Value when Deviations Are Taken from the Mean (*Ref:* Section 6.10)

Let A be the point about which the deviation of each score is taken, and define it as a point which differs from the mean by an amount, d: $A = \overline{X} + d$. Then,

$$\sum(X - A)^2 = \sum[X - (\overline{X} + d)]^2$$

$$= \sum[(X - \overline{X}) - d]^2$$

$$= \sum[(X - \bar{X})^2 - 2d(X - \bar{X}) + d^2]$$
$$= \sum(X - \bar{X})^2 - 2d\sum(X - \bar{X}) + nd^2$$

From Note 5.2, $\sum(X - \bar{X}) = 0$, so

$$\sum(X - A)^2 = \sum(X - \bar{X})^2 + nd^2$$

Inspection of the right side of the above equation shows that $\sum(X - A)^2$ is smallest when $d = 0$. From the definition of d, this occurs when $A = \bar{X}$. Since $S = \sqrt{\sum(X - \bar{X})^2/n}$, it is apparent that S has a minimum value when deviations are taken from $\bar{X}$.

PROBLEMS AND EXERCISES

Identify:

measures of variability	x
range	$A.D.$
semiinterquartile range	σ^2
average deviation	S^2
variance	σ
standard deviation	S
Q	S_c

1. Find (a) the range, and (b) the semiinterquartile range for the data of Table 4.1.

2. We want to compare the variability of the two sets of reaction time scores in Data 4A. (a) Find the range of both distributions. (b) Find the semiinterquartile range for both distributions. What can we say about relative variability under the two stimulus conditions?

3. Given these scores: X: 5, 8, 3, 5, 7; Y: 4, 2, 7, 4, 7. (a) What is the range of the X scores? The Y scores? (b) Find the standard deviation of the X scores by the deviation score method. Keep all work to 1 decimal. (c) Find S_X by raw score Method I. Keep all work to one decimal. (d) Find S_X by raw score Method II. (e) Comment on the relative ease of calculation of the three methods.

4. Repeat parts (b), (c), and (d) of Problem 3, but as applied to the Y scores.

5. The standard deviation of a set of scores is 20. What would the standard deviation be if (a) 15 points were added to each score? (b) each score was divided by 5? (c) ten points were subtracted from each score and the resulting scores were divided by 2? (d) each score was multiplied by 2 and then 10 points were added to those resulting scores?

6. Assume you have a group of scores whose values range from .300 to .342 and you wish to find the standard deviation. These scores could be doubly coded to simplify computation. How? After coding and finding the standard deviation of the coded scores, how would you then find the standard deviation of the original scores?

7. Find the mean and standard deviation of the scores in Table 4.1 by the coded score method.

8. Does the value obtained for the standard deviation in Problem 7 appear reasonable in view of the range of scores? Explain.

9. Show how the x' values used in Problem 7 may be obtained by a double coding process.

10. Find the mean and standard deviation of the two sets of scores in Data 4A. What can we say about the differences between the two distributions?

11. Do the values obtained for the standard deviations in Problem 10 appear reasonable in view of the range of scores? Explain.

12. After the mean, median, range, Q, and S of a set of 40 scores had been computed, the researcher found that the highest score was in error, and, in fact, was slightly lower than originally recorded. Which of the measures would be affected by the change? Explain.

13. What are the advantages of the standard deviation over the other measures of variability?

14. An elementary statistics student decided to calculate the mean and standard deviation of a set of scores so that he could see if they followed the normal distribution. Comment.

15. What measure of variability do you suggest for the data of Problem 11, Chapter 5? Explain.

16. A junior high school science teacher gives a standard test of knowledge of science to his class. The data for his students and for a national sample are as follows: Instructor's class: $\bar{X} = 90$, $S = 8$; National sample: $\bar{X} = 75$, $S = 14$. What is the meaning of these findings? What implication is suggested for teaching science to this class?

17. An instructor teaches three statistics classes, and gives each class a test of mathematical skill on the first day. Data for the three classes are as follows: Class A: $\bar{X} = 32$, $S = 6$, $n = 30$; Class B: $\bar{X} = 38$, $S = 8$, $n = 40$; Class C: $\bar{X} = 29$, $S = 9$, $n = 20$. (*a*) What is the mean if all cases are combined in one distribution? (*b*) What is the standard deviation of the combined distribution?

7
The Normal Curve

7.1 Introduction

In the development so far, there has been frequent reference to the *normal curve*. This stands as testimony to the pervasive significance of that function for statistical procedures. It is now time to examine it more closely. We need to know what the normal curve is, what its properties are, the ways in which it is useful as a statistical model, and how to put it to work in answering questions. Some consideration of its history is in order because of its intrinsic interest and because it throws some light on the character and widespread use of the normal curve as a model.

7.2 The Nature of the Normal Curve

It is important to make a distinction between data which are normally distributed (or approximately so), and the normal curve itself. The normal curve is a mathematical abstraction having a particular defining equation (given in the Note at the end of this chapter). As a mathematical abstraction, it is not, of necessity, associated with (or determined by) any event or events in the real world. It is not, therefore, a "law of nature," contrary to the thought and terminology associated with it a century ago. Nevertheless, a specific normal curve may be useful in describing a given set of natural events under appropriate circumstances. In the same way, the equation of a circle is a mathematical abstraction, and not a law of nature. We may find a boulder which has a circumference approximated by a circle having a particular equation, or observe that the circumference of the earth roughly conforms to the equation of another circle, or cut out a table top to agree with a third such equation. Nevertheless, the circular objects do not of necessity exist because of the mathematical abstraction called a circle. We shall return to this point in Section 7.4.

95

Just as the equation of a circle describes a family of circles, some big and some small, so the equation of the normal curve describes a family of normal curves. The family of normal curves may differ with regard to their means, standard deviations, or area under the curve. In other respects, members of this family have the same characteristics. Figure 7.1 illustrates three possibilities:

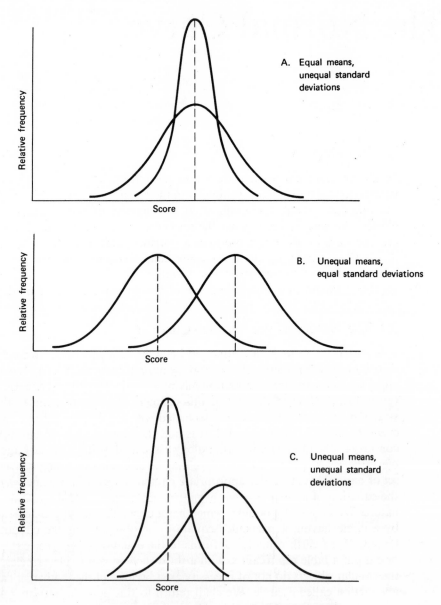

FIGURE 7.1 Variations in Normal Distributions.

equal means and unequal standard deviations, unequal means and equal standard deviations, and unequal means and unequal standard deviations.†

All normal curves are *symmetrical*; that is, the left half of the normal curve is a mirror image of the right half. They are *unimodal*, with the mode at the center. Indeed, mean, median, and mode all have the same value. Starting at the center of the curve and working outward, the height of the curve descends gradually at first, then faster, and finally slower. A curious and important situation exists at the extremes of the curve. Although the curve descends promptly toward the horizontal axis, it never actually touches it, no matter how far out one goes. Such a curve is said to be *asymptotic* to the horizontal axis. One might think that if the curve never touches the X axis, a large proportion of the total area under the curve must lie in the extremes, but this is not so. For example, the area included within the range of $\mu \pm 3\sigma$ comprises approximately 99.7% of the total area under the curve, as we learned in Section 6.13.

The normal curve is *continuous*. This is of interest, because we remember that recorded values of observations always form a discrete series (see Section 2.5). It is our first indication that when the normal curve is used as a model for events of the "real world," it must be expected to be only approximate.

Finally, for all members of the family of normal curves, the proportion of area under the curve relative to a particular location on the horizontal axis is the same when the location is stated on a comparable basis. For example, approximately two-thirds (68%) of the area under a normal curve lies within the range of $\mu \pm 1\sigma$. Thus in a normal curve characterized by $\mu = 100$ and $\sigma = 20$, two-thirds of the area falls between the values of 80 and 120, and in a normal curve characterized by $\mu = 500$ and $\sigma = 100$, two-thirds of the area falls between the values of 400 and 600.

7.3 Historical Aspects of the Normal Curve‡

The substantial beginnings of the development of statistical theory occurred in the middle of the 17th century. At that time, the first significant contributions were made to the principles associated with chance events, and hence to the theory of probability. To illustrate one such problem, suppose we toss eight coins and take as our observation the number of heads. We shall suppose that each coin is as likely to come up heads as tails, and that the outcome of the toss of one of the eight coins in no way affects the outcome of the toss of another. Because of the operation of chance factors, we can not say precisely how many heads will appear on any one toss. But suppose we ask another question: if the

†When it is appropriate to use the normal curve as a model for real events, it is most often the population of such events which is so modeled. Consequently, we shall use μ and σ in connection with the normal curve throughout this chapter, rather than $\bar{X}$ and S.

‡Those who wish to study further the historical development of statistical concepts will find the following reference of interest: H. M. Walker, *Studies in the History of Statistical Method*, The Williams & Wilkins Co., Baltimore, 1929.

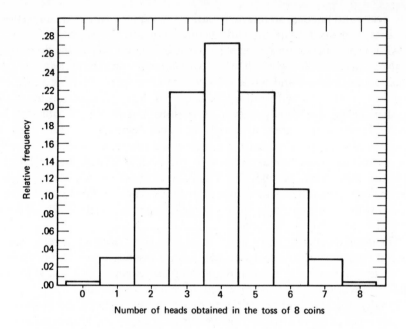

FIGURE 7.2 Relative Frequency of Occurrence of Heads in Tossing 8 Coins.

act of tossing eight coins is repeated an extremely large number of times, what relative frequency of heads will occur? These early mathematicians developed a theory which provides the answer. The relative frequency distribution, derived from that theory, is shown in Figure 7.2. By inspection of the figure, we note that *on the average* there will be four heads, and that the more divergent the number of heads and tails on any one toss (e.g., 7 heads and 1 tail), the lower the relative frequency of its occurrence.

We also see that if a normal curve were superimposed on the histogram in Figure 7.2, it would afford an approximate fit to the data. If 16 coins were tossed, rather than eight, there would be more bars in the histogram, and the normal curve would be an even better fit, as illustrated in Figure 7.3. It is apparent that the normal curve affords a good approximation to the relative frequency distribution generated by the operation of chance factors in a situation such as the one described. If the number of coins were increased indefinitely, the number of bars in the histogram would similarly increase and their outline, as represented in a histogram, would grow smoother and smoother.

Indeed, in 1733 Abraham De Moivre discovered the formula for the normal curve as the limiting case characterizing an infinite number of such independent events. Because of this origin, the normal curve has frequently been connected

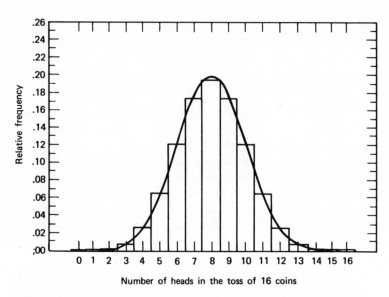

FIGURE 7.3 Relative Frequency of Occurrence of Heads in Tossing 16 Coins.

with the notion that it occurs as a description of nature when a large number of factors are operating, each independent of the others and governed by chance.

Further significant development awaited the beginning of the 19th century. Indeed, it seems that Pierre-Simon (the Marquis de Laplace) and Carl Friedrich Gauss rediscovered the normal curve independently of De Moivre's work. Gauss's interest was associated with problems in astronomy; for example, determination of the orbit of a planet from a number of measurements (observations) which are subject to error. These problems led to the consideration of a theory of errors of observation with such strength that the normal curve came in that century to be known as the *"normal law of error"* (the name is now obsolete).†

Promotion of the applicability of the normal curve as a model for other situations is due primarily to Adolphe Quetelet, a Belgian, in the middle part of the 19th century. He was a teacher of mathematics and astronomy, originator of the basic methods of physical anthropometrics, and perhaps the founder of sociology. He believed that the normal curve could be extended to apply to problems in meteorology, anthropology, and human affairs. It was his opinion that "mental and moral traits," when measured, would conform to the "normal law." One of his conceptions was *l'homme moyen*, or "average man." He compared the normal distribution to the notion that nature, in aiming at a mark *(l'homme moyen)*, missed, and so produced a distribution of "error" in her effort.

†Vestiges of this terminology hang on. Note, in Chapter 13, the current term, *Standard Error*.

In the latter part of the 19th century, Sir Francis Galton began the first serious study of individual differences, a domain so significant for psychology and education. He found that many mental and physical traits conformed reasonably to the normal curve, and was greatly impressed by the applicability of the normal curve to natural phenomena. In 1889, he wrote:

"I know of scarcely anything so apt to impress the imagination as the wonderful form of cosmic order expressed by the 'Law of Frequency of Error.' The law would have been personified by the Greeks and deified, if they had known of it. It reigns with serenity and in complete self-effacement amidst the wildest confusion. The huger the mob and the greater the apparent anarchy, the more perfect is its sway. It is the supreme law of Unreason. Whenever a large sample of chaotic elements are taken in hand and marshalled in the order of their magnitude, an unsuspected and most beautiful form of regularity proves to have been latent all along."†

His enthusiasm is understandable and well worthy of our appreciation. His theory, however, must be tempered in light of current knowledge. A more balanced view will emerge in the next section.

7.4 Theorems, Laws, and Models

In science, a *theorem* is a statement derived logically from postulates and is subject to confirmation through observation; a *law* is a well-confirmed theorem.‡

Should we assign the character of a law to the normal curve? It may be appropriate to do so when the data under observation are produced by a very great number of independent factors, each of which operates in accordance with chance. We do find many situations in which a specific set of data appear to form a distribution approximating the normal curve, as Galton has indicated. It is by no means clear, however, that the data are produced by chance operations of the type specified above. For example, the distribution of intelligence test scores of a reasonably homogeneous group, such as 12-year-old Scottish children, tends to follow the normal curve rather closely. It is, however, nothing more than a speculation that differences in intelligence are due to the chance arrangement of a great many equally important and independently operating factors. Indeed, the little that we do know about the factors involved suggests that it is most unlikely that the strict requirements are met which would give the normal curve the character of a law in this situation. It is no wonder that investigators like Quetelet and Galton were so delighted with their discoveries and so enthusiastic about possible formulation of laws, but more sober evaluation has led to the view that too much has been expected from our theorems, and, in particular, from the normal curve.

†F. Galton, *Natural Inheritance*, MacMillan and Co., London, 1889, p. 66.
‡Not all theorists agree with the above definitions. No matter, we shall plunge ahead.

This point of view has been reflected in the growing use of the term *model*. A model is an *as if* proposition, having only the character of an analogy. A model may be very useful in organizing, describing, and predicting the behavior of a set of empirical observations, but it claims to be less than a theorem. It does not have postulates which must be subjected to the test, nor does it pretend to owe its origin to "causal" principles. The justification of a model lies in its utility in assisting organization and thought about data, and it may be readily modified as circumstances dictate. In general, we find it more appropriate to assign to the normal curve the role of model, rather than law, in problems of psychology and education.

7.5 The Normal Curve as a Statistical Model

One role of the normal curve is as a model for distributions of populations of observations. It appears to be a rather good fit to many (but not all) distributions of physical measurements made in biology and anthropology. For example, in reasonably homogeneous populations, the distribution of stature follows the normal curve closely. As the mathematical astronomers found, it fits errors of observation in many circumstances. Again, it is often a good fit to the distribution of errors made in skill performance, such as shots aimed at a target. Many measures of mental traits (e.g., intelligence) tend to be normally distributed. These examples by no means exhaust the list, and there is every reason to understand Galton's enthusiasm in uncovering so many variables for which the normal curve is a satisfactory model.

Several words of caution are in order. First, the normal curve as a model best describes an infinity of observations which are on a continuous scale of measurement. As we know, recorded observations are discrete rather than continuous, and, among concrete data, we do *not* have an infinity of observations. Real populations may be large, but they are not of infinite size. Although the normal curve closely approximates distributions of data of many kinds, it is a fair speculation that *no* real variable is *exactly* normally distributed. We conclude that this does not matter too much; it is the utility of the model that counts. We *are* reminded to examine the evidence and to decide whether the model is a close enough fit to warrant use.

Second, many variables are *not* normally distributed. Some variables which tend to show at least a degree of skewness are: human body weight, size of family income, reaction time, and frequency of accidents. Even variables which can exhibit a normal distribution in homogeneous populations may fail to do so under changed circumstances. The distribution of stature of a mixed group of men and women is bimodal, and a mental test which might yield a normal distribution of scores if appropriately constructed may produce distributions skewed to the right or left if the test is too easy or too hard for the group measured.

The second way in which the normal curve functions as a model is for distributions of sample statistics, rather than for the raw observations. For instance, if one were to draw a very great number of random samples from a population and compute the mean of each sample, it would be found that the distribution of this large number of means tends to approximate the normal curve. In situations of this type, the fit of the normal curve is often very good indeed. This is a property of utmost importance in statistical inference, because the shape of such distributions must be known in order to provide information necessary to make the appropriate inference. We will give it closer attention in Chapter 13.

There is another dimension to the role of the normal curve in relation to data. First, it can serve as a *relative frequency distribution*, descriptive of events which have occurred. Second, it can serve as a *probability distribution*, giving information about expected values. In the first sense, the normal curve, for example, provides the information that half of a population obtain intelligence test scores above the mean. In the second sense, it provides the basis for stating that if a person is selected at random from the population, the chances are one out of two that he will score above the mean. Again, this concept will be explored in more detail in Chapter 13.

7.6 Standard Scores (*z* Scores) and the Normal Curve

A question of the following type occurs frequently in statistical work: Given a normally distributed variable with a mean of 100 and a standard deviation of 20, what proportion of scores will fall above the score of 120? This question can be answered if we can find the area under the normal curve beyond the position of the score of 120, because *area under the curve is proportional to frequency of scores in the distribution.* By the methods given in the next section, we can determine that 16% of the area falls above the given point, and therefore we know that 16% of the scores fall above the same point. This is illustrated in Figure 7.4.

Tables have been constructed which specify the area under the normal curve relative to particular locations along the horizontal axis. However, a way must be found to express location of a score in terms which are comparable for *all* normal curves. Raw scores will not do, since, for example, the score of 120 does not represent the same position in a normal distribution having a mean or standard deviation different from the values cited in the example above.

The solution is to convert the raw score to a *standard score*. A standard score, or *z* score, states the position of the score in relation to the mean of the distribution, using the standard deviation as the unit of measurement. In a distribution which has $\mu = 100$ and $\sigma = 20$, the score of 120 may be expressed as a *z* score of $+1$, indicating that the score is one standard deviation above the mean of the distribution. Similarly, a score of 85 is expressed as a *z* score of $-.75$,

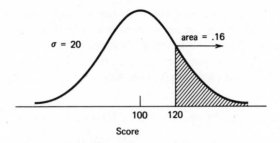

FIGURE 7.4 Proportion of Scores Exceeding a Score of 120 in a Normal Distribution Characterized by $\mu = 100$ and $\sigma = 20$.

since it is three-quarters of a standard deviation below the mean. The *z* score may be stated in terms of a formula:

z Score: *Deviation Score Form* $z = \dfrac{x}{\sigma_X}$ †   (7.1)

z Score: *Raw Score Form* $z = \dfrac{X - \mu}{\sigma_X}$ †   (7.2)

The *z* score makes it possible to report scores from different normal distributions on a single, comparable basis. Consider a normal distribution which has $\mu = 50$ and $\sigma = 10$. In this distribution, a score of 60 lies one standard deviation above the mean; it may therefore be reexpressed as $z = +1.00$. This score, in its distribution, therefore falls at the same relative position as a score of 120 in a distribution which has $\mu = 100$ and $\sigma = 20$. Granted that both distributions follow the normal curve, we shall find that 16% of scores exceed the score of 60 in its distribution, just as 16% of scores exceed the score of 120 in its distribution. A single table of areas under the normal curve will therefore suffice for work with *all* normal distributions, irrespective of their means and standard deviations. All that is needed is to translate the relevant raw score to a *z* score in order to enter the table.

    The idea of a *z* score is of great importance in statistical work, and it will appear again and again in this book. It is well to know Formula 7.2 by heart, and to know that *a z score states how many standard deviations the score lies above or below the mean of the distribution.*

    Because the notion of a *z* score has been introduced in connection with the

†In dealing with a sample rather than with a population, the formula for a *z* score is:

$$z = \frac{x}{s_X} \quad \text{or} \quad z = \frac{X - \bar{X}}{s_X}$$

normal curve, one might be tempted to conclude that z scores are necessarily normally distributed. This is not so; a score from any distribution may be stated in this form. A distribution of z scores has whatever shape is characteristic of the set of raw scores from which they were derived. This point is given further consideration in the next chapter (Section 8.2).

7.7 Finding Areas when the Score Is Known

This section and the next is concerned *only* with distributions which follow the normal curve; in other situations the outcomes presented would differ. Let us begin with the problem stated in the previous section: *Given a normally distributed variable with a mean of 100 and a standard deviation of 20, what proportion of scores will fall above a score point of 120?* The problem is illustrated in Figure 7.5.

The first step is to translate the score of 120 to a z score; its value is: $z = +1.00$. Table B (in the appendix) is now of use. It gives the area under the normal curve which falls above or below a particular point when that point is expressed in standard score form. In this table, locate the value $z = 1.00$ in the first column and look across that row for the entry in the column marked "area beyond z." This entry is .1587, or if rounded, .16. The total area under the curve is defined as unity in this table, so the value, .16, may be interpreted as the proportion of the total area falling in the tail. As we noted in the last section, area under the curve is proportional to frequency of scores, so the question above is answered: .16 of the scores fall above the score point 120.

Suppose the problem had been to determine the proportion of scores lying below 80. Figure 7.5 also illustrates this problem. The z-score equivalent of 80 is -1.00. Negative z scores do not appear in the table. Because the normal curve is symmetrical, as many scores fall below a z of -1.00 as fall above a z of

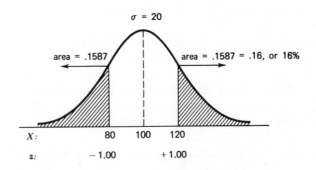

FIGURE 7.5 Proportion of Scores Exceeding a Score of 120 and Falling Below a Score of 80 in a Normal Distribution Characterized by $\mu = 100$ and $\sigma = 20$.

+1.00. The distinction between positive and negative values is therefore not needed. The column heading, "area beyond z" takes care of both situations, and our answer is the same, .16.

Consider another type of problem: *assuming a mean of 100 and a standard deviation of 20, what proportion of scores falls within the score range of 90 to 120?* This problem is shown in Figure 7.6. Again, the first step is to obtain the z-score equivalents of these two scores. Using Formula 7.2, the values are found to be $z = -.50$ and $z = +1.00$, respectively. If we find the area under the curve between the z score of $-.50$ and the mean, and add this to the area between the mean and the z score of $+1.00$, we will have the proportion of scores which fall within the given range. In Table B, the second column, "area between mean and z," gives the appropriate values:

area between $z = -.50$ and the mean: .1915

area between the mean and $z = +1.00$: .3413
total area: .5328

To two decimal places, the answer is .53, or 53%.

A third type of problem is illustrated by this question: *What proportion of scores falls between the values of 110 and 120?* We shall assume the same mean and standard deviation as before. One way to answer is to determine the proportion of scores falling above 110, and subtract from this value the proportion of scores falling above 120. The problem and its solution are illustrated in Figure 7.7. We begin, as usual, by converting the raw score values to z scores: $X = 110$

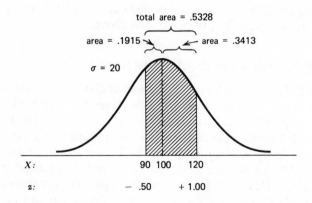

FIGURE 7.6 Proportion of Scores Falling between 90 and 120 in a Normal Distribution Characterized by $\mu = 100$ and $\sigma = 20$.

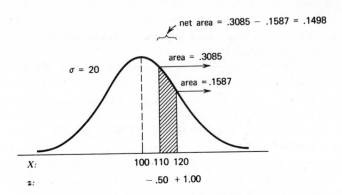

FIGURE 7.7 Proportion of Scores Falling between 110 and 120 in a Normal Distribution Characterized by $\mu = 100$ and $\sigma = 20$.

becomes $z = +.50$, and $X = 120$ becomes $z = +1.00$. Using Table B, the solution is:

$$\text{area above } z = +.50: \quad .3085$$
$$\text{area above } z = +1.00: \quad -.1587$$
$$\underline{}$$
$$\text{difference:} \quad .1498$$

or, to two decimals, .15 of the scores.†

If the number of scores rather than the proportion of them is required, we have but to multiply the proportion by the total number of scores in the distribution. Thus, in the last problem, if there are 2000 scores in the distribution, $(.1498)(2000) = 299.6$ or 300 of them fall between the two points, 110 and 120.

In solving problems of the sort described in this section, many students find it helpful to draw a picture of the kind used above.

7.8 Finding Scores when the Area Is Known

Consider the following problem: *Given a normal distribution, find the score which separates the upper 20% of scores from the lower 80%.* It is like some of the problems in the previous section, except that its form is inverted. There, the score was known and the area required; here, the area is known and the score required. We *could* solve it by reading Table B "backward," locating the value in the column entitled "area beyond z" closest to .20 and then identifying the z score associated with it. However, Table C (in the appendix) will facilitate this work. Consulting Table C, we look for the value of .20 in the column headed "the

†In solving problems of this kind, beginners are sometimes tempted to subtract one z score from the other, and find the area corresponding to that difference. A moment's thought shows that this will not work. *It is the difference between the two areas which is required.*

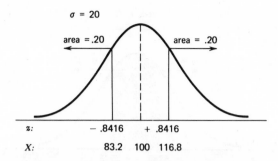

FIGURE 7.8 The Score Dividing the Upper 20% of Observations (or the Lower 20%) from the Remainder in a Normal Distribution Characterized by $\mu = 100$ and $\sigma = 20$.

smaller area," and note that the z score associated with it is .8416. As before, the table does not distinguish between positive and negative z scores: we must supply that information. Noting that it is the *top* 20% which is to be distinguished from the remainder, it is clear that the value of the z score is positive: $z = +.8416$, or, to two decimals, $+.84$. Figure 7.8 presents this problem.

We can go no farther in answering this question unless the mean and standard deviation of the distribution concerned are known. If, for example, the mean is 100 and the standard deviation is 20, we may proceed as follows. A z score of $+.84$ states that the score is 84/100 of a standard deviation above the mean. The value sought is therefore:

$$
\begin{array}{rcr}
\text{mean} & = & 100.0 \\
(+.84)(20) & = & +\ 16.8 \\
\hline
& & 116.8
\end{array}
$$

If the question asked for the point separating the *lower* 20% of scores from the remainder, the z score would be $-.84$, and the raw score equivalent:

$$
\begin{array}{rcr}
\text{mean} & = & 100.0 \\
(-.84)(20) & = & -\ 16.8 \\
\hline
& & 83.2
\end{array}
$$

Another kind of question arises: *What are the limits within which the central 50% of scores fall?* Figure 7.9 illustrates this problem. If 50% of the cases fall between the two symmetrically located scores, 25% must fall above the upper limit and 25% below the lower limit. What is the score beyond which 25% of the cases fall? From Table C, it is found to be a z score of .6745. The scores are therefore located .6745 of a standard deviation above and below the mean.

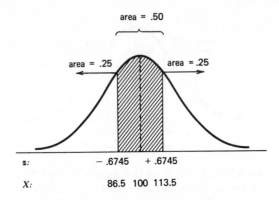

FIGURE 7.9 The Limits Which Include the Central
50% of Observations in a Normal Distribution
Characterized by $\mu = 100$ and $\sigma = 20$.

If the mean is 100 and the standard deviation is 20, the limits are as follows:

Lower Limit	Upper Limit
$z = -.6745$	$z = +.6745$
mean = 100.0	mean = 100.0
$(-.6745)(20) = -13.5$	$(+.6745)(20) = +13.5$
raw score = 86.5	raw score = 113.5

In the illustrations above, the transitions from z score to raw score have
been made in recognition of the meaning of a z score. The equivalent formula for
making this transition may be obtained by solving Formula 7.2 for z; it is:

Formula for Translating a $\quad\quad X = \mu + z\sigma$ † $\quad\quad\quad\quad\quad\quad$ (7.3)
z Score to a Raw Score

Applying it to the solution of the upper limit in the problem above, we find:

$$X = 100 + (+.67)(20) = 113.5$$

the same value obtained previously.

NOTE

The Equation of the Normal Curve (*Ref:* Section 7.2)

The equation of the normal curve is:

$$Y = \frac{N}{\sigma\sqrt{2\pi}}e^{-(X-\mu)^2/2\sigma^2}$$

†For samples, rather than populations, Formula 7.3 becomes: $X = \bar{X} + zS_X$.

As a model for a frequency distribution, it may be interpreted as follows:

$$Y = \text{frequency}$$
$$N = \text{number of cases}$$
$$X = \text{a raw score}$$
$$\mu = \text{mean of the set of scores}$$
$$\sigma = \text{standard deviation of the set of scores}$$
$$\left.\begin{array}{l} \pi = 3.1416 \\ e = 2.7183 \end{array}\right\} \text{mathematical constants}$$

The variables which determine what Y will be are: X, μ, σ, and N. Basically, the area under the curve is determined by N, the location of the center of the curve by μ, and the rapidity with which the curve approaches the abcissa by σ.

If one chooses to speak of a normal curve of unit area and in which the scores are standard scores, then: $N = 1$, $\mu = 0$, $\sigma = 1$, and the equation becomes:

$$Y = \frac{1}{\sqrt{2\pi}} e^{-(z^2/2)}$$

In this form, the value of z is the only variable which determines Y, the relative frequency. It is this function for which areas are tabled in Table B, in the appendix.

Strictly speaking, Y in the normal curve is not interpretable as frequency; it is simply the height of the curve corresponding to a particular (point) value of X. Frequency *is* interpretable as the area under the normal curve which falls between two values of X (the frequency of scores within that range). The frequency of scores between limits of given width differs depending on where such an interval is located on the abcissa. If the distance between the two values of X is decreased to a very small but finite quantity, the area between these limits becomes approximately proportional to the height of the curve at the midpoint of the limits. It is in this sense that we suggest that Y in the normal curve may be taken as an indication of frequency.

PROBLEMS AND EXERCISES

Identify:

normal curve	Gauss
normally distributed data	Quetelet
symmetrical distribution	Galton
unimodal distribution	normal law of error
asymptotic curve	theorem
continuous distribution	law
discrete distribution	model
De Moivre	standard score
Laplace	z score

1. For normally distributed scores, what proportion of scores would fall: (*a*) above $z = +1.00$? (*b*) above $z = +2.00$? (*c*) above $z = +3.00$? (*d*) below $z = -2.00$? (*e*) below $z = -3.00$?

2. For normally distributed scores, what proportion of scores would fall: (*a*) above $z = -1.00$? (*b*) below $z = 0$? (*c*) below $z = +2.00$?

3. For normally distributed scores, what proportion of scores would fall: (a) between $z = +.25$ and $z = +1.25$? (b) between $z = -1.00$ and $z = -2.00$? (c) between $z = -1.00$ and $z = +1.00$? (d) between $z = -2.00$ and $z = +2.00$? (e) between $z = -3.00$ and $z = +3.00$?

4. If the distribution consists of 400 scores, what is the answer to each part of Problem 3 in terms of the number of scores involved?

5. For normally distributed scores, what proportion of scores would fall: (a) between $z = -1.25$ and $z = -.50$? (b) between $z = -.75$ and $z = +.25$? (c) outside the limits: $z = -.40$ and $z = -.20$? (d) outside the limits: $z = -1.00$ and $z = +2.00$?

6. If college entrance examination scores are normally distributed with a mean of 500 and a standard deviation of 100, what proportion of the scores fall: (a) above 550? (b) above 600? (c) below 420? (d) above 350? (e) between 550 and 750? (f) between 300 and 625? (g) between 625 and 725? (h) between 380 and 480?

7. In a normal distribution of 1000 aptitude test scores, with a mean of 60 and a standard deviation of 8, how many scores fall: (a) above 76? (b) below 80? (c) above 50? (d) below 46? (e) between 48 and 52? (f) between 58 and 70?

8. Among normally distributed scores, what z score (a) divides the upper 5% of scores from the remainder? (b) divides the upper 2.5% of scores from the remainder? (c) divides the upper 1% of scores from the remainder? (d) divides the upper .5% of scores from the remainder?

9. Among normally distributed scores, what are the z score limits which identify the central: (a) 99% of scores? (b) 95% of scores? (c) 50% of scores?

10. In a normal distribution of scores, what is (are) the z score(s): (a) above which 20% of the scores fall? (b) below which 65% of the scores fall? (c) above which 70% of the scores fall? (d) below which 6% of the scores fall? (e) between which the central 64% of the scores lie.

11. In a normal distribution of 200 scores, what is (are) the z score(s): (a) above which 20 scores fall? (b) below which 124 scores fall? (c) above which 156 scores fall? (d) below which 12 scores fall? (e) between which the central 100 scores lie?

12. In a normal distribution of employment screening test scores, with a mean of 25 and a standard deviation of 5, what is (are) the score(s): (a) above which 5% of the scores fall? (b) below which 52% of the scores fall? (c) above which 88% of the scores fall? (d) below which 10% of the scores fall? (e) between which the central 30% of the scores lie?

13. In a normal distribution of 500 intelligence test scores, with a mean of 100 and a standard deviation of 15, what is (are) the score(s): (a) above which 10 scores fall? (b) below which 175 scores fall? (c) above which 355 scores fall? (d) below which 32 scores fall? (e) between which the central 80% of scores lie?

8

Derived Scores

8.1 The Need for Derived Scores

A student friend has been worried about his performance in a history examination. You see him for the first time in two weeks; the examination period is now over. "How did you do on the history examination?", you ask. "I got a score of 123," he replies. You consider his answer, not knowing whether to rejoice with him or to sympathize. "What was the class average?", you inquire. "One hundred and five," he responds. You are happy for him, but press the inquiry further: "What was the range?" "The low score was 80, and the high score was 125," he replies.

The example above illustrates the problem of meaning which is typical of scores obtained in psychological and educational measurement. The raw score, by itself, is really uninterpretable. A frame of reference is needed to decide whether a given score is indicative of a good performance or a poor one. In the example above, learning the value of the mean of the distribution contributed to understanding of his level of performance. Additional information was acquired by asking about the range; his answer indicated that his performance was very near to the best in the class. In this instance, the raw score, originally without meaning, became interpretable by relating it to a measure of central tendency and a measure of variability of a reference distribution.

The problem of making scores meaningful, in any dimension, is one of providing an adequate frame of reference. If we measure the length of an object in feet, the measurement obtained is meaningful first because the length obtained is the same whether measured by your yardstick or mine, and second, because we have some understanding of how long a foot is. In mental measurement, the problem is different. In measuring achievement in history, or intelligence, or mechanical aptitude, there is

111

no standard raw score unit of measurement, nor should we expect one. On tests of these functions, the size and spread of scores that result depend on the number of test items, the number of points assigned to each test item, the difficulty of the items, and other factors. The problem is aggravated by two related matters. First, a test of intelligence, for example, is a *sample* of questions designed to tap this function. Another test of the same function will therefore constitute a somewhat different sample, with somewhat different outcome. Second, since we are not in perfect agreement as to what intelligence is, two test constructors may sample domains which are not exactly alike. All of these factors mean that, unlike the measurement of distance, one "yardstick" of intellectual functioning is not necessarily the same as another.

With measures of this kind, meaningfulness is contributed by relating the position of individual scores to the distribution of scores obtained by a group whose characteristics are known.† We have already met two kinds of *derived scores* that serve this function: centile ranks and z scores.

The advantage of derived scores, then, is that they provide a standard frame of reference within which the meaning of a score can be better understood. Derived scores also make possible, under certain conditions, the comparison of scores from different measures. This property will be explained in Section 8.8.

8.2 Standard Scores: The z Score

One kind of derived score is the *standard score*. What is "standard" about standard scores is that they have a specified mean and standard deviation. There is more than one kind of standard score. Foremost among them is the z score, considered in this section. Other kinds will be taken up in the next section and in Sections 8.9 and 8.10.

The z score has been defined in Section 7.6. For ready reference, we repeat here its definition and its formula (Formula 7.2) in the form suited to samples. *A z score states how many standard deviations the score lies above or below the mean of the distribution.*

$$z = \frac{x}{S_X} = \frac{X - \overline{X}}{S_X}$$

The mean of any set of z scores is always zero. This is apparent from the above definition, since the value of the mean is also the value of a score which is "no standard deviations away from the mean," and hence is represented by $z = 0$. *The standard deviation of any set of z scores is always one.* Again, study of the definition of the z score reveals that it sets the standard deviation as the

---

†A reference group of individuals with known characteristics is called a *norm group*, and the distribution of test scores obtained from such a group is known as the *test norms*.

unit of measurement, and therefore defines the standard deviation as unity. The z score of $+1$, for example, lies one standard deviation above the mean.

As indicated in Section 7.6, the shape of the distribution is unchanged by transformation of raw scores to z scores. If the original distribution is positively skewed, the z-score equivalents of the scores will form a distribution which is positively skewed, and to the same degree. In short, the z-score transformation preserves the proportionality of interscore distances existing in the original distribution. For example, consider the following scores and their z-score equivalents:

four scores from a distribution where $\overline{X} = 80$ and $S_X = 10$:   70 75 85 100

interscore differences among raw scores: 5   10 15

equivalent z scores: -1 $-\frac{1}{2}$ $+\frac{1}{2}$ $+2$

interscore differences among z scores: $\frac{1}{2}$ 1 $1\frac{1}{2}$

Note the relation between the interscore distances exhibited for the above raw scores and the z scores. The proportional magnitude of difference between successive raw scores, $5:10:15$, is exactly the same in z-score terms, $\frac{1}{2}:1:1\frac{1}{2}$.

Knowledge of the z score does not, by itself, give us precise information about the centile rank of the score.† That depends, additionally, on the shape of the distribution. If it is reasonable to assume normality of the distribution, precise information becomes available through the methods described in the previous chapter. We know, for instance, that approximately 98% of scores lie below the value of $z = +2$ in a normal distribution.

8.3 Standard Scores: Other Varieties

There are minor inconveniences associated with the use of z scores. First, both negative and positive values will occur in any given distribution. Second, it is generally necessary to report the scores to one or two decimal places in order to achieve sufficient refinement in indicating location. Third, there can be a communication problem in dealing with a public unused to them. Imagine, if you will, a conference in which the teacher is attempting to explain to a mother that her son's performance in spelling, indicated by a score of zero, is for him really rather good.

To circumvent these difficulties, other varieties of standard scores have been devised. Each of them is like the z score in that it has a fixed mean and standard

†Centile rank is defined in Section 3.9.

deviation; this is what is "standard" about them. The following are examples of those most commonly used:

Type	Mean	Std Dev	Example of Use
1	50	10	(Various)
2	100	20	Army General Classification Test, World War II
3	100	15	Wechsler Intelligence Scale IQ's
4	500	100	College Entrance Examination Board Scores (CEEB)

On the scale having a mean of 50 and a standard deviation of 10, a z score of -1.00 is represented by a score of 40. On the remaining scales, that same location is represented by scores of 80, 85, and 400, respectively.

Scores of the first type, with a mean of 50 and a standard deviation of 10, offer sufficient discrimination for most purposes without resort to decimals. They are also convenient for further statistical treatment since scores are, in general, limited to two-digit values. This type of score is sometimes called a T score. This is unfortunate, because that name was originally given to another kind of score, one described in Section 8.9. The T score described there also has a mean of 50 and a standard deviation of 10, but in addition the distribution of scores has been altered to conform to the normal curve. The scores discussed in the present section share with z scores the property that they form a distribution which retains the same shape as the raw score distribution from which they were derived.

Despite the convenient features of these standard scores, the z score is in no danger of being replaced by them entirely, because it conveys directly the meaning which is only indirectly given by the others. For example, the meaning of a score of 120 on a standard score scale where the mean is 100 and the standard deviation is 20 is that this score lies one standard deviation above the mean. However, that information is given *directly* by its z-score equivalent, $z = +1.00$.

It should be noted that the term *standard score* is used indiscriminately for z scores and for other types. It is easy to tell from context when the z score is meant, since its values hover close to zero.

8.4 Translating Raw Scores to Standard Scores

There are two ways of translating a raw score to a standard score. The first might be called the "common sense" method, and the second the "formula" method. With the first method, the principle can be carried in one's head; it is convenient to use when only a few scores are to be translated. The second is better if a larger set of scores is involved, but the formula is not so easily remembered. Both procedures will be illustrated.

Suppose we have a score of 68, obtained from a distribution having a mean of 80 and a standard deviation of 8. What score is equivalent to this in a distribution where the mean is 100 and the standard deviation is 20? We need a principle of equivalence to solve this problem: *Two scores will be considered equivalent if they are the same number of standard deviations above (or below) the mean in their respective distributions.* The score of 68 is 1.5 standard deviations below the mean (80) of its distribution. In the new distribution, an equivalent score will be 1.5 standard deviations below the mean of 100. Since the standard deviation is 20, this amounts to 30 points below 100, or 70.

The question, "How many standard deviations is this score away from the mean?", is answered directly by the z score. Consequently, the transformation procedure converts the score from the original distribution to a z score and, from the information thus made available, to an equivalent score in the new distribution. A second illustration utilizing this point of view appears below:

Problem: In a distribution with a mean of 71 and a standard deviation of 18, there exists a score of 85. What is the equivalent score in a distribution with a mean of 50 and a standard deviation of 10?

Procedure: 1. Translate the score in the original distribution to a z score:

$$z = \frac{X - \overline{X}}{S_X} = \frac{85 - 71}{18} = +.78$$

2. The score is therefore .78 of a standard deviation above its mean. Find 78/100 of the standard deviation of the new distribution, add that amount to the mean of the new distribution, and round the value as desired:

$$\text{mean} = \quad 50$$
$$(+.78)(10) = \underline{+ \ 7.8}$$
$$57.8 \approx 58$$

The principle of equivalence can be stated in terms of a formula:

$$\frac{X_n - \overline{X}_n}{S_n} = \frac{X_o - \overline{X}_o}{S_o}$$

In this formula, the subscripts n and o identify characteristics of the new distribution and the original distribution, respectively. Notice the nature of the formula. Both sides of it are in z-score form. In effect, it says that scores in two distributions are equivalent when their z-score position is the same. The formula is not in its most convenient form for use in translating scores from one distribution to another. When solved for X_n, it becomes Formula 8.1, and is easier to use in practice:

Formula for Translating Scores in One Distribution to Equivalent Scores in Another
$$X_n = \left(\frac{S_n}{S_o}\right) X_o + \overline{X}_n - \left(\frac{S_n}{S_o}\right) \overline{X}_o \qquad (8.1)$$

As indicated above, this formula is most useful when a number of scores are to be translated. In such use, it is better to refrain from inserting the first score until the constants (means and standard deviations) have been substituted and the equation simplified. The procedure is illustrated below with the data of the immediately previous example:

$$X_n = \left(\frac{10}{18}\right) X_o + 50 - \left(\frac{10}{18}\right) 71$$

$$= .56 X_o + 10.24$$

The set of new scores may now be obtained by substituting the several values for X_o. In our example, the score of 85 is converted as follows:

$$X_n = (.56)(85) + 10.24$$

$$= 57.8$$

This answer is the same as obtained by the earlier "common sense" method.

If scores are already in z-score form, equivalent values in a different standard score system may be found by the following modification of Formula 7.3:

*Formula for Translating z scores
to Equivalent Scores in* $\qquad X_n = \bar{X}_n + z S_n$ $\qquad\qquad$ (8.2)
Another Distribution

In the example illustrated above, the z-score equivalent of the score of 85 is $+.78$. Hence $X_n = 50 + (+.78)(10) = 57.8$.

8.5 The Linear Function

An equation which when graphed yields a straight line is called a *linear function*. This concept has several important applications in statistics. A basic review of the linear function is presented in Section A.9 (Appendix A), and should be studied now. What follows here assumes that you understand that material.

Any transformation of a variable involving adding, subtracting, multiplying, or dividing by constants can be expressed by the equation of a linear function, i.e., the equation of a straight line. Earlier, we found that coding scores in this manner could ease the job of hand computation of the mean and standard deviation (Sections 5.6, 5.7, 6.8, and 6.9). The several ways of coding are therefore examples of linear transformations of the original variable.

The several types of standard scores considered so far in this chapter are also linear transformations; that is, the standard scores are related to the raw scores by a linear function. You will find it instructive to examine the formula for a z score (Formula 7.2) and the formula for the general transformation equation (Formula 8.1) in relation to the characteristics of a linear function as stated in Section A.9.

In Section 8.2, it was pointed out that the z-score transformation preserved the proportionality of interscore distances, and hence the shape of the original distribution. This is characteristic also of the other kinds of standard scores which we have met so far. Indeed, it is a characteristic of *any* linear transformation. This property is illustrated in Figure 8.1. In Sections 8.7, 8.9, and 8.10, we will meet derived scores which do not have this property (except under special circumstances).

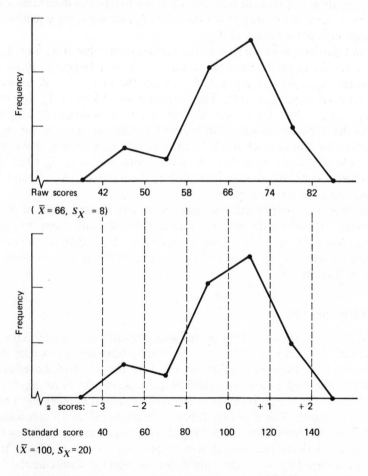

FIGURE 8.1 Comparison of Shape of a Raw Score Distribution and a Standard Score Distribution.

8.6 Conversion of Raw Scores to Standard Scores: A Graphic Solution

When a number of raw scores are to be converted to standard scores, one may use the "formula" method, described earlier in this chapter. Alternatively, it may be convenient to turn to a graphic solution. We shall illustrate this method in terms of the general transformation equation (Formula 8.1), using once again the data of Section 8.4. The first step is to substitute the constants (means and standard deviations) in the equation and simplify the expression. That process was described in Section 8.4; the result was the equation: $X_n = .56X_o + 10.24$. Since this is an equation of a straight line, and since any two points determine a straight line, we may select arbitrarily two values for X_o and solve the equation to find the corresponding two values of X_n.

To find the first point, we shall select a convenient value of X_o (say, $X_o = 40$), insert it into the equation, and solve for X_n: $X_n = (.56)(40) + 10.24 = 32.6$. These values, $X_o = 40$ and $X_n = 32.6$, identify the first point. A second value of X_o is selected (say, $X_o = 100$). The corresponding value of X_n, found in the same way, is $X_n = 66.2$. On a sheet of graph paper, X_o is assigned to the abcissa, and X_n to the ordinate, as shown in Figure 8.2. Choose the scale for the graph so as to allow for scores which might be three standard deviations above or below the mean. On the graph, locate the two points, and draw a straight line through them. As a check, see if the point identified by the intersection of $\overline{X}_o$ and $\overline{X}_n$ falls on the line; an error has been made if it does not.

Once this is accomplished, one may locate any desired value of X_o on the abcissa, read vertically to the line, and then read horizontally from the line to the ordinate to learn the equivalent value of X_n. Figure 8.2 illustrates the procedure for finding X_n from an X_o value of 85, the same problem used to illustrate the methods of Section 8.4.

8.7 Centile Scores

The basic characteristics of centile scores were presented in Chapter 3 (beginning with Section 3.9). They are also derived scores, but their properties differ in some respects from those of standard scores. Like the standard scores described so far, the centile rank of a score describes its location relative to other scores in the distribution. It has an advantage in terms of directness of meaning, a property always to be desired. The idea that Johnny's centile rank of 75 in a science test means that he performs better than 75% of comparable students is easy to comprehend, and relatively meaningful even to persons without statistical training. If ease of intelligibility were the only criterion, derived scores in the form of centile ranks would easily be the winner.

Unfortunately, there are certain disadvantages. Primarily, the problem is that *changes in raw scores are not necessarily reflected by proportionate changes in*

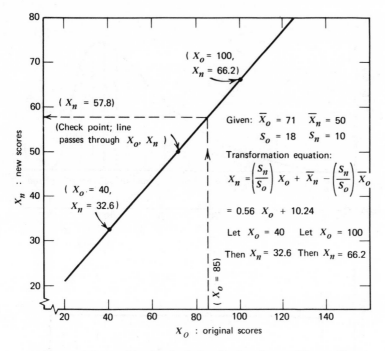

FIGURE 8.2 Graphic Method for Performing a Linear Transformation.

centile rank. When one centile rank is higher than another, the corresponding raw score of the one is higher than that of the other, but we do not know by how much. Indeed, changes in raw score are accompanied by proportionate changes in centile rank only when the distribution of scores is rectangular. Figure 8.3 illustrates this. For example, in the illustrated rectangular distribution, a change of ten points in centile rank reflects a change of five score points. In the other distribution, a change of ten points in centile rank reflects a change in score which may be larger or smaller than five points, depending on the location in the distribution.

In the normal distribution, the frequency of scores is greatest near the center of the distribution. The distance between two scores near the center is therefore represented by a relatively large difference in centile rank. On the other hand, as one approaches the extremes of the distribution, that same interscore distance is represented by a smaller and smaller difference in centile rank. This is illustrated in Figure 8.4. This figure shows, *in the normal distribution*, the relative scale for a wide variety of commonly used derived scores. It is worth close study, not only in connection with the matter currently under discussion, but in relation to the various types of derived scores discussed in other sections of this chapter.

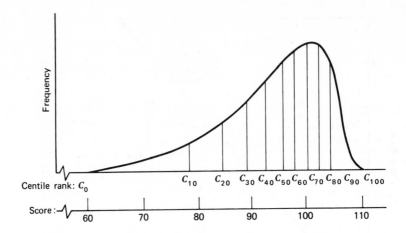

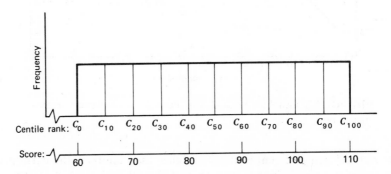

FIGURE 8.3 Comparative Location of Centile Ranks in Two Distributions.

Some of the scores presented in this illustration will be introduced in later sections, e.g., *T* scores (Section 8.9) and stanines (Section 8.10).

To return to the problem of disproportionality of centile ranks in the normal distribution, Figure 8.4 shows, for example, the actual score distance between two students who stand respectively at the fortieth and sixtieth centile rank. It is actually *smaller* than that between two students who stand respectively at the ninety-fifth and ninety-ninth centile rank. The standard scores discussed earlier do not suffer from this type of deficiency.

In summary, the centile scale is likely not to reflect proportionate raw score distances. When the basic raw score scale approaches the character of a normal distribution, expression of scores in terms of centile ranks tends to leave the impression that there is a greater difference in performance between two individuals who fall near the center of the distribution than is actually warranted.

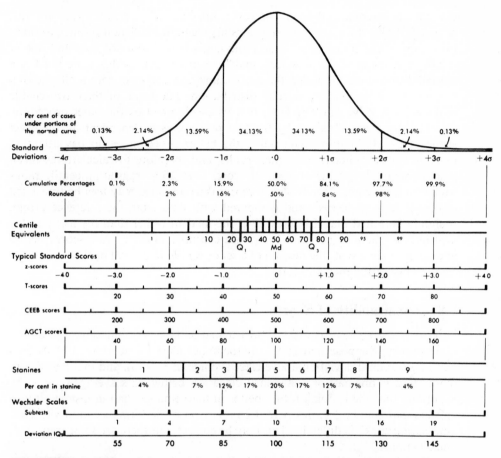

FIGURE 8.4 Centiles and Standard Scores in a Normal Distribution (Adapted with Permission from Test Service Bulletin No. 48, The Psychological Corporation, New York).

On the other hand, individuals near the extremes tend to be inadequately differentiated. Note that $z = +2$ and $z = +4$ would be represented by C_{98} and C_{99}, respectively. If this system of derived scores is used, it is recommended that centile ranks beyond C_{99} be reported to at least one decimal.

A related problem arises when we wish to compare the performance of a particular group of individuals with that of another. For example, suppose a history teacher has scores for each member of his class on a standard test of achievement in history. He wants to know how the average of his class compares with standards developed on a national sample. This can be done in straightforward fashion if the scores are in raw score or standard score form; he can compute the mean for his class and observe where that value falls in the distribution for the reference group. If, however, his students' scores are cast in terms of centile ranks, the mean of *these* values may lead to a different result. Consider, for example, the problem of finding the mean of a z score of zero and one of $+2.00$. The mean is a z of $+1.00$, and the centile rank of this score is 84 in a normal distribution. However, the centile rank of a z score of zero is 50, and of a z score of $+2.00$, 98, in a normal distribution. The mean of these two centile ranks is 74, a value differing from that of 84 obtained by the other procedure.

The difference obtained by the two procedures is dependent on the exact shape of the distribution. Generally, the better procedure is to pay attention to score values rather than to their ranks, and therefore to calculate the mean (and standard deviation) of a set of scores *only* after translating centile ranks back into raw scores. Means of raw scores thus obtained may *then* be translated to centile rank if desired, and compared with data from the reference group. It should be noted that if interest is in the median rather than the mean of the distribution, there is no need to translate centile ranks to raw scores before finding this value, since the median of a set of centile ranks will be the same as the centile rank of the median score.

8.8 Comparability of Scores

Mary may earn a raw score of 37 in her mathematics examination, and one of 82 in history. Suppose that in her mathematics class the score of 37 falls one-half of a standard deviation above class average ($z = +.5$), and that her history score of 82 is one-half of a standard deviation below class average ($z = -.5$). It appears that she is doing rather better in mathematics than in history. It also appears that standard scores permit comparison of performance even when the "measuring stick" is different. This may be correct, but there are some important qualifications.

If both courses were required of all freshmen, it is possible that the interpretation of Mary's performance stated above is correct. On the other hand, the picture is not so clear if the mathematics course is a remedial course required of freshmen who are deficient in that subject, but the history course is subject to enrollment only by honors students. *One element necessary for appropriate comparison is, therefore, that the reference groups used to generate the standard scores are comparable.* The prerequisite of comparable groups is just as important for comparison of centile ranks as it is for standard scores.

Even if the two norm groups are similar, standard scores will not be comparable unless the shapes of the distributions from which they arose are similar. The illustration in Figure 8.5 shows two distributions which are skewed in opposite directions. In the upper distribution, a score located at $z = +2$ is the top score in the distribution. In the other, a score having the same z-score value is not the top score; some scores fall substantially beyond this point. Unless distributions from which standard scores are computed have the same shape,

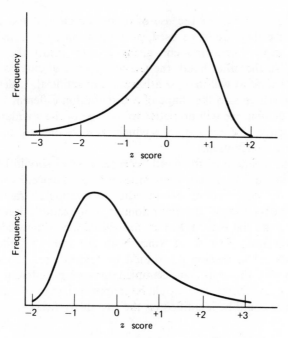

FIGURE 8.5 Noncomparability of Standard Scores when Distributions Differ in Shape.

we will find that equal standard scores may not have equal rank in their respective distributions. Thus, *standard scores should be used for comparing scores from two different distributions only if the two distributions have roughly the same shape.*

There is no satisfactory way in which the problem of noncomparable groups may be circumvented, but there is a solution to the problem of varying shape. One possibility is to use centile ranks. They are independent of the shape of the original distributions and thus may be used for comparison purposes even though the distributions differ in shape. Another solution is to convert scores to derived score distributions which have identical shapes, as well as identical means and standard deviations. The next two sections describe transformations which do precisely this. In each case, scores are forced into a normal distribution, in addition to being given standard values for the mean and standard deviation. Distributions treated in this fashion yield scores which are equal in rank as well as in score value, and in addition have the well-known properties of the normal distribution. The latter characteristic may be particularly useful when it is desired to use advanced statistical procedures based on the assumption of normally distributed data.

If the departure from normality of the original distribution is due only to an oddity in the construction of the measuring device, such as differences in difficulty of the test items or the use of items too easy or too difficult for the group with which they are to be used, normalization may actually improve the nature of the scale of measurement, giving it more nearly the character of an interval scale. On the other hand, the use of the normal curve as a Procrustean bed to stretch and fit at will may be arbitrary and artificial. Unless there is good reason to force scores into the shape of a distribution different from that which they naturally exhibit, we will do better to use one of the standard score devices described in Sections 8.2 and 8.3, ones which preserve the original characteristics of the raw score distribution.

The limited meaning of the word "comparability" should be clearly recognized. It will not do to stretch it to include "equivalence," for example. The temptation to do so sometimes occurs when evaluating characteristics in what we perceive to be the "same" behavior domain. For example, it might be thought possible to estimate the Binet IQ of an individual from knowledge of his Army General Classification Test score, since both are tests of "intelligence." The cautions introduced in Section 8.1 should be remembered in such a situation. Those constructing the tests have sampled somewhat different aspects of the general domain, and therefore it would be inappropriate to presume that equivalent performance could be identified on the two instruments.

8.9 Normalized Standard Scores: The T Score†

The T score is a standard score based on a distribution with a mean of 50, a standard deviation of 10, *and the shape of the normal curve.* Figure 8.4 shows the scale of T scores. When raw scores are converted to T scores, their distribution is automatically altered to assume a shape approximating that of a normal distribution, irrespective of the shape of the original raw score distribution. Figure 8.6 shows first a skewed distribution of raw scores, and second, the normal distribution which results when these scores have been translated to T scores.

To translate raw scores to T scores, the first step is to find the proportion of scores falling below (the midpoint of) each score in the distribution. These values are best computed to two, or perhaps to three decimal places. In effect, we are finding the centile rank of each score. This may be done by procedures described in Section 3.11, or by the graphic method described in Section 4.6. Next, look in Table C (in the appendix) to find the z score in the normal curve below which that particular percent of scores fall. Since that z score tells us how many standard deviations the score is above or below the mean, it is straightforward to compute the equivalent score in a distribution having a mean of 50 and a standard deviation of 10 by the procedures of Section 8.4. In terms of a formula, we would compute:

$$T = 10z + 50$$

We may try a simple example for purposes of illustration.

†Named after an early leader in educational measurement, E. L. Thorndike.

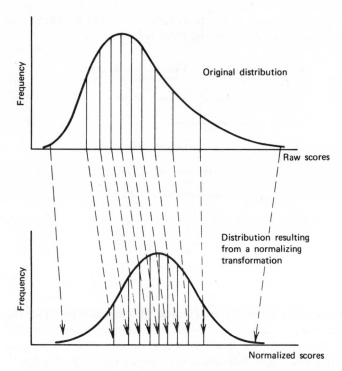

FIGURE 8.6 Effect of Using a Normalized Standard Score Transformation.

Given the following scores: 30, 32, 38, 39, 40.
Find: The *T*-score equivalent of the score of 32.
Procedure: One and one-half of the five scores fall below the score point of 32.0.†
In terms of a decimal fraction, .30 of the scores fall below this point. Consulting Table C, we find that this corresponds to a z score of $-.52$. Therefore, $T = (10)(-.52) + 50 = 44.8$.

8.10 Normalized Standard Scores: The Stanine

The term *stanine* was devised by research workers in World War II. It is a contraction of "standard nine," and refers to standard scores expressed in digits ranging from 1 to 9. Like the *T*-score system, translation of raw scores to stanines normalizes the distribution. The mean of a distribution of stanines is 5.0, and the standard deviation is 1.96, or approximately 2.0. One can translate raw scores

†The score of 32 is considered to extend from 31.5 to 32.5. Therefore, half of the score lies below its midpoint, 32.0.

to stanines by converting scores to centile ranks and assigning stanine values according to the limits shown in the table below.

Stanine	Centile Rank Limits
9	
	→ 95.99
8	
	→ 89.44
7	
	→ 77.34
6	
	→ 59.87
5	
	→ 40.13
4	
	→ 22.66
3	
	→ 10.56
2	
	→ 4.01
1	

The stanine is a relatively coarse unit of measurement, since the difference between successive stanines is one-half of a standard deviation. Its advantage is that of simplicity; only a single digit is required to express its value. In many situations, this amount of differentiation is adequate to the purpose. On the other hand, differentiation of performance is particularly poor at the extremes of the distribution. Stanines of 1 and 9 cover the scores of the lower and upper 4% of individuals. Within the range of each, a substantial difference in performance may exist. Figure 8.4 illustrates the scale of stanine scores. It shows that under the umbrella of a stanine of 9, we could find both an individual of very good attainment, and one of truly unusual ability. In guidance counseling, for example, the counselor might be unwilling to let such a difference go undiscovered.

The description of derived scores which appears so far in this chapter by no means exhausts the kinds of standard scores, whether of the linear function type or the normalized type. Those chosen for discussion include those most commonly used, and serve to illustrate the general nature of the problem. Further consideration, systematically presented, can be found in other volumes. Particularly recommended is one by Lyman.†

8.11 The Mean of Measures from Different Distributions

Suppose Instructor A has given his class a quiz, a midterm, and a final examination, and now wishes to combine these measures to obtain an index of performance for each student. We shall suppose the score for each measure is recorded

†H. B. Lyman, *Test Scores and What They Mean*, Prentice-Hall, Inc., Englewood Cliffs, N. J., 1963.

in numerical form. Two thoughts may occur to him. First, he may feel that each measure ought to be counted equally. If so, he will probably think that the correct approach is to find the mean of the three scores for each student, and to take this value as the appropriate index of performance. Second, he may wish to give differential weight to the several measures. Let us suppose he feels that the final ought to count twice as much as the midterm, and the midterm twice as much as the quiz. In this case, he may wish to find the *weighted mean*:

$$\text{Weighted Mean} \qquad \overline{X}_W = \frac{W_X X + W_Y Y + \cdots}{W_X + W_Y + \cdots} \qquad (8.3)$$

where: $\overline{X}_W$ is the weighted mean; $W_X, W_Y, \ldots$ are the weights assigned to each score; and $X, Y, \ldots$ are the individual's scores from the different distributions. In line with his intentions, he will assign a weight of 1 to the score on the quiz, a weight of 2 to the score on the midterm, and a weight of 4 to the score on the final examination. Unfortunately, neither of these procedures (simple mean or weighted mean) is likely to carry out his intent. To explore the problem, let us consider the case in which it is desired to have the measures count equally.

The basic difficulty is that when scores are taken from different distributions and averaged, each one does *not* necessarily count equally in determining their total, and therefore their mean. It can be shown that *if the several scores are independent* (i.e., if knowledge of standing in one variable is not predictive of standing in one of the others), the calculation of the simple mean of the scores actually weights the scores implicitly according to the magnitude of the standard deviation of the distribution from which each came.

A simple example may help to convey an intuitive grasp of this state of affairs. Suppose Instructor B gave two tests, and determined student status by the mean of the two performances on the assumption that each should count equally. Let us further suppose that scores on the first test range from 20 to 60, and on the second test, from 50 to 70. In view of the proposition that both tests should count equally, a student who is at the lowest position on the first test and at the highest position on the second test should receive a mean score which is the same as that of a student who is at the highest position on the first test and at the lowest on the second. We can see that this is not the case. The first student's mean is 45, whereas that of the second student is 55. The second student obtained the superior index because he had the good fortune to perform better on the test with the greater variability and less well on the test with the smaller variability, whereas the opposite is true of the first student. Note that the mean of each distribution has nothing to do with the outcome; it is solely a function of the variability of performance. In this case, the first test had the lower mean but the greater variability, and its contribution counted more than that of the second test.

This situation can be rectified by assuring that all of the test distributions from which scores are to be averaged have the same standard deviation. Usually, the simplest way to accomplish this is to translate scores from the several distributions to standard scores. The scores may *then* be averaged or an appropriate weighted average found, as desired. In this way one may be assured that the scores are receiving the weight intended.

One might wish that this were the end of the problem, but it is not. The careful reader will note that the above procedure was offered on the assumption that the several scores were independent. Most usually, this is not the case. For example, in the case of the instructor's two tests, it is likely that persons who score well on the first test will tend to do better than average on the second. If so, the two tests can not be considered to be completely independent.

This is not a problem when only two measures are to be combined, but it is when there are more than two. With more than two measures, the procedure recommended above does not ensure that the weights assigned will result in the intended proportional importance of the contribution of each to the whole. Nevertheless, it is better to follow the procedure outlined above than to allow the scores to be weighted by the amount of variability inherent in the distribution of each, since this is often a factor of irrelevant origin. Still more sophisticated alternatives exist but they are beyond the scope of elementary statistics.

PROBLEMS AND EXERCISES

Identify:

norm group	principle of equivalence
test norms	linear function
derived scores	linear transformation
standard score	centile rank
mean and standard deviation	T score
of z scores	stanine
equivalent score	weighted mean

1. A student's grade on a very difficult English exam is 85. What can you say about the merits of the student's performance? Explain.

2. A distribution has a mean of 57.0 and a standard deviation of 12.0. Translate, by the "common sense" method, the following scores to equivalent scores in a distribution having a mean of 100 and a standard deviation of 20: (*a*) $X = 63$ (*b*) $X = 72$ (*c*) $X = 48$ (*d*) $X = 30$.

3. A distribution has a mean of 108.0 and a standard deviation of 30.0. Translate, by the "common sense" method, the following scores to equivalent scores in a distribution having a mean of 500 and a standard deviation of 100: (*a*) $X = 120$ (*b*) $X = 100$ (*c*) $X = 90$ (*d*) $X = 105$.

4. (*a*) Write the transformation equation required to solve Problem 2 by the "equation" method, and simplify it. (*b*) Use the equation to solve the several parts of Problem 2. (*c*) Graph the equation and show by dotted lines the graphic solution to Problems 2*a* and 2*d*.

5. (*a*) Write the transformation equation required to solve Problem 3 by the "equation" method and simplify it. (*b*) Use the equation to solve the several parts of Problem 3. (*c*) Graph the equation and show by dotted lines the graphic solution to Problem 3*a* and 3*d*.

6. $\bar{X} = 500$ and $S = 100$ for a set of normally distributed college entrance examination scores. What is the centile rank of a score of: (*a*) 450? (*b*) 700? (*c*) 550? (*d*) 625?

7. A high school principal wishes to compare the scores of his students on a standard achievement test with the scores of high school students in the adjacent district on the same test. Only the centile ranks of the students are available to him. What measure of central tendency would you suggest he use? Explain.

8. An instructor wants to compare his students' mathematics aptitude test score with their mathematics achievement score. The following are the means and medians for each of the two distributions: Math aptitude: $\bar{X} = 100$, $Mdn = 90$; Math achievement: $\bar{X} = 70$, $Mdn = 80$. How do you suggest that the comparison be made? Explain.

9. At the end of the school year, student A's science achievement score has changed from C_{50} to C_{70}, student B's score has changed from C_5 to C_{25}, and student C's score has changed from C_{65} to C_{85}. Assuming achievement test scores to be normally distributed, what can we say about the relative raw score gain of the three students?

10. Given the following set of scores: 10, 12, 13, 18, 19, 23, 24, 25; find the T score equivalent for 24.

11. From Table 3.7, find the T score corresponding to a score of (*a*) 59 (*b*) 80 (*c*) 87.

12. From Figure 4.4, find the T score corresponding to a score of (*a*) 60 (*b*) 77 (*c*) 83.

13. What are the equivalent stanines of the three scores listed in Problem 11?

14. From Figure 4.4, find the raw score limits of a stanine of (*a*) 3 (*b*) 5 (*c*) 8.

15. Two students score as follows on Text X and Test Y:

	mean	std dev	Mary's score	Beth's score
Test X:	70	8	58	82
Test Y:	60	20	90	30

(*a*) Find Mary's mean raw score and Beth's mean raw score. (*b*) Translate the four scores into z scores. Find Mary's mean z score and Beth's mean z score. (*c*) Explain the discrepancy in outcome of (*a*) and (*b*).

16. A professor gave a midterm and a final examination to his students. The following data are available: midterm: $\bar{X} = 50$, $S = 9$; final: $\bar{X} = 65$, $S = 18$. He wants to base his course grade on the average test score, but he feels the final examination should count twice as much as the midterm. What is the simplest way to find an average score for each student that will accomplish his aim?

17. Interpret Formula 5.4 in terms of Formula 8.3.

9
Correlation

9.1 Measurement of Association and Prediction

What relation exists between stature and weight? Certainly taller persons tend to weigh more. On the other hand, we do not expect the tallest person to be the heaviest, the next tallest the next heaviest, and so on down to the shortest person. There is plainly a degree of association which exists between these two variables. Just how great is it?

We know that score earned on an academic aptitude test is related, to a degree, to the grade point average which the student will earn in college. A student who is relatively bright is therefore a better bet to do well in college than one who is not so talented. What grade point average shall we predict for a student who earns a particular score on the test? And what margin of error shall we attach to that prediction? If the relationship is not perfect, a particular prediction can only be considered to be a "good bet."

The first question concerns the degree of association between stature and weight, and illustrates a problem in *correlation*. The *correlation coefficient*, for instance, is a way of stating the degree of association between two variables. In this chapter and the next, we shall explore the problem of measuring the degree of association between two variables. The second question concerns the estimation of academic performance from knowledge of aptitude, and illustrates a problem in *prediction*. In Chapters 11 and 12, we shall explore the problem of prediction. The two problems are closely related. For example, we shall find that the closer the degree of association as measured by the correlation coefficient, the more accurately it is possible to predict standing in one variable from knowledge of standing in the other.

Determining degree of correlation and establishing rules of prediction are important in many areas of psychology and education. They are of particular importance in the study of individual differences. In this domain, two major problems are measuring traits in which individuals differ and determining the extent of relation between different kinds of characteristics. The notion of correlation is basic to the theory and practice of trait measurement. For example, many students will have encountered correlation in connection with the problem of test reliability (e.g., to what extent is initial performance on a test indicative of performance on the same test at a subsequent time?), and test validity (e.g., to what extent is score on a mechanical aptitude test related to on-the-job performance of machinists?). The second problem, that of interrelationship of individual differences, is illustrated by the two examples cited at the beginning of this section. Other examples: Is there a relation between reading speed and reading comprehension? To what extent, if any, are physical factors, such as stature, related to mental characteristics, such as intelligence?

9.2 Some Historical Matters

Fatherhood of the study of individual differences should without doubt be assigned to Sir Francis Galton, gentleman scholar of England during the latter part of the nineteenth century, man of astounding genius, and avid investigator of natural phenomena. In 1859, Galton's distinguished cousin, Charles Darwin, spelled out the theory of evolution and offered unimpeachable evidence in its behalf. This theory pointed to the importance of understanding the dimensions in which organisms differ, and to the necessity for studying the role of heredity in transmission of these characteristics. These problems interested Galton. To study the inheritance of stature, for example, he put parent's height on one coordinate of a graph and offspring's height on the other coordinate, essentially in the manner illustrated in Table 9.1. In fact, the data are Galton's.† Distributions of this type are called *bivariate distributions*, and their representation in the manner of Table 9.1, *scatter diagrams*. In this table, each cell entry is a frequency. For example, consider the entry in the cell at the intersection of the column headed 68–69 (midparent height), and the row 66–67 (height of children). It is 25. Of those parents whose midparent height was between 68 and 69 in., there were 25 children whose adult height was between 66 and 67 in. In diagrams of this kind, Galton perceived that a trend line could be fitted which would show the rate of increase in height of offspring as a function of increase in height of parent. He saw that a *straight line* was most often reasonably characteristic of the relationship observed, and that, other things being equal, the steepness of slope of the line was an indicator of the closeness of the relationship between the two variables. Some time later (1896), Karl Pearson, a scientist associated with

---

†F. Galton, "Regression Towards Mediocrity in Hereditary Stature," *Journal of the Anthropological Institute*, XV, 246–263 (1885–1886).

TABLE 9.1 Bivariate Distribution of Midparent Height and Height of Adult Children (All Female Heights Multiplied by 1.08).

Height of adult children (in.)	Below 64	64–65	65–66	66–67	67–68	68–69	69–70	70–71	71–72	72–73	Above 73
						Midparent height (in.)					
Above 74							5	3	2	4	
73–74						3	4	3	2	2	3
72–73			1		4	4	11	4	9	7	1
71–72			2		11	18	20	7	4	2	
70–71			5	4	19	21	25	14	10	1	
69–70	1	2	7	13	38	48	33	18	5	2	
68–69	1		7	14	28	34	20	12	3	1	
67–68	2	5	11	17	38	31	27	3	4		
66–67	2	5	11	17	36	25	17	1	3		
65–66	1	1	7	2	15	16	4	1	1		
64–65	4	4	5	5	14	11	16				
63–64	2	4	9	3	5	7	1	1			
62–63		1		3	3						
Below 62	1	1	1			1		1			

Galton's laboratory, provided the mathematical basis now used to find the straight line of best fit, and the fundamental formula for the correlation coefficient. These procedures, as finally developed by Pearson, are the ones considered in this book.

Before leaving the subject of history, it is worth noting that Pearson was the outstanding contributor to the development of statistical techniques around the turn of the century. Many indispensable techniques are owed to him.

9.3 Association: A Matter of Degree

According to the development owed to Galton and Pearson, the degree of association shared by two variables is indicated by the coefficient of correlation; its symbol is r_{XY}, although it is often written without the subscripts. Again, we distinguish between the symbol for the population value of this coefficient and that for a sample drawn from the population. We shall let the Greek letter ρ (*rho*) stand for the population value, and r_{XY} for a sample value.† In this chapter the descriptive nature of the correlation coefficient is basic, and to avoid confusion

---

†The Greek letter ρ_{XY} is often used to designate a variant of Pearson r; namely, Spearman's rank order correlation coefficient. When reading in other sources, be alert to possible variation in meaning assigned to this symbol.

the symbol r_{XY} will be used consistently wherever possible. The principles and procedures for calculation described here apply equally to samples and to populations.

The coefficient is, in fact, a constant in the equation of Pearson's straight line of best fit, and it has properties convenient for expressing degree of relationship. When no relationship exists, its value is zero. When a perfect relationship exists, its value is one. An intermediate degree of relationship is represented by an intermediate value of r. The sign of the coefficient may be positive or negative. A positive value of r indicates that there is a tendency for high values of one variable (X) to be associated with high values of the other variable (Y), and low values of the one to be associated with low values of the other. The correlation between stature and weight is an example of such a relationship. A negative value of r indicates that high values of X are associated with low values of Y, and vice versa. For example, we should expect IQ and number of errors made on a spelling test to be negatively correlated, i.e., the higher the IQ, the lower the number of errors. The sign of the coefficient indicates the direction of the association; it has nothing to do with its strength. For example, if the correlation between IQ and number of errors on the spelling test is $-.50$, the correlation between IQ and number of words correctly spelled would be $+.50$ (assuming that an "error" includes both misspelled words and words not attempted). For some variables, a high score is indicative of good performance, whereas for others a low score has the same meaning. The sign of the coefficient, therefore, will reflect the nature of the measure as well as the nature of the relationship. The scatter diagrams in Figure 9.1 illustrate various degrees of correlation. In these illustrations, each dot represents a pair of scores, one for X and one for Y. In those diagrams characterized by a moderate positive correlation, note that although there is a general *tendency* for higher values in X to be associated with higher values of Y, it is easy to find specific instances of inversion. Such inversions may be seen by comparing points indicated at a and b in three of the diagrams. Note also that when $r = +1.00$ or -1.00 every point lies *exactly* on a straight line. This means that if we know the value of X, we can predict the value of Y without *any* error. It will not come as a surprise, therefore, to learn that in the "real world" of variables to be investigated, we do not encounter such perfect relationships, except in trivial instances (e.g., the correlation will be -1.00 between the number of correct answers on a spelling test and the number of errors plus omissions).

9.4 A Measure of Correlation

This section introduces formulas for computing the coefficient of correlation. As indicated above, the formulas are Pearson's, and are intended for situations where two variables are involved and both are expressed in quantitative form. Other measures of association exist, and many of them are derived from Pearson's

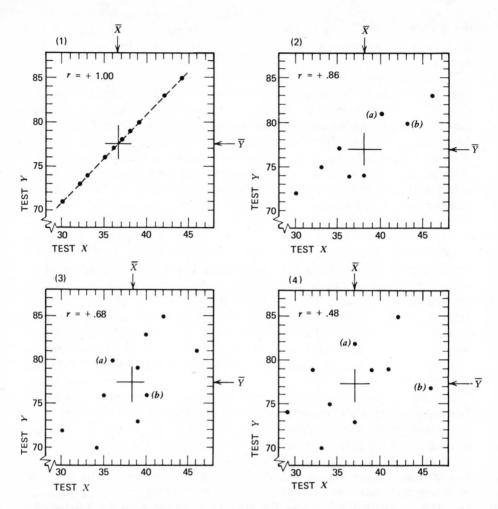

FIGURE 9.1 Scatter Diagrams Illustrating Various Degrees of Correlation.

basic formula, but are adapted to special situations. Some of these other measures are also represented by the symbol *r*, e.g., *biserial r*. In research literature, when any question exists about what coefficient is meant, it is common to refer to the coefficient described in this chapter as *Pearson r*, or *product-moment correlation*.

We may consider the formula below (Formula 9.1) as the defining formula for the coefficient of correlation.

Correlation Coefficient;
Deviation Score Formula
$$r_{XY} = \frac{\sum xy}{nS_X S_Y} \qquad (9.1)$$

where: $x = (X - \bar{X})$, $y = (Y - \bar{Y})$, $\sum xy$ is the sum of the products of the paired

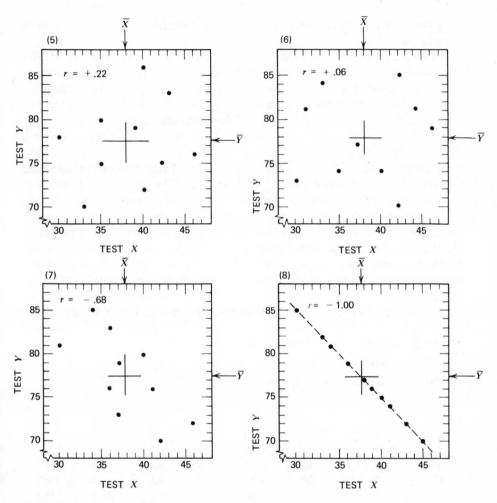

FIGURE 9.1 (*Continued*)

deviation scores, n = number of *pairs* of scores, and S_X, S_Y are the standard deviations of the two distributions. Note that the numerator consists of the sum of the products of pairs of scores (expressed in deviation score form). We meet two "old friends" in this equation. Implicit in the numerator is the mean ($x = X - \bar{X}$), and the standard deviation, S, appears explicitly in the denominator. We shall illustrate the process of computation of r by this method, because it should help in understanding the nature of the formula. However, this formula is of interest mainly because of its simplicity of expression, and because it is useful in certain further derivations. In almost all situations of practical computation, the raw score method (described in the next section) or the grouped data method (Section 9.8) have substantial advantages in ease of computation.

Table 9.2 illustrates computation of r by the deviation score formula. This table shows the midterm (X) and final examination (Y) test scores for each of ten students. First, the mean of each variable must be found. Then each raw score is translated to a deviation score (columns 3 and 4). To obtain the two standard deviations, we find the squares of the deviation scores (columns 5 and 6). For the numerator of the formula, the product of the pairs of deviation scores is obtained (column 7). For example, the xy value for student A is $+3.1$, obtained by multiplying his x score (-1.2) by his y score (-2.6). From the sums of the values in columns 5, 6, and 7, we obtain Σx^2, Σy^2, and Σxy. The two standard deviations are then computed by the usual deviation score formula (see Section 6.6), and the correlation coefficient is found by substituting the appropriate values in Formula 9.1. Note that the order in which the pairs of scores appear makes no difference; the means, standard deviations, and sum of cross-products would remain the same. However, any shifting about requires that *both* members of a particular pair be moved at the same time. To do otherwise would affect the value of Σxy.

The data of Table 9.2 have been represented graphically in Figure 9.2. In

TABLE 9.2 Calculation of r_{XY}: Deviation Score Method.

Student	(1) First test: X	(2) Second test: Y	(3) x	(4) y	(5) x²	(6) y²	(7) xy
A	37	75	-1.2	-2.6	1.4	6.8	$+3.1$
B	41	78	$+2.8$	$+.4$	7.8	.2	$+1.1$
C	48	88	$+9.8$	$+10.4$	96.0	108.2	$+101.9$
D	32	80	-6.2	$+2.4$	38.4	5.8	-14.9
E	36	78	-2.2	$+.4$	4.8	.2	$-.9$
F	30	71	-8.2	-6.6	67.2	43.6	$+54.1$
G	40	75	$+1.8$	-2.6	3.2	6.8	-4.7
H	45	83	$+6.8$	$+5.4$	46.2	29.2	$+36.7$
I	39	74	$+.8$	-3.6	.6	13.0	-2.9
J	34	74	-4.2	-3.6	17.6	13.0	$+15.1$
$n = 10$	$\Sigma X = 382$ $\overline{X} = 38.2$	$\Sigma Y = 776$ $\overline{Y} = 77.6$			$\Sigma x^2 =$ 283.2	$\Sigma y^2 =$ 226.8	$\Sigma xy =$ $+188.6$

$$S_X = \sqrt{\frac{\Sigma x^2}{n}} = \sqrt{\frac{283.2}{10}} = 5.3 \qquad r_{XY} = \frac{\Sigma xy}{nS_X S_Y} = \frac{+188.6}{(10)(5.3)(4.8)} = +.74$$

$$S_Y = \sqrt{\frac{\Sigma y^2}{n}} = \sqrt{\frac{226.8}{10}} = 4.8$$

this figure, each dot represents one of the ten pairs of scores. Beside each dot is a number indicating the product of the x value and the y value of the point expressed in deviation score form (the xy product). This diagram is divided into four quadrants by two lines, one located at the mean of X and one at the mean of Y. Points located to the right of the vertical line are therefore characterized by positive values of x, and those to the left by negative values of x. Those points lying above the horizontal line are characterized by positive values of y, and those below by negative values of y. For any point, the xy product may be positive or negative, depending on the sign of x and the sign of y. As shown in Figure 9.2, the xy products will be positive for points falling in quadrants I and III, and will be negative for points falling in quadrants II and IV. On examination of the deviation score formula, $r = \Sigma xy/nS_X S_Y$, it is apparent that the sum of the products, Σxy, determines whether the coefficient will be negative, zero, or positive. Moreover, if other things are equal, the larger its magnitude the larger the magnitude of the correlation coefficient. In studying Figure 9.2, the substantial positive correlation ($r = +.74$) is owed to the relatively large positive contribution to Σxy made by those points lying in quadrants I and III, while at the same time the negative contribution made by those points lying in quadrants II and IV is small.

More generally, the correlation coefficient will be zero when the sum of the negative xy products from quadrants II and IV equals the sum of the positive

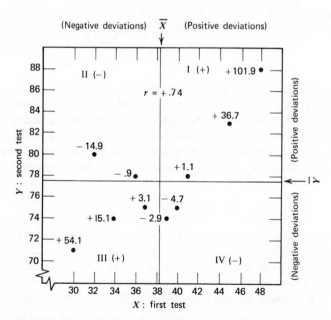

FIGURE 9.2 Scatter Diagram of the Data from Table 9.2, Showing the xy Product of Each Pair of Scores.

products from quadrants I and III, the coefficient will be negative when the contributions from quadrants II and IV exceed those from quadrants I and III, and the coefficient will be positive when the reverse is true. The greater the predominance of the sum of products bearing one sign over those bearing the other, the greater the magnitude of the coefficient. It should be instructive for you to return to Figure 9.1, mentally identify the perpendicular lines located at the means of the distributions which divide each diagram into quadrants, and observe the points falling into each quadrant relative to the indicated value of r. To make this easier, the location of $\overline{X}$ and $\overline{Y}$ has been identified in each of the diagrams of Figure 9.1.

9.5 Computation of r_{XY}: Raw Score Method

In calculating the standard deviation (Chapter 6), we found the raw score formula more convenient for practical computation than the deviation score formula. The same is true in calculating the correlation coefficient. From the deviation score formula for r, it is possible to derive an equivalent raw score formula. Its derivation is given in Notes 9.1 and 9.2. This formula makes it possible to begin calculation without the bother of first translating each score into a deviation score. Its use is particularly convenient when a desk calculator is available. The raw score formula for r is:

Correlation Coefficient; Raw Score Formula

$$r_{XY} = \frac{n\sum XY - (\sum X)(\sum Y)}{\sqrt{n\sum X^2 - (\sum X)^2}\,\sqrt{n\sum Y^2 - (\sum Y)^2}} \tag{9.2}$$

where: ΣXY is the sum of the products of the paired raw scores.

Ordinarily, when the correlation coefficient is calculated, one also wants to know the values of the means and standard deviations. Inspection of Formula 9.2 shows that these values are easily recovered from the components required to be found in the calculation of r_{XY}. The quantity ΣX has only to be divided by n to yield $\overline{X}$, and S_X is readily found by Formula 6.6, repeated here for convenience:

$$S_X = \frac{1}{n}\sqrt{n\sum X^2 - (\sum X)^2}$$

Calculation of r_{XY}, together with $\overline{X}$, $\overline{Y}$, S_X, and S_Y is illustrated in Table 9.3. The data from Table 9.2 are used once again. For "hand" calculation, it will be convenient to set up the computing routine as shown in this table. Again, it does not matter in which order the pairs of scores appear, but the two members of a given pair must remain as originally paired. The steps are as follows:

1. Set down the paired values of X and Y (columns 1 and 2).
2. Square each of these values (columns 3 and 4).

TABLE 9.3 Calculation of r_{XY}: Raw Score Method.

Student	(1) First test X	(2) Second test Y	(3) X^2	(4) Y^2	(5) XY
A	37	75	1369	5625	2775
B	41	78	1681	6084	3198
C	48	88	2304	7744	4224
D	32	80	1024	6400	2560
E	36	78	1296	6084	2808
F	30	71	900	5041	2130
G	40	75	1600	5625	3000
H	45	83	2025	6889	3735
I	39	74	1521	5476	2886
J	34	74	1156	5476	2516
$n = 10$	$\Sigma X = 382$	$\Sigma Y = 776$	$\Sigma X^2 =$ 14,876	$\Sigma Y^2 =$ 60,444	$\Sigma XY =$ 29,832

$$\bar{X} = \frac{\Sigma X}{n} = \frac{382}{10} = 38.2$$

$$\bar{Y} = \frac{\Sigma Y}{n} = \frac{776}{10} = 77.6$$

$$S_X = \frac{1}{n}\sqrt{n\Sigma X^2 - (\Sigma X)^2}$$

$$S_X = \left(\frac{1}{10}\right)(53.4) = 5.3$$

$$S_Y = \frac{1}{n}\sqrt{n\Sigma Y^2 - (\Sigma Y)^2}$$

$$= \left(\frac{1}{10}\right)(47.6) = 4.8$$

$$r_{XY} = \frac{n\Sigma XY - (\Sigma X)(\Sigma Y)}{\sqrt{n\Sigma X^2 - (\Sigma X)^2}\sqrt{n\Sigma X^2 - (\Sigma Y)^2}}$$

$$= \frac{(10)(29832) - (382)(776)}{\sqrt{(10)(14876) - (382)^2}\sqrt{(10)(60444) - (776)^2}}$$

$$= \frac{+1888}{\sqrt{2836}\sqrt{2264}}$$

$$= \frac{+1888}{(53.4)(47.6)} = +.74$$

3. Find the product of each X with its paired Y (column 5). For example, the first entry in column 5 is 2775, the product of the first pair of scores, 37 and 75.
4. Sum the values for each column.
5. Substitute these values in the formula for r_{XY}, and complete the calculation as shown in Table 9.3.
6. Find means and standard deviations as required, using the components calculated for r_{XY}.

9.6 Effect of Coding on r_{XY}

In the chapters on central tendency and variability, we considered the effect of coding on the mean (Section 5.6) and standard deviation (Section 6.8). How will the correlation between X and Y be affected if X is coded by adding a constant to, or subtracting a constant from each score? And what is the effect of multiplying X by a constant or dividing it by a constant before obtaining the correlation between that variable and Y? The answer, though not intuitively obvious, is most interesting: nothing happens. In each of the instances described above, the correlation between the altered variable and the remaining variable remains just as it was before the adjustment was made. In symbolic terms:

$$r_{(X+C)(Y)} = r_{XY} \qquad r_{(X-C)(Y)} = r_{XY}$$

$$r_{(CX)(Y)} = r_{XY} \qquad r_{(X/C)(Y)} = r_{XY}$$

Proof of these propositions appears in Note 9.3 at the end of this chapter.

Furthermore, two-stage coding is possible without affecting the value of r_{XY}. For example, one may subtract 10 points from each X score and then divide each of these altered scores by 5, and the correlation between those doubly altered scores and the Y variable will be just the same as though the modifications of X had not taken place.

Also, X can be coded in one way (perhaps by adding a constant), and Y in another (say by multiplying by a constant), and the value of the coefficient remains unaltered. It follows that if each variable is doubly coded, even though in a different way, the value of r_{XY} will remain unaffected.

This remarkable property has consequences which are at once useful in simplifying the work of computation and of significance in understanding what a correlation coefficient means. Let us consider the latter proposition first.

Suppose we obtain the correlation between stature and weight as measured by inches and pounds, respectively. These propositions tell us that if the measurements were translated into centimeters and kilograms, the value of r would be unaffected.† Similarly, the correlation will remain the same whether the scores are expressed in raw score form, in deviation score form, or in z-score form. In fact, *as long as the translation of either (or both) variable(s) is a linear one (see Section 8.5) the correlation will be unaltered.* Again, consider the correlation between test and retest, as might be used to evaluate the consistency (reliability) of the measure. If practice results in some *constant* amount of improvement of performance on the occasion of the retest, this factor has, *per se*, no effect on the correlation between the two performances. What matters is whether those who had high scores on the first performance tend on the second testing to have scores which, *as compared with others on the second test*, are also high. To

---

†A centimeter, for example, may be thought of as a "coded inch." If measurements in inches are divided by .3937, the distances are expressed in centimeters.

clarify this point, note that if scores on the first administration were augmented by adding 10 points to each score, and these values were correlated with the unaugmented scores, the correlation coefficient would be $+1.00$.

These principles can be put to good use in easing the work of computation. If the X scores range from 506 to 548, for example, 500 may be subtracted from each score, and the resulting scores correlated with Y. The same answer will be obtained as if the alteration had not been made. Again, if scores are reported to one decimal point, we may multiply each by 10 (removing the decimal), and the subsequent correlation will be unaffected.

Full use of the property described above is made in the coded score method of calculation of r, described in the next section. By a procedure identical with that used in coded score calculation of the mean (Section 5.7) and standard deviation (Section 6.9), scores in X and Y may both be doubly coded to yield simple numbers which take the place of the original (and less simple) raw score values. The correlation between these values may then be obtained, and the resulting r will be *exactly* the same as though this set of operations had not been performed.

9.7 Scatter Diagram (Coded Score) Method of Finding r_{XY}: Introduction

The scatter diagram method of calculating r_{XY} is particularly attractive when the scores are numerous, when the values of the scores are expressed in two or more digits, and when no calculating machine is available. The method combines grouping of data into class intervals for ease of handling, use of coded scores to simplify the handling of awkward numbers, and visual presentation of the data in the form of a two-way plot.

The special advantage of this method is that one gets to "see" the way the data are related by studying the graphic representation afforded by the scatter diagram. For the neophyte, this offers one of the very best ways to learn what is meant by a given magnitude of correlation. For the experienced data analyst, the scatter diagram provides a means of making an "eye check" on a number of factors which may influence the value of the coefficient or which should be taken into account in interpreting its meaning. This point will be better appreciated when we have studied these factors. For the present, note that inspection of a scatter diagram gives a rough check on the accuracy of computation of the correlation coefficient. If, for instance, the scatter plot looks like that in Figure 9.1 which corresponds to an r of $+.68$, but the computational outcome yields an r of $+.22$, we would be aware of the discrepancy and begin a recheck of our calculations. Using the raw score method, one would be unlikely to observe that something was wrong. When experienced workers are using the raw score method (or obtaining their results from a computer), they frequently find it helpful to construct a scatter diagram in order to study situations of particular interest, or to check values which appear unusual or dubious. For those who have access to a computer, it should be noted that the more sophisticated programs for computing correlation also make a provision for construction (by the computer) of the scatter plot. If there is an option, be sure to select one of these.

9.8 Computation of r_{XY}: Coded Score Method

Computation begins with a set of paired scores, just as with the raw score method. Table 9.4 shows the faculty rating accorded to 40 psychology seniors, together with the scores for the same students on a comprehensive test of psychological knowledge. By the methods described in Section 3.5, class intervals are chosen in which to group the X scores. As usual, there should be 10 to 20 class intervals. When the number is between 10 and 15, the interests of accuracy are usually satisfactorily served, and convenience is maximized (in the illustration to follow, fewer intervals are used because of space limitations). The same kind of decision is then made about the scores in Y. It is not necessary to have exactly the same number of class intervals in X as in Y, nor is it necessary to use the same interval width in both variables. Indeed, if inches of rainfall were correlated with wheat

TABLE 9.4 Scores on an Achievement Test in Psychology (X), and Mean Faculty Rating of Potential as a Graduate Student (Y) ($n = 40$ Senior Psychology Students).

Student	X	Y	Student	X	Y
1	106	2.3	21	107	3.8
2	101	2.4	22	124	4.8
3	129	5.0	23	126	4.8
4	128	4.1	24	133	4.0
5	113	2.6	25	132	4.9
6	116	2.9	26	116	3.3
7	117	4.0	27	112	2.8
8	138	4.0	28	103	3.0
9	131	4.2	29	103	3.2
10	132	3.8	30	128	4.6
11	111	3.1	31	135	4.2
12	96	4.0	32	103	2.1
13	100	3.7	33	101	2.7
14	100	1.9	34	105	3.2
15	102	3.3	35	119	4.2
16	114	3.3	36	122	3.4
17	122	4.3	37	112	2.6
18	118	4.5	38	120	3.7
19	102	3.0	39	132	3.2
20	106	2.5	40	109	1.7

yield in bushels, the range of the scores would be so different that it would be quite impossible to consider equating class interval width in X and Y.

The next step is to construct a grid in the manner exhibited in Tables 9.5 and 9.6. Table 9.5 shows the initial steps in constructing the diagram, and Table 9.6 shows the additional columns and rows which will be needed for the full computing routine. Graph paper with $\frac{1}{4}$ in. or 1 cm divisions is often convenient to use. First, the class intervals are recorded at the two margins of the graph, as shown in Table 9.5. Remember to place the high score values of X to the right, and the high values of Y toward the top (if done otherwise, the coding process will be confused).

The tally of the scores is done next. Referring to Table 9.4, we find that the first student had a test score (X) of 106, and rating (Y) of 2.3. On the grid (Table 9.5), we locate the class interval in X in which the score of 106 will fall (105–109), and the class interval in Y in which the rating of 2.3 will fall (2.3–2.6).

TABLE 9.5 Initial Steps in Construction of a Scatter Diagram (Data from Table 9.4).

Comprehensive test of psychological knowledge

Average faculty rating	95–99	100–104	105–109	110–114	115–119	120–124	125–129	130–134	135–139
4.7–5.0						/	⌐	/	
4.3–4.6				/	/	/			
3.9–4.2	/				⌐		/	⌐	⌐
3.5–3.8		/	/			/		/	
3.1–3.4		⌐	/ ⌐		/	/		/	
2.7–3.0		⊓		/	/				
2.3–2.6		/ ⌐	⌐						
1.9–2.2		⌐							
1.5–1.8			/						

(See Table 9.6 for computing cells to be entered here)

(See Table 9.6 for computing cells to be entered here)

TABLE 9.6 Calculation of the Correlation Coefficient (r_{XY}) between Performance on Psychological Achievement Test Score and Rating of the Student by the Faculty: Scatter Diagram (Coded Score) Method.

Comprehensive test of psychological knowledge

Average faculty rating	95–99	100–104	105–109	110–114	115–119	120–124	125–129	130–134	135–139	f_Y	y'	fy'	fy'^2	row Σfx'y' +	row Σfx'y' −
4.7–5.0					+4 1 +4	+8 2 +16	+12 1 +12			4	+4	+16	64	32	
4.3–4.6				0 1 0	+3 1 +3	+6 1 +6				3	+3	+9	27	9	
3.9–4.2	−8 1 −8			0 2 0		+4 1 +4	+6 2 +12	+8 2 +16		8	+2	+16	32	32	8
3.5–3.8	−3 1 −3	−2 1 −2			+1 1 +1		+3 1 +3			4	+1	+4	4	4	5
3.1–3.4	0 2 0	0 1 0	0 2 0	0 1 0	0 1 0		0 1 0			8	0		+45 −25		
2.7–3.0	+3 3 +9		+1 1 +1	0 1 0						5	−1	−5	5	10	
2.3–2.6	+6 1 +6	+4 2 +8	+2 2 +4							5	−2	−10	20	18	
1.9–2.2	+9 2 +18									2	−3	−6	18	18	
1.5–1.8		+8 1 +8								1	−4	−4	16	8	
										40	+20	186		+131 +118	−13
										n	$\Sigma fy'$	$\Sigma fy'^2$		$\Sigma fx'y'$	

TABLE 9.6 (*Continued*)

f_X	1	9	5	5	5	4	4	5	2	40	n
x'	-4	-3	-2	-1	0	$+1$	$+2$	$+3$	$+4$		
fx'	-4	-27	-10	-5	$+35$ / -46	$+4$	$+8$	$+15$	$+8$	-11	$\Sigma fx'$
fx'^2	16	81	20	5		4	16	45	32	219	$\Sigma fx'^2$
$+$		33	16	5		8	26	27	16	$+131$	
$^{col}\Sigma fx'y'$	$-$	$-$	$-$	$-$	$-$	$-$	$-$	$-$	$-$	$+118$	$\Sigma fx'y'$
$-$	8	3	2							-13	

$$r_{XY} = \frac{n\Sigma fx'y' - (\Sigma fx')(\Sigma fy')}{\sqrt{n\Sigma fx'^2 - (\Sigma fx')^2}\ \sqrt{n\Sigma fy'^2 - (\Sigma fy')^2}}$$

$$r_{XY} = \frac{(40)(+118) - (-11)(+20)}{\sqrt{(40)(219) - (-11)^2}\ \sqrt{(40)(186) - (+20)^2}}$$

$$= \frac{4720 + 220}{\sqrt{8760 - 121}\ \sqrt{7440 - 400}}$$

$$= \frac{+4940}{(92.9)(83.9)} = +.63$$

$$\overline{X} = A.O. + i_X\left(\frac{\Sigma fx'}{n}\right)$$

$$= 117.0 + 5\left(\frac{-11}{40}\right)$$

$$= 115.6$$

$$S_X = \frac{i_X}{n}\sqrt{n\Sigma fx'^2 - (\Sigma fx')^2}$$

$$= \frac{5}{40}(92.9) = 11.6$$

$$\overline{Y} = A.O. + i_Y\left(\frac{\Sigma fy'}{n}\right)$$

$$= 3.25 + .4\left(\frac{+20}{40}\right)$$

$$= 3.45$$

$$S_Y = \frac{i_Y}{n}\sqrt{n\Sigma fy'^2 - (\Sigma fy')^2}$$

$$= \frac{.4}{40}(83.9) = .84$$

At the cell located at the intersection of this column and row, enter a tally mark. This process is then repeated for each successive pair of scores until all pairs have been accounted for. The result will then look like Table 9.5. If the work of tallying has been done in pencil, the tally may then be erased, and the appropriate frequency indicated by the usual Arabic numerals, as shown in Table 9.6. Assuming that the computing columns to the right of the grid and the rows below the grid have been constructed (see Table 9.6), we may proceed as follows:

1. Sum the frequencies in each row of the main grid, entering the total in the appropriate f_Y cell (located immediately to the right of the main grid).
   (Steps 2–5 are performed in a manner identical with that used in finding the standard deviation by the coded score method; see Section 6.9.)
2. Assign to y' the value of zero for a class interval in Y approximately midway between the top and bottom class interval. In Table 9.6, this value has been assigned to the class interval of 3.1–3.4, and the value of zero has therefore been entered in the y' column opposite this class interval.
3. Assign additional values of y' ($+1$, $+2$, etc.; -1, -2, -3, etc.) as required to complete the entries in the y' column. Successive positive values are assigned to cells above that to which zero was assigned, and successive negative values are assigned to the cells lying below this point.
4. Multiply each value of y' by the accompanying value of f_Y. Enter the result in the appropriate cell in the column headed fy'. For example, in the row corresponding to the class interval 4.7–5.0, we multiply $+4$ by 4 and enter the product of $+16$ in the fy' cell at the right.
5. Similarly, the entries in the column headed fy'^2 are found by multiplying together the entries in the two cells lying immediately to the left (in the y' column and fy' column). Thus for the class interval 4.7–5.0, we multiply $+4$ by $+16$, obtaining $+64$.
6. Repeat steps 1–5, but as applied to the other axis of the diagram. This will complete the entries for the first four rows lying below the scatter diagram proper.
7. We now calculate the *moments* for each cell. For each cell of the bivariate distribution, find the value of x' and y' corresponding to its location, and record the product of these two values in the upper left corner of the cell. For example, consider the cell lying at the intersection of the 120–124 class interval in X and the 4.7–5.0 class interval in Y. The value of x' for this column is $+1$, and the value of y' for this row is $+4$. The product of these two numbers, $+4$, has been entered in the upper corner of the cell. (Note that (1) all such products will be zero in the column where x' is zero, and in the row where y' is zero, (2) the products need not be found for cells which contain no frequencies, and (3) if the diagram is considered to be divided into quadrants as indicated in Table 9.6, all products located in the lower left and upper right quadrants will be positive, and those located in the lower right and upper left quadrants will be negative.)

8. For each cell, multiply the value of the moment by the frequency recorded in the cell, and write the product in the lower right corner of the cell. The symbolic equivalent of these values is $fx'y'$.
9. These values of $fx'y'$ are now summed for each row, and the total entered in the double column at the far right. For example, in the top row, the three values, $+4$, $+16$, and $+12$ sum to $+32$; this sum is therefore entered under the $+$ sign in the double column at the far right. Since it is easier to sum all the positive values and then all the negative values, rather than to keep track of changing signs as one adds, a double column has been provided to accommodate this process.
10. The same cell values ($fx'y'$) are now summed for each column, rather than each row, and the values entered in the double row at the bottom of the computing diagram.
11. We now find the sum of the figures in each computing *column* (except for the y' column), taking proper account of the algebraic sign of the entries. These sums are shown at the bottom of the columns. In the example shown, they are: $n = 40$, $\Sigma fy' = +20$, $\Sigma fy'^2 = 186$, and $\Sigma fx'y' = +118$.
12. Step number 11 is repeated, but with application to the computing *rows*, as shown in the illustration. Note that the values of n and $\Sigma fx'y'$ have been found two ways; a partial check is thus afforded for these two figures.

At this point, we have obtained all of the component values needed to find r_{XY}, and it remains only to substitute them in the appropriate equation given as Formula 9.3.

Correlation Coefficient; Coded Score Formula

$$r_{XY} = \frac{n\sum fx'y' - (\sum fx')(\sum fy')}{\sqrt{n\sum fx'^2 - (\sum fx')^2}\ \sqrt{n\sum fy'^2 - (\sum fy')^2}} \tag{9.3}$$

In most cases where the correlation coefficient is calculated, we also want to know the values of the two means and the two standard deviations. Finding these additional values requires very little additional work, since the basic components are available as a byproduct of the calculation of r_{XY}. We may use the coded score formulas (Formulas 5.3 and 6.7) which were given in earlier chapters for finding these values. The complete calculation of the correlation coefficient, means, and standard deviations is shown in Table 9.6.

9.9 The Correlation Coefficient: Some Cautions and a Preview of Some Aspects of Its Interpretation

One might think that interpretation of a given correlation coefficient would be a straightforward matter. Actually, this question is somewhat elusive. For the moment, we shall try to identify some of the more significant aspects pertinent to its understanding.

1. The degree of association is not ordinarily interpretable in direct proportion to the magnitude of the coefficient. For example, if we propose that "a correlation coefficient of $+.50$ means that there is 50% association between the two variables," a close analysis reveals that there are no objective referents by which this statement could be considered true; it turns out to be a nonsense statement. In general, a change of $.10$ point in the coefficient has greater consequence when applied to coefficients having high values than when applied to those having low values. For instance, accuracy of prediction is benefited more by an increase in the coefficient from $.80$ to $.90$ than by an increase from $.20$ to $.30$.
2. It is tempting to think that if two variables are substantially correlated, that one must be, at least in part, the *cause* of the other. This is not so. Mere association is insufficient to claim a causal relation between the two variables.
3. The strength of the association between two variables depends, among other things, upon the nature of the measurement of the two variables as well as on the kind of subjects studied. It is not possible, then, to speak of *the* correlation between two variables without taking these factors into consideration.
4. You remember that Pearsonian correlation is based on the *straight* line of best fit to the bivariate distribution. Although a straight line is reasonably considered to be the line of best fit in many situations, sometimes it is not. When it is not, the strength of association is likely to be underestimated by Pearson r.
5. The correlation coefficient is affected by the *range of talent* (variability) characterizing the measurements of the two variables. In general, the smaller the range of talent in X and/or Y, the lower the correlation coefficient, other things being equal. For example, in a given school the correlation between academic aptitude test score and grade point average may be $+.50$ for students in general. However, if the same correlation is determined using only those students who achieved a superior grade record, the correlation will be substantially lower.
6. Finally, the correlation coefficient, like other statistics, is subject to sampling variation. Depending on the characteristics of a particular sample, the obtained coefficient may be higher or lower than it would be if a different sample had been employed.

These, and other factors, will be discussed in some detail in the next chapter and in Chapter 12.

NOTES

Note 9.2 shows the derivation of the raw score formula for the correlation coefficient from the deviation score formula. However, we first derive the raw score equivalent of Σxy (shown in Note 9.1), as it will simplify the development in Note 9.2.

NOTE 9.1 The Raw Score Equivalent of Σxy

$$\Sigma xy = \Sigma(X - \bar{X})(Y - \bar{Y})$$
$$= \Sigma(XY - \bar{X}Y - \bar{Y}X + \bar{X}\bar{Y})$$
$$= \Sigma XY - \bar{X}\Sigma Y - \bar{Y}\Sigma X + n\bar{X}\bar{Y}$$
$$= \Sigma XY - \frac{(\Sigma X)(\Sigma Y)}{n} - \frac{(\Sigma Y)(\Sigma X)}{n} + \frac{n(\Sigma X)(\Sigma Y)}{(n)(n)}$$
$$= \Sigma XY - \frac{(\Sigma X)(\Sigma Y)}{n}$$

NOTE 9.2 Derivation of the Raw Score Formula for r_{XY} from the Deviation Score Formula (*Ref:* Section 9.5)

The deviation score formula for r_{XY} is:

$$r_{XY} = \frac{\Sigma xy}{nS_X S_Y}$$

Substituting the raw score equivalent of Σxy (see Note 9.1) in the numerator, and the raw score equivalents of S_X and S_Y (Formula 6.6) in the denominator, we have:

$$r_{XY} = \frac{\Sigma XY - \dfrac{(\Sigma X)(\Sigma Y)}{n}}{n\left[\dfrac{1}{n}\sqrt{n\Sigma X^2 - (\Sigma X)^2}\right]\left[\dfrac{1}{n}\sqrt{n\Sigma Y^2 - (\Sigma Y)^2}\right]}$$

$$= \frac{\dfrac{1}{n}[n\Sigma XY - (\Sigma X)(\Sigma Y)]}{\dfrac{1}{n}\sqrt{n\Sigma X^2 - (\Sigma X)^2}\sqrt{n\Sigma Y^2 - (\Sigma Y)^2}}$$

$$= \frac{n\Sigma XY - (\Sigma X)(\Sigma Y)}{\sqrt{n\Sigma X^2 - (\Sigma X)^2}\sqrt{n\Sigma Y^2 - (\Sigma Y)^2}}$$

NOTE 9.3 Correlation between Coded Scores (*Ref:* Section 9.6)

A. Let $r_{(X+C)Y}$ be the correlation between one variable (X) which has been altered by adding a constant (C) to each score, and another variable (Y).

$$r_{(X+C)Y} = \frac{\Sigma[(X + C) - \overline{X + C}]y}{nS_{(X+C)}S_Y}$$

From Note 5.1A, $\overline{X + C} = \bar{X} + C$, and from Note 6.2A, $S_{(X+C)} = S_X$. Making these substitutions, we have:

$$r_{(X+C)Y} = \frac{\Sigma[(X + C) - (\bar{X} + C)]y}{nS_X S_Y}$$

$$= \frac{\sum [X - \overline{X}]y}{nS_X S_Y}$$

$$= \frac{\sum xy}{nS_X S_Y}$$

$$= r_{XY}$$

If C may take negative values, we have without further proof:

$$r_{(X-C)Y} = r_{XY}$$

    B. Let $r_{(CX)Y}$ be the correlation between one variable (X) which has been altered by multiplying each score by a constant (C) and another variable (Y)

$$r_{(CX)Y} = \frac{\sum [CX - \overline{CX}]y}{nS_{CX} S_Y}$$

From Note 5.1B, $\overline{CX} = C\overline{X}$, and from Note 6.2B, $S_{CX} = CS_X$. Making these substitutions, we have:

$$r_{(CX)Y} = \frac{\sum [CX - C\overline{X}]y}{nCS_X S_Y}$$

$$= \frac{C\sum [X - \overline{X}]y}{nCS_X S_Y}$$

$$= \frac{\sum xy}{nS_X S_Y}$$

$$= r_{XY}$$

If C may take fractional values, we have without further proof:

$$r_{(X/C)Y} = r_{XY}$$

PROBLEMS AND EXERCISES

Identify:

correlation	Pearson
correlation coefficient	negative value of r
prediction	$r = \pm 1$
Galton	product-moment correlation
bivariate distribution	quadrants I, II, III, IV
scatter diagram	cell moment

    1. Seven students made the following scores on two tests, X and Y:

Student:	A	B	C	D	E	F	G
Score on X:	3	9	7	8	4	7	5
Score on Y:	2	7	8	6	6	5	7

(a) Compute r to two decimals using the deviation score method. (b) Compute r to two decimals using the raw score method. (c) Did you get exactly the same answer in (a) and (b)? Explain. (d) Which method was easier? Why?

2. Five students made the following scores on two tests, X and Y:

Student:	H	I	J	K	L
Score on X:	9	4	5	3	5
Score on Y:	4	8	4	8	7

(a) Compute r, using the raw score method. (b) Compute $\bar{X}$, $\bar{Y}$, S_X, and S_Y, making the best use of quantities already found in computing r.

3. In Figure 9.1, one of the scatter diagrams is described by: $r = +.68$. The 10 pairs of scores are:

X:	30	34	35	36	39	39	40	40	42	46
Y:	72	70	76	80	73	79	76	83	85	81

(a) Verify, by the raw score method, that $r = +.68$. (b) Find $\bar{X}$, $\bar{Y}$, S_X, and S_Y.

Data 9A

In a statistics class, the instructor gave a test of elementary mathematics skills (X) on the first day. At the end of the course, he had available the score on the final examination (Y) for the same students. The data were as follows:

Student	X	Y	Student	X	Y	Student	X	Y	Student	X	Y
1	29	56	16	14	37	31	6	29	46	9	32
2	9	26	17	21	41	32	18	56	47	27	53
3	14	43	18	14	25	33	16	52	48	19	22
4	28	38	19	22	44	34	6	20	49	14	35
5	21	53	20	16	24	35	22	49	50	34	41
6	10	36	21	19	42	36	32	38	51	15	51
7	16	33	22	12	39	37	27	53	52	14	28
8	11	38	23	9	36	38	21	34	53	21	42
9	18	48	24	10	33	39	7	28	54	21	53
10	27	42	25	19	36	40	14	43	55	20	23
11	23	42	26	34	42	41	29	45	56	35	44
12	11	37	27	23	34	42	27	46	57	27	53
13	12	37	28	34	56	43	15	36	58	39	48
14	16	34	29	19	38	44	31	57	59	21	52
15	23	49	30	18	44	45	18	29	60	24	40

4. (a) Using a desk calculator, find r for the 60 pairs of scores in Data 9A. (b) Calculate $\bar{X}$, $\bar{Y}$, S_X, and S_Y for the same data.

5. An r of $+.60$ was obtained between points earned on a spelling test and IQ for all current members of the sixth grade in a particular school. For each of the following, state whether the correlation would be affected, and if so, how. If it would be affected in an unpredictable manner, say so. Treat each question as independent of the others. (*a*) Score in spelling is changed to number of answers not correct, rather than the number correct. (*b*) Each IQ is divided by 10. (*c*) Ten points are added to each spelling score. (*d*) Ten points are added to each spelling score *and* each IQ is divided by 10. (*e*) Ten points are subtracted from each spelling score and these scores are multiplied by 2. (*f*) Spelling scores are converted to *z* scores. (*g*) Spelling scores are converted to *z* scores *and* IQ to standard scores with a mean of 50 and a standard deviation of 10. (*h*) *r* is calculated using only those paired scores for students whose IQ exceeds 100.

    6. (*a*) Construct a scatter diagram for the data in Data 9A, using 6–8 for the bottom class interval in X and 20–22 for the bottom class interval in Y. (*b*) From the appearance of the scatter diagram, estimate *r*. (*c*) Compute *r*, using the coded score method. (*d*) Compute $\overline{X}$, $\overline{Y}$, S_X, and S_Y, using the coded score methods. Make as much use as possible of the calculations required to find *r*.

10

Factors Influencing the Correlation Coefficient

10.1 Correlation and Causation

The meaning of the word *causation* has given wise men many hours of contemplation and debate. We cannot consider its subtleties here, but shall take a common sense approach, as in the statement that fly spray kills flies. In this sense, if variation in X is responsible for variation in Y, this must be reflected by evidence of some degree of association between X and Y, when the effect of interfering variables is appropriately controlled. However, the converse of this proposition is not true. The fact that X and Y vary together is a necessary, but not a sufficient condition for one to make a statement about causal relationship between the two variables. In short, evidence that two variables vary together is not necessarily evidence of causation. *If one is to speak of causation, it must be on grounds over and above those merely demonstrating association between the two variables.*

There is, for instance, a high correlation between length of left arm and length of right arm, but one is not the cause of the other. Again, if a sample of children ranging in age from 6 to 12 years is drawn and the correlation obtained between their scores on a test of reading comprehension and lengths of their big toes, a substantial positive correlation would be found. Of course, physical and mental maturity are parallel processes of growth, and the variation in state of growth affects the relationship. If the study were redone with children of *one particular age level*, the correlation coefficient would drop to a level close to zero. To speculate a bit, suppose that age has been held constant, and that the correlation between length of big toe and reading comprehension is reliably found to be low and positive (but not zero). How could this occur? The following argument is speculative but possible and is offered for purposes of illustration. In a given cultural environment, it could be that differences in physique are due in part to the diet of the children, that their diet may be associated with the economic condition of the family, that the economic condition in turn is associated with intelligence of the parents, that intelligence of the parents is related to intelligence of their children, and hence with the reading comprehension scores which were obtained.

Figure 10.1 shows schematically four of the possibilities which may exist when the variables X and Y are correlated. First, it may be that the condition of Y is determined (in part, at least), by the condition of X. Second, the situation may be reversed, and Y is causing X to vary. Third, there may be a third factor which is influencing both X and Y, thus producing the observed association between the two. Fourth, the "third factor" may not be a unitary characteristic, but in fact a complex of interrelated variables. This is certainly the case in the example given above concerning the association between reading comprehension and length of big toe. To invoke the concept of maturation makes it appear as though one were speaking of a single factor, but in fact it is a process of considerable complexity. To analyze the nature of the mechanism by which the particular physical traits and mental characteristics are associated through increase in age requires knowledge of substantial depth.

In correlational studies, the investigator must be particularly alert to the possible presence of extraneous variables (such as maturation in the example above), in order to exert an appropriate degree of control so that the interpretation of the obtained correlation coefficient may be as straightforward as possible.

10.2 Linearity of Regression

Figure 10.2 shows a scatter diagram in which the correlation between X and Y is moderately low, and another in which the correlation is high. In each, the

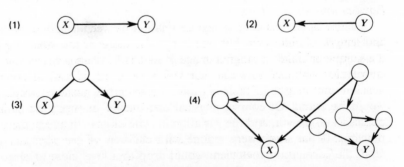

FIGURE 10.1 Diagrammatic Representation of Causal Relationships.

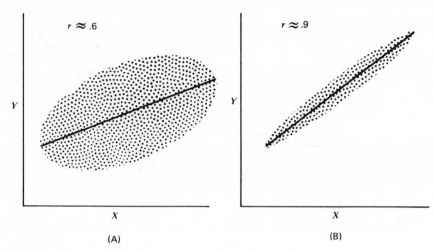

FIGURE 10.2 Scatter Diagrams Corresponding to a Moderate and High Degree of Correlation.

straight line of best fit has been included. In the diagram depicting the lower correlation, notice that the points scatter rather widely about the line. In the other picture, the points tend to hug the line quite closely. *In general, the more closely the scores hug the straight line of best fit, the higher the value of r.* A review of Figure 9.1 (in the previous chapter) offers further verification of this point. It shows scatter diagrams corresponding to correlation coefficients ranging in value from 0 to 1. In looking at those diagrams, one sees that if a straight line were fitted to each, the "hugging principle" described above would hold. When r is 0, the scores scatter as widely about the line as possible, and when r is 1, the scores hug the line as closely as possible (since they all fall exactly on the line). One meaning of this principle is that prediction of Y from knowledge of X can be made with greater accuracy when the correlation is high than when it is low. This consequence will be explored in detail in the next chapter. At the moment, our concern is with the relation between this principle and the notion of fitting a *straight* line to the bivariate distribution.

Pearson's solution to the problem of finding a measure of association (Sections 9.2 and 9.3) lay in fitting a straight line to the data; the correlation coefficient is a constant in the equation of this line. In a given set of data, a straight line may or may not reasonably describe the relationship between the two variables. When a straight line is appropriate, X and Y are said to be *linearly related.* More formally, the data are said to exhibit the property of *linearity of regression.* What happens when X and Y are not linearly related? Figure 10.3 illustrates two sets of data in which a curved line is apparently a better fit than a straight line. In the first picture, the curvature is pronounced, but a straight line has been fitted nonetheless. This therefore represents a situation in which

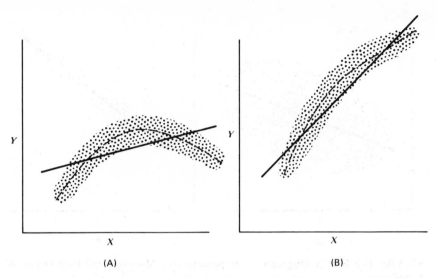

FIGURE 10.3 Scatter Diagrams of Data Which are Curvilinearly Related.

Pearson r has been computed, but linearity of regression does not hold. How well do the scores hug the straight line? Obviously, not very well. As a result, when the correlation coefficient is calculated using the Pearsonian method, the obtained coefficient will reflect this fact, and will have a low value. On the other hand, if the proper curved line had been fitted (illustrated by the dotted line), the scores would hug this line rather closely, reflecting a higher degree of association.

It can therefore be expected that *when the correlation is other than zero and the relationship is nonlinear, Pearson r will underestimate the degree of association.* Further, the greater the degree to which the data depart from a straight-line relationship, the more Pearson r will underestimate the strength of the association. In the second illustration of Figure 10.3, the relationship departs only slightly from a linear one, and the points hug the straight line better than in the first illustration. In this instance, Pearson r will underestimate the degree of association slightly, rather than to a great extent.

Rather surprisingly, it has been found (as Galton earlier observed) that a great number of variables tend to exhibit a linear relationship, or one that is nearly so. Of course, this is why Pearsonian r is so useful in measuring association. Still, other types of relationship do occur, and their instance is not negligible. For example, score on a test of mental ability (or a measure of physical strength) would be curvilinearly related to age, if the span of age were taken, say, from 5 to 80 years. There are statistical tests which can be applied to determine whether the hypothesis of linearity is a reasonable one,† but the "eyeball test," made by inspecting the scatter diagram, is both a good and an easy way to

†Q. McNemar, *Psychological Statistics*, 4th ed., John Wiley & Sons, Inc., New York, 1969.

learn whether a problem exists which should be examined with greater precision. Remember to allow for chance variation from a linear relationship.

10.3 Homoscedasticity

In the last section, we found that if the scores scattered widely about the straight line of best fit, the value of r_{XY} would be low, whereas if the scores hugged the line closely, r_{XY} would be high. Look at Figure 10.4. In the first scatter diagram, no matter what value of X is chosen, the corresponding values of Y scatter to

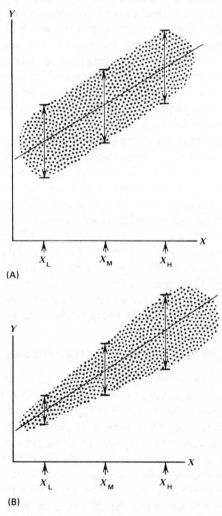

FIGURE 10.4 Variability in Y as a Function of the Value of X.

about the same extent. In the second diagram this is not so. Although Y does not vary much about the line when the value of X is low, it varies more when X has an intermediate value, and it varies greatly when X has a high value. Since r is a function of the degree to which the points hug the regression line, the value obtained for it has a meaning of general significance in the first diagram: it describes the closeness of association of X with Y *irrespective of the specific value of X (or Y)*.

In the second diagram, according to the "hugging criterion," there is a close association between X and Y for low values of X, a lesser degree of association when X has an intermediate value, and very little association when the values of X are high. It follows that if Pearsonian r is computed on the data in the second situation, it will reflect the "average" degree to which the scores hug the line, and will characterize properly only the degree of relationship appropriate to intermediate values of X and Y. The strength of association as measured by r_{XY} will not, in these circumstances, have the general meaning that it does for the data of the first diagram. In the specific illustration (the second diagram), r_{XY} will underestimate the extent of the relationship for low values of X, and will over-estimate the relationship for high values.

When the amount of scatter is the same throughout, the bivariate distribution is said to exhibit the property of *homoscedasticity*, or, roughly translated from the classic tongue, equal variability. This property implies that if the data were sectioned into columns, the variability of Y would be the same from column to column, or if sectioned into rows, the variability of X would be the same from row to row. This characteristic is illustrated in Figure 10.5.

Obviously, the meaning to be attached to r_{XY} will depend on whether the hypothesis of homoscedasticity is appropriate to the data. Once more, tests of this property exist, but a simple way to make a preliminary check is to inspect the scatter diagram. One must allow, of course, for departure from perfect equality attributable to random sampling fluctuation. Fortunately, a reasonably homoscedastic relationship holds for many kinds of data.

10.4 The Correlation Coefficient in Discontinuous Distributions

Suppose someone in the admissions office of a university wants to know the relation between entrance aptitude test score and freshman grade point average for last year's freshman class. At lunch with a friend from the student personnel office, he learns that a readymade sample of personnel records awaits him; his friend is sending disqualification notices to those who failed during their first year, and also sending notices of election to the Gold Star Society to those who qualified for that scholastic honor during their first year. His friend offers to pass on to him the records of these students when he is through, thus saving the effort of pulling records from the file. If the man from the admissions office accepts the offer, pools the two sets of personnel records, and computes the

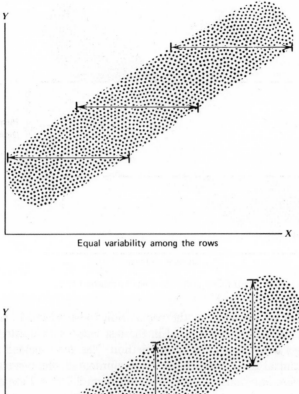

Equal variability among the rows

Equal variability among the columns

FIGURE 10.5 A Homoscedastic Relationship.

coefficient of correlation between test score and grade point average, his data might look like those pictured in Figure 10.6. Note that distributions which normally would be continuous have been rendered discontinuous because of the exclusion of students whose grade point average was at an intermediate level.

A sample constituted in this manner will generally yield a correlation coefficient higher than that obtained by drawing a sample in a manner giving an

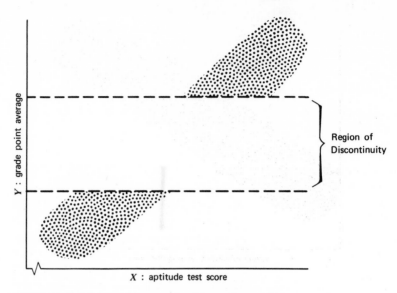

FIGURE 10.6 Scatter Diagram for Discontinuous Data.

opportunity for all elements in the population to be selected. As an example, consider the data of Table 9.6, used in the last chapter to illustrate the process of calculating r_{XY} by the coded score method. The data yielded an r of $+.63$. If the three central class intervals in X are eliminated, the correlation becomes $+.67$. If the class intervals covering Y scores from 2.7 to 4.2 are eliminated, the value obtained is $+.94$.

This matter may be put in proper perspective by considering it from the point of view of adequacy of sampling. What population does the man from the admissions office want to study? Apparently, he intends to draw conclusions about the entire freshman class. Accordingly, he should draw a fair sample of such persons. The readymade sample is a very special sample, composed only of students who made either outstandingly good or outstandingly bad records. It is appropriate only if one wants to draw conclusions about a population so constituted.

10.5 Shapes of the Distributions and r_{XY}

If the correlation coefficient is to be calculated purely as a descriptive measure, nothing need be assumed about the shape of the distribution of X or Y. In particular, there is no requirement that the distributions be normal. However, two points must be mentioned concerning distribution shape. First, if one or both distributions are skewed, they may also be curvilinearly related. Therefore when the distributions are not symmetrical, it is particularly desirable to examine the data with an eye to the correctness of the linear hypothesis.

Second, obtaining the coefficient is often only the first step in analysis. When additional steps are undertaken, the assumption frequently must be made that X and Y are normally distributed. For example, this assumption is needed in making inferences about the population value of the coefficient (Chapter 18) and in establishing limits of error in prediction (Chapter 11).

10.6 Random Variation and r_{XY}

Sometimes we are interested only in describing how things are in the particular group of observations under study; in this case the correlation coefficient obtained with that group is exactly what we want to know. Most often, however, interest is in a population, but only a sample is available for study. The industrial psychologist is interested in how well job performance can be predicted from an aptitude test for employees-in-general of the type studied, rather than for the specific workers with whom the correlation between these two variables was obtained. The educator wants to know what relation exists between intelligence and achievement in English among 12-year-olds in general, rather than just among the particular 12-year-olds whom he studied.

In these circumstances, we want to make an inference about the state of affairs in the population from knowledge of the state of affairs in the sample. Like all statistics, the value of r_{XY} varies from sample to sample, depending on the chance factors associated with selection of the particular sample. Suppose that for all eighth grade pupils in a large city, the correlation is $+.45$ between achievement test scores in history and mathematics. If by random selection we choose 35 of these students and obtain the correlation between these two measures, its value may be, say, $+.30$. Another sample selected in the same way may yield a value of $+.53$, and a third sample still a different value.

How to make appropriate inferences about conditions in the population from evidence obtained with a sample is a very important problem, but adequate consideration of it must be postponed until the principles and procedures of statistical inference are properly developed. This problem, with specific reference to correlation coefficients, is treated in Chapter 18. Two general aspects of the question must be considered here.

The first point has already been made and is now summarized: when a coefficient has been obtained from a particular set of paired observations, it does not represent *the* correlation between the two variables; another sample will yield a somewhat different value. The second point concerns how big "somewhat" is. In general, large samples yield values of r_{XY} which are similar from sample to sample, and thus the value obtained from a sample of this type will probably be close to the population value. For very small samples, r_{XY} is quite unstable from sample to sample, and its value can not be depended upon to lie close to the population value. Table 10.1 illustrates this point. It shows, for selected sample sizes, the limits within which 80% of sample coefficients will fall if the samples

TABLE 10.1 Limits within Which 80% of Sample Values of r_{XY} Will Fall when the True Correlation Is Zero.

Sample size	80% limits for r_{XY}
5	$-.69$ to $+.69$
15	$-.35$ to $+.35$
25	$-.26$ to $+.26$
50	$-.18$ to $+.18$
100	$-.13$ to $+.13$
200	$-.09$ to $+.09$

of that size are drawn at random from a population in which the true correlation is zero. Note, therefore, that 20% of such coefficients would actually fall *farther* away from the "true" value than the points indicated by the limits. Note also that great variation characterizes the smaller sample sizes. Estimation of the degree of association from study of a sample is really not very satisfactory unless *n* is large enough to produce reasonably stable results.

10.7 The Correlation Coefficient and the Circumstances under Which It Was Obtained

The influence of random sampling variation is but one reason why the obtained correlation coefficient is not *the* coefficient between the two variables under study. Consider the correlation between intelligence and achievement in a mathematics course. The extent of the relationship may depend upon a variety of moderating circumstances. It may differ depending on the specific measures of "intelligence" and "achievement" which are used,† it may differ among fourth-grade pupils as compared with those in the eighth grade, it may differ among students from middle class families as compared with those from economically deprived families or among children who are bilingual, and it may differ for students learning in an atmosphere of anxiety as compared with those operating in a more normal learning situation.

Suppose that, in a given industrial plant, score on a mechanical aptitude test correlates to the extent of $+.45$ with measures of job proficiency of assembly workers. The test would be useful in selecting assembly workers. However, it is quite possible that the nature of the job will change substantially over a period of 5 years or so; worker characteristics required for success on the job may then be different. The mechanical aptitude test may then no longer satisfactorily

†See Section 8.1.

predict job success, despite the fact that the job title is the same. It is all too easy to think that "the correlation between mechanical aptitude and job performance *is* $+.45$ for assembly workers in factory X." Obviously, what is needed is a periodic review to ascertain whether the fundamental situation has changed sufficiently that a restudy is in order.

The degree of association between two variables depends (1) on the specific measure taken for each of the two variables, (2) on the kinds of subjects used for the investigation, and (3) on the particular circumstances under which the variables are operative. If any of these factors changes over time, the extent of the association may also change. Consequently, it is of utmost importance that a correlation coefficient be interpreted in the light of the particular conditions by which it was obtained. Any report of research, therefore, should include a careful description of the measures used and the circumstances under which the coefficients were obtained. Similarly, research results reported by others may or may not be directly applicable to the circumstances with which you are concerned. Such results should be taken only as a working hypothesis, subject to confirmation under the present circumstances.

10.8 Other Factors Influencing the Correlation Coefficient

Two important factors which influence the magnitude of the correlation coefficient remain to be discussed: *range of talent* and *heterogeneity of samples*. Their influence can best be understood after the development of certain concepts. Since these concepts will be presented in Chapter 11, consideration of these two factors is deferred until the beginning of Chapter 12 (see Sections 12.1 and 12.2).

PROBLEMS AND EXERCISES

Identify:

linearity of regression	discontinuous distribution
homoscedasticity	range of talent

1. In one transit company, the correlation between frequency of accidents and age of the bus drivers was $r = -.50$. It was recommended that the transit company try to hire older men for the job. Identify several factors that might suggest caution in adopting this recommendation.

2. Among a group of children selected at random from an elementary school, the correlation between strength of grip and score on an arithmetic achievement test was $r = +.65$. The study was repeated on a group of college seniors, and r was found to be $+.10$. Assuming both are representative findings, what is the likely explanation?

3. Given the following 20 pairs of scores:

Pair	X	Y	Pair	X	Y	Pair	X	Y
1	79	51	8	86	45	15	89	39
2	77	47	9	81	45	16	89	44
3	74	49	10	80	48	17	92	38
4	58	37	11	63	39	18	82	49
5	58	40	12	87	47	19	90	42
6	85	42	13	60	37	20	62	42
7	65	40	14	75	46			

(a) The bivariate distribution formed by these 20 pairs of scores exhibits two interesting features. Can you guess what they are from inspection of the above data? (b) On graph paper, plot the 20 points indicated by the pairs of scores. What two features appear? Would these be likely to affect the value of Pearson r? Explain.

4. Given the following 20 pairs of scores:

Pair	X	Y	Pair	X	Y	Pair	X	Y
1	64	45	8	85	71	15	62	45
2	63	43	9	83	62	16	71	47
3	66	50	10	56	38	17	59	39
4	66	44	11	62	42	18	70	57
5	63	47	12	60	42	19	77	67
6	73	50	13	79	52	20	89	56
7	60	41	14	58	41			

(a) The bivariate distribution formed by these 20 pairs of scores exhibits two interesting features. Can you guess what they are from inspection of the data above? (b) On graph paper, plot the 20 points indicated by the pairs of scores. What two features appear? Which one is more important for understanding the strength of the relationship? Explain.

5. A statistics instructor has a class of 30 students, half male and half female. Among the males, he finds the correlation between aptitude score and achievement in statistics to be $r = +.50$; among the females, the correlation is $r = +.35$. One observer suggests that apparently the relationship is different among men than among women. Any objection?

6. The personnel director for Company A often has lunch with the personnel director for Company B. This noon, he mentions that they are having trouble selecting good assembly workers. The second man replies that they have had great luck with Aptitude Test X, and that the correlation, established on 400 of their assembly workers, is $+.60$ between test score and job performance. Have you any caution to offer Company A's man before he rushes out to adopt the test as a selective device?

11

Regression and Prediction

11.1 The Problem of Prediction

There is a substantial positive correlation between stature and weight. Therefore, if a man is tall, we expect that his weight will be above average. In general, if two variables are correlated, it is possible to predict, with better than chance accuracy, standing in one of them from knowledge of standing in the other. We know that when the correlation coefficient is zero, knowledge of X is of no help in predicting Y, and if the coefficient is ± 1, we can predict Y with perfect accuracy. Clearly, the degree of correlation is indicative of the predictive possibilities, yet knowing the value of the coefficient, by itself, does not tell us how to make the prediction.

Consider the bivariate distribution pictured in Figure 11.1. Suppose we wish to predict the value of Y which might be expected if X is 87. Taking the simplest possible approach to prediction, we could erect a column at the location of that value of X, and inquire as to the mean Y value of each of the points falling within the borders of the column. As shown in Figure 11.1, this would lead us to take $Y = 52$ as the predicted Y for those scoring 87 in X.

This method of prediction is satisfactory, but it has one handicap. This prediction is based *only* on the Y values of those scores falling in the particular column, a rather small number of cases. Other values of paired scores are ignored. As might be expected, predictions based on a small number of cases tend to be unstable, since another sample from the population of paired scores may yield different values in the particular column. If we follow this method, considerable instability attributable to random sampling fluctuation will be encountered.

165

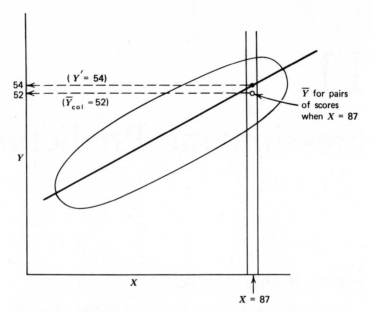

FIGURE 11.1 Prediction of Y from Column Mean and from
Line of Best Fit.

How can the situation be improved? We note that for the data indicated,
the hypothesis of linearity of relation between X and Y appears to be reasonable.†
It is therefore possible to find the straight line of best fit to the Y values, a line
determined by *all* of the scores in the bivariate distribution. Such a line is called
a *regression line*, and its equation, a *regression equation*. *The prediction may then
be made by noting the Y value of the point on the line which corresponds to the
particular value of X.* Figure 11.1 shows that, following this procedure, the predicted value of Y (which we shall call Y') is 54 when X is 87. Prediction made in the
simpler way (first described) would be better if one were concerned only with the
present set of paired scores, i.e., if this set of points constitutes the population of
paired values. However, in this case "prediction" would have little meaning,
since we would *know* the Y value for each X. When the data are only a sample
of the larger population of interest (the usual situation), sampling fluctuation
must be taken into account, and a prediction more resistant to this factor is
obviously preferable. A prediction made by taking into account *all* the data is
therefore a superior solution to the problem.

Two limitations still remain. First, the straight line fitted to the sample is
probably not quite the same as the straight line that would be obtained if the
population were available for study. Other things being equal, the larger the

†The hypothesis of linearity states that the line best describing the relationship between X and Y is
a straight line. See Section 10.2.

sample, the closer the approximation. Second, the adequacy of the procedure depends on the assumption that a straight line *is* a reasonable description of the interrelationship of X and Y. Fortunately, the linear hypothesis is often satisfactory; inspection of the scatter diagram is useful in checking possible exceptions. The present chapter will deal only with situations in which a linear relation between X and Y is a reasonable assumption.

11.2 The Criterion of Best Fit

It is all very well to speak of finding the straight line of best fit to the data, but how is one to know when the "best fit" has been achieved? There are, in fact, several possible (and reasonable) ways in which "best fit" could be defined. Karl Pearson's solution to this problem was to apply the *least-squares criterion*. Let us consider the problem of predicting Y from X. Figure 11.2 shows a bivariate distribution in which the discrepancy (in the Y dimension) between each point and the corresponding point on the straight line is indicated by the symbol d. The least-squares criterion calls for the straight line to be laid down in such a manner that the sum of the squares of these discrepancies is as small as possible (Σd_Y^2 is a minimum value).

Paradoxically, there is *another* straight line of best fit. If one wishes to predict X from Y, rather than the other way around, the deviations in X should be minimized, rather than the deviations in Y. Figure 11.3 illustrates this situation. *There are therefore two regression lines.* One is called the *line of regression of Y on X*, and is used when predicting Y from X. The other is the *line of regression of X on Y*, and is used when predicting X from Y. When one thinks about it,

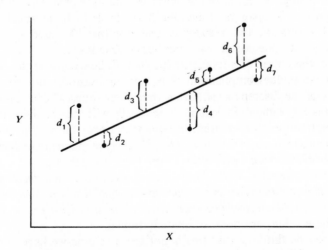

FIGURE 11.2 Discrepancies between Y Values and the Line of Regression of Y on X.

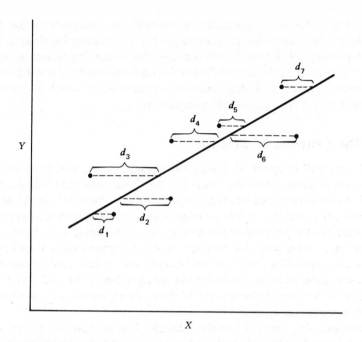

FIGURE 11.3 Discrepancies between X Values and the Line of Regression of X on Y.

it is sensible that there should be two lines. In predicting Y from X, X is known and Y is estimated. In this case, we wish to minimize error in estimating Y. In the other case, it is error in estimating X which is to be as small as possible. Figure 11.4 shows the two regression lines for the data used to illustrate the calculation of r by the coded score method (Table 9.4).

At first, the notion of minimizing the sum of the *squares* of the discrepancies seems to be an undue complication. Why not minimize the sum of the absolute magnitudes of the discrepancies, rather than their squares? The answer has two parts: (1) it is very difficult to deal mathematically with the absolute discrepancies, whereas the treatment of squared discrepancies opens the way to mathematical developments which are of practical value in interpreting the regression equation, and (2) desirable statistical properties follow from using the least-squares criterion. One important property of the least-squares solution is that *the location of the regression lines and the value of the correlation coefficient will fluctuate less under the influence of random sampling than would occur if another criterion were used.* In short, these values are more stably determined.

You may be thinking that this is not the first time we have dealt with the sum of squared discrepancies, and that, indeed, one property of the mean is that the sum of the squares of the deviations of each score from the mean is a minimum

(Σx^2 is a minimum; see Section 6.10). Is there some connection between these facts and the current issues concerning correlation?

First, just as the regression line is a least-squares solution to the problem of the straight line of best fit, so the mean is a least-squares solution to the problem of finding a measure of central tendency. Both are chosen so as to minimize the sum of squares of discrepancies. It may be expected, therefore, that both will have analogous properties. Indeed, we note that resistance to the influence of sampling fluctuation characterizes them both.

Second, the regression line may actually be thought of as a kind of mean. One way to think of it is as a "running mean," a line which tells us the mean, or expected value of Y, for a particular value of X. Looked at another way, $\overline{Y}$ is the "unconditional" mean of Y, the mean of *all* values in the set, whereas the regression line (of Y or X) gives the "conditional" mean of Y, an estimate of the mean of Y *given the condition that X has a particular value.*

11.3 A Practical Resolution to the Problem of Two Regression Equations

In the last section, we observed that there were two regression equations, one for predicting Y from X, and the other for predicting X from Y. This state of affairs has consequences of theoretical interest which we shall want to pursue at a later time. However, for practical problems in prediction this complication

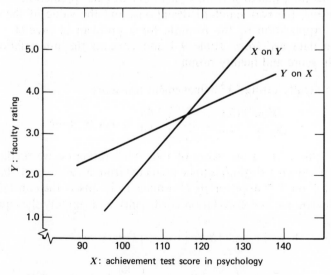

FIGURE 11.4 The Two Regression Lines for the Data of Table 9.4.

can be avoided. In normal application, interest is in predicting in one direction, not both. Therefore, *it is always possible to define the variable to be predicted as Y, and the variable used to make the prediction as X.* Consequently, it will suffice to discuss only the prediction of Y from X. At the end of the chapter (Section 11.13), we shall explain how to obtain the formulas appropriate to prediction of X from Y, should they be needed.

11.4 The Regression Equation: Raw Score Formula

The equation of the line of best fit can be cast in raw score form, deviation score form, or standard score form. Each equation has its use, but for practical application the raw score form is the most useful. It is given here; consideration of the other forms appears in Section 11.6:

Regression of Y on X:
Raw Score Formula
$$Y' = \left(r_{XY}\frac{S_Y}{S_X}\right)X - \left(r_{XY}\frac{S_Y}{S_X}\right)\overline{X} + \overline{Y} \qquad (11.1)$$

where:
$\quad$ Y' is the predicted raw score in Y
$\quad$ S_X and S_Y are the two standard deviations
$\quad$ $\overline{X}$ and $\overline{Y}$ are the two means
$\quad$ r_{XY} is the correlation coefficient between X and Y.

$\quad$ The formula looks more complicated than it really is. To predict Y, we need to know the value of X from which the particular prediction is to be made, the two means, the two standard deviations, and the value of the correlation coefficient. Application of the formula for a problem in prediction is shown below. The data are from Table 9.4 and concern the interrelation between achievement score and faculty rating.

Given: $\quad$ Y: faculty rating; X: achievement test score

$$\overline{X} = 115.6 \qquad \overline{Y} = 3.45$$
$$S_X = 11.6 \qquad S_Y = .84 \qquad r_{XY} = +.63$$

Problem: $\quad$ John earns a test score of 130. What rating do we predict for him?
Solution: $\quad$ 1. Since Y (rating) is to be predicted from X (test score), the regression equation of Y on X is appropriate (Formula 11.1). Insert the constants (means, standard deviations, and correlation coefficient), and simplify the equation:

$$Y' = \left(r_{XY}\frac{S_Y}{S_X}\right)X - \left(r_{XY}\frac{S_Y}{S_X}\right)\overline{X} + \overline{Y}$$

$$= (.63)\left(\frac{.84}{11.6}\right)X - (.63)\left(\frac{.84}{11.6}\right)(115.6) + 3.45$$

$$= .0456X - 1.82$$

2. Insert the value of X from which the prediction is to be made, and find Y' (the predicted value of Y):

$$Y' = .0456X - 1.82$$
$$= (.0456)(130) - 1.82$$
$$= 4.1$$

Note that the particular value of X from which Y is to be predicted has not been inserted until the equation has first been simplified. This is particularly desirable if more than one prediction is to be made, as is usually the case. For example, if we now wish to predict Y when $X = 100$, it is possible to insert that value of X in the formula $Y' = .0456X - 1.82$, whereas if the equation were not first reduced to its simplest form, one must back up to an earlier point in the calculation before inserting the new value of X, and the ensuing series of calculations would be more of a nuisance.

11.5 A Graphic Solution to the Problem of Prediction†

If a certain amount of inaccuracy inherent in the construction and reading of a graph can be tolerated, and if numerous predictions are to be made, graphic representation of the regression of Y on X can be quite convenient.

Since any two points determine a straight line, we may find two such values, connect them with a straight line, and read off the predictions to be made. Using the data of the illustration of the previous section, we take a convenient value of X (say, $X = 100$), insert it into the simplified equation ($Y' = .0456X - 1.82$), and obtain $Y' = 2.74$. These two values ($X = 100$, $Y' = 2.74$) locate the first point. Choosing a second value of X ($X = 120$), we find $Y' = 3.65$. The two points are then plotted on the bivariate axes, as illustrated in Figure 11.5, and a straight line is drawn through them. The regression line will pass through the intersection of the mean of X and the mean of Y; this affords a check on accuracy of graphic construction. This property is explored further in Section 11.7.

When the line is constructed, we may select any value of X, read vertically up to the regression line, and then read horizontally over to the Y axis to find the predicted value of Y. In the previous section we found that the predicted faculty rating (Y') was 4.1 for a student who earned a score of 130 on an achievement test (X). The graphic solution to this problem is illustrated by dotted lines in Figure 11.5.

Remember to make the graph big enough to afford reasonable accuracy. It is a good idea to provide room on each axis for scores ranging from three standard deviations below the mean to an equal distance above.

†It will be helpful to review Section A.9 (Appendix A) as background for this section.

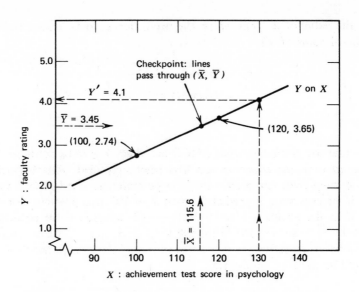

FIGURE 11.5 Construction of Regression Lines; Data from Table 9.4.

11.6 Other Forms of the Regression Equation: Deviation Score and Standard Score Form

In Section 11.4 the raw score form of the regression equation was given. Repeating that formula (Formula 11.1) here, the development of the deviation score form is not difficult:

$$Y' = \left(r_{XY}\frac{S_Y}{S_X}\right)X - \left(r_{XY}\frac{S_Y}{S_X}\right)\overline{X} + \overline{Y}$$

Factoring out the term in brackets, we have:

$$Y' = \left(r_{XY}\frac{S_Y}{S_X}\right)(X - \overline{X}) + \overline{Y}$$

And subtracting $\overline{Y}$ from each side of the equation:

$$Y' - \overline{Y} = \left(r_{XY}\frac{S_Y}{S_X}\right)(X - \overline{X})$$

This leaves both sides of the equation in deviation score form, and so we may write:

Regression of Y on X: $\qquad y' = \left(r_{XY}\dfrac{S_Y}{S_X}\right)x$ $\qquad\qquad$ (11.2)
Deviation Score Formula

The deviation score form of the regression equation is useful for certain algebraic transformations, but the raw score form is more useful in practical prediction.

The standard score form of the regression equation is readily obtainable from the deviation score formula. We begin with that formula.

$$y' = \left(r_{XY}\frac{S_Y}{S_X}\right)x$$

Dividing both sides of the equation by S_Y:

$$\frac{y'}{S_Y} = \left(r_{XY}\frac{S_Y}{S_YS_X}\right)x$$

and rearranging the terms:

$$\frac{y'}{S_Y} = r_{XY}\frac{x}{S_X}$$

Since $z_X = x/S_X$, etc.:

Regression of Y on X:
Standard Score Formula $$z_Y' = r_{XY}z_X \qquad\qquad (11.3)$$

This formula is now in the simplest form possible. Although of limited use in the practical work of prediction, it affords valuable insight into what is going on. We will make reference to it in subsequent sections.

11.7 The Regression of Y on X and the Mean of Y

When we learned how to graph the regression equation of Y on X (Section 11.5), we found that the regression line always passed through the point located at the intersection of $\overline{Y}$ and $\overline{X}$. Examination of the equation verifies that this will always be so. Consider the raw score form of the regression equation:

$$Y' = \left(r_{XY}\frac{S_Y}{S_X}\right)X - \left(r_{XY}\frac{S_Y}{S_X}\right)\overline{X} + \overline{Y}$$

If X has the value of its mean, we may substitute $\overline{X}$ for X in the above equation:

$$Y' = \left(r_{XY}\frac{S_Y}{S_X}\right)\overline{X} - \left(r_{XY}\frac{S_Y}{S_X}\right)\overline{X} + \overline{Y}$$

It is apparent that the first two terms on the right side of the equation reduce to zero, and we have:

$$Y' = \overline{Y}$$

Examining the other two formulas for the regression of Y on X (the deviation score formula and the standard score formula), we find the same characteristic.

For example, the standard score formula is: $z_Y' = r_{XY}z_X$. If X is at the mean, $z_X = 0$, and $z_Y' = r_{XY}(0) = 0$, which is the mean of the Y variable when expressed in z-score form.

What happens to the regression equation when $r_{XY} = 0$? In its raw score form, the regression equation is, when $r_{XY} = 0$:

$$Y' = \left[0\left(\frac{S_Y}{S_X}\right)\right]X - \left[0\left(\frac{S_Y}{S_X}\right)\right]\overline{X} + \overline{Y}$$

$$= \overline{Y}$$

If the correlation is zero, it is apparent that the predicted value of Y is the mean of Y no matter what value of X is used to predict Y. The implications are both interesting and logical. If knowing the value of X affords no advantage in predicting Y, what value of Y shall we predict? The mean of Y is not only an intuitively reasonable prediction, but it satisfies the least-squares criterion; the sum of the squares of errors of prediction will be minimized. Figure 11.6 shows the line of regression of Y on X when $r = 0$.

11.8 The Regression Line as a Linear Function†

Figure 11.7 shows the graphic representation of two different straight lines (they could be, but are not necessarily, regression lines). Of course, it is possible to draw many more straight lines, each one different. If we have a particular straight

†Section A.9 (Appendix A) provides the background for this section.

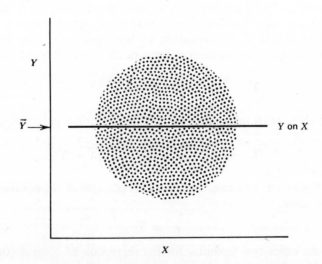

FIGURE 11.6 The Line of Regression of Y on X when $r = 0$.

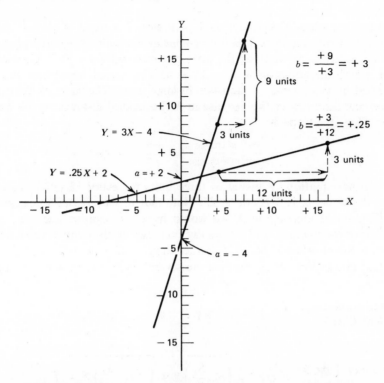

FIGURE 11.7 Graphs of Two Straight Lines, Showing Slope and Y Intercept of Each.

line in mind, how can it be identified so as to distinguish it from others? One way is to specify two points which lie on the line. Any two points completely specify the particular line, since one and only one straight line can be drawn through them. Another way is to specify the *slope of the line* and the *point at which the line intersects the Y axis*. Again, one and only one straight line can be drawn when these two characteristics are fixed.

The equation for any straight line can be put into the following form:

General Equation of $Y = bX + a$ (11.4)
a Straight Line

In this equation, a is a constant which identifies the point on the Y axis at which the line crosses it. It is known as the Y *intercept*. For the two lines in Figure 11.7, the equation of one is $Y = 3X - 4$, and the equation of the other is $Y = .25X + 2$. Note that in each case the value of a identifies the point on the Y axis at which the line crosses it.

The other constant in the equation is b; and it is called the *slope* of the line. It will be positive when the value of Y increases with increasing values of X, as is the case with the two lines pictured. It will be negative if the line slants the other way, i.e., when Y *decreases* as X increases. *The slope of the line specifies the amount of increase in Y which accompanies one unit of increase in. X.* This can be appreciated by studying the lines pictured in Figure 11.7. Consider the line for which the equation is $Y = 3X - 4$. The dotted lines show that if X is increased by three units, Y increases by nine units. The ratio of the increase in Y (vertical distance) to the increase in X (horizontal distance) is the slope of the line. Thus, the slope is:

$$b = \frac{\textit{vertical change}}{\textit{horizontal change}} = \frac{+9}{+3} = +3.0$$

In the second equation, Y increases three units for every 12 units of increase in X, so the slope, b, is 3/12, or $+.25$. Note that if Y *decreased* three units for every 12 units of increase in X we would have a "negative increase" in the numerator of the fraction, and a "positive increase" in the denominator, and the resultant value of b would be $-.25$, rather than $+.25$.

Using this model, let us examine the several forms of the line of regression of Y on X.

General Equation of
a Straight Line $\qquad Y = \qquad bX \qquad + \qquad a$

Regression of Y on X:
Raw Score Formula $\qquad Y' = \overbrace{\left(r_{XY}\frac{S_Y}{S_X}\right)}^{b}X + \overbrace{\left(-r_{XY}\frac{S_Y}{S_X}\right)\overline{X} + \overline{Y}}^{a}$

Regression of Y on X:
Deviation Score Formula $\qquad y' = \overbrace{\left(r_{XY}\frac{S_Y}{S_X}\right)}^{b}x + \overbrace{0}^{(a=0)}$

Regression of Y on X:
Standard Score Formula $\qquad z'_Y = \overbrace{r_{XY}z_X}^{b} + \overbrace{0}^{(a=0)}$

The values of a and b are most interesting when the regression equation is cast in standard score form. In this case, the correlation coefficient *is* the slope of the regression line. *One interpretation of the correlation coefficient, therefore, is that it states the amount of increase in Y which accompanies unit increase in X when both measures are expressed in standard score units.* It indicates how much of a standard deviation Y will increase for an increase of one standard deviation in X. Next, note that the value of a is zero. This is as it should be, since the regression line passes through the point of intersection of the mean of X and the mean of Y. In z-score terms, this is the point at which $z_X = 0$ and $z_Y = 0$. Consequently, the Y intercept, a, is zero.

The Y intercept is also zero when the regression equation is cast in deviation score form, since the mean of any set of deviation scores (whether X or Y) is zero (see Section 5.8 and Note 5.2). However, r_{XY} is no longer the slope of the regression line. In deviation score form and in raw score form, the slope of the line of regression of Y on X is $r_{XY}(S_Y/S_X)$, and is therefore not only a function of the correlation coefficient but also of the relative magnitude of the two standard deviations.

Note that the slope of a very steep line is a very large number. It approaches ∞ (infinity) as the line approaches the vertical. As the line approaches the horizontal, the slope approaches zero. Depending on the relative magnitude of the two standard deviations, the line of regression of Y on X could have any slope between these two limits. In standard score form, the slope is r_{XY}, and can take values only between zero and ± 1. Under these conditions the maximum slope corresponds to a 45° angle.

11.9 Error of Prediction: The Standard Error of Estimate

The regression equation states what value of Y is expected (Y') when X has a particular value. Of course, Y' is not likely to be the *actual* value of Y which corresponds to the particular X. If a man is six feet tall, the appropriate regression equation may predict his weight to be 175 lb, but we do not expect a given six-footer to have exactly that weight. *The predicted value is but an estimate of mean value of weights of persons who are that height*, a "best estimate" of the person's weight. If the correlation is low, considerable variation of actual values about the predicted value may be expected. If the correlation is high, the actual values will cluster more closely about the predicted value. Figure 10.2 (in the last chapter) illustrates this. *Only when the correlation is unity will the actual values regularly and precisely equal the predicted values.*

What is needed is a way to measure the predictive error, the variability of the actual Y values about the predicted value (Y'). Such a measure would have desirable properties if it were cast in the form of a standard deviation (see Chapter 6). The *standard error of estimate* is exactly that kind of measure; its formula (with, for comparison, that of the standard deviation) is presented below.

Standard Deviation
$$S_Y = \sqrt{\frac{\sum(Y - \overline{Y})^2}{n}}$$

Standard Error of Estimate of Y on X
$$S_{YX} = \sqrt{\frac{\sum(Y - Y')^2}{n}} \tag{11.5}$$

Figure 11.8 illustrates the discrepancies, $(Y - Y')$, on which Formula 11.5 is based. These are, in fact the same values we called "d_Y" in Section 11.2, and illustrated in Figure 11.2.

The standard error of estimate is a kind of standard deviation: it is the standard

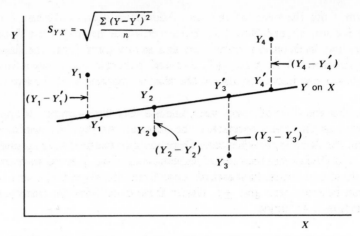

(a) These Large Values of $(Y - Y')$ Are Characteristic of a Low Correlation; They Will Lead to a Large Value of S_{YX}.

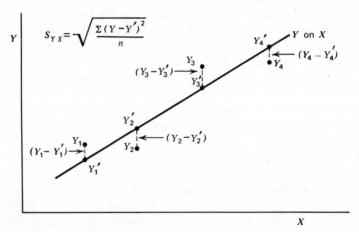

(b) These Small Values of $(Y - Y')$ Are Characteristic of a High Correlation; They Will Lead to a Small Value of S_{YX}.

FIGURE 11.8 The Standard Error of Estimate (S_{YX}) as a Function of the Magnitude of the $(Y - Y')$ Discrepancies.

deviation of the distribution of obtained Y scores about the predicted Y score. There is another way to look at this quantity. Suppose that for each value of X, we record the discrepancy between the actual value of Y and the value of Y predicted by the regression equation: $(Y - Y')$. This set of values may be thought of as the set of predictive errors. If the standard deviation of this set is then calculated, its value will be exactly S_{YX} (Note 11.2 at the chapter's end gives proof of this proposition). S_{YX} *is therefore the measure we are seeking; it is a measure of the magnitude of errors of prediction.*

When the correlation is perfect, every value of $(Y - Y')$ is zero, and therefore S_{YX} is zero. In short, there is *no* error of prediction. When the correlation is zero, $Y' = \overline{Y}$ for all values of X. We may therefore substitute $\overline{Y}$ for Y' in Equation 11.5, and it becomes $\sqrt{\Sigma(Y - \overline{Y})^2/n}$, or S_Y. *The value of* S_{YX} *therefore ranges from zero when the correlation is perfect to* S_Y *when there is no correlation at all.* Table 11.1 shows the calculation of S_Y and S_{YX} for data taken from Table 9.2. The first two columns present the paired raw scores. Columns 3 and 4 contain the values needed for the calculation of S_Y. Column 5 presents the value of Y predicted by the regression equation from each value of X. Columns 6 and 7 contain the values needed for the calculation of S_{YX}. For these data, the correlation coefficient is $+.74$. As expected from the foregoing discussion, the value $S_{YX} = 3.2$ is less than that of $S_Y = 4.8$, but greater than zero.

Is S_{YX} really a standard deviation? Formula 11.5 looks very much like the formula for the standard deviation. In fact, the form of the equations for S_Y and S_{YX} are the same, except that Y' (rather than $\overline{Y}$) has been subtracted from

TABLE 11.1 Calculation of S_Y and S_{YX}: Data from Table 9.2.

(1)	(2)	(3)	(4)	(5)	(6)	(7)
X	Y	$(Y - \overline{Y})$	$(Y - \overline{Y})^2$	Y'	$(Y - Y')$	$(Y - Y')^2$
37	75	-2.6	6.8	76.8	-1.8	3.2
41	78	$+.4$	.2	79.4	-1.4	2.0
48	88	$+10.4$	108.2	84.1	$+3.9$	15.2
32	80	$+2.4$	5.8	73.4	$+6.6$	43.6
36	78	$+.4$	.2	76.1	$+1.9$	3.6
30	71	-6.6	43.6	72.1	-1.1	1.2
40	75	-2.6	6.8	78.8	-3.8	14.4
45	83	$+5.4$	29.2	82.1	$+.9$	.8
39	74	-3.6	13.0	78.1	-4.1	16.8
34	74	-3.6	13.0	74.8	$-.8$	.6
Σ 382	776	0	227	776	0	101
Σ/n 38.2	77.6	0	22.7	77.6	0	10.1

$$S_Y = \sqrt{\frac{\Sigma(Y - \overline{Y})^2}{n}} \qquad S_{YX} = \sqrt{\frac{\Sigma(Y - Y')^2}{n}}$$

$$= \sqrt{22.7} \qquad\qquad = \sqrt{10.1}$$

$$= 4.8 \qquad\qquad = 3.2$$

each score in calculating S_{YX}. However, Y' is indeed a kind of mean (Section 11.2); it is the estimated mean of Y when X has a particular value. S_{YX} is therefore a genuine standard deviation.

If S_{YX} is really a standard deviation, it should have the properties of one. One such property is that the sum of the squares of the deviations of each score from the mean is a minimum (Section 6.10). Indeed, this is precisely the way in which the regression line is laid down. It is to be so located that the sum of the squares of the discrepancies between each value of Y and the corresponding value of Y' given by the regression line, $\Sigma(Y - Y')^2$, is minimized. A second property of the standard deviation is that the sum of the deviations of each score from the mean of the scores must be zero (Section 5.8). Consider the third and sixth columns in Table 11.1. The quantity $\Sigma(Y - Y')$ is zero, just as $\Sigma(Y - \overline{Y})$ is zero. Note 11.1 shows this property to be a general one, and not just an accident.

11.10 An Alternate (and Preferred) Formula for S_{YX}

The formula given in the previous section for the standard error of estimate, $S_{YX} = \sqrt{\Sigma(Y - Y')^2/n}$, is in a form more convenient for studying the nature of the statistic than it is for actual work in prediction. For this purpose, it is better to use Formula 11.6.

Standard Error of Estimate
of Y on X $$S_{YX} = S_Y \sqrt{1 - r_{XY}^2} \qquad\qquad (11.6)$$

It can be shown (see Note 11.3) that Formula 11.6 is the exact algebraic equivalent of Formula 11.5. Note, for example, that if $r = 0$, $S_{YX} = S_Y$, and that if $r = \pm 1$, $S_{YX} = 0$. In the previous section, calculation of S_{YX} by Formula 11.5 was illustrated in Table 11.1. The value is the same if recalculated by Formula 11.6: $S_{YX} = 4.8 \sqrt{1 - (.74)^2} = 3.2$.

11.11 Error in Estimating Y from X

From earlier study of the standard deviation, we learned certain useful facts that applied when confronted with a normal distribution. For example, in a normal distribution:

$$68\% \text{ of scores fall within the limits: } \overline{X} \pm 1S_X$$
$$95\% \text{ of scores fall within the limits: } \overline{X} \pm 1.96S_X$$
$$99\% \text{ of scores fall within the limits: } \overline{X} \pm 2.58S_X$$

These values can be easily verified by consulting Table C, in the appendix.

Since the standard error of estimate is a kind of standard deviation, the same kind of interpretation can be made if it is reasonable to assume that the obtained scores are normally distributed about the predicted scores, and that variability of Y about Y' is similar for all values of Y'. Thus,

> 68% of obtained Y values fall within the limits: $Y' \pm 1S_{YX}$
> 95% of obtained Y values fall within the limits: $Y' \pm 1.96S_{YX}$
> 99% of obtained Y values fall within the limits: $Y' \pm 2.58S_{YX}$

This type of interpretation is illustrated in Figure 11.9. One part of the picture shows schematically the limits within which 95% of obtained Y values would be expected to fall when predicting Y from a low value of X. The other shows the limits resulting from a prediction made from a higher value of X.

Specific application is best shown in a concrete example. The examples presented below illustrate the solution of two types of problems which may arise. It may be helpful to review Sections 7.6, 7.7, and 7.8, since the procedures described there are needed to solve the problems presented here.

Given: $\overline{X} = 80$ $\overline{Y} = 100$ $r_{XY} = +.60$
           $S_X = 10$ $S_Y = 20$

Problems: 1. For those who score 90 in X, what proportion may be expected to score 120 or better in Y? 2. For those who score 90 in X, within what central limits may we expect 50% of their Y scores to fall? (These two problems are illustrated in Figure 11.10.)

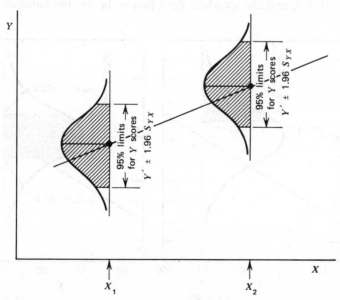

FIGURE 11.9 Ninety-five Percent Limits for Actual Y Scores of Subjects Scoring at Particular Levels in X.

Solutions: For both problems, the first step is to find the predicted value of Y.

$$Y' = \left(r_{XY}\frac{S_Y}{S_X}\right)X - \left(r_{XY}\frac{S_Y}{S_X}\right)\bar{X} + \bar{Y}$$

$$= (+.60)\left(\frac{20}{10}\right)X - (+.60)\left(\frac{20}{10}\right)(80) + 100$$

$$= 1.20X + 4.00$$

For $X = 90$, we have

$$Y' = (1.20)(90) + 4.00$$

$$= 112.00$$

Next, S_{YX} is calculated.

$$S_{YX} = S_Y \sqrt{1 - r^2}$$

$$= 20 \sqrt{1 - (.60)^2}$$

$$= 16.00$$

Solution to Problem 1.   As Figure 11.10 shows, the problem is to find, in the distribution of obtained Y scores for those who score 90 in X, the proportion of Y scores which exceed 120. We take the mean of this distribution to be 112 (the value of Y'), and the standard deviation to be 16 (the value of S_{YX}). The

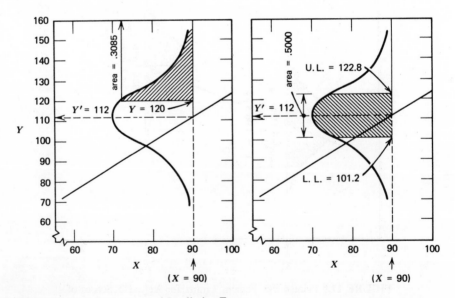

FIGURE 11.10 Estimation of Predictive Error.

problem now becomes one of the type described in Section 7.7. We must therefore translate the score of 120 to z-score terms, and find the area which would lie above this point in a normal curve. Remembering that a z score is *(score − mean)/(standard deviation)*, we have:

$$z = \frac{Y_{\text{obt}} - Y'}{S_{YX}}$$

$$= \frac{120 - 112}{16}$$

$$= +.50$$

Consulting Table B in the appendix, it is found that .3085 of the cases will fall beyond a z of $+.50$ in a normal distribution (see Figure 11.10). This is the answer to the problem: For those who score 90 in X, 31 per cent may be expected to have Y scores of 120 or better.

Solution to Problem 2.　　The second problem is also concerned with the distribution of obtained Y scores for those who score 90 in X, a distribution in which the mean (Y') is 112, and the standard deviation (S_{YX}) is 16. We are to find the limits within which the central 50% of Y scores will be found, a problem of the type discussed in Section 7.8. The points desired are therefore those in the normal curve beyond which .25 of the cases fall. Table C, in the appendix, shows these points to be:

Upper Limit: $z = +.6745$
Lower Limit: $z = -.6745$

Translating these limits to raw score values,

$$Y = (z)(standard\ deviation) + (mean)$$

Upper Limit: $Y_{\text{UL}} = (+.6745)(16) + 112$

$$= 122.8$$

Lower Limit: $Y_{\text{LL}} = (-.6745)(16) + 112$

$$= 101.2$$

　　Procedures of the kind illustrated above may be useful in various practical situations. For example, a university admissions officer may wish to predict the likelihood of academic success (as defined by achieving a given grade point average or better) for those who score at a given level on the institution's scholastic aptitude test. Using the procedures illustrated above, he may find, say, that 65% of students who make the particular score on the aptitude test may be expected to earn a grade point average of 2.5 or better. Similarly, a personnel officer for an industrial organization might use this procedure to estimate the percentage of applicants who would succeed on the job when they score at a given level on a selection test. Information of this kind would also be useful in counseling.

11.12 Cautions Concerning Estimation of Predictive Error

Correct application of the procedures described in the preceding section requires that several assumptions be satisfied. First, the regression equation was used to obtain the predicted value of Y; we must assume that a straight line *is* the line of best fit, or this predicted value may be too high or low. The first picture in Figure 11.11 shows that, with these curvilinearly related data, the straight line of best fit will make the right prediction for Y from X for only two values of X. For other values, Y' will underestimate or overestimate the correct value.

Second, S_{YX} is taken as the standard deviation of the distribution of obtained Y scores about Y', *irrespective of the value of X from which the prediction has been made*. It is therefore necessary to assume that variability is the same from column to column (the assumption of homoscedasticity; see Section 10.3). The formula, $S_{YX} = \sqrt{\Sigma(Y - Y')^2/n}$, shows that S_{YX} is a function of the *average* magnitude of the squared discrepancies between each Y value and Y'. If the data are like those pictured in the second part of Figure 11.11, S_{YX} will approximate the standard deviation of Y values when X is at an intermediate level, but

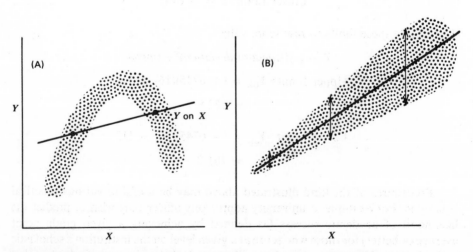

FIGURE 11.11 Bivariate Distributions in Which the Properties of Linearity and Homoscedasticity Do Not Hold.

will overestimate Y variation when X is low, and will underestimate Y variation when X is high.

Third, the procedures of the previous section depend on the assumption that the distribution of obtained Y scores (for a particular value of X) is normal. Remember that the obtained value of z was taken to the table of areas under the *normal* curve in order to find the proportion of cases expected to fall above or below the value of z.

The assumptions listed above must sound formidable. Fortunately, there are numerous occasions on which it is reasonable to assume that these conditions are sufficiently closely approximated that an estimate of predictive error made by the procedures of Section 11.11 is sensible. One hopes that it is not too much of a blow to add one more warning.

Procedures of Section 11.11 do not take into account the influence of random sampling variation. Since in any realistic prediction situation we are not dealing with the population of paired scores (why predict if you know?), but with a sample from that population, the "true" correlation coefficient, regression line, and standard error of estimate will probably differ somewhat from those characterizing the sample with which we are confronted. More sophisticated approaches which take this factor into account may be found in texts such as those by Hays and by Armore.† We cannot pursue them here, because they require an understanding of statistical inference which has yet to be developed in this book. However, a certain kind of comfort can be offered: if the assumptions listed above hold for the *population* of paired values, and if sample size is reasonably large, the procedures here described will yield results close to those resulting from application of the more advanced procedures.

As might be expected, taking account of the additional variability attributable to sampling fluctuation will increase the width of the limits within which the actual values may be expected to be found. If sample size is 100, the more accurate procedures will yield limits for Problem 2 of the previous section which range from about 3% to 7% greater, depending on whether the value of X from which the prediction is made is centrally located or in the outer limits of the distribution. If sample size is greater than 100, the amount of error will be less. Suffice it to say that prediction and estimating error of prediction are best made when sample size is large enough to reduce the margin of error to a tolerable amount. One hundred cases is really rather small for this purpose.

11.13 Formulas Appropriate to the Regression of X on Y

So far, we have considered only the problem of predicting Y from X, since it is always possible to define Y as the variable to be predicted, and X as the predictor

†W. L. Hays, *Statistics for Psychologists*, Holt, Rinehart, and Winston, New York, 1963, Chapter 15.
S. J. Armore, *Introduction to Statistical Analysis and Inference*, John Wiley & Sons, Inc., New York, 1966, Chapter 14.

(see Section 11.3). However, it is easy enough to generate the formulas for predicting in the other direction. Each of the formulas (Formulas 11.1–11.6) may be converted to suit prediction of X from Y by the simple expedient of substituting the letter X wherever the letter Y appears, and vice versa (including subscripts). In the case of the general equation of a straight line (Formula 11.4), b will now refer to change in X relative to unit change in Y, rather than the other way around, and a will designate the X intercept, rather than the Y intercept.

NOTES

NOTE 11.1 Sum of the Deviations of Scores about Their Predicted Values (*Ref:* Section 11.9)

Substituting the raw score equivalent of Y' (from Formula 11.1) in the expression $\Sigma(Y - Y')$, we have:

$$\Sigma(Y - Y') = \Sigma\left[Y - \left(r\frac{S_Y}{S_X}\right)X + \left(r\frac{S_Y}{S_X}\right)\overline{X} - \overline{Y}\right]$$

$$= \Sigma\left[(Y - \overline{Y}) - \left(r\frac{S_Y}{S_X}\right)(X - \overline{X})\right]$$

$$= \Sigma(Y - \overline{Y}) - r\frac{S_Y}{S_X}\Sigma(X - \overline{X})$$

Since $\Sigma(Y - \overline{Y}) = 0$ and $\Sigma(X - \overline{X}) = 0$ (see Note 5.2), $\Sigma(Y - Y') = 0$.

NOTE 11.2 S_{YX} as the Standard Deviation of the Errors of Prediction (*Ref:* Section 11.9)

Define $(Y - Y')$ as an error of prediction. Then:

$$S_{Y-Y'} = \sqrt{\frac{\Sigma[(Y - Y') - \overline{Y - Y'}]^2}{n}}$$

From Note 11.1, $\Sigma(Y - Y') = 0$, so $\overline{Y - Y'} = 0$, and

$$S_{Y-Y'} = \sqrt{\frac{\Sigma[Y - Y']^2}{n}}$$

$$= S_{YX} \text{ (Formula 11.5)}$$

NOTE 11.3 Equivalence of Formula 11.5 and Formula 11.6 for S_{YX} (*Ref:* Section 11.10)

$$S_{YX}^2 = \frac{1}{n}\Sigma(Y - Y')^2 \text{ (from Formula 11.5)}$$

$$= \frac{1}{n}\Sigma[(Y - \overline{Y}) - (Y' - \overline{Y})]^2$$

$$= \frac{1}{n}\Sigma[y - y']^2$$

From Formula 11.2, $y' = r\dfrac{S_Y}{S_X}x$, and

$$S_{YX}^2 = \frac{1}{n}\sum\left[y - r\frac{S_Y}{S_X}x\right]^2$$

$$= \frac{1}{n}\sum\left[y^2 - 2r\frac{S_Y}{S_X}xy + r^2\frac{S_Y^2}{S_X^2}x^2\right]$$

$$= \frac{\sum y^2}{n} - 2r\frac{S_Y}{S_X}\frac{\sum xy}{n} + r^2\frac{S_Y^2}{S_X^2}\frac{\sum x^2}{n}$$

Since $r = \Sigma xy/nS_XS_Y$, $\Sigma xy/n = rS_YS_X$, and

$$S_{YX}^2 = S_Y^2 - 2r^2\frac{S_Y^2\mathcal{S}_X}{\mathcal{S}_X} + r^2\frac{S_Y^2}{\mathcal{S}_X^2}\mathcal{S}_X^2$$

$$= S_Y^2 - r^2 S_Y^2$$

$$= S_Y^2(1 - r^2)$$

and therefore

$$S_{YX} = S_Y\sqrt{1 - r^2} \quad \text{(Formula 11.6)}$$

PROBLEMS AND EXERCISES

Identify:

regression equation	linear function
least-squares criterion	Y intercept
regression of Y on X	slope of a line
regression of X on Y	standard error of estimate
conditional mean of Y	

1. Under what two circumstances is prediction of Y from X better made from the linear regression equation than from the mean of the Y column corresponding to the particular value of X?

2. Identify two advantages of using the least-squares criterion of "best fit."

3. Look ahead to Table 13.1. What is the modal grade for the 507 statistics students? What is the modal grade for statistics students given the condition that they score below 30 on the mathematics test?

4. The following data are for freshman students at Spartan University:

Aptitude score: X Freshman grade point average (gpa): Y

$$\bar{X} = 560 \qquad\qquad \bar{Y} = 2.65$$
$$S_X = 75 \qquad\qquad S_Y = .35$$
$$r_{XY} = +.50$$

(*a*) Write the raw score regression equation for predicting Y from X and simplify it. (*b*) John and Will score 485 and 710, respectively, on the aptitude test. Predict the freshman gpa for each. (c) What assumption is necessary for this prediction to be valid? (d) What is the Y intercept of this regression equation? (e) What is the slope of this regression equation? (f) On graph paper, plot the line of regression for predicting gpa from aptitude score. (g) On the graph, show the solution to part (b), above. (h) What is the value of the standard error of estimate of Y on X? (i) For students whose aptitude score is the same as John's: 1. What proportion will be expected to obtain a gpa equal to the freshmen mean or better? 2. What proportion will be expected to obtain a gpa of 2.0 or below? 3. Within what central gpa limits will 95% of students with aptitude scores like John's be likely to be found? (j) For students whose aptitude score is the same as Will's: 1. What proportion will be expected to obtain a gpa equal to 2.5 or better? 2. What proportion will be expected to obtain a gpa of 3.0 or below? 3. Within what central gpa limits will 50% of students with aptitude scores like Will's be likely to be found? (k) What assumptions are necessary for the answers to 4i and 4j to be valid?

5. For the general data of Problem 4, write the regression equation of Y on X in deviation score form.

6. For the general data of Problem 4, write the regression equation of Y on X in z-score form.

7. Given the following data: $\bar{X} = 50$, $S_X = 15$, $\bar{Y} = 100$, $S_Y = 20$, and $r_{XY} = +.70$, (a) Write the raw score regression equation for predicting Y on X and simplify it. (b) Mary and Alice score 60 and 30, respectively, in X. What Y score do we predict for each? (c) Graph the line of regression of Y on X. (d) Use the graph to make the predictions requested in (b), above. (e) For persons whose X score is the same as Mary's: 1. What proportion will be expected to equal or exceed a score of 90 in Y? 2. What proportion will be expected to obtain a Y score of 100 or below? 3. Within what central limits will 99% of Y scores for such students be likely to be found? (f) For persons whose X score is the same as Alice's: 1. What proportion will be expected to equal or exceed a score of 90 in Y? 2. What proportion will be expected to obtain a Y score of 80 or below? 3. Within what central limits will 75% of Y scores of such students be likely to be found?

8. Given the following data: $\bar{Y} = 50$, $S_Y = 10$, $\bar{X} = 150$, $S_X = 20$, $r = +.60$. For each of the following questions, use the standard score form of the regression equation to develop your answer, and try working the problems in your head: (a) Find z'_Y when $z_X = +2.00$. (b) Find Y' when $X = 190$. (c) Find Y' when $X = 170$. (d) Find Y' when $X = 130$. (e) Find Y' when $X = 110$. (f) Find Y' when $X = 150$.

9. If $r = 0$, then $Y' = \bar{Y}$, no matter what the value of X. What justification is there for such a prediction, aside from intuition?

10. If Y increases 3 units for every 4 units increase in X, what is the slope of the line of regression of Y on X?

11. If Y decreases 4 units for every 3 units increase in X, what is the slope of the line of regression of Y on X?

12. If the regression equation of Y on X reads: $Y' = -.25X + 40$, (a) Could it be that the X and Y scores were expressed in z-score form? Explain. (b) Could the correlation be positive? Explain. (c) Could it be that $r = 0$? Explain. (d) Is $r = -.25$? Explain.

13. Write the general regression equation for predicting X from Y (a) in raw score form, (b) in deviation score form, (c) in z-score form.

12

Interpretive Aspects of Correlation and Regression

12.1 Factors Influencing r_{XY}: Range of Talent

The problem of range of talent is very important in understanding what a correlation coefficient means (or does not mean). First, let us lay a little groundwork.

According to Formula 11.6, $S_{YX} = S_Y \sqrt{1 - r_{XY}^2}$. This equation can be solved for r_{XY}, expressing the value of r_{XY} in a form which we have not seen before:

Alternate Formula for r_{XY} $$r_{XY} = \sqrt{1 - \frac{S_{YX}^2}{S_Y^2}}$$ (12.1)

This is not a practical formula for computing the correlation coefficient, but it is quite helpful in understanding the meaning of r. You will remember (Section 10.2) that it was contended that if the Y scores "hugged" the regression line closely, the correlation would be high, and if not, it would be low. We now have a more precise expression of this "hugging principle." Notice that *the magnitude of r is not solely a function of the size of S_{YX}*, the absolute measure of the variation of Y about the regression line, *but rather of the relative size of S_{YX} to S_Y*. If S_{YX} is zero, there is no error of prediction, and the correlation coefficient, according to Formula 12.1, is ± 1. On the other hand, if S_{YX}

has the same value as S_Y, the correlation will be zero. It is of no consequence, therefore, to the determination of the degree of correlation, to state that the standard error of estimate "is small." What matters is whether it is small *in relation to S_Y.*

Figure 12.1 illustrates a bivariate distribution and shows the consequences of restriction of range. First, when the entire distribution is included, the measure of Y variability is given by S_{Y_2}, and r is a function of the ratio, $S_{YX}{}^2/S_{Y_2}{}^2$. What happens if X is restricted in range by removing those pairs of scores which fall to the left of the vertical line? On the assumption of homoscedasticity, the value of S_{YX} remains the same, but overall Y variability shrinks to the value of S_{Y_1}, and r is a function of the ratio, $S_{YX}{}^2/S_{Y_1}{}^2$. This ratio is larger than that for the data as a whole, and therefore, according to Formula 12.1, r will be smaller.

The immediate consequence of this knowledge is that the value of the correlation coefficient depends on the degree of variation characterizing the two variables, as well as on the relationship present. It is common to find that the correlation coefficient between score on an academic aptitude test and academic achievement is highest among grade school children, lower among high school seniors, and still lower among college students. These differences may not so much indicate that something different is going on among the three groups as that the range of ability is greatest among the students in the lower grades, and successively less as one progresses into the realms of higher education.

In a given situation, restriction of range may take place in X, in Y, or in

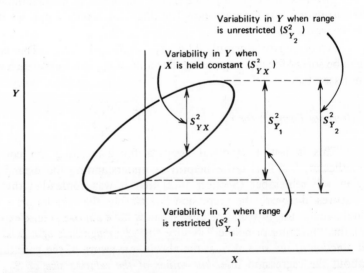

FIGURE 12.1 Relation between $S_{YX}{}^2$ and $S_Y{}^2$ when Range of Talent Differs.

both. The value of r will be smaller in those situations in which the range of either X or Y (or both) is less, other things being equal. This means that there is no such thing as *the* correlation between two variables, and that the value obtained must be interpreted in the light of the variability of the two variables in the circumstances in which it was obtained. *Other things being equal, the greater the restriction of range in X and/or Y, the lower the correlation coefficient.* When reporting a correlation coefficient, one should state the standard deviation of X and Y, so that others may judge whether the range of talent is similar to that with which they are concerned, or whether some allowance must be made.

It is possible to predict what the correlation will be in a situation characterized by a given degree of variability from knowledge of the correlation in a situation characterized by a different degree of variability. Guilford† offers a good discussion of this problem.

12.2 Factors Influencing r_{XY}: Heterogeneity of Samples

Section 10.7 cautioned that the correlation coefficient should be interpreted in terms of the circumstances under which it was obtained. One aspect of this warning was explored in Section 12.1. Another is considered here.

Suppose Professor Haggerty, a natural science instructor, obtains the correlation between academic aptitude test score and grade given in his course in natural science; let us say that it is $+.50$. He persuades Professor Eagan, a colleague of his who also teaches the same course, to repeat the study in his class to verify the result. Professor Eagan does so, and also finds the correlation to be $+.50$. In a moment of idle curiosity, Haggerty decides to pool the pairs of scores from the two classes and recalculate the correlation coefficient. He does so, and obtains a value of $+.30$! How could this be?

The answer lies in something well known to natural science students, although perhaps inadequately appreciated by the instructors. The fact of the matter is that the first instructor is known as "Hard Nosed Haggerty," and the second as "Easy Aces Eagan." Professor Haggerty is a hard grader; once, 8 years ago, he had a student whom he thought deserved an "A." Professor Eagan, on the other hand, thinks all students are wonderful, and rarely gives a grade below "C." Consequently, the scatter diagrams obtained from the two samples are like those shown in the first illustration of Figure 12.2. Note that the ability of the students appears to be about the same in the two classes (the X distributions), but the distributions of grades (the Y distributions) are not. The reason for the different correlation coefficient is that when the data are pooled, the scores no longer hug the regression line (which now must be a line lying amidst the two distributions) as closely as they do in either distribution considered by itself.

†J. P. Guilford, *Fundamental Statistics for Students of Psychology and Education*, 4th ed., McGraw-Hill Book Co., New York, 1965, pp. 341–345.

In terms of our more recent knowledge, the ratio of S_{YX}^2 to S_Y^2 is smaller in either sample taken by itself than it is among the data when they are pooled.

In the particular case illustrated, the distributions differed, between samples, in the mean of X but not in the mean of Y. Other types of differences are quite possible. The second illustration in Figure 12.2 shows a situation in which a second sample differs in that *both* the mean of X and the mean of Y are higher than in the first sample. In this case, the fraction S_{YX}^2/S_Y^2 is *smaller* when the data are pooled than when each sample is considered separately, and the correlation will therefore be greater among the pooled data than among the separate samples.

12.3 Interpretation of r_{XY}: The Regression Equation

In Section 9.9, we observed that there was no simple way in which to interpret the meaning of the correlation coefficient; that, for example, it was not meaningful to say that a coefficient of $+.50$ indicates "50% association" between the two variables. We are now in a better position to say what the correlation coefficient does mean.

One interpretation can be made in terms of the regression equation. In Section 11.8, we found that r_{XY} was the slope of the equation of regression of Y on X when both variables were cast in z-score form, and therefore indicates how much of a standard deviation Y will change for one standard deviation of change in X. Let us see what the standard score form of the regression equation says about the consequences of three possible values of r: 0, $+.50$, and $+1.00$. A graphic representation of the regression of Y on X is shown in Figure 12.3 for each of these situations, together with the regression equation appropriate to each. As the figure shows, when the correlation is $+1$, the predicted standard score in Y is the same as the standard score in X from which the prediction is

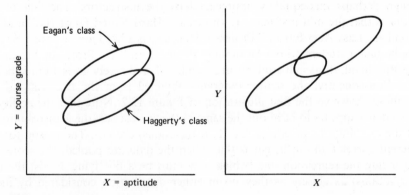

FIGURE 12.2 Correlation Resulting from Pooling of Data from Heterogeneous Samples.

made. When the correlation is zero, the mean of Y ($z = 0$) is predicted, no matter what value X has. This is logical because information about X supplies no information which would improve over a sheer guess as to the value of Y. The most interesting of the three situations is where r_{XY} has an intermediate value. Think, for example, of the correlation between intelligence of parents and offspring, which indeed has a value close to $+.50$. If parental intelligence is two standard deviations above the mean, the predicted intelligence of their offspring is one standard deviation above the mean. On the other hand, if the parents' intelligence is two standard deviations below the mean, the predicted intelligence of their offspring is only one standard deviation below the mean. To put it in other words, bright parents will tend to have children who are

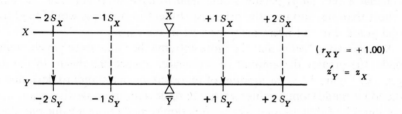

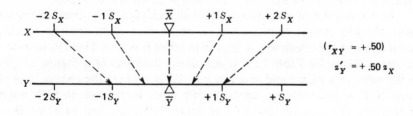

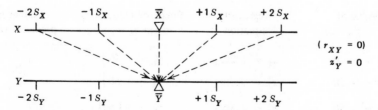

FIGURE 12.3 Regression for Three Values of r_{XY}.

brighter than average, but not as bright as they, and dull parents will tend to have children who are dull, but not as dull as their parents. Remember that the predicted value is to be thought of as an *average* value; it is quite possible for bright parents to have a child brighter than they or one whose intelligence is below average.

This phenomenon is precisely what Sir Francis Galton observed in his studies of inheritance. He first referred to it as "reversion," and later, as "regression." Today we refer to it as *regression on the mean*. You understand now why the straight line of best fit is called a regression line, and why the symbol r was chosen for the correlation coefficient.

The fact of regression on the mean is, of course, characteristic of *any* relationship in which the correlation is less than perfect. Consequently, we would expect that a very short person would tend to have short children, but children less short than he, and that the brightest student in the class would tend to earn a good grade, but not necessarily the best in the class.

An interesting fact is that the more extreme the value from which prediction is made, the greater the amount of regression toward the mean. In the middle diagram of Figure 12.3, the amount of regression is one standard deviation when prediction is made from a value two standard deviations above the mean, whereas regression is half that amount when prediction is made from a value one standard deviation above the mean.

As the z-score form of the regression equation ($z_Y' = r_{XY}z_X$) shows, the higher the value of r, the less the amount of regression. For $z_X = +1$, $z_Y' = +.9$ when $r = +.90$, $+.5$ when $r = +.50$, and $+.2$ when $r = +.20$.

In Section 9.9, it was contended that a change of a given amount in the value of r has greater consequences (in most ways of interpreting r) when the initial value of the coefficient is high than when it is low. There is, however, one exception. Consider Table 12.1, which shows the effect of a change of .10 point in the value of a high r and in a low one. As is evident, the change in predicted value of Y, as measured in standard score units, is the same in both situations. In Sections 12.6 and 12.7 we will encounter interpretations in which the effect differs as a function of the level of r.

TABLE 12.1 Effect of Change in r on Predicted Value.

Value of r	Regression equation	Predicted value of z_Y when $z_X = +2$	Change in predicted value
$r = +.20$	$z_Y' = +.20z_X$	$z_Y' = +.40$	.20
$r = +.30$	$z_Y' = +.30z_X$	$z_Y' = +.60$	
$r = +.80$	$z_Y' = +.80z_X$	$z_Y' = +1.60$	.20
$r = +.90$	$z_Y' = +.90z_X$	$z_Y' = +1.80$	

12.4 Two Apparent Paradoxes in Regression

Assume that the correlation between IQ of parents and offspring is $+.50$, as we did in the previous section. If parents' IQ is 120, the predicted value for their children is 110, a value regressed halfway back to the mean. Now consider children whose IQ is 110; what shall we predict the intelligence of their parents to be? It is not 120, as one might at first suppose, but 105. The answer to this apparent paradox lies in the fact that we must remember to use the right regression equation of the two available (see Section 11.2). If Y represents IQ of the child and X the IQ of the parents, then the first prediction is made according to the regression of Y on X. To make a prediction in the opposite direction, we must deal with the regression of X on Y. When this is done, regression will once again take the predicted value halfway back to the mean, at 105.

This point may be clearer if we look at Figure 12.4 which describes the situation discussed above. If parent IQ is 120, it is necessary to consider the IQ's of all children of such parents. These are the Y values of the points to be found in the column which lies directly above the value $X = 120$. The mean of these values is represented by the small circle at the center of the column, and, reading horizontally to the Y axis, its value is found to be $Y = 110$. If we now wish to study parental IQ for children whose IQ is 110, it is necessary to consider the IQ's of all parents of such children. These are represented by the X values of the points falling in the row directly to the right of the value $Y = 110$. The mean of these values is represented by the small square at the center of the row, and

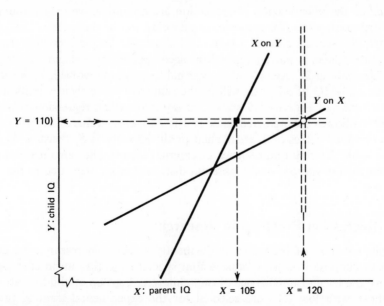

FIGURE 12.4 Regression of Y on X, and X on Y.

reading vertically down to the X axis, its value is found to be $X = 105$. Figure 12.4 shows very clearly that different sets of scores are involved in making the two predictions, excepting only those lying at the intersection of the column and the row. In the first prediction, for example, we are talking about parents whose IQ is exactly 120, and therefore of offspring whose *mean* IQ is 110. In the second prediction, we are not speaking of children whose mean IQ is 110, but those who have an IQ of *exactly* 110.

The second apparent paradox is one which attracted Galton's attention. If parents with extreme characteristics tend to have offspring with characteristics less extreme than themselves, how is it that, after a few generations, we do not find everybody at the center? The answer to this one is that *regression of predicted values toward the mean is accompanied by variation of obtained values about the predicted values, and the greater the degree of regression toward the mean, the greater the amount of variation.* The inward movement of regression is therefore accompanied by the expansive action of variability, which makes it possible for the more extreme values of Y to occur. Specifically, Y', the predicted value of Y, is only the predicted *mean* of Y for those who obtain a particular score in X. The obtained Y values corresponding to that value of X will be distributed about Y' with a standard deviation equal to S_{YX}. The lower the value of the correlation coefficient, the greater the value of S_{YX}, so that the greater the degree of regression on the mean, the greater the variation of obtained Y values about their predicted values.

Figure 12.5 illustrates the situation. The first part of this figure shows that when $r = 1$, each obtained Y exactly equals its predicted value. Unless factors *external* to the phenomenon of regression are operative, we may presume that the distribution of IQ (for example) of offspring will be the same as that of their parents. The second part of Figure 12.5 illustrates an intermediate degree of correlation. There is partial regression, accompanied by a degree of variability of Y values about Y'. Again, unless external factors are involved, we see that the distribution of IQ of offspring will be the same as that of their parents. Finally, the third part of Figure 12.5 shows the situation when regression is complete $(r = 0)$. Although the predicted value of Y is $\overline{Y}$ for every value of X, the variability of the obtained values of Y about their predicted value is S_Y (because $S_{YX} = S_Y$ when $r = 0$). Barring the influence of external factors, the same features (mean and standard deviation) of the parental distribution are recreated in that of the offspring.

12.5 Regression Problems in Research

The phenomenon of regression is frequently a factor in research design. For example, suppose it is hypothesized that special education at an early age can improve the level of intelligence of dull children. A group of children are tested, and those with low IQ's are selected for the experimental training program.

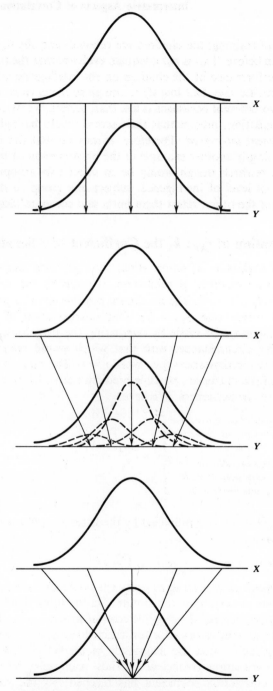

FIGURE 12.5 Regression and Variation of Obtained Values about the Regressed Values.

On completion of training, the children are retested, and the mean IQ is found to be higher than before. This is *not* adequate evidence that the training program improved the performance of the children on the intelligence test. The children were selected because they had low IQ's, and since the correlation between test scores on the two different occasions is less than perfect, we would, according to the regression equation, predict that their scores would be higher on retesting *even if no treatment intervened*. Therefore, it may be that the improvement in performance is simply another example of the phenomenon of regression on the mean. A better research design would be to select two groups of children of comparable initial level of intelligence, subject one group to the experimental treatment but not the other, retest them both, and compare these scores.

12.6 Interpretation of r_{XY}: k, the Coefficient of Alienation

The measure of variability of scores about the regression line, or as we might call it, the measure of error of prediction, is given by the standard error of estimate, $S_{YX} = S_Y \sqrt{1 - r^2}$. The maximum possible error of prediction occurs when $r = 0$, in which case $S_{YX} = S_Y$. One interpretation of the correlation coefficient can therefore be made by comparing the magnitude of error in the present predictive circumstances with that which would obtain in the worst possible predictive circumstances, i.e., when $r = 0$. The ratio of S_{YX} to S_Y gives the proportion of the maximum possible predictive error which characterizes the present predictive circumstances. We have:

$$\frac{\begin{bmatrix} \textit{magnitude of predictive error} \\ \textit{characterizing our predictive} \\ \textit{situation} \end{bmatrix}}{\begin{bmatrix} \textit{magnitude of predictive error} \\ \textit{in the worst possible predic-} \\ \textit{tive situation } (r = 0) \end{bmatrix}} = \frac{S_{YX}}{S_Y} = \frac{S_Y \sqrt{1 - r^2}}{S_Y} = \sqrt{1 - r^2}$$

This quantity, $\sqrt{1 - r^2}$, is symbolized by the letter k, and it is called the *coefficient of alienation*:

Coefficient of Alienation $k = \sqrt{1 - r^2}$ (12.2)

When the value of k is close to unity (its maximum value), the magnitude of predictive error is close to its maximum. On the other hand, when the value of k is close to zero, most of the possible error of prediction has been eliminated.

Table 12.2 presents values of k for selected values of r. In examining this table, a striking fact is that the magnitude of predictive error decreases very slowly as the correlation coefficient ascends from zero. For instance, note that when the correlation coefficient has reached .50, the standard error of estimate is 87% of the size that it would be if the correlation were zero. To put it the other way, the reduction in variability in predictive error amounts only

TABLE 12.2 Values of Several Indicators of Utility of r for Different Levels of the Correlation Coefficient.

r_{XY}	k	r^2	A	B
1.00	.00	1.00	.50	1.00
.95	.31	.90	.40	.80
.90	.44	.81	.35	.71
.85	.53	.72	.32	.65
.80	.60	.64	.30	.59
.75	.66	.56	.27	.54
.70	.71	.49	.25	.49
.65	.76	.42	.23	.45
.60	.80	.36	.20	.41
.55	.84	.30	.19	.37
.50	.87	.25	.17	.33
.45	.89	.20	.15	.30
.40	.92	.16	.13	.26
.35	.94	.12	.11	.23
.30	.95	.09	.10	.19
.25	.97	.06	.08	.16
.20	.98	.04	.06	.13
.15	.99−	.02	.05	.10
.10	.99+	.01	.03	.06
.05	1.00−	.00+	.02	.03
.00	1.00	.00	.00	.00

k: coefficient of alienation (see Section 12.6)
r^2: coefficient of determination (see Section 12.7)
A: proportion of correct placements in excess of chance (see Section 12.8)
B: proportion of improvement in correct placement relative to the chance proportion of .50 (see Section 12.8)

to 13% for a coefficient of this magnitude. Note also that a change in r from .20 to .30 results in a reduction of .03 in the size of the coefficient of alienation, whereas a change in r from .80 to .90 results in a change of .16. This shows that a given change in the magnitude of a correlation coefficient has greater consequences when the correlation is high than when it is low.

12.7 Interpretation of r_{XY}: r^2, the Coefficient of Determination

When a number of scores are assembled, it is found that their values are not all the same. What is the source of this variation? If the question is applied to the Y scores in a bivariate distribution, the answer has two parts. First, some of the variation in Y is associated with changes in X. That is, assuming some degree of correlation between X and Y, Y takes different values depending on whether the associated value of X is high or low. However, if we settle on any single value of X, there is still some variability in Y (this second kind of variability is measured by S_{YX}). Total variation in Y may therefore be thought of as having two component parts: variation in Y which is associated with or attributable to changes in X, and variation in Y which is inherent in Y, and hence independent of changes in X.

It is possible to partition the total Y variation in such a way as to reflect the contribution of these two components. This partition must be done in terms of the *variance* of Y, which can be partitioned into additive components, rather than in terms of the standard deviation of Y, which cannot.† We may begin by dividing the deviation of any Y score from its mean into two components:

$$(Y - \overline{Y}) = (Y - Y') + (Y' - \overline{Y})$$

This equation says that the difference between a score and its mean may be expressed in terms of the difference between the score and its predicted value, and the difference between its predicted value and the mean.‡ Note that the equation above is an algebraic identity, since on the right side of the equation the two values of Y' will cancel, if we wish, leaving the expression on the right the same as that on the left. Figure 12.6 illustrates this way of expressing the location of a score in Y. Consider Point 1 in that illustration. It lies 15 points above the mean of Y. It may be reexpressed as the deviation of the point from Y' ($+5$), plus the deviation of Y' from the mean ($+10$). Point 2 illustrates a position which is the combination of two deviations, one positive and the other negative.††

If both sides of the above equation are squared, and if these values are then summed over all scores and the resulting expression simplified, we have:

$$\sum(Y - \overline{Y})^2 = \sum(Y - Y')^2 + \sum(Y' - \overline{Y})^2$$

Proof of this development appears in Note 12.1. If both sides of the equation are divided by n, we obtain the following expression.

$$\frac{\sum(Y - \overline{Y})^2}{n} = \frac{\sum(Y - Y')^2}{n} + \frac{\sum(Y' - \overline{Y})^2}{n}, \text{ or}$$

---

†Variance is the term used for the square of the standard deviation, $S_Y{}^2$ (see Section 6.5). It gets at the same basic characteristic as does the standard deviation, namely, variation in Y.

‡This may at first seem to be an arbitrary and uninvited complication of an originally simple expression. In fact, it is a way of stating location which is handy in everyday life. "You will find a stop sign five blocks down this street; the grocery store is two blocks beyond" is the same kind of statement.

††This is comparable to saying: "There is a stop sign five blocks down this street; the grocery store is one block short of it."

*Partition of Y Variance
into Two Components*

$$S_Y{}^2 \quad = \quad S_{YX}{}^2 \quad + \quad S_{Y'}{}^2 \qquad (12.3)$$

$$\begin{bmatrix} \text{total } Y \\ \text{variance} \end{bmatrix} = \begin{bmatrix} \text{variance in } Y \\ \text{independent of} \\ \text{changes in } X \end{bmatrix} + \begin{bmatrix} \text{variance in } Y \\ \text{associated with} \\ \text{changes in } X \end{bmatrix}$$

Each of these elements is a variance of some kind. The expression on the left side of the equation is $S_Y{}^2$, the total variance of Y. The first component on the right is $S_{YX}{}^2$, the variance of Y which is inherent in Y, and the remaining component is $S_{Y'}{}^2$, the variance in Y associated with changes in X. This last quantity we have not met before. Note that it is a function of the discrepancies between each predicted value of Y and the mean of Y. As close inspection of its formula shows, it is the variance (square of the standard deviation) of the set of predicted Y values. If $r = 0$, the predicted value of Y is $\overline{Y}$, no matter what the value of X, and each discrepancy, $(Y' - \overline{Y})$, becomes zero. Consequently, $\Sigma(Y' - \overline{Y})^2/n$ becomes $0/n$, and $S_{Y'}{}^2 = 0$. In this case, *none* of the variance in Y is associated with changes in X. On the other hand, if $r = \pm 1.00$, each predicted value of Y is the actual value of Y, and $\Sigma(Y' - \overline{Y})^2/n$ becomes $\Sigma(Y - \overline{Y})^2/n$. In this case, $S_{Y'}{}^2 = S_Y{}^2$. This would mean that *all* of the variation in Y is contributed by reason of the association with X.

In Section 11.9, the calculation of S_Y and S_{YX} was illustrated for a set of bivariate data (Table 11.1). The same illustration is extended in Table 12.3 to

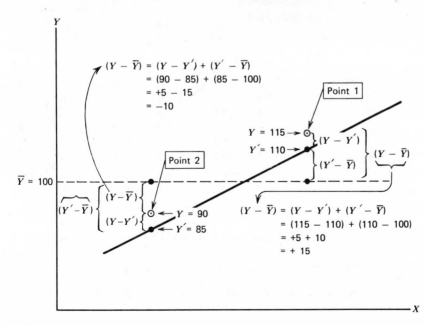

FIGURE 12.6 Partition of a Deviation Score $(Y - \overline{Y})$ into Component Deviations: $(Y - Y')$, $(Y' - \overline{Y})$.

show direct calculation of $S_{Y'}^2$, and to permit comparison of the three quantities, S_Y^2, S_{YX}^2, and $S_{Y'}^2$. Contents of Table 12.3 are as follows:

Columns 1 and 2: paired values of the raw scores
Columns 3 and 4: values needed for calculation of S_Y^2
Column 5:   values of Y predicted from each
                value of X by means of the
                regression equation
Columns 6 and 7: values needed for calculation of S_{YX}^2
Columns 8 and 9: values needed for calculation of $S_{Y'}^2$

Note that the two sums of squares of deviation scores developed by the partition (columns 7 and 9) are, when added together, exactly equal to the unpartitioned sum of squares of deviation scores (column 4). Similarly, the variances derived from these sums of squares are equated in the same way: $S_Y^2 = S_{YX}^2 + S_{Y'}^2$. Note also that the sum of the *unsquared* deviations (columns 3, 6, and 8) each comes to zero.

TABLE 12.3 Calculation of S_Y, S_{YX}, and $S_{Y'}$: Data from Table 9.1.

(1) X	(2) Y	(3) $(Y - \overline{Y})$	(4) $(Y - \overline{Y})^2$	(5) Y'	(6) $(Y - Y')$	(7) $(Y - Y')^2$	(8) $(Y' - \overline{Y})$	(9) $(Y' - \overline{Y})^2$
37	75	-2.6	6.8	76.8	-1.8	3.2	$-.8$	.6
41	78	$+.4$	.2	79.4	-1.4	2.0	$+1.8$	3.2
48	88	$+10.4$	108.2	84.1	$+3.9$	15.2	$+6.5$	42.2
32	80	$+2.4$	5.8	73.4	$+6.6$	43.6	-4.2	17.6
36	78	$+.4$	.2	76.1	$+1.9$	3.6	-1.5	2.2
30	71	-6.6	43.6	72.1	-1.1	1.2	-5.5	30.2
40	75	-2.6	6.8	78.8	-3.8	14.4	$+1.2$	1.4
45	83	$+5.4$	29.2	82.1	$+.9$	.8	$+4.5$	20.2
39	74	-3.6	13.0	78.1	-4.1	16.8	$+.5$	.2
34	74	-3.6	13.0	74.8	$-.8$	.6	-2.8	7.8
Σ 382	776	0	227	776	0	101	0	126
Σ/n 38.2	77.6	0	22.7	77.6	0	10.1	0	12.6

EQUATIONS FOR TABLE 12.3

Basic Data $\overline{X} = 38.2$ $\overline{Y} = 77.6$ $r_{XY} = +.74$

                    $S_X = 5.3$ $S_Y = 4.8$ $Y' = .664X + 52.2$

Equations continued on following page

Partition of Sum of Squares of Deviation Scores

$$\sum(Y - \overline{Y})^2 = \sum(Y - Y')^2 + \sum(Y' - \overline{Y})^2$$

$$227 \quad = \quad 101 \quad + \quad 126$$

Partition of
Variance

$$S_Y^2 \quad = \quad S_{YX}^2 \quad + \quad S_{Y'}^2$$

$$22.7 \quad = \quad 10.1 \quad + \quad 12.6$$

Sum of Deviations

$$\sum(Y - \overline{Y}) = 0 \qquad \sum(Y - Y') = 0 \qquad \sum(Y' - \overline{Y}) = 0$$

One interpretation of the correlation coefficient can be made in terms of the *proportion of the total Y variance which is associated with changes in X*. This proportion is given by:

$$\frac{\left[\begin{array}{c}\textit{variance in Y associated}\\ \textit{with changes in X}\end{array}\right]}{[\textit{total variance in Y}]} = \frac{S_{Y'}^2}{S_Y^2}$$

This expression can be simplified by appropriate substitution. Since

$$S_Y^2 = S_{YX}^2 + S_{Y'}^2$$

then

$$S_{Y'}^2 = S_Y^2 - S_{YX}^2$$

and

$$\frac{S_{Y'}^2}{S_Y^2} = \frac{S_Y^2 - S_{YX}^2}{S_Y^2}$$

$$= \frac{S_Y^2 - (S_Y\sqrt{1 - r^2})^2}{S_Y^2}$$

$$= \frac{S_Y^2 - S_Y^2(1 - r^2)}{S_Y^2}$$

$$= \frac{S_Y^2 - S_Y^2 + S_Y^2 r^2}{S_Y^2}$$

$$= r^2$$

So r^2 *gives the proportion of Y variance which is associated with changes in X.* r^2 is called the *coefficient of determination.* If $r = .50$, $r^2 = .25$. This means, for example, that 25% of Y variance is associated with changes in X (and 75% is not).

Values of r^2 are given for selected values of r in Table 12.2. Note, once more, that the proportion of Y variance accounted for by variation in X increases more slowly than does the magnitude of the correlation coefficient. Not until $r = .71$ does $r^2 = .50$.

12.8 Interpretation of r_{XY}: Proportion of Correct Placements

The interpretation of the meaning of r according to k or r^2 is certainly not very encouraging as to the value of r's of moderate magnitude. However, in practical problems of prediction, we are often interested in estimating, from knowledge of a person's score in X, the likelihood that he will "succeed" (i.e., score above a given point in Y). In these terms we can often do much better by using the predictor than by not doing so, even when the correlation is modest. Consequently, a somewhat more cheerful outlook may be had by considering the proportion of correct placements which occur when the regression equation is used to predict success. Assume a normal bivariate distribution, that success is defined as scoring above the median on the criterion variable (Y), and that those who are selected as potentially successful are those who score above the median on the predictor variable (X). If $r = 0$, 50% correct placement will be achieved by using score on the predictor for selection. Look at the first picture in Table 12.4. Successful predictions have been made for the 50 individuals who were predicted to succeed and did, plus the 50 who were predicted to fail and did, i.e., those individuals who fall in the first and third quadrants of the diagram. The proportion of successful placements is therefore 100 out of the 200 candidates, or 50%. Now look at the second picture in Table 12.4. In this case, the correlation

TABLE 12.4 Proportion of Successful Placements for Two Levels of r_{XY}.

	($r = .00$) Below $\bar{X}$	Above $\bar{X}$			($r = +.50$) Below $\bar{X}$	Above $\bar{X}$
Above $\bar{Y}$	II 50	I 50		Above $\bar{Y}$	II 33	I 67
Y: Criterion				Y: Criterion		
Below $\bar{Y}$	III 50	IV 50		Below $\bar{Y}$	III 67	IV 33
		$n = 200$				$n = 200$
	X: Predictor				X: Predictor	

coefficient is $+.50$, and the number of correct placements is $67 + 67 = 134$. The proportion of correct placements is therefore $134/200$, or $.67$. The proportion of correct placements in excess of chance proportion of such placements ($.50$) is $.17$. The proportion of improvement in correct placement relative to the proportion for chance placement ($.50$) is $.17/.50$, or $.33$.† Viewed this way, a correlation coefficient of $.50$ appears to have greater utility than some other interpretations suggest. The last two columns of Table 12.2 present, for selected values of r, the proportion of correct placements in excess of chance and the proportion of improvement in correct placements relative to the chance proportion of $.50$.‡

It should be remembered that the interpretation offered above is dependent on splitting the two variables at the median, and on the assumption of a normal bivariate distribution. If these conditions are varied, a somewhat different result will follow. Some years ago, Taylor and Russell pointed out that effectiveness of prediction depended not only on the magnitude of the correlation coefficient, but also where the cut was made on the predictor variable.†† Indeed, their work shows that a rather low coefficient may be quite useful in improving the quality of performance on the criterion when there are a large number of "applicants" but a small number to be selected. Their article is recommended for those who are concerned with this problem.

NOTE

Partition of the Sum of Squares of Deviation Scores into Two Components
(*Ref:* Section 12.7)

$$(Y - \overline{Y}) = (Y - Y') + (Y' - \overline{Y})$$

and squaring both sides,

$$(Y - \overline{Y})^2 = (Y - Y')^2 + (Y' - \overline{Y})^2 + 2(Y - Y')(Y' - \overline{Y})$$

Summing across all scores,

$$\sum(Y - \overline{Y})^2 = \sum(Y - Y')^2 + \sum(Y' - \overline{Y})^2 + 2\sum(Y - Y')(Y' - \overline{Y})$$

We now proceed to evaluate the expression on the far right:

$$\sum(Y - Y')(Y' - \overline{Y}) = \sum[(Y - \overline{Y}) - (Y' - \overline{Y})][Y' - \overline{Y}]$$
$$= \sum[y - y']y'$$

---

† $.17/.50$ actually equals $.34$, but $.33$ is the right value; the discrepancy is due to rounding.

‡ This interpretive approach, and the entries for columns A and B of Table 12.2, are owed to: W. B. Michael, "An Interpretation of the Coefficients of Predictive Validity and of Determination in Terms of the Proportions of Correct Inclusions or Exclusions in Cells of a Fourfold Table," *Educational and Psychological Measurement*, **26**, No. 2, 419–424 (1966).

†† H. Taylor, and J. Russell, "The Relationship of Validity Coefficients to the Practical Effectiveness of Tests in Selection: Discussion and Tables," *Journal of Applied Psychology*, **23**, 565–578 (1939).

From the deviation score formula for y' (Formula 11.2),

$$\sum(Y - Y')(Y' - \overline{Y}) = \sum\left[y - \frac{S_Y}{S_X}rx\right]\left[\frac{S_Y}{S_X}rx\right]$$

$$= \sum\left[\frac{S_Y}{S_X}rxy - \frac{S_Y^2}{S_X^2}r^2x^2\right]$$

$$= \frac{S_Y}{S_X}r\sum xy - \frac{S_Y^2}{S_X^2}r^2\sum x^2$$

Since $r = \sum xy/nS_XS_Y$, $\sum xy = rnS_XS_Y$, and since $S_X^2 = \sum x^2/n$, $\sum x^2 = nS_X^2$; making these substitutions we have:

$$\sum(Y - Y')(Y' - \overline{Y}) = \frac{S_Y}{\mathscr{S}_X}r^2n\mathscr{S}_XS_Y - \frac{S_Y^2}{\mathscr{S}_X^2}r^2n\mathscr{S}_X^2$$

$$= 0$$

and therefore

$$\sum(Y - \overline{Y})^2 = \sum(Y - Y')^2 + \sum(Y' - \overline{Y})^2$$

If both sides of the equation are divided by n, we have:

$$S_Y^2 \quad = \quad S_{YX}^2 \quad + \quad S_{Y'}^2$$

PROBLEMS AND EXERCISES

Identify:

range of talent   regression on the mean
homoscedasticity   coefficient of alienation
heterogeneity of samples   coefficient of determination

    1. Solve the equation $S_{YX} = S_Y\sqrt{1 - r^2}$ for r, thus obtaining Formula 12.1.

    2. Among a group of retarded 10-year-old children, it is found that the correlation between IQ and reading achievement is $+.25$. However, on a school-wide basis, the correlation is $+.50$. Assuming these results to be typical, what explanation do you suggest?

    3. To study the phenomenon of creativity, a number of outstandingly creative persons are assembled and tested. It is found that rating on creativity and IQ correlate to the extent of $r = +.20$ among this group. It is concluded that creativity is really quite different from intelligence. Any objections?

    4. It is common to find that the correlation between airplane pilot aptitude test score and pilot proficiency is higher among aviation cadets than among experienced pilots. What could account for this?

    5. One way to learn whether an aptitude test works is to test applicants for the particular job, hire them all, and subsequently correlate test score with a measure of job proficiency. Another way, usually more practical, is to test all currently employed workers of the particular type, and obtain the same correlation. Is there any reason to think that the coefficient might be different when obtained in these two ways? Explain.

6. At certain stages in school, girls tend to be superior to boys in verbal skills. Suppose the correlation between spelling score and IQ is $+.50$ for a sample of girls, and the same among a sample of boys. If the two sets of subjects were pooled and the coefficient computed on the total group, would you expect r to be about the same? Explain.

7. Suppose the correlation is $-.30$ between strength of grip and time in the 100-yard dash for a sample of men and the same among a sample of women. If the two samples are combined and r is recomputed, would it be about the same? Explain.

8. If $r = -.50$, and Pete scores $\frac{1}{2}$ standard deviation below the mean in X, what (a) z score do we predict for him in Y? (b) score do we predict for him in Y if $\overline{Y} = 100$ and $S_Y = 20$? (c) score do we predict for him in Y if $\overline{Y} = 82$ and $S_Y = 16$?

9. It is proposed that those with an IQ below 70 be sterilized, in order to eliminate feebleminded children. Any objection, other than humanitarian?

10. Someone proposes a "hot-house" treatment for gifted children. Four-year-olds are tested, and those whose IQ appears to be above 140 are selected for special treatment. Before treatment, mean IQ of this group is 150. Let us suppose that the treatment has no effect on IQ. What mean IQ would you expect when the children are retested one year later? Explain.

11. In one company, it is found that frequency of accidents correlates about $+.40$ from one year period to the next. It institutes a safety course for the 10% least safe of workers last year. This year, the accident record of these men is distinctly better. Your comment?

12. Interpret the correlation coefficients $.10, .30, .60,$ and $.90$ in terms of (a) the coefficient of alienation, (b) the coefficient of determination, (c) the proportion of correct placements when the split is at the median in X and Y.

13. By revising a test, we are able to increase the correlation between it and the criterion from $.25$ to $.50$. Interpret the gain made by revision according to (a) the coefficient of alienation, (b) the coefficient of determination, (c) the proportion of correct placements when the split is at the median in X and Y. (d) Do any of these interpretations suggest that the increase from $.25$ to $.50$ doubled the strength of the relationship?

14. When $r = \pm 1.00$, what value would $\Sigma(Y - Y')^2/n$ have? Explain.

15. When $r = 0$, what value would $\Sigma(Y - Y')^2/n$ have? Explain.

16. Under what conditions will $S_Y = S_{Y'}$? Explain.

13

The Basis of Statistical Inference

13.1 A Problem in Inference: Testing Hypotheses

A basic aim of statistical inference is to form a conclusion about a characteristic of a population from study of a sample taken from that population. In inference, the fundamental factor which must be taken into account is that sample outcomes vary. There are two types of inferential procedures: *hypothesis testing* and *estimation*. We will consider hypothesis testing in this section, and estimation in the next.

Mr. Jones, wondering whether the coin he holds in his hand is a "fair" coin (i.e., is as likely to come up heads as tails), decides to put it to a test. He tosses the coin 100 times and observes the number of heads obtained in this series of trials.

Dr. Brown, director of institutional research at a large university, is aware of a nationwide survey of academic aptitude of college and university freshmen. He would like to know if the level of aptitude of the current freshman class at his institution is, as measured on the same test, the same as that obtained in the survey. In his institution, there are 5000 freshmen, too many to study conveniently. He therefore selects 250 students from among the 5000, finds their mean aptitude test score, and compares it with the mean of the nationwide group.

Dr. Smith, a psychologist, wants to know if reaction time is equally fast to red and green light. He chooses two groups of 50 subjects each, and measures their reaction time when one group is exposed to the green stimulus and the other to the red. He then compares the mean reaction time of the two groups.

Jones, Brown, and Smith each have problems for which hypothesis testing procedures are appropriate. In each case we might first think of the problem in terms of a question, but the procedure for answering is easier if the question is translated into an hypothesis; that is, a statement to be subjected to test, and, on the outcome of the test, to be accepted or rejected. For example, Mr. Jones wants to know if the number of heads obtained in the sample of 100 tosses is in line with what could be expected if, in the population of all possible tosses, heads will occur half the time. For purposes of statistical examination, this question is rephrased as an hypothesis: *in the population of possible tosses, the proportion of heads is .50.* He then proceeds to compare the results for his sample of 100 tosses with the type of results that would be expected if the hypothesis were true. If the result obtained is in line with the results expected when the hypothesis is true, he will accept the hypothesis. If the result obtained differs greatly from what would be expected, he will reject the hypothesis. To be concrete about the matter, let us complete the example on intuitive terms. Suppose Mr. Jones obtained 54 heads in the 100 tosses. This is a reasonable result if the coin is fair, and therefore he has no reason to reject the hypothesis. On the other hand, suppose he obtained 95 heads in the 100 tosses. If the coin were fair, this outcome would be possible, but extremely unlikely. It is more reasonable to believe that the coin is not fair, and so he will reject the hypothesis.

Dr. Brown and Dr. Smith will also cast their questions in the form of hypotheses. Dr. Brown will hypothesize that the mean of the population of freshman test scores at his institution is equal to the mean characterizing the national group. Dr. Smith wants to draw conclusions about the reaction times of subjects in general like the ones he studied, not just about the 100 subjects in his experiment. He will therefore hypothesize that the mean of the *population* of responses to a red light is the same as the mean of the *population* of responses to a green light. To evaluate their hypotheses, both men will ask what type of sample results one would expect to obtain if the hypothesis is correct. If their sample outcome is not in accord with what they would expect, they will reject their hypotheses.

In the three examples of hypothesis testing, the first two illustrate what is called the *one-sample case*. In each instance, there is a single sample, and the question is whether the population parameter has the hypothesized value. The third example, concerning reaction time to red and green light, illustrates the *two-sample case*. In this instance, there is a sample from one population, and a second sample from another. The question is not about location of a specific population value (parameter), but about the relation between the two population values. The two-sample case is of great importance because it is the basic model for evaluating the outcome of an experiment, where one group is treated one way and the second, another. Not illustrated above is the *multisample case*, where more than two populations are involved. For example, Dr. Smith might have hypothesized that there is no difference in reaction time to red, green, yellow, or blue light, and conducted his experiment accordingly.

13.2 A Problem in Inference: Estimation

In hypothesis testing, we have a particular value in mind; we hypothesize that the value we have in mind characterizes the population of observations. The question is whether that value is reasonable in the light of the evidence from the sample. In the problem of estimation, on the other hand, there is no particular *a priori* population value to be examined. Rather, the question is, what *is* the population value?

What proportion of the eligible voters favor, at this point in time, passing of the bond issue? What is the mean IQ of students who attend school in the Fremont District? What is the mean amount of time required for experienced airplane pilots to note some abnormal flight condition and to take appropriate remedial action? These are examples of problems in estimation. In each case it is impractical to study the characteristic of interest in the entire population. Instead, a sample is drawn, studied, and an inference made about the population characteristic.

It has been stated that the object of inference is to form a conclusion about the nature of a characteristic of a population. We should be explicit. The characteristic may be a proportion, a mean, a median, a standard deviation, a correlation coefficient, or any other of a number of statistical parameters. Furthermore, inference may, according to the two-sample model, be concerned with the difference between two populations with regard to a given parameter. In the development to follow, emphasis will first be placed on inference about means because of the basic utility of that measure in answering questions about data.

13.3 Basic Issues in Inference

In the discussion of inference so far, the dominant theme is uncertainty. It is not possible to know *for sure* what is characteristic of a population from study of only a portion of it. What remains? Only probable knowledge. But, the value of probable knowledge is great indeed. Most of our lives are based on such information, and we live with it in reasonable comfort. Having done as well as we have in undergraduate college years, shall we aspire to a graduate degree? We have some notion as to what the odds are. Is there any point in applying for that position listed in the job announcement? We have some idea of the degree to which our qualifications fit the description of requirements. Will the sun come up tomorrow morning? We do not know for sure, but is a good bet.

A characteristic of any statistical inference is that it may be right or wrong. Accepting that proposition, the question then becomes how to establish a *known* risk of being wrong. This question is both important and legitimate. Under appropriate circumstances, it is quite capable of being answered.

The fundamental fact of sampling is that the value of the characteristic we are studying will vary from sample to sample. If Mr. Jones repeated his coin-tossing experiment, and if both the coin and the method of tossing were fair, it would not be surprising to find that he obtained 54 heads on the first series of 100 tosses, 49 heads on the second, and 44, 57, and 52 heads on the third, fourth, and fifth series. Similarly, if Dr. Smith repeated his experiment about reaction time to red and green light on several occasions, and *even if there were really no differential effect of color on reaction time*, the means of his two samples would not be identical on each occasion. Sometimes the mean of the green group would be higher, and sometimes the mean of the red group would hold that honor.

Why would this be? Dr. Smith's case is analyzed because it is more relevant to research in psychology and education. First, any given subject will vary from time to time in the score achieved on a particular trial. If tested Monday, he may do a little better or a little worse than if tested Tuesday, for a variety of reasons. Second, the constituency of Dr. Smith's sample will differ from experiment to experiment. After all, he selected two samples of subjects from among the population about which he wished to draw conclusions, and the subjects, being nonidentical, will differ somewhat in ability.

The key to any problem in statistical inference is to discover what values may be expected to occur (and with what frequency) under repeated sampling. For example, a sample is drawn and the mean is computed. A second sample yields a mean of somewhat different value. A third, still another value. What kind of distribution will be formed by these means when sampling is repeated time after time? We must be able to describe it completely if we are to say what would happen in sampling circumstances like ours.

Now there are many ways in which samples could be drawn in which it would be quite impossible to predict the distribution formed by repeated sampling. The casual sampling method is one of these. The problem with casual sampling is that the "rule" by which samples are drawn is not accurately specified, and is likely to change in unknown ways with repeated application. What is needed is a systematic way to draw samples, one resulting in a known distribution of the sample statistic. Fundamentally, the answer is to draw *probability samples*, samples in which the probability for inclusion in the sample of each element of the population is known. One kind of probability sample, the random sample, is of preeminent importance. It is the kind considered in this book. If a random sample has been drawn, certain facts are known about the distribution of the statistic under consideration. These facts permit inference of the type illustrated earlier.

It should be obvious that we are getting ahead of ourselves. Certain concepts need clarification and definition. First, if inference is to be understood, the notion of population and sample must be thoroughly understood. These concepts were presented in Section 2.1. It is important that you review that section now, because a precise understanding of these concepts is most important in the work to follow. For summary reference here, we offer the reminder that a population consists of the complete set of observations about which it is desired to draw conclusions, and a sample is a part of a population.

Second, we must examine closely what is meant by probability. It is, indeed, out of the theory of probability that principles and procedures for statistical inference have been developed. For example, characteristics of the distribution of the sample statistic, formed by repeated sampling, can be known *only* when the values comprising the distribution are obtained by drawing probability samples. We will begin examination of the nature of probability in the next section.

Third, it is necessary to understand the nature of a random sample. An introduction to this concept was given in Section 2.2, and it should be reviewed. It is so basic to inference that further consideration is needed; we will turn to it again after discussing probability.

Once these concepts have received adequate attention, we will be prepared to study the nature of *sampling distributions*, the distributions of sample statistics formed through repeated sampling from a specified population.

13.4 Probability

The essence of *probability* lies in the idea of *uncertainty* of occurrence of an event. We buy a raffle ticket from the little boy who comes to our door, but the probability of winning the color TV seems low. On going to the airport, we allow extra time; the probability of a traffic jam is always present, and the probability of a flat tire, though remote, urges caution.

A quantitative statement of probability is an expression of degree of *assurance* relative to the occurrence of the event. The probability that our small son will leave his sweater on the playground sometime this month is high; the probability of having an accident while driving to work tomorrow is low.

Although the concepts of uncertainty and degree of assurance are the basic attributes of probability, they do not indicate with precision what is meant by this term. When it comes to definition, there are several useful ways of looking at probability. We shall consider two of them. Let us start with some examples of problems in probability. What is the probability that when:

A coin is tossed, it will come up heads?
A die is tossed, it will come up six?
A score is selected blindly from a distribution, its value will exceed C_{75}?

In each case, it is possible to think of a single trial (e.g., a particular toss of a coin), and of a series of trials extending indefinitely.† Furthermore, rational considerations lead us to specify the state of expectation in each instance. For example, in the first question, it appears that heads will come up as often as tails. A die has six sides, and if it is a fair die, one side is as likely to come up as another. In the third situation, three-quarters of the scores fall below C_{75}, and one-quarter above. On any given trial, the outcome may be one way or the other. But, if the number of trials is increased indefinitely, the relative number of events which satisfy the condition specified in each question approaches, respectively, one-half, one-sixth, and one-quarter. We may, therefore, offer the first definition of probability:

> *The probability of an event, A, occurring on a single trial is the proportion of times that the event would occur in an infinite series of trials, when each trial is conducted in a like manner.*

Probability, then, can be ascribed a numerical value. The values which it may take vary from zero to one. The probability is *zero* that the coin will come up *neither* heads nor tails, and it is *one* that it will come up *either* heads or tails, to use a trivial example.

Some events appear to be equally likely. In the toss of a fair coin, heads and tails are equally likely to occur. In the toss of a fair die, the values 1, 2, 3, 4, 5, and 6 are equally likely to occur. In selecting a score blindly from a distribution, we are equally likely to obtain a score above the median as below. This idea leads to a second definition of probability:

> *Given a population of possible outcomes, each of which is equally likely to occur, the probability of an event, A, occurring on a single trial is equal to the number of outcomes which yield A, divided by the total number of possible outcomes.*

In a deck of 52 cards, there are 13 spades. If a card is drawn at random, there are 52 equally likely ways in which a card may be drawn. Since there are 13 ways in which a spade may be drawn out of the 52 possible ways, the probability of drawing a spade is 13/52, or 1/4. Similarly, the probability of drawing an Ace is 4/52, the probability of drawing an Ace in a red suit is 2/52, and the probability of drawing a card (of any denomination) in a red suit is 1/2. In a distribution of 100 scores, there are 25 scores above C_{75} and 75 below. In drawing blindly, each score is equally likely to be selected. Therefore, there are 25 ways to select a score above C_{75}, out of the 100 ways in which a score can be selected. The probability of selecting a score above C_{75} is, then, 1/4.

A distinction can be made between *theoretical probability* and *empirical probability*. In the former case, rational grounds lead us to the probability value.

---

†In selecting a score from the distribution, the outcome is noted but the score is returned to the distribution. Thus on each trial the set of scores from which selection is to be made remains identical, and the possible number of trials is indefinitely large.

Thus, we assume that if a fair coin is tossed fairly, the probability that it will come up heads is 1/2. An empirical probability value, on the other hand, is obtained by observation of the relative frequency of occurrence of an event over a finite series of trials, short or long. An empirical probability is but an estimate of the true value, and confidence is to be placed in it according to the number of observations on which it is based. For example, a survey of 1000 homes selected at random in a city may show that 85% have telephones. We therefore presume that a home selected at random has a probability of .85 of having a phone.

As noted above, probability refers to uncertainty of outcome of an event. It is the event that is important, and not our knowledge of it. If we are *about* to toss a coin, the probability is one-half that it will come up heads. If the coin *has* been tossed, but the outcome not revealed, the probability of heads is no longer one-half; it is one or zero, but we do not know which.

13.5 Two Theorems in Probability

Let us look again at a problem used to illustrate the second definition of probability, presented in the previous section. In a deck of 52 cards, what is the probability of drawing an Ace? We observed that there were four ways of drawing an Ace out of the 52 ways in which a card might be drawn. According to the principle of relative frequency among equally likely events, the probability of drawing an Ace is 4/52.

The same problem may be viewed another way. The probability of drawing an Ace of Spades is 1/52, and the same is true for the Ace of Hearts, the Ace of Diamonds, and the Ace of Clubs. The probability of drawing the Ace of Spades *or* the Ace of Hearts, *or* the Ace of Diamonds, *or* the Ace of Clubs is the sum of the probabilities of the individual events, i.e., $1/52 + 1/52 + 1/52 + 1/52 = 4/52$. Similarly, the probability of obtaining a 5 *or* a 6 on a single toss of a die is $1/6 + 1/6 = 2/6$.

These examples illustrate the *addition theorem* of probability:

> The probability of occurrence of any one of several events is the sum of the probabilities of occurrence of the individual events, provided that the events are mutually exclusive.

Note that this proposition is valid only when the events are *mutually exclusive*; that is, when the occurrence of one event precludes the possibility of the occurrence of any of the others. In the examples above, the card drawn may be the Ace of Spades *or* the Ace of Hearts, but it can not be both. Similarly, a die may come up five *or* six, but we can not have it both ways.

Of the students at a given college, suppose that (1), 60% are men and 40% are women and (2), that 50% of the students are in the lower division, 40% in the upper division, and 10% in the graduate division. The addition theorem may be applied to state that in selecting a student at random, the probability that he will be either a lower division or an upper division student is .50 + .40 = .90. However, the same theorem may *not* be applied to obtain the probability that the student will be either a graduate student or a male; these are not mutually exclusive events. A modification of the addition theorem appropriate to events which are not mutually exclusive is presented in Note 13.1.

Another useful theorem concerns joint events. Two coins are tossed. What is the probability that both will come up heads? Let us view the tossing of two coins as an experiment which is to be repeated indefinitely. In the long run, the first coin will come heads half of the time. The second coin will come heads in but half of those trials in which the first coin came heads. Therefore, the proportion of *all* trials in which both coins will come up heads is $(\frac{1}{2})(\frac{1}{2}) = \frac{1}{4}$. The probability of obtaining two heads on a single trial is therefore $\frac{1}{4}$.

This illustrates the *multiplication theorem* of probability:

> *The probability of several events occurring jointly is the product of the separate probabilities of each event, provided that each event is independent of the others.*

Again, we have a qualification; the events must be independent. *Independence* of events means that the outcome of one event must in no way alter the probability of occurrence of the other event (or events).† In the example cited, the way the first coin falls has no influence on the way the second coin will fall. The outcome of the toss of two coins is therefore the outcome of two independent events. Note that the rule, as stated, is extended to more than two independent events. If we ask the probability of obtaining three heads when three coins are tossed, it is $(\frac{1}{2})(\frac{1}{2})(\frac{1}{2}) = \frac{1}{8}$.

Man being what he is, it is not unusual for him to act as though events are not independent when in fact they are. This failure occurs often enough that it has been given a name: the Gambler's Fallacy. If we look over the shoulder of a person playing roulette, we may find him keeping track of the numbers which have come up, with the idea that he will bet on one which has not appeared recently, and so is "due." Such a system comes to naught. Assuming a fair wheel, fairly spun, there is no way in which the outcome of an earlier trial may affect the outcome of the present trial.

Many events are, of course, *not* independent. What is the probability of selecting a student who is above the median in intelligence *and* above the median in spelling? If the one is true, the other is more likely to occur. The multiplication theorem does not apply. Indeed, any two sets of events which are correlated (see Chapter 9) are necessarily dependent events, to some extent. A modification of the multiplication theorem appropriate to dependent events is presented in Note 13.4 (but read Notes 13.2 and 13.3 first for the necessary background).

---

†Formal consideration of independence in a probability sense is given in Note 13.3. To understand this note, Note 13.2 must be read first.

13.6 The Probability Distribution and Expectancy Tables

Any frequency distribution may be considered as a *probability distribution*. Suppose an instructor has a statistics class of (Heaven forbid!) 200 students, and at the end, he has assigned course grades as follows:

Grade	f	$\%f$
A	30	15
B	60	30
C	80	40
D	20	10
F	10	5
	$n = 200$	$\% = 100$

Considered as a frequency distribution, the data above indicate, for example, that 15% of the students made an A grade. As a probability distribution, the same information tells us that if a student is selected at random, the probability is .15 that his course grade is that of A. According to the addition theorem, the probability of so selecting a student who earned a grade of B or better is .15 + .30 = .45. Suppose a student knows that his professor has graded his last class in this manner. On the assumption that the professor views students' performance in the same way and that the next group of students are of similar ability, the student may use the outcome of the last semester as an *empirical* probability distribution to help estimate his chances. The actual distribution of grades which the professor will dispense may, if these assumptions are correct, reasonably approximate what occurred in the previous semester.

A slightly more sophisticated form of the empirical probability distribution is useful in many instances where it is desired to predict future performance in one dimension from knowledge of present performance in a related dimension. For example, what does a person's level of mathematical skill tell us about the likelihood of his success in a statistics course? To what extent does performance on a mechanical aptitude test predict performance in a machinist training course? To what extent is IQ predictive of successful performance in college?

In one institution, students enrolled in the several sections of a course in elementary statistics were given, on the first day, a test of basic mathematical skills. Their progress was then followed to learn what happened to them. Table 13.1 shows the results of this inquiry.† Note first that there was some relation between performance on the test and grade received in statistics. Of those scoring above 39, 75% of them emerged with grades of A or B, whereas of those who scored within the range 30–39, 45% did that well, and for those whose score fell below 30, only 25% achieved at that level. So far, Table 13.1 is simply a report of what happened to 507 students. However, if we may assume

†These data are genuine.

TABLE 13.1 Expectancy Table, Showing the Likelihood of Achieving a Particular Grade in Elementary Statistics as a Function of Score on a Test of Mathematics Fundamentals (Based on Performance of 507 Students).[a]

Grade achieved in statistics course	Score on mathematics test			Number of students
	Below 30	30–39	Above 39	
A	5%	10%	30%	101
B	20%	35%	45%	178
C	40%	30%	20%	152
D or F	20%	10%	0%	25
Incomplete or Withdrew	15%	15%	5%	51
n^b = 114		174	219	507

[a]Percents are rounded to the nearest 5%. [b]Number of students in each score range.

that course content is similar, and that behavior of future students and of the instructors is similar, the table may be interpreted as an empirical probability distribution. A distribution of this particular form is often called an *expectancy table*. Suppose you are a student who earned a score of 25 on the mathematics test. You belong in the group scoring below 30 on this test. What is your likelihood of success? This can be answered in several ways, depending on your interest. What is the most likely thing that will happen? That you will receive a grade of C, since that occurred with greater frequency than anything else (40% of students achieving a score of this kind met this fate). What are the chances of earning a grade of B or better? Twenty-five percent of similar students did this well. What is the probability of receiving a grade of D or F? Twenty percent of similar students met this fate.

Expectancy tables can be very useful in counseling, in the sense that they show what the chances are, *other things being equal*, for success in a given area as a function of performance in previous indicators. In problems of selection, they give the employing agency some indication of the probability of success of the candidate on the basis of performance on tasks which are predictive of success. Of course, other things are *not* always equal. A student with a low score may study hard and achieve a superior grade, and one who comes well equipped may be unmotivated.

Those students who have studied correlation (Chapters 9–12), will recognize that the expectancy table is very similar to the bivariate frequency distribution encountered there. The basic difference is in interpretation. Any bivariate distribution may be interpreted as an (empirically derived) expectancy table, just as any relative frequency distribution may be considered as a probability distribution. Remember, however, that if past experience is to be the guide for future performance, assumptions must be made that the future situation is similar to that of the past.

So far, we have discussed empirical probability distributions. In statistical inference, the sampling distribution is treated as a *theoretical probability distribution*. This idea will be developed after we have had an opportunity to get better acquainted with the sampling distribution.

13.7 The Random Sample

A random sample is a sample so drawn that each possible sample of that size has an equal probability of being selected. Note that it is the method of selection, and not the particular sample outcome, which defines a random sample. If we were given a population and a sample from that population, it would be impossible to say whether the sample was random without knowing the method by which it was selected. Although characteristics of random samples *tend* to resemble those of the population, those of a particular random sample may not. If we deal 13 cards from a 52-card deck, each of the four suits (clubs, hearts, diamonds, spades) will usually be represented. Somewhat infrequently, a hand of 13 cards will contain cards from only three suits, and even less frequently, only two suits. It is possible that the hand might consist of cards from just one suit, but this is indeed a rare random sampling result: the probability is approximately .000000000006.

One important characteristic of a random sample is that every element in the population has an equal probability of inclusion in the sample. Suppose a sample of five scores is to be selected from a population of 50 scores. We write the value of each score on a ticket, place the 50 tickets in a can, shake the can thoroughly, and make a blindfold selection of five tickets, withdrawing them one at a time.† The sample so selected is a random sample, and each ticket (and therefore each element) has an equal opportunity for inclusion in the sample. If done with care, the "tickets in a can" method results in a random sample. In most practical statistical work, better reliability and convenience can be guaranteed by using a table of random numbers. This technique is described in Section 13.17, the last section in this chapter. Further discussion of problems in drawing a random sample will be found in Section 14.12.

13.8 Two Sampling Plans

Actually, there are two *sampling plans* which yield a random sample. In the example of the previous section, one ticket was withdrawn and set aside, then another, and so on until five tickets were selected. This method is called *sampling without*

---

†*Each* of the 50 scores is an element of the population. If, therefore, several scores have the same value, there must still be a ticket for each.

replacement, because as each of the five elements is selected, it is removed from the population, and becomes unavailable for subsequent selection. After selection of the first score, for example, there remain only 49 scores from which the second may be chosen.

Suppose the same procedure for selection had been used, with one modification: a ticket is selected, the score noted, and the ticket returned to the can before the next ticket is selected. This sampling plan is called *sampling with replacement*. Under this plan, it is possible to draw a sample in which the same element of the population appears more than once.

Both of these plans satisfy the condition of random sampling, but certain sample outcomes possible when sampling with replacement are not possible under the other method. This is illustrated in the following example. Suppose a population consists of three scores: 2, 4, 6, and samples of size two are drawn from this population. Table 13.2 shows the possible samples which could result when sampling is done with and without replacement. Note that when sampling without replacement, the samples are the same as when sampling with replacement except for those in which the same element appears more than once. In the table, the sample in which 2 was obtained on the first draw and 4 on the second is treated as a different sample from that in which 4 was obtained on the first draw and 2 on the second. *Both* are possible samples, and account must be taken of each. This point will be clarified in the next section.

The model that will be developed here, because of its usefulness and sim-

TABLE 13.2 Possible Samples of Size 2 Drawn from a Population of Three Scores under Two Sampling Plans.

Population: 2, 4, 6

Possible samples: sampling with replacement		Possible samples: sampling without replacement	
1st draw	2nd draw	1st draw	2nd draw
2	2	———	
2	4	2	4
2	6	2	6
4	2	4	2
4	4	———	
4	6	4	6
6	2	6	2
6	4	6	4
6	6	———	

plicity in statistical inference, is that of sampling *with* replacement. The fact remains that, in practice, most sampling is done *without* replacement. When 100 students are drawn from among 4000 freshmen, it is typical that once a student is selected, he is not given a subsequent chance of inclusion of the same sample. The sample therefore always consists of 100 *different* freshmen.

How could the argument for simplicity possibly be acceptable in the face of an admittedly incorrect assumption about the sampling plan? If the size of the sample is quite small relative to that of the population, the chance of including the same element more than once in a given sample is also quite small. When this condition holds, the characteristics which follow from sampling without replacement closely approximate those which follow from sampling with replacement. As a rule of thumb, if sample size is less than 5% of population size, we will not be in serious trouble. In certain instances (particularly in survey sampling), this criterion may not be met, and the more exact procedures appropriate to sampling without replacement should be used.†

In general, this approximation is not a consequential problem. In the example cited above, a sample of 100 from a population of 4000 constitutes a sample which is 2.5% of the population. More typical of most research problems is that of Dr. Smith, presented in Section 13.1. He was investigating the possibility of a different reaction time to lights of different color. Although his two samples totaled 100 subjects, the population which he assumed he was sampling consisted of young adults in general who have similar physiological characteristics. The population he believes he is sampling is, although difficult to enumerate precisely, obviously quite large.‡

The limiting case is that of the population of *infinite* size. In sampling from such a population, the two sampling plans produce identical results. After all, if the population is infinite, the chance of drawing the same element more than once for a given sample is infinitely small. The "sampling with replacement" model therefore characterizes both situations equally well.

13.9 The Random Sampling Distribution of Means: Introduction

In what follows, we shall assume the characteristic of interest to be the mean. It could be another summary statistic, such as the standard deviation, the proportion of times an event occurs, the correlation coefficient, etc. (see Section 13.2).

What sample means occur when samples are drawn at random from a specified population, and what is their relative frequency of occurrence? The method of random sampling specifies that each possible sample be given an equal opportunity of selection. We will therefore first inquire as to the samples which would

†See: W. J. Dixon and F. J. Massey, *Introduction to Statistical Analysis*, 2nd ed., McGraw-Hill Book Co., Inc., New York, 1957. pp. 42–43.

‡We *can* criticize his sampling procedure on the grounds that it is not, strictly speaking, a random sample from a fully defined population. More will be said about this in Section 14.12.

occur, and next as to the means of these samples. To begin, we will confine the question to a simple situation, because it can be explored concretely.

Consider a population of four scores: 2, 4, 6, 8, from which samples of size two are to be selected. What are the possible samples? When sampling is done with replacement, there are four ways in which the first score may be chosen, and also four ways in which the second may be chosen. Consequently, there are $4 \times 4 = 16$ possible samples. These are shown at the left in Table 13.3.

What is the probability of drawing the sample (2, 2)? When each score is given an equal opportunity of selection, the probability that the first element will be 2 is $\frac{1}{4}$, and, when the score is replaced before selecting the second element, the probability that the second element will be 2 is also $\frac{1}{4}$. Selection of the second element is in no way dependent on the outcome of selection of the first element, and the two events are independent. The probability, therefore, of obtaining the sample (2, 2) is the product of the two probabilities: $(\frac{1}{4})(\frac{1}{4}) = \frac{1}{16}$, according to the multiplication rule for independent events (see Section 13.5). By similar reasoning, the probability of occurrence of any one of the other samples is also $\frac{1}{16}$. These probabilities are shown in the second column of Table 13.3. It is apparent that if samples are selected in this manner, each of the 16 possible samples is equally likely to occur, and the basic condition of random sampling is satisfied.

TABLE 13.3 Possible Samples and Sample Means for Samples of Size Two (Sampling with Replacement).

Population: 2, 4, 6, 8

Sample	Probability of occurrence	Mean
2, 2	1/16	2.0
2, 4	1/16	3.0
2, 6	1/16	4.0
2, 8	1/16	5.0
4, 2	1/16	3.0
4, 4	1/16	4.0
4, 6	1/16	5.0
4, 8	1/16	6.0
6, 2	1/16	4.0
6, 4	1/16	5.0
6, 6	1/16	6.0
6, 8	1/16	7.0
8, 2	1/16	5.0
8, 4	1/16	6.0
8, 6	1/16	7.0
8, 8	1/16	8.0

Our fundamental interest is in the means of these samples, rather than in the samples themselves. The mean of each sample is given in the third column of Table 13.3. Note that, although there are 16 different samples, each equally likely, this does *not* result in 16 different means, each equally likely. For example, there is only one sample (2, 2) which yields the mean of 2.0, but there are two samples for which the mean is 3.0: (2, 4), and (4, 2).† The probability of obtaining a sample with a mean of 2.0 is therefore $\frac{1}{16}$, whereas the probability of obtaining a sample with a mean of 3.0 is $\frac{1}{8}$, twice as great. This reminds us that *random sampling results in equal probability of occurrence of any possible sample, not in equal probability of occurrence of any possible sample mean.*

The 16 means may be cast in a relative frequency distribution, as shown in Table 13.4. Such a distribution is called the *random sampling distribution of means*, or simply the *sampling distribution of means*. In general, *the random sampling distribution of means is the relative frequency distribution of means obtained from all possible samples of a given size*.‡ In Section 13.11, we will explore the properties of this distribution.

TABLE 13.4 Sampling Distribution of Means:
Data from Table 13.3.

Sample means	Relative frequency
8.0	1/16
7.0	2/16
6.0	3/16
5.0	4/16
4.0	3/16
3.0	2/16
2.0	1/16

13.10 The Sampling Distribution: An Alternate Approach

There is another way of looking at the sampling distribution of means which may be helpful in understanding its nature. The random sampling distribution of means may be generated as follows:

1. A particular method is adopted for drawing samples from a population: random sampling.
2. A sample of given size is selected.
3. The mean of the sample is calculated and recorded.

†It is apparent that the sample (2, 4) must be treated as distinct from the sample (4, 2). Each is possible, and each yields a sample mean which must be accounted for.

‡This definition holds whether sampling is with or without replacement.

4. The observations constituting the sample are returned to the population.
5. Steps 2, 3, and 4 are repeated for an infinity of trials.
6. The sample means thus obtained are cast in a relative frequency distribution.

The relative frequency distribution thus obtained is identical with the relative frequency distribution of means obtained from all possible samples, as described in the previous section.

13.11 Characteristics of the Sampling Distribution

In Section 13.9, samples of size two were drawn at random from a population of four observations. Sixteen equally likely samples resulted, and the mean of each was computed. The distribution of these means, shown in Table 13.4, constitutes the sampling distribution of means for this situation; it is shown graphically in Figure 13.1. For comparative purposes two features have been added. First, the distribution of the population of scores appears in the same figure. Second, a normal curve has been fitted to the sampling distribution of means.† What features appear in this sampling distribution?

†The process of fitting a normal curve involves equating the mean and standard deviation of the normal curve to those characterizing the actual sampling distribution of means. The resulting curve shows the relative frequency of occurrence of means if the sampling distribution had been precisely normal in form.

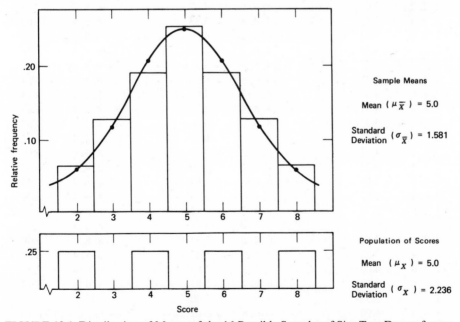

FIGURE 13.1 Distribution of Means of the 16 Possible Samples of Size Two Drawn from a Population of Four Scores: Data from Table 13.4. Population: 2, 4, 6, 8.

1. The mean of the sampling distribution of means is the same as the mean of the population of scores, that is, $\mu_{\bar{X}} = \mu_X = 5.0$.
2. The variability of the sampling distribution of means is *less* than the variability of the population of scores. The standard deviation of the population of scores is 2.236 ($\sigma_X = 2.236$), but the standard deviation of the distribution of means is 1.581 ($\sigma_{\bar{X}} = 1.581$).
3. The distribution of sample means tends to resemble the normal curve, although the population of scores is more like a rectangular distribution.

What happens if sample size is larger? Suppose that samples of size three are selected, rather than samples of size two. In this case, there are four ways to select the first element of the sample, four ways for the second, and again four ways for the third. There are, therefore, $4 \times 4 \times 4 = 64$ distinct samples of size three which may be chosen from a population of four elements. The 64 possible samples and their means are shown in Table 13.5. Again, each of the 64 samples

TABLE 13.5 Possible Samples and Sample Means for Samples of Size Three (Sampling with Replacement).

Population: 2, 4, 6, 8

Sample	Mean	Sample	Mean	Sample	Mean
2, 2, 2	2.00	4, 4, 6	4.67	6, 8, 2	5.33
2, 2, 4	2.67	4, 4, 8	5.33	6, 8, 4	6.00
2, 2, 6	3.33	4, 6, 2	4.00	6, 8, 6	6.67
2, 2, 8	4.00	4, 6, 4	4.67	6, 8, 8	7.33
2, 4, 2	2.67	4, 6, 6	5.33	8, 2, 2	4.00
2, 4, 4	3.33	4, 6, 8	6.00	8, 2, 4	4.67
2, 4, 6	4.00	4, 8, 2	4.67	8, 2, 6	5.33
2, 4, 8	4.67	4, 8, 4	5.33	8, 2, 8	6.00
2, 6, 2	3.33	4, 8, 6	6.00	8, 4, 2	4.67
2, 6, 4	4.00	4, 8, 8	6.67	8, 4, 4	5.33
2, 6, 6	4.67	6, 2, 2	3.33	8, 4, 6	6.00
2, 6, 8	5.33	6, 2, 4	4.00	8, 4, 8	6.67
2, 8, 2	4.00	6, 2, 6	4.67	8, 6, 2	5.33
2, 8, 4	4.67	6, 2, 8	5.33	8, 6, 4	6.00
2, 8, 6	5.33	6, 4, 2	4.00	8, 6, 6	6.67
2, 8, 8	6.00	6, 4, 4	4.67	8, 6, 8	7.33
4, 2, 2	2.67	6, 4, 6	5.33	8, 8, 2	6.00
4, 2, 4	3.33	6, 4, 8	6.00	8, 8, 4	6.67
4, 2, 6	4.00	6, 6, 2	4.67	8, 8, 6	7.33
4, 2, 8	4.67	6, 6, 4	5.33	8, 8, 8	8.00
4, 4, 2	3.33	6, 6, 6	6.00		
4, 4, 4	4.00	6, 6, 8	6.67		

is equally likely under random sampling, and so the relative frequency distribution of means of these samples forms the sampling distribution of means. This distribution is shown in Table 13.6 and is graphically represented in Figure 13.2. The mean of the distribution is again the same as for the population of scores: 5.0. The standard deviation of the distribution is again smaller than that of the population of scores; it is 1.291. Once more, the shape of the distribution more closely resembles the normal distribution than the distribution of the population of scores.

TABLE 13.6 Sampling Distribution of Means: Data from Table 13.5.

Sample means	Relative frequency
8.00	1/64
7.33	3/64
6.67	6/64
6.00	10/64
5.33	12/64
4.67	12/64
4.00	10/64
3.33	6/64
2.67	3/64
2.00	1/64

Indeed, close comparison suggests that this sampling distribution is even more like the normal distribution than that generated by drawing samples of size two. In both Figure 13.1 and Figure 13.2, a normal curve has been fitted. Both are rather good fits, despite small sample size. In judging goodness of fit, pay particular attention to the height of each rectangle in comparison with the height of the point of the fitted normal curve corresponding to the center of each rectangle. The average discrepancy is a little less for the distribution resulting from samples of size three.

One notable difference between the two sampling distributions is that variability is less when means are based on larger sample size. $\sigma_{\bar{X}} = 1.581$ for samples of size two, but $\sigma_{\bar{X}} = 1.291$ for samples of size three. This is intuitively reasonable; we would expect sample means based on a larger number of cases to be more stable, i.e., to fluctuate less with random sampling variation.

We may, therefore, add two more observations to the list of findings derived from study of miniature sampling distributions:

4. The sampling distribution of means more closely approximates the normal distribution when sample size is larger.
5. Variability of the sampling distribution is less when sample size is larger.

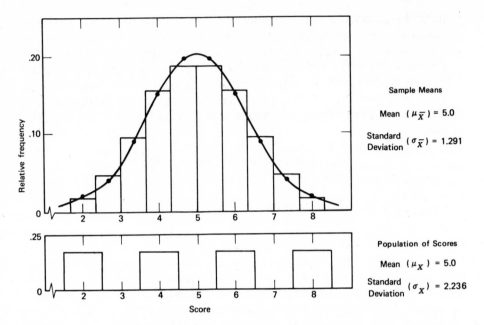

FIGURE 13.2 Distribution of the Means of the 64 Possible Samples of Size Three Drawn from a Population of Four Scores: Data from Table 13.6. Population: 2, 4, 6, 8.

The several characteristics which are noted here in examining very simple distributions exemplify the basic properties of the random sampling distribution of means in general. We turn next to the general case.

13.12 The Sampling Distribution: General Case

In inference about means, the population is typically much larger than the four observations characterizing the previous examples. When the population is large, it is no longer practicable to specify the sampling distribution of means by enumeration of the possible samples. For example, there are 100,000 different samples of size five which may be selected with replacement from a population of ten observations! For populations of any considerable size, therefore, we must depend on the theoretical analysis provided by mathematical statistics for knowledge of the properties of the sampling distribution of means. These properties are essentially those summarized in the previous section, but by making use of the result of mathematical analysis, we can be even more specific in some instances. Let us specify the available knowledge.

First, the mean of any random sampling distribution of means is the same as the mean of the population scores. To put it symbolically:

Mean of the Sampling
Distribution of Means $\qquad\qquad \mu_{\bar{X}} = \mu_X$ $\qquad\qquad\qquad\qquad$ (13.1)

Second, the standard deviation of any random sampling distribution of means (when sampling with replacement) is given by the following formula:

Standard Error of the Mean $\qquad \sigma_{\bar{X}} = \dfrac{\sigma_X}{\sqrt{n}}$ $\qquad\qquad\qquad\qquad$ (13.2)

This formula is called the *standard error of the mean*. It calculates the standard deviation of the sampling distribution of means based on samples of a specified size. The term *standard error* is used in place of *standard deviation*. This term serves notice that theory leads us to its value, rather than actual calculation of the standard deviation of the multitudinous means which would occur with random sampling.† Nevertheless, its value is the same as if that had been done, and it behaves just like a standard deviation. Note that, according to its formula, variation among sample means will be greater when variation among the population of scores is greater. On the other hand, variation among sample means will be less when sample size is greater. In the sampling distributions obtained from the population of four observations, the standard deviation of each sampling distribution was calculated by the usual method. Using the new formula for the standard error of the mean, we obtain identical results: for $n = 2$, $\sigma_{\bar{X}} = 2.236/\sqrt{2} = 1.581$, and for $n = 3$, $\sigma_{\bar{X}} = 2.236/\sqrt{3} = 1.291$. When sampling without replacement, the mean of the sampling distribution is unaffected, but its standard deviation will be smaller. The larger the sampling fraction, n/N, the smaller it will be.

Although knowledge of the mean and standard deviation of the sampling distribution of means provides important information, the shape of this distribution must also be known if we are to put it to use in statistical inference. Now if the population of scores is normally distributed, the sampling distribution of means will also be normally distributed. But if the population of scores is *not* normally distributed, the sampling distribution of means may not be normally distributed. Fortunately, a remarkable bit of statistical theory comes to the rescue in most situations: the Central Limit Theorem.

13.13 The Central Limit Theorem

The *Central Limit Theorem* states, in effect, that the random sampling distribution of means tends toward a normal distribution, *irrespective of the shape of the population of observations sampled*, and that the approximation to the normal distribution becomes increasingly close with increase in sample size. With many

---

†The mathematical derivation of this formula depends on the assumption of random sampling with replacement. It is valid whether or not the scores are normally distributed in the population.

populations, the distribution of scores is sufficiently similar to a normal distribution that little assistance from the Central Limit Theorem is required. But even when the population of scores differs substantially from a normal distribution, the sampling distribution of means may be treated as though it were normally distributed when sample size is reasonably large.

Even when sample size is quite small, the approximation is fairly close in many situations. In Section 13.11 we studied the sampling distributions based on $n = 2$ and $n = 3$, generated from a population which resembled a rectangular distribution rather than a normal one. Those sampling distributions, while not normal, showed a remarkable resemblance to that theoretical normal distribution (see Figures 13.1 and 13.2).

Happily, the trend toward normality increases rather rapidly as sample size increases. For example, when the population is skewed, skewness of the sampling distribution of means is inversely proportional to the square root of sample size. This means that the sampling distribution of means will exhibit only one-third as much skewness as does the population of scores when $n = 9$, one-fifth as much when $n = 25$, and one-tenth as much when $n = 100$. As a practical consequence, the normal curve will serve as a satisfactory model when samples are small and the population is close to a normal distribution, or when samples are large and the population markedly skewed.

The Central Limit Theorem is a remarkable proposition of great generality. Its value for inference about means can hardly be overestimated, because it makes possible use of the normal curve as a statistical model for the sampling distribution of means in a wide variety of practical situations. If this were not so, many problems in inference would be very awkward to solve, to say the least.

13.14 The Sampling Distribution as a Theoretical Probability Distribution

The sampling distribution of means may be considered as a probability distribution. It is a theoretical probability distribution, rather than an empirical probability distribution, because theory specifies the relative frequency of occurrence of particular sample means when sampling at random from a given population.

In Section 13.9, the sampling distribution of means was illustrated by drawing all possible samples of size two from a population of four scores. That sampling distribution is repeated here as Table 13.7; we will use it to illustrate the probability interpretation. For example, when sampling is random, the probability of obtaining a sample mean of 2.0 is 1/16, the probability of obtaining a mean of 3.0 or less is 3/16, and the probability of obtaining a mean between 4.0 and 6.0, inclusive, is 10/16. In general, the probability of selecting at random a sample mean exceeding a particular value, or one which falls within certain limits, is equal to the relative frequency of occurrence of means of that type.

TABLE 13.7 Sampling Distribution of Means:
Data from Table 13.3.

Sample means	Relative frequency
8.0	1/16
7.0	2/16
6.0	3/16 ⎫
5.0	4/16 ⎬ Pr = 10/16
4.0	3/16 ⎭
3.0	2/16 ⎫ Pr = 3/16
2.0	1/16 ⎭

13.15 The Fundamentals of Inference and the Random Sampling Distribution of Means: A Review

Let us return, for review, to the issues stated at the beginning of this chapter. A basic aim of statistical inference is to draw conclusions about a characteristic of a population from study of a sample taken from that population. The value of the population characteristic is fixed, if unknown, but the value of that characteristic, as observed in the sample, will vary from sample to sample. The key to the problem of inference is to discover what sample values may be expected to occur in repeated sampling. More precisely, we must know the nature of the sampling distribution of that characteristic. To make this knowledge possible, a method of drawing samples must be specified, and used consistently. Random sampling is the fundamental method which makes it possible to discover the properties of the sampling distribution. When sampling is random, it is possible to know the properties of the sampling distributions of many different statistics, e.g., the mean, standard deviation, proportion, etc.

In this chapter, we have developed the properties of the random sampling distribution of means. Its mean is μ_X, the mean of the population of observations, and its standard deviation is $\sigma_X/\sqrt{n}$, the standard error of the mean. If the population of observations is normally distributed, so will be the sampling distribution of means. If not, the normal distribution will still be a close, and therefore usable approximation, if sample size is not too small, due to the good offices of the Central Limit Theorem.

13.16 Putting the Sampling Distribution of Means to Use

From Chapter 7, we know that many useful questions can be answered when confronted with a normal distribution of known mean and standard deviation.

Those procedures are applied here to answer some questions of typical interest about the sampling distribution of means. It is assumed that the methods of Chapter 7 (see especially Sections 7.7 and 7.8) are understood.

Given: A normally distributed population, with $\mu_X = 70$ and $\sigma_X = 20$. (Assume sample size is 25.)

Problem 1: How often would sample means of 80 or higher occur?

Solution; Step 1.   Calculate the standard deviation of the sampling distribution, i.e., the standard error of the mean.

$$\sigma_{\bar{X}} = \frac{\sigma_X}{\sqrt{n}} = \frac{20}{\sqrt{25}} = 4.00$$

Step 2.   Restate the location of the sample mean of 80 as a z score. The general formula for a z score is: *(score − mean)/(standard deviation)*. In a sampling distribution of means, the sample mean is the score, the mean of the population of scores is the mean, and the standard error of the mean is the standard deviation. Therefore,

$$z = \frac{80 - 70}{4} = +2.50$$

Step 3.   Take the z score to the table of areas under the normal curve (Table B, in the appendix), and determine the proportionate area beyond z. It is .0062. In random sampling, therefore, means of 80 or higher would occur with a relative frequency of .0062, or .6% of the time for samples of size 25. The probability of obtaining such a mean in random sampling is therefore .0062. Figure 13.3 illustrates the problem.

Problem 2: How often would sample means differ from the population mean, the "expected value," by 10 points or more? In Problem 1, the mean of 80 fell 10 points above the mean (70) of the sampling distribution. Since the normal curve is symmetrical, the same area lies below a mean of 60 (10 points below 70) as above one of 80 (10 points above 70). The z score will have the same magnitude;

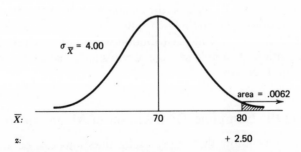

FIGURE 13.3 Finding the Proportion of Sample Means Exceeding a Given Value.

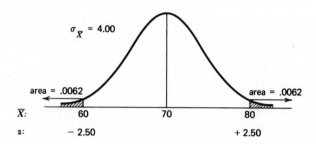

FIGURE 13.4 Finding the Proportion of Sample Means Which Differ from the Population Mean by More Than a Given Amount.

we must double the corresponding area to find the required probability. The probability of obtaining a sample mean differing from the population mean by 10 points or more is therefore $(2)(.0062) = .0124$. The problem is illustrated in Figure 13.4.

Problem 3: Above what value will 5% of means fall?

Solution; Step 1.   From Table C in the appendix find the z score above which .05 of the area under the normal curve falls; it is $z = +1.6449$, or, to three decimals, $+1.645$.

Step 2.   The value of z informs us that the desired value is 1.645 standard deviations above the mean of the distribution. Therefore (remembering that our concern is with the sampling distribution, and that *its* standard deviation is $\sigma_{\overline{X}}$, not σ_X):

$$\overline{X} = \mu_{\overline{X}} + z\sigma_{\overline{X}}$$

$$= 70 + (+1.645)(4.00)$$

$$= 70 + 6.58$$

$$= 76.58$$

Five percent of sample means will have a value of at least 76.58; the probability is .05 of selecting such a mean. The problem is illustrated in Figure 13.5.

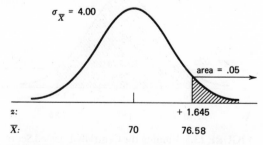

FIGURE 13.5 Finding the Value Above Which a Given Proportion of Sample Means Will Fall.

Problem 4: Within what limits would the central 95% of sample means fall? If 95% of the values are to fall in the center, the remaining 5% must be divided equally between the two tails of the distribution. Therefore, we must find the value of z beyond which 2.5% of the area is located. The method is the same as for Problem 3, and the solution is outlined below:

Lower Limit	Upper Limit
$z_{LL} = -1.96$	$z_{UL} = +1.96$
$\overline{X}_{LL} = \mu_{\overline{X}} + z_{LL}\sigma_{\overline{X}}$	$\overline{X}_{UL} = \mu_{\overline{X}} + z_{UL}\sigma_{\overline{X}}$
$= 70 + (-1.96)(4.00)$	$= 70 + (+1.96)(4.00)$
$= 70 - 7.84$	$= 70 + 7.84$
$= 62.16$	$= 77.84$

Ninety-five percent of sample means fall between 62.16 and 77.84. In random sampling, the probability is .95 of obtaining a mean within these limits, and .05 of obtaining one beyond these limits. The problem is illustrated in Figure 13.6.

13.17 Using a Table of Random Numbers

How shall we select "at random"? Numerous experiments have demonstrated that human judgment can not be depended upon to perform this function, even when no apparent bias is present. The several variations of the "numbered tags in a box" scheme are at the very least awkward, and under some circumstances unreliable. By far the most convenient and reliable procedure is to use a table of random numbers, such as Table I, in the appendix. Such tables are usually constructed by computer, according to a program which insures that each digit has an equal probability of occurrence.

A table of random numbers may be read as successive single digits, as successive two-digit numbers, as three-digit numbers, or otherwise. Thus, in

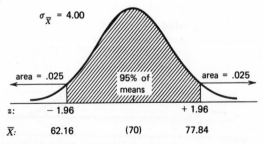

FIGURE 13.6 Finding the Centrally Located Score Limits between Which a Given Proportion of Sample Means Will Fall.

Table I in the appendix, if we begin at the top left on the first page and read down, the random order of single digit numbers would be: 1, 9, 0, 7, 3, ... If we wish to read two-digit numbers, they would be: 11, 96, 07, 71, 32, ...

Since the digits in the table are random, many schemes for selecting a set of random numbers are acceptable. For example, the desired numbers may be read vertically (in either direction), or horizontally (in either direction). To use them properly, some scheme must be adopted *in advance*. It should specify how the desired group of numbers (e.g., two-digit numbers) will be formed, and how they will be read from the table (including how to proceed when the end of a column or row has been reached). In addition, it should specify how to enter the table. Well-shuffled slips of paper may be used to identify the page, column, and row which should mark the beginning.

To begin, each element of the population should be assigned an identification number. The order of the elements does not matter, since subsequent randomization will take care of that. Suppose 30 scores are to be selected at random from a population of 700. Each element may be given a three-digit identification number, from 000 to 699, or 001 to 700, if preferred.† For the sake of simplicity, suppose our scheme requires that we start at the upper left of the first page of the table and read down. The first random number is 113, and the first element to be included in the sample is therefore that bearing the identification number 113. The next random number is 969; it is skipped because it identifies no element of the population. The next number is 077, and identifies the second score to be included in the sample. We continue until 30 elements have been selected. If sampling is *with* replacement and the same element is selected twice, it must be included again. If sampling is *without* replacement, and an identification number appears a second time, it should be skipped.

†In a table of random numbers, the three-digit number 000 is as likely to occur as any other three-digit number.

NOTES

NOTE 13.1 Probability of Occurrence of A or B when A and B Are Not Mutually Exclusive Events (*Ref:* Section 13.5)

$$Pr (A \text{ or } B) = Pr (A) + Pr (B) - Pr (AB)$$

where: Pr (A) is the probability of A
Pr (B) is the probability of B
Pr (AB) is the probability of A
and B occurring together

The event, (A *or* B), is satisfied if A occurs, if B occurs, or, when A and B are not mutually exclusive events, if both A and B occur. Note the accompanying illustration, in which A and B are *not* mutually exclusive events. If the number of events characterized by A is

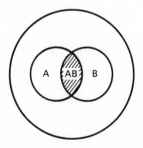

added to the number of events characterized by B, their sum includes *twice* the number of events characterized by the joint occurrence of A and B. To determine the number of events characterized by A *or* B, this total must therefore be reduced by the number of events characterized by A *and* B, so that the latter quantity will be counted only once. Similarly, the probability of (A or B) ought to include but once the probability of (AB). When A and B *are* mutually exclusive events, Pr (AB) = 0, and the formula for Pr (A or B) reduces to the addition theorem given in Section 13.5: Pr (A or B) = Pr (A) + Pr (B).

NOTE 13.2 Conditional Probability (*Ref:* Section 13.5)

Pr (A|B) is the symbolic representation for the probability of occurrence of A, *given that* B has occurred.† Probabilities of this type are called *conditional probabilities*. Consider the selection of a card, without replacement, from a 52 card deck. If we ask in advance as to the probability that the second card will be an Ace, it is 1/13 (or 4/52). But with additional knowledge, the probability changes. According to the above definition, Pr (2nd card is an Ace | 1st card is an Ace) = 3/51, whereas Pr (2nd card is an Ace | 1st card is not an Ace) = 4/51.

∤ The notion of conditional probability is important in defining independence of events (see Note 13.3), in finding the probability of joint events (see Note 13.4), and in considering sampling without replacement (see Note 13.4). It is also relevant to an understanding of the likelihood of occurrence of error in testing hypotheses (see Section 15.7).

NOTE 13.3 Independence in a Probability Sense (*Ref:* Section 13.5)

(*N.B.* Note 13.2 provides proper background for this note.)

In Section 13.5, it was stated that independence of events means that the outcome of one event must in no way alter the probability of occurrence of the other. Symbolically, we may say that A and B are independent if Pr (A) = Pr (A|B). For example, in tossing coins, Pr (2nd coin comes heads) = Pr (2nd coin comes heads | 1st coin comes heads), and the two events are independent. However, in a given university, Pr (admission of an applicant) ≠ Pr (admission of an applicant | applicant's high school record is straight "A"); these two events are not independent.

The property of independence is pertinent in sampling *with* replacement. Consider a population of three scores: 2, 4, 6. What is the probability of selecting the sample (2, 6)?‡ The probability that the first element of the sample will be 2 is 1/3. When that element has been replaced before selecting the second element, the probability that the second element will be 6 is also 1/3; selection of the second element is independent of the outcome of selection of the first element. In terms of the definition of independence, Pr (second element is 6 | first element is 2) = Pr (second element is 6) = 1/3. The probability, then, of selecting the sample (2, 6) follows the multiplication theorem for independent events (Section 13.5): Pr (2, 6) = (1/3)(1/3) = 1/9. See Note 13.4 for a comparable problem in sampling without replacement.

NOTE 13.4 Probability of Joint Occurrence of Dependent Events (*Ref:* Section 13.5)

(*N.B.* Notes 13.2 and 13.3 provide proper background for this note.)

When A and B are dependent events, probability of occurrence of both A *and* B is given by the product of the two probabilities: Pr (AB) = [Pr (A|B)][Pr (B)]. This concept can be

†The vertical bar is therefore to be read "given that," or perhaps "given the condition that."
‡The sample (2, 6) is considered to be one sample, and the sample (6, 2) another.

illustrated in application to sampling without replacement (see Section 13.8). Consider a population of three scores: 2, 4, 6. What is the probability of selecting the sample (2, 6)? The probability that the first element of the sample will be 2 is 1/3. Given that 2 has been selected (and removed from further selection), the probability that the second element will be 6 is 1/2. Since the outcome of selection of the first element affects the probability of occurrence of the second element, the two events are not independent. In terms of the definition of the probability of joint occurrence of dependent events, Pr (2, 6) = [Pr (second element is 6 | first element is 2)][Pr (first element is 2)] = (1/2)(1/3) = 1/6. Compare this with the probability of occurrence of the same sample drawn with replacement (see Note 13.3).

According to Note 13.3, A and B are independent if Pr (A|B) = Pr (A). When A and B are independent, the expression for probability of joint occurrence of A and B therefore reduces to the multiplication theorem given in Section 13.5: Pr (AB) = [Pr (A)][Pr (B)].

PROBLEMS AND EXERCISES

Identify:

hypothesis testing

estimation

population

sample

one-sample case

two-sample case

multisample case

probability sample

theoretical probability

empirical probability

mutually exclusive events

addition theorem of probability

multiplication theorem of probability

independence of events

expectancy table

random sample

sampling without replacement

sampling with replacement

random sampling distribution of means

standard error of the mean

Central Limit Theorem

random numbers

1. The principal notes that the mean reading test score of Miss Bates's class is 35.5 this year, but was 37.5 last year. Any question before we recommend that he have a talk with her about "shaping up"?

2. Two dice are tossed. (*a*) List the 36 ways the dice may fall (remember to distinguish between the outcome of die #1 and die #2). (*b*) Consider the sum of the points on the two dice; they may be from 2 to 12. With what relative frequency does each possible sum occur? (*c*) What is the probability of obtaining a 1 with the first die and a 3 with the second die? (*d*) What is the probability of obtaining a sum of points equal to 4? (*e*) What is the probability of obtaining a sum of points equal to 7 on one toss? (*f*) What is the probability of obtaining a sum of points greater than 7? Greater than 4? (*g*) What is the probability of obtaining a sum of points equal to 7 on two successive throws? Of 2 points on two successive throws?

3. An instructor gives a 100-item multiple choice examination. Each question has four alternatives. If the student knows nothing about the subject and selects answers by chance, (*a*) What is the probability for a given question that it will be answered correctly? (*b*) What is the expected number of correct answers for a given student (assume he attempts all questions)?

4. From a deck of 52 cards, 2 cards are drawn *with* replacement. What is the probability that (*a*) Both cards will be the jack of diamonds? (*b*) Both cards will be jacks? (*c*) Both cards will be diamonds? (*d*) The first card will be an ace and the second a king? (*e*) The "hand" of two cards will contain an ace and a king?

5. (*Based on Notes*) From a deck of 52 cards, 2 cards are drawn *without* replacement. What is the probability that (*a*) Both cards will be the jack of diamonds? (*b*) Both cards will be jacks? (*c*) Both cards will be diamonds? (*d*) The first card will be an ace, and the second a king?

6. Consider Table 13.6. In random sampling, what is the probability of obtaining a sample mean (*a*) of 2.67 or less? (*b*) between 3.33 and 6.67, inclusive? (*c*) greater than 5.00?

7. Consider Table 9.6. If a student scores 120 or above in the comprehensive examination, what is the probability that he will be rated (*a*) 3.85 or better by the faculty? (*b*) 3.45 or below by the faculty?

8. Consider a population of five scores: 1, 2, 4, 7, 11. (*a*) Find the mean and standard deviation of this set of scores. (*b*) List the 25 possible samples of size 2 which may be composed from this population by sampling with replacement. (*c*) Calculate the mean of each of the 25 samples found in (*b*). (*d*) Cast the 25 means into a frequency distribution. (*e*) Find the mean and standard deviation of the distribution formed in (*d*). (*f*) Calculate the standard error of the mean of samples of size 2: $\sigma_{\bar{X}} = \sigma_{pop}/\sqrt{2}$. (*g*) Does $\mu_{\bar{X}} = \mu_X$? (*h*) Is $\sigma_{\bar{X}}$ as calculated in (*f*) the same as the standard deviation calculated in (*e*)? (*i*) The population of five scores does not form a symmetrical distribution. Does the distribution of means found in (*d*) appear to follow the normal curve? If not, does it seem closer to a normal distribution than the distribution formed by the population of five scores? What principle is involved?

9. Given: a normally distributed population, with $\mu_X = 150$, and $\sigma_X = 24$. If samples of size 36 are drawn at random, what is the probability of obtaining (*a*) a sample mean of 154 or higher? (*b*) a sample mean which differs from 150 by 6 points or more?

10. For the data of question 9, (*a*) What sample mean is so great that it would be exceeded but 1% of the time in random sampling? (*b*) Within what central limits would 99% of sample means fall?

11. Consider the X scores in Data 9A. Using the table of random numbers and the without replacement sampling plan, select a sample of 20 scores from this set of 60 scores. Describe the steps in your procedure, including how you used the table of random numbers.

12. (*Based on Notes*) Look ahead to Table 21.8. If a student were selected at random from among the 190, (*a*) What is the probability that the student will be male? (*b*) What is the probability that the student will aspire to the doctorate? (*c*) What is the probability that the student will aspire to the doctorate given the condition that he is male? (*d*) By inspection of Table 21.8, what is the probability that the student will be a male who aspires to the doctorate? Verify this by the theorem presented in Note 13.4, using the answers to earlier parts of this question. (*e*) If aspiring to a particular higher degree were independent of sex, what would be the expected probability that the student would be a male who aspires to the doctorate? (*f*) By inspection of Table 21.8, what is the probability that the student will be male *or* will aspire to the doctorate? Verify this by the theorem presented in Note 13.1.

14

Inference about Single Means: Large Samples

14.1 Introduction

In this chapter we shall learn how knowledge of the characteristics of the random sampling distribution of means can be used to test hypotheses about single means and to estimate the location of the mean of a population. We shall study both the basic logic of the inferential process and the procedural steps in its accomplishment. The procedures described in this chapter are suited to problems where a reasonably large sample ($n \geq 40$) is available. As is usual in use of statistical models, there are some complications in applying the theoretical model to practical problems. These will receive attention in the last two sections of the present chapter.

As you study this chapter, you will probably find the question "Why?" frequently comes to mind. Indeed, a number of aspects of inferential procedure require further thought and explanation. Chapter 15 gives a commentary on the major questions which arise. The aspects of inference discussed there apply generally, and are therefore not limited to problems concerning means.

In Chapter 16 we shall present the large sample approach to problems of inference about two means. It is of particular importance because it forms the model for evaluating the outcome of an experiment in which two groups of subjects are treated differently and the question is whether the difference in treatment resulted in a difference in performance.

In Chapter 17 we shall discuss inference about means when sample size is small.

A number of factors must be considered in designing a study so that the risk of error in inference is known, the efficiency of the study is as high as possible, and the conclusions drawn at the outcome follow logically from the evidence. Problems of experimental design, such as those listed above, are discussed in Chapter 19.

14.2 Testing an Hypothesis about a Single Mean

Dr. Baker, the research director of a large school district, reads in the test manual that the national norm for sixth-grade students on a particular test of achievement in mathematics is 85. He would like to know if the students in his district are performing at the same level. He selects at random 100 students from all the sixth-grade students in the district, and arranges to have the same test administered to them. The population of interest to him consists of the test scores of all currently enrolled sixth-grade students in the district. From study of the sample, he wants to draw an inference as to whether or not μ_X, the mean of his population, is the same as the national norm, i.e., 85.

To answer this question, he will use the statistical model for testing hypotheses about single means. He will translate his question into a statistical hypothesis: that the mean of the population of sixth graders in his district is 85. This hypothesis will then be subjected to examination, and, at the end, accepted or rejected. To examine its validity, he will ask what sample means would occur if many samples of the same size were drawn at random from his population if the hypothesis that the population mean is 85 is true. The random sampling distribution of means appropriate to his problem provides this information. He will compare his sample mean with those which would result if the hypothesis were true. The relation between his sample mean and those of the random sampling distribution of means might look like that pictured at the left in Figure 14.1. If so, his mean is one which could reasonably occur if the hypothesis were true, and he will "accept" the hypothesis. If the relationship is like that pictured at

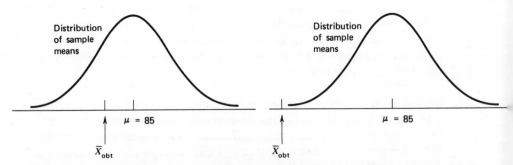

FIGURE 14.1 Possible Locations of the Obtained Sample Mean Relative to the Distribution of Expected Sample Means when the Hypothesis Is True.

the right, his mean is so deviant that it would be quite unusual to obtain such a value when the hypothesis is true. In this case, he will "reject" the hypothesis, believing it more likely that the mean of his population is not 85, as specified in the hypothesis.

14.3 Generality of the Procedure for Hypothesis Testing

The general logic and procedure for testing *all* statistical hypotheses, whether about means, frequencies, or other population characteristics, is essentially the same as described in the previous section. It is also the same for the two-sample case and the multisample case (see Section 13.1). Let us set off the steps for ready reference:

1. *A specific hypothesis is formulated about a parameter of the population (e.g., about the population mean).*
2. *A random sample is drawn from the population of observations, and the value of the sample statistic (e.g., the value of the sample mean) is obtained.*
3. *Characteristics of the random sampling distribution of the statistic under consideration are examined to learn what sample outcomes would occur (and with what relative frequency) if the hypothesis were true.*
4. *The hypothesis is accepted if the particular sample outcome is in line with the outcomes expected if the hypothesis were true; otherwise, it is rejected.*†

In this chapter, we will continue to concentrate on the problem of inference about single means. It is not appropriate at this time to illustrate in detail the universality of the four steps given above. However, Section 13.1 outlined three problems (those of Mr. Jones, Dr. Brown, and Dr. Smith) which illustrate different types of problems in inference. It would be good to reread that section, noting the applicability of the four steps to each situation. Particular attention should be given to Mr. Jones's question about the fairness of his coin, since that problem was outlined in some detail.

14.4 Estimating the Standard Error of the Mean when σ_X Is Unknown

In Section 14.6 we will evaluate Dr. Baker's problem (as outlined in Section 14.2). One point should have the benefit of preliminary comment. Specifically, it will be necessary to find the standard deviation of the random sampling distribution of means. As we learned in Section 13.12, this quantity is called the standard error of the mean, and is given by Formula 13.2.

$$\sigma_{\overline{X}} = \frac{\sigma_X}{\sqrt{n}}$$

†To "accept" the hypothesis has a special meaning. See Sections 14.6 and 15.5.

If we know the value of σ_X, well and good. But in most cases, σ_X, the standard deviation of the population of scores, is *not* known. In that event, it must be estimated from the sample. One would think that the sample standard deviation, S_X, provides the proper estimate, but it is, on the average, a little too small.

This problem can be solved by use of a new statistic, s_X, which provides a better estimate of σ_X. The formula for this statistic is given in Equation 14.1.

Estimate of the Standard
Deviation of the Population $s_X = \sqrt{\dfrac{\sum x^2}{n-1}}$ (14.1)

The quantity s_X differs only slightly from S_X. Recall that the defining formula for the sample standard deviation is: $S_X = \sqrt{\Sigma x^2/n}$. The only difference is that in finding s_X the sum of the squares of the deviation scores is divided by $n-1$, rather than by n. Note that this tends to make the value of s_X slightly larger than that of S_X. To return to the problem of estimating the standard error of the mean when σ_X is unknown, we may substitute s_X for σ_X in Formula 13.2.

Estimate of the Standard
Error of the Mean $s_{\overline{X}} = \dfrac{s_X}{\sqrt{n}}$ (14.2)

Note that we have changed the symbol for the standard error of the mean from $\sigma_{\overline{X}}$ to $s_{\overline{X}}$. *This serves as a reminder that the standard error of the mean is estimated from the data of the sample.*

Substituting an estimate, even though corrected, for the true value of σ_X introduces a degree of variable error into the procedure. In general, this error is negligible for reasonably large samples (say, $n \geq 40$). For this reason, the methods developed in this chapter are sometimes called *large sample procedures*. Methods have been developed which take precise account of the error introduced, and which are preferable when sample size is small. They will be described in Chapter 17.

14.5 A Note on the Calculation of s_X

A few words are in order concerning the calculation of s_X. If calculation is to be done by the raw score method, one may obtain Σx^2 by calculating its raw score equivalent according to Formula 6.5:

$$\sum x^2 = \sum X^2 - \frac{(\sum X)^2}{n}$$

Σx^2 may then be inserted in Formula 14.1 to complete the calculation of s_X. To understand the details of the calculation, it may be helpful to review Section 6.7. Give special attention to Method I as described in Table 6.2.

If it is more convenient to use the coded score method, probably the simplest procedure is to calculate S_X by the method described in Section 6.9, and to use an alternate formula for estimating the standard error of the mean:

Estimate of the Standard Error of the Mean; Alternate Formula $$s_{\bar{x}} = \frac{S_X}{\sqrt{n-1}}$$ (14.3)

In this alternate formula, adjustment for the tendency of S_X to underestimate σ_X is incorporated in the denominator of the formula for the standard error of the mean rather than directly in the estimate (s_X) of σ_X. It can readily be shown that Formulas 14.2 and 14.3 are algebraically identical. *Consequently, Formula 14.3 may be used at any time that S_X is available and s_X is not.* On first encounter, it is curious that the sample standard deviation should tend to underestimate the population standard deviation. Closer study of the matter is definitely in order, but will be postponed until Section 15.8 in the next chapter.

14.6 Dr. Baker's Problem: An Example of Testing an Hypothesis about a Single Mean

We now return to Dr. Baker's problem, outlined in Section 14.2. He selected a sample of 100 cases; we shall suppose that the mean of his sample is 81, and the estimate of the population standard deviation, as calculated from the sample, is 18. He wants to know if the mean of the population from which his sample came is 85. Therefore, he will hypothesize that the mean of the population *is* 85. Formally, his hypothesis is expressed as follows:

$$H_0: \mu = 85$$

$$H_A: \mu \neq 85$$

H_0 is called the *null hypothesis*; it is the hypothesis he will subject to test, and which he will decide to accept or reject. H_A is the *alternative hypothesis*. If the evidence is contrary to H_0 *and points with sufficient strength to the validity of H_A*, he will reject H_0; otherwise he will accept it.

Next, Dr. Baker selects the criterion by which he will decide to accept or reject the null hypothesis. If the sample mean is so different from what is expected when H_0 is true that its appearance would be unlikely, H_0 should be rejected. What degree of rarity of occurrence is so great that it seems better to reject the null hypothesis than to accept it? Common research practice is to reject H_0 if the sample mean is so deviant that its probability of occurrence in random sampling is .05 or less, or alternatively, .01 or less. Such a criterion is called the *level of significance*, and is symbolized by the Greek letter α (alpha). Issues governing the choice of level of significance are discussed in Section 15.4. In the present illustration, we shall assume that Dr. Baker wishes to adopt the .05 level.

What sample means would occur if the hypothesis were true? Figure 14.2

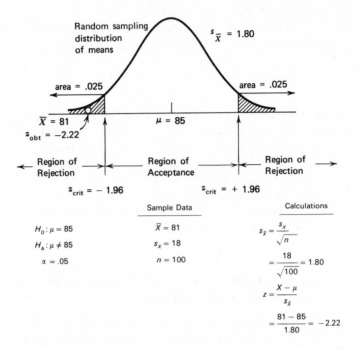

FIGURE 14.2 Dr. Baker's Problem: The Random Sampling Distribution of Means when H_0 Is True, Together with Data and Calculations Needed for Testing $H_0 : \mu = 85$.

shows the random sampling distribution of means and also presents the data and calculations characterizing the present problem. If the conditions described in Section 13.15 have been met, the sampling distribution may be treated as a normal distribution and if H_0 is true, its mean will be 85. Although the standard deviation of the sampling distribution is best given by $\sigma_{\bar{X}} = \sigma_X/\sqrt{n}$, Dr. Baker has available only s_X, and therefore he must estimate $\sigma_{\bar{X}}$ by Formula 14.2: $s_{\bar{X}} = s_X/\sqrt{n} = 18/\sqrt{100} = 1.80$.

What is the relative position of the obtained mean among those expected if the hypothesis were true? He calculates the z-score position of the obtained mean.† z has the form: *(score — mean)/(standard deviation)*. In the distribution of sample means, the sample mean is the score, the hypothesized population mean is the mean, and the standard error of the mean is the standard deviation. Consequently, the location of the sample mean is expressed by:

Location of Sample Mean in the
Sampling Distribution of Means, $\qquad z = \dfrac{\bar{X} - \mu}{s_{\bar{X}}}$ $\qquad\qquad$ (14.4)
Expressed as z

---

†Strictly speaking, this formula is not a true z, because an estimate, $s_{\bar{X}}$, replaces the true standard deviation, $\sigma_{\bar{X}}$, in the denominator. However, when samples are large enough, we will treat $(\bar{X} - \mu)/s_{\bar{X}}$ as though it were z, since its properties are then very similar.

In the present problem, $z = (81 - 85)/1.80 = -2.22$

According to the decision criterion adopted, H_0 should be rejected if the obtained sample mean is of the kind so deviant that its probability of occurrence, if the hypothesis were true, would be .05 or less. The critical magnitude of z is therefore that which separates the outer 5% of sample means from the remainder, as shown in Figure 14.2. From Table C in the appendix, this value is found to be: $z = \pm 1.96$. The space between the two critical values of z (for Dr. Baker's problem, $z = -1.96$ and $z = +1.96$) is called the *region of acceptance*, because H_0 will be accepted if the obtained sample mean falls within these limits. Similarly, the space outside of these limits is called the *region of rejection*. These regions are illustrated in Figure 14.2.

Since Dr. Baker's z is -2.22, his mean falls in the region of rejection, and so his decision is to reject the null hypothesis. In short, he concludes that it is *not* reasonable to believe that the mean of the population from which this sample came is 85. Under the circumstances, it seems reasonable to go a step farther, and say that the mean of the population is very likely less than 85.

If Dr. Baker had used $\alpha = .01$ as his decision criterion rather than $\alpha = .05$, the values of z which would separate the regions of rejection from the region of acceptance are: $z = \pm 2.58$. Figure 14.3 shows the sampling distribution of means, the location of these critical values of z, and the location of his sample mean. When this decision criterion is used, it is apparent that the sample mean falls in the region of acceptance, and therefore the decision would be to accept H_0. *The decision to "accept" H_0 does not mean that it is likely that H_0 is true, but only that it could be true.*† For example, if Dr. Baker had chosen to test the hypothesis that $\mu = 83$ at the .01 level of significance, his sample would have led him also to accept that hypothesis. His hypothesis, that $\mu = 85$, is but one

---

†For this reason, some statisticians prefer to say "fail to reject," rather than "accept." For a fuller discussion of the meaning of the statistical decision, see Section 15.5.

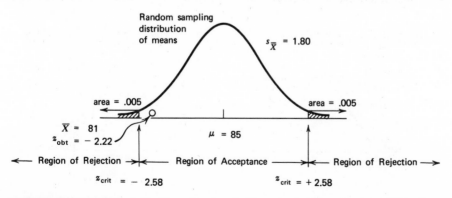

FIGURE 14.3 Dr. Baker's Problem: Testing the Hypothesis that $\mu = 85$ According to the .01 Significance Level.

of many possible hypotheses about which the decision to "accept H_0" would result, given Dr. Baker's sample mean.

14.7 Directional and Nondirectional Alternative Hypotheses

In Dr. Baker's problem, H_A was stated: $\mu \neq 85$. Such an alternative hypothesis is said to be nondirectional. Use of a *nondirectional alternative* allows the investigator to reject the null hypothesis if the evidence points with sufficient strength to the possibility that μ is greater than the value hypothesized, *or* to the possibility that it is less. Dr. Baker chose this form of the alternative hypothesis because if the mean of his population of school children differed from the national norm in either direction, he would want to know it.

Sometimes a *directional alternative* hypothesis is better suited to the problem at hand. For example, Dr. Baker might have adopted the following alternative hypothesis: $H_A: \mu < 85$. If he had done so, he would reject $H_0: \mu = 85$ only in the face of evidence that μ is *less* than 85. Consequently, he would place the entire region of rejection in the *left* tail of the sampling distribution, rather than dividing it between the two tails. The illustration at the left in Figure 14.4 shows how the test would be conducted. If $\alpha = .05$, the critical value of z is -1.645. Dr. Baker's calculated value of z ($z = -2.22$) falls in the region of rejection. However, if he had adopted the alternative hypothesis: $H_A: \mu > 85$, the region of rejection would be placed entirely in the *right* tail of the distribution. This is illustrated at the right in Figure 14.4. In this event, his sample mean falls in the region of acceptance, and his decision must be to accept H_0.

A directional alternative hypothesis is appropriate when, if the null hypothesis should be false, it is only of interest to learn that the true value of μ differs from the hypothesized value *in a particular direction*. For example, if Dr. Baker's inquiry was initiated solely by the thought that he should take some action if the mean of the population of sixth graders was *below* the national norm, and that otherwise no action was necessary, the appropriate alternative hypothesis would

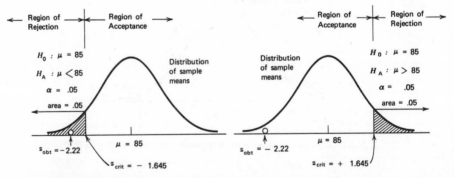

FIGURE 14.4 Location of Regions of Acceptance and Rejection when H_A Is Directional.

be: $H_A: \mu < 85$. Note that if μ_{true} actually fell *above* μ_{hyp}, it is unlikely that a sample mean would be obtained which would lead to rejection of H_0. In view of Dr. Baker's interest (as suggested immediately above), this does not matter because he is interested only in learning whether his population is *below* the norm or not.

One must choose, therefore, between a directional alternative and a nondirectional one. The choice should be determined by the rationale that gave rise to the study, and should be made *before* the data are gathered. Further discussion of the issues involved in the choice appear in Section 15.3.

When a nondirectional alternative hypothesis is stated, the resulting test is referred to as a *two-tailed test*, because H_0 will be rejected if the obtained sample mean is located in an extreme position in *either* tail of the sampling distribution. Similarly, a directional alternative leads to a *one-tailed test*.

14.8 Summary of Steps in Testing an Hypothesis about a Mean

1. Specify the statistical hypothesis to be tested (H_0). It is determined according to the substantive question to be studied (see Sections 1.6 and 14.2), and stated in terms of a specific value of the population parameter, e.g., $H_0: \mu = 100$.
2. Specify the alternative hypothesis (H_A). A choice must be made between a directional and a nondirectional alternative, depending on the rationale of the substantive inquiry.
3. Specify the level of significance (α) to be used as the criterion for decision.
4. Calculate $\overline{X}$ and, if $\sigma_{\overline{X}}$ cannot be determined, calculate its estimate, $s_{\overline{X}}$ (see Sections 14.4 and 14.5).
5. If $\sigma_{\overline{X}}$ is estimated by $s_{\overline{X}}$ and $n < 40$, complete the test by the methods of Chapter 17. If $n \geq 40$ *or* if $\sigma_{\overline{X}}$ is known, proceed with the method indicated below.†
6. Calculate, in z-score terms, the position of $\overline{X}$ in that sampling distribution of means which would result when sampling from a population in which H_0 is true.
7. Determine the z-score value or values which differentiate the region of rejection from the region of acceptance in the sampling distribution of means. Location is determined according to the specified level of significance and the directional or nondirectional nature of H_A.
8. Reject H_0 if $\overline{X}$ is located in the region of rejection; otherwise accept H_0.

14.9 The Problem of Estimation

The problem of estimation has been defined and illustrated in Section 1.2 and

---

†The procedures of Chapter 17 are *always* appropriate when $s_{\overline{X}}$ must be used in place of $\sigma_{\overline{X}}$, but those described here are quite satisfactory when n is large.

(especially) in Section 13.2. It will be helpful to review these sections as a prelude to the development of this section and the next.

The problem of estimation may take two forms: *point estimation* and *interval estimation*. Sometimes it is required to state a single value as an estimate of the population value. Such estimates are called point estimates. What percentage of voters will vote for candidate X? What is the mean aptitude test score of applicants for admission to Spartan University? If it is impractical to find the proportion in the entire population (in the first example), or the mean of the population (in the second example), an estimate of the population characteristic may be made from a random sample.

Point estimates alone are made reluctantly, because they may be considerably in error without one being aware of it. Interval estimates are more practical when conditions permit. In interval estimation, limits are set within which it appears reasonable that the population parameter lies. In the question about Candidate X, a point estimate might state that 49% of the population of voters favor him. If an interval estimate were made, the outcome might state that we are 95% confident that the porportion of voters (in the population) who favor him is not less than 46% and not greater than 52%.

Of course, we may be wrong in supposing that the stated limits contain the population value. Other things being equal, if wide limits are set, the likelihood that the limits will include the population value is high, and if narrow limits are set, there is greater risk of being wrong.† Because the option exists of setting wider or narrower limits, any statement of limits must be accompanied by indication of the degree of confidence that the population parameter falls within the limits. The limits themselves are usually referred to as a *confidence interval*, and the statement of degree of confidence as a *confidence coefficient*.

14.10 Interval Estimates of μ_X

Figure 14.5 shows the possible sample means which could occur when drawing samples of size 100 from a population in which $\mu = 100$ and $\sigma_X = 20$. We shall assume that these means are normally distributed. Suppose each sample mean was taken in turn, and the statement made that μ lay somewhere within the range: $\overline{X} \pm 1.96\sigma_{\overline{X}}$. For example, if $\overline{X} = 103$, it would be claimed that μ lies somewhere within the interval $103 \pm (1.96)(2.00)$, or between 99.08 and 106.92. We note that this claim is correct. On the other hand, if $\overline{X} = 95$, it would be claimed that μ lies within the interval $95 \pm (1.96)(2.00)$, or between 91.08 and 98.92. This time the claim is incorrect. These two intervals are shown at (*a*) and (*b*) in Figure 14.5.

If the sample mean is not farther away from μ than $\pm 1.96\sigma_{\overline{X}}$, the claim that μ falls within the interval will be correct. Otherwise, it will not. In Figure 14.5,

†Indeed, one might consider the point estimate as the ultimate in narrow limits, and the risk of being wrong is great indeed.

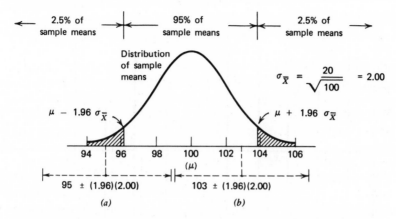

FIGURE 14.5 Distribution of Sample Means Based on $n = 100$. Drawn from a Population Characterized by $\mu = 100$, $\sigma = 20$. (*a*) Interval Estimate of μ Constructed about $\overline{X} = 95$; Estimate Does Not Cover μ. (*b*) Interval Estimate of μ Constructed about $\overline{X} = 103$; Estimate Covers μ.

the sample means which are not farther away from μ than $\pm 1.96\sigma_{\overline{X}}$ are those found in the unshaded part of the distribution. They constitute 95% of all sample means. The remaining 5% of means, shown in the tails of the distribution (the shaded portion), will lead to intervals which are *not* correct.

Figure 14.6 shows some of the intervals which might result if samples were selected at random from a particular population, and intervals constructed about the sample mean by the procedure described above. In this illustration, the tick at the center of each vertical line represents the sample mean, and the extent of the vertical line represents the band within which it is claimed that μ lies. In the illustration, all of the intervals cover μ except one. According to the procedure specified, we may expect that 95 out of every 100 estimates will include μ within their range. If a sample is drawn at random, the probability is therefore .95 that the sample will yield a mean such that, when an interval estimate is constructed according to the rule:

$$\overline{X} \pm 1.96\sigma_{\overline{X}}$$

μ will be covered by the interval.

We may wish to be even more sure that our estimate includes μ. Suppose that a probability of .99 is preferred to that of .95. Since 99% of sample means fall between $\mu \pm 2.58\sigma_{\overline{X}}$, an estimate may be made for which the probability is .99 that the interval will cover μ by the rule:

$$\overline{X} \pm 2.58\sigma_{\overline{X}}$$

Note that a wider interval results than when a probability of .95 was used.

The two levels of probability, .95 and .99, are the ones commonly used in

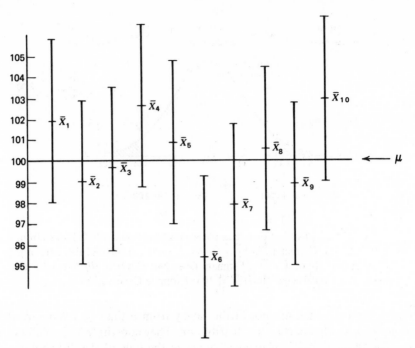

FIGURE 14.6 Interval Estimates of μ Constructed from Means of Several Successive Random Samples: σ_X Known.

interval estimation. But, it is possible to construct an interval estimate according to any desired level of probability. Suppose it is desired to find an interval such that the probability is .50 that μ is included within its limits. What is the value of z such that 50% of means are included within $\mu \pm z\sigma_{\bar{X}}$? From Table C in the appendix, this value is found to be: $z = .6745$.† Consequently, the rule for constructing intervals such that the probability is .50 that the interval will contain μ is:

$$\bar{X} \pm .6745\sigma_{\bar{X}}$$

In general, intervals may be constructed according to a specified level of probability by the rule (Formula 14.5):

Rule for Constructing an $\bar{X} \pm z_p\sigma_{\bar{X}}$ (14.5)
Interval Estimate of μ_X

where:

$\bar{X}$ is the sample mean, obtained by random sampling

$\sigma_{\bar{X}}$ is the standard error of the mean

†Procedures for finding the value of z corresponding to a specified probability are described in Section 7.8.

z_p is the magnitude of z for which the probability is p of obtaining a value so deviant or more so (in either direction)

The procedure so far described requires knowledge of $\sigma_{\overline{X}}$, which in turn requires that σ_X be known. As usual, most frequently $s_{\overline{X}}$ must be substituted as an estimate of $\sigma_{\overline{X}}$ (see Section 14.4). Accordingly, a rule less nearly correct, but more likely to be applicable in practical situations is:

Approximate Rule for Constructing an $\overline{X} \pm z_p s_{\overline{X}}$ (14.6)
Interval Estimate of μ

When $n \geqq 40$, little error will be introduced by substituting $s_{\overline{X}}$ for $\sigma_{\overline{X}}$. When sample size is smaller, procedures described in Chapter 17 (Section 17.14) are in order.

The procedure for establishing confidence limits is illustrated below. Because σ_X is commonly unknown, the problems suppose that only a sample estimate is available. The sample problems, together with their solution, are presented in Table 14.1.

TABLE 14.1 Construction of Confidence Intervals Concerning μ when σ_X Is Unknown and Sample Size Is Large.

Given: $\overline{X} = 121.0$

$s_X = 18.0^a$ Therefore, $s_{\overline{X}} = \dfrac{s_X}{\sqrt{n}} = \dfrac{18.0}{\sqrt{144}} = 1.50$

$n = 144$

Problem 1: Estimate, at the 95% level of confidence, the location of μ.

Solution: $\overline{X} \pm (z_{.05})(s_{\overline{X}})$

$121.0 \pm (1.96)(1.50)$

118.06 to 123.94   Therefore, $C(118.06 \leq \mu \leq 123.94) = .95$
$\begin{pmatrix}\text{Lower}\\\text{Limit}\end{pmatrix}$ $\begin{pmatrix}\text{Upper}\\\text{Limit}\end{pmatrix}$

Problem 2: Estimate, at the 99% level of confidence, the location of μ.

Solution: $\overline{X} \pm (z_{.01})(s_{\overline{X}})$

$121.0 \pm (2.58)(1.50)$

117.13 to 124.87   Therefore, $C(117.13 \leq \mu \leq 124.87) = .99$
$\begin{pmatrix}\text{Lower}\\\text{Limit}\end{pmatrix}$ $\begin{pmatrix}\text{Upper}\\\text{Limit}\end{pmatrix}$

---

^{a}Calculation of s_X is explained in Section 14.5.

When intervals are constructed according to the rule used in Problem 1, it is proper to say that the probability is .95 that an interval so constructed will include μ. *However, once the specific limits are established for a given set of data, the interval thus obtained either does or does not cover μ.* The probability is, at this stage, either 1.00 or 0 that the interval covers μ; we do not know which.† Consequently, it is usual to substitute the term *confidence* for probability in speaking of a specific interval. Thus, the outcome of Problem 1 is usually written as a *confidence interval*:

$$C(118.06 \leqq \mu \leqq 123.94) = .95$$

and the outcome of Problem 2:

$$C(117.13 \leqq \mu \leqq 124.87) = .99$$

The level of confidence is symbolized by C, the confidence coefficient. The first of these two statements may be translated as follows: we are 95% confident that μ falls between 118.06 and 123.94. But what does it mean to say that we are "95% confident"? We do not know whether the *particular* interval covers μ, but when intervals are constructed according to the rule, 95 of every 100 of them (on the average) will include μ. Note that, as illustrated in Figure 14.6, *it is the interval that varies from estimate to estimate, and not the value of μ. μ is a fixed value, if unknown, and therefore does not vary.*

For a given confidence coefficient, a small sample results in a wide confidence interval, and a large sample in a narrower one. How to choose sample size so that the resulting interval is of a desired width is discussed in Section 19.12.

14.11 Review of Assumptions in Inference about Single Means

In Chapters 13 and 14, we have encountered a number of conditions necessary for use of the statistical model of inference about single means to be *precisely* correct. These conditions apply whether the problem is one of hypothesis testing or of estimation. Because these assumptions are scattered about, they are listed together here, with a brief comment on each. They are:

1. A random sample has been drawn from the population.
2. The sample has been drawn by the "with replacement" sampling plan.
3. The sampling distribution of means follows the normal curve.
4. The standard deviation of the population of scores is known.

A truly random sample is often difficult to achieve in practice. Violation of this assumption may affect the mean and standard deviation of the sampling distribution in unpredictable ways. This problem is of sufficient importance that fuller discussion of it is reserved for the next section.

†See Section 13.4.

For the model of inference about single means described in this chapter to be strictly correct, it is assumed that sampling is with replacement. However (see Section 13.8), common practice is to sample without replacement. The consequent error in inference is quite small as long as sample size is a small fraction of population size (say, .05 or less). The effect of the error is to over-estimate the standard error of the mean, which in turn tends to increase the probability of accepting H_0 when it should be rejected.

The third assumption is that the sampling distribution of means may be treated as a normal curve. As indicated in Section 13.11, this assumption is quite reasonably approximated in all but very small samples, and when the scores in the population are reasonably close to a normal distribution. When the scores in the population are *not* normally distributed, the Central Limit Theorem comes to the rescue when sample size is reasonably large (Section 13.13). In this situation, assuming that the sampling distribution follows the normal curve results in minimal error.

The fourth assumption is that σ_X is known. In fact, we must frequently estimate σ_X from the sample (see Section 14.4). If sample size is large, there is no substantial problem. As sample size decreases, the error thus introduced is in-tensified. With the procedures of this chapter, as sample size decreases there is an increasing probability of rejecting H_0 when it is in fact true. In general, when sample size drops below 40, an alternate approach which takes the error into account is desirable. A suitable method and further explanation of the issue involved are presented in Chapter 17.

14.12 Problems in Selecting a Random Sample

Of all of the problems in matching reality to the model of statistical inference, perhaps the one that hurts the most is that of aligning the requirement of a random sample with what is possible in the real world of data. To refer once again to the principal's problem, our principal may wish to draw conclusions about those students now in attendance and those who will come in the next five years. To follow the statistical model exactly, he must give an equal oppor-tunity for *every* element of that population to be included in the sample. Obviously this is impossible, but he must make his decision now. Consequently, he assumes that those students now present are not importantly different from those of a random sample from the population that he really wishes to consider. If change in the community is not occurring too rapidly, his assumption has some justifica-tion. On the other hand, it cannot be justified with exactitude. Consequently, he does what he can, since a decision must be made at the moment, and he hopes that the error will not be so large as to be disastrous. It will be important for him to check on the adequacy of his assumption as future years unfold.

Similarly, the theoretical scientist who is conducting a study of the behavior of "laboratory rats in general" cannot draw a truly random sample of this population, but must study the behavior of those rats sent to him in the latest shipment from Superba Breeding Laboratories.

As a consequence, the proper scientist realizes that he is dealing with a problem in limitation of generalization. To be sure, just as every son has a mother, every sample might be considered a random sample from *some* population. The question remains as to whether the referent population is appropriate to the substantive question posed. This is one reason why it is so necessary, in scientific work, to describe adequately the characteristics of the sample studied, and the circumstances under which it was drawn.

Another aspect of the problem often occurs with human subjects. If a scientist is studying a problem in learning, perception, etc., he may reach for a convenient group of subjects to begin his exploration. This often turns out to be, for example, students currently enrolled in a general psychology class. He does not really wish to draw conclusions about a population of such students, but that is, at best, the population for which it is appropriate to generalize the outcome. In situations of this kind, it is common to refer to sampling from an *hypothetical population*, which really means a population chosen for convenience. This may be satisfactory for many pilot studies. Results found in such groups can be, if of interest, verified by restudy in a population of greater importance. The major point is that *it is possible to generalize only to a population from which the sample may be considered to be a random sample.*

When the elements of the population can actually be enumerated, the possibility exists of a closer degree of fulfillment of the random sampling requirement of the statistical model. Even under these circumstances, it is not uncommon to use procedures which approximate, rather than guarantee, a true random sample. For example, one may decide to draw a sample of the students currently enrolled in the school by selecting every tenth one in an alphabetical list. In many cases, such a procedure probably closely approximates a truly random sample. However, this method will *not* do so if there is a cyclical trend in the data which happens to coincide with the periodicity of selection of the cases. Another difficulty occurs when scores are placed in order from high to low before selection is made by this method. In this case, the sample will be more nearly a *representative* one than a random one.† Consequently, successive samples chosen in the same way would tend to resemble the population more closely than would successive random samples. As a result, the usual standard error formula, expressing the variation among means of random samples, will overestimate variation among means obtained by this sampling method by an unknown amount.

When it is possible to enumerate elements of the population, by far the best

---

†A *representative* sample is the term usually used to refer to a sample drawn in such a way as to guarantee its resemblance to the population. Unless special precautions are taken, the sampling distribution for such samples is not known. Although characteristics of a random sample *tend* to resemble those of the population, particular random samples may not. For example, obtaining ten heads is a rare, but possible, random sampling result of tossing ten coins.

method is to refer to a table of random numbers in order to select the sample. This method was described in Section 13.17.

PROBLEMS AND EXERCISES

Identify:

s_X, S_X, σ_X	one-tailed test
$s_{\bar{X}}$, $\sigma_{\bar{X}}$	two-tailed test
null hypothesis	point estimation
alternative hypothesis	interval estimation
level of significance	confidence interval
region of acceptance	confidence coefficient
region of rejection	hypothetical population
directional hypothesis	representative sample
nondirectional hypothesis	

1. A sample consists of four scores: 3, 3, 5, 7. (*a*) Find Σx^2 by the raw score equivalent method described in Section 14.5. (*b*) Find s_X from Formula 14.1. (*c*) Find $s_{\bar{X}}$ from Formula 14.2. (*d*) Find S_X from Formula 6.4b. (*e*) Find $s_{\bar{X}}$ from Formula 14.3. (*f*) Is your answer to (*c*) and (*e*) the same, within rounding error?

2. If H_0 is rejected at the 5% significance level, can we be reasonably confident that H_0 is false? Explain.

3. If H_0 is accepted at the 5% significance level, can we be reasonably confident that H_0 is true? Explain.

4. Given the following data: $\bar{X} = 63$, $s_X = 12$, $n = 100$, $H_0: \mu = 60$, $H_A: \mu \neq 60$. (*a*) Test the null hypothesis at the 5% significance level, and state your conclusions. (*b*) Test the null hypothesis at the 1% significance level, and state your conclusions. (*c*) What is the probability, in random sampling, of obtaining a mean of 63 or higher when samples of this size are drawn from a population in which $\mu = 60$? Of obtaining a sample mean which differs by three points or more (in either direction) from $\mu = 60$?

5. Repeat parts (*a*) and (*b*) of Problem 4, but assume that the alternative hypothesis reads $H_A: \mu > 60$.

6. Assume the same data as are given in Problem 4. Suppose that the alternative hypothesis reads $H_A: \mu < 60$. Test the null hypothesis at the 5% significance level, and state your conclusions.

7. The eighth-grade national norm for a social science test is a score of 123. The research director of a school district wants to know how knowledge of pupils in his district compares with this standard. He selects a random sample of 81 students, and finds that: $\bar{X} = 117$; $s_X = 36$. State the null hypothesis and alternative hypothesis best suited to the nature of his inquiry. Test the null hypothesis (*a*) at the 5% level of significance, and state your conclusions; (*b*) at the 1% level of significance, and state your conclusions. (*c*) What is the probability of obtaining, through random sampling, a sample mean so deviant (in either direction) from μ as his sample mean is?

8. Repeat Problem 7, but assume that $\bar{X} = 112$.

9. A training director for a large company has been told that on completion of the training course, average score of his trainees on the final evaluation should be 100. He will need to institute remedial procedures if the evidence points to poorer performance. A sample of 49 scores of recent trainees shows: $\bar{X} = 94$; $s_X = 21$. State the null hypothesis and alternative hypothesis best suited to the nature of his inquiry. Test the null hypothesis (a) at the 5% level of significance, and state your conclusions; (b) at the 1% level of significance, and state your conclusions. (c) What is the probability of obtaining, through random sampling, a sample mean so low or lower if μ is as stated in the null hypothesis?

10. For the data of Problem 4 ($\bar{X} = 63$, $s_X = 12$, and $n = 100$), construct an interval estimate of μ according to (a) $C = .95$ (b) $C = .99$ (c) $C = .90$.

11. Repeat parts (a) and (b) of Problem 10, but with the condition that n is four times as large. Compare the size of the intervals obtained in the two problems. State your conclusion.

12. For the data of Problem 7, construct an interval estimate of μ according to (a) $C = .95$ (b) $C = .99$ (c) $C = .50$.

13. A poll is designed to study habits of library usage among students at Spartan University. Various suggestions are made as to how to conduct the survey, as indicated below. What particular objection (or objections) might be made to each idea? (a) The survey is to be conducted just before midterms. (b) A booth is to be set up in front of the library, and those who pass by will be polled. (c) Freshman English is mandatory, so all students currently enrolled in those classes will be polled. (d) The Division of Humanities and Arts volunteers to poll all of its majors, so it is suggested that these students constitute the sample. (e) All students in 8:00 am classes will be polled.

15

Further Considerations in Hypothesis Testing

15.1 Introduction

In the last chapter, we learned the basic steps which characterize inference about single means. Embedded in the process of testing an hypothesis are a number of concepts which deserve further analysis. The purpose of the present chapter is to afford a commentary on major aspects of hypothesis testing. Although the last chapter concerns testing hypotheses about single means, and although the commentary offered here is oriented toward the same problem, the principles involved are quite general. As you study further problems in hypothesis testing, you may expect to find that the discussion presented here retains much of its relevance in those other contexts.

15.2 Statement of the Hypothesis

There are two parts to the hypothesis: H_0, the hypothesis to be subjected to test, and H_A, the alternative hypothesis. H_0 is always a statement about the population parameter (or parameters, in the two- or multisample cases). It is never a statement about the sample statistic. For example, if the hypothesis had been that the *sample* mean was 85, Dr. Baker would simply deny it because the sample mean is 81, and no inference is involved.

Second, the hypothesis to be tested, H_0, is expressed in terms of a point value, rather than a range. If the hypothesis is expressed as a point value, a single random sampling distribution of means applies, and the

255

consequences of this particular distribution can be explored. If the hypothesis were expressed as a range, a multitude of sampling distributions would be relevant, each with a slightly different mean, and the problem of exploration becomes most awkward.

Third, the decision to accept or reject "the hypothesis" always has reference to H_0, and never to H_A. It is H_0 which is the subject of the test. The role of H_A is explained below.

Finally, H_0 is often referred to as the "null hypothesis." No special significance should be attached to this term; it is simply whatever hypothesis is to be subjected to test.

The alternative hypothesis describes the condition which, if the evidence of our sample is contrary to H_0 *and points toward it* with sufficient strength, leads us to reject H_0. We shall reject H_0, then, *only* when the evidence substantially favors H_A.

15.3 Choice of H_A: One-Tailed and Two-Tailed Tests

The alternative hypothesis may be directional or nondirectional, depending on the purpose of the study. When the alternative hypothesis is nondirectional, a two-tailed test results, and it is possible to detect a discrepancy between the true value of the parameter and the hypothesized value irrespective of the direction of the discrepancy. This capability is often desirable in examining research questions. For example, in most cases in which performance of a group is compared with a known standard, it would be of interest to discover that the group is superior *or* to discover that the group is substandard.

Sometimes a one-tailed test is more appropriate. Examples of situations in which a one-tailed test is indicated are:

1. A manufacturer wishes to test the length of life of light bulbs made by a new process. He wants to adopt the new process only if mean length of life is greater than 1500 hours.
2. The physical fitness of school children is tested. If mean performance is substandard, it will be necessary to institute a special physical training program.
3. The claim is made that when a particular hormone is ingested, more hair will grow.
4. A new teaching method is proposed; it is decided that the new method should be instituted if it can be demonstrated that learning accomplished under the new method is superior to that under the standard method.

In each of these situations, interest is in discovering whether there is a difference *in a particular direction* or not. For instance, in Example 2, the question is whether or not the children are substandard with regard to physical fitness. This may be tested by hypothesizing that the mean physical fitness score of the population of school children equals the standard value versus the alternative that it is less than this value. Note that if the children's physical fitness equals or exceeds the standard, no action is necessary. A special training program will be instituted *only* if their performance is substandard. Similarly, in the case of the Hairy Hormone Hypothesis, a finding of normal incidence of hair, or less hair than normal are equal in meaning: the research hypothesis is unsupported by the evidence. In this instance, one might test the hypothesis of normal hair, versus the alternative of more hair.

In general, *a directional alternative hypothesis is appropriate when there is no practical difference in meaning between finding that the hypothesis is true and finding that a difference exists in a direction opposite to that stated in the directional alternative hypothesis.* The reason for this advice is apparent in Figure 15.1. This figure illustrates the design for decision when testing $H_0: \mu = 100$ against the alternative hypothesis $H_A: \mu < 100$. As we see, the region of rejection is entirely at the left. A value of $\overline{X}$ which falls above 100 *cannot* lead to rejection of the null hypothesis, *no matter how deviant.* If this state of affairs is unacceptable, it means that a directional alternative is inappropriate, and that a two-tailed test should be used.

The decision to use a one-tailed alternative must always flow from the logic of the substantive question, as illustrated above. The time to decide on the nature of the alternative hypothesis is therefore at the beginning of the study, before the data are collected. It will not do to observe the sample outcome and then set the region of rejection in the tail of the sampling distribution toward which the sample outcome tends. For example, if we adopt the 5% level of significance and follow this erroneous procedure systematically, we are really, in the long run, conducting two-tailed tests at the 10% significance level. Likewise, it is not satisfactory to set our one-tailed trap in the direction in which we *think* the outcome might go, only to switch to a two-tailed test if the sample mean appears in the opposite direction. If tests are conducted in this manner, using $\alpha = .05$, they are equivalent to two-tailed tests at $\alpha = .075$, with an area of .05 in one tail, and .025 in the other—but with the larger area located by the prejudice of preconception. It is

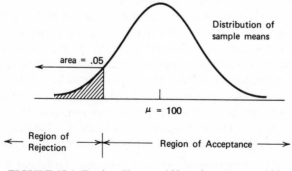

FIGURE 15.1 Testing $H_0: \mu = 100$ against $H_A: \mu < 100$; $\alpha = .05$.

much better to decide in advance what kind of discrepancy is important to discover and to choose H_A accordingly.

15.4 The Criterion for Acceptance or Rejection of H_0

The decision to accept or reject the null hypothesis is dependent on the criterion of rarity of occurrence adopted, commonly known as the *level of significance* (α). Two questions deserve our further attention. First, what is the meaning of the term "significance"?

The value of an obtained mean may depart from the value expected under the null hypothesis because of chance variation when the hypothesis is true, *or* because there is a real (and therefore *significant*) difference between the true mean of the population and the hypothesized mean. Research workers commonly speak of the outcome of a test as being (for example) "significant at the .05 level." This means, in our terms, that $\alpha = .05$ was adopted as the decision criterion, that the sample statistic fell in the region of rejection, and therefore H_0 is believed to be false.

Second, the choice of α is in the hands of the person conducting the test. How shall he choose? The more extreme the position in the sampling distribution, the less the probability of occurrence of so deviant a mean when the null hypothesis is true. At what point is the probability of occurrence so low that it seems better to reject the null hypothesis than to accept it?

Let us consider the consequence of setting the level of significance relatively high, say $\alpha = .25$. When α is set at .25, *and the null hypothesis is true*, 25% of sample means will fall in the region of rejection thus established. Therefore, when the null hypothesis is true, one test in four will lead to the erroneous conclusion that the hypothesis is false. The risk of committing this error seems uncomfortably high.

To reduce the risk, we may set α at a lower level. Suppose it is set very low, say $\alpha = .001$ (one in one thousand). Now suppose a test is conducted and a mean obtained which is so deviant that it would occur but once in five hundred times if the null hypothesis were true. According to the criterion adopted, we have insufficient evidence to reject the null hypothesis, and therefore must accept it. In this case, we run a substantial risk of accepting the hypothesis when it is false. To turn to an intuitive example, suppose you are testing the honesty of a pair of dice belonging to the gentleman with the waxed mustache. In 20 out of 30 tosses, the dice come up seven. Are you willing to say, "Well, that *could* be chance; I have insufficient reason to reject the hypothesis of fair dice"?†

Two facts emerge. First, settling on any particular value of α as the criterion for decision is basically arbitrary, since rarity of occurrence is a matter of degree.

†In this paragraph and in the preceding one, we meet the two types of errors that may occur in testing hypotheses: rejecting H_0 when it is true, and accepting H_0 when it is false. These errors will be explored in Section 15.7.

Second, there are substantial disadvantages in selecting either a very low or a very high value of α. In recent years, it has become common for research workers to evaluate the outcome of tests according to the 5% level of significance, or, alternatively, according to the 1% level. These values tend to give reasonable assurance that the null hypothesis will not be rejected unless it really should be. At the same time, they are not so stringent as to raise unnecessarily the likelihood of accepting false hypotheses.

When a two-tailed test is conducted and α is set at .05, the critical values of z are -1.96 and $+1.96$. For the same test, but with $\alpha = .01$, the critical values of z are -2.58 and $+2.58$. For a one-tailed test, the critical magnitude of z is 1.64 (or 1.645) when $\alpha = .05$, and 2.33 when $\alpha = .01$. *The need for these values occurs often enough that it is well to commit them to memory.*

Research workers sometimes evaluate the outcome of tests of hypotheses by applying *both* the 5% criterion and the 1% criterion. Figure 15.2 illustrates three possible values of z resulting from a two-tailed test of significance. If the obtained value is z_1, the outcome fails to reach significance according to either criterion; H_0 will be accepted. If the obtained value is z_2, it is so deviant that its prior probability of occurrence is less than .05, but not less than .01. The outcome is therefore significant at the .05 level, but not at the .01 level. To put it another way, according to $\alpha = .05$, H_0 will be rejected, but according to $\alpha = .01$, it will not. The outcome, z_3, is so deviant that its prior probability of occurrence is less than .01, and H_0 will be rejected by either criterion.

Although the 5% and the 1% criteria are useful for general purposes, there are circumstances when selecting other values would make better sense. If it were important to be quite sure that the hypothesis was wrong before acting on that conclusion, we might wish to adopt an α even lower than .01. For example, if a change in educational procedure is implied by the rejection of the hypothesis, and if the change were costly (in time, effort, and/or money), we would want to be quite certain of our conclusions before making the change. On the other hand, if we were trying to uncover a possible difference with the idea of subjecting it to

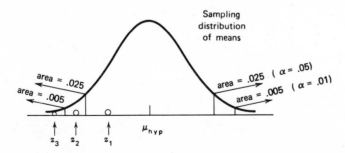

FIGURE 15.2 Three Possible Outcomes of a Two-Tailed Test when $\alpha = .05$ and $\alpha = .01$.

further confirmatory exploration, it might be desirable to set the value of α at .10 or perhaps .20. Such a situation might occur in preliminary stages of test construction, when it is more important to discover items of possible value than to be certain of eliminating the "duds."

Whatever the level of significance adopted, the decision should be made in advance. If, so to speak, we "peek" at the outcome of the sample data before arriving at this decision, there is a temptation to set the level of significance at a point which permits the conclusion to be in line with whatever preconception we may have. In any event, setting the level of significance should flow from the substantive logic of the study, and not from the specific outcome obtained in the sample.

15.5 The Statistical Decision

At the outcome of the test of an hypothesis, the decision is either to accept H_0 or to reject it. When testing the hypothesis that $\mu = 100$ versus the alternative that it is not, a decision to reject H_0 means that we do not believe the mean of the population to be 100. Moreover, the lower the probability of obtaining a sample mean of the kind that occurred when the hypothesis is true, the greater the confidence we have in the correctness of our decision to reject the hypothesis.

On the other hand, accepting the hypothesis does not mean that we believe the hypothesis to be true. Rather, *this decision merely reflects the fact that we do not have sufficient evidence to reject the hypothesis.* To put it another way, the decision to accept H_0 means simply that the hypothesis is a tenable one. Certain other hypotheses which might have been stated would also have been accepted if subjected to the same criterion. Consider the example above, where the hypothesis is: $\mu = 100$. If our sample mean is 101, and is related to the hypothesized sampling distribution as illustrated at the left in Figure 15.3, our decision will be to accept the hypothesis. But suppose the hypothesis had been: $\mu = 102$. If the same sample result had occurred, $\overline{X} = 101$, we would be led equally to accept the hypothesis that $\mu = 102$. This is shown at the right in

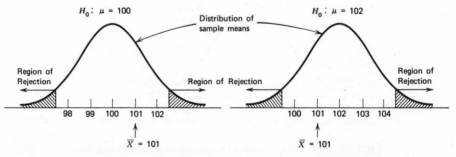

FIGURE 15.3 Testing the Hypothesis that $\mu = 100$, or that $\mu = 102$ when $\overline{X} = 101$.

Figure 15.3. In short, rejecting the hypothesis means that it does not seem reasonable to believe that it is true, but accepting the hypothesis merely means that we believe that the hypothesis *could* be true. It does *not* mean that it must be true, *or even that it is probably true,* for there would be many other hypotheses that if tested with the same sample data would also be accepted.

15.6 A Statistically Significant Difference versus a Practically Important Difference

To test the hypothesis that $\mu = 100$, we calculate z as

$$z = \frac{\overline{X} - \mu_{\text{hyp}}}{\dfrac{s_X}{\sqrt{n}}}$$

If z is large enough, the hypothesis will be rejected. Now the magnitude of z depends both on the quantity in the numerator *and* on the quantity in the denominator. Other things being equal, if sample size is very large, the denominator, $s_X/\sqrt{n}$, will be quite small. In this event, a relatively small discrepancy between $\overline{X}$ and μ_{hyp} may produce a value of z large enough to lead us to reject the hypothesis.† In cases of this kind, we may have a result which is "statistically significant," but one in which the difference between μ_{true} and μ_{hyp} is so small as to be unimportant.

Recall Dr. Baker's problem. He asked if the mean of the population of his sixth grade students' achievement test scores could be 85. To study this question, he drew a sample of 100 students. Suppose that the state director of educational research asked the same question about the state's sixth grade students, and drew a sample of 2500 students. Assuming the standard deviation of test scores to be the same as in Dr. Baker's case, the estimated standard error of the mean is $s_{\overline{X}} = 18/\sqrt{2500} = .36$. Adopting the 5% level of significance (as before), the director of research will reject the hypothesis that the mean is 85 if z is 1.96 or larger. This value will be reached when the sample mean differs from $\mu = 85$ by only .71 score points. Although a value this discrepant is reasonably indicative that the mean of the population of sixth graders is not 85, it remains that a difference of this order is not worth bothering with. It is apparent that once a significant difference has been found, according to whatever criterion has been adopted, one must evaluate the importance of this finding in terms of its meaning for the substantive situation.

---

†The discrepancy between $\overline{X}$ and μ_{hyp} depends on random variation, and, when the hypothesis is false, on the additional discrepancy between μ_{hyp} and μ_{true}. When samples are very large, the first component (due to random sampling) is small, and the second component, when present, is more "noticeable." A relatively small difference between μ_{hyp} and μ_{true} may therefore be detected in the test of significance with large samples.

The converse of the above proposition is also of interest. If very small samples have been used, the standard error of the mean will be large, and if the null hypothesis is false, it will be difficult to discover that it is, unless the difference between μ_{true} and μ_{hyp} is quite large. This suggests that an important consideration in experimental design is the size of the sample which should be drawn. The question of minimum sample size for tests of hypotheses about means is explored in Section 19.10.

15.7 Error in Hypothesis Testing

There are, so to speak, two "states of nature": either the hypothesis, H_0, is true, or it is false. Similarly, there are two possible decisions: to accept the hypothesis or to reject it. Taken in combination, there are four possibilities. They are diagrammed in Table 15.1. If the hypothesis is true and we accept it, or if it is false and we reject it, a correct decision has been made. Otherwise, we are in error. Note that there are two kinds of error. They are identified as Type I error and Type II error.

TABLE 15.1 Two Types of Error in Hypothesis Testing.

State of Nature

		H_0 false	H_0 true
Decision	Accept H_0	**Type II Error**	*correct decision*
	Reject H_0	*correct decision*	**Type I Error**

A Type I error is committed when H_0 is rejected and in fact it is true. Consider the picture of the sampling distribution shown in Figure 15.4. It illustrates a situation which might arise in testing the hypothesis that $\mu = 150$ (against the alternative that it is not) when the 5% significance level has been adopted. Suppose the sample mean is 146, which, when the test has been conducted in the usual way, leads us to reject H_0. The logic in rejecting H_0 is that if the hypothesis were true, sample means this deviant would occur less than 5% of the time, and therefore it seems more reasonable to believe that this sample mean arose through random sampling from a population with a mean different from that specified in H_0. However, this sample mean *could* be one of those deviant values obtained through the vagaries of random sampling from a population where the hypothesis is true. By definition, the region of rejection identifies a degree of deviance such

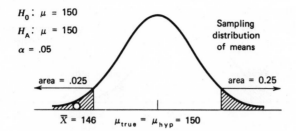

$H_0: \mu = 150$
$H_A: \mu = 150$
$\alpha = .05$

Sampling
distribution
of means

area = .025

area = 0.25

$\bar{X} = 146$ $\mu_{true} = \mu_{hyp} = 150$

FIGURE 15.4 Testing $H_0: H_0$ Is True but $\bar{X}$ Leads to Type I Error.

that, when the hypothesis is true, 5% of sample means will reach or exceed it. Therefore, when conducting tests according to this criterion, *and when the hypothesis is true*, 5% of sample means will lead us to an erroneous conclusion: rejection of the hypothesis.

When faced with true hypotheses, therefore, we take a certain risk of coming to the wrong conclusion. The magnitude of the risk is given by the probability of committing a Type I error, and is symbolized by the lower case Greek letter, alpha (α). Stated formally, it is:

$$\alpha = \text{Pr (Type I error)} = \text{Pr (rejecting } H_0 | H_0 \text{ is true)} \dagger$$

Note that the same symbol, α, has been given to the probability of committing a Type I error and to the level of significance. Of course, they are the same. The 5% level of significance specifies that the probability of rejecting the hypothesis when the hypothesis is true (committing a Type I error) is .05.

Note that the probability of committing a Type I error exists *only* in situations where the hypothesis is true. If the hypothesis is false, it is impossible to commit this kind of error.

A Type II error is committed when H_0 is accepted and in fact it is false. As in the previous example, suppose that the hypothesis is tested that $\mu = 150$, against the alternative that it is not. Again, the 5% level of significance is adopted. A sample is drawn, and its mean is found to be 152. Now it may be that, unknown to us, the mean of the population is really 154. This situation is pictured in Figure 15.5. In this figure, two sampling distributions are shown. The true distributions is shown with a dotted line, and centers about 154, the true population mean. The other is the sampling distribution which would occur if H_0 were true; it centers about 150, the hypothesized mean. The sample mean actually belongs to the true sampling distribution. But, to test the hypothesis that $\mu = 150$, the mean is evaluated according to its position in the sampling distribution shown

---

†The upright bar in the expression (rejecting $H_0 | H_0$ is true) is to be read: "give the condition that." Probabilities of this type are known as conditional probabilities; see Note 13.2.

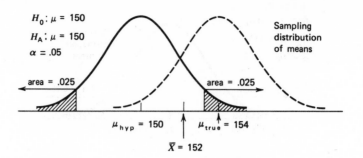

$H_0: \mu = 150$

$H_A: \mu = 150$

$\alpha = .05$

area = .025

area = .025

Sampling distribution of means

$\mu_{hyp} = 150$ $\mu_{true} = 154$

$\bar{X} = 152$

FIGURE 15.5 Testing H_0: H_0 Is False but $\bar{X}$ Leads to Type II Error.

with a solid line. Relative to *that* distribution, it is not so deviant (from the mean of 150) as to call for rejection of H_0. The decision will therefore be to accept the hypothesis that $\mu = 150$. It is, of course, an erroneous decision; we have committed a Type II error. To put it another way, we have failed to claim that a real difference existed when in fact it did.

The probability of committing a Type II error is given by:

$$\beta = \text{Pr (Type II error)} = \text{Pr (accepting } H_0 | H_0 \text{ is false)}$$

The Greek letter β (beta) is used to indicate this probability. Note that the probability of committing a Type II error exists *only* in situations where the hypothesis is false. If the hypothesis is true, it is impossible to commit this kind of error.

Several factors affect the probability of committing Type II errors. These are explored in Chapter 19 (see Sections 19.5–19.9).

15.8 The Problem of Bias in Estimating σ_X^2

The standard error of the mean is:

$$\sigma_{\bar{X}} = \frac{\sigma_X}{\sqrt{n}}$$

When σ_X is unknown, which is most often the case, it must be estimated from the sample. Intuition suggests substituting S_X, the sample standard deviation, as an estimate, but it tends to be a little too small (see Section 14.4).

The basic problem is that the sample variance, S_X^2, is a *biased estimator* of the population variance, σ_X^2. *When an estimator is* unbiased, *the mean of the estimates made from all possible samples equals the value of the parameter estimated.* For example, the sample mean is an unbiased estimator of the population mean, because the average of the means computed from all possible samples exactly equals μ. The same relationship does *not* hold between S_X^2, and σ_X^2: the mean value of S_X^2, calculated from all possible samples, is a little smaller than σ_X^2.

The formula for the sample variance (Formula 6.3b) is:

$$S_X^2 = \frac{\sum(X - \overline{X})^2}{n}$$

It has been shown that the tendency toward underestimation will be corrected if $\sum(X - \overline{X})^2$ is divided by $n - 1$, rather than by n. Formula 15.1 incorporates this correction.

Unbiased Estimate of the
Population Variance $s_X^2 = \dfrac{\sum(X - \overline{X})^2}{n - 1}$ (15.1)

The lower case letter, s^2, distinguishes this formula from that of S^2. Taking the square root of the formula, we have an estimate of the standard deviation of the population (Formula 14.1; see Section 14.4):

$$s_X = \sqrt{\frac{\sum(X - \overline{X})^2}{n - 1}}$$

TABLE 15.2 Possible Samples, Together with Estimates of the Population Variance Computed from Each (Data from Table 13.3).

Population: 2, 4, 6, 8
Population Variance: $\sigma^2 = 5.0$

Sample	Estimate of population variance (s^2)
2, 2	0
2, 4	2
2, 6	8
2, 8	18
4, 2	2
4, 4	0
4, 6	2
4, 8	8
6, 2	8
6, 4	2
6, 6	0
6, 8	2
8, 2	18
8, 4	8
8, 6	2
8, 8	0

Mean value of s^2: 5.0

Dividing by $n - 1$, rather than by n, will make little difference when n is large, but the smaller the sample, the greater the effect.

The characteristics described above may be demonstrated in one of the miniature populations described in Chapter 13. Table 13.3 presented the 16 possible samples arising when samples of size two are drawn from a population of four observations. Calculation of the variance of the four scores yields: $\sigma_X^2 = 5.0$. An estimate of the variance of the population may be calculated from each of the 16 possible samples, in accord with Formula 15.1. The 16 samples, together with the 16 variance estimates, are shown in Table 15.2. We observe that these estimates range in magnitude from zero to 18, and that their mean is 5.0, the true value of the quantity being estimated. Obviously, if the 16 estimates had been made by dividing by $n = 2$ rather than by $n - 1 = 1$, their mean would have been less than 5.0.

To return to the problem of estimating the standard error of the mean when σ_X is unknown, we may substitute s_X for σ_X in Formula 13.2. This yields Formula 14.2:

$$s_{\overline{X}} = \frac{s_X}{\sqrt{n}}$$

Although the correction introduced in estimating the standard error of the mean makes for a better estimate *on the average*, we should recognize that any particular sample will probably yield an estimate too large or too small. No explanation has been offered, so far, as to *why* S_X^2 tends to underestimate σ_X^2. The note at the end of the chapter explains this matter.

NOTE

Further Comments on Unbiased Estimates of σ_X^2 (*Ref:* Section 15.8)

The variance of a population of scores is given by Formula 6.3a: $\overset{N}{\Sigma}(X - \mu)^2/N$, where N is the number of scores in the population. The best unbiased estimate of this quantity may be made by calculating: $\sigma_{X(\text{est})}^2 = \overset{n}{\Sigma}(X - \mu)^2/n$. Note that the deviation of each score in the sample is taken from μ. Demonstration of the unbiasedness of this estimate may be had by calculating variance estimates according to this formula for each of the 16 samples shown in Table 15.2. It will be found that the mean of the 16 estimates is 5.0, precisely the value of σ_X^2.

When μ is unknown, it becomes necessary to take the deviation of each score from its own sample mean: $\overset{n}{\Sigma}(X - \overline{X})^2$. Recall (Section 6.10) that the sum of the squares of deviation scores is a minimum when the deviations are taken from the mean of *that set of scores*, i.e., $\overline{X}$. But we should, if we could, compute $\overset{n}{\Sigma}(X - \mu)^2$. Since $\overline{X}$ and μ will not ordinarily be identical, $\overset{n}{\Sigma}(X - \overline{X})^2 < \overset{n}{\Sigma}(X - \mu)^2$, and therefore $S_X^2 < \sigma_{X(\text{est})}^2$. To obtain an unbiased estimate of $\sigma_X{}^2$, $\overset{n}{\Sigma}(X - \bar{X})^2$ must be divided by $n - 1$ rather than by n. This adjustment is incorporated in Formula 15.1: $s_X{}^2 = \overset{n}{\Sigma}(X - \bar{X})^2/(n - 1)$.

It is tempting to think that $S_X{}^2$ tends to underestimate $\sigma_X{}^2$ because, when sampling from a normal distribution, very deviant scores are less likely to be present in any particular small sample than in a large one. Like most temptations, it should be resisted. Although the *number* of rare scores is expected to be less in small samples, their *proportional frequency* of occurrence is unaltered if sampling is random. Also, the shape of the population sampled is fundamentally irrelevant. Underestimation stems from use of $\bar{X}$, rather than μ, as the point about which deviations are taken.

One interesting point remains. Although $s_X{}^2$ is an unbiased estimator of $\sigma_X{}^2$, s_X still tends to underestimate σ_X, although s_X is an improved estimate. This does not cause important trouble in testing hypotheses about means. First, the degree of underestimation is quite small for samples in which $n > 10$. Second, when sample size is small, the procedures of Chapter 17 are indicated. These procedures take *exact* account of the substitution of s_X for σ_X, and so no error is involved.

This result is due to the fact that the mean of the values of a variable tends to be less than the square root of the mean of the same squared values, a fact which follows from the nonlinear relation between numbers and their squares.

PROBLEMS AND EXERCISES

Identify:

reject H_0
accept H_0
α
$z = 1.96, 2.58$
$z = 1.64, 2.33$
statistical significance

practical significance
Type I error
Type II error
β
unbiased estimator

1. A friend hands us a mysterious coin, saying that he thinks it is biased in favor of heads. We take as our null hypothesis that the coin is fair, and as the alternative hypothesis that it is biased in favor of heads. On tossing the coin 100 times we obtain 98 tails and 2 heads. If we make an intuitive significance test, what is our proper conclusion?

2. Why should the choice of a one- or two-tailed test be made before the data are gathered?

3. Why is it inadequate to choose a one-tailed test on the basis that we expect the outcome to be in that direction?

4. The meaning of "accepting H_0" is not exactly the opposite of "rejecting H_0." Explain.

5. Some investigators have praised the use of small samples in hypothesis testing, saying that such usage is better for the development of their science. (*a*) Explain the merit of this position. (*b*) Explain the limitations and/or defects of this position.

6. There are three urns. One urn contains two white balls, and the others each contain one white ball and one black ball. (*a*) Unable to see into the urns, we hypothesize that each urn contains at least one white ball. We will select one urn at random, and accept the hypothesis if it contains at least one white ball; otherwise we reject it. What is α? (*b*) We hypothesize that each urn contains at least one black ball. Selecting an urn at random, we accept the hypothesis if it contains at least one black ball; otherwise we reject it. What is β?

7. Given: some hypotheses are true and some are false. A man rejects all hypotheses. (a) What is α? (b) What is β?

8. Given: some hypotheses are true and some are false. A man rolls a die. If it comes up 1 or 2 he accepts the hypothesis, otherwise he rejects it. (a) What is α? (b) What is β?

9. A connoisseur of cigars claims that he can tell Puerto Rican cigars from Cuban cigars. We blindfold him, and offer him two Cuban cigars and one Puerto Rican cigar. His task is to identify the Puerto Rican cigar. We hypothesize that the man is always right, and establish the alternative hypothesis that he is right by chance. We give him one trial, and accept H_0 if he correctly identifies the Puerto Rican cigar; otherwise we reject H_0. (a) What is α? (b) What is β?

10. (*Based on the Note*) In Table 15.2, we showed that the mean of the 16 variance estimates made by calculating $\overset{2}{\Sigma}(X - \overline{X})^2/1$ equalled $\sigma^2 (5.0)$. For each of the 16 samples, calculate $\overset{2}{\Sigma}(X - \mu)^2/2$, and verify that the mean of these values also equals σ^2.

16

Inference about Two Means: Large Samples

16.1 Introduction

In many fields of inquiry, including psychology and education, one of the most important ways of increasing knowledge is to ask whether it makes a difference when some characteristic is measured under two different conditions. Does supplementing the diet with extra quantities of vitamin A make a difference in ability to see under conditions of dim illumination? Is speed of reaction to a light stimulus the same as to a sound stimulus? Is ability to spell equal for male and female high school seniors? Is the error rate of typists the same when work is done in a noisy environment as in a quiet one?

Each of these questions is an example of a problem for which the test of the hypothesis of the equality of two means may be helpful in finding the answer. Consider the first question. Two sets of 50 subjects may be selected at random, and one fed a normal diet while the other receives the normal diet plus supplementary vitamin A. After a suitable period under this regimen, each individual can be tested for visual acuity in conditions of dim illumination. A visual acuity "score" is thus obtained for each subject, and the mean score may be calculated for each group. We may imagine that the mean of the group receiving the vitamin A supplement is 47, and the mean of the other group is 43. However, *it is not particularly instructive to compare the two sample means, because we would expect two samples to yield different means even if the two groups had been treated alike.*

The important question is not about the samples, but about the populations from which the samples came. Is it possible that the mean of the population of visual acuity scores obtained under normal diet is the same as the mean of the population of observations obtained under normal diet plus supplementary vitamin A? The two *population* means should be the same if vitamin A had no effect. This question may be expressed as a statistical hypothesis to be subjected to test. If scores obtained under the vitamin A condition are designated by X and those under normal diet by Y, we have:†

$$H_0: \mu_X - \mu_Y = 0$$

$$H_A: \mu_X - \mu_Y \neq 0$$

H_A may be directional or nondirectional. If interest were only in discovering whether vitamin A *improved* vision, $H_A: \mu_X - \mu_Y > 0$ would be the appropriate alternative. However, presumably we would want to know it if the effect were *either* to improve vision or to impair it. Consequently, a two-tailed test is in order.

From this point on, the procedure for testing the hypothesis follows the same basic principles outlined in Chapter 14. First, the criterion for decision, α, must be chosen. Next, the characteristics of the pertinent sampling distribution are examined so that the present sample outcome can be compared with those outcomes expected when the hypothesis is true. In the sampling distribution, a region of rejection is established according to the nature of H_A and the value of α. In the present problem, if the difference between the two sample means is so great, in either direction, that it could not reasonably be accounted for by chance variation when the population means are the same, the hypothesis will be rejected.

In short, the logic and general procedure for testing an hypothesis about the difference between two means is the same as for testing an hypothesis about a single mean. There are, however, two characteristics of the test of two means which deserve special attention. The first is the nature of the relevant sampling distribution, and the second is the question as to whether the two samples are dependent or independent. We will consider these issues in the next three sections.

16.2 The Random Sampling Distribution of the Differences between Two Sample Means

The random sampling distribution of *single* means described the sample means which occur when sampling at random from a population having the mean specified in H_0. Here we are concerned with the *difference* between two means, and the pertinent reference distribution is the *random sampling distribution of differences between two sample means*. Just what *is* this distribution?

---

†The test of the difference between two means always involves the question of the difference between measures of the *same* variable when taken under two conditions. For example, in the example above, X stands for vision scores of subjects treated one way, and Y stands for vision scores of subjects treated another way.

Suppose one sample is drawn at random from the population of X scores and another from the population of Y scores. The mean of each is computed, and the difference between these two means obtained and recorded. Let the samples be returned to their respective populations, and a second pair of samples be selected in the same way. Again the two means are calculated and the difference between them noted and recorded. If this experiment is repeated indefinitely, the differences (values of $(\overline{X} - \overline{Y})$ thus generated) form the random sampling distribution of differences between two sample means.

The use to which the sampling distribution is put is, of course, to describe what differences would occur between $\overline{X}$ and $\overline{Y}$ when H_0 is true. In inquiry about the difference between two means, H_0, the hypothesis to be tested, is almost always that μ_X and μ_Y do not differ.† Now if pairs of samples are drawn at random from two populations *and the means of the two populations are the same*, we will find that sometimes $\overline{X}$ is larger than $\overline{Y}$ [leading to a positive value for $(\overline{X} - \overline{Y})$], and sometimes it is the other way around [leading to a negative value for $(\overline{X} - \overline{Y})$]. It is easy to see that when all possible differences are considered, their mean will be zero. Hence, the mean of the sampling distribution of differences is zero when $\mu_X - \mu_Y = 0$.‡

In Section 13.9, we found that another way of looking at the random sampling distribution of means is to consider it as the distribution of means of all possible samples. The same is true for the random sampling distribution of differences between $\overline{X}$ and $\overline{Y}$. If we specify sample size for X and Y, enumerate each possible sample which can be formed from the two populations, calculate the mean of each, couple in turn each sample mean of X with all of the possible sample means of Y, and obtain the difference between each resulting pair, we will have the complete set of possible differences between pairs of sample means. The distribution of differences thus formed is equivalent to that formed by repeated sampling over an infinity of trials in that both lead to the same conclusions when interpreted as relative frequency, or probability distributions.††

16.3 An Illustration of the Sampling Distribution of Differences between Means

The set of differences between pairs of possible means is extremely large unless the populations are quite small. It is instructive to explore by actual enumeration the nature of the distribution of differences, but to do so, we shall have to confine our attention to miniature populations.

---

†H_0 *could* state that $\mu_X - \mu_Y = +5$, for example, and this hypothesis is capable of being tested. However, the nature of inquiry seldom leads to such a question.

‡In general, the mean of the sampling distribution of differences between two means, $\mu_{\overline{X} - \overline{Y}}$, is equal to the difference between the means of the two populations: $\mu_X - \mu_Y$.

††The sampling distributions described above are those which would be formed when the two random samples are selected *independently* from their respective populations. Sometimes samples are selected which do not meet this criterion. See Section 16.4 for further discussion.

Suppose the population of X scores consists of three scores: 3, 5, 7. Because the usual inquiry asks what would happen if the "treatment" had no effect, we shall also suppose that the population of Y scores consists of the same three scores: 3, 5, 7. If samples of two cases are drawn with replacement from either population, there are nine possible samples, and therefore nine possible means which may occur. These are shown in Table 16.1. Note that we say that there are nine possible means, even though some of them have the same value. All must be taken into account.

TABLE 16.1 Possible Samples and Sample Means for Samples of Size Two (Sampling with Replacement).

Population of X scores: 3, 5, 7 $\mu_X = \mu_Y = 5$
Population of Y scores: 3, 5, 7 $\sigma_X = \sigma_Y = 1.633$

Sample from X population	$\overline{X}$	Sample from Y population	$\overline{Y}$
3, 3	3	3, 3	3
3, 5	4	3, 5	4
3, 7	5	3, 7	5
5, 3	4	5, 3	4
5, 5	5	5, 5	5
5, 7	6	5, 7	6
7, 3	5	7, 3	5
7, 5	6	7, 5	6
7, 7	7	7, 7	7

To inquire as to what differences may occur between sample means in X and sample means in Y, we must consider that there are nine sample means in X, and that each may be coupled with any one of the nine sample means in Y. Thus, there are 81 possible pairings of means of X with means of Y. The possible sample means are shown on the margins of Table 16.2, and the 81 differences between each pair $(\overline{X} - \overline{Y})$ are shown in the body of the same table. *If samples are drawn independently and at random, each of the listed differences is equally likely to appear.* If we collect these differences in a frequency distribution, the result is as given in Table 16.3, and is graphically illustrated in Figure 16.1.

Several features of the resulting frequency distribution are notable. First, the mean of the distribution is zero, the difference between μ_X and μ_Y. Second, the distribution is very reasonably approximated by the normal curve. In Figure 16.1, a normal curve has been fitted to the distribution, and it is apparent that the expected frequencies of the normal curve (shown by points on the curve) are close to the actual frequency of particular means (shown by the height of the

TABLE 16.2 Differences between Pairs of Sample Means $(\overline{X} - \overline{Y})$ for All Possible Paired Samples of X and Y (Data from Table 16.1).[a]

				$\overline{Y}$					
$\overline{X}$	3	4	4	5	5	5	6	6	7
7	4	3	3	2	2	2	1	1	0
6	3	2	2	1	1	1	0	0	−1
6	3	2	2	1	1	1	0	0	−1
5	2	1	1	0	0	0	−1	−1	−2
5	2	1	1	0	0	0	−1	−1	−2
5	2	1	1	0	0	0	−1	−1	−2
4	1	0	0	−1	−1	−1	−2	−2	−3
4	1	0	0	−1	−1	−1	−2	−2	−3
3	0	−1	−1	−2	−2	−2	−3	−3	−4

[a] The body of the table contains values of $(\overline{X} - \overline{Y})$.

TABLE 16.3 Distribution of Differences between All Possible Pairs of Sample Means (Data from Table 16.2).

$(\overline{X} - \overline{Y})$	f	
4	1	
3	4	
2	10	$\mu_{\overline{X}-\overline{Y}} = 0$
1	16	$\sigma_{\overline{X}-\overline{Y}} = 1.633$
0	19	
−1	16	
−2	10	
−3	4	
−4	1	
	$n = 81$	

bars in the histogram). If the sampling distribution of means for X and Y is approximately normal, the distribution of differences between pairs of means selected at random will also be approximately normal. In the present situation, the distribution of the population of scores in X and Y resembles a rectangular distribution more than it does a normal distribution. Yet the distribution of differences between pairs of sample means resembles the normal curve. Thus the effect predicted for single means by the Central Limit Theorem (see Section 13.13) also has important bearing on the distribution of differences between sample means. The normal curve, therefore, remains as an important model for the

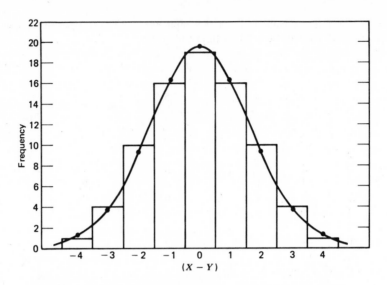

FIGURE 16.1 Distribution of Differences between All Possible Pairs of Sample Means: Data from Table 16.3.

sampling distribution of differences between means even when population distributions depart to some extent from normality.

16.4 Independent and Dependent Sample Means

The standard deviation of the random sampling distribution of differences between means depends on whether the pairs of sample means are *independent* or *dependent*, although the mean of the sampling distribution is $\mu_X - \mu_Y$ in either case. Independent random samples exist when the selection of elements comprising the sample of Y scores is in no way influenced by the selection of elements comprising the sample of X scores, and vice versa. In ordinary random selection from two populations, this would be true. For example, the experiment concerning the influence of vitamin A, described in Section 16.1, falls in this category.

In what circumstances would the sample means be dependent? Suppose the vitamin A experiment had been conducted by selecting a group of 50 subjects at random, feeding them a normal diet, testing their vision under dim illumination, *and then feeding them a normal diet plus supplementary vitamin A and retesting them.* In this case, we would have 50 pairs of observations, but each pair would be measured on the same subject. Presumably, a subject who was relatively good under one condition would tend to be relatively good on the other, aside from possible difference due to vitamin A.† Thus, with a given pair of observations,

†If the subjects differ in basic visual acuity, a man whose vision is 20–20 might be expected to perform better (relatively) under both conditions than one whose visual acuity was 20–40.

the value of Y is in part determined by (or related to) the particular value of X, and the samples cannot be said to be independent.

Samples may be dependent even when different subjects have been used. In an experiment with the same objective, it might occur to the experimentor that an extraneous source of variation is contributed by differences in basic visual acuity among individuals selected at random. He could eliminate this source of variation by pairing individuals matched on pretest performance in basic visual acuity. Thus the two members of the first pair of subjects may each have 20–40 vision, the members of the second pair 20–20 vision, etc. When paired in this way, the value of any particular Y score will be in part related to the value of its paired X score, and so the values of X and Y cannot be said to be completely independent.

Indeed, using the same subjects twice may be considered as a special case of matched observations. For example, using the same subjects in the experiment described above certainly matches the pairs of observations in terms of basic visual acuity of the respondents, in that they are made on the same person. The pairs of observations are also matched on many more variables than that of basic visual acuity when the same subjects are used. The merits and disadvantages of this experimental design will be explored in Section 16.12 and Section 16.13.

To summarize, there are three common ways of conducting a study: one leads to independent samples, and the other two lead to dependent samples. If two samples are selected at random from their respective populations, the samples are independent. If the same subjects are used for both conditions of the study, or if they are matched on some variable related to performance on the variable being observed, the samples are dependent.

The standard deviation of the sampling distribution of differences between two means is called the *standard error of the difference between two means*. Its symbol is $\sigma_{\bar{X}-\bar{Y}}$. If the sampling distribution is composed of the differences between means of *dependent* samples, its standard deviation is given by Formula 16.1:

Standard Error of the Difference between Two Dependent Means
$$\sigma_{\bar{X}-\bar{Y}} = \sqrt{\sigma_{\bar{X}}{}^2 + \sigma_{\bar{Y}}{}^2 - 2\rho_{XY}\sigma_{\bar{X}}\sigma_{\bar{Y}}} \qquad (16.1)$$

where:
   $\sigma_{\bar{X}}$ = standard error of the mean of X
   $\sigma_{\bar{Y}}$ = standard error of the mean of Y
   ρ_{XY} = correlation coefficient of the population
      of pairs of X and Y measures†

If X and Y are *independent*, $\rho_{XY} = 0$, the term $2\rho_{XY}\sigma_{\bar{X}}\sigma_{\bar{Y}}$ disappears, and Formula 16.2 applies.

†See Chapter 9 for the nature and computation of the correlation coefficient.

Standard Error of the Difference
between Two Independent Means $\qquad \sigma_{\bar{X}-\bar{Y}} = \sqrt{\sigma_{\bar{X}}^2 + \sigma_{\bar{Y}}^2}$ $\qquad\qquad$ (16.2)

Like the formula for the standard error of the mean, Formulas 16.1 and 16.2 have been derived through theoretical considerations, and on the assumption of random sampling with replacement. When sampling is done without replacement, as is usually the case, the error is negligible when the size of each sample is a small fraction of its population size or ($n/N \leq .05$).

In the illustration of Section 16.3, the distribution of possible differences was constructed on the assumption of independence of sample means. According to Formula 16.2, its standard deviation should be

$$\sigma_{\bar{X}-\bar{Y}} = \sqrt{\left(\frac{1.633}{\sqrt{2}}\right)^2 + \left(\frac{1.633}{\sqrt{2}}\right)^2} = 1.633$$

Note that actual calculation of the standard deviation (see Table 16.3) yields the same value, 1.633.†

16.5 Estimating $\sigma_{\bar{X}-\bar{Y}}$ from Sample Values

As usual, the population values required for Formulas 16.1 and 16.2 are not likely to be known, and formulas must be used which estimate these quantities. Formula 16.3 is appropriate for dependent samples.

Estimate of $\sigma_{\bar{X}-\bar{Y}}$,
Dependent Case $\qquad s_{\bar{X}-\bar{Y}} = \sqrt{s_{\bar{X}}^2 + s_{\bar{Y}}^2 - 2r_{XY}s_{\bar{X}}s_{\bar{Y}}}$ $\qquad\qquad$ (16.3)

Formula 16.4 is suited to independent samples.

Estimate of $\sigma_{\bar{X}-\bar{Y}}$,
Independent Case $\qquad s_{\bar{X}-\bar{Y}} = \sqrt{s_{\bar{X}}^2 + s_{\bar{Y}}^2}$ $\qquad\qquad$ (16.4)

Because population values are usually unknown, these formulas will be used to illustrate procedures for testing hypotheses about two means in subsequent sections. Substitution of these formulas for the more accurate ones introduces a degree of error. In general, the error is negligible if the size of each sample equals or exceeds 20 when samples are independent, or when the number of *pairs* of scores equals or exceeds 40 when samples are dependent. If these conditions are not met, the procedures described in Chapter 17 are to be preferred.

†It is a coincidence that in this problem $\sigma_X = \sigma_Y = \sigma_{\bar{X}-\bar{Y}}$.

16.6 The Vitamin A Experiment: An Illustration of the Procedure for Testing the Hypothesis of No Difference between Two Means (Independent Samples)

Did vitamin A make a difference in ability to see under conditions of dim illumination? We will test the hypothesis that:

$$H_0: \mu_X - \mu_Y = 0$$

$$H_A: \mu_X - \mu_Y \neq 0$$

using the 5% significance level ($\alpha = .05$). We need to know the two means, the two standard deviations, and the size of each sample. Suppose they are:†

supplementary vitamin A	normal diet
$\bar{X} = 47.0$	$\bar{Y} = 43.0$
$s_X = 14.0$	$s_Y = 12.0$
$n_X = 49$	$n_Y = 49$

We need to calculate the standard error of the difference between the two means. Since the samples are independent and only sample estimates are available for computation of the two standard errors of the mean, Formula 16.4 is appropriate:

$$s_{\bar{X}-\bar{Y}} = \sqrt{s_{\bar{X}}^2 + s_{\bar{Y}}^2}$$

and from Formula 14.2,

$$s_{\bar{X}-\bar{Y}} = \sqrt{\frac{s_X^2}{n_X} + \frac{s_Y^2}{n_Y}} \ddagger$$

$$= \sqrt{\frac{(14)^2}{49} + \frac{(12)^2}{49}}$$

$$= 2.63$$

If the hypothesis is true, the sampling distribution of differences between two means is as illustrated in Figure 16.2. How deviant is our particular difference? The difference is calculated in the form of a z score. Remember that $z = (score - mean)/(standard\ deviation)$. In this distribution, our difference is the score, the hypothesized difference is the mean, and $s_{\bar{X}-\bar{Y}}$ is the standard deviation. Hence, z may be calculated by Formula 16.5.

†In the illustration, it is assumed that the two sample means and standard deviations have previously been calculated. When starting with raw data, the means may be calculated by one of the methods described in Chapter 5. Calculation of s_X is discussed in Section 14.5.

‡If S_X is available, rather than s_X, one may calculate: $s_{\bar{X}-\bar{Y}} = \sqrt{S_X^2/(n_X - 1) + S_Y^2/(n_Y - 1)}$. See Section 14.5.

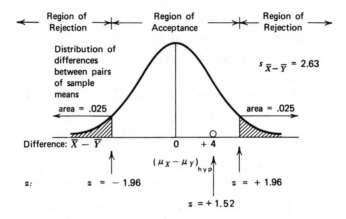

FIGURE 16.2 The Random Sampling Distribution of Differences between Two Sample Means when H_0 is True.

Location of $\bar{X} - \bar{Y}$ in the Sampling Distribution, Expressed as a z Score

$$z = \frac{(\bar{X} - \bar{Y}) - (\mu_X - \mu_Y)_{\text{hyp}}\dagger}{s_{\bar{X}-\bar{Y}}}$$

(16.5)

So,

$$z = \frac{(47 - 43) - 0}{2.63}$$

$$= +1.52$$

Since the decision criterion is the 5% level of significance and the test is non-directional, the critical values of z are -1.96 and $+1.96$. The obtained difference is located within the region of acceptance, and the decision is to accept H_0. We conclude that H_0 *could* be true. The outcome is illustrated in Figure 16.2.

16.7 The Conduct of a One-Tailed Test

Suppose it had been important, in the problem of the previous section, only to discover if supplementary feedings of vitamin A *improved* vision. In this case, a one-tailed test is in order. The null hypothesis and the alternative hypothesis would then be:

$$H_0: \mu_X - \mu_Y = 0$$

$$H_A: \mu_X - \mu_Y > 0$$

†Strictly speaking, this formula is not a true z, because an estimate replaced the true standard deviation ($\sigma_{\bar{X}-\bar{Y}}$) in the denominator. However, when samples are large enough we will treat it as z, since its properties are then very similar.

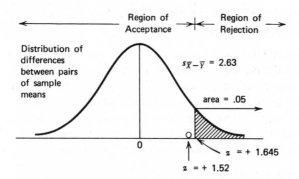

FIGURE 16.3 Testing the Hypothesis that $\mu_X - \mu_Y = 0$ against the Alternative that $\mu_X - \mu_Y > 0$; Data from Section 16.6.

The region of rejection must, consequently, be placed entirely in the upper tail of the sampling distribution. Figure 16.3 illustrates the situation. The calculation of z is exactly the same as for a two-tailed test, and the obtained value remains: $z = +1.52$. In the normal distribution, $z = +1.645$ identifies the point above which 5% of the values will be found. The obtained z is not so deviant, and therefore falls in the region of acceptance.

16.8 Sample Size in Inference about Two Means

When inference concerns two independent sample means, the samples may be of different size. However, if σ_X and σ_Y are equal, the *total* of the sample sizes $(n_X + n_Y)$ is used most efficiently when $n_X = n_Y$. This will result in a smaller value for $\sigma_{\bar{X}-\bar{Y}}$ than otherwise. For example, when one sample is twice as large as the other, $\sigma_{\bar{X}-\bar{Y}}$ is about 6% larger than if the same total sample size were distributed equally between the two samples.† The inflation of $\sigma_{\bar{X}-\bar{Y}}$ continues at an accelerated pace as the relative sample size becomes increasingly more discrepant.

The advantage of a smaller $\sigma_{\bar{X}-\bar{Y}}$ is that, if there *is* a difference between μ_X and μ_Y, the probability of claiming it (rejecting H_0) is increased. In estimation, a smaller value of $\sigma_{\bar{X}-\bar{Y}}$ means that the confidence interval will have narrower limits for the same confidence coefficient.

The discussion above relates to the *relative* size of the two samples. But what about the *absolute* magnitude of sample size? Other things being equal, large samples increase the probability of detecting a difference when a difference exists. The question of minimum sample size required for testing hypotheses about two means is given detailed consideration in Section 19.10.

---

†This statement assumes that $\sigma_X^2 = \sigma_Y^2$.

16.9 Common Aspects of Testing Hypotheses about One and Two Means

It has been stressed that the logic and the basic character of the procedures for testing hypotheses (and for estimation) are essentially the same, irrespective of the particular parameter or parameters about which the inference is made. In the last chapter, many aspects of the process were discussed in detail, because they were met for the first time. The following characteristics, discussed in detail in Chapter 15, have equal applicability to the problems of the present chapter (reference is made to section numbers for convenience):

> The nature of H_0 and H_A (Section 15.2)
> The criterion for decision (Section 15.4)
> The meaning of the decision about H_0 (Section 15.5)
> The relative merit of a one- or two-tailed test (Section 15.3)
> Significance versus importance of a discrepancy (Section 15.6)
> The two types of error in hypothesis testing (Section 15.7)

A review of these sections is recommended, keeping in mind applicability to the two-sample problem.

16.10 Testing the Hypothesis of No Difference between Two Means (Dependent Samples)

Is reaction time different to a red light than to a green light? Suppose a group of subjects has been selected at random and given a preliminary test to determine the reaction time of each individual to a white-light stimulus. From among this group, pairs of subjects are formed such that the two members of any given pair are equal in speed of reaction to white light. Taking each pair in turn, one member is tested with a green light as the stimulus, and the other with a red light. Which member of each pair receives which stimulus is determined at random. Reaction times are recorded in milliseconds. The two groups of subjects so selected constitute two dependent samples.

We shall test: $H_0: \mu_X - \mu_Y = 0$ (where X represents reaction time of those exposed to green light and Y reaction time of those exposed to red light), against: $H_A: \mu_X - \mu_Y \neq 0$, using the 5% significance level. The procedure for testing the hypothesis of no difference between the two treatment means is exactly the same as given in Section 16.6, except that allowance must be made for use of dependent rather than independent samples. This is done by using Formula 16.3 for the standard error of the difference, rather than Formula 16.4. To illustrate the procedure, we shall suppose that ten pairs of subjects have been selected. This number of subjects is much too small for proper application of the procedures described in this chapter; the procedures of Chapter 17 (small sample procedures) are more nearly appropriate.† We shall persist only for the sake of simplicity in demonstrating the necessary calculations.

The details of the test are shown in Table 16.4. This table contains the basic data, the calculations necessary for the test when raw score formulas are used, and the statistical decision. First, we must calculate $\Sigma X, \Sigma Y, \Sigma X^2, \Sigma Y^2$, and ΣXY, the sums of the products of the paired X and Y values. The subsequent calculations, keyed to numbers appearing in Table 16.4, are:‡

(1) Calculation of $\bar{X}$ and $\bar{Y}$
(2) Calculation of S_X and S_Y
(3) Calculation of r_{XY}
(4) Calculation of $s_{\bar{X}}$ and $s_{\bar{Y}}$
(5) Calculation of $s_{\bar{X}-\bar{Y}}$
(6) Calculation of z

The accompanying illustration, Figure 16.4, shows the relevant sampling distribution, and the basis for the conclusion. Once again, z is calculated in step (6) as: ($score - mean$)/($standard\ deviation$). In the present instance, the score is the difference between the two sample means, the mean is the hypothesized difference between the two population means, and the standard deviation is the standard error of the difference between two (dependent) means.

In Table 16.4 we find that the calculated value of z is $+.65$. Since the test is two-tailed and conducted at the 5% level of significance, the critical values of z are -1.96 and $+1.96$, respectively. The obtained z therefore falls in the region of acceptance (see Figure 16.4), and the decision is to accept the hypothesis.

The new factor, required for this test but not required for the test of independent means, is the Pearsonian correlation coefficient (r_{XY}) between the set of paired observations. In the present example, the means, standard deviations, and the correlation coefficient have been obtained by raw score formulas. Other formulas may be used if desired (see Chapters 5, 6, and 9).

16.11 An Alternate Approach to the Problem of Two Dependent Means

An alternative method is available for calculating z for the test of two dependent means. Depending on circumstances, it may save much computational labor. The outcome is identical with that of the method described in the previous section. That method dealt explicitly with the characteristics of the distribution of X and Y, and required the correlation coefficient between the paired values of

†The same example, properly evaluated by small sample procedures, is treated in Section 17.13.

‡In this illustration, values of S_X and S_Y are calculated rather than values of s_X and s_Y, primarily because these calculations are more compatible with the raw score formula for r_{XY} which we learned in Chapter 9. If it is desired to know s_X and s_Y, they may be found from: $s = S\sqrt{n/(n-1)}$.

TABLE 16.4 Test of the Hypothesis of the Difference of Two Dependent Means.

Pair	Reaction to green light stimulus X	Reaction to red light stimulus Y	X^2	Y^2	XY
1	28	25	784	625	700
2	26	27	676	729	702
3	33	28	1089	784	924
4	30	31	900	961	930
5	32	29	1024	841	928
6	30	30	900	900	900
7	31	32	961	1024	992
8	18	21	324	441	378
9	22	25	484	625	550
10	24	20	576	400	480
	$\Sigma X =$ 274	$\Sigma Y =$ 268	$\Sigma X^2 =$ 7718	$\Sigma Y^2 =$ 7330	$\Sigma XY =$ 7484

(1) $\bar{X} = \dfrac{\Sigma X}{n} = \dfrac{274}{10} = 27.4$ $\qquad\qquad \bar{Y} = \dfrac{\Sigma Y}{n} = \dfrac{268}{10} = 26.8$

(2) $S_X = \dfrac{1}{n}\sqrt{n\Sigma X^2 - (\Sigma X)^2} = \dfrac{1}{10}\sqrt{10(7718) - (274)^2} = \dfrac{1}{10}(45.9) = 4.59$

$S_Y = \dfrac{1}{n}\sqrt{n\Sigma Y^2 - (\Sigma Y)^2} = \dfrac{1}{10}\sqrt{10(7330) - (268)^2} = \dfrac{1}{10}(38.4) = 3.84$

(3) $r_{XY} = \dfrac{n\Sigma XY - (\Sigma X)(\Sigma Y)}{\sqrt{n\Sigma X^2 - (\Sigma X)^2}\ \sqrt{n\Sigma Y^2 - (\Sigma Y)^2}}$

$= \dfrac{10(7484) - (274)(268)}{(45.9)(38.4)} \quad \begin{cases} \text{obtained from calculations} \\ \text{of } S_X \text{ and } S_Y \end{cases}$

$= \dfrac{+1408}{(45.9)(38.4)} = +.80$

(4) $s_{\bar{X}} = \dfrac{S_X}{\sqrt{n-1}} = \dfrac{4.59}{\sqrt{10-1}} = 1.53 \qquad s_{\bar{Y}} = \dfrac{S_Y}{\sqrt{n-1}} = \dfrac{3.84}{\sqrt{10-1}} = 1.28$

(5) $s_{\bar{X}-\bar{Y}} = \sqrt{s_{\bar{X}}^2 + s_{\bar{Y}}^2 - 2r_{XY}s_{\bar{X}}s_{\bar{Y}}}$

$= \sqrt{(1.53)^2 + (1.28)^2 - 2(+.80)(1.53)(1.28)}$

$= \sqrt{3.98 - 3.12} = \sqrt{.86} = .93$

(6) $z = \dfrac{(\bar{X} - \bar{Y}) - (\mu_X - \mu_Y)_{\text{hyp}}}{s_{\bar{X}-\bar{Y}}} = \dfrac{(27.4) - (26.8) - 0}{.93} = +.65$

Since the region of acceptance falls between $z = -1.96$ and $+1.96$, the decision is to accept H_0.

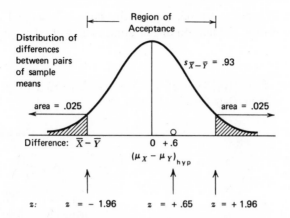

FIGURE 16.4 The Random Sampling Distribution of Differences between Two Sample Means when H_0 is True.

X and *Y. The present method focuses on the characteristics of the distribution of differences between the paired X and Y scores.*

Consider the hypothesis that $\mu_X - \mu_Y = 0$. If the hypothesis is true, then it is also true that the mean of the population of differences between paired values of *X* and *Y* is zero (see Note 16.1 for proof). If the difference between paired *X* and *Y* scores is designated by *D*, the initial hypothesis may be restated: $H_0: \mu_D = 0$. In the present method, we shall find $\overline{D}$, the mean of the sample set of difference scores, and inquire whether it differs significantly from the hypothesized mean of the population of difference scores, μ_D.†

To conduct the test by the alternate method, the paired scores are recorded in tabular form, as shown in Table 16.5. Then each value of *Y* is subtracted from its paired value of *X*, and the difference recorded in a new column, *D*. We must find the mean and (estimate of the) standard deviation of these difference scores ($\overline{D}$, and s_D). The raw score methods are used in the present illustration.

To find the standard deviation, the square of each difference score is required. These values are shown in the column headed: D^2. Computation of $\overline{D}$ and s_D is shown in the table. Next, we find the standard error of the mean of the difference scores, $s_{\overline{D}} = s_D/\sqrt{n}$. *z* may then be calculated by Formula 16.6.

Location of $\overline{D}$ in the Sampling Distribution, Expressed as a z Score

$$z = \frac{\overline{D} - \mu_{D\,(hyp)}}{s_{\overline{D}}}$$ (16.6)

†Note that this transforms the test from a two-sample test to a one-sample test. Compare the test made here with that illustrated in Section 14.6.

Note (Table 16.5) that $z = +.65$, exactly the same as obtained by the method of the previous section. Evaluation of z is done as usual to determine significance of the outcome.

TABLE 16.5 Test of the Hypothesis of the Difference between Two Dependent Means: Difference Score Method (Data from Table 16.4).

Pair	X	Y	D	D^2	Calculations
1	28	25	3	9	
2	26	27	-1	1	$\bar{D} = \dfrac{\sum D}{n} = \dfrac{+6}{10} = +.6$
3	33	28	5	25	
4	30	31	-1	1	Let $d = (D - \bar{D})$, a deviation
5	32	29	3	9	score in D. Then:
6	30	30	0	0	
7	31	32	-1	1	$\sum d^2 = \sum D^2 - \dfrac{(\sum D)^2}{n}$
8	18	21	-3	9	
9	22	25	-3	9	$= 80 - \dfrac{(+6)^2}{10} = 76.4$
10	24	20	4	16	

$$\sum D = +6 \quad \sum D^2 = 80 \qquad \text{And:}$$

$$s_{\bar{D}} = \frac{s_D}{\sqrt{n}} = \frac{2.91}{\sqrt{10}} = .92 \qquad\qquad s_D = \sqrt{\frac{\sum d^2}{n-1}} = \sqrt{\frac{76.4}{9}} = 2.91$$

$$z = \frac{\bar{D} - \mu_{D(\text{hyp})}}{s_{\bar{D}}} = \frac{+.6 - 0}{.92} = +.65$$

Although the simpler method, described in this section, reduces the computational burden substantially, it also yields less information. When we are done, we know the size of the difference between the two sample means $(\bar{D})$, and whether the difference was or was not significant according to the decision criterion adopted. Often we wish to know the actual value of each of the means and standard deviations, and perhaps also the extent of the correlation between the two sets of measures. This short method provides none of that information.

One last caution: the method described in this section is suited *only* to the case of *dependent* means of large samples.

16.12 An Advantage in Using Dependent Samples

From a statistical standpoint, there can be an advantage in electing to use paired observations rather than independent random samples, when a choice is available. Pairing observations makes possible elimination of an extraneous source of variation. For example, in the vitamin A study, variation between the two samples in basic visual acuity can be eliminated by pairing subjects in terms of this capability (see Section 16.4).

The effect of doing so is to reduce the expected variation between the two *sample* means when in fact there is no difference between the two population means. Compare Formula 16.1 with Formula 16.2; the former will yield the smaller value of $\sigma_{\bar{X}-\bar{Y}}$. In testing the hypothesis that $\mu_X - \mu_Y = 0$, whether z reaches significance depends in part on the influence of random variation on the two sample means, and in part on the difference (if any) between the two population means.† If there *is* a difference between the means of the two populations, it is more likely to be discovered (i.e., more likely that z will be large enough to lead to rejection of H_0) when it is accompanied by a small amount of random variation than by a large amount. To put it more formally, a reduction in $\sigma_{\bar{X}-\bar{Y}}$ reduces the probability of committing a Type II error (see Section 15.7).

Note that the reduction in $\sigma_{\bar{X}-\bar{Y}}$ induced by pairing observations depends on the value of ρ_{XY} (see Formula 16.1). In general, when pairing is on the basis of a variable importantly related to performance of the subjects, the correlation will be higher than otherwise, and the reduction in $\sigma_{\bar{X}-\bar{Y}}$ will consequently be greater. For example, matching subjects on the basis of visual acuity will probably be beneficial in the vitamin A study, and so will matching subjects to be used in an experiment on rate of learning on their intelligence test scores or, better, on pretest performance on a learning task similar to that used in the main experiment.

16.13 Disadvantages in Using Dependent Samples

The general assumptions required for inference about two means are discussed in Section 16.15. However, there are some special considerations which apply when the test between two means is conducted on dependent samples. These will be discussed here.

The special requirements for (entirely satisfactory) use of matched observations are as follows:

1. There exists a population of paired subjects, matched on the basis of a characteristic related to the observation to be measured.
2. A sample of pairs is selected at random from this population.
3. The two conditions of the "treatment" (e.g., vitamin A versus normal diet) are assigned *at random* to the members of each pair, and *random assignment is made independently for each pair.*
4. ρ_{XY}, the correlation between pairs of observations among the population of pairs, is known (as well as the values of σ_X and σ_Y).

In practical work, we can not abide strictly by the first two conditions.

---

†Note 16.2, at the end of this chapter, compares the algebraic values of z when the hypothesis is true, and when it is not.

Ordinarily, it will be satisfactory to identify the kind of subjects that it is desired to study, select a random sample from among them, form as many matched pairs as possible from this sample, and assign the two conditions of the treatment at random among the members of each pair.

It must be confessed that problems in psychology and education have frequently been approached through the paired sample design under circumstances which do not even conform to the practice just described. The outcome of such tests is not easy to interpret with confidence. Sometimes it is necessary to brave the hazards involved because there is no reasonable alternative, but it remains that this design has often been used when better alternative approaches are available.

It may be helpful to identify two common applications which often lead to difficulty in interpretation. Suppose it is desired to compare certain characteristics of juvenile delinquents with those of nondelinquent children. We may think it appropriate to choose two groups matched on IQ, since juvenile delinquents tend to be substantially lower in this regard than children in general. That may improve the study, but a basic difficulty remains: *the "treatment condition" is not (and cannot be) assigned at random to members of a pair.* In the vitamin A experiment, condition of diet may be assigned at random to members of a pair. In the delinquency study, the "treatment" is delinquency–nondelinquency, and condition of delinquency is "built in" to each member of a pair; it cannot be assigned at random. A host of problems arise in attempting to interpret the outcome of such a study. For example, it is likely that the two groups will differ in socioeconomic status, as well as in delinquency. If differences are discovered in the variables under study, it may be associated with differences in this dimension, rather than with differences in delinquency *per se.* Randomization affords control over extraneous factors; use of *intact groups* (i.e., "assigning" subjects to groups *before* matching) does not. The role of randomization in achieving control over extraneous factors is explored further in Section 19.14.

A second problem concerns use of repeated measures on the *same* subjects. *This design leads to trouble when administration of the first treatment changes the subject in some way so that he performs differently on administration of the second treatment.* For example, a study of the effectiveness of learning under two different methods is likely to be subject to practice effect, an influence extraneous to the study. A subject may therefore perform better on the second trial than on the first, irrespective of the relative merits of the two methods of learning. Further discussion of problems associated with the dependent samples design appears in Sections 19.15 and 19.16.

Two further points may be made here. First, the advantage of the paired elements design is proportional to the size of the correlation induced by pairing. *If the correlation is low, little benefit ensues.* Second, *when the correlation must be estimated from the pairs of scores in the sample, error is introduced to the extent that the sample correlation coefficient differs from the population coefficient.* For example, it might be that the correlation in the population is actually zero, and yet the sample coefficient is, say, $+.20$. Consequently, we ought to be sure that the coefficient is substantial enough that the loss in efficiency through the introduction of error is more than recovered through the degree of dependency induced by pairing. As a rule of thumb, it is suggested that the correlation coefficient ought at least to be significantly above zero (see Section 18.3 for the means of conducting this test).

The last of the four requirements is that ρ_{XY} be known. When it is not (the ordinary case), the procedures described here will be reasonably satisfactory when the number of pairs of scores ≥ 40. When it is less, the exact procedures of Chapter 17 (see Section 17.13) apply.

16.14 An Interval Estimate of $\mu_X - \mu_Y$

Just as an interval estimate may be made of the value of μ_X, so also is it possible to estimate the true difference between μ_X and μ_Y. The logic of doing so, and the general nature of the procedure is the same as for the case of the single mean (see Section 14.9 and 14.10). Figure 16.5 shows the random sampling distribution of differences between pairs of sample means when the true difference between μ_X and μ_Y is $+5$ points, and $\sigma_{\bar{X}-\bar{Y}} = 3.00$. Suppose each sample difference, $(\bar{X} - \bar{Y})$, was taken in turn, and the claim made that $\mu_X - \mu_Y$ lay somewhere within the range: $(\bar{X} - \bar{Y}) \pm 1.96\sigma_{\bar{X}-\bar{Y}}$. For example, if $(\bar{X} - \bar{Y}) = +1.00$, it would be claimed that $\mu_X - \mu_Y$ lay somewhere within the interval: $+1 \pm (1.96)(3.00)$ or between -4.88 and $+6.88$. We note that this claim is correct. This interval is shown in Figure 16.5.

If the difference between the two sample means is not farther away from the difference between the two population means than $\pm 1.96\sigma_{\bar{X}-\bar{Y}}$, the claim will be correct. Otherwise, it will not. Since 95% of the obtained differences (under random sampling) between the two sample means will be within this range, 95% of claims made by following this procedure will be correct. Accordingly, if a pair of samples are drawn at random, the probability is .95 that an interval estimate constructed by the procedure outlined above $[(\bar{X} - \bar{Y}) \pm 1.96\sigma_{\bar{X}-\bar{Y}}]$ will include the true value of $\mu_X - \mu_Y$. An interval constructed in this way is called a 95% confidence interval, and the confidence coefficient, C, corresponding to an interval so constructed is .95.

If we wish to be even more sure that the true difference between the two population means lies within the interval, a different confidence coefficient may be selected. For $C = .99$, the interval would be constructed according to the rule: $(\bar{X} - \bar{Y}) \pm 2.58\sigma_{\bar{X}-\bar{Y}}$. Probabilities other than .95 and .99 may be selected if desired. See Section 14.10 for the procedure.

In general, intervals may be constructed according to a specified level of probability by the rule of Formula 16.7.

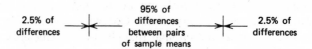

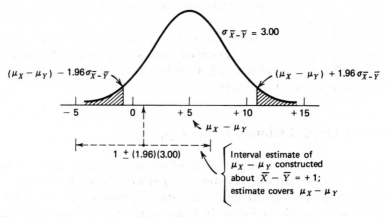

FIGURE 16.5 Distribution of Differences between Two Sample Means, Drawn from Populations in Which $\mu_X - \mu_Y = +5$ and $\sigma_{\overline{X}-\overline{Y}} = 3.00$.

Rule for Constructing an Interval Estimate of $\mu_X - \mu_Y$ $(\overline{X} - \overline{Y}) \pm z_p \sigma_{\overline{X}-\overline{Y}}$ (16.7)

where:

$(\overline{X} - \overline{Y})$ is the difference between the two sample means

$\sigma_{\overline{X}-\overline{Y}}$ is the standard error of the difference between two means

z_p is the magnitude of z for which, in the normal distribution, the probability is p of obtaining a value so deviant or more so (in either direction)

$p = 1 - C$, where C is the confidence coefficient

Once again, the procedure described above is dependent on knowledge of $\sigma_{\overline{X}}$ and $\sigma_{\overline{Y}}$ (and ρ_{XY}, in the case of dependent samples), the values needed to obtain $\sigma_{\overline{X}-\overline{Y}}$. If only sample estimates are available (the usual case), $s_{\overline{X}-\overline{Y}}$ must be substituted for $\sigma_{\overline{X}-\overline{Y}}$. Accordingly, a rule less nearly correct is given in Formula 16.8.

Approximate Rule for Constructing an Interval Estimate of $\mu_X - \mu_Y$ $(\overline{X} - \overline{Y}) \pm z_p s_{\overline{X}-\overline{Y}}$ (16.8)

When the size of each of the two samples equals or exceeds 20 for independent samples, or when the number of pairs of scores equals or exceeds 40 when samples are dependent, the error in such a substitution is minimal.

The procedure of establishing confidence limits is illustrated in Table 16.6. Because the population values are commonly unknown, the problem supposes that only sample estimates are available. It is usual to express the outcome of calculation of a confidence interval in the general form: $C[\text{Lower Limit} \leq (\mu_X - \mu_Y) \leq \text{Upper Limit}] = value\ of\ the\ confidence\ coefficient$. Thus, for the problem in Table 16.6, $C[-1.15 \leq (\mu_X - \mu_Y) \leq +9.15] = .95$.

TABLE 16.6 Construction of a Confidence Interval Concerning $\mu_X - \mu_Y$ when σ_X and σ_Y Are Unknown, Samples Are Independent, and Sample Size Is Large.

Given: Independent random samples, where:

$$\bar{X} = 74.0 \qquad \bar{Y} = 70.0$$
$$s_X = 14.0 \qquad s_Y = 12.0$$
$$n_X = 49 \qquad n_Y = 49$$

Problem: Estimate, at the 95% level of confidence, the value of $\mu_X - \mu_Y$.

Solution; Step 1: Calculate s_{X-Y} according to Formula 16.4.

$$s_{\bar{X}-\bar{Y}} = \sqrt{s_{\bar{X}}^2 + s_{\bar{Y}}^2} = \sqrt{\frac{s_X^2}{n_X} + \frac{s_Y^2}{n_Y}}$$

$$= \sqrt{\frac{(14.0)^2}{49} + \frac{(12.0)^2}{49}}$$

$$= 2.63$$

Step 2: Calculate limits of the interval according to Formula 16.8.

$$(\bar{X} - \bar{Y}) \pm (z_{.05})(s_{\bar{X}-\bar{Y}})$$
$$(74.0 - 70.0) \pm (1.96)(2.63)$$
$$-1.15 \text{ to } +9.15$$
$$\begin{pmatrix}\text{Lower}\\\text{Limit}\end{pmatrix} \quad \begin{pmatrix}\text{Upper}\\\text{Limit}\end{pmatrix}$$

Therefore, $C[-1.15 \leq (\mu_X - \mu_Y) \leq +9.15] = .95$

The procedure described above is applicable to estimation of the difference between two population means for dependent samples as well as for independent samples. Of course, the formula for the standard error of the difference between two dependent means must be used. See Table 16.4 (Section 16.10) for an illustration of its calculation.

For a given confidence coefficient, a small sample results in a wide confidence interval and a large sample in a narrower one. How to choose sample size so that the resulting interval is of a desired width is discussed in Section 19.13.

16.15 Review of Assumptions in Inferences about Two Means

The general assumptions required for inference about two means to be precisely correct (according to the models presented in the present chapter) are basically those pertaining to inference about single means. These were described in Section 14.11. For convenient reference here, the major points are summarized below in terms suited to inference about two means.

1. Each sample is drawn at random from its respective population.
2. The samples are drawn with replacement.
3. The sampling distribution of differences between pairs of sample means follows the normal curve.
4. The standard deviation of the population of each set of scores is known.

Section 14.11 contained a commentary on each of these points. These comments are just as applicable here as there; it would be a good idea to reread them now. In addition, there are a few considerations which are special to the problem of inference about two means.

First, if inference concerns two *independent* means, the first assumption listed above must be further qualified by specifying that the two random samples be *independently* selected. For the dependent sample design, the four requirements given in Section 16.13 apply.

The third point listed at the beginning of this section states that the sampling distribution of differences between pairs of sample means should follow the normal curve. When the distributions of both populations are normal and sampling is random, this condition will hold. As we saw in the case of the miniature sampling distribution constructed in Section 16.3, when these distributions are not normal, the Central Limit Theorem makes its influence felt, and the sampling distribution of differences tends toward normality. Since the procedures described in this chapter are appropriate for large samples, and since increased sample size tends to facilitate the benefits of the Central Limit Theorem, there is seldom need to worry about moderate degrees of departure from normality in the two populations.

Similarly, the assumption that σ_X and σ_Y (and, if required, ρ_{XY}) are known is not critical for large samples since the estimates of these values made from the samples will tend to be reasonably close.

NOTES

NOTE 16.1 Proof that $\mu_{X-Y} = \mu_X - \mu_Y$ when X and Y Are Paired (*Ref:* Section 16.11)

Let: μ_{X-Y} = mean of the population of difference scores formed by subtracting a score in Y from a score in X, μ_X = mean of the population of X scores, μ_Y = mean of the population of Y scores, N = the number of X scores, Y scores, or $(X - Y)$ scores.

Then:

$$\mu_{X-Y} = \frac{\sum(X - Y)}{N}$$

$$= \frac{\sum X - \sum Y}{N}$$

$$= \frac{\sum X}{N} - \frac{\sum Y}{N}$$

$$= \mu_X - \mu_Y$$

(In the terminology of Section 16.11, $\mu_D = \mu_X - \mu_Y$.)

NOTE 16.2 Comparison of z when the Hypothesis (H_0) Is True, and when It Is Not (*Ref:* Section 16.12)

To test H_0, z is calculated as follows:

$$z = \frac{(\overline{X} - \overline{Y}) - (\mu_X - \mu_Y)_{hyp}}{\sigma_{\overline{X} - \overline{Y}}}$$

When H_0 is *true*, z is in fact:

$$z = \frac{(\overline{X} - \overline{Y}) - (\mu_X - \mu_Y)_{true}}{\sigma_{\overline{X} - \overline{Y}}}$$

But when H_0 is *false*, the values of $(\overline{X} - \overline{Y})$ are distributed about $(\mu_X - \mu_Y)_{true}$ rather than about $(\mu_X - \mu_Y)_{hyp}$. In this case, z *as calculated to test H_0* is actually:

$$z = \frac{[(\overline{X} - \overline{Y}) - (\mu_X - \mu_Y)_{true}] + [(\mu_X - \mu_Y)_{true} - (\mu_X - \mu_Y)_{hyp}]}{\sigma_{\overline{X} - \overline{Y}}}$$

Now the element at the left in the numerator tends to be proportionate to the denominator (the ratio of these two elements exceeds ± 1.96 only 5% of the time). Consequently, the larger the element at the right in the numerator, the more likely it will be that z is large (specifically, large enough to lead to rejection of H_0).

PROBLEMS AND EXERCISES

Identify:

sampling distribution of
   difference between means
independent samples

dependent samples
intact groups

1. We wish to compare mechanical aptitude scores of male high school seniors with female high school seniors. We draw a random sample of males, and another of females to conduct the test. Should we consider these to be dependent samples because both groups are equated in the sense that they are high school seniors? Or are they independent samples? Explain.

2. Given: $\bar{X} = 165.0$, $s_X = 24.0$, $n_X = 36$, and $\bar{Y} = 175.0$, $s_Y = 21.0$, $n_Y = 49$; assume the samples are independent. (*a*) State formally the hypotheses necessary to conduct a nondirectional test of no difference between the two population means. (*b*) Calculate $s_{\bar{X}-\bar{Y}}$. (*c*) Calculate z. (*d*) Evaluate z according to $\alpha = .05$ and .01, and state your conclusions.

3. In Problem 2, suppose H_A was: $H_A: \mu_X - \mu_Y < 0$. Evaluate z according to $\alpha = .05$ and $\alpha = .01$, and state your conclusions.

4. In Problem 2, suppose H_A was: $H_A: \mu_X - \mu_Y > 0$. Evaluate z according to $\alpha = .05$ and $\alpha = .01$, and state your conclusions.

5. Repeat the steps of Problem 2, but as applied to these data: $\bar{X} = 97.0$, $s_X = 16.0$, $n_X = 64$; $\bar{Y} = 90.0$, $s_Y = 18.0$, $n_Y = 81$.

6. (In this problem, the samples are much too small for the procedures of this chapter to be appropriate; the problem is offered this way to eliminate lengthy computation.) Given the following scores from two independent samples:

$$X: \quad 6, 7, 8, 8, 11 \qquad Y: \quad 3, 4, 4, 7, 7$$

(*a*) State formally the hypotheses necessary to conduct a nondirectional test of no difference between the two population means. (*b*) Calculate s_X and s_Y (see Section 14.5). (*c*) Complete the test at the .05 and .01 levels of significance, and state your conclusions.

7. Repeat the steps of Problem 6, but as applied to these data:

$$X: \quad 2, 2, 5, 5, 6 \qquad Y: \quad 8, 8, 8, 9, 12$$

8. Given the following data from two dependent samples: $\bar{X} = 88.0$, $s_X = 16.0$, $\bar{Y} = 85.0$, $s_Y = 12.0$, $n = 64$, $r = +.50$. (*a*) State formally the hypotheses necessary to conduct a nondirectional test of no difference between the two population means. (*b*) Calculate $s_{\bar{X}-\bar{Y}}$. (*c*) Complete the test at the .05 and .01 levels of significance, and state your conclusions.

9. (See parenthetical introduction to Problem 6.) Given the following pairs of scores from dependent samples:

$$
\begin{array}{lccccc}
\text{Pair:} & 1 & 2 & 3 & 4 & 5 \\
X: & 4 & 4 & 6 & 5 & 9 \\
Y: & 5 & 2 & 3 & 1 & 6
\end{array}
$$

(*a*) State formally the hypotheses necessary to conduct a nondirectional test of no difference between the two population means. (*b*) Calculate $\bar{X}$, $\bar{Y}$, S_X, S_Y. (*c*) Calculate r_{XY}. (*d*) Calculate $s_{\bar{X}-\bar{Y}}$. (*e*) Complete the test at the .05 and .01 levels of significance, and state your conclusions.

10. Using the data of Problem 9, test the hypothesis of no difference between population means by the difference method described in Section 16.11: (*a*) Calculate $\bar{D}$ and $s_{\bar{D}}$. (*b*) Calculate z and compare it with that obtained in Problem 9. (*c*) Evaluate z according to $\alpha = .05$ and .01, and state your conclusions.

11. For the data of Problem 2, construct an interval estimate of $\mu_X - \mu_Y$ according to: (*a*) $C = .95$ (*b*) $C = .99$ (*c*) $C = .50$.

12. Repeat Problem 11, but use the data of Problem 5.

13. Repeat Problem 11, but use the data of Problem 8 (remember that these data are for dependent samples).

17

Inference about Means: Small Sample Approach

17.1 Introduction

In Chapters 14 and 16, models were developed for inference about single means and about two means, respectively. For these models to be exactly correct, the relevant standard errors must be calculated from the population parameters (Formulas 13.2, 16.1, and 16.2). For example, the formula for the standard error of the mean is: $\sigma_{\overline{X}} = \sigma_X/\sqrt{n}$, which requires knowledge of the standard deviation of the population of X scores. In most practical applications, the required population parameters are not known, and the standard errors must be estimated from the data of the sample (Formulas 14.2, 16.3, and 16.4). To continue the example, the standard error of the mean must, in these circumstances, be estimated by a formula such as: $s_{\overline{X}} = s_X/\sqrt{n}$.

Substitution of sample estimates introduces a degree of error into the procedure for inference. The amount of error is a function of sample size: the larger the sample, the less the error. When sample size is reasonably large, error is minimal, and if one chooses to use the methods of Chapters 14 and 16, no substantial harm is done. When sample size is small, the error may be substantial. It then becomes desirable to turn to alternate procedures. In the present chapter we will discuss the issues involved and present these procedures.

The techniques of the preceding chapters are often called "*large sample procedures*," and those to be described here, "*small sample procedures*." These designations are appropriate, but sometimes they lead students to believe that the basic question is that of sample size. We should make it clear at the outset that this is not so. The *fundamental* issue is whether the formulas for the standard errors are based on population parameters or on sample estimates of those parameters. If based on population parameters, the procedures of Chapters 14 and 16 are exactly correct *irrespective of sample size*. If based on *estimates* of population parameters, the procedures of this chapter are exactly correct.

17.2 Inference about a Single Mean when σ_X Is Known: Role of the Normal Distribution

Suppose the hypothesis that $\mu_X = 100$ is to be tested against the alternative that it is not, *and σ_X is known*. To do so, we calculate z:

$$z = \frac{\overline{X} - \mu_X}{\sigma_{\overline{X}}}$$

The value of z is then taken to the normal distribution for evaluation. For example, if the test is two tailed and $\alpha = .05$, the hypothesis will be rejected if the calculated value of z exceeds a magnitude of 1.96.

Is it right to treat z as a normally distributed variable? If the assumptions of Section 14.11 are satisfied, values of $\overline{X}$ will be normally distributed as we move from random sample to random sample, but the values of μ_X and $\sigma_{\overline{X}}$ will remain fixed. Consequently, values of z may be considered to be formed as follows:

$$z = \frac{(normally\ distributed\ variable) - (constant)}{(constant)}$$

where:
  $\overline{X}$ is the normally distributed variable
  μ_X is a constant
  $\sigma_{\overline{X}}$ is a constant

Subtracting a constant from each score in a normal distribution does not change the shape of the distribution, nor does dividing by a constant.† Consequently, z will be normally distributed when $\overline{X}$ is normally distributed, and the normal distribution is therefore the correct distribution to which to refer z for evaluation.

17.3 Inference about a Single Mean when σ_X Is Unknown: Inadequacy of the Normal Distribution

Once more, suppose the hypothesis that $\mu_X = 100$ is to be tested against the alternative that it is not. *This time we shall assume that σ_X is unknown.* When σ_X

---

†The mean and standard deviation are affected by these operations, but the relative distances between scores (i.e., the "shape" of the distribution) remain unaltered. (See Section 8.5.)

is unknown the exact value of the standard error of the mean can not be found; it must be estimated from the sample. Then, to evaluate the position of the sample mean, we calculate the statistic known as t :†

t Required for Testing Hypotheses About Single Means

$$t = \frac{\overline{X} - \mu_X}{s_{\overline{X}}} \qquad (17.1)$$

This statistic differs from the z of the previous section in that *the denominator of the expression is a variable.* As we move from random sample to random sample, not only will values of $\overline{X}$ vary, but *each sample will yield a different estimate* $(s_{\overline{X}})$ *of* $\sigma_{\overline{X}}$.‡ The resulting statistic may be considered to be formed as follows:

$$t = \frac{(normally\ distributed\ variable) - (constant)}{(variable)}$$

where:
$\overline{X}$ is the normally distributed variable
μ_X is a constant
$s_{\overline{X}}$ is a variable

Because of the presence of the variable in the denominator, this statistic does *not* follow, with exactitude, the normal distribution. Just what distribution does it follow? Shortly after the turn of the century, William S. Gosset, writing under the name of "Student," solved this problem, and presented the proper distribution for it. Since that time, the statistic has been called "t," and its distribution has been referred to as "Student's distribution," or "*Student's distribution of* t;" we shall do the same.

Before turning to Student's distribution, one comment seems in order. Beginners sometimes think that it is the sampling distribution of means which becomes nonnormal when $\sigma_{\overline{X}}$ must be estimated from the sample. This is not so. If the assumptions of Section 14.11 are met, $\overline{X}$ will be normally distributed *regardless of sample size. However, the position of* $\overline{X}$ *is not evaluated directly; rather, it is the value of the statistic* $t = (\overline{X} - \mu)/s_{\overline{X}}$. *Although* $\overline{X}$ *is normally distributed, the resulting value of t is not, for the reason cited above.*††

17.4 Characteristics of Student's Distribution of t

What may we expect of Student's distribution of t? When samples are large, the values of $s_{\overline{X}}$ will be close to that of $\sigma_{\overline{X}}$, and t will be much like z. Its distribution

†The expression here identified as t is the same as that offered earlier as z (see Formula 14.4). It is not a true z (see footnote, Section 14.6), but its properties are so close to those of z for large samples that we chose to treat it as such. Since small samples are now at issue, the conventional symbol, t, will now be used.

‡It can be shown that the sampling distribution of $s_{\overline{X}}$ tends to be positively skewed.

††Indeed, $\overline{X}$ *must* be normally distributed for Student's distribution to be exactly applicable.

is, consequently, very nearly normal. Indeed, the recommendations of Chapters 14 and 16 that we treat t as normally distributed z were based on this fact. On the other hand, when sample size is small, the values of $s_{\bar{x}}$ will vary substantially about $\sigma_{\bar{x}}$. The distribution of t will then depart significantly from that of normally distributed z.

It is becoming clear that *Student's distribution of t is not a single distribution, but rather a family of distributions.* The exact shape of a particular member of that family depends on sample size, or, more accurately, on the number of *degrees of freedom (df)*, a quantity closely related to sample size.† When the number of degrees of freedom is infinite ($df = \infty$), the distribution of Student's t is exactly the same as that of normally distributed z. As the number of degrees of freedom decreases, the characteristics of the t distribution begin to depart from those of normally distributed z. Figure 17.1 illustrates this point. It shows the normalized z distribution, and, in contrast, Student's distribution of t for $df = 12$ and $df = 4$.

When the number of degrees of freedom is less than infinite, the theoretical distribution of t and the normal distribution of z are alike in some ways, and different in others. They are alike in that both distributions:

1. have a mean of zero
2. are symmetrical
3. are unimodal

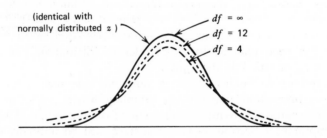

FIGURE 17.1 The Distribution of Student's t for Three Levels of Degrees of Freedom.

The two distributions differ in that the distribution of t:

1. is more *leptokurtic* than the normal distribution (a leptokurtic curve has a greater concentration of area in the center *and* in the tails than does a normal curve)
2. has a larger standard deviation (remember that $\sigma_z = 1$)
3. depends on the number of degrees of freedom

---

†For example, $df = n - 1$ for problems of inference about single means. The concept of degrees of freedom will receive more explicit treatment in Section 17.5.

The different characteristics of Student's t have an important consequence in statistical inference. For example, if we test an hypothesis at $\alpha = .05$, the critical value of z is ± 1.96 for a two-tailed test. But, the magnitude of t for which the probability is .05 of obtaining a value so deviant or more so (in either direction) is *larger* than 1.96. One can see that this will be so from study of Figure 17.1. The tails of the t distribution descend less rapidly to the horizontal axis than do those of the normal distribution, and so in the t distribution it will be necessary to go to a more extreme location to find the point beyond which .025 of the area (in one tail) falls.

How much larger t must be than z to correspond to the same infrequency of occurrence depends on sample size (or, more accurately, on the number of degrees of freedom). Table 17.1 illustrates this. It shows, for selected values of df, the critical magnitude of t corresponding to a two-tailed test conducted according to the decision criterion: $\alpha = .05$. Note that:

1. For an infinite number of degrees of freedom, the critical magnitude of t is the same as the critical magnitude of z: 1.96.
2. The smaller the number of degrees of freedom, the larger the critical magnitude of t.
3. The behavior of t is extremely similar to that of z until the number of degrees of freedom drops below 100.
4. As the number of degrees of freedom decreases, the change in Student's distribution of t, slight at first, progresses at an increasingly rapid rate.

TABLE 17.1 Magnitude of t for Which, in Student's Distribution, the Probability Is .05 of Obtaining a Value at Least as Deviant (in Either Direction).

df:	5	10	25	50	100	500	∞
$t_{.05}$:	2.571	2.228	2.060	2.008	1.984	1.965	1.960

17.5 Degrees of Freedom and Student's Distribution

Basically, the term "degrees of freedom" refers to the freedom of scores to vary. In general, the number of degrees of freedom corresponds to the number of scores which are completely free to vary. One might at first suppose that this would be the same as the number of scores in the sample (or samples), but often conditions exist which impose restrictions so that the number of degrees of freedom is less. We shall illustrate the concept of degrees of freedom in connection with the calculation of s_X.

Suppose a sample consists of three scores: 33, 35, 40. If s_X is calculated by the deviation score formula, $s_X = \sqrt{\Sigma(X - \bar{X})^2/(n - 1)}$, we begin by listing the scores, finding the mean ($\overline{X} = 36$), and forming the deviation scores by subtracting the mean from each score. This is shown below.

$$X \qquad (X - \overline{X})$$

$$33 \qquad (33 - 36) = -3 \qquad \Sigma X = 108$$

$$35 \qquad (35 - 36) = -1 \qquad \overline{X} = 36$$

$$40 \qquad (40 - 36) = +4$$

The illustration will not be completed, because we have gone far enough for the present purpose.

In figuring degrees of freedom for this problem, the value of $\overline{X}$ is considered to be fixed. The first score, 33, could have a different value. It is "free to vary." The same is true of the second score, 35. But, if any values we wish are assigned to the first two scores, we are then *not* free to specify the value of the third score. Remember that the mean of the three scores, 36, is subtracted from each score. Consequently, as soon as the values of any two scores are determined, the third score must have whatever value is required so that the total of the three scores will equal 108, the figure which, when divided by three, yields $\overline{X} = 36$. The number of degrees of freedom in this problem is, therefore, 2.

There are several points worth noting. First, in the example above, the first and second scores were said to be free to vary, the third one fixed by the "choice" exercised relative to the first two. Actually, *any* two of the three are free to vary in the manner indicated; the one that remains will be fixed.

Second, if there had been *four* scores (rather than three), any *three* of them would be free to vary. In general, for a problem of the type presented, the number of degrees of freedom will be one less than sample size; i.e., $df = n - 1$. The number of degrees of freedom is not always $n - 1$; it depends on the type of problem. This will be considered as we turn to each type of problem.

17.6 Using Student's Distribution of *t*

The theoretical distribution of t appears in Table D in the appendix. In using this table, it is important to remember that the area under a given distribution of t is taken to be 1.00, just as in the normal curve tables. The table makes no distinction between negative and positive values of t, since the area falling above a given positive value of t is the same as the area falling below the same negative value. This is illustrated in Figure 17.2.

Each row of the table specifies, according to the particular number of degrees of freedom, the value of t beyond which lies the area (in the tail of the curve) indicated at the top of the table. Characteristic use of the table may be best shown by some examples. Consider the following problem.

Problem: When $df = 20$, what value of t is so great that it will be equaled or exceeded but 5% of the time?

Solution: Consult Table D, and identify the row corresponding to $df = 20$. Then find the column corresponding to *area in one tail* = .05. At the intersection of this row and column, read the entry of $t = 1.725$. Since, in effect, we are looking for the 95th centile point of the t distribution, its value is positive: $t = +1.725$. This is illustrated in Figure 17.2.

If we had been testing the hypothesis that $\mu = 100$ against the directional alternative that $\mu > 100$, and were using the decision criterion, $\alpha = .05$, this would be the critical value of t when $df = 20$. Note that, according to the normal curve, the critical value of z would be: $z = +1.645$, a lesser value.

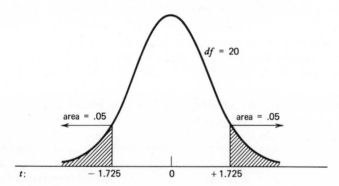

FIGURE 17.2 The Value of t, for $df = 20$, Which Corresponds to Area in Each Tail of Student's Distribution = .05.

A second example explores another problem typically useful in inference.

Problem: When $df = 20$, and a two-tailed test is conducted at $\alpha = .05$, what values of t differentiate the region of rejection from the region of acceptance?

Solution: We must identify the values of t such that the central 95% of obtained t's will be included within these limits. These are (1) the value of t below which 2.5% of t's will be located, and (2) the value of t above which 2.5% of t's will be located. The requisite magnitude of t may be read according to the heading *area in one tail* = .025. For $df = 20$, the value is: $t = \pm 2.086$. The problem is illustrated in Figure 17.3.

It should be clear that the distribution of t may be interpreted as a probability distribution, just as may be done with the normal distribution. For example, when $df = 20$, and when sampling is random, the probability of obtaining a value of t exceeding the limits ± 2.086 is .05.

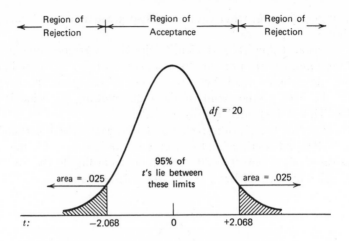

FIGURE 17.3 Student's Distribution: Values of t, for $df = 20$, between Which the Central 95% of t's Will Fall.

17.7 Application of the Distribution of t to Problems of Inference about Means

Student's distribution is applicable to the problems of testing hypotheses about single means, testing hypotheses about two means (both the dependent and the independent case), interval estimation of μ, and interval estimation of $\mu_X - \mu_Y$. In short, it is pertinent for all of the problems described in Chapter 14 and Chapter 16 in circumstances where the relevant standard error must be estimated from data contained in the sample.

The following sections of this chapter show how Student's distribution applies to these problems. The exposition is based on the assumption that the logic and procedures of Chapters 14, 15, and 16 are understood. A review of pertinent parts of those chapters may be desirable as collateral to study of the remainder of this chapter.

A distinction must be made between values of t calculated from sets of data, and the theoretical distribution of t as given in the appendix. Just as calculated values of z follow the normal distribution only under certain conditions, so calculated values of t follow Student's distribution of t only when certain assumptions are met. The assumptions for small sample procedures are essentially those for large sample procedures, except that it is not required that population variance(s) be known. One exception occurs in connection with the test of the difference between two independent means. It is discussed at the time that problem is explored (Section 17.9). The question of assumptions is given explicit attention in the closing section (Section 17.17).

17.8 Testing an Hypothesis about a Single Mean

Suppose the claim has been made that the height of adult males is greater than it used to be, and that we wish to test this hypothesis. From a nationwide survey made 20 years ago, it is learned that the mean height of 21 year old males was, at that time, 69.5 inches.† To study the question, 25 males of the same age are selected at random, and measurements of height obtained. The research question is then translated into a statistical hypothesis, and the decision made to test the hypothesis at the 5% significance level:

$$H_0: \mu = 69.5$$
$$\alpha = .05$$
$$H_A: \mu > 69.5$$

We find the mean and standard deviation of the 25 measurements of stature. The standard error of the mean is also required, and, lacking the standard deviation of the population of scores, it is estimated according to Formula 14.2. The sample data, together with calculation of the standard error of the mean, are shown below:

$$\overline{X} = 70.4$$

$$s_X = 3.15 \qquad s_{\overline{X}} = \frac{s_X}{\sqrt{n}} = \frac{3.15}{\sqrt{25}} = .63$$

$$n = 25$$

To test the hypothesis, we calculate t:

$$t = \frac{\overline{X} - \mu}{s_{\overline{X}}} = \frac{70.4 - 69.5}{.63} = +1.43$$

Since $s_{\overline{X}}$, the estimate of the standard error of the mean, was based on 25 observations, the number of degrees of freedom associated with t is: $df = n - 1 = 24$.

The distribution of t for 24 degrees of freedom is shown in Figure 17.4. Because the alternative hypothesis specifies that μ is greater than 69.5, the region of rejection must be placed in the right tail of the distribution. According to the decision criterion adopted, H_0 should be rejected if the obtained sample mean leads to a value of t so deviant (and in the *particular* direction) that the probability of its occurrence, if the hypothesis were true, would be .05 or less. The critical value of t is therefore that which divides the upper 5% of the t distribution from the remainder. From Table D in the appendix, we learn that, for 24 degrees of freedom, the critical value is: $t = +1.711$. Figure 17.4 shows the critical value of t, the region of rejection thereby established, and the location of the obtained value of t. Since the sample mean of 70.4 was not sufficiently discrepant to lead to a t of $+1.711$ or higher, our decision must be to accept H_0.

†The data of this example, like others in this book, are hypothetical.

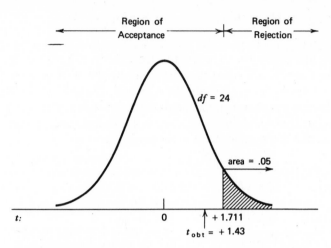

FIGURE 17.4 Testing an Hypothesis about μ againsт a Directional Alternative: $\alpha = .05$.

In the example worked above, it was assumed that s_X had already been calculated. When the problem is begun with only the raw scores at hand, s_X must be found; the method of its calculation is discussed in Section 14.5.

17.9 Testing an Hypothesis about the Difference between Two Independent Means

To test the difference between two independent means, the large sample procedure presented in Section 16.6 called for calculation of z according to the following formula:

$$z = \frac{(\overline{X} - \overline{Y}) - (\mu_X - \mu_Y)_{\text{hyp}}}{s_{\overline{X} - \overline{Y}}}$$

where:

$$s_{\overline{X} - \overline{Y}} = \sqrt{s_{\overline{X}}^2 + s_{\overline{Y}}^2}$$

When sample size is relatively large, z is very nearly normally distributed. As sample size decreases, its distribution departs from the normal, but, unfortunately, *neither is it distributed exactly as Student's t.*

An eminent British statistician, the late Sir Ronald A. Fisher, showed that a slightly different approach in figuring the standard error of the difference between two means, $s_{\overline{X} - \overline{Y}}$, results in a statistic which *is* distributed as Student's t. To understand Fisher's approach to this problem, it will be helpful to rewrite the formula for $s_{\overline{X} - \overline{Y}}$. According to Formula 14.2, s_X^2/n may be substituted for $s_{\overline{X}}^2$, and s_Y^2/n for $s_{\overline{Y}}^2$.† The result is given as Formula 17.2.

†Recall that s_X^2 and s_Y^2 are unbiased estimates of, respectively, σ_X^2 and σ_Y^2 (see Section 15.8).

Estimate of the Standard Error
of the Difference between $s_{\bar{X}-\bar{Y}} = \sqrt{\dfrac{s_X^2}{n_X} + \dfrac{s_Y^2}{n_Y}}$ (17.2)
Two Independent Means

Note, in the formula above, that *each* sample is allowed to estimate its *own* population variance. Thus, s_X^2 estimates σ_X^2, and s_Y^2 estimates σ_Y^2. This is quite correct if σ_X^2 and σ_Y^2 may have different values.

The change that Fisher introduced was, in effect, to assume that $\sigma_X^2 = \sigma_Y^2$. This is often called the *assumption of homogeneity of variance*. Now *if the two population variances are equal, both s_X^2 and s_Y^2 are estimates of the same population variance*. Rather than make two separate estimates, each based on a small sample, it is preferable to combine the information from both samples, and make a single, pooled estimate of *the* population variance. In general, the "best estimate" of a population variance (see Section 15.8) is made by:

$$\sum x^2/(n-1)$$

where: x is the deviation of each score from the mean of that set of scores, and $n-1$ is the number of degrees of freedom associated with $\sum x^2$. A pooled estimate, made from the two samples, can be made by pooling the sums of squares of deviation scores from each sample and dividing by the total number of degrees of freedom associated with the pooled sum of squares. Thus, s_p^2 is:

Estimate of σ^2 Made by Pooling $s_p^2 = \dfrac{\sum x^2 + \sum y^2}{(n_X - 1) + (n_Y - 1)}$ (17.3)
Information from Two Samples

This quantity may be substituted for s_X^2 *and* for s_Y^2 in Formula 17.2. Thus:

$$s_{\bar{X}-\bar{Y}} = \sqrt{\dfrac{s_p^2}{n_X} + \dfrac{s_p^2}{n_Y}}$$

Factoring s_p^2, the formula may be rewritten:

$$s_{\bar{X}-\bar{Y}} = \sqrt{s_p^2\left(\dfrac{1}{n_X} + \dfrac{1}{n_Y}\right)}$$

If the expression for s_p^2 given by Formula 17.3 is substituted in this formula, we have:

Estimate of Standard Error of the Difference between
Two Independent Means when $\sigma_X^2 = \sigma_Y^2$

$$s_{\bar{X}-\bar{Y}} = \sqrt{\dfrac{\sum x^2 + \sum y^2}{(n_X - 1) + (n_Y - 1)}\left(\dfrac{1}{n_X} + \dfrac{1}{n_Y}\right)}$$ (17.4)

When t is calculated according to the following formula, *and $s_{\bar{X}-\bar{Y}}$ is calculated* *according to Formula 17.4, t will be distributed according to Student's distribution:*

t Required for Testing Hypotheses about the Difference between Two Means

$$t = \frac{(\bar{X} - \bar{Y}) - (\mu_X - \mu_Y)_{\text{hyp}}}{s_{\bar{X} - \bar{Y}}} \tag{17.5}$$

17.10 Finding Σx^2: A Computational Note

Formula 17.4 requires Σx^2, a quantity most awkward to compute if attempted by direct calculation of deviation scores. There are roundabout routes which will ease the labor of computation.

First, the values of Σx^2 and Σy^2 may be found directly from their raw score equivalents, as given by Formula 6.5:

$$\Sigma x^2 = \Sigma X^2 - \frac{(\Sigma X)^2}{n} \quad \text{and} \quad \Sigma y^2 = \Sigma Y^2 - \frac{(\Sigma Y)^2}{n}$$

Examples of the use of these computational procedures appear in the next section.

It may be that we will want the values of the two sample standard deviations, S_X and S_Y, or the two estimates of the population standard deviations, s_X and s_Y. These values are useful to know, since inspection of them offers an eye-check on the assumption of homogeneity of variance. If knowledge of either of these two quantities is desired, and Σx^2 and Σy^2 have been computed as above, the standard deviations may be found from the deviation score formulas (Formula 6.4*b* and Formula 14.1): $S_X = \sqrt{\Sigma x^2/n}$ and $S_Y = \sqrt{\Sigma y^2/n}$, or $s_X = \sqrt{\Sigma x^2/(n-1)}$ and $s_Y = \sqrt{\Sigma y^2/(n-1)}$.

A second way to find Σx^2 and Σy^2 begins by calculating the two sample standard deviations, S_X and S_Y, by any of the methods of Chapter 6. Then, according to Formula 6.3*b*, $S_X{}^2 = \Sigma x^2/n$, and it follows that:

$$\Sigma x^2 = nS_X{}^2 \quad \text{and} \quad \Sigma y^2 = nS_Y{}^2$$

Thus the sum of the squares of the deviation scores can be found without determining each deviation score individually.†

Third, it may be that s_X and s_Y are known. Because $s_X{}^2 = \Sigma x^2/(n-1)$, it follows that:

$$\Sigma x^2 = (n-1)s_X{}^2 \quad \text{and} \quad \Sigma y^2 = (n-1)s_Y{}^2$$

17.11 Testing Hypotheses about Two Independent Means: Examples

In learning foreign language vocabulary, a 2-hour study period may be arranged as one continuous session, or as four half-hour sessions with rest periods between

---

†If S has been calculated, but s is desired, it may be found by the relationship: $s = S\sqrt{n/(n-1)}$.

sessions. Is there any difference between the two methods of study in the amount learned? We shall suppose that an appropriate experiment has been designed to test this question, that two groups of subjects have been randomly and independently selected, and that one group learned according to the "massed practice" study condition and the other according to the "spaced practice" condition. The (hypothetical) data for the two samples are given below:

massed practice	spaced practice
$\bar{X} = 75.0$	$\bar{Y} = 86.0$
$s_X = 12.0$	$s_Y = 10.0$
$n_X = 15$	$n_Y = 13$

We shall test the hypothesis of no difference between the two population means against a nondirectional alternative, at the 5% significance level:

$$H_0: \quad \mu_X - \mu_Y = 0$$
$$\alpha = .05$$
$$H_A: \quad \mu_X - \mu_Y \neq 0$$

To calculate t, we need Σx^2 and Σy^2. These may be found by a method described in the previous section:

$$\Sigma x^2 = (n_X - 1)s_X{}^2 \qquad \Sigma y^2 = (n_Y - 1)s_Y{}^2$$
$$= (14)(12.0)^2 \qquad = (12)(10.0)^2$$
$$= 2016 \qquad = 1200$$

Then, t is calculated according to Formula 17.5:

$$t = \frac{(\bar{X} - \bar{Y}) - (\mu_X - \mu_Y)_{\text{hyp}}}{\sqrt{\dfrac{\Sigma x^2 + \Sigma y^2}{(n_X - 1) + (n_Y - 1)}\left(\dfrac{1}{n_X} + \dfrac{1}{n_Y}\right)}}$$

$$= \frac{(75.0 - 86.0) - 0}{\sqrt{\dfrac{2016 + 1200}{(15 - 1) + (13 - 1)}\left(\dfrac{1}{15} + \dfrac{1}{13}\right)}} = -2.61$$

In calculating t, the denominator, $s_{\bar{X}-\bar{Y}}$, is based on s^2_{pooled}. Since this quantity has associated with it $(n_X - 1) + (n_Y - 1)$ degrees of freedom, the calculated value of t must be evaluated relative to the distribution of t corresponding to $(15 - 1) + (13 - 1) = 26$ degrees of freedom. The position of the calculated value of t relative to the sampling distribution of this statistic is shown in Figure 17.5. Since $\alpha = .05$ and the test is two tailed, the critical values of t, for $df = 26$, are ± 2.056. The obtained t exceeds these limits, so the decision is to reject H_0. There is, apparently, a real difference between performance under the two conditions of practice.

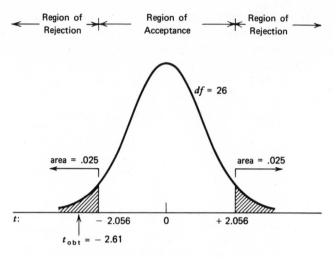

FIGURE 17.5 Testing an Hypothesis about the Difference between Two Means against a Nondirectional Alternative: $\alpha = .05$.

A second example illustrates conduct of the test beginning with the raw scores of the two samples. A psychologist is interested in the effect of social pressure. He selects two groups of subjects at random. Each subject is asked to estimate by eye the length of a stick. In one group, the subject is placed in the presence of four other persons who, unknown to him, have been instructed to give estimates which are too large. Each of these persons gives his estimate orally to the experimenter before the subject is asked for his estimate. In the other group, the same procedure is employed, except that the four persons present (in addition to the subject) are instructed to make honest estimates. Estimates (in inches) made by each subject are given in Table 17.2.

The hypothesis to be tested is:

$$H_0: \quad \mu_X - \mu_Y = 0$$
$$\alpha = .01$$
$$H_A: \quad \mu_X - \mu_Y \neq 0$$

We shall assume that the researcher has selected $\alpha = .01$ as the decision criterion. To conduct the test, the two sample means and the values of Σx^2 and Σy^2 are required. These calculations may be made by raw score procedures; they are illustrated in Table 17.2. The remaining steps in conducting the test are likewise shown in this table. Apparently, social pressure makes a difference in this study.

17.12 Some Comments on the Assumption of Homogeneity of of Variance

In testing hypotheses about the difference between two *independent* means, the assumption of homogeneity of variance is, in principle, required any time the

TABLE 17.2 Small Sample Test of the Difference between Two Independent Means.

Estimates made in unbiased environment		Estimates made in biased environment	
X	X^2	Y	Y^2
38	1444	47	2209
35	1225	45	2025
37	1369	42	1764
40	1600	45	2025
45	2025	47	2209
34	1156	40	1600
40	1600	43	1849
36	1296	45	2025
43	1849	40	1600
41	1681	48	2304
$\Sigma X = 389$	$\Sigma X^2 = 15245$	$\Sigma Y = 442$	$\Sigma Y^2 = 19610$

$$\bar{X} = \frac{389}{10} = 38.9 \qquad\qquad \bar{Y} = \frac{442}{10} = 44.2$$

$$\Sigma x^2 = \Sigma X^2 - \frac{(\Sigma X)^2}{n} = 15245 - \frac{(389)^2}{10} = 113$$

$$\Sigma y^2 = \Sigma Y^2 - \frac{(\Sigma Y)^2}{n} = 19610 - \frac{(442)^2}{10} = 74$$

$$t = \frac{(\bar{X} - \bar{Y}) - (\mu_X - \mu_Y)_{\text{hyp}}}{\sqrt{\frac{\Sigma x^2 + \Sigma y^2}{(n_X - 1) + (n_Y - 1)}\left(\frac{1}{n_X} + \frac{1}{n_Y}\right)}}$$

$$= \frac{(38.9 - 44.2) - 0}{\sqrt{\frac{113 + 74}{(10 - 1) + (10 - 1)}\left(\frac{1}{10} + \frac{1}{10}\right)}}$$

$$= -3.68$$

$$df = (10 - 1) + (10 - 1) = 18$$

$$t_{\text{crit}} = \pm 2.878 \qquad \textbf{Decision:} \quad \text{Reject } H_0$$

standard errors cannot be obtained from population parameters, but must be estimated from the samples. Of course, violation of this assumption might be expected to make more difference when the difference between σ_X^2 and σ_Y^2 is large than when it is small. Fortunately, there is help from several quarters.

First, practical experience suggests that the assumption of homogeneity of variance appears to be reasonably satisfied in many cases. It is relatively rare that a striking difference in variance occurs. Second, violation of the assumption makes less disturbance when samples are large than when they are small. As a rule of thumb, it might be hazarded that moderate departure from homogeneity of variance will probably have little effect when each sample consists of 20 or more observations.

Finally, the problem created by heterogeneity of variance is minimized when the two samples are chosen to be of equal size. Since there are other benefits from using equal sample size (see Section 16.8), this procedure is recommended. If sample size is small and it is suspected that the assumption of homogeneity of variance may not be satisfied, it is possible to test the significance of the difference between the two variance estimates ($s_X{}^2$ and $s_Y{}^2$). Other volumes present the details of conducting such a test, and describe the manner of conducting a proper test of the difference between two means when the assumption of homogeneity of variance is not justified.† It should be noted that tests of homogeneity of variance are not always entirely satisfactory in small sample situations. To combat the influence of nonhomogeneity of variance, the best bet is to select samples of equal (or approximately equal) size, and the larger the better.

17.13 Testing an Hypothesis about Two Dependent Means

To test an hypothesis about the difference between two related means, t is calculated as:

$$t = \frac{(\overline{X} - \overline{Y}) - (\mu_X - \mu_Y)_{\text{hyp}}}{s_{\overline{X} - \overline{Y}}}$$

This is Formula 17.5, the same basic formula used for the test of two unrelated means. However, *for the test between dependent means, a different formula must be used to find $s_{\overline{X} - \overline{Y}}$, one which takes account of the correlation between the pairs of scores.* The appropriate formula is that first presented in Section 16.5 (Formula 16.3):

$$s_{\overline{X} - \overline{Y}} = \sqrt{s_{\overline{X}}{}^2 + s_{\overline{Y}}{}^2 - 2r_{XY}s_{\overline{X}}s_{\overline{Y}}}$$

Note that calculation of t, described above, is exactly the same as the calculation of z required for the large sample test of two related means. Because it is the same, an adequate account of the procedure may be found in Section 16.10 (see especially Table 16.4); it will not be repeated here.

An alternative (and equivalent) method is described in Section 16.11. This

†See, for example: Allen L. Edwards, *Experimental Design in Psychological Research*, 3rd ed., Holt, Rinehart and Winston, Inc., New York, 1968, pp. 99–104.

method, sometimes computationally advantageous, yields the same value of z (and hence, t) as the first method. To be explicit, if this method is adopted, t is calculated as:

$$t = \frac{\bar{D} - \mu_{D\,(hyp)}}{s_{\bar{D}}}$$

Details of the method are found in Section 16.11, and the steps of calculation are illustrated in Table 16.5.

Once t is obtained, it should be evaluated with $df = n - 1$, where n is the number of *pairs* of scores. Note that this is but half of the $(n_X - 1) + (n_Y - 1)$ degrees of freedom which would obtain if the same study were conducted using independent samples. Why fewer degrees of freedom for dependent samples?

When samples are independent, the score recorded for the first subject in the first group and for the first subject in the second group are completely unrelated. But, when subjects are matched (or when the same subjects are used under both treatment conditions), this is not so. If a subject does very well as compared with others under one condition, his matched counterpart will tend to do well as compared with others under the other condition, if matching has been on a relevant variable. For example, suppose the study compares two methods of learning and pairs of subjects have been formed on the basis of level of intelligence. We may expect that a pair of bright subjects will both tend to perform relatively well, each in his own group. In short, performance of one "member" of the pair is *not* independent of that of the other "member." Thus, when the score of one member of the pair is specified, that of the other is not completely "free to vary." Consequently, only one degree of freedom can be ascribed to each *pair* of scores. Since there are n pairs of scores, there will be $n - 1$ degrees of freedom.

The loss of degrees of freedom relative to the test of two independent means represents the price to be paid for error in estimating ρ_{XY}. When samples are independent, we *know* that ρ_{XY} is zero; the formula for the standard error reflects this knowledge. The dependent samples design ought not to be considered unless pairing of measures produces a substantial correlation. When the correlation is reasonably substantial, the resulting reduction in error will more than make up for the error introduced in estimating ρ_{XY}. (See Sections 16.12 and 16.13 for further comment on this problem, and for discussion of the advantages and disadvantages of the dependent samples design.)

Evaluation of an obtained t may be illustrated with reference to the example given in Table 16.4, which appears in Section 16.10. In that example, a two-tailed test is to be conducted at the 5% level of significance. The obtained value of t is $+.65$ (the value given there as z). Since there are ten pairs of scores, $df = 9$, and the critical values of t are ± 2.262. Figure 17.6 shows the relation of the obtained t to the sampling distribution of t. The obtained t falls within the critical limits, and H_0 must be accepted.

The small sample test of the difference between two *independent* means

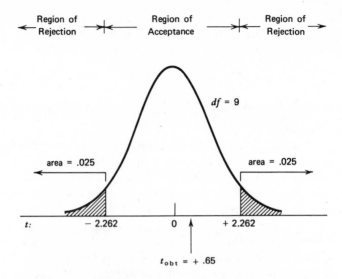

FIGURE 17.6 Testing an Hypothesis about the Difference between Two Means against a Nondirectional Alternative: $\alpha = .05$.

required the assumption of homogeneity of variance. It should be noted that this assumption is *not* required for the small sample test of the difference between two *dependent* means.

17.14 Interval Estimates of μ

The logic of constructing an interval estimate of the location of μ has been discussed in detail in Section 14.10. The procedures described there are suited to large sample situations. Those described here are the correct ones when $\sigma_{\overline{X}}$ is unknown, and the estimate, $s_{\overline{X}}$, must be substituted. The manner of constructing an interval estimate according to small sample procedures is identical with that described in Section 14.10, except that the appropriate value of t is substituted for z.

To be specific, the upper and lower limits may be found according to the desired confidence coefficient (C) by calculating:

Rule for Constructing an $$\overline{X} \pm t_p s_{\overline{X}} \qquad\qquad (17.6)$$
Interval Estimate of μ

where:
$\overline{X}$ is the sample mean
$s_{\overline{X}}$ is the estimate of the standard error of the mean

t_p is the magnitude of t for which the probability is p of obtaining a value so deviant or more so (in either direction)

p is $1 - C$

t_p must be identified according to $df = n - 1$, the number of degrees of freedom associated with s_X.

As an example, suppose it is desired to estimate the location of μ_X according to the 95% level of confidence when the sample data are:

$$\overline{X} = 85.0, \quad s_X = 15.0, \quad n = 25$$

We first calculate the estimated standard error of the mean.†

$$s_{\overline{X}} = \frac{s_X}{\sqrt{n}} = \frac{15.0}{\sqrt{25}} = 3.00$$

The number of degrees of freedom associated with s_X is $n - 1$, or 24 for the present problem. From Table D in the appendix, the value of t so great that the probability is .05 of equalling or exceeding its magnitude is:

$$t_p = 2.064$$

The limits are, therefore:

$$\overline{X} \pm t_{.05}s_{\overline{X}}$$

$$85.0 \pm (2.064)(3.00)$$

$$78.81 \quad \text{to} \quad 91.19$$

$$\text{(Lower Limit)} \quad \text{(Upper Limit)}$$

Stated formally:

$$C(78.81 \leq \mu_X \leq 91.19) = .95$$

In the problem above, the confidence coefficient is .95. If, instead, we desire an interval according to $C = .99$, the appropriate value of t for $df = 24$ is: $t_{.01} = 2.797$.

Once again, it is important to remember that μ_X, though unknown, is fixed. It is the *interval*, as constructed from sample data, which is the random variable, not μ. Figure 17.7 shows some of the intervals which might result if samples were selected at random and intervals constructed about the sample means by the procedures described above. We may expect that 95% of such estimates will include μ within their range when t_p is selected to agree with $C = .95$.

It is interesting to compare the intervals shown in Figure 17.7 with those

---

†If s_X is not already available, it (or, what is more important, $s_{\overline{X}}$) may be found by several means. (See Sections 14.4 and 14.5.)

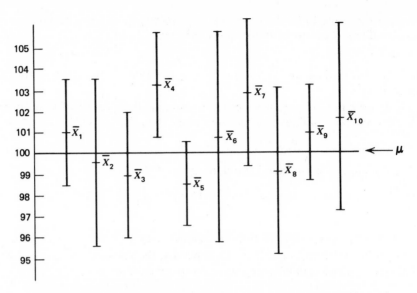

FIGURE 17.7 Interval Estimates of μ Constructed from Means of Several Random Samples: σ_X Unknown.

shown in Figure 14.6. In the earlier illustration, intervals were constructed according to the rule: $\overline{X} \pm z_p \sigma_{\overline{X}}$. As one moves from sample to sample (drawn at random from the same population), $\overline{X}$ varies, but z and $\sigma_{\overline{X}}$ do not. Consequently, intervals made from different samples *all have the same width*, although their location differs. However, the intervals shown in Figure 17.7 are derived from the rule: $\overline{X} \pm t_p s_{\overline{X}}$. As we move from sample to sample, the estimate, $s_{\overline{X}}$, varies, as well as $\overline{X}$. *This results in intervals of different width.* Nevertheless, if both rules are in accord with $C = .95$ and if the assumptions appropriate to each have been met, it is true for each that the probability is .95 that an interval constructed according to the rule will include μ.

17.15 Interval Estimates of $\mu_X - \mu_Y$

The story of small sample estimates of the difference between two population means closely parallels that of estimates similarly made of a single population mean. In short, the rules earlier presented for large samples are followed, except for the substitution of t for z. (See Section 16.14 for discussion of the logic of the process of estimation and for description of the large sample approach.) On the assumption that matters discussed in that section are understood, an example should suffice to clarify the procedure.

Suppose it is desired to estimate $\mu_X - \mu_Y$, the difference between two population means, according to the 99% level of confidence. We shall assume that the two samples are independent, and that the following information is available:

$$\bar{X} = 87.0 \qquad \bar{Y} = 92.0$$

$$s_X = 10.0 \qquad s_Y = 12.0$$

$$n_X = 13 \qquad n_Y = 15$$

An estimate can be made, according to the desired confidence coefficient (C) by the rule of Formula 17.7:

Rule for Constructing an
Interval Estimate of $\mu_X - \mu_Y$ $\qquad (\bar{X} - \bar{Y}) \pm t_p s_{\bar{X} - \bar{Y}}$ $\qquad\qquad$ (17.7)

where:
$(\bar{X} - \bar{Y})$ is the difference between the two sample means
$s_{\bar{X} - \bar{Y}}$ is the estimate of the standard error of the difference
between two means
t_p is the magnitude of t for which the probability is p of
obtaining a value so deviant or more so (in either direction)
p is $1 - C$

For independent samples, $df = (n_X - 1) + (n_Y - 1)$, and t_p must be determined accordingly. In the present problem, $df = 26$, and the critical value of t is:

$$t_{.01} = 2.779$$

The standard error of the difference between the means is given by Formula 17.4.

$$s_{\bar{X} - \bar{Y}} = \sqrt{\frac{\sum x^2 + \sum y^2}{(n_X - 1) + (n_Y - 1)} \left(\frac{1}{n_X} + \frac{1}{n_Y} \right)}$$

This quantity is found by methods described earlier (see Sections 17.10 and 17.11). Following those methods, we find that $s_{\bar{X} - \bar{Y}} = 4.21$.

The 99% confidence interval is therefore constructed as follows:

$$(\bar{X} - \bar{Y}) \pm t_{.01} s_{\bar{X} - \bar{Y}}$$

$$(87.0 - 92.0) \pm (2.779)(4.21)$$

$$-5 \pm 11.70$$

$$-16.70 \quad \text{to} \quad +6.70$$

$$\text{(Lower Limit)} \quad \text{(Upper Limit)}$$

Formally, this is expressed as:

$$C(-16.70 \leq (\mu_X - \mu_Y) \leq 6.70) = .99$$

This example illustrated procedures appropriate to *independent* samples. When samples are *dependent*, the procedure is the same except for calculation of $s_{\overline{X}-\overline{Y}}$. For dependent samples, Formula 16.3 should be used. For convenient reference, it is reproduced below.

$$s_{\overline{X}-\overline{Y}} = \sqrt{s_{\overline{X}}^2 + s_{\overline{Y}}^2 - 2r_{XY}s_{\overline{X}}s_{\overline{Y}}}$$

The method of its calculation is described in Section 16.10 (see especially Table 16.4). When samples are dependent, $df = n - 1$, where n is the number of *pairs* of scores (see Section 17.13). The value of t_p should be identified accordingly.

17.16 Estimating Sample Size in Problems of Inference about Means

It is possible to select sample size such that there is a known probability that the population parameters (μ or $\mu_X - \mu_Y$) will be no farther away from their sample values than a specified amount (see Sections 19.12 and 19.13 for the procedure). Determination of appropriate sample size for testing hypotheses about single means and about the difference between two means may be made by methods described in Section 19.10. These procedures (for testing hypotheses) are based on the concept of achieving a given protection level against committing Type I and Type II errors (see Section 15.7).

17.17 Assumptions Associated with the Small Sample Approach to Problems of Inference about Means

With but one exception, all of the assumptions required for the large sample approach to inference about means are also required for the small sample procedures described in this chapter. This is true for inference about single means and about two means, and applies both to interval estimation and tests of hypotheses. Attention is therefore especially invited to the earlier, detailed discussions of these assumptions. These may be found in Section 14.11 (inference about single means), and in Sections 16.13 and 16.15 (inference about two means).

The single exception applies to the calculation of the relevant standard errors. To be strictly correct, the "large sample approach" requires that the standard errors be determined from population parameters. As we have seen, when parameters are known this approach is exactly correct *irrespective* of sample size. The procedures of the present chapter are correct when all other assumptions are met, but when the standard errors have been obtained from sample estimates of the population parameters.†

---

†One *additional* assumption is required for the small sample test of two independent means: homogeneity of variance (see Section 17.9).

One point deserves special mention. A requirement, as you will remember, is that the sampling distribution of means, or of differences between two means, follows the normal distribution.† Strictly speaking, the sampling distribution will be normal only when the distribution of the population of scores is also normal. However, according to the Central Limit Theorem, the sampling distribution of means tends toward normality even when the population of scores in not normally distributed (see Section 13.13). *The strength of this tendency toward normality is pronounced when samples are large, but less so when samples are small.*

Now the Central Limit Theorem, *only*, offers aid in this problem. The small sample procedures here described have no remedial effect; they do not make allowance for nonnormality in the population of scores. Since the effect of the Central Limit Theorem is weakest when samples are small, it is particularly important to inquire as to the shape of the population (or populations) of scores when working with small samples.

Fortunately, the normalizing effect of the Central Limit Theorem is rather pronounced unless sample size is quite small indeed. For example, a moderate degree of skewness in the population can probably be tolerated if sample size is, say, 20 or more. Indeed, empirical investigations have shown that the *t* test gives remarkably good results when applied in situations characterized by nonnormality, and, in the case of independent means, characterized by nonhomogeneity of variance.‡

When serious question still exists about the propriety of conducting tests about means because of nonnormality of the parent population, certain of the so-called "nonparametric" statistical tests may be considered. These techniques are, in some circumstances, less responsive to the totality of information conveyed by the data, but they are free of assumptions about the specific shape of the distribution of the population of scores. Some of these techniques are described in Chapter 21. A more extended collection is readily available elsewhere.††

PROBLEMS AND EXERCISES

Identify:

Student

Student's distribution

leptokurtic distribution

degrees of freedom

Fisher

homogeneity of variance

s^2_{pooled}

†Remember that it is the distribution of *t* which is leptokurtic, not the sampling distribution of means, or of differences between means (see Section 17.3).

‡See, for example: C. A. Boneau, "The Effects of Violations of Assumptions Underlying the *t* Test," *Psychological Bulletin*, **57**, 49–64 (1960).

††For example, see: W. L. Hays, *Statistics for Psychologists*, Holt, Rinehart, and Winston, New York, 1963, Chapter 18. S. Siegel, *Nonparametric Methods for the Behavioral Sciences*, McGraw-Hill Book Company, New York, 1956.

1. For a sample of three scores, the quantity $\Sigma(X - \bar{X})^2$ has associated with it 2 degrees of freedom. For the same sample, the quantity $\Sigma(X - \mu)^2$ is characterized by 3 degrees of freedom. Explain.

2. From Table D in the appendix, identify the value of t which, for 15 degrees of freedom, (a) is so high that only 1% of t's would be higher, (b) is so low that only 10% of t's would be lower.

3. From Table D, identify the centrally located limits, for 8 degrees of freedom, which would include (a) 50% of t's, (b) 90% of t's, (c) 95% of t's, (d) 99% of t's.

4. From Table D, and for 25 degrees of freedom, what proportion of t's would be (a) less than $t = -1.316$? (b) less than $t = +1.316$? (c) between $t = -2.060$ and $t = +2.060$? (d) between $t = -1.708$ and $t = +2.060$?

5. We adopt $\alpha = .05$ and test the hypothesis that $\mu = 50$ according to the small sample approach. What conclusion should we draw if (a) $n = 10$, $t_{calcd} = +2.10$ and $H_A: \mu \neq 50$? (b) $n = 20$, $t_{calcd} = +2.10$ and $H_A: \mu \neq 50$? (c) $n = 10$, $t_{calcd} = +2.10$ and $H_A: \mu > 50$? Show the critical value of t for each problem.

6. Given the following data: $\bar{X} = 50.0$, $s_X = 12.0$, $n = 16$. Test, using $\alpha = .05$, (a) $H_0: \mu = 44.0$ versus $H_A: \mu \neq 44.0$ (b) $H_0: \mu = 55.0$ versus $H_A: \mu < 55.0$. Show the critical value of t for each problem.

7. Given the following scores: 2, 4, 4, 7, 8. (a) Calculate s_X by the raw score formula (see Section 14.5). (b) Calculate t required to test $H_0: \mu = 8.0$ versus $H_A: \mu \neq 8.0$. (c) Evaluate t for $\alpha = .05$ and state your conclusions. (d) Evaluate t for $\alpha = .01$ and state your conclusions.

8. Given the following data from two independent samples: $\bar{X} = 82.0$, $\Sigma x^2 = 120.0$, $n_X = 11$; $\bar{Y} = 88.0$, $\Sigma y^2 = 220.0$, $n_Y = 21$; (a) Calculate $s_{\bar{X}-\bar{Y}}$ according to Formula 17.4. (b) Test the hypothesis of no difference between the two population means against a nondirectional alternative using $\alpha = .05$.

9. Do Problem 6 of Chapter 16 by the method of the present chapter.

10. Do Problem 7 of Chapter 16 by the method of the present chapter.

11. Given the following data from two dependent samples: $\bar{X} = 40.0$, $s_X = 8.0$, $\bar{Y} = 36.0$, $s_Y = 12.0$, $n = 16$, $r = +.60$. (a) State formally the hypotheses necessary to conduct a nondirectional test of no difference between the two population means. (b) Calculate $s_{\bar{X}-\bar{Y}}$. (c) Complete the test at the .05 and .01 levels of significance, and state your conclusions.

12. Do Problem 9 of Chapter 16 by the method of the present chapter.

13. Given: independent samples, and $s_X = s_Y = 10$. (a) Calculate $s_{\bar{X}-\bar{Y}}$ from Formula 17.2; assume $n_X = n_Y = 15$. (b) Calculate $s_{\bar{X}-\bar{Y}}$ from Formula 17.2; assume $n_X = 20$ and $n_Y = 10$. (c) Compare the two values of $s_{\bar{X}-\bar{Y}}$. What principle does this outcome illustrate?

14. For the data of Problem 6, construct an interval estimate of μ according to: (a) $C = .95$ (b) $C = .99$ (c) $C = .50$.

15. Do what is required in Problem 14, but use the data of Problem 7.

16. For the data of Problem 8, construct an interval estimate of $\mu_X - \mu_Y$ according to: (a) $C = .95$ (b) $C = .99$ (c) $C = .50$.

17. Do what is required in Problem 16, but use the data of Problem 6 in Chapter 16.

18. For the data of Problem 11, construct an interval estimate of $\mu_X - \mu_Y$ according to: (a) $C = .95$ (b) $C = .99$ (c) $C = .90$.

19. Do what is required in Problem 18, but use the data of Problem 9 in Chapter 16.

18

Inference about Pearson Correlation Coefficients

18.1 Introduction

The Pearsonian correlation coefficient (see Chapter 9), like other statistics, varies from sample to sample under the influence of random sampling variation. In most practical situations, we have knowledge only of the sample coefficient, but we want to know the state of affairs in the population. The two basic techniques of statistical inference, hypothesis testing and estimation, are therefore frequently pertinent to inquiries concerning degree of relationship as expressed by Pearson r.

In this chapter, we will consider procedures for inference about single coefficients and about the difference between two coefficients. An understanding of the basics of inference, such as may be found in Chapters 13, 14, and 15, is assumed. In addition, some of the procedures require knowledge of the distribution of Student's t. The characteristics of this distribution were presented in Chapter 17.

18.2 The Random Sampling Distribution of r

Consider a population of pairs of scores (X and Y) which form a bivariate distribution. The Pearsonian correlation coefficient, calculated from the complete set of paired scores, is ρ_{XY}. When the coefficient is calculated from a sample, it is r_{XY}. If we draw a sample of given size at random from the population, calculate r, return the sample to the population, and repeat this operation indefinitely, the multitude of sample r's will form the *random sampling distribution of r* for samples of the particular size. The mean of this sampling distribution is approximately ρ, and the standard deviation is $\sigma_r = (1 - \rho^2)/\sqrt{n - 1}$. As we might expect (and can see from this formula), *the values of r will vary less from sample to sample when sample size is large.* Something that might not be anticipated is also apparent on study of the formula: *The values of r will vary less from sample to sample when the true correlation, ρ, is high than when it is low.*

If the sample values of r formed a normal distribution, we could proceed to solve problems of inference by methods already familiar (see Chapter 14). *Unfortunately, the sampling distribution of r is not normally distributed.* When $\rho = 0$, the sampling distribution of r is symmetrical and nearly normal. But, when ρ has a value other than zero, the sampling distribution is skewed. In fact, the larger the value of ρ (either positively or negatively), the greater the skewness. Figure 18.1 shows the sampling distribution for $\rho = -.8$, 0, and $+.8$ when $n = 8$. It is not difficult to understand why the distribution is skewed when the value of r is high. When $\rho = +.8$, for example, fluctuations of random sampling might yield a sample coefficient as much as .2 point higher ($r = +1.0$), but it could be substantially lower than .2 point below $r = +.8$. Indeed, the lower absolute limit is -1.0.

The degree of skewness of the sampling distribution of r is also a function of sample size. When $\rho \neq 0$, the smaller the size of the sample, the greater the skewness of the sampling distribution.

Because the distribution of sample r's is not normal, alternative solutions must be sought to provide a practical frame for inference. For some problems, the t distribution affords an appropriate model. For others, transformation of r

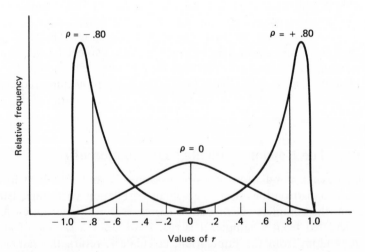

FIGURE 18.1 The Random Sampling Distribution of r for Three Values of $\rho: n = 8$.

to a variable which *is* (approximately) normally distributed offers the best solution.

18.3 Testing the Hypothesis That $\rho = 0$

Without doubt, the most frequent question of inference about problems of association is whether there is any relationship at all between two variables. For example, if we are developing a test with the hope of predicting success in the job of insurance salesman, the primary question is whether the test has *any* relationship to a measure of job success. If, among a sample of salesmen, $r = +.30$ between test performance and job performance rating, it may still be that the true correlation (ρ) is zero, and that this value of r has occurred simply as a matter of random sampling variation. To answer this question, we test the hypothesis that $\rho = 0$ against the alternative that it is not.

The late Sir Ronald A. Fisher showed that when $\rho = 0$, the expression given in Formula 18.1 is distributed as Student's t with $n - 2$ degrees of freedom:†

$$t\ Required\ for\ Testing\ the \qquad t = \frac{r}{\sqrt{(1 - r^2)/(n - 2)}} \qquad\qquad (18.1)$$
$$Hypothesis\ That\ \rho = 0$$

where: r is the *sample* coefficient and n is the number of *pairs* of scores in the sample. To test the hypothesis that $\rho = 0$, we calculate t according to Formula 18.1, and evaluate it, according to the significance level adopted and $(n - 2)$ degrees of freedom, with reference to the values of t found in Table D, in the appendix.‡ In the illustration given below, it is assumed that a two-tailed test at the 5% level of significance is desired. From the table of t, we learn that the critical value of t is ± 2.069, and since our obtained t does not reach that magnitude, we have no reason to reject the hypothesis. The calculated value of t would equal or exceed that critical magnitude only when, in sampling at random from a population in which $\rho = 0$, the sample value of r is so deviant from zero that its probability of occurrence would be .05 or less. The findings in the following problem are illustrated in Figure 18.2.

Problem: A sample of 25 pairs of scores yields $r = +.30$. Is it possible that there is really no relation between the two variables?

Solution; Step 1: State the hypothesis, the alternative hypothesis, and the desired significance level:

$$H_0: \quad \rho = 0$$
$$\qquad\qquad\qquad \alpha = .05$$
$$H_A: \quad \rho \neq 0$$

---

†The note at the chapter's end explains why $df = n - 2$.

‡Section 17.6 is particularly pertinent for those who wish to review use of the t distribution.

Step 2: Calculate, from the sample data, the obtained value of t:

$$t = \frac{+.30}{\sqrt{[1 - (.30)^2]/(25 - 2)}} = +1.51$$

Step 3: Determine the number of degrees of freedom:

$$df = 25 - 2 = 23$$

Step 4: From Table D, in the appendix, and according to the number of degrees of freedom, find the magnitude of t so deviant from zero that it will be exceeded but 5% of the time. That critical value is:

$$t_{crit} = \pm 2.069$$

Step 5: Compare the obtained value of t with the critical magnitude of t required to reject H_0. Since t_{obt} is smaller in magnitude than t_{crit}, we come to the following conclusion:

Decision: Accept H_0

The method of testing the hypothesis that $\rho = 0$, described above, is quite general. It can be used for a variety of levels of significance, and for one- or two-tailed tests. A special table is provided which eliminates the computational labor when conducting one- or two-tailed tests at the 5 or 1% significance level. Table E, in the appendix, gives the critical values of r required to reach significance under these circumstances. To use this table, enter it with the appropriate value of df, and read the critical value of r according to the desired significance level. If r_{obt}

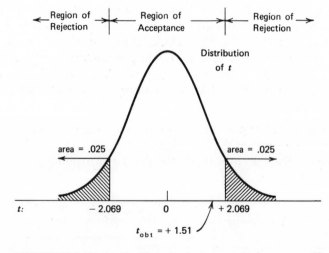

FIGURE 18.2 Testing the Hypothesis that $\rho = 0$ when $r = +.30$ and $df = 23$.

exceeds the tabled value, H_0 is rejected; otherwise not. For the example illustrated above, $df = 23$ and $r_{crit} = .396$. Since $r_{obt} = .30$, it falls short of the degree of deviance from zero required to reject the hypothesis.

In terms of the *research* question posed, the finding of a significant r is only a preliminary. The next question is whether the correlation is large enough to be of practical or theoretical use. With large samples, an *un*usefully small r may prove to be "statistically significant" (see Section 18.9 for further consideration of this problem.)

18.4 Fisher's z' Transformation

Although the technique described in the previous section serves to test the hypothesis that $\rho = 0$, it can not be used for other types of problems. Another approach is required, and, once more, it is the result of work by R. A. Fisher.

The fundamental problem is that the sampling distribution of r departs from the normal when $\rho \neq 0$. Moreover, the degree of skewness varies with the magnitude of ρ. Fisher derived a logarithmic function of r, which we shall call z', which exhibits certain desirable properties:

1. The sampling distribution of z' is approximately normal irrespective of the value of ρ.
2. The standard error of z', unlike the standard error of r, is essentially independent of the value of ρ.

Because of these properties, we can, for several problems of inference about correlation coefficients, translate r to z' and conduct inference in terms of these converted values. We are then able to use the familiar properties of the normal curve in conducting the evaluation, and the outcome is the same as though we were able to conduct inference directly in terms of r.

The formula for z' is:

Formula for Translating
r to Fisher's z'
$$z' = \tfrac{1}{2}[\log_e (1 + r) - \log_e (1 - r)] \qquad (18.2)$$

Note that the value of z' depends *wholly* on the value of r. The z' translation is therefore simply a mathematical reformulation which changes the scale of r. Note, also, that *Fisher's z' is not a z score, nor is it related in any way*. The similarity in symbolism is unfortunate; another symbol would be better. Fisher originally called his statistic z, which is completely unacceptable because of the wide use of that symbol for a standard score (z score). Usage has perpetuated Fisher's symbolism, at least as closely as possible without creating utter confusion. We will shortly be using the symbols z and z' in close proximity; watch for the difference.

The improvement in scale can be most readily shown pictorially. Figure 18.3

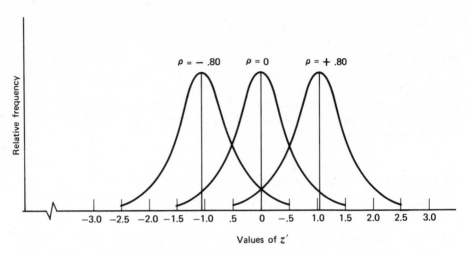

FIGURE 18.3 The Random Sampling Distribution of z' Corresponding to Three Values of $\rho: n = 8$.

shows the sampling distribution of z' which corresponds to $\rho = -.8$, $\rho = 0$, and $\rho = +.8$ when $n = 8$. Compare these distributions with those of r for the same values of ρ (Figure 18.1). Note that the sampling distribution of z' is essentially similar in shape and variability under these three conditions, whereas the sampling distribution of r is not.

It would be awkward to work through the formula for z' to translate an r to z', or vice versa. Fortunately, Table F, in the appendix, makes the conversion easy. In this table, if r is positive, read the value of z' as positive, and if negative, read z' as negative.

It is rewarding to give this table a few moments of study, because it reveals what is accomplished by Fisher's translation. Note that when r is zero, z' is also zero, and that the two values are essentially equivalent up to, say, $r = .25$. As r progresses from zero to one, a discrepancy between r and z' begins to appear, z' being larger than its parent, r. The discrepancy increases more rapidly the higher the value of r. What is accomplished is that the scale of r (ranging from -1.00 through 0 to $+1.00$) is being stretched, very little at the center but increasingly more so at the extremes. Note that the original scale of r becomes, in terms of z', a scale ranging from approximately -3 to $+3$ (or even farther, if it is allowed that r might exceed $\pm.995$).

In the suggested uses of the z' transformation which follow, keep in mind that reasonable results will obtain unless sample size (n) is very small, or ρ is very high. Actually, we have no justification for finding Pearsonian r among very small samples (see Section 18.9), nor do we ordinarily encounter correlation coefficients much above .9. Thus, the limitations are more academic than practical.

18.5 Testing the Hypothesis That ρ Is Some Value Other Than Zero

Suppose we have obtained a correlation coefficient of $+.65$ between two variables based on a sample of 60 subjects. Previous research indicates that the typical correlation is $+.45$ between these variables. Is our value to be considered within random sampling fluctuation from this figure? We test:

$$H_0: \quad \rho = +.45$$
$$H_A: \quad \rho \neq +.45 \qquad \alpha = .05$$

To do so, we translate r and ρ to z', calculate the position of the sample z' in its sampling distribution, and reject H_0 if the obtained z' is so deviant from what would be expected if H_0 were true that its probability of occurrence would be .05 or less. We therefore calculate z (not z') as follows:

Calculation of z to Test the Hypothesis That ρ is a Specified Value
$$z = \frac{z' - Z'}{\sigma_{z'}} \qquad (18.3)$$

where:

z' is the value of z' corresponding to r_{obt}
Z' is the value of z' corresponding to the hypothesized value of ρ
$\sigma_{z'}$ is the standard error of z'

Unexplained so far is $\sigma_{z'}$, the standard error of z'. It is:

Standard Error of z'
$$\sigma_{z'} = \frac{1}{\sqrt{n - 3}} \qquad (18.4)$$

where n is the number of pairs of scores in the sample. Note that this quantity is solely a function of n, whereas σ_r is a function of both n and ρ (see Section 18.9).

To continue with the example, Table F shows that values of z' corresponding to r's of $+.65$ and $+.45$ are $+.78$ and $+.49$, respectively. Making use of Formulas 18.3 and 18.4, we have:

$$\sigma_{z'} = \frac{1}{\sqrt{60 - 3}} = .13$$

$$z = \frac{(+.78) - (+.49)}{.13} = +2.23$$

Since the test is two tailed and at the 5% level of significance, the critical value of z is ± 1.96. The obtained value of z is more deviant, and H_0 is rejected. The problem is illustrated in Figure 18.4.

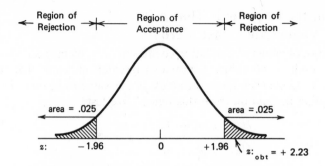

FIGURE 18.4 Testing the Hypothesis that $\rho = +.45$ when $r = +.65$ and $n = 60$.

The same procedure *could* be used to test the hypothesis that the population coefficient is zero. Fisher's t test, described in Section 18.3, is *exactly* correct when the assumptions have been met (see Section 18.9), but the method described in this section will give results which are very close to those of the t test. As noted at the beginning of Section 18.4, the t test is appropriate *only* for testing the hypothesis that $\rho = 0$.

18.6 Testing the Hypothesis of No Difference between ρ_1 and ρ_2: Independent Samples

In the course of studying factors involved in academic success in Spartan University, an investigator wonders whether intelligence test score is related to freshman grade point average to the same degree for male and female students. Drawing a sample of 100 male students, he finds the correlation between these two variables to be: $r_1 = +.50$, and for a sample of 100 female students, the correlation between the same two variables is: $r_2 = +.35$.

We are faced with the problem that the two sampling distributions of r, corresponding to ρ_1 and ρ_2, are unknown and probably skewed. Hence, the sampling distribution of differences between pairs of coefficients will tend to be nonnormal. Again, Fisher's z' transformation provides the avenue for solution, normalizing the sampling distribution. We shall therefore convert r to z', and conduct the test in terms of z'.

We first state the hypothesis and the desired significance level:

$$H_0: \quad \rho_1 - \rho_2 = 0$$
$$\alpha = .01$$
$$H_A: \quad \rho_1 - \rho_2 \neq 0$$

From Table F in the appendix, we find the z' equivalents of r_1 ($z' = +.55$) and r_2 ($z' = +.37$). Then z (not z') is calculated according to Formula 18.5:

z Required to Test the Hypothesis That $\rho_1 = \rho_2$ when Samples Are Independent
$$z = \frac{(z_1' - z_2') - (Z_1' - Z_2')_{hyp}}{\sigma_{z_1' - z_2'}} \qquad (18.5)$$

To use this formula, the equation for the standard error of the difference between two values of z', $\sigma_{z_1' - z_2'}$, is required. It is given by Formula 18.6:

Standard Error of the Difference between Two Independent z''s
$$\sigma_{z_1' - z_2'} = \sqrt{\frac{1}{n_1 - 3} + \frac{1}{n_2 - 3}} \qquad (18.6)$$

To conclude the test, we have:

$$\sigma_{z_1' - z_2'} = \sqrt{\frac{1}{100 - 3} + \frac{1}{100 - 3}} = .14$$

and,
$$z = \frac{(.55 - .37) - 0}{.14} = +1.29$$

Treating the obtained value of z ($+1.29$) as a normal deviate, we find that it falls short of the critical value of z ($z = \pm 2.58$) required to declare significance at the 1% level. The grounds are insufficient to reject the hypothesis; H_0 is accepted.

The procedure described above is suited *only* to situations involving two independent random samples. It is not appropriate, for example, when the two correlation coefficients have been obtained on the same set of subjects. (See Section 16.4 for fuller discussion of independent versus dependent samples.)

18.7 Testing the Hypothesis of No Difference between ρ_1 and ρ_2: Dependent Samples

Is intelligence test score related to grade point average to the same degree for freshmen as for seniors? If the correlation between these variables is found among a sample of freshmen, and, 3 years later, among the *same* subjects when they are seniors, we have a problem involving dependent, rather than independent samples. Again, suppose we have two predictors of job success, and want to know if the two are equally related to the criterion. If the two correlations (between predictor and criterion) have been obtained on the *same* sample of subjects, the samples are dependent. The method of the previous section is inappropriate to either of the above circumstances, suited as it is to independent samples.

For dependent samples, we may distinguish two cases. In Case I, the problem is to compare the correlation between a set of two measurements with the correlation between another set of two measurements obtained on the same (or matched) subjects. The first of the two examples in the previous paragraph illustrates the problem. Curiously, there is no entirely satisfactory test of the difference between two correlation coefficients obtained in such circumstances. Attempts have been made to solve this problem. Some proposals are of incompletely evaluated validity, and others are satisfactory but involve rather restrictive assumptions which may not be met in practical work. More detailed consideration of this problem may be found in a text by Johnson and Jackson.†

In Case II, the problem is to compare the correlation between one predictor and a criterion measure with the correlation between a second predictor and the *same* criterion measure when both correlations have been obtained on the same (or matched) subjects. In this case, there are just three sets of measures, since the criterion measure consists of the *same* set of scores in both correlations. The second example in the first paragraph illustrates Case II. This problem *does* have a solution, but because Case II is somewhat special we will omit its development here and make reference to other sources such as Johnson and Jackson, cited above.

18.8 Estimating ρ

Rather than testing the hypothesis that ρ is some specific value, it may be desirable to ask within what limits the population coefficient may be found. Accordingly, a confidence interval may be constructed corresponding to a selected level of confidence. The basic logic of formation of confidence intervals was developed in Sections 14.9 and 14.10. The discussion here assumes that knowledge.

The problem of the nonnormal sampling distribution of r is again with us (see Section 18.2), and again it is solved by making use of Fisher's normalizing z' transformation. A confidence interval may be constructed by translating the sample r to z', and following the rule:

*Rule for Constructing an
Interval Estimate of ρ*
$$z' \pm z_p \sigma_{z'} \tag{18.7}$$

   where:
   z' is the value of z' corresponding to the sample r
   z_p is the magnitude of z for which the probability is p of obtaining a value
      so deviant or more so (in either direction)
   p is $(1 - C)$, where C is the confidence coefficient

Application of the above rule will result in a lower limit and an upper limit, both expressed in terms of z'. These must then be converted to r's by means of Table F, in the appendix.

The procedure is illustrated with the same data used in Section 18.3. The sample r is $+.30$, based on 25 pairs of observations. What are the limits in which we can be 95% confident that they include ρ, the population value of the

---

†P. O. Johnson, and R. W. B. Jackson, *Modern Statistical Methods*, Rand McNally & Co., Chicago, 1959, pp. 353–356.

correlation coefficient? From Table F, we find that $z' = +.31$ corresponds to $r = +.30$. $\sigma_{z'} = 1/\sqrt{25-3} = .21$, and in a normal distribution, $z = \pm 1.96$ is the value so deviant that it would be exceeded but .05 of the time. According to the rule given in Formula 18.7, the limits of the 95% confidence interval are:

$$+.31 \pm (1.96)(.21)$$

$$-.10 \quad \text{to} \quad +.72$$

$$\begin{pmatrix}\text{Lower} \\ \text{Limit}\end{pmatrix} \quad \begin{pmatrix}\text{Upper} \\ \text{Limit}\end{pmatrix}$$

Using Table F, these values of z' are translated back to values of r, and the limits are:

$$r_{LL} = -.10 \qquad r_{UL} = +.62$$

Formally, the confidence interval is expressed:

$$C(-.10 < \rho < +.62) = .95$$

Note that these limits are not equidistant from $r = +.30$. The upper limit is closer to $r = +.30$, as might be expected (see Section 18.2).

18.9 Concluding Comments

From earlier chapters, you may recall that no assumption about the shape of the bivariate distribution is required when the correlation coefficient is used purely as a descriptive index. However, *all of the procedures for inference about coefficients described in this chapter are based on the assumption that the population of pairs of scores form a normal bivariate distribution*. This implies that X is normally distributed, Y is normally distributed, and that the relation between X and Y is linear. If we are not dealing with a normal bivariate population, then these procedures for inference must be considered to yield approximate results.

Studies designed to ascertain the degree of association between two variables should be planned with an eye to adequacy of sample size. In many circumstances, the correlation coefficient can not be stably determined from small samples. In evidence of this, Table E in the appendix is worth study. This table may be interpreted to state the range which would include 95% (or 99%) of sample coefficients when the true correlation is zero. Note, for instance, that when n is 10 ($df = 8$), and $\rho = 0$, the 95% limits for r are $\pm.63$, and the 99% limits, $\pm.77$. Suppose, unknown to us, $\rho = +.60$, and our sample r happened to have exactly the same value. Nevertheless, if we were testing the hypothesis that $\rho = 0$, we would find no cause to reject it. Even when $df = 30$, the 95% limits are $\pm.35$, and the 99% limits are $\pm.45$. It should be obvious that a good-sized sample is needed to determine the extent of relationship with any degree of accuracy.

It is true that if ρ is nonzero, random sampling variation of r will be less. The otherwise relatively useless formula for the standard error of a correlation coefficient, $\sigma_r = (1 - \rho^2)/\sqrt{n - 1}$, helps to show this. Note that, according to this formula, if ρ were near ± 1.00, sampling variability in r would indeed be quite small. *In general, it would be good practice to make interval estimates of ρ (according to the procedures of Section 18.8) much more often than is commonly done in research.* Such intervals call attention more directly to the inherent amount of sampling variation. It seems likely that research workers are often tempted to think that the population value of the coefficient is closer to the sample r at hand than inspection of the actual interval estimate would warrant.

Large samples are always better than small ones, from the standpoint of precision. However, large samples may create a problem in interpretation unless we are careful to make the distinction between a significant difference and an important one. This concept was discussed in Section 15.6, and it would be desirable to review it. Rejection of the hypothesis that ρ is zero depends not only on the magnitude of the sample coefficient, but also importantly on sample size. *If samples are very large, a relatively small coefficient may lead to the conclusion that there is a real relationship between the two variables.* For instance, a coefficient of $+.10$, based on a sample of 1000 cases would lead to rejection of the hypothesis of no correlation. However, a correlation of that magnitude, genuine though it may be, is of little value for any purpose, practical or theoretical, that an investigator might have in mind.

NOTE

Degrees of Freedom and the Correlation Coefficient (*Ref:* Section 18.3)

When the t test is used to examine the hypothesis that $\rho = 0$, we learned that $df = n - 2$. Why? Recall (Section 9.3) that the correlation coefficient is a constant in the equation of the straight line of best fit to the bivariate distribution. Now if this "distribution" consists of but *one* pair of scores, a single point is identified, and any number of "best fitting" straight lines can be drawn through that point. Therefore, the correlation coefficient is indeterminate since its slope is indeterminate. When there are *two* pairs of scores, there are two points, and a straight line can be fitted to two points with no error. Consequently, the correlation is either $+1.00$ or -1.00. With three pairs of scores (and therefore three points), there is at last freedom for the correlation coefficient to take values which may range from -1.00 to $+1.00$. So, 1 degree of freedom is acquired only when $n = 3$ is reached. To put it another way, we have lost 2 degrees of freedom by reason of the two points (or slope and intercept) needed to determine the location of a straight line amid the data.

PROBLEMS AND EXERCISES

Identify:

sampling distribution of r Fisher's z' transformation

1. Given: $H_0: \rho = 0$, $H_A: \rho \neq 0$, $r = +.30$, $n = 24$. Test the null hypothesis at $\alpha = .10$, and $\alpha = .05$.

2. Using Table E, in the appendix, test the hypothesis that $\rho = 0$ when: (a) $r = +.40$, $n = 28$, $H_A: \rho \neq 0$, $\alpha = .05$ (b) $r = -.55$, $n = 18$, $H_A: \rho \neq 0$, $\alpha = .01$ (c) $r = -.40$, $n = 22$, $H_A: \rho < 0$, $\alpha = .05$ (d) $r = +.45$, $n = 25$, $H_A: \rho < 0$, $\alpha = .05$. Show the critical value of r for each problem.

3. Given: $r = +.40$, $n = 28$, $\alpha = .05$, and that the alternative hypothesis is non-directional. Test the hypothesis that: (a) $\rho = +.50$ (b) $\rho = +.60$.

4. Professor Smith wants to know whether academic aptitude test score is related to freshman grade point average to the same extent for male college students as it is for female students. He obtains the following data from samples obtained at his institution: Males: $r = +.45$, $n = 103$; Females: $r = +.30$, $n = 103$. (a) State the null hypothesis and the alternative hypothesis appropriate to his question. (b) Test the hypothesis using $\alpha = .05$ and .01, and state your conclusions.

5. Given: $r = .65$, $n = 103$. Construct an interval estimate of ρ according to: (a) $C = .95$ (b) $C = .99$ (c) $C = .90$.

6. Repeat Problem 5, but assume these data: $r = .45$, $n = 19$.

7. In a particular study, it is reported that $r = +.75$ between predictor and criterion. Reading on, we find that this value was obtained on a sample of six cases. Comment.

8. In another study, it is reported that $r = +.12$ between predictor and criterion. This correlation is based on 500 cases. Is it significantly different from zero? Your comment?

19

Some Aspects of Experimental Design

19.1 Introduction

At the beginning of this book (Section 1.6), we attempted to identify the role of applied statistics in the pursuit of empirical knowledge. Now that we have become better acquainted with some of the statistical devices, we should review that role and consider some aspects of statistical application which are related to the strategy of inquiry.

The normal course of inquiry may be outlined as follows:

1. *Stating the question.* (Is there a difference in speed of learning when learning is accomplished under Method *A* as compared with Method *B*?)
2. *Refining the question, rendering it amenable to empirical investigation.* (What kind of subjects, what kind of learning task, what measure of learning, etc.?)
3. *Deciding on the means of comparison of the measures obtained.* (What statistical model will best illuminate the condition of the data relative to the substantive question?)
4. *Collecting the evidence.* (What is the speed-of-learning score for each subject?)
5. *Analyzing the data, and stating the statistical conclusion.* (Assuming that Step 3 led to the significance test between two means, shall the hypothesis that $\mu_A = \mu_B$ be rejected?)
6. *Stating the substantive conclusion.* (If the null hypothesis is rejected, is it reasonable to attribute the difference in mean learning speed to difference in method?)

In the entire list, the only *purely* statistical step is the fifth one. It should be evident that several steps demand an interplay between substantive knowledge and statistical knowledge. For example, in refining the question (Step 2), the investigator will do well to keep in mind how the data are to be analyzed (Step 3). In many instances, lack of forethought may result in closing the door to efficient methods of analysis, or even in inability to analyze the data in any meaningful way. No study should be designed with data analysis as the *foremost* consideration; this tends to lead to rigorous conclusions about trivia (see Section 1.8). At the same time, failure to take analytic factors into account in designing a study is inexcusable.

In itself, determining the nature of the analysis (Step 3) affords exercise of both substantive and statistical knowledge. We must know the properties of the several available statistical tools to choose the procedure which (1) is appropriate to the condition of the data (are the assumptions of the technique reasonably met?), (2) illuminates best the substantive meaning of the data, and (3) provides the most efficient analysis.

Finally, we must emphasize that there is a substantial difference between a statistical conclusion (Step 5) and a substantive conclusion (Step 6). If the analytic statistical model was inappropriately selected, or if conditions required for it to be correctly applied do not hold, the proper substantive conclusion may not correspond to the statistical one. For example, if the study of two methods of learning is conducted by assigning volunteer subjects to one method and drafted subjects to the other, the factors of motivation and method will be hopelessly entangled.† The hypothesis, $\mu_A = \mu_B$, will probably be rejected, but for what reason we may not hope to know from such a study.

These considerations make it abundantly clear that it is not only necessary to understand the properties of statistical methods, but also to interpret them in the light of the particular substantive inquiry. In any exposition of statistics, primary emphasis must be accorded to fundamental properties of statistical devices. Nevertheless, it is important to clarify the relationships between experimental logic and statistical logic, and between substantive concerns and statistical properties. On numerous occasions we have considered such aspects of statistical practice. Definition of a population, selection of sample size, choice of α, and choice of the alternative hypothesis are examples of acts which must be performed by the investigator in the light of his knowledge of the consequences of these decisions relative to the adequacy of the substantive conclusions which are the end product of his inquiry. A number of areas of such interaction remain underdeveloped relative to their importance. The purpose of this chapter is to give better treatment to certain of these matters.

19.2 Type I Error and Type II Error

In Section 15.7, we learned that two types of error may occur in testing hypoth-

---

†"Confounded" is the well-chosen statistical term for such a situation.

eses: Type I error and Type II error. The probability of committing each is defined as follows:

Type I Error $\alpha = \text{Pr}(\text{rejecting } H_0 | H_0 \text{ is true})$

Type II Error $\beta = \text{Pr}(\text{accepting } H_0 | H_0 \text{ is false})$

In arranging the test of an hypothesis, the probability of committing a Type I error is relatively "visible," because the investigator must select the value of α he wishes to use. Issues to be faced in choice of α are discussed in Section 15.4. The risk of a Type II error is much less likely to receive direct attention. Often it is only faced indirectly, as in the question, "Is my sample large enough?" Because of the importance of the Type II error, it deserves further consideration. Section 19.4 will show how to calculate its probability of occurrence. The succeeding five sections examine the influence of factors affecting its probability, and Section 19.10 shows how to face directly the risk of this error in selecting sample size.

19.3 The Power of a Test

The decision to accept a false hypothesis is the complement of that to reject a false hypothesis. Since the probability of the former is β, the probability of the latter is $(1 - \beta)$:

$$(1 - \beta) = \text{Pr}(\text{rejecting } H_0 | H_0 \text{ is false})$$

In other words, $(1 - \beta)$ is the probability of claiming a significant difference when a true difference really exists. The probability of doing so, $(1 - \beta)$, is called the *power of the test*. Among several ways of conducting a test, the most powerful one is that offering the greatest probability of rejecting H_0 when it should be rejected.

In succeeding sections, we shall examine the several conditions which affect β, the probability of committing a Type II error. Since β and power are complementary, it must be remembered that any condition which decreases β increases the power of the test.

19.4 The Probability of Committing a Type II Error

Suppose the following hypothesis is to be subjected to examination:

$$H_0: \quad \mu_X = 80$$
$$H_A: \quad \mu_X \neq 80 \qquad \alpha = .05$$

If sample size is 25, and it is known that $\sigma_X = 20$, then $\sigma_{\bar{X}} = \sigma_X / \sqrt{n} = 4.00$. To test the hypothesis, we inquire as to the sampling distribution of means which occurs when the hypothesis is true. This sampling distribution is shown in solid outline in Figure 19.1. If, relative to this distribution, a sample mean is obtained that falls within the limits $z = \pm 1.96$, H_0 will be accepted.

Let us suppose that the hypothesis is false, and that in fact $\mu_{\text{true}} = 84$. In random sampling, the values of $\overline{X}$ actually obtained will follow the true sampling distribution, shown in dotted outline in Figure 19.1. If the obtained sample mean is one of those shown in the shaded portion of this distribution, the decision will be to accept H_0: a Type II error will be committed. What is the probability of committing this error? Taking the total area under the curve shown in dotted outline as unity, it will be equal to the shaded area under that curve.

To find the area in the shaded portion of the curve, its boundaries must be expressed in z-score terms. We already know what the boundaries are in z-score terms *relative to the hypothesized sampling distribution*: $z_{\text{LL}} = -1.96$ and $z_{\text{UL}} = +1.96$. The path to the solution is to note the difference between μ_{hyp} and μ_{true}, and convert it to z-score units: $(\mu_{\text{hyp}} - \mu_{\text{true}})/\sigma_{\overline{X}} = 4.00/4.00 = 1.00$. The lower boundary, 1.96 z-score units below μ_{hyp}, is $(1.96 + 1.00)$ z-score units below μ_{true}. Its location *relative to the true distribution*, is therefore: $z_{\text{LL}} = -2.96$. The upper boundary, 1.96 z-score units above μ_{hyp}, is $(1.96 - 1.00)$ z-score units above μ_{true}. Its location, relative to the true distribution, is therefore: $z_{\text{UL}} = +.96$. Finding the area between these boundaries may now be accomplished by the

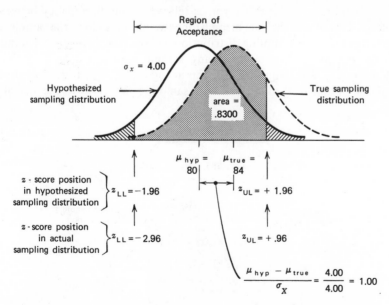

FIGURE 19.1 Probability of Type II Error when Testing the Hypothesis that $\mu = \mu_{\text{true}}$.

methods of Section 7.7, on the assumption of normality of the sampling distribution. The area between z_{LL} and the mean is .4985 and the area between the mean and z_{UL} is .3315, according to the table of areas under the normal curve. The sum of these two areas is .8300, the probability of obtaining a sample mean falling within the two boundaries, and is, therefore, β. The final phases of this solution are shown in Figure 19.2.

Several observations are worth noting. First, β *can not be calculated unless the value of* μ_{true} *can be specified.* Although this value is unknown, the ability to calculate β according to different values of μ_{true} makes it possible to see the consequences of hypothesis testing under various circumstances, and thus to plan the test accordingly. Second, calculation of β was illustrated above in the test of an hypothesis about a single mean. The idea, of course, applies to tests of other hypotheses. For example, a similar analysis can be made for a test of the difference between two means. Third, in the example used, it was assumed that σ_X is known. When σ_X must be estimated from the sample, the normal curve is only an approximate model, growing worse as sample size is reduced. Other models are available for these circumstances, but in the present elementary exposition they can not be given systematic treatment.

19.5 Factors Affecting Type II Error: Discrepancy between the True Mean and the Hypothesized Mean

β, the probability of a Type II error, is related to the discrepancy between the hypothesized mean and the true mean. If the two are very close, the sample means obtained from the true sampling distribution will overlap the region of acceptance to a large extent. Consequently, many sample values will lead to the false acceptance of H_0. The diagram at the top in Figure 19.3 illustrates this situation. The means obtained through random sampling will follow the distribution

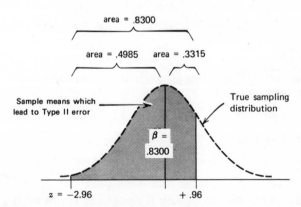

FIGURE 19.2 Probability of Type II Error.

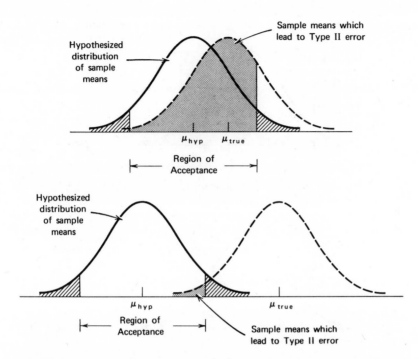

FIGURE 19.3 Probability of Type II Error as a Function of the Size of the Difference between μ_{hyp} and μ_{true}.

shown in dotted outline, and, in the case illustrated, over half of them will lead to the false acceptance of the hypothesis that $\mu = \mu_{hyp}$.

In the illustration at the bottom in Figure 19.3, the true mean and the hypothesized mean are substantially different. Here, few samples will lead to the acceptance of H_0. *In general, when the hypothesis is false, the greater the discrepancy between μ_{true} and μ_{hyp}, the less the probability of falsely accepting the hypothesis.*

19.6 Factors Affecting Type II Error: Choice of Level of Significance (α)

β is also related to the choice of α. In Figure 19.4, the illustration at the top shows the probability of accepting H_0 when it is false, and $\alpha = .05$. The illustration at the bottom shows the identical situation, except that $\alpha = .01$. In both diagrams, the sample means represented by the shaded area in the distributions shown in dotted outline are those which fall in the region of acceptance. The proportionate frequency of such means is greater when $\alpha = .01$ than when it is .05. There is, therefore, a greater chance of obtaining a sample mean which will

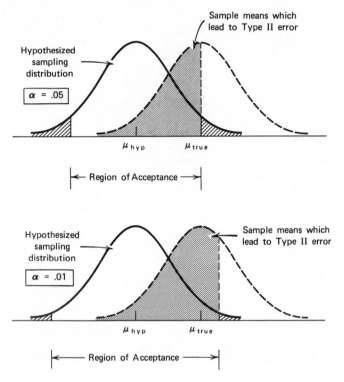

FIGURE 19.4 Probability of Type II Error as a Function of α.

lead to the false acceptance of H_0 when α is smaller. *In general, reducing the risk of a Type I error increases the risk of committing a Type II error.*

Recognition of the relationship between α and β is reflected in the change in research practice from that of 40 years ago. In the "old days," it was common to require that $z \geq \pm 3$ before declaring the hypothesis to be rejected. This z is so discrepant that it would occur less than three times in one thousand in a normal distribution. In current practice, it is common to reject the hypothesis when the discrepancy is so great that it would occur 5% of the time or less ($z_{crit} = \pm 1.96$), or 1% of the time or less ($z_{crit} = \pm 2.58$). The modern view is more satisfactory; it takes better account of the necessity of keeping Type II error under control, and still maintains an adequate watch over Type I error. Sometimes the older view is thought to be more "conservative," but it is now understood that conservatism in setting α is paid for by being a spendthrift with regard to β. See Section 15.4 for an earlier discussion of this point.

The primary consideration in selecting α should be, of course, the logic of the experiment, as discussed in Section 15.4. But unthinking conservatism in minimizing α will have an *unnecessarily* adverse influence on β. Actually, proper control over the probability of a Type II error can be exerted by choice of sample size. It is to this subject that we now turn.

19.7 Factors Affecting Type II Error: Sample Size

The probability of committing a Type II error is related to sample size. Consider the test of the hypothesis that $\mu = \mu_{hyp}$ when sample size is 100. The standard error of the mean will be $\sigma_{\bar{X}} = \sigma_X/\sqrt{100} = \frac{1}{10}\sigma_X$. If sample size were 400, the standard error of the mean would be $\sigma_{\bar{X}} = \sigma_X/\sqrt{400} = \frac{1}{20}\sigma_X$, only half as large. Figure 19.5 shows how the sampling distributions might appear when all factors are the same except for sample size. In general, the larger the size of the samples, the smaller the standard deviation ($\sigma_{\bar{X}}$) of the sampling distribution of $\bar{X}$. Comparison of the two situations illustrated shows that when sample size is larger, there is less overlap between the two distributions. Consequently, the risk is less of drawing a sample that leads to (false) acceptance of the hypothesis. *Other things being equal, the larger the size of the sample, the lower the probability of committing a Type II error.*

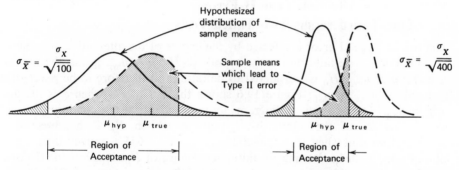

FIGURE 19.5 Probability of Type II Error as a Function of Sample Size.

The regulation of sample size offers the simplest avenue of controlling risk of a Type II error. In Section 19.10, we will consider how to take account of β in selecting sample size for tests of hypotheses about means.

19.8 Factors Affecting Type II Error: Variability of the Measure

In the previous section, we saw that increase in sample size reduced the risk of Type II error by reason of its action in reducing the standard error of the mean. Since the standard error of the mean is $\sigma_X/\sqrt{n}$, another way to make it smaller is to reduce the size of σ_X. At first glance, one might think that this is beyond the control of the investigator. Actually, this opportunity is often open, but advance planning is necessary.

The standard deviation of the set of measures reflects variation attributable to the factors we wish to study, but it also reflects variation attributable to extraneous and irrelevant sources. Any source of extraneous variation tends to increase σ_X over what it would be otherwise, so an effective effort to eliminate such sources will tend to decrease σ_X and thus reduce β. For example, measures in behavioral science (e.g., tests, ratings) suffer from inconsistency to some degree.† Some are really rather poor in this regard. Improving the reliability of the measuring instrument will have the effect of reducing σ_X, other things being equal.

In comparing means of two groups, the matched sample design offers another example of the reduction of variation through elimination of sources of extraneous error. Comparison of the formula for the standard error of the difference between two correlated means, $\sigma_{\bar{X}-\bar{Y}} = \sqrt{\sigma_{\bar{X}}^2 + \sigma_{\bar{Y}}^2 - 2\rho_{XY}\sigma_{\bar{X}}\sigma_{\bar{Y}}}$, with that of the difference between two independent means, $\sigma_{\bar{X}-\bar{Y}} = \sqrt{\sigma_{\bar{X}}^2 + \sigma_{\bar{Y}}^2}$, shows the statistical improvement that can be accomplished by this method. (See Section 16.12 for other comment on the merit of this design.)

19.9 Factors Affecting Type II Error: One-Tailed versus Two-Tailed Tests

The risk of Type II error is affected by the choice of the alternative hypothesis. In conducting a one-tailed test of the hypothesis $H_0: \mu = \mu_{hyp}$ against the alternative $H_A: \mu > \mu_{hyp}$, H_0 is considered to be false (and therefore to be rejected) if and only if $\mu_{true} > \mu_{hyp}$. Figure 19.6 shows the test of H_0 when α is .05 and $\mu_{true} > \mu_{hyp}$. The two sets of diagrams represent identical test conditions except for the nature of the alternative hypothesis. When H_A is nondirectional, $z_{crit} = \pm 1.96$, and when H_A is directional, $z_{crit} = +1.645$. Compare the proportion of sample means leading to (false) acceptance of H_0. It is less for the one-tailed test. *Other things being equal, the probability of committing a Type II error is less for a one-tailed test than for a two-tailed test.*

The fact that a one-tailed test is more powerful (i.e., carries lower risk of Type II error) has sometimes been advanced in support of the proposition that one-tailed tests ought to be used more often. The position taken in this volume is that the choice of the alternative hypothesis ought to derive from the logic of the investigation. If that logic points to use of a one-tailed alternative, then the increase in power comes with it as an extra, or bonus benefit. See Section 15.3 for issues to be considered in making the choice.

19.10 Estimating Sample Size for Tests of Hypotheses about Means

In testing hypotheses about means, convenience suggests the desirability of a small sample, but accuracy suggests a large one. Means of small samples vary

---

†Inconsistency means "rubber in the yardstick," or, in its technical sense, unreliability of measurement.

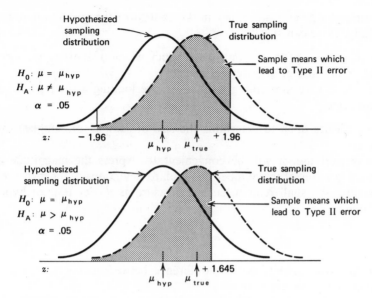

FIGURE 19.6 Type II Error in a One- and Two-Tailed Test when $\alpha = .05$.

widely from the mean of the population and so β, the probability of accepting a false hypothesis, is larger for small samples. But how large a sample is really needed? There is no point in taking a sample of 500 cases if 100 will do.

To answer this question, we must first decide what magnitude of discrepancy between the hypothesized value and the true value of the parameter is so great that, if one of this size or larger existed, we would want to be reasonably certain of discovering it. To put it another way, certain discrepancies are sufficiently small that if the hypothesis were (falsely) accepted, the error is one that we would be willing to overlook. For example, suppose a school principal tests the hypothesis that $\mu_{IQ} = 100$ for his population of school children. If he accepts that hypothesis when the mean IQ of the population is really 102, he might feel that the error was of no practical consequence. On the other hand, he would probably be quite unwilling to accept that hypothesis if the mean of the population were really 110.

Now it is fair to say that very likely *all* statistical hypotheses are false. The hypothesis is stated as a point value, and it is most unlikely, for example, that any real population has a mean IQ of *exactly* 100. *The value of hypothesis testing is that it can be used to reveal discrepancies which are large enough that we care about them.* (See Section 15.6 for another discussion of "important" discrepancies.)

The decision as to just how big a discrepancy between the parameter's hypothesized value and its true value is important is fundamentally a substantive question, and not a statistical one. It can only be made by a person who knows the meaning of a given discrepancy in the context of the question that gave rise to the study. If we can specify:

1. the magnitude of the *smallest* discrepancy which, if it exists, we wish to be reasonably sure of discovering, and
2. the risk (β) we are willing to take of overlooking a discrepancy of that magnitude,

then the path lies open to determine the size of sample (or samples) that will be necessary.

For general use, it will be convenient to express the magnitude of this discrepancy in terms of the number of standard deviations of the measure under consideration. We shall refer to such a measure as d. For tests of hypotheses about single means:

$$d = \frac{\mu_{\text{true}} - \mu_{\text{hyp}}}{\sigma_X}$$

For tests of hypotheses about the difference between two means, *and on the assumption that $\sigma_X = \sigma_Y$*:

$$d = \frac{(\mu_X - \mu_Y)_{\text{true}} - (\mu_X - \mu_Y)_{\text{hyp}}}{\sigma}$$

where: $\sigma_X = \sigma_Y = \sigma$. In each case, *note that d expresses the discrepancy relative to the standard deviation of the set of measures, not to the standard error.*

If $d = .5$, this means that the discrepancy between the true value and that hypothesized is one-half of a standard deviation of the variable measured. For example, for a common individual test of intelligence, mean IQ is 100, and the standard deviation is 16. If one were to decide that a discrepancy between μ_{true} and μ_{hyp} as large as eight IQ points should not be overlooked, then for this problem, $d = .5$. Table 19.1 presents information suited to one-tailed or two-tailed tests of hypotheses about single means for the two common levels of α, three levels of β, and several magnitudes of d. When these values are specified for the problem at hand, the table may be entered to find the required sample size.

As an example of its use, suppose we have used the intelligence test described above, and hypothesize that the mean IQ is 100. We have further decided on a two-tailed test, and that if the true mean is as high as 108 or as low as 92, we wish to be quite certain of uncovering that discrepancy. Since the difference of eight IQ points is half of the standard deviation, $d = .5$. To guard against rejecting the hypothesis when it is true, we adopt $\alpha = .05$, and in order to be equally careful about accepting the hypothesis when it is false, we adopt $\beta = .05$. Entering the table with these values of α, β, and d, we find that 55 cases are required.

If the problem is that of testing the difference between two means, Table 19.2 is applicable. *Each* of the two samples must be of the size indicated. Entries in this table are based on the assumption that $\sigma_X = \sigma_Y$, that $n_X = n_Y$, and that the

TABLE 19.1 Approximate Sample Size Required for Testing an Hypothesis about a Single Mean.

d	$\beta = .05$		$\beta = .10$		$\beta = .20$	
	$\alpha = .05$	$\alpha = .01$	$\alpha = .05$	$\alpha = .01$	$\alpha = .05$	$\alpha = .01$
			Two-Tailed Test			
1.50	8	12	7	10	6	9
1.00	15	22	13	19	10	15
.75	25	36	21	31	16	25
.50	55	74	43	64	34	51
.25	208	285	168	238	126	187
			One-Tailed Test			
1.50	7	10	6	9	5	7
1.00	13	19	10	16	8	13
.75	22	31	17	26	13	21
.50	46	65	36	54	27	42
.25	173	252	137	208	99	161

TABLE 19.2 Approximate Sample Size Required for Testing an Hypothesis about the Difference between Two Independent Means.[a]

d	$\beta = .05$		$\beta = .10$		$\beta = .20$	
	$\alpha = .05$	$\alpha = .01$	$\alpha = .05$	$\alpha = .01$	$\alpha = .05$	$\alpha = .01$
			Two-Tailed Test			
1.50	14	20	12	17	9	14
1.00	28	40	23	34	18	27
.75	48	69	40	58	31	46
.50	106	150	87	125	66	100
.25	416	570	336	476	251	374
			One-Tailed Test			
1.50	11	17	9	15	7	12
1.00	23	34	19	29	14	23
.75	40	59	32	50	23	38
.50	90	130	71	108	51	85
.25	346	505	274	417	198	321

[a] The tabled values indicate required size for *each* of the two samples. It is assumed that $\sigma_X = \sigma_Y$ and that $n_X = n_Y$. For dependent samples, see text.

samples are independent. To find approximate sample size for a test between two dependent samples, find sample size from the table, multiply by $(1 - \rho_{XY})$, and increase this value by a few cases to compensate for the loss of degrees of freedom when ρ must be estimated from r.

For both tables, entries are derived on the assumption that populations of scores are normally distributed. Reasonable departure from this assumption will not seriously invalidate usage (see Sections 14.11 and 16.15). Both tables are appropriate when small sample procedures are indicated (see Chapter 17), as well as for large sample situations.†

Frequently, studies are performed by setting the level of significance, and then deciding intuitively on sample size. The tables above make possible a more rational approach to this problem. Using the tables, one faces directly the question of maximum acceptable risk of committing a Type II error, and then selects sample size according to that decision. One practical defect in this approach is that σ_X must be known to determine accurately the value of d. Often a reasonable estimate can be made from results of other studies using the same variable, or from a pilot study. Or, in some instances it may be appropriate to "think in terms of σ units" directly, in which case the problem is avoided.

19.11 Some Implications of Table 19.1 and Table 19.2

Close examination of the tables presented in the previous section points up a number of issues in experimental design. Some have been previously discussed in this chapter. To illustrate, reference is made to Table 19.1, in conjunction with the test of a single mean.

1. If it is satisfactory to discover a discrepancy only when it is large, fewer cases are required. In the example of the previous section ($\alpha = .05$, $\beta = .05$, $d = .5$), if it is required to reject the hypothesis only when the discrepancy is as great as 16 IQ points ($d = 1.00$), a sample of 15 cases would be adequate, rather than one of 55 cases.
2. If it is important to discover a discrepancy as small as one-quarter of a standard deviation of the variable measured, sample size must be rather large. For the same circumstances as above, 208 cases are required.
3. If it is acceptable to increase the risk of a Type II error, smaller sample size is needed. If $\beta = .10$ is adequate (rather than $\beta = .05$) for the problem cited earlier, sample size of 43, rather than 55, will do the job.
4. If α is set at .01 rather than .05, a larger sample will be required to maintain the same protection level for β. For the problem cited, changing α from .05 to .01 means that 74 cases will be required, rather than 55.
5. If a one-tailed test is appropriate, a smaller sample will be required to main-

†In both tables, values for $d = .25$ derive from the properties of the normal curve; others from the properties of noncentral t.

tain the same level of protection for β. In the same problem, if $H_A: \mu < 100$, rather than $H_A: \mu \neq 100$, a sample of 46 cases, rather than 55, will be required.

6. If the problem involves the difference between two means, rather than an hypothesis about a single mean, approximately *twice* as many cases will be required in *each* of the two samples to achieve the same level of protection against committing a Type II error. Compare values in the two tables for equal values of α, β, and d.

19.12 Sample Size Required for Interval Estimates of μ

If certain facts are known, it is possible to find the sample size required to estimate μ with a given degree of precision. For example, suppose it is desired to estimate μ with 95% confidence that it will not be farther away from $\overline{X}$ than four points, and it is known that $\sigma = 16$. The required sample size may be found by Formula 19.1:

Sample Size Required for an Interval
Estimate of Given Width on μ
$$n = \frac{\sigma^2 z_p^2}{w^2}$$
(19.1)

where:
  n = required sample size
  σ^2 = variance of the population of scores
  z_p = magnitude of z for which, in the normal distribution, the probability
     is p of obtaining a value so deviant or more so (in either direction)
  $p = 1 - C$, where C is the confidence coefficient
  w = maximum distance desired between $\overline{X}$ and μ.

For the data of the problem above:

$$n = \frac{(16)^2 (1.96)^2}{4^2} = 62$$

The assumptions for the validity of this estimate are the same as for estimating μ; they are stated in Section 14.11. Note that the formula requires knowledge of σ. Often an approximate estimate of σ can be made from other studies using the same variable.

When construction of the interval depends on estimating σ from the sample, and when an estimate of sample size has been made by the procedure described above, there are two points to remember. First, if the required sample size is small, the interval estimate should be made by the small sample procedures described in Chapter 17 (Section 17.14), rather than by those of Chapter 14 (Section 14.10). Second, when the estimated sample size is small, it tends to be an underestimate. Consequently, when small sample procedures are in order, it is also desirable to use a sample larger by a few cases than that estimated by Formula 19.1.

19.13 Sample Size Required for Interval Estimates of $\mu_X - \mu_Y$

Suppose it is desired to estimate $\mu_X - \mu_Y$ with 95% confidence that it will not be farther away from $(\overline{X} - \overline{Y})$ than four score points, and it is known that $\sigma_X = \sigma_Y = 16$. What sample size will be required? *The method of estimation given below assumes that the two samples are independent, that the size of both samples is the same, and that σ_X and σ_Y are known and equal.* In practical application, an approximate estimate of the population standard deviations can be made from other studies using the same variables. Aside from these special considerations, the assumptions for the validity of the estimate of sample size are the same as for the estimate of $\mu_X - \mu_Y$ itself (see Section 16.15).

The required size of *each* of the two samples may be found by Formula 19.2:

Sample Size Required
for an Estimate $n = \dfrac{2\sigma^2 z_p{}^2}{w^2}$ (19.2)
of Given Width on $\mu_X - \mu_Y$

where:
  n = required size of *each* sample
  σ^2 = variance of the population of X (or Y) scores
  z_p = magnitude of z for which, in the normal distribution, the probability
        is p of obtaining a value so deviant or more so (in either direction)
  $p = 1 - C$, where C is the confidence coefficient
  w = maximum desired discrepancy between $(\overline{X} - \overline{Y})$ and $(\mu_X - \mu_Y)$.

For the data of the problem above:

$$n = \frac{2(16)^2(1.96)^2}{4^2} = 123$$

It is of interest to note that (within rounding error) *twice* as many cases are required for *each* sample to maintain the same distance, w, for the two-sample estimate as were required for the one-sample estimate illustrated in the previous section.

If the estimated sample size is small, the procedures of Chapter 17 should be used (Section 17.15), and sample size should be larger than that indicated by the estimate by a few cases. The procedure described is for independent samples. If samples are dependent, the number of *pairs* of elements may be found by the same procedure, except that the resulting value of n should be multiplied by $(1 - \rho_{XY})$.

19.14 Randomization as Experimental Control

The importance of randomization for statistical inference has been stressed on many occasions (see, especially, Section 13.3). With randomization, it is possible to know the properties of the sampling distribution of the statistic under examination; without it, we are lost. Randomization serves a second function, not always fully appreciated: experimental control.

Consider a study of accuracy of perception. Two samples of subjects are drawn, one experimental condition is imposed upon one group, a second upon the other, and the perception score of each subject is recorded. If subjects are assigned by casual methods to one group or the other, there may well be factors associated with the assignment which are related to the performance being tested. If subjects first to volunteer are placed in one group, the two groups may differ in level of motivation, and so subsequently in performance. If subjects are inspected as they report for the experimental chore and assigned by whim, the experimenter may unconsciously tend to assign those without glasses to the condition where better performance is expected.

The primary experimental (as opposed to statistical) benefit of randomization lies in the chance (and therefore impartial) assignment of extraneous influence among the groups to be compared. The beauty of randomization is that it affords this type of experimental control over extraneous influences whether or not they are known by the experimenter to exist. Note that randomization does not pretend to render the two samples *equal* with regard to such factors. However, if the same procedure were applied in repeated samplings, equality would be achieved in the long run. Thus, randomization insures a lack of bias, whereas other methods of assignment may not.

Inequality of extraneous factors in the samples need not concern us unduly when it is attributable to randomization, since *such variation is taken into account in the standard error formulas*. A happy effect of increasing sample size is that inequality tends to be lessened. Sometimes it is possible to exert tighter control over extraneous factors than can be achieved through randomization alone. The dependent samples design is one such technique (see Section 16.10).

One caution is in order. Inspection of the outcome of randomization sometimes tempts the experimenter to exchange a few subjects from group to group before proceeding with the treatment, in order to obtain groups more nearly alike. Such a move leads to disaster. The standard error formulas are based on the assumption of randomization, and casual adjustment of this kind makes them inappropriate. If they are used anyway, the long run effect is to lower the actual value of α from its nominal value by an unknown amount, and to lower the power of the test by an unknown amount.

19.15 The Experiment versus the *In Situ* Study

In the classic pattern of the experiment, all variables are controlled except the one subject to inquiry. The variable to be studied is then manipulated and the effect on the variable under observation is then examined. For example, one may vary the form of motivation and observe its effect on speed of learning or length of retention. In an experiment, the variable subject to manipulation is called the *independent variable*, and that under observation is called the *dependent variable*.

The two primary characteristics of the experiment are (1) manipulation of the independent variable, and (2) control of extraneous factors. In the example above, the experimenter selects the kind of motivation, and arranges conditions of the test so that if motivation does make a difference its effect will not be clouded by group differences in kinds of subjects, learning task employed, circumstances of learning (other than motivation), etc.

In the basic two-group experiment, control may be achieved in a number of ways. One fundamental technique is to hold the condition of a possible interfering factor constant for every subject in the study. For example, the learning task should be the same for every subject in the learning study, irrespective of motivational treatment. Other means of control are possible. For example, the matched-groups design (see Section 16.10) equates subjects in the two groups on some characteristic, rather than holding the characteristic constant for all subjects. As we learned in the previous section, another important means of control is randomization.

The significance of adequate control can not be overstressed. Only through such control is it possible to move from a statistical conclusion to a substantive conclusion without ambiguity. Statements of causal relationship, in the sense of asserting that certain antecedents lead to certain consequences, can be made with confidence only in such circumstances.

Many independent variables of potential interest are not subject to manipulation by the experimenter. Some are unmanipulable because we are unwilling to do so. For example, the effect of varying brain damage among human subjects must be studied by examining individuals to whom damage has occurred through injury or disease. Other variables are unmanipulable because they are inherent characteristics of the organism. Among such variables are stature, level of intelligence, ethnic group of origin, sex, and age. To study the effect of differences in such a variable, it may be possible to identify subpopulations possessing the desired differences. For example, to study the effect of differences in IQ on a particular learning task, the correlation between IQ and task performance may be obtained, or subpopulations described as high IQ, medium IQ, and low IQ may be identified, sampled, and their mean performance on the learning task compared.

Studies conducted in this manner can not be called experiments, because the element of manipulation of the independent variable is absent. There is no universal name for this type of investigation; we may refer to them as *in situ* studies, in reference to the fact that the characteristic must be taken as we find it in the intact individual. The important difference between experiment and *in situ* study is that in the latter, a significant degree of control is lost. This loss of control makes it difficult to interpret the outcome of such studies. For example, suppose we learn that 50% of female chemistry majors marry, whereas 90% of female home economics majors do so. It is completely unjustified to conclude that marital practice is owed to differential educational experience. What about factors of personality, interest, and intellect which led these women to these educational paths? Had it been possible to assign women at random to the two majors, interpretation of the outcome of the study would be clearer.

When individuals are selected according to differences which they possess in the variable we wish to investigate, they inevitably bring with them associated differences in other dimensions. If differences in these extraneous dimensions are related to the dependent variable we may well find that the different "treatment" groups are significantly different with regard to the dependent variable, but the origins of these differences may be so entangled that it is extremely difficult or even hopeless to sort them out. In short, it is most difficult to develop statements of causal relationship in studies of this type.

This is not to say that *in situ* studies are worthless. Many important empirical questions do not appear approachable in any other way, and there are numerous instances in which such studies have made important contributions to knowledge. Advancement of knowledge through *in situ* studies often calls upon the highest degree of substantive knowledge, and the most skillful devisement of investigatorial tactics.

19.16 Hazards of the Dependent Samples Design

Comparison between means of dependent samples was introduced in Chapter 16. Because of its frequent use in psychology and education, and because a number of hazards are involved in its application, it deserves more detailed consideration. Some of the advantages and disadvantages of this design were considered in Sections 16.12 and 16.13. The present development assumes that background; review may be desirable.

Application and interpretation of the matched pairs design is straightforward when used as an adjunct to the experiment; a single population is sampled, matched pairs of subjects are formed, and the treatment conditions are randomly assigned to the two members of each pair. If matching has been on a variable strongly related to the observation being recorded (the dependent variable), the standard error of the difference between the two means will be smaller, and the power of the test will be increased (see Section 19.8).

Trouble begins when the design of the study departs from these conditions. Three problem situations may be identified.

1. Pairs of observations are formed by repeated observations on the *same* subjects. Assignment of treatment condition is random with regard to the two trials for a given subject.

When repeated measurements are made on the same subjects, it is possible that exposure to the treatment condition assigned *first* may change the subject in some way which will affect his performance on the treatment condition assigned *second*. An influence of this sort is called an *order effect*. Practice, fatigue, and change in set or attitude are examples of such influences. When an order effect is present *and* it can be assumed that the influence of one treatment upon the other is the same as that of the other upon the one, the outcome of the experiment may be interpretable, if treatment condition has been assigned at random with regard to order of treatment. However, the disturbing order effect will introduce an additional source of variation in each set of scores, according to the magnitude of its influence. This tends to increase the standard error, and consequently to decrease the power of the test. The purpose of choosing the dependent-data design is ordinarily to *reduce* extraneous error, but the effect may be quite opposite. If the influence of one treatment upon the other is *not* the same as that of the other upon the one, *bias will be introduced*, as well as unwanted variation. The outcome then becomes difficult or impossible to interpret. For example, if the two treatment conditions are mild and heavy shock, a subject receiving heavy shock first may have a different outlook toward the second trial than one who receives mild shock first.

2. Pairs of observations are formed by repeated observations on the *same* subjects. Assignment of treatment condition to the two trials for a given subject is nonrandom. (This design is typical of "growth" studies of the same subjects.)

If the design utilizes repeated observations on the same subjects but assignment of the treatment condition is not random with regard to order, we are in even graver difficulty. Any order effect will bias the comparison. In many investigations, it is not possible to avoid this problem. For example, it occurs in studies where the object is to determine what change has taken place in subjects over a period of time. Is a particular type of psychotherapy effective? The subjects condition may be evaluated before and after therapy, and the results compared. "Before" and "after" can not be randomly assigned to a subject. The results of comparison are, of course, ambiguous. If there is improvement, is it the result of therapy, the person's belief that he is *supposed* to feel better, the mere fact that someone paid attention to him, or simply a natural recovery that would have taken place without therapy? To be meaningful, the study must include a comparison group, chosen in the same way and treated alike except for the therapy to be evaluated.

Studies of this type may also be subject to another source of bias: the *regression effect*. If subjects are selected *because* of their extreme scores on some measure, we expect remeasurement on the same variable to yield scores closer to the mean. Discussion of this effect and an illustration of it will be found in Section 12.5.

3. The two groups consist of *different* subjects, matched on an extraneous but

related variable. Assignment of treatment condition to members of a matched pair is nonrandom.

These conditions are likely to arise when studying the effect of a non-manipulable variable in intact groups. For example, one may wish to compare attitude test score of men and women who have been matched for level of education, or to compare personality characteristics of delinquent and nondelinquent children matched on parents' socioeconomic level. Such investigations fall in the category of *in situ* studies, described in the last section. They are open to all of the difficulties described there. There are several additional hazards:

1. Matching may reduce, and therefore obscure, the influence of other important variables associated with the variable on which matching took place.
2. When the two intact populations differ widely on the matching variable, it may be possible to form matched pairs only from among those in one group who have low scores on the matching variable and those in the other group who have (among members of that group) relatively high scores on the matching variable. Under these conditions, any conclusion reached will be generalizable only to peculiarly constituted subgroups of the two target populations. The restriction of generalization is diagrammed in Figure 19.7.
3. When subjects are selected for pairing because of their extreme scores on the matching variable, a regression effect may be expected. This is likely to

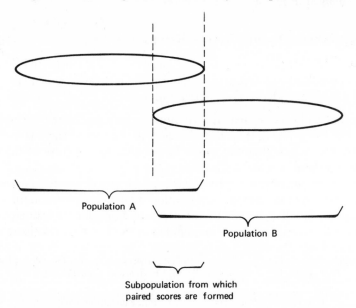

FIGURE 19.7 Restriction of Generalization Resulting from Matching in Discrepant Populations.

occur in studying two intact populations which differ widely on the matching variable. Suppose we wish to compare the effect of educational counseling on mentally retarded students with that on students of normal intelligence, and decide to match subjects on achievement test score. To form matched pairs, students from the mentally retarded population will be selected *because* they have (relatively) high achievement test scores, and students from the normal population *because* they have (relatively) low achievement test scores. Since they were selected because of their extreme scores, a regression effect may be expected. If their achievement were remeasured, we would expect lower scores in the mentally deficient group, and higher scores in the normal group. To the extent that this mismatch affects the outcome of counseling, bias has been introduced.

This section has touched upon some, but not all of the problems in dependent analysis. A most comprehensive and valuable analysis of this problem may be found in the work of Campbell and Stanley.† Their treatment not only covers analysis of dependent samples, but considers systematically many problems of experimental design, and is highly recommended to those who wish to explore this important matter. Two other useful works are those by Kerlinger and by Van Dalen.‡ Although the approach of all of these authors is oriented primarily to problems of design of educational research, their message is just as important for those engaged in psychological research.

19.17 Hypothesis Testing versus Estimation

In statistical analysis of research data, it has been characteristic that hypothesis testing has been used very frequently, and interval estimation much less. There is much to be said for wider use of interval estimation:

1. Its conclusions are stated in terms of the measure of the variable under consideration, rather than in terms of a derived score such as z or t. This brings the investigator into closer terms with the structure of the variable of his concern.
2. Because the outcome is stated in terms of the measure of the variable under consideration, the amount of variation attributable to random sampling fluctuation is called directly to our attention. For example, estimation shows that the limits within which the population value of a correlation coefficient

†D. T. Campbell, and J. C. Stanley, "Experimental and Quasi-experimental Designs for Research on Teaching," in: N. L. Gage, Ed., *Handbook of Research on Teaching*, Rand McNally & Co., Chicago, 1963.

‡F. N. Kerlinger, *Foundations of Behavioral Research*, Holt, Rinehart and Winston, Inc., New York, 1963, Part 4. D. B. Van Dalen, *Understanding Educational Research*, rev. ed., McGraw-Hill Co., New York, 1966, Chapter 11.

may lie are very wide when an estimate of its value is made from a small sample.

3. Estimation helps to do away with the confusion between a statistically significant difference and an important difference (see Section 15.6), a problem arising in interpretation of significance when very large samples are used. It does so because it focuses on the variation in the measure under consideration rather than on the magnitude of a derived variable, such as z or t.

4. Since the null hypothesis is a *point* hypothesis, it is most likely not precisely true in *any* circumstance (see Section 19.10), and therefore interval estimation is more realistic.

5. It helps to avoid the error of thinking that accepting H_0 means that H_0 is true, or probably true (see Section 15.5).

In reports of research, hypothesis testing predominates over interval estimation by a very wide margin. Sometimes hypothesis testing is the preferable procedure, as in an investigation which must lead to a decision for action. (Are the children subnormal in physical fitness? If so, the physical training program should be revised.) But it appears that interval estimation could profitably be used much more often than it is. A thoughtful examination of some of the defects of the hypothesis testing approach has been provided by Bakan.†

PROBLEMS AND EXERCISES

Identify:

Type I error	experiment
Type II error	*in situ* study
power of the test	order effect
independent variable	regression effect
dependent variable	

1. Give an example illustrating the difference between a substantive hypothesis and a statistical hypothesis.

Data 19A

$$H_0: \mu = 80.0 \qquad \sigma_X = 20.0$$
$$H_A: \mu \neq 80.0 \qquad n = 100$$

2. With regard to Data 19A, (*a*) If $\alpha = .05$ and $\mu_{true} = 81.0$, what is β? (*b*) If $\alpha = .05$ and $\mu_{true} = 82.0$, what is β?

3. With regard to Data 19A, (*a*) If $\alpha = .05$ and $\mu_{true} = 83.0$, what is β? (*b*) If $\alpha = .01$ and $\mu_{true} = 83.0$, what is β?

†D. Bakan, "The Test of Significance in Psychological Research," *Psychological Bulletin*, **66**, 423–437 (1966).

4. With regard to Data 19A, (a) If $\alpha = .05$ and $\mu_{true} = 82.0$, what is β? (b) If $\alpha = .05$, $\mu_{true} = 82.0$, but $\sigma_X = 10.0$, what is β?

5. With regard to Data 19A, (a) If $\alpha = .05$ and $\mu_{true} = 84.0$, what is β? (b) If $\alpha = .05$, $\mu_{true} = 84.0$, but $H_A : \mu > 80.0$, what is β?

6. A school research director notes that the norm for an eighth-grade reading test is 80.0. He would like to know whether his eighth-grade students may be considered to perform at this level, or whether they differ. He feels that the risk of making a Type I error should be .05, and that a risk of .10 of making a Type II error would be acceptable. From the data of the norm group, he estimates that the standard deviation of reading test scores is 12.0, and he feels that if the mean of his students is 6 points (or more) away from the norm, it would be important to know it. (a) State the hypothesis and the alternative hypothesis appropriate to his interest. (b) What sample size should he select to test this hypothesis?

7. In reference to Problem 6, what should sample size be if the research director felt that: (a) The risk of a Type II error should be .05? (b) It was important to know it if the mean of his students was 3 points (or more) away from the norm? (c) He would take action only if his students were significantly below the norm. (Consider the three parts of this question to be independent.)

8. A psychologist wonders whether midsemester warning notices improve performance. He decides to select a sample of delinquent students, and, at random, to send such notices to half of them, and no notice to the other half. Experience suggests that among such delinquent students, $\sigma_{gpa} = .30$. He decides to adopt $\alpha = .05$, and $\beta = .05$. If the difference between warned and unwarned students is as great as .075 grade point, he would want to know it. (a) State the hypothesis and the alternative hypothesis appropriate to his interest. (b) What should the size of each sample be to test this hypothesis?

9. In reference to Problem 8, what should sample size be if the psychologist felt that: (a) He should choose $\alpha = .01$ and $\beta = .20$? (b) It was important to know it if the difference between the means was .15 point (or more)? (c) It was only desired to discover if the warning system were different from the nonwarning system, rather than superior to it? (Consider the three parts of this question to be independent.)

10. A psychologist wishes to estimate mean reaction time such that he can be 95% confident that μ is not farther than 3 milliseconds (msec) away from his sample mean. He estimates that the standard deviation of reaction times is 15 msec. What size of sample should he draw?

11. Repeat Problem 10, but with the condition that the confidence coefficient should be .99.

12. With reference to Problem 10, our psychologist now wishes to change the nature of the reaction task and to compare mean reaction time on the original task with that on the altered task. He assumes that the standard deviation will be the same on both tasks, and wants to estimate at the 95% level of confidence the difference between the two population means. He wants this difference to be within 5 msec of the difference between the sample means. (a) If he selects two random samples, what should be the size of each? (b) If he uses subjects matched on a pretest of reaction time and ρ is estimated to be $+.40$ between pairs of measurements, what should be the size of each sample?

13. Repeat Problem 12, but with the condition that the confidence coefficient should be .99.

20

Elementary Analysis
of Variance

20.1 Introduction

In Chapters 16 and 17, we learned how to test for the significance of the difference between two means. This procedure is of great importance because it provides a statistical model for evaluating the outcome of the two-group investigation, the most basic weapon in the researcher's arsenal. For example, in the simplest form of the classic experiment, two groups are treated differently, and examined with regard to the variable under observation to discover if the difference in treatment had an effect.

What if we wish to know about the relative effect of three or more different "treatments"? Does color of a light stimulus make a difference in speed of reaction time? We should want to use more than two colors in examing this question. Is there a difference in effectiveness among three methods of conducting psychotherapy? Among five different genetic strains of rats available for laboratory use, is there a difference in speed of learning?

In each of these examples, the *t* test of the difference between two means could be pressed into service, making comparisons among each possible combination of two means. This method is inadequate in several ways. Consider the example involving five strains of rats. First, there must be ten tests of difference if each strain is to be compared with each of the others. Second, in any one comparison, use is made only of the information provided by the two groups compared; the remaining groups contain information which could make the tests stronger. Third, with so many tests, there is an increased likelihood of declaring that a

353

difference exists among one or more of the comparisons when in fact there is no difference. Fourth, when the ten tests are completed, there are but ten bits of information, but not a single, direct answer as to whether, taken as a whole, there is evidence of difference in performance among the five kinds of animals.

To provide a better answer in the face of these problems, we turn to *analysis of variance*, originally developed by the late Sir Ronald A. Fisher. Analysis of variance is a powerful aid to the investigator. It enables him to design studies more efficiently, to generalize more broadly, and to take account of the complexities of interacting factors. Analysis of variance is actually a class of techniques, designed to aid in hypothesis testing; entire volumes have been written about the subject. In this chapter, we shall develop its details only in its two simplest forms. The first is appropriate to the problems posed earlier in this section; it is variously called *simple analysis of variance*, *one-way analysis of variance*, or the *completely randomized design*. We shall consider it in the next few sections. The second is a form of the *factorial design*, and may be called *two-way analysis of variance*. Its consideration is begun in Section 20.12.

To follow the discussion of this chapter, certain background is needed. Particularly important is a basic understanding of sampling distributions (Chapter 13) and hypothesis testing (Chapters 14 and 15). Specific topics of pertinence, which you may wish to review, include:

1. the concept of variance (Section 6.5)
2. calculation of $\Sigma(X - \overline{X})^2$ (Sections 6.6 and 6.7)
3. $s_X{}^2$ as an estimate of $\sigma_X{}^2$ (Sections 15.8 and 17.9)
4. degrees of freedom in a variance estimate (Section 17.9)
5. independent samples (Section 16.4)
6. t test of the difference between two means (Sections 17.9 and 17.11)
7. homogeneity of variance (Sections 17.9 and 17.12)
8. Type II error (Section 15.7).

20.2 One-Way Analysis of Variance: The Hypothesis

One-way analysis of variance proceeds on the assumption that k samples have been selected independently and at random. The several samples may be designated D, E, F, etc., and the population values of the subgroup means μ_D, μ_E, μ_F, etc. If the different treatment applied to the subgroups has no differential effect on the variable under observation, then we may expect these subgroup means to be equal. To inquire as to whether variation in treatment made a difference, we therefore test the null hypothesis:

$$H_0: \mu_D = \mu_E = \mu_F = \cdots$$

against the alternative that they are unequal in some way. In testing the hypothesis of no difference between *two* means, a distinction was made between directional and nondirectional alternative hypotheses. Such a distinction no longer makes sense when the number of subgroups exceeds two. In the multigroup analysis of variance, H_0 may be false in any one of a number of ways. For example, two or more subgroup means may be alike while the remainder differ, all may be different, etc.

One-way analysis of variance is very closely related to the t test of the difference between two independent means (described in Sections 17.9 and 17.11). In fact, the outcome of analysis of variance applied to the special case of two subgroups is identical with that of the t test. The t test, therefore, may be thought of as a special case of one-way analysis of variance, or, conversely, one-way analysis of variance may be considered as an extension of the t test between independent groups to problems involving more than two subgroups.

In earlier chapters, a distinction was made between approaches to hypothesis testing which were satisfactory for large samples, and others more appropriate for small samples. The t test of the difference between two means was one of those procedures adapted to small samples, but also quite correct for large samples. Because of the relationship between the t test and analysis of variance, one might conclude that analysis of variance is suited to samples of any size. This is quite right.

20.3 The Effect of Differential Treatment on Subgroup Means

Suppose three subgroups of ten cases each have been selected independently and at random, and differential treatment applied. If the difference in treatment has no effect, the distribution of scores in the three subgroups might appear as shown in Figure 20.1. Note that:

1. Scores vary about their subgroup means, and to a similar extent in each subgroup.
2. The subgroup means are similar but not identical.

Both of these observations are in accord with what we have learned about the influence of random sampling variation.

Now suppose that the three treatments *did* have a differential effect. In this case, the distribution of scores in the three subgroups might appear as shown in Figure 20.2. By inspection, we note the following:

1. Within each subgroup, scores vary about their subgroup means, and to an extent similar to that when there was no treatment effect.
2. The subgroup means do not form as close a cluster as they did when there was no treatment effect.

A key to inquiry about the possible differential effect of the three treatments lies in the amount of variation shown among the several subgroup sample means. Of course, we would not expect $\overline{X}_D$, $\overline{X}_E$, and $\overline{X}_F$ all to have the same value even

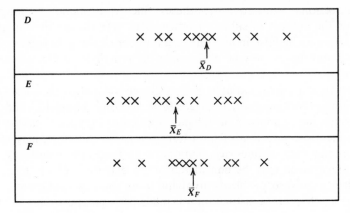

FIGURE 20.1 Distribution of Ten Scores in Three Subgroups: No Treatment Effect.

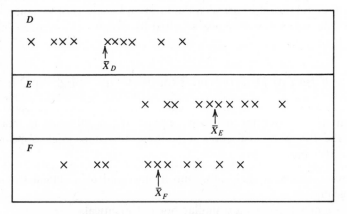

FIGURE 20.2 Distribution of Ten Scores in Three Subgroups: Treatment Effect Present.

when $\mu_D = \mu_E = \mu_F$. These means are subject to random sampling variation. But *how much variation is expected when the subgroup population means are equal?* Fortunately, we have ways of finding out.

If there is no treatment effect, $\mu_D = \mu_E = \mu_F$, and we may treat the three samples as though they came from the same population. Remember that the standard error of the mean measures the amount of variation expected among means of random samples drawn from the same population. If $\mu_D = \mu_E = \mu_F$, we should find the actual variation of our three sample means to be similar, within limits of random sampling fluctuation, to that predicted by the standard error of the mean. On the other hand, if the three subgroup population means are unequal, we should find rather greater variation among the three sample means than that predicted by the standard error of the mean.

20.4 Measures of Variation: Three Sources

The comparison we are after could be conducted quite satisfactorily along the lines developed in the previous section. However, the traditional procedures of analysis have followed a slightly different viewpoint, although one wholly consonant with the reasoning of the previous section. We shall follow this viewpoint because of its universality and because it is more adaptable when one considers advanced forms of the analysis of variance.

Careful study of the examples of the last section will reveal three situations in which an index of variability might be obtained. They are:

1. Variability of scores about their subgroup means.
2. Variability of subgroup means about the mean of the combined distribution.
3. When scores of the several subgroups are combined, variability of the scores about the mean of the combined distribution.

The first two are of particular importance in analysis of variance. *Variability of scores about their subgroup means is of interest because it is a measure of inherent variation, free from the influence of differential treatment which may affect the several groups.*† *Within* a given subgroup, conditions are homogeneous insofar as treatment effect is concerned.

Variability of subgroup means is also of interest, because it reflects *two* sources of variation:

1. *Inherent variation*, free from the influence of treatment effect.
2. Variation attributable to differences between subgroup population means, if any, and therefore *variation attributable to treatment effect, if any*.

We need to develop (1) a measure of variation which reflects only inherent variation, and (2) a measure which reflects inherent variation plus treatment effect, if present, and (3) a means of comparing the two measures. We would expect the two measures to be of the same order if the subgroup population means were equal. However, if the subgroup population means were not equal, we would expect the second measure to be larger than the first.

20.5 Within-Groups and Among-Groups Variance Estimates

True to its name, analysis of variance is concerned with the *variance* as a measure of variability. You will remember (Section 6.5) that the variance of a set of scores is the square of the standard deviation. Thus, σ_X^2 is the variance of a population

---

†In analysis of variance, variance of this kind is sometimes called *error variance*.

of scores, and $\sigma_{\overline{X}}^2$ is the variance of the sampling distribution of means. It is also important to know that an unbiased estimate of a population variance is made by calculating the sum of the squares of the deviations of each score from the sample mean, and *dividing by the number of degrees of freedom associated with that sum of squares* (see Section 17.9).

We will use the symbol σ^2 to mean the variance inherent in the population of scores, *free from the influence of treatment effect*. In the example of Section 20.3, an estimate of σ^2 could be made from any one of the three subgroups by taking the sum of the squares of the deviations of scores in that group from the subgroup mean, and dividing by the appropriate number of degrees of freedom. However, on the assumption that the subgroup population variances are the same for all subgroups (the *assumption of homogeneity of variance*), a better estimate may be made by combining information from these several subgroups. Following the line of thought first described in Section 17.9, such an estimate may be made by pooling the sums of squares of deviation scores from the several subgroups and dividing by the sum of the degrees of freedom characterizing each of the subgroups. This estimate is called the *within-groups variance estimate*; we shall symbolize it by s_W^2. Formula 20.1 shows this variance estimate in deviation score form:

Within-Groups Variance Estimate
$$s_W{}^2 = \frac{\sum(X_D - \overline{X}_D)^2 + \sum(X_E - \overline{X}_E)^2 + \cdots}{(n_D - 1) + (n_E - 1) + \cdots} \tag{20.1}$$

where:
  X_D is a score in subgroup D, etc.
  $\overline{X}_D$ is the mean of subgroup D, etc.
  n_D is the number of elements in subgroup D, etc.

Another estimate of σ^2 is required, one which will reflect influence of the treatment effect (if any) as well as inherent variation. Such an estimate can be derived from the formula for the square of the estimated standard error (variance) of the mean, $s_{\overline{X}}{}^2 = s_X{}^2/n$. Solving this equation for $s_X{}^2$, it reads:

$$s_X{}^2 = ns_{\overline{X}}{}^2$$

An estimate of the variance of the means, $s_{\overline{X}}{}^2$, may be made by finding the deviations of each of the k subgroup means from the mean of the combined distribution, squaring them, summing the squares, and dividing that sum by $k - 1$, the number of degrees of freedom associated with that sum of squares. Substitution of this value in the above equation produces the desired estimate of the variability. This estimate is called the *among-groups variance estimate* and is symbolized by $s_A{}^2$. When the subgroups are of equal size, the formula for this estimate, in deviation score form, is:

Among-Groups Variance Estimate:
Subgroups of Equal Size
$$s_A{}^2 = n\left[\frac{\sum\limits^{k}(\overline{X} - \overline{\overline{X}})^2}{k - 1}\right] \qquad (20.2)$$

where:

$\overline{X}$ is the mean of a subgroup
$\overline{\overline{X}}$ is the mean of the combined distribution of scores
k is the number of subgroups
n is the number of scores in each subgroup

If there is no treatment effect, the subgroup sample means will tend to cluster about $\overline{\overline{X}}$ as predicted by the standard error of the mean, and $s_A{}^2$ will be an unbiased estimate of inherent variation, σ^2. It will, therefore, estimate the same quantity as that estimated by $s_W{}^2$. On the other hand, if there is a treatment effect, the sum of squares of the deviations of the $\overline{X}$'s about $\overline{\overline{X}}$ will tend to be larger, and $s_A{}^2$ will tend to be larger than $s_W{}^2$.

The formula above is appropriate when n, the number of scores in a subgroup, is the same for all subgroups. When sample size differs among subgroups, the appropriate formula is:

Among-Groups Variance Estimate:
Subgroups of Unequal Size
$$s_A{}^2 = \frac{\sum n_i(\overline{X}_i - \overline{\overline{X}})^2}{k - 1} \qquad (20.3)$$

where: n_i is the number of scores in the ith subgroup and $\overline{X}_i$ is the mean of the ith subgroup.

20.6 Partition of Sums of Squares and Degrees of Freedom

To complete the analysis of variance, we require a means of comparing $s_W{}^2$ and $s_A{}^2$. But first, it will be instructive to work a simple example, showing the procedure for finding these two variance estimates. The example will not only help to make the procedure more concrete, but will demonstrate two rather surprising and useful facts.

Suppose there are three treatment groups, D, E, and F, and that the first consists of three scores while the others are comprised of two scores each.†
The scores in each group are shown in the table. First, calculate the mean of

	D	E	F
$\overline{X}_D = 6$	3	4	2
$\overline{X}_E = 7$	5	10	8
$\overline{X}_F = 5$	10		
$\overline{\overline{X}} = 6$			

†The number of scores will serve for explanatory purposes, but is much too small for a practical study.

each subgroup and the mean of all scores combined. These values are shown at the left of the table. Next, calculate s_W^2 according to Formula 20.1:

$$s_W^2 =$$

$$\frac{[(3 - 6)^2 + (5 - 6)^2 + (10 - 6)^2] + [(4 - 7)^2 + (10 - 7)^2] + [(2 - 5)^2 + (8 - 5)^2]}{(3 - 1) + (2 - 1) + (2 - 1)}$$

$$= \frac{62}{4} = 15.5$$

We now calculate s_A^2 according to Formula 20.3:

$$s_A^2 = \frac{3(6 - 6)^2 + 2(7 - 6)^2 + 2(5 - 6)^2}{(3 - 1)}$$

$$= \frac{4}{2} = 2.0$$

Although these two variance estimates are all that are needed to conduct the analysis of variance, it is instructive to calculate a third estimate, made by treating all scores as though they belonged to a single group. This estimate is found by calculating the deviation of each of the seven scores from their mean, $\overline{\overline{X}}$, squaring them, summing the squares, and dividing by $\Sigma n_i - 1$ (which is $7 - 1 = 6$ for this example), the number of degrees of freedom associated with that sum of squares. You will recognize this procedure as the normal one for calculating an estimate of population variance from a sample. We may call this estimate s_T^2; its formula is given below:

Variance Estimate
From from All Scores $$s_T^2 = \frac{\Sigma(X - \overline{\overline{X}})^2}{\Sigma n_i - 1}$$ (20.4)

where: $\overline{\overline{X}}$ is the mean of all scores and n_i is the number of scores in the ith subgroup.

To continue with our example, we calculate s_T^2 according to Formula 20.4:

$$s_T^2 = \frac{(3 - 6)^2 + (5 - 6)^2 + (10 - 6)^2 + (4 - 6)^2 + (10 - 6)^2 + (2 - 6)^2 + (8 - 6)^2}{(7 - 1)}$$

$$= \frac{66}{6} = 11.0$$

Each of the variance estimates is formed by dividing a "sum of squares" by the number of degrees of freedom associated with that sum of squares. In analysis of variance, the sum of squares is usually symbolized by the letters SS; we shall follow that practice.†

†It is also common to refer to s_W^2, s_A^2, and s_T^2 as *mean squares*; thus: MS_W, MS_A, and MS_T. We shall continue to use the former designations in this chapter.

In our example, $SS_W = 62$, $SS_A = 4$, and $SS_T = 66$, the sum of the first two values. This relationship holds in *any* analysis of variance: *the within-groups sum of squares plus the among-groups sum of squares equals the total sum of squares.* Thus:

$$SS_T = SS_W + SS_A$$

In our example, $df_W = 4$, $df_A = 2$, and $df_T = 6$, the sum of the first two values. This relationship also holds in *any* analysis of variance: *the number of degrees of freedom associated with SS_W plus the number of degrees of freedom associated with SS_A equals the number of degrees of freedom associated with SS_T.* Thus:

$$df_T = df_W + df_A$$

These are the characteristics which give rise to the name, analysis of variance. The sum of squares which contributes to total variance, and the number of degrees of freedom, may be analyzed, or partitioned, into component parts, each attributable to different sources.

In analysis of variance, it is convenient to present a summary table indicating source, and the corresponding sum of squares, degrees of freedom, and variance estimate. Such a table is shown in Table 20.1. One advantage of such a table is that it shows the basic result of the analysis very clearly. Another is that it makes clear that the several sums of squares add to equal the total sum of squares, and that the several degrees of freedom add to equal the total number of degrees of freedom. Note that the table does not show s_T^2. Although SS_T and df_T are of interest in analysis of variance, s_T^2 is of no use, and is therefore ordinarily not computed.

TABLE 20.1 Table of Analysis of Variance, Showing the Partition of Sums of Squares and Degrees of Freedom.

Source	df	SS	(MS) s^2
Within Groups	4	62.00	15.50
Among Groups	2	4.00	2.00
Total	6	66.00	

20.7 Raw Score Formulas for Analysis of Variance

So far, we have discussed analysis of variance in terms of sums of squares of deviation scores. This approach helps to see what is happening. When the goal is ease of computation, rather than understanding, raw score formulas are more practical than those expressed in deviation scores. The raw score formulas for SS_W, SS_A, and SS_T appear below:

Within-Groups Sum of Squares: Raw Score Formula

$$SS_W = \overset{\overset{\text{all}}{\text{scores}}}{\sum} X^2 - \left[\frac{(\sum X_D)^2}{n_D} + \frac{(\sum X_E)^2}{n_E} + \cdots \right] \tag{20.5}$$

Among-Groups Sum of Squares: Raw Score Formula

$$SS_A = \left[\frac{(\sum X_D)^2}{n_D} + \frac{(\sum X_E)^2}{n_E} + \cdots \right] - \frac{(\overset{\overset{\text{all}}{\text{scores}}}{\sum} X)^2}{\sum n_i} \tag{20.6}$$

Total Sum of Squares: Raw Score Formula

$$SS_T = \overset{\overset{\text{all}}{\text{scores}}}{\sum} X^2 - \frac{(\overset{\overset{\text{all}}{\text{scores}}}{\sum} X)^2}{\sum n_i} \tag{20.7}$$

SS_W and SS_A yield the desired variance estimates when divided by the appropriate number of degrees of freedom:

Within-Groups Variance Estimate $\qquad s_W{}^2 = \dfrac{SS_W}{\sum (n_i - 1)} \tag{20.8}$

Among-Groups Variance Estimate $\qquad s_A{}^2 = \dfrac{SS_A}{k - 1} \tag{20.9}$

where: n_i is the number of cases in the ith subgroup and k is the number of subgroups. According to Formulas 20.5 and 20.6, the basic quantities which require computational labor are (1) the sum of the squares of all the scores, (2) the sum of all the scores, and (3) the sum of the scores in each subgroup. It is easy to arrange computational routine to find the third quantity as part of the procedure of finding the second.

We may apply these formulas to the problem of the previous section, by way of illustration. Once again, the distribution of scores:

D	E	F
3	4	2
5	10	8
10		

$$SS_W = 3^2 + 5^2 + 10^2 + 4^2 + 10^2 + 2^2 + 8^2$$
$$- \left[\frac{(3 + 5 + 10)^2}{3} + \frac{(4 + 10)^2}{2} + \frac{(2 + 8)^2}{2} \right]$$

$$= 318 - 256 = 62$$

$$SS_A = \frac{(3 + 5 + 10)^2}{3} + \frac{(4 + 10)^2}{2} + \frac{(2 + 8)^2}{2}$$

$$- \frac{(3 + 5 + 10 + 4 + 10 + 2 + 8)^2}{3 + 2 + 2}$$

$$= 256 - 252 = 4$$

Note that the values obtained for SS_W and SS_A are exactly the same as those obtained by the deviation score formulas in the previous section.

It is easier to see what number of degrees of freedom corresponds to each sum of squares when working with deviation scores than when working with raw scores. For reference, let us summarize:

$$df_W = \sum(n_i - 1)$$
$$df_A = k - 1$$
$$df_T = \sum n_i - 1$$

where: n_i is the number of cases in the ith subgroup and k is the number of subgroups. In the problem illustrated above, these values are: $df_W = 4$, $df_A = 2$, and $df_T = 6$.

20.8 The *F* Distribution

To compare the two estimates, s_W^2 and s_A^2, we must consider the probability distribution of the *F* ratio, a statistic devised by R. A. Fisher, and named in his honor. *F* is formed by the ratio of two unbiased variance estimates:

F Ratio $\qquad\qquad F = s_1^2/s_2^2$ $\qquad\qquad$ (20.10)

The tabled values of *F* describe the distribution of *F* when:

1. The population of scores is normally distributed.
2. Two sample estimates, s_1^2 and s_2^2 have been made of the same population variance, σ^2.
3. The scores comprising each estimate have been selected at random from the population.
4. The two samples from which the estimates arise are independent.

If these conditions have been met, *F* will have the distribution characteristics given in Table H, in the appendix. To use this table, we enter it with the number of degrees of freedom associated with the estimate appearing in the numerator of *F*, and the number of degrees of freedom associated with the estimate appearing in the denominator. Like the *t* distribution, the *F* distribution is actually a family

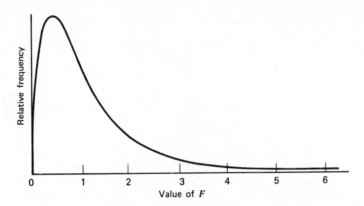

FIGURE 20.3 Distribution of F for 4 Degrees of Freedom in the Numerator and 20 Degrees of Freedom in the Denominator. From: *Statistical Inference* by Helen M. Walker and Joseph Lev. Copyright 1953 by Holt, Rinehart and Winston, Inc. Reprinted by permission of Holt, Rinehart and Winston, Inc.

of curves, depending on the number of degrees of freedom associated with the variance estimates. The distribution of F is shown in Figure 20.3 for 4 degrees of freedom in the numerator and 20 degrees of freedom in the denominator.

Note that this distribution is skewed positively. This is intuitively reasonable. If two estimates are made of the same value (σ^2), the estimate placed in the numerator may be smaller than that in the denominator, in which case F will be less than 1.00, but not less than zero. But if the estimate placed in the numerator is larger than that in the denominator, the F ratio may be much larger than 1.00.

20.9 Comparing s_W^2 and s_A^2 According to the F Test

From the analysis of variance of the data of our sample (Section 20.6), we have two estimates of σ^2: s_W^2 and s_A^2. We form them into an F ratio:

$$F_{\text{calcd}} = \frac{s_A^2}{s_W^2} = \frac{2}{15.5} = .13$$

Now s_A^2 estimates variance inherent in the scores, plus variance attributable to treatment differences (if any), whereas s_W^2 estimates only variance inherent in the scores. If the assumptions have been satisfied, *and there is no treatment effect*, both s_A^2 and s_W^2 estimate the same quantity, σ^2, and F_{calcd} will be distributed as F_{tabled}.† If, on the contrary, there is a treatment effect, this will tend to inflate s_A^2, and F_{calcd} will be larger than otherwise.

†You may recall that F follows the tabled distribution of F only if the two variance estimates are independent. s_W^2 and s_A^2 *are* independent, despite the fact that the same scores form the source of both estimates.

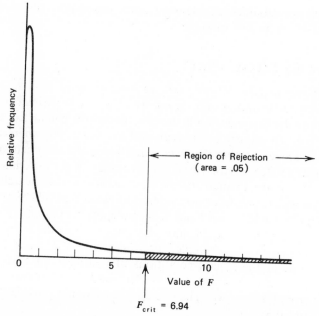

FIGURE 20.4 Distribution of F for 2 and 4 Degrees of Freedom.

To test the hypothesis that $\mu_D = \mu_E = \mu_F$, we must compare the calculated value of F with the values of F which would occur through random sampling if the hypothesis were true. Now if s_A^2 is *always placed in the numerator of F, as is customary, the hypothesis of equality of subgroup means will be rejected only if the calculated value of F is larger than expected.* Consequently, the region of rejection is placed entirely in the *upper* tail of the F distribution. In our example, there were 2 degrees of freedom associated with s_A^2 and 4 degrees of freedom associated with s_W^2. Turn to Table H, and locate the entries corresponding to $df = 2$ in the numerator and $df = 4$ in the denominator.† Assuming that we wish to adopt the 5% significance level, the critical value of F is 6.94. This is the value of such magnitude that it would be equalled or exceeded but 5% of the time in random sampling when the hypothesis is true. Beyond this value, therefore, lies the region of rejection, as shown in Figure 20.4. It is clear that the obtained value of $F = .13$ lies much below that critical value, and the null hypothesis will be accepted.

The rather low value of F brings up a point of interest. To what are we to attribute a very *low* value of F? If the assumptions are correct, a low F simply means that the subgroup means are closer together than might ordinarily be

†Be sure to keep straight which df characterizes the numerator and which the denominator. Note that tabled entries are not the same for 4 and 2 df as they are for 2 and 4 df.

expected. Other possibilities include error in the calculations, or selection of the wrong model of analysis of variance.

20.10 After the *F* Test, What?

In discussing the analysis of variance, we have assumed that the question of overall equality of the subgroup means was the one of primary importance. This is certainly the first question if the experiment was conducted as a "fishing expedition;" i.e., an inquiry in the region of the unknown, where the primary purpose is to discover whether the several conditions of a treatment do or do not have a differential effect on the variable under study. If the experiment has been conducted with this idea in mind and the outcome is to accept the null hypothesis, the study is complete: we have no evidence to claim that differential treatment made a difference. On the other hand, if the outcome is to reject the null hypothesis, we may well wish to inquire more specifically as to the source of the significant *F*. It could be, for example, that the difference is owed to the errant effect of but one of the several conditions of treatment, or that among four conditions of treatment, two are alike in effect, and the other two are also alike but different from the first two. The overall *F* test can not provide the answer to questions of this type.

Other circumstances may also point to the desirability of inquiring about relationships between certain subgroup means, rather than to an overall test of significance. Suppose that the study has been organized not as a wide-open fishing expedition, but with some particular questions in mind. For example, one subgroup may be subjected to a standard treatment and the remainder to several varieties of experimental treatment. In these circumstances there may be two questions of primary importance: (1) Is there a difference between the effect of the standard treatment and the average effect of the experimental treatments, and (2) is there a difference among the several varieties of the experimental treatment?

Procedures exist for making more specific analyses than that provided by the overall *F* test, and which are appropriate for answering questions of the type posed above. On first thought, one might consider that individual *t* tests between subgroup means (in the manner of Chapter 17) might be the proper way to answer many of these questions. Actually, this is the *least* satisfactory of the several approaches which have been developed. Because there are several approaches, and because development of an understanding needed to make the best selection for a particular problem takes more space than can be afforded in this book, it must suffice to make reference to other sources. Two reasonably full treatments of this subject may be found in the works of Edwards and of Hays.†

†A. L. Edwards, *Experimental Design in Psychological Research*, 3rd ed., Holt, Rinehart and Winston, Inc., New York, 1968, Chapter 8. W. L. Hays, *Statistics for Psychologists*, Holt, Rinehart and Winston, Inc., New York, 1963, Chapter 14.

20.11 Review of Assumptions

Several assumptions have been mentioned as necessary for the analytic model presented to be entirely correct. We collect them here for purposes of review:

1. The subgroup populations are normally distributed.
2. Samples are drawn at random.
3. Selection of elements comprising any subgroup is independent of selection of elements of any other subgroup.
4. The variances of the several subgroup populations are the same for all subgroups (homogeneity of variance).

As with the *t* test for independent means, moderate departure from conditions specified in the first and fourth requirements will not unduly disturb the outcome of the test. Resistance to such disturbance is enhanced when sample size rises. In any event, tiny samples are hardly worth while because of the substantial risk of committing a Type II error. If there is a choice, it is desirable to select samples of equal size for the subgroups. This will make computation a little simpler, minimize the effect of failing to satisfy the condition of homogeneity of variance, and, for a given Σn_i, minimize the probability of committing a Type II error.

The most troublesome problem is probably that of obtaining random samples. Attention is called to an earlier discussion of this problem in Sections 14.11 and 14.12.

The third assumption (independent samples) reminds us that the analysis described in this chapter is not appropriate for repeated measures on the same subjects, nor when matched subjects have been assigned to treatment groups. Other techniques of analysis of variance are designed to handle problems of this sort.

20.12 Two-Way Analysis of Variance

One analysis of variance design, a step up in complexity, permits the simultaneous study of the effect of two types of treatment conditions. For example, we may wish to study the relative legibility of three styles of type under two levels of illumination. We form six subgroups, one for each combination of style of type and level of illumination, and assign at random, say, ten subjects to each subgroup. Table 20.2 illustrates the subgroup means which might result.

An analysis of variance may be performed on the data, and three basic *F* tests of significance may be performed. First, it is possible to inquire whether style of type made a difference in the legibility score. There is greater generality to the outcome of this test than if it were conducted in the form of a "basic" experiment. In a basic experiment, illumination would be fixed at some arbitrarily chosen level, and the conclusions would apply only to situations characterized by *that* level of illumination. In this experiment, conclusions are not so restricted.

TABLE 20.2 Two-Way Analysis of Variance: Subgroup Means.

Level of illumination	Style of type		
	A	B	C
High	$\bar{X} = 33$	$\bar{X} = 40$	$\bar{X} = 33$
Low	$\bar{X} = 23$	$\bar{X} = 35$	$\bar{X} = 8$

Second, it is possible to inquire whether level of illumination made a difference in the subjects' legibility score. Once again, the conclusions are broader than would obtain if a study of the effect of illumination had been conducted using only a single type style. Another benefit of this design now appears: we have been able to answer *two* questions for the price of *one*. If the two questions had been conceived separately, and a one-way analysis of variance conducted (each based on the same number of observations), *twice* the number of observations would have been required.

Third, we are able to examine a new and important question, one which can not be answered by the simple *t* test or by the one-way analysis of variance: *whatever the difference among the several styles of type, is it the same for both levels of illumination?* In analysis of variance, this question is referred to as one of *interaction* effect. If the *F* test for interaction is significant, it means that differences attributable to styles of type are *not* the same for both levels of illumination. This can be illustrated more clearly by graphic representation of the several subgroup means, as shown in Figure 20.5. In this figure, straight lines connect those subgroup means characterized by a particular level of illumination. According to Figure 20.5, it appears that legibility is somewhat improved by greater illumination irrespective of style of type. However, if the effect of level of illumination was the *same* for all type styles, we would expect the two lines to be parallel (within limits of random sampling fluctuation). This does not seem to be the case.† Specifically, type style C appears especially to suffer under the condition of low illumination.

This question of interaction of factors is easy to overlook when the approach is through the design of the basic experiment, but it is obviously very important. As a further example, suppose that teaching method A has been shown to be

---

†In effect, in the problem illustrated, the *F* test for interaction examines the question of whether the two lines depart significantly from a parallel relationship.

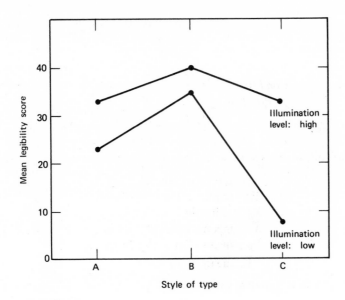

FIGURE 20.5 Interaction Effect: Two-Way Analysis of Variance.

superior to teaching method B among children of superior intelligence. Will the same superiority of method hold for children of inferior intelligence? The question is one of interaction of method and level of intelligence.

20.13 A Problem in Two-Way Analysis of Variance

Analysis of variance (of whatever type) is often referred to by a contraction of its name: *anova*. We shall use this term from time to time. Now let us begin the step-by-step development of two-way analysis of variance.

In a learning experiment, we may want to know whether there is a difference in performance among three kinds of motivation and also whether there is a difference between two conditions of practice. The table below shows the 12 scores which might be obtained in such a study, if two subjects were assigned at random to each of the six possible combinations of kind of motivation and condition of practice.† We shall designate the three conditions of motivation as C_1, C_2, and C_3, (column effect), and the two conditions of practice as R_1 and R_2 (row effect).

†(a) The number of cases is too small for a practical study, but will serve to illustrate the calculations involved; (b) in the two-way design, it is important to have an equal number of cases in each cell (see Section 20.19).

Kind of Motivation

	C_1	C_2	C_3
R_1	4,4	2,3	8,6
R_2	6,8	5,4	10,13

Condition of Practice (labels R_1, R_2 appear at left)

In what is to follow, we shall use the following symbolism:

X: scores in general
X_{C_i}: scores in the ith column
X_{R_i}: scores in the ith row
$\overline{X}_{C_i}$: mean of the ith column
$\overline{X}_{R_i}$: mean of the ith row
$\overline{X}$: mean of all scores

We will develop four variance estimates:

$s_{WC}{}^2$ (*within cells estimate*), derived from the discrepancy between scores within each cell. This measure is of interest because it is free from the influence of possible differences between columns (column effect), possible differences between rows (row effect), and also free from any interaction effect, if present. It therefore measures only inherent variation, and is analogous to $s_W{}^2$ in one-way anova.

$s_C{}^2$ (*column estimate*), derived from the differences between column means. If the difference in kind of motivation has no effect, then $\mu_{C_1} = \mu_{C_2} = \mu_{C_3}$, and variation among column means ($\overline{X}_{C_1}$, $\overline{X}_{C_2}$, and $\overline{X}_{C_3}$) will be affected only by inherent variation. Under these circumstances, $s_C{}^2$ will estimate the same quantity estimated by $s_{WC}{}^2$. If there is a difference among kinds of motivation, $s_C{}^2$ will tend to be larger than otherwise. It is therefore analogous to $s_A{}^2$ in one-way anova.

$s_R{}^2$ (*row estimate*), derived from the differences between row means. If the difference in condition of practice has no effect, then $\mu_{R_1} = \mu_{R_2}$, and variation among row means ($\overline{X}_{R_1}$ and $\overline{X}_{R_2}$) will be affected only by inherent variation. It is therefore just like $s_C{}^2$, except that it is sensitive to row effect rather than to column effect.

$s_{R \times C}{}^2$ (*interaction estimate*), derived from the discrepancy between the means of the several cells and the values predicted for each on the assumption of no interaction.† If there is no interaction, $s_{R \times C}{}^2$ will be responsive only to inherent variation, and will estimate the same

---

†It is customary to read $R \times C$ as R by C; thus we speak of the "row by column interaction."

quantity estimated by s_{WC}^2. If interaction is present, it will tend to be larger.

Each of three variance estimates, s_C^2, s_R^2, and $s_{R \times C}^2$, is responsive (1), to the presence of the effect for which it is named (column effect, row effect, and interaction effect), and (2), to inherent variation. s_{WC}^2, on the other hand, is responsive only to inherent variation. When the three estimates are at hand, F's may be formed by placing each in turn in the numerator and s_{WC}^2 in the denominator. A significantly large F will then serve as an indicator of the presence of the effect specially associated with the kind of estimate placed in the numerator.

20.14 Partition of the Sum of Squares for Two-Way Anova

In two-way analysis of variance, we divide the total sum of squares (SS_T) into four components:

$$SS_T = SS_C + SS_R + SS_{R \times C} + SS_{WC}$$

where:
SS_T is the total sum of squares, generated from the deviation of each score from the mean of all scores, $(X - \overline{\overline{X}})$
SS_C is the sum of squares for columns, generated from the deviation of each column mean from the mean of all scores, $(\overline{X}_{C_i} - \overline{\overline{X}})$
SS_R is the sum of squares for rows, generated from the deviation of each row mean from the mean of all scores, $(\overline{X}_{R_i} - \overline{\overline{X}})$
$SS_{R \times C}$ is the sum of squares for interaction, generated from the deviation of each cell mean from the value predicted for that cell on the assumption of no interaction
SS_{WC} is the sum of squares within cells, generated from the deviation of each score from its cell mean, $(X - \overline{X}_{\text{cell}})$

This time, we will bypass the deviation score formulas, since the raw score formulas are more practical for actual computation.
SS_T is calculated in the same way as for one-way anova:

Total Sum of Squares

$$SS_T = \sum^{\substack{\text{all} \\ \text{scores}}} X^2 - \frac{\left(\sum^{\substack{\text{all} \\ \text{scores}}} X \right)^2}{n_{\substack{\text{all} \\ \text{scores}}}} \tag{20.7}$$

SS_C is calculated from the column totals and the grand total:

Column Sum of Squares

$$SS_C = \frac{\left(\sum X_{C_1} \right)^2}{n_{C_1}} + \frac{\left(\sum X_{C_2} \right)^2}{n_{C_2}} + \cdots - \frac{\left(\sum^{\substack{\text{all} \\ \text{scores}}} X \right)^2}{n_{\substack{\text{all} \\ \text{scores}}}} \tag{20.11}$$

Similarly, SS_R is calculated from the row totals and the grand total:

Row Sum of Squares

$$SS_R = \frac{(\sum X_{R_1})^2}{n_{R_1}} + \frac{(\sum X_{R_2})^2}{n_{R_2}} + \cdots - \frac{(\overset{\text{all}}{\underset{\text{scores}}{\sum}} X)^2}{n_{\underset{\text{scores}}{\text{all}}}} \qquad (20.12)$$

SS_{WC} is calculated from the individual scores and from the cell totals:

Within Cells Sum of Squares

$$SS_{WC} = \overset{\text{all}}{\underset{\text{scores}}{\sum}} X^2 - \overset{\text{all}}{\underset{\text{cells}}{\sum}} \left[\frac{(\overset{\text{cell}}{\sum} X)^2}{n_{\text{cell}}} \right] \qquad (20.13)$$

The second half of the last expression means that we are to find the total of the scores in a given cell, square it, and divide by the number of cases in the cell. Repeating this operation for each cell, the resultant quantities are summed and that sum is subtracted from ΣX^2. It is really rather easier than it sounds. Let us illustrate with the data of the table in the previous section:

$$SS_T = 4^2 + 4^2 + 6^2 + 8^2 + \cdots + 13^2$$

$$- \frac{(4 + 4 + 6 + 8 + \cdots + 13)^2}{12} = 110.92$$

$$SS_C = \frac{(4 + 4 + 6 + 8)^2}{4} + \frac{(2 + 3 + 5 + 4)^2}{4} + \cdots$$

$$- \frac{(4 + 4 + 6 + 8 + \cdots + 13)^2}{12} = 68.17$$

$$SS_R = \frac{(4 + 4 + 2 + 3 + 8 + 6)^2}{6} + \frac{(6 + 8 + 5 + 4 + 10 + 13)^2}{6}$$

$$- \frac{(4 + 4 + 6 + 8 + \cdots + 13)^2}{12} = 30.09$$

$$SS_{WC} = 4^2 + 4^2 + 6^2 + 8^2 + \cdots + 13^2$$

$$- \left[\frac{(4 + 4)^2}{2} + \frac{(6 + 8)^2}{2} + \frac{(2 + 3)^2}{2} + \cdots \right] = 9.50$$

Since the several components (SS_C, SS_R, $SS_{R \times C}$, and SS_{WC}) sum to equal SS_T, we may most easily find $SS_{R \times C}$ by subtraction:

$$SS_{R \times C} = SS_T - (SS_C + SS_R + SS_{WC})$$

$$= 110.92 - (68.17 + 30.09 + 9.50)$$

$$= 3.16$$

20.15 Degrees of Freedom in Two-Way Analysis of Variance

The total number of degrees of freedom also may be divided into components associated with each sum of squares:

$$df_T = df_C + df_R + df_{R \times C} + df_{WC}$$

In counting degrees of freedom, we shall let C equal the number of columns, R equal the number of rows, and n_{WC} equal the number of scores within each cell. Since there are C deviations involved in the computation of SS_C, $df = C - 1$; similarly, $df_R = R - 1$. In computing SS_{WC}, we consider the deviation of each score in the cell from the cell mean. Consequently, each cell contributes $n_{WC} - 1$ degrees of freedom, and

$$df_{WC} = \overset{\substack{\text{all} \\ \text{cells}}}{\sum}(n_{WC} - 1)$$

Computation of SS_T involves as many deviations as there are scores, or $(R)(C)(n_{WC})$ of them; consequently, df_T is one less than this number. Finally, $df_{R \times C} = (R - 1)(C - 1)$. Applying this information to the present problem, we have:

$$df_C = (C - 1) = 2$$
$$df_R = (R - 1) = 1$$
$$df_{R \times C} = (R - 1)(C - 1) = 2$$
$$df_{WC} = \sum(n_{WC} - 1) = 6$$
$$df_T = (R)(C)(n_{WC}) - 1 = 11$$

Note that the degrees of freedom for the first four components sum to 11, the number of degrees of freedom accorded to SS_T.

20.16 Completing the Analysis

To complete the analysis, each variance estimate (s^2) is calculated by dividing each component sum of squares by the number of degrees of freedom associated with it, as in one-way anova. Then, the three F's are calculated according to the principle described at the end of Section 20.13. The resultant values are shown in Table 20.3.

We now turn to the tabled values of F (Table H, in the appendix) to learn what magnitude must be reached or exceeded to declare significance. We shall assume that $\alpha = .05$ has been selected for all tests. Since the F for column effect and the F for interaction have 2 df associated with the numerator and 6 df associated with the denominator, the critical value of F is 5.14. The F row effect has 1 and 6 df associated with it, and the critical value is 5.99. These values are shown at the right in Table 20.3. The obtained F's for column effect and row effect both exceed

TABLE 20.3 Outcome of the Two-Way Analysis of Variance.

Source	df	SS	s^2	Calcd. value of F	Crit. value of $F\,(\alpha = .05)$
Columns	2	68.17	34.09	$F = s_C{}^2/s_{WC}{}^2 = 21.58$	5.14
Rows	1	30.09	30.09	$F = s_R{}^2/s_{WC}{}^2 = 19.04$	5.99
Columns × rows	2	3.16	1.58	$F = s_{R \times C}{}^2/s_{WC}{}^2 = 1.00$	5.14
Within cells	6	9.50	1.58		
Total	11	110.92			

their critical values; consequently, the hypotheses that $\mu_{C_1} = \mu_{C_2} = \mu_{C_3}$ and that $\mu_{R_1} = \mu_{R_2}$ are rejected. The obtained F for interaction, on the other hand, is not significant.

To return to the substantive problem, the analysis gives reason to believe that the differences in motivation (column effect) made a difference in performance and that the difference in condition of practice also made a difference in performance. The nonsignificant outcome of the test for interaction means that there are no grounds for believing that the relative effect of the three kinds of motivation differed between the two practice conditions, or, if we wish to put it the other way around, that there are no grounds for believing that the relative effect of the two conditions of practice differed among the three motivational conditions.

20.17 Studying the Outcome of Two-Way Anova

If the outcome of any of the three F tests is significant, it will generally be useful to calculate the several cell means and study them. To see what is going on, these may be cast in a table, as in the earlier example shown in Table 20.2, or, even better, in graphic form, as in Figure 20.5. For the present problem, Figure 20.6 shows the six cell means. The line labeled R_1 shows the means for the R_1 condition of practice under the several kinds of motivation (C_1, C_2, and C_3). The line labeled R_2 shows the means for the R_2 condition of practice under the same circumstances. This figure shows that one condition of practice was consistently superior to the other. Similarly, we see that there were differences in performance according to the several kinds of motivation employed. The nonsignificant interaction component is reflected by the fact that the two lines are reasonably parallel.

20.18 Interaction and the Interpretation of Main Effects

The column effect and the row effect are called *main effects*. In our example, the tests for both main effects were significant. Interpretation of such an outcome is

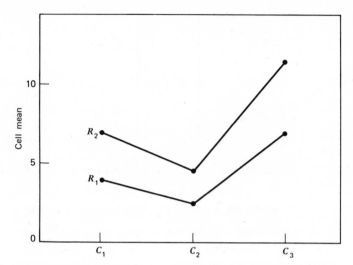

FIGURE 20.6 Cell Means for a 2 × 3 Analysis of Variance: Data from Section 20.13.

clear when there is no interaction. However, when interaction is present, the outcome of tests for main effects may be clouded. Consider Figure 20.7, which shows two possible outcomes in which significant interaction is present in a 2 × 2 analysis of variance. In the first part of this picture (at the left), it is apparent that one row condition (R_1) results in rather higher scores than the other. At the same time, it appears that the difference between R_1 and R_2 is greater under the condition C_2 than under C_1.

The second part of Figure 20.7 shows an interesting possibility. The average effect of R_1 (under condition C_1 and C_2) is not different from the average effect of R_2, a fact which would be reflected by a nonsignificant F in the test for row effect. Similarly, the average effect of C_1 (under conditions R_1 and R_2) is not different from the average effect of C_2. At the same time, the nonparallel lines show the strong interaction effect which is present. According to the data, high performance may be expected when R_1 occurs in combination with C_1, *or* when R_2 occurs in combination with C_2.

A hypothetical situation may help in understanding the meaning of such a finding. Suppose we wish to compare the effectiveness of two teachers and of two teaching methods. It might be that one teacher is quite effective when using one method and not so effective when using the other, whereas just the reverse is true for the other teacher.

It should be clear that it is particularly important to study the several values of the cell means when the test for interaction is significant. As Figure 20.7 shows, the meaning of the outcome of the tests for main effects is highly dependent on the particular nature of the interaction effect.

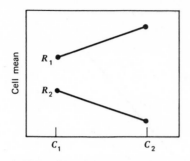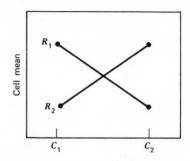

FIGURE 20.7 Cell Means for 2 × 2 Analyses of Variance: Interaction Present.

20.19 Some Comments on Two-Way Analysis of Variance

Two-way analysis of variance is by no means limited to a 2 × 2 or 3 × 2 design. Each variable may be represented by two conditions, or any number of conditions greater than two. A review of the computational procedure will make it plain that any such arrangement may be easily accommodated.

It is quite important, in two-way analysis of variance, to assign at random an *equal* number of cases to each cell. If this is not the case, the procedure illustrated may not apply. Indeed, it may be necessary to make new assumptions (which cannot be easily verified) in order to finish the analysis, and a decision must be made as to how to proceed. Advanced texts describe the hazards and offer approximate solutions for this situation. As the authors of one such volume say, "The point of advice will become painfully evident . . . when the student tries to struggle through the morass of arithmetic and interpretative difficulties that threaten to engulf him when dealing with data for which the numbers in the subclasses are unequal."†

PROBLEMS AND EXERCISES

Identify:

one-way analysis of variance	*F* distribution
within-groups variance estimate	two-way analysis of variance
among-groups variance estimate	interaction effect
F ratio	main effect

1. With reference to Table H, what tabled value of *F* is so great that it would be exceeded in random sampling only 5% of the time when there are: (*a*) 5 degrees of freedom in the numerator and 20 in the denominator? (*b*) 20 degrees of freedom in the numerator and 5 in the denominator? (*c*) 3 degrees of freedom in the numerator and 40 in the denominator? (*d*) 6 degrees of freedom in the numerator and 100 in the denominator?

†P. O. Johnson and R. W. B. Jackson, *Modern Statistical Methods*, Rand McNally & Company, Chicago, 1959, p. 234.

Data 20A

There are three subjects in each of three treatment groups. Scores are as follows:

Group L:	2,	7,	3
Group M:	7,	9,	5
Group N:	9,	12,	9

2. Approach the following problems through the deviation score formulas. For Data 20A: (a) Find SS_W, SS_A, and SS_T. Does $SS_W + SS_A = SS_T$? (b) What are the values of df_W, df_A, and df_T? Does $df_W + df_A = df_T$? (c) Find s_W^2 and s_A^2. (d) Present the outcome developed so far in an analysis of variance table. (e) Test the hypothesis that $\mu_L = \mu_M = \mu_N$ at $\alpha = .05$ and state your conclusions.

3. Repeat Problem 2 using the raw score formulas.

4. In the analysis of variance F test, why is it that only the area in the upper tail of the F distribution is of interest?

Data 20B

Group O:	2,	5,	6		
Group P:	4,	7,	11,	8	
Group Q:	8,	8,	12,	15,	15

5. Approach the following problem through the deviation score formulas. For Data 20B: (a) Find SS_W, SS_A, and SS_T. (b) What are the values of df_W, df_A, and df_T? (c) Find s_W^2 and s_A^2. (d) Present the outcome so far developed in an analysis of variance table. (e) Test the hypothesis that $\mu_O = \mu_P = \mu_Q$ at $\alpha = .05$ and $\alpha = .01$, and state your conclusions.

6. Repeat Problem 5 using the raw score formulas.

7. Which approach do you recommend for Data 20B: the raw score approach or the deviation score approach? Explain.

8. An experimenter wishes to evaluate the effectiveness of four teaching methods among three kinds of students. The study is conducted as a two-way analysis of variance, and each combination of method and type of student is represented by five subjects. (a) What df characterizes each of the SS's which will be calculated? (b) If the tests are conducted at the 5% level of significance, what is the critical value of F for testing difference among methods? For difference among types of students? For interaction?

Data 20C

	Col 1	Col 2
Row 1	2,4	1,5
Row 2	3,6	3,4

9. Suppose the eight numbers shown in the body of the table entitled Data 20C represent scores obtained in a two-way analysis of variance. (a) Find df_T, df_C, df_R, df_{WC}, and $df_{R \times C}$. (b) Find SS_T, SS_C, SS_R, SS_{WC}, and $SS_{R \times C}$. (c) Calculate the several variance estimates appropriate to two-way anova, and present the results so far developed in a table. (d) Calculate the F's required to test the main effects and the interaction effect. Draw the statistical conclusions appropriate when $\alpha = .05$.

10. "A good way to begin computation of two-way anova is to find, for each cell, the number of raw scores, the sum of them, and the sum of their squares." Would you agree? Explain.

Data 20D

	Teaching machine	Conventional method
Bright students	5, 7, 9	10, 11, 15
Ordinary students	5, 10, 9	4, 8, 6

11. An experiment is designed to test the relative effectiveness of the teaching machine method of instruction as compared with the conventional method. Two samples of three subjects each were selected from among students of good aptitude, and assigned to the two methods of instruction, as shown in Data 20D. Two samples of the same size were selected from among students of ordinary ability, and assigned to the same methods of instruction (also shown in Data 20D). In the test trial, the 12 students earned the scores shown in Data 20D. (a) Find df_T, df_C, df_R, df_{WC}, and $df_{R \times C}$. (b) Find SS_T, SS_C, SS_R, SS_{WC}, and $SS_{R \times C}$. (c) Calculate the several variance estimates appropriate to two-way anova, and present the results so far developed in an analysis of variance table. (d) Calculate the F's required to test the main effects and the interaction effect. Draw the statistical conclusions appropriate when $\alpha = .05$ and $\alpha = .01$. (e) Construct a graph of the cell means in the manner of Figure 20.7. (f) In the light of the statistical outcome (d), and the graph (e), what appears to be the essential sense of the study?

21

Inference about Frequencies

21.1 Introduction

In previous chapters, problems in hypothesis testing have been concerned with hypotheses about summary characteristics of a distribution (or distributions), such as the mean, or the correlation coefficient. In this chapter, we introduce the *chi-square statistic*, which may be used to test hypotheses about entire frequency distributions. The central question is how to make an inference about a population distribution from the evidence contained in a sample distribution. To approach this question, one compares the obtained (sample) frequencies characterizing the several categories, or class intervals, of the distribution with those frequencies expected according to the researcher's hypothesis. The methods of this chapter, then, are used to test hypotheses about frequencies, and, since proportions may be converted to frequencies, about proportions.

As originally developed, this approach was intended for distributions of a categorical nature, i.e., those in which the several classes consist of unordered, qualitative categories, such as eye color, sex, or political affiliation. However, it may also be used with continuous, quantitative variables by treating the several class intervals as "categories."

21.2 A Problem in Discrepancy between Expected and Obtained Frequencies

Is there a difference, among four brands of cola drink, in the proportion of consumers who prefer the taste of each? This question might be

379

answered by allowing subjects to taste each of the four brands and then declare their preference. Of course, suitable experimental conditions must be provided to control for possible extraneous influences, such as knowledge of brand name or order of presentation. Suppose an appropriately designed experiment is conducted among 100 subjects selected at random, and the *obtained frequencies* of preference (f_o's) are as indicated in Table 21.1. To answer the question, we shall hypothesize that the cola drinks do not differ in regard to the proportion of people who prefer each. According to this null hypothesis, the expected proportionate preference for each cola is $1/4$, and the *expected frequency* of preference (f_e) for each is $(1/4)(100) = 25$.

TABLE 21.1 Expected and Obtained Frequency of Preference for Four Brands of Cola (100 Subjects).

	Brand A	Brand B	Brand C	Brand D	
Observed frequency	$f_o = 20$	$f_o = 31$	$f_o = 28$	$f_o = 21$	$\Sigma f_o = 100$
Expected frequency	$f_e = 25$	$f_e = 25$	$f_e = 25$	$f_e = 25$	$\Sigma f_e = 100$

The expected frequencies are those which would, *on the average*, occur in indefinite repetitions of such an experiment when no differential preference exists. In any one experiment, we anticipate that the obtained frequency of choices will vary from the expected frequencies in accord with random sampling variation. But how much variation is reasonable to expect? Some measure of discrepancy is needed, and a means of testing whether the obtained discrepancy is within the bounds of random sampling variation.

21.3 Chi-Square (χ^2) as a Measure of Discrepancy between Expected and Obtained Frequencies

The *chi-square* statistic, χ^2, provides a measure of the discrepancy between expected and obtained frequencies. Its basic formula, suited to this task, is:

Chi-Square
$$\chi^2 = \Sigma \left[\frac{(f_o - f_e)^2}{f_e} \right] \qquad (21.1)$$

where: f_e is the expected frequency and f_o is the obtained frequency and summation is over the number of discrepancies characterizing a given problem.

For the data of Table 21.1 there are four discrepancies, and chi-square is calculated as follows:

$$\chi^2_{calcd} = \frac{(20-25)^2}{25} + \frac{(31-25)^2}{25} + \frac{(28-25)^2}{25} + \frac{(21-25)^2}{25}$$

$$= \frac{(-5)^2 + 6^2 + 3^2 + (-4)^2}{25} = 3.44$$

Examination of the formula and the illustrated calculation reveals several points of interest about χ^2:

1. χ^2 can not be negative since all discrepancies are squared; both positive and negative discrepancies make a positive contribution to the value of χ^2.
2. χ^2 will be zero only in the unusual event that each obtained frequency exactly equals the expected frequency.
3. Other things being equal, the larger the discrepancy between the f_e's and their corresponding f_o's, the larger χ^2 will be.
4. *But*, it is not the size of the discrepancy alone which accounts for a contribution to the value of χ^2; it is the size of the discrepancy *relative to the magnitude of the expected frequency*.

    This is intuitively reasonable. For example, if we toss a number of coins and inquire as to the number of "heads," f_e is 6 when 12 coins are tossed, and 500 when 1000 coins are tossed. If 11 heads are obtained in 12 tosses, the discrepancy is 5, most unusual. However, if 505 heads are obtained in 1000 tosses, the discrepancy is also 5, hardly a rarity.
5. The value of χ^2 depends on the *number* of discrepancies involved in its calculation. For example, if the experiment described above had been limited to three brands of cola instead of four, there would be one less discrepancy to contribute to the total of χ^2. The method of evaluating χ^2 must therefore take this factor into account. This is done by considering the number of *degrees of freedom* (*df*) associated with the particular χ^2, as explained in Section 21.5.

21.4 The Logic of the Chi-Square Test

Although the chi-square test is conducted in terms of frequencies, *it is best viewed conceptually as a test about proportions*. For example, in the cola experiment we explore the possibility that in the population of consumers, the *proportion* of individuals preferring each brand is 1/4. The hypothesized proportions are derived from a substantive question of interest to the researcher, and, as usual, *the hypothesis concerns the population proportions*, not sample proportions. Our concern with the sample is simply to see whether it is in reasonable accord with what is hypothesized to be true of the population.

To conduct the test, we must generate expected frequencies, and these are obtained for each category by multiplying the proportion hypothesized to characterize that category in the population by sample size. Thus, the expected frequency of preference for Brand A is $(1/4)(100) = 25$. An expected frequency is the mean of the obtained frequencies which would occur on indefinite repetitions of such an experiment when the hypothesis is true and sampling is random.

When the hypothesis is true, the several obtained frequencies will vary from their corresponding expected frequencies according to the influence of random sampling fluctuation. The calculated value of χ^2 will be smaller when agreement between f_o's and f_e's is good and larger when it is not.

When the hypothesized f_e's are *not* the true ones, the set of discrepancies between f_o and f_e will tend to be larger than otherwise, and, consequently, so will the calculated value of χ^2. To test the hypothesis, we must learn what calculated values of χ^2 would occur under random sampling when the hypothesis is true. Then we will compare the χ^2 calculated from our particular sample with this distribution of values. If it is so large that such a value would rarely occur when the hypothesis is true, the hypothesis will be rejected. For example, if the 5% significance level is adopted, the hypothesis will be rejected for values of χ^2 so large that their prior probability of occurrence is .05 or less.

21.5 Chi-Square and Degrees of Freedom

To evaluate a given χ^2, the number of degrees of freedom (*df*) associated with it must be taken into account. The concept of degrees of freedom has been encountered earlier (Chapter 17). In that setting, *df* proved to be a function of sample size. However, *in χ^2 problems with frequency data, the number of degrees of freedom is determined by the number of ($f_o - f_e$) discrepancies which are independent of each other*, and are therefore "free to vary."

In considering what this means, it may be easier to think of the number of obtained frequencies which may be written independently. The key to understanding is that the *total* number of observations must be considered as fixed. In the cola problem, for example, there are 100 responses. In the four cells corresponding to the four brands of cola, any three of the f_o's are free to vary. But, once three are determined, the fourth is fixed since the total of all four must be 100. There are, therefore, 3 degrees of freedom for the cola problem. If the experiment had been conducted with three colas rather than four, there would be 2 degrees of freedom. In general, the number of degrees of freedom for problems of this type will be $C - 1$, where C is the number of categories involved.

The cola problem is an example of one general class of problems which may be approached through the chi-square test. Other classes of problems exist, as we shall see. For these, determination of the number of degrees of freedom proceeds somewhat differently, although according to the same general principle. This question will be considered as it arises.

21.6 The Random Sampling Distribution of Chi-Square

When the hypothesis to be tested is true *and certain conditions hold*, the sampling distribution formed by the values of χ^2 calculated from repeated random samples closely follows a known theoretical distribution. These conditions will be discussed in Section 21.7. Actually, there is a *family* of sampling distributions of χ^2, each member corresponding to a given number of degrees of freedom. Figure 21.1 shows several of the theoretical models of the sampling distribution for differing values of *df*.

Table G in the appendix may be used to determine the probability of obtaining a sample χ^2 greater than a specified amount. To use this table, it must be entered with the appropriate *df*. For example, the table shows that when *df* = 1, the probability is .05 of obtaining a χ^2 equal to or greater than 3.84.

We may return to the cola problem to illustrate the table's use in conducting a test. If the test is conducted at the 5% significance level, we must identify the value of χ^2 so large that it will be equaled or exceeded but 5% of the time in random sampling when the null hypothesis is true. In the cola problem, *df* = 3, and entering Table G with this value, we find that the critical value is 7.82. The test situation is illustrated in Figure 21.2. The value of χ^2 calculated from the

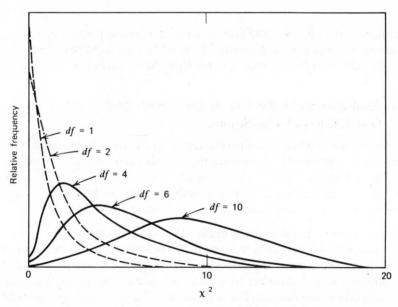

FIGURE 21.1 Approximate Forms of the χ^2 Distribution for Certain Degrees of Freedom. Reproduced with permission from: E. F. Lindquist, *Design and Analysis of Experiments in Psychology and Education*, Houghton Mifflin Co., Boston, 1953.

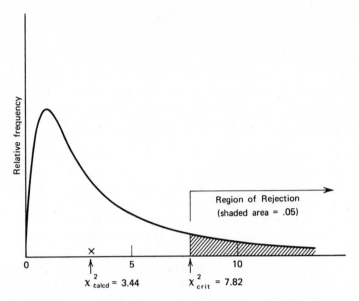

FIGURE 21.2 Location of the Calculated Value of χ^2 Relative to the Expected Sampling Distribution of χ^2 when $df = 3$.

experimental data is 3.44, and falls short of the critical point. The $(f_o - f_e)$ discrepancies are therefore of a magnitude small enough to be reasonably expected when the null hypothesis is true, and the hypothesis will not be rejected.

21.7 Assumptions in the Use of the Theoretical Distribution of Chi-Square

The percentage points of the distribution of χ^2, as recorded in Table G, follow from certain theoretical considerations. The distribution of χ^2, owed to Karl Pearson, is therefore a theoretical model, and obtained values of χ^2 may be expected to follow this distribution exactly only when the assumptions appropriate to this model are satisfied. What are these assumptions?

1. It is assumed that the sample drawn is a random sample from the population about which inference is to be made. In practice, this requirement is seldom fully met because of the difficulty in identifying each element of the target population and therefore in giving each element an equal opportunity for inclusion in the sample. The discussion in Section 14.12 is quite as relevant here as there. We are often reduced to limiting our conception of the target population to what we may hope we have adequately sampled, taking precautions to exclude obvious sources of bias, and hoping that our sampling procedure, though not strictly random, has been sufficiently carefully done

that the sample is *like* what would have occurred under true random sampling.

2. It is assumed that observations are independent. For example, in the cola experiment, utilizing 100 randomly selected subjects, the preference of one individual is not predictable from that of any other. But suppose each subject had been given three trials. There would then be 300 responses from the 100 subjects. In all likelihood the three responses of each subject are not independent of each other. If so, the chi-square model is not appropriate. In general, the set of observations will not be completely independent when their number exceeds the number of subjects.

3. It is assumed that, in repeated experiments, observed frequencies will be normally distributed about expected frequencies. With random sampling, this *tends* to be true. There are two important ways in which this assumption may be violated:

   (a) When f_e is small, the distribution of f_o's about f_e tends to be positively skewed. For instance, when $f_e = 3$, f_o can be no more than three points lower, but it may range to a greater distance above. In subsequent discussion of the χ^2 model, suitable cautionary rules of thumb will be offered according to the particular circumstances.

   (b) Pearson's theoretical distribution of chi-square is smooth and continuous. In other words, the theoretical distribution makes allowance for the possibility that a particular χ^2 may have *any* fractional value, such as 3.645, 3.646, etc. On the other hand, the obtained values of χ^2 actually form a discrete distribution.† The reason is that adjacent values of f_o can differ *only* in terms of full units. For example, in the cola problem, the first discrepancy is: $f_o - f_e = 20 - 25$. The *least* amount by which this discrepancy can be greater is: $f_o - f_e = 19 - 25$, a full unit larger. Comparing the obtained values of χ^2, which form a discrete series, with the continuous distribution of theoretical values may result in a degree of error. The importance of this discrepancy is, fortunately, minimal unless both n and df are small. A correction exists when $df = 1$, and will be explained as the circumstance arises.

21.8 The Alternative Hypothesis

In the chi-square test, the null hypothesis is that in the population distribution the proportional frequency in each subcategory equals a specified value. In the cola experiment, these values were predicated upon equal preference among the four brands. In this experiment, if the hypothesis is false, it could be that a preference exists for the first of the colas, but that the remainder are equally,

†See Section 2.5 for discussion of discrete and continuous measures.

if less, attractive. It could also be false in that the first two are preferred above the second two, or that a difference in preference exists in numerous other ways. As we have found, when the true expected frequencies differ from the hypothesized expected frequencies *in any way*, the obtained value of χ^2 tends to be enlarged. It is for this reason that *the region of rejection always appears in the* upper tail *of the sampling distribution of χ^2*.

What, then, is the nature of the alternative hypothesis?† It simply specifies that the null hypothesis is untrue in some (any) way. Note that the distinction between a directional test and a nondirectional one, encountered in connection with tests about means (see Section 14.7), is no longer pertinent. The chi-square test is, so to speak, "nondirectional."

What of the other tail of the chi-square distribution? A very low obtained value of χ^2 means that, *if the assumptions have been met and the calculation is correct*, the obtained frequencies are rather closer to the expected frequencies than chance would ordinarily allow. A very small value of χ^2 has no significance other than to remind us to check on the adequacy of our procedure.

21.9 Chi-Square and the 1 × C Table

The development of the cola problem has taken place over several sections; it is now time to consider the general problem which that application exemplifies, and to summarize the procedure. That problem illustrates one of the several classes of problems for which χ^2 may be useful in testing the discrepancy between expected and obtained frequencies. The class of problems to which the cola problem belongs may be termed the "*one-variable case*," because it always involves the categories of a single variable. Problems of this class are sometimes said to be characterized by a 1 × C table, where C is the number of categories or class intervals.

In the 1 × C table, χ^2 may be used to test whether the relative frequencies characterizing the several categories (or class intervals) of a sample frequency distribution are in accord with the set of such values hypothesized to be characteristic of the population distribution. In any such problem, the hypothesized relative frequency of occurrence in each class interval is dictated by the substantive hypothesis of interest. In the cola problem, the hypothesized proportions derive from interest in the possibility that the four brands are equally attractive.

The hypothesized proportions need not be equal. For example, one of Mendel's finding regarding heredity holds that plants bred in a particular way will show one of four characteristics, and that the relative frequency of those characteristics will occur according to the ratio 9:3:3:1. In an experiment designed to test this hypothesis, the ratios will be converted into relative fre-

†The concept of the "alternative hypothesis" is discussed in Sections 15.2 and 15.3.

quencies such that their sum equals 1.00. Thus, the relative frequencies, or proportions, are: $p_1 = 9/16$, $p_2 = 3/16$, $p_3 = 3/16$, and $p_4 = 1/16$. Suppose plants are bred in the specified manner, and a sample of 256 seedlings is obtained. Upon examining the characteristics of these seedlings, some exhibit one characteristic and some another, as indicated in Table 21.2. The expected frequencies, obtained by multiplying each of the above-hypothesized relative frequencies by 256, are also shown in the table. Calculating χ^2 according to Formula 21.1 we have:

$$\chi^2 = \frac{(130 - 144)^2}{144} + \frac{(55 - 48)^2}{48} + \frac{(50 - 48)^2}{48} + \frac{(21 - 16)^2}{16} = 4.03$$

For problems of this general class, the number of degrees of freedom is one less than the number of categories, and here, therefore, $df = 3$. Is the discrepancy between expected and obtained frequencies so great as to be beyond the realm of chance? We turn to Pearson's function (Table G), and find that when $df = 3$, a χ^2 of 7.82 or greater would occur by chance 5% of the time when the hypothesis is true. Our χ^2 is not so rare an event (the table shows that its probability of occurrence is between .20 and .30). If the test is conducted at the 5% significance level, we have therefore no reason to reject the statistical hypothesis. The sample outcome offers no reason to refute Mendel's hypothesis.

TABLE 21.2 Expected and Obtained Frequency of Occurrence of Four Inherited Plant Characteristics.

Type 1	Type 2	Type 3	Type 4	
$f_o = 130$	$f_o = 55$	$f_o = 50$	$f_o = 21$	$\Sigma f_o = 256$
$f_e = 144$	$f_e = 48$	$f_e = 48$	$f_e = 16$	$\Sigma f_e = 256$

It should be mentioned that the chi-square test is not satisfactory when the expected frequencies are very small. Discussion of the issues involved and recommendations for practice will be found in Section 21.12.

21.10 The 1 × 2 Table and the Correction for Discontinuity

Suppose we want to know if light or dark enters into a preference of rats when given two alternative routes at a choice point in a maze. A study may be designed which incorporates controls designed to guard against extraneous factors such as a tendency for the animal always to choose alternatives which are on a particular side. If then 50 rats are afforded the opportunity of choosing between two routes, one light and the other dark, the obtained frequencies may appear as follows:

$$\text{light}: \quad f_o = 15 \qquad \text{dark}: \quad f_o = 35$$

If illumination makes no difference, the proportionate preference should be $1/2$ for each side, and the two f_e's are each $(1/2)(50) = 25$. By Formula 21.1:

$$\chi^2 = \frac{(15 - 25)^2}{25} + \frac{(35 - 25)^2}{25} = \frac{(-10)^2}{25} + \frac{10^2}{25} = 8.00$$

In this problem, the number of degrees of freedom is equal to one. In the special circumstance that $df = 1$, a correction may be applied to compensate for the error involved in comparing calculated values of χ^2, which form a discontinuous distribution, with the theoretical tabled values of χ^2, which form a continuous distribution. This correction is known as *Yates' correction*, or the *correction for discontinuity*, and consists in reducing the discrepancies between f_o and f_e by .5 before squaring. Thus, the corrected value of χ^2 is:

$$\chi^2 = \frac{(|15 - 25| - .5)^2}{25} + \frac{(|35 - 25| - .5)^2}{25}$$

$$= \frac{(9.5)^2}{25} + \frac{(9.5)^2}{25} = 7.22$$

The vertical bars in the formula indicate that $1/2$ unit is to be subtracted from the *absolute* discrepancy (discrepancy taken without regard to sign) before squaring.

We have 1 degree of freedom, and if the test is conducted at the 5% significance level, $\chi^2_{\text{crit}} = 3.84$. Since χ^2_{calcd} exceeds that value, the hypothesis will be rejected. Apparently, light or dark is a factor in the rat's choice.

Yates' correction is always applicable to chi-square tests of hypotheses about frequencies when $df = 1$. It makes less difference when the number of observations is large, but because it is easy to apply and improves the accuracy of the test, it ought always to be used. It is *not* a satisfactory correction when $df > 1$; there is no simple alternative. Fortunately, the need for a correction is slight when $df > 1$, so we need not be concerned.

Earlier (Section 21.7), we learned that the chi-square test is not satisfactory when expected frequencies are very small. When $df = 1$, both f_e's ought to equal or exceed 5. Further discussion appears in Section 21.12.

21.11 The Sign Test

Let us suppose that an investigator wishes to study the effect of the physical arrangements in a sorting task. Each of 20 subjects is given a shuffled deck of 52 playing cards, and asked to sort them according to suit, putting them into four labeled boxes placed in front of him. The time required for the subject to complete the sort is recorded. We shall suppose that speed of performance improves with practice, but not generally beyond the 15th trial. Our investigator gives his subjects 20 trials, rearranges the order in which the sorting boxes are placed before the subject, and conducts another trial. Let us suppose that the sorting times for trial 20 and 21 are those indicated in Table 21.3.

To inquire as to whether rearrangement of the sorting boxes made a difference in performance, one might elect to test the significance of the difference of mean sorting time for trial 20 and trial 21. If so, the appropriate procedure is that for dependent samples, since both trials involve the same subjects.

A different approach is possible. Let us assign the symbol "+" to a pair of observations when the sorting time on trial 21 is higher than for trial 20, and "−" when the opposite occurs. Such a classification is indicated in Table 21.3.

TABLE 21.3 Time (in Seconds) for Two Trials in a Card Sorting Task for 20 Subjects.

	Time				Time		
Subject	Trial 20	Trial 21	Difference	Subject	Trial 20	Trial 21	Difference
1	51	53	+	11	39	45	+
2	40	47	+	12	48	50	+
3	42	40	−	13	50	55	+
4	54	63	+	14	47	52	+
5	48	55	+	15	51	50	−
6	42	48	+	16	42	46	+
7	39	40	+	17	47	50	+
8	50	54	+	18	54	58	+
9	47	46	−	19	58	60	+
10	57	61	+	20	51	54	+

Now if the conditions under which the two trials were conducted make no difference, we would expect that there would be as many "pluses" as "minuses," within limits of sampling fluctuation. This question is open to interpretation in terms of chi-square. The expected and obtained frequencies of "plus" and "minus" are shown below.

$$
\begin{array}{ccc}
 & (-) & (+) \\
f_o: & 3 & 17 \\
f_e: & 10 & 10
\end{array}
$$

Chi-square is calculated with Yates' correction, since $df = 1$.

$$\chi^2 = \frac{(|17 - 10| - .5)^2}{10} + \frac{(|3 - 10| - .5)^2}{10} = \frac{(6.5)^2}{10} + \frac{(6.5)^2}{10} = 8.45$$

With 1 degree of freedom, χ^2 must reach or exceed 3.84 to be significant at the 5% level, and 6.64 to be significant at the 1% level. Our χ^2 surpasses both of these critical values. It is clear that reordering the position of the sorting boxes made a difference in performance.

This application of the 1×2 chi-square table is sometimes known as the *sign test*. It is not as sensitive as the test of the difference between means, since it disregards some information which the other procedure takes into account. Specifically, each "plus" simply indicates that the sorting time on trial 21 is higher than that for the same subject on trial 20, but no account is taken of how much higher.

In conducting a test according to these principles, it will occasionally occur that some of the differences will be zero, and cannot, therefore, be categorized as $+$ or $-$. This dilemma may be solved in one of several ways. Probably the simplest is to ignore such cases, reduce n accordingly, and proceed with the test on the remaining values.

21.12 Small Expected Frequencies and the Chi-Square Test

In Section 21.7, we learned that the χ^2 test is dependent on the assumption that the f_o's will be normally distributed about their f_e's. When f_e is quite small, the distribution of f_o's will tend to be skewed, and the theoretical chi-square model will not be adequate. The matter is of greater consequence when df is small than when it is large.

Knowledgeable statisticians vary in their recommendations, but none argues that the test is satisfactory when $df = 1$ *and* when any f_e is less than 5 (some propose 10). We shall support the more liberal criterion: *all f_e's should equal or exceed 5 when $df = 1$.* Please note that the requirement concerns *expected* frequencies and not obtained frequencies.

There is even less agreement when $df > 1$. One suggestion frequently offered for contingency tables (see Section 21.13) is that if no more than 1/5 of the expected frequencies are less than 5, then an expected frequency as low as 1 is allowable.†

For problems involving one degree of freedom, procedures alternative to chi-square are available when expected frequencies fall below permissible levels. These procedures are described in other volumes. Several appropriate references are listed in Section 21.19.

21.13 Contingency Tables and the Hypothesis of Independence

So far, we have considered the application of chi-square to the one-variable case. It also has important application to the analysis of bivariate frequency distribu-

---

†W. G. Cochran, "Some methods for strengthening the common χ^2 tests," *Biometrics*, **10**, 417–451 (1954).

tions. For example, suppose we poll 400 students on a college campus and ask what role they feel students should have in determining the college curriculum. We may wish to analyze the nature of their response in relation to college major of the respondents. Do students with different majors see their role in the same way?

To study this question, the data are classified in a bivariate distribution, as indicated in Table 21.4. As an example of the information conveyed by the table, note that of the 400 students, 200 were majors in Humanities and Arts, and of the 200 Humanities and Arts majors, 72 thought that students should be voting members of the college curriculum committee.

In many ways, this table is similar to the bivariate frequency distributions encountered in the study of correlation (see Chapter 9). Indeed, the major difference is that the two variables (student's major and student's role) are both qualitative variables rather than quantitative variables.† As with a correlation table, we may ask whether there is a relationship between the two variables. That is, is classification of response independent of classification of the respondent's major, or is one contingent upon the other in some way?

TABLE 21.4 Classification of Responses of 400 College Students to the Question: "How Should Students Participate in Determining the Curriculum?"

Role of Students

College Major of Respondents		Recommendation through student association	Nonvoting membership on college curriculum committee	Voting membership on college curriculum committee	
	Humanities and Arts	46	82	72	$f_{row} = 200$
	Science	42	38	20	$f_{row} = 100$
	Business	52	40	8	$f_{row} = 100$
		$f_{col} = 140$	$f_{col} = 160$	$f_{col} = 100$	$n = 400$

†For ordinary Pearson r, both variables are continuous and quantitative. For the chi-square test, either or both *may* be unordered, qualitative variables.

Bivariate frequency distributions of the type illustrated in Table 21.4 are known as *contingency tables*. From such a table we may inquire what cell frequencies would be expected if the two variables are independent of each other. Then, chi-square may be used to compare the obtained cell frequencies with those expected under the hypothesis of independence.

21.14 Finding Expected Frequencies in a Contingency Table

How shall we determine the expected frequency for a given cell when it is hypothesized that the two variables are independent? In Section 13.5, we learned that the probability of the joint occurrence of two events is the product of the separate probabilities of the two events, provided that the two are independent. If the two variables of classification are independent, the probability that a response will fall in a given cell is the product of the probability of a response falling in the column in which that cell appears and the probability of a response falling in the row in which that cell appears. Symbolically, we have:

$$p_{\text{cell}} = (p_{\text{col}})(p_{\text{row}})$$

The probability of a response falling in a particular column or row may be found by dividing the frequency of responses in that column or row by total number of responses:

$$p_{\text{row}} = \frac{f_{\text{row}}}{n} \quad \text{and} \quad p_{\text{col}} = \frac{f_{\text{col}}}{n}$$

The expected *frequency* of response for a particular cell may be found by multiplying the cell probability by total number of responses:

$$f_{e\,\text{cell}} = (p_{\text{cell}})(n)$$

Combining the information developed so far, we have:

$$f_{e\,\text{cell}} = \left(\frac{f_{\text{col}}}{n}\right)\left(\frac{f_{\text{row}}}{n}\right)(n)$$

It is apparent that this formula may be simplified; the result is shown below as Formula 21.2:

Expected Cell Frequency under $\quad f_{e\,\text{cell}} = \dfrac{(f_{\text{col}})(f_{\text{row}})}{n}$ $\qquad\qquad$ (21.2)
the Hypothesis of Independence

To illustrate its use, let us calculate the expected frequency for the upper right cell in Table 21.4:

$$f_e = \frac{(100)(200)}{400} = 50$$

This value, and those for each of the other eight cells, appear in Table 21.5. Note that, in any row or column, the total of the expected frequencies equals that of the observed frequencies. This fact affords a useful check on accuracy of calculation of the f_e's.

TABLE 21.5 Expected and Obtained Frequency of Response to a Question Asked of College Students (Data from Table 21.4).

Role of Students

		Recommendation through student association	Nonvoting membership on college curriculum committee	Voting membership on college curriculum committee	
	Humanities and Arts	$f_o = 46$ $f_e = \dfrac{(140)(200)}{400} = 70$	$f_o = 82$ $f_e = \dfrac{(160)(200)}{400} = 80$	$f_o = 72$ $f_e = \dfrac{(100)(200)}{400} = 50$	$f_{row} = 200$
	Science	$f_o = 42$ $f_e = \dfrac{(140)(100)}{400} = 35$	$f_o = 38$ $f_e = \dfrac{(160)(100)}{400} = 40$	$f_o = 20$ $f_e = \dfrac{(100)(100)}{400} = 25$	$f_{row} = 100$
	Business	$f_o = 52$ $f_e = \dfrac{(140)(100)}{400} = 35$	$f_o = 40$ $f_e = \dfrac{(160)(100)}{400} = 40$	$f_o = 8$ $f_e = \dfrac{(100)(100)}{400} = 25$	$f_{row} = 100$
		$f_{col} = 140$	$f_{col} = 160$	$f_{col} = 100$	$n = 400$

(College Major of Respondents)

21.15 Calculation of χ^2 and Determination of Significance in a Contingency Table

Now that the expected and obtained frequencies are at hand for each cell (Table 21.5), χ^2 may be calculated according to Formula 21.1. As usual, each $(f_o - f_e)$ discrepancy is squared and divided by f_e. The sum of these nine components is the calculated value of χ^2.

$$\chi^2 = \frac{(46 - 70)^2}{70} + \frac{(42 - 35)^2}{35} + \frac{(52 - 35)^2}{35} + \frac{(82 - 80)^2}{80} + \frac{(38 - 40)^2}{40}$$

$$+ \frac{(40 - 40)^2}{40} + \frac{(72 - 50)^2}{50} + \frac{(20 - 25)^2}{25} + \frac{(8 - 25)^2}{25} = 40.28$$

How many degrees of freedom are associated with this χ^2? To figure degrees of freedom in a contingency table, we consider that the column totals and the row totals are fixed, and ask how many cell frequencies are free to vary. In general, for an $R \times C$ contingency table, their number (and therefore the number of degrees of freedom) is $(C - 1)(R - 1)$, where C is the number of columns and R is the number of rows. For the problem currently under consideration, $df = (3 - 1)(3 - 1) = 4$.

If the hypothesis of independence is true, we should expect that random sampling will produce obtained values of χ^2 which are in accord with the tabled distribution of that statistic. If the hypothesis is false in any way, the calculated value of χ^2 will tend to be larger than otherwise. As before, then, the region of rejection is placed in the upper tail of the tabled distribution. For $df = 4$, Table G shows that when the test is conducted at $\alpha = .05$, $\chi^2_{crit} = 9.49$, and when $\alpha = .01$, $\chi^2_{crit} = 13.28$. The calculated χ^2 is 40.28, a value exceeding both critical points. Accordingly, the hypothesis of independence is rejected.

The same cautions voiced earlier concerning small expected frequencies apply to χ^2 as calculated from contingency tables. See Section 21.12 for advice on this matter.

Since the contingency table is analogous to the correlation table, it might be thought that χ^2, like r, provides a measure of strength of association. Although χ^2 may be converted into such a measure, it does not, by itself, serve this function. The purpose of the chi-square test as applied to a contingency table is to examine the hypothesis of independence between the two variables. Consequently, it is more nearly analogous to the test of the hypothesis, in a correlation table, that the true correlation is zero.

21.16 Another View of the Hypothesis of Independence

In the study of student attitude, we tested the hypothesis that view of student's role was independent of the student's major. Suppose these two variables *were* independent; what would we expect? The expected frequencies in Table 21.5 provide the key to this question. Let us take the expected frequency in each cell and divide it by the corresponding row frequency. The resulting proportions are shown in Table 21.6. At the bottom of the table, we also show each column total expressed as a proportion of the total number of cases. Note that the sequence of proportions (.35, .40, .25) is the same for all rows, *including that at the bottom of the table*. This illustrates another way of looking at the hypothesis of independence: it states that, *on a proportional basis*, the role assigned to students is the same for students from each of the three college majors.

In general, the hypothesis of independence in a contingency table is equivalent to hypothesizing that *the proportionate distribution of frequencies for any row is the same for all rows*, or that *the proportionate distribution of frequencies for any column is the same for all columns*.

TABLE 21.6 Expected Frequencies Expressed as Proportions of the Row Totals (Data from Table 21.5).

Student Role

	Advisory	Nonvoting member	Voting member	
Humanities and Arts	$\dfrac{70}{200} = .35$	$\dfrac{80}{200} = .40$	$\dfrac{50}{200} = .25$	1.00
Science	$\dfrac{35}{100} = .35$	$\dfrac{40}{100} = .40$	$\dfrac{25}{100} = .25$	1.00
Business	$\dfrac{35}{100} = .35$	$\dfrac{40}{100} = .40$	$\dfrac{25}{100} = .25$	1.00
	$\dfrac{140}{400} = .35$	$\dfrac{160}{400} = .40$	$\dfrac{100}{400} = .25$	

Student Major

21.17 Interpretation of the Outcome of a Chi-Square Test

Finding that χ^2 is significant only opens the door to explanatory analysis. *It is often helpful to convert the obtained frequencies to proportions*, in order to study what is happening. This is particularly true for the two-variable analysis, as exemplified by the contingency table. In the study of student attitude, the number of students was not the same for the three majors. It is easier to compare the trend under these circumstances if frequencies are converted to proportions, which puts each category of student on a common basis. The process is illustrated with the data of Table 21.5.

We want to compare the responses of students from the three different majors. Taking each *obtained* frequency and dividing it by the corresponding row frequency, we obtain the proportions shown in Table 21.7. For comparison, we also divide each column total by n, as shown at the bottom of the table. As indicated in the previous section, the proportions at the bottom of the table are the *expected proportions for each row if the classifications are independent.*

Now let us inspect this table. We take each column in turn, and *within the column* compare each proportion with the others and with the expected proportion as shown at the bottom of the table. Although the center column shows little variation from row to row, the story is different in the two outer columns. Tentatively, it appears that Humanities and Arts majors differ from Business

TABLE 21.7 Obtained Frequencies Expressed as Proportions of the Row Totals (Data from Table 21.5).

Student Role

		Advisory	Nonvoting member	Voting member	
Student Major	Humanities and Arts	$\dfrac{46}{200} = .23$	$\dfrac{82}{200} = .41$	$\dfrac{72}{200} = .36$	1.00
	Science	$\dfrac{42}{100} = .42$	$\dfrac{38}{100} = .38$	$\dfrac{20}{100} = .20$	1.00
	Business	$\dfrac{52}{100} = .52$	$\dfrac{40}{100} = .40$	$\dfrac{8}{100} = .08$	1.00
		$\dfrac{140}{400} = .35$	$\dfrac{160}{400} = .40$	$\dfrac{100}{400} = .25$	

majors in favoring more strongly the fullest student participation, and that Science majors fall somewhere in between.

This conclusion should be taken as a tentative hypothesis rather than as a confirmed fact. Remember that a significant outcome of the chi-square test is directly applicable *only to the data taken as a whole*. The χ^2 which we obtained is inseparably a function of the nine contributions (one from each cell) composing it. We can not say for sure whether one group is responsible for the finding of significance or whether all are involved.

We should also remember that when large samples are involved, *proportionately* small differences may be responsible for statistically significant differences. This does not appear to be a vital factor in the present example, but it could be if n were substantially larger. Paying attention to proportions rather than frequencies will help curb undue excitement upon obtaining a significant outcome in a large sample.

21.18 The 2 × 2 Contingency Table

Although the 2 × 2 contingency table is one kind of $R \times C$ table, it deserves special consideration. The 2 × 2 table affords one degree of freedom. Consequently, Yates' correction is applicable (see Section 21.10). We may, if we wish, proceed to treat this table in exactly the same way as afforded an $R \times C$ table, except that each $(f_o - f_e)$ discrepancy would be reduced by .5 before squaring. However, the formula for calculating χ^2 given below will produce a result exactly equivalent, and with less work. Because the test is improved by Yates' correction, the formula incorporates that feature:

Chi-Square for $\qquad \chi^2 = \dfrac{n[|AD - BC| - (n/2)]^2}{(A + B)(C + D)(A + C)(B + D)}$ $\qquad$ (21.3)
a 2 × 2 Table

where A, B, C, and D are the obtained frequencies in the four cells of the contingency table.

A	B	$(A + B)$
C	D	$(C + D)$

$(A + C)$ $\quad$ $(B + D)$

Note that the four quantities in parentheses in the denominator are the marginal totals of the table. In the numerator of Formula 21.3 the vertical bars indicate that $n/2$ (Yates' correction) is to be subtracted from the *absolute* difference between AD and BC before squaring.

We illustrate the procedure with analysis of answers of undergraduate psychology majors who contemplate graduate study to a question about their degree objective. Responses are cross-classified according to sex of the respondent, as indicated in Table 21.8. Following the procedure just described, χ^2 is calculated as follows:

$$\chi^2 = \frac{190[|(42)(32) - (58)(58)| - (190/2)]^2}{(42 + 58)(58 + 32)(42 + 58)(58 + 32)}$$

$$= \frac{190[|1344 - 3364| - 95]^2}{(100)(90)(100)(90)}$$

$$= \frac{190(1925)^2}{(9000)^2} = 8.69$$

When $\alpha = .01$ and $df = 1$, the critical value of χ^2 is 6.64. The obtained value of χ^2 exceeds this value, and the hypothesis must therefore be rejected. The obtained frequencies could be converted to proportions in the manner described in the previous section, but in this case the conclusion seems reasonably clear without doing so: male students differ from female students in that they more frequently aspire to the doctorate.

Remember the cautions applicable when *expected* frequencies are small; see Section 21.12.

TABLE 21.8 Educational Objective of 190 Undergraduate Psychology Students Who Contemplate Graduate Study.

Master's Degree   Doctorate

Male	*A* 42	*B* 58	$(A + B) = 100$
Female	*C* 58	*D* 32	$(C + D) = 90$

$(A + C) = 100$ $(B + D) = 90$ $n = 190$

21.19 Other Applications of Chi-Square

If you pursue advanced studies in statistics, you will find that Pearson's chi-square function is a useful mathematical model for a surprising variety of statistical questions, some having to do with frequencies and some not. We have considered its application only to problems involving discrepancies between obtained and expected frequencies. Even in this realm, two major classes of problems were selected for consideration from among a larger group. Some indication of the richness of application of this technique is owed before closing.

As a special application of the one-variable case, chi-square may be used to test goodness-of-fit. Is it possible that scores in a given distribution may be considered as a random sample from a normally distributed population? The degrees of freedom must be calculated in a special way for this test.

We have used chi-square to test hypotheses about proportions among independent samples. It may also be used to test hypotheses about proportions obtained from dependent samples.

In Section 21.15, it was mentioned that chi-square is not in itself a measure of association when applied to a contingency table, but that it is possible to derive measures of association from it. The *contingency coefficient* is such a measure; it applies to contingency tables in which the dimensions are greater than 2 × 2. In 2 × 2 tables, the *phi coefficient* (derived also from chi-square) serves the same function.

Finally, the chi-square distribution may be used in a test that has nothing to do with the discrepancy between expected and obtained frequency. Specifically, it may be used to test the hypothesis that the population variance equals some specified quantity. Alternatively, it may be used to provide an estimate of the population variance, based on the obtained sample value.

Description of the application of chi-square to such problems may be found in other books. Among them are volumes by Guilford, Hays, McNemar, and Siegel.†

PROBLEMS AND EXERCISES

Identify:

categorical data	$R \times C$ table
obtained frequency	correction for discontinuity
expected frequency	sign test
chi-square statistic	contingency table
chi-square distribution	hypothesis of independence
$1 \times C$ table	

1. One hundred students take a multiple-choice test. There are 80 questions, and each has five alternatives. To Question 36, the frequency of responses was as follows:

Alternative:	A	B	C	D	E
Frequency of response:	15	40	5	12	28

(*a*) Test the hypothesis, at $\alpha = .05$ and $.01$, that the students were just guessing on this item. (*b*) Suppose Alternative B is the correct answer: (1) What is the obtained frequency of correct and incorrect answers? (2) What is the expected frequency of correct and incorrect answers if the students are just guessing? (3) Test the hypothesis, at $\alpha = .05$ and $.01$, that the frequency of correct and incorrect answers is in accord with chance.

2. A student took the test described in Problem 1, and answered all the questions. Twenty-five of his answers were correct. (*a*) If he were just guessing, and if his answers to the questions are independent of each other, how many questions would we expect he would answer correctly? (*b*) Test the hypothesis, at $\alpha = .05$ and $.01$, that his frequency of correct and incorrect answers is in accord with chance.

3. In a grocery store, customers who pass by are asked to sample three cheese spreads and to declare their preference for one. Frequency of choice is as follows:

Spread:	A	B	C
Frequency of choice:	20	39	25

(*a*) Test the hypothesis of equal preference, using $\alpha = .05$ and $.01$. (*b*) Test the hypothesis that spread B is as popular as the other two combined, using $\alpha = .05$ and $.01$. (*c*) It is argued that it is proper to examine the question raised in part (*b*) of this problem if it were hypoth-

---

†J. P. Guilford, *Fundamental Statistics in Psychology and Education*, 4th ed., McGraw-Hill Book Co., New York, 1965.
W. L. Hays, *Statistics for Psychologists*, Holt, Rinehart and Winston, New York, 1963.
Q. McNemar, *Psychological Statistics*, 4th ed., John Wiley & Sons, Inc., New York, 1969.
S. Siegel, *Nonparametric Methods for the Behavioral Sciences*, McGraw-Hill Book Co., New York, 1956.

esized in advance of collecting the data, but that if the hypothesis were generated by the finding that spread B was more popular than the rest, it would be improper. Explain.

4. In the χ^2 test, why is it that only the area in the upper tail of the χ^2 distribution is of interest?

5. A standard of physical strength is set for men, and it is claimed that 50% of men will meet it. In a sample of eight men, one surpasses the standard, and seven fall short. It is proposed to use χ^2 to test whether these results are significantly discrepant from those claimed. Any objection?

6. In a given problem situation, 12 children are praised on one occasion, and blamed on another. Their reactions, subsequent to the problem situation, are judged for aggressive reactions toward others. Ratings of aggressive behavior are as follows:

Children:	A	B	C	D	E	F	G	H	I	J	K	L
Praise:	6	8	2	1	4	5	6	9	8	7	7	3
Blame:	7	11	4	5	3	7	9	8	9	11	9	6

Examine, by the sign test, the hypothesis of no difference between the two treatments. Use $\alpha = .05$ and .01.

7. To a question of attitude, the responses of men and women are categorized as follows:

	disagree	undecided	agree
males	40	25	70
females	25	20	30

Test the hypothesis that attitude is independent of the sex of the respondent. Use $\alpha = .05$ and .01.

8. The mechanical aptitude scores of different types of workers were as follows:

	30–49	50–69	70 and above
unskilled	20	30	10
semiskilled	10	40	30
skilled	5	10	20

(a) Test the hypothesis that test score is independent of job classification. Use $\alpha = .05$ and .01. (b) Translate each obtained frequency into proportion relative to its row frequency. Do the same for the expected frequencies. Comparing the two, and in view of your answer to (a), what interpretation appears likely?

9. Senior psychology majors were asked about their plans for a job. Those who said they wanted to teach the subject are represented below:

	teach in a junior college	teach in a college or university
male	32	28
female	24	4

(a) Test the hypothesis that teaching aspiration is independent of sex of the respondent, using Formula 21.3. Use $\alpha = .05$. (b) What are the expected proportions of teaching preference for each sex under the hypothesis of independence? (c) What are the obtained proportions? (d) The lower right cell frequency is small. Is it really legitimate to use the χ^2 test of independence with these data? Explain.

   10. χ^2 as described in this chapter would be appropriate for testing equality of accident liability among four divisions of an industry, but not for testing equality of accident liability of the industry's workers among the months of January, February, March, and April. Why not?

APPENDIX A

Review of Basic Mathematics

Contents

A.1 Introduction

This appendix offers information about basic skills which are useful in an introductory course in statistics. It is not intended to be a comprehensive compendium, nor should it be considered as an initial unit of instruction for those who have no knowledge of the subject. It is intended primarily as a reminder of principles formerly learned, but possibly covered with mental cobwebs.

A pretest appears below, covering many (*but not all*) of the principles stated in the remaining sections. If you can answer all of these questions correctly, you would do well to skim the subsequent sections, looking for principles which seem unfamiliar. Questions are keyed to particular sections in this appendix, so if you miss a question you will know where to look to review the principles involved. Answers to the pretest questions will be found at the end of this appendix.

Listed below are three books which may be helpful for those who desire further review. They are listed in order of increasing comprehensiveness. All are designed for self-instruction.

1. A. R. Baggaley, *Mathematics for Introductory Statistics*, John Wiley & Sons, Inc., New York, 1969 (paperback).
2. V. A. Clark, and M. E. Tarter, *Preparation for Basic Statistics*, McGraw-Hill Book Co., New York, 1968 (paperback).
3. H. M. Walker, *Mathematics Essential for Elementary Statistics*, rev. ed., Holt, Rinehart and Winston, Inc., New York, 1951.

A.2 Pretest of Mathematical Skills

Reference for questions 1–4: Section A.3.

1. What symbol, inserted between 3 and 2, indicates that 3 is greater than 2? _____

2. The reciprocal of 2/3 is _____

3. $(2)(3)^2 = ?$ _____

4. Write $(ab)^2$ another way _____

Reference for questions 5–11: Section A.4.

5. $2 - (-4) = ?$ _____

6. $(3)(-4) = ?$ _____

7. $(-3)(-4) = ?$ _____

8. $(2)(-3)(-2)(-2) = ?$ _____

9. $(2)(-3)(0)(-1) = ?$ _____

10. $2 - 4(3/4) = ?$ _____

11. $-4/-2 = ?$ _____

Reference for questions 12–18: Section A.5.

12. Does $(abc)^2 = abc^2$? _____

13. Does $a^2 + b^2 = (a + b)^2$? _____

14. Does $\dfrac{a^2}{b^2} = \left(\dfrac{a}{b}\right)^2$? _____

15. Does $\sqrt{4b} = 2\sqrt{b}$? _____

16. Does $\sqrt{a^2 + b^2} = a + b$ _____

17. Does $\sqrt{\dfrac{a^2}{b^2}} = \dfrac{a}{b}$? _____

18. The square of $\sqrt{a} = ?$ _____

Reference for questions 19–23: Section A.6.

19. $3/12 =$ what percent? _____

20. Simplify: $\dfrac{2ab^2}{a}$ _____

21. Simplify: $\dfrac{a}{\dfrac{ab}{c}}$ _____

22. Does $\dfrac{a - b}{c} = \dfrac{a}{c} - \dfrac{b}{c}$? _____

23. Can you tell *easily* that $12/15 = 4/5$? _____

Reference for questions 24–29: Section A.7.

24. $a - (b - a) = ?$ _____

25. $a(X + Y) = ?$ _____

26. $2ab^2 - 2b$ may be expressed as the product of what two quantities? _____

27. $(X + 4)(Y - 2) = ?$ _____

28. $(X - Y)^2 = ?$ _____

29. $\left\{ 20 - 3\left[3 + \left(\dfrac{12}{4}\right) \right] \right\}^2 = ?$ _____

Reference for questions 30–36: Section A.8.

30. $Y - 3 = 2$ $Y =$ _____

31. $2Y = -6$ $Y =$ _____

32. $(3/4)Y = 12$ $Y =$ _____

33. $\dfrac{2}{Y} = 3$ $Y =$ _____

34. $2(Y - 2) = 4$ $Y =$ _____

35. $3Y - 3 = 2Y + 5$ $Y =$ _____

36. $\sqrt{Y^2 - 9} = k$ $Y =$ _____

Reference for questions 37–44: Section A.9.

37. The graph of a linear function is what kind of line? _____

38. Among the following, which are linear equations? Write the *letters* corresponding to those equations which are linear functions on the line provided at the end of this question.

    (*a*) $Y = 3X - 4$
    (*b*) $3Y = 4X + 2$
    (*c*) $Y - 3 = (7 + 2X)/3$
    (*d*) $Y/2 = 20 - 4(X - 1)$
    (*e*) $Y^2 = 3X + 2$

(f) $\sqrt{Y} = X - 3$
(g) $Y = X^2 - 2X + 1$
(h) $Y = -4$ _____

If $Y = bX + a$, what are the values of b and a for:

39. $Y = -X + 20$ $b =$ _____ ; $a =$ _____

40. $Y = 3X - 14$ $b =$ _____ ; $a =$ _____

41. $Y = -7X$ $b =$ _____ ; $a =$ _____

42. $Y = -3$ $b =$ _____ ; $a =$ _____

If $Y = 2X - 30$, then

43. When $X = 20$, $Y = ?$ _____

44. When $X = 10$, $Y = ?$ _____

Reference for questions 45 and 46: Section A.10.

$100^2 = 10,000$ and $102^2 = 10,404$. If we assumed that change in the square proceeded at the same rate as change in the number to be squared, we would estimate that:

45. $101^2 = ?$ _____

46. $(100.5)^2 = ?$ _____

Questions 47–50 are to be answered without the aid of tables.

Reference for questions 47 and 48: Section A.11.

47. $800^2 = ?$ _____

48. $.8^2 = ?$ _____

Reference for questions 49 and 50: Section A.12.

49. $\sqrt{90,000} = ?$ _____

50. $\sqrt{1.44} = ?$ _____

A.3 Symbols and Their Meaning

Symbol	Meaning
$X \neq Y$	X is not equal to Y.
$X > Y$	X is greater than Y.
$X < Y$	X is less than Y.
$X \geq Y$	X is equal to, or greater than Y.
$X < W < Y$	W is greater than X, but less than Y.
$X \leq W \leq Y$	W is not less than X, nor greater than Y.
$X \pm Y$	As used in this book, it always identifies two limits: $X + Y$ and $X - Y$.
XY or $(X)(Y)$	Alternative ways of indicating the product of X and Y; X times Y.
$\dfrac{X}{Y}$ or X/Y	Alternative ways of indicating X divided by Y.
$\dfrac{Y}{X}$	The *reciprocal* of $\dfrac{X}{Y}$.

$\dfrac{1}{Y}$

The *reciprocal* of Y $\left(\text{reciprocal of } \dfrac{Y}{1}\right)$.

$(X)\left(\dfrac{1}{Y}\right)$

The product of X and the reciprocal of Y; an alternative way of writing X/Y.

$(XY)^2$

The square of the product of X and Y.

$X^2 Y^2$

The product of X^2 and Y^2; it is the same as $(XY)^2$.

XY^2

The product of X and Y^2; *the "square" sign modifies Y but not X.*

∞

Infinity; a number indefinitely large.

4 or $+4$

When a *specific* number is written without a sign in front of it, a positive number is intended. Negative numbers are so indicated, e.g., -4.

A.4   Arithmetic Operations Involving Positive and Negative Numbers

Problem	Comment
$3 - 12 = -9$	To subtract a larger number from a smaller one, subtract the smaller from the larger and reverse the sign.
$3 + (-12) = -9$	Adding a negative number is the same as subtracting that number.†
$3 - (-12) = 15$	Subtracting a negative number is the same as adding it.†
$-3 - 12 = -15$	The sum of two negative numbers is the negative sum of the two numbers.
$(3)(-12) = -36$	The product of two numbers is negative when *one* of the two is negative.
$(-3)(-12) = 36$	The product of two numbers is positive when *both* are negative.
$(-2)^2 = 4$	The square of a negative number is positive, since to square is to multiply a number by itself.
$(-2)(3)(-4) = 24$	The product of more than two numbers is obtained by finding the product of any two of them, multiplying that product by one of the remaining numbers, and continuing this process as needed. Thus: $(-2)(3) = -6$, and $(-6)(-4) = 24$.
$(2)(0)(4) = 0$	The product of several terms is zero if any one of them is zero.

†An equivalent instruction is: "When a positive sign precedes parentheses, the parentheses may be removed without changing the sign of the terms within, but when a negative sign precedes, reverse the signs of these terms." (See Section A.7.)

$2 + 3(-4) = 2 - 12 = -10$

In an additive sequence, reduce each term before summing. In the example, obtain the product *first*, then add it to the other term.

$\dfrac{-4}{2} = -2$

When *one* of the numbers in a fraction is negative, the quotient is negative.

$\dfrac{-4}{-2} = 2$

When *both* numbers in a fraction are negative, the quotient is positive.

A.5   Squares and Square Roots

Problem   Comment

$[(2)(3)(4)]^2 = (2^2)(3^2)(4^2)$

The square of a product equals the product of the squares.

$24^2 \quad\quad = \quad (4)(9)(16)$

$576 \quad = \quad\quad 576$

$(2 + 3 + 4)^2 \neq 2^2 + 3^2 + 4^2$

The square of a sum does *not* equal the sum of the squares.

$9^2 \quad\quad \neq \quad 4 + 9 + 16$

$81 \quad\quad \neq \quad\quad 29$

$\left(\dfrac{4}{16}\right)^2 = \dfrac{4^2}{16^2}$

The square of a fraction equals the fraction of the squares.

$\left(\dfrac{1}{4}\right)^2 = \dfrac{16}{256}$

$\dfrac{1}{16} \quad = \dfrac{1}{16}$

$\sqrt{(4)(9)(16)} = \sqrt{4}\sqrt{9}\sqrt{16}$

The square root of a product equals the product of the square roots.

$\sqrt{576} \quad = \quad (2)(3)(4)$

$24 \quad = \quad\quad 24$

$\sqrt{9 + 16} \neq \sqrt{9} + \sqrt{16}$

The square root of a sum does *not* equal the sum of the square roots.

$\sqrt{25} \quad \neq \quad 3 + 4$

$5 \quad \neq \quad\quad 7$

$\sqrt{\dfrac{4}{16}} = \dfrac{\sqrt{4}}{\sqrt{16}}$

The square root of a fraction equals the fraction of the square roots.

$$\sqrt{\frac{1}{4}} = \frac{2}{4}$$

$$\frac{1}{2} = \frac{1}{2}$$

$(\sqrt{4})^2 = 4$

$2^2 = 4$

$4 = 4$

The square of a square root is the same quantity found under the square root sign. Another example: $(\sqrt{x^2 - c})^2 = x^2 - c$.

A.6 Fractions

| Problem | Comment |

$\frac{1}{4} = .25$

To convert the ratio of two numbers to a decimal fraction, divide the numerator by the denominator.

$.25 = (100)(.25)\%$

$= 25\%$

To convert a decimal fraction to percent, multiply by 100.

$\left(\frac{3}{5}\right)(16) = \frac{(3)(16)}{5}$

$= \frac{48}{5}$

$= 9.6$

To multiply a quantity by a fraction, multiply the quantity by the numerator of the fraction, and divide that product by the denominator of the fraction.

$\frac{16}{4} = \left(\frac{1}{4}\right)(16) = 4$

To divide by a number is the same as multiplying by its reciprocal.

$\frac{16}{\frac{4}{5}} = \left(\frac{5}{4}\right)(16) = 20$

To divide by a fraction, multiply by its reciprocal.

$\frac{3 + 4 - 2}{8} = \frac{3}{8} + \frac{4}{8} - \frac{2}{8}$

$= \frac{5}{8}$

When the numerator of a fraction is a sum, the numerator may be separated into component additive parts, each divided by the denominator.

$\frac{3}{8} + \frac{4}{8} - \frac{2}{8} = \frac{3 + 4 - 2}{8}$

$= \frac{5}{8}$

When the several terms of a sum are fractions having a common denominator, the sum may be expressed as the sum of the numerators, divided by the common denominator.

$$\frac{(3)(15)}{5} = \frac{(3)(3)(\cancel{5})}{\cancel{5}}$$

$$= 9$$

When the numerator and/or denominator of a fraction is the product of two or more terms, identical terms appearing in the numerator and denominator may be cancelled.

$$\left(\frac{1}{5}\right)\left(\frac{2}{7}\right)\left(\frac{3}{11}\right) = \frac{(1)(2)(3)}{(5)(7)(11)}$$

$$= \frac{6}{385}$$

The product of several fractions equals the product of the numerators divided by the product of the denominators.

A.7   Operations Involving Parentheses

Problem | Comment

$2 + (4 - 3 + 2)$

$= 2 + 4 - 3 + 2$

$= 5$

When a positive sign precedes parentheses, the parentheses may be removed without changing the signs of the terms within.

$2 - (4 - 3 + 2)$

$= 2 - 4 + 3 - 2$

$= -1$

When a negative sign precedes parentheses, they may be removed if signs of the terms within are reversed.

$a(b + c) = ab + ac$

A numerical example:

$2(3 + 4) = 2(3) + 2(4)$

$2(7) = 6 + 8$

$14 = 14$

When a quantity within parentheses is to be multiplied by a number, *each* term within the parentheses must be so multiplied.

$2a + 4ab^2 = (2a)(1) + (2a)(2b^2)$

$= 2a(1 + 2b^2)$

A numerical example:

$(6 + 8) = (2)(3) + (2)(4)$

$14 = 2(3 + 4)$

$14 = (2)(7) = 14$

When all terms of a sum contain a common multiplier, that multiplier may be factored out as a multiplier of the remaining sum.

$3 + (1 + 2)^2 = 3 + 3^2$

$= 3 + 9 = 12$

When parentheses are modified by squaring or some other function, take account of the modifier before combining with other terms.

$$\left[100 - 40\left(\frac{20}{10}\right)\right] + \left[\frac{20}{10} + (40 - 30)\right]$$

When an expression contains nesting parentheses, *perform those operations required to remove the*

$$= [100 - 40(2)] + [2 + 10]$$

$$= [100 - 80] + 12$$

$$= 20 + 12$$

$$= 32$$

most interior parentheses first. Simplify the expression by working outward.

$(a + b)(c - d)$

$$= ac - ad + bc - bd$$

A numerical example:

$(2 + 3)(5 - 4)$

$$= (2)(5) + (2)(-4) + (3)(5) + (3)(-4)$$

$$= 10 - 8 + 15 - 12$$

$$= 5$$

The product of two sums may be obtained by multiplying each element of one term by each element of the other term.

$(a - b)^2 = a^2 - 2ab + b^2$

A numerical example:

$(2 - 4)^2 = 2^2 + 2(2)(-4) + (-4)^2$

$(-2)^2 = 4 - 16 + 16$

$4 = 4$

The square of a binomial equals the square of the first term, plus two times the product of the two terms, plus the square of the second term.

A.8 Equations in One Unknown

To solve an equation in an unknown, we must work to isolate the unknown, unmodified and by itself, on one side of the equation, and everything else on the other side of the equation. In working toward this goal, one side of the equation may be altered if the other side is altered in the *same* way. Alteration by adding, subtracting, multiplying, dividing, squaring, taking the square root, or taking the reciprocal may each be useful, depending on circumstances. *In each of the problems illustrated below, we shall suppose that it is required to solve for Y.*

Problem	Comment
$Y + 3 = 4$ *Operation*: subtract 3 from both sides $Y = 1$	Subtracting 3 isolates Y on one side of the equation.
$3Y = 12$ *Operation*: divide both sides by 3 $Y = 4$	Dividing by 3 isolates Y.
$\dfrac{Y}{3} = 4$ *Operation*: multiply both sides by 3 $Y = 12$	Multiplying by 3 isolates Y.

Many problems require two or more successive operations to isolate the unknown. Several examples are given below. The order of operations is generally important, although sometimes there is more than one economical solution. Steps in a solution should be thought out in advance, as if it were a miniature chess game.

Problem	Comment

$\dfrac{3}{Y} = 4$

1st Operation: take the reciprocal of both sides

$\dfrac{Y}{3} = \dfrac{1}{4}$

2nd Operation: multiply both sides by 3

$Y = \dfrac{3}{4}$

Y must be dug out of the denominator, and taking the reciprocal is one way to do it. Can you think of another way?

$2Y - 4 = 8$

1st Operation: add 4 to both sides

$2Y = 12$

2nd Operation: divide both sides by 2

$Y = 6$

In this problem, the two operations could be performed in reverse order with no loss of efficiency.

$2(4 - Y) = 12$

1st Operation: perform the indicated multiplication

$8 - 2Y = 12$

2nd Operation: subtract 8 from both sides

$-2Y = 4$

3rd Operation: divide both sides by -2

$Y = -2$

There is another way to isolate Y; can you think of it?

$5Y - 3 = Y + 5$

1st Operation: subtract Y from both sides

$4Y - 3 = 5$

2nd Operation: add 3 to both sides

$4Y = 8$

Like terms must be collected in solving an equation.

3rd Operation: divide both sides by 4

$Y = 2$

Sometimes it is required to solve an equation for an unknown when the constants are expressed by letters, rather than numbers (e.g., A, B, C, etc.). The same principles hold. Here are two examples (we are to solve for Y):

$$\frac{C}{Y + K} = A$$

A different solution is possible.

1st Operation: take the reciprocal of both sides

$$\frac{Y + K}{C} = \frac{1}{A}$$

2nd Operation: multiply both sides by C

$$Y + K = \frac{C}{A}$$

3rd Operation: subtract K from both sides

$$Y = \frac{C}{A} - K$$

$$\sqrt{Y^2 - C^2} = A$$

This problem becomes a nightmare unless the first operation is to square both sides.

1st Operation: square both sides
$$Y^2 - C^2 = A^2$$
2nd Operation: add C^2 to both sides
$$Y^2 = A^2 + C^2$$
3rd Operation: take the square root of both sides
$$Y = \sqrt{A^2 + C^2}$$

A.9 The Linear Function: An Equation in Two Variables

The equation, $Y = 2X + 20$, is really a sentence expressing the functional relation between two variables. It states: "If X is . . . , then Y is . . . ." Table A.1 shows several ways in which that sentence may be completed, each of which is in agreement with the above equation.

TABLE A.1 Values of Y Corresponding to Particular Values of X when $Y = 2X + 20$.

If X is	Then Y is
$+20$	$+60$
$+15$	$+50$
$+10$	$+40$
$+5$	$+30$
0	$+20$
-5	$+10$
-10	0
-15	-10
-20	-20

When the graph of an equation is a straight line, the equation is said to express a *linear function*. $Y = 2X + 20$ is an equation of a straight line, so we may say that Y is a linear function of X. It is easy to tell when an equation describes a straight line; the variables in such an equation are always expressed as an additive (but not multiplicative) function of "just plain X and Y". Thus the equations below at the left are linear functions, whereas those at the right are not:

Linear Functions	Nonlinear Functions
$Y - 3X = 12$	$Y - 3X^2 = 12$
$\dfrac{2Y + 3}{4} = 16X$	$\dfrac{2Y + 3}{4} = 16\sqrt{X}$
$2Y + 1 = \dfrac{2X - 3}{7}$	$\dfrac{4}{5(2Y - 3)} = \dfrac{2 \, log \, X - 3}{7}$
$Y = 4$	$2XY = 3$

The equation at the bottom on the left is of special importance. Although it does not contain the variable X, it is still the equation of a straight line. If we think of it as a sentence relating X and Y, it says: "Y has the value $+4$ for any and all values of X." Its graph would be a horizontal line lying 4 units above the intersection of the two axes.

A linear function expressing the relation between two variables can always be reduced to the form: $Y = bX + a$, where a and b are *constants*, and X and Y are *variables*. In the equation $Y = 2X + 20$, $b = +2$, and $a = +20$. Here are several other linear functions, together with the values of a and b:

Equation	Values of a and b
$Y = -3X - 20$	$b = -3, \quad a = -20$
$Y = -X + 2$	$b = -1, \quad a = +2$
$Y = 4$	$b = 0, \quad a = +4$
$Y = 3X$	$b = +3, \quad a = 0$

In elementary statistics, we encounter linear functions which are not initially expressed in this simplest form. In statistical computation, it is often required to simplify the expression, and put it in this form. For example (see Section 8.4):

$$X_n = \left(\frac{S_n}{S_o}\right)X_o + \overline{X}_n - \left(\frac{S_n}{S_o}\right)\overline{X}_o$$

where: X_n and X_o are variables and the other symbols stand for constants. If the values of the constants are:

$$\overline{X}_o = 70 \qquad S_o = 10$$
$$\overline{X}_n = 100 \qquad S_n = 20$$

the equation becomes:

$$X_n = \left(\frac{20}{10}\right)X_o + 100 - \left(\frac{20}{10}\right)(70)$$

$$X_n = 2X_o + 100 - 140$$

$$X_n = 2X_o - 40$$

It is now apparent that the equation is in the form: $Y = bX + a$, where $b = +2$ and $a = -40$. The constants b and a have particular meanings which help to interpret a given linear function. This aspect is explored in Section 11.8.

Since two points determine a straight line, the graph of a linear function is easy to construct. Let X be any convenient numerical value, substitute that value in the equation, and determine the corresponding numerical value of Y. The pair of numerical values for X and Y identify one point on the line. Repeat this operation, using another convenient value for X. These values identify a second point on the line. Find the location of each point on the graph, and draw a straight line through them.

This process may be illustrated with the equation $Y = 2X + 20$, described at the beginning of this section. Referring to Table A.1, we find that when $X = 0$, $Y = +20$. The point thus identified is shown in Figure A.1. When $X = +15$, $Y = +50$; this point is also shown in Figure A.1. In practical work, it is a good idea to find a third point as a check on com-

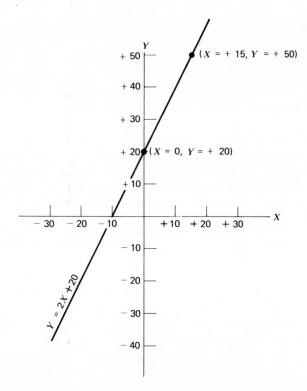

FIGURE A.1 Graph of the Linear Function: $Y = 2X + 20$.

putational accuracy. If the third point does not lie on the line drawn through the other two, a mistake has been made. Compare other pairs of values appearing in Table A.1 with the graph. For example, Table A.1 states that when $X = -15$, $Y = -10$. Does this point fall on the line?

A.10   Linear Interpolation

Suppose Johnny is 64 inches tall on his sixteenth birthday, and 68 inches tall on his seventeenth birthday. If we wish to estimate how tall he was at sixteen and a half, we might assume that growth proceeded at a constant rate during the year, and conclude that he was probably 66 inches tall at that time. If we wished to estimate his height at age sixteen and three-quarters, we would proceed on the assumption that three-quarters of the growth had taken place when three-quarters of the time interval had passed. His height at that time is therefore estimated to be 64 in. + (3/4)(4 in.) = 67 in.

The means of estimating Johnny's height described above is called *linear interpolation*. The term "interpolation" implies that values exterior to the one desired are known, and that this knowledge is used to help estimate it. The adjective "linear" tells us that the rate of change is assumed to be constant. If it is, the equation relating the variable used to assist in prediction to the variable being predicted is one which describes a straight line. In the example above, it is assumed that age and stature are linearly related.

In evaluating this procedure, we must focus on the assumption that the relationship is really linear. Indeed, as with the height–age relationship, it is often known that it is not. *This will not matter much if the relation is close to a linear one, or if the two values between which interpolation takes place are close together.*

A.11   How to Use a Table of Squares of Numbers

Finding the squares of numbers is a problem occurring frequently in statistical calculation. Most statistics books, including this one, include a table of squares in the appendix. The table in this book gives squares of numbers from 1.00 to 10.00, in intervals of .01. If the number is one of these, the square may be read directly from the table. However, the table is useful even when the number is not one of those tabulated.

The rule is: Consider the number to be squared. Move the decimal point whatever number of places, and in whatever direction is required to produce a number which may be found in the table. Read the square of this number from the table. With regard to this answer, *shift the decimal point two places for every one place it was moved in the original number, and in the opposite direction.*

Example: Find 670^2.
Step 1:   Shift the decimal *two places to the left*, and find the square from the table:

$$6{\underset{\curvearrowleft}{\,}}70.^2 = 6.70^2 = 44.8900$$

Step 2:   Shift the decimal *four places to the right*:

$$670^2 = 44.8900{\underset{\curvearrowright}{\,}} = 448900$$

Example: Find $.21^2$.
Step 1:   Shift the decimal *one place to the right*, and find the square from the table:

$$.2{\underset{\curvearrowright}{\,}}1^2 = 2.10^2 = 4.4100$$

Step 2: Shift the decimal *two places to the left*:

$$.21^2 = \underset{\smile}{.04}.4100 = .0441$$

A.12   How to Use a Table of Square Roots

Finding square root is also a problem frequent in statistical calculation. The table in this book gives the square root of numbers from 1.00 to 10.00, in intervals of .01. If the number is one of these, the root may be read directly from the table in the column headed $\sqrt{N}$. The table also gives the square root of numbers from 10.0 to 100.0, in intervals of .1. These values may be found by using the column headed $\sqrt{10N}$. For example, to find $\sqrt{25}$ we observe that $25 = \sqrt{(10)(2.5)}$; it may be found in the column headed $\sqrt{10N}$ opposite the entry $N = 2.50$. However, the table is also useful when the number is not one of those tabulated in the $\sqrt{N}$ or $\sqrt{10N}$ columns.

The rule is: Consider the number for which the square root is desired. Move the decimal point *two places at a time* in whatever direction is required to produce a number which may be found in the table. Read the square root of this number from the table. With regard to this answer, *shift the decimal point one place in the opposite direction for every two places it was moved in the original number*.

Example: Find $\sqrt{670}$.
Step 1: Shift the decimal *two places to the left*, and find the square root from the table:

$$\sqrt{6\underset{\smile}{.70}.} = \sqrt{6.70} = 2.58844$$

Step 2: Shift the decimal *one place to the right*:

$$\sqrt{670} = 2.\underset{\smile}{5}.8844 = 25.8844$$

Example: Find $\sqrt{6700}$.
Step 1: Shift the decimal *two places to the left*, and find the square root from the $\sqrt{10N}$ column in the table:

$$\sqrt{67\underset{\smile}{.00}.} = \sqrt{67.00} = 8.18535$$

Step 2: Shift the decimal *one place to the right*:

$$\sqrt{6700} = 8.\underset{\smile}{1}.8535 = 81.8535$$

Example: Find $\sqrt{.00067}$.
Step 1: Shift the decimal *four places to the right*, and find the square root from the table:

$$\sqrt{.0006\underset{\smile}{.7}} = \sqrt{6.70} = 2.58844$$

Step 2: Shift the decimal *two places to the left*:

$$\sqrt{.00067} = \underset{\smile}{.02}.58844 = .0258844$$

These rules are based on the principle stated in Section A.5 that $\sqrt{ab} = \sqrt{a}\sqrt{b}$. For example, $\sqrt{.00067} = \sqrt{(.0001)(6.70)} = \sqrt{.0001}\sqrt{6.70} = .01\sqrt{6.70} = .01(2.58844) = .0258844$. Similarly, $\sqrt{670} = \sqrt{(100)(6.70)} = \sqrt{100}\sqrt{6.70} = 10(2.58844) = 25.8844$.

Sometimes a number contains more significant digits than can be used in finding square root by the table. If the loss in accuracy is tolerable, the solution is to round the number to three significant digits before entering the table. For example:

$$\sqrt{6275.41} \text{ may be rounded to } \sqrt{6280}$$
$$\sqrt{.03214} \text{ may be rounded to } \sqrt{.0321}$$

When a greater degree of accuracy is desired, methods such as those described by Walker may be used.†

One point in finding square roots is worth special attention; inadequate recognition of it often leads to error. We expect the square root of a number to be a smaller number. *This is so only when the number of which the root is required is greater than one.* When the number is between zero and one, its square root is larger (but less than one). For example, $\sqrt{25} = 5$, but $\sqrt{.25} = .5$.

A.13   Answers to Pretest Questions

1. $>$
2. 3/2
3. 18
4. a^2b^2
5. 6
6. -12
7. 12
8. -24
9. zero
10. -1
11. 2
12. no
13. no
14. yes
15. yes
16. no
17. yes

18. a
19. 25
20. $2b^2$
21. c/b
22. yes
23. —
24. $-b$
25. $aX + aY$
26. $2b$ and $(ab - 1)$
27. $XY + 4Y - 2X - 8$
28. $X^2 - 2XY + Y^2$
29. 4
30. 5
31. -3
32. 16
33. 2/3
34. 4

35. 8
36. $\sqrt{k^2 + 9}$
37. straight line
38. $a, b, c, d,$ and h
39. $b = -1, a = 20$
40. $b = 3, a = -14$
41. $b = -7, a = 0$
42. $b = 0, a = -3$
43. 10
44. -10
45. 10,202
46. 10,101
47. 640,000
48. .64
49. 300
50. 1.2

†H. M. Walker, *Mathematics Essential for Elementary Statistics*, rev. ed., Holt, Rinehart and Winston, Inc., New York, 1951, Chapter 15.

APPENDIX B

Summation Rules

In the algebraic transformation of statistical equations, there are three basic rules of summation which come into frequent play. The first is:

Rule 1: *When a quantity which is itself a sum or difference is to be summed, the summation sign may be distributed among the separate terms of the sum.* That is:

$$\sum(X + Y) = \sum X + \sum Y \tag{B.1}$$

Proof of this proposition is:

$$\sum(X + Y) = (X_1 + Y_1) + (X_2 + Y_2) + \cdots + (X_n + Y_n)$$
$$= (X_1 + X_2 + \cdots + X_n) + (Y_1 + Y_2 + \cdots + Y_n)$$
$$= \qquad \sum X \qquad + \qquad \sum Y$$

By extension of the proof, it follows that:

$$\sum(X + Y + W) = \sum X + \sum Y + \sum W, \text{ etc.}$$

The second rule is:

Rule 2: *The sum of a constant equals the product of the constant and the number of times the constant appears.* That is:

$$\sum a = na \tag{B.2}$$

Proof of this proposition is apparent from the consequences of proposition B.1:

$$\sum(X + a) = (X_1 + a) + (X_2 + a) + \cdots + (X_n + a)$$
$$= (X_1 + X_2 + \cdots + X_n) + (a + a + \cdots + a)$$
$$= \qquad \sum X \qquad + \qquad \sum a$$

which follows from proposition B.1. Since the number of a's to be summed is the same as the number of scores to be summed, it is clear that there are n of them, and that $\Sigma a = na$.

419

The third rule is:

Rule 3: *The sum of the product of a constant and a variable is equivalent to the product of the constant and the sum of the variable.* That is:

$$\sum aX = a\sum X \tag{B.3}$$

Proof of this proposition is:

$$\sum aX = aX_1 + aX_2 + \cdots + aX_n$$
$$= a(X_1 + X_2 + \cdots + X_n)$$
$$= a\sum X$$

These three rules can be combined, and extended. Several illustrations are given below, and the rules involved are listed at the right. In the illustrations, a and b represent constants, and X and Y are variables.

1. $\Sigma(X + 2) = \Sigma X + 2n$ B.1, B.2
2. $\Sigma(X^2 - 1) = \Sigma X^2 - n$ B.1, B.2
   Note: If X is a variable, so is X^2.
3. $\Sigma 2a = 2an$ B.2
4. $\Sigma ab^2 XY^2 = ab^2 \Sigma XY^2$ B.3
5. $\Sigma a(Y + 3)^2 = a\Sigma(Y + 3)^2$ B.3
   Note: If Y is a variable, so is $(Y + 3)^2$.
6. $\Sigma(2X - 3) = 2\Sigma X - 3n$ B.1, B.2, B.3
7. $\Sigma(Y - a)^2 = \Sigma(Y^2 - 2aY + a^2)$
          $= \Sigma Y^2 - 2a\Sigma Y + na^2$ B.1, B.2, B.3

APPENDIX C

List of Symbols

Symbols used in this book are identified below. Numbers in parentheses indicate the page on which each symbol is introduced and defined.

Greek Letter Symbols

α	level of significance, probability of a Type I error (241, 263)
β	probability of a Type II error (264)
$1 - \beta$	power of a test (332)
Σ	the sum of (56)
σ, σ_X	standard deviation of a population (78)
$\sigma^2, \sigma_X{}^2$	variance of a population (78)
σ_r	standard error of r (318)
$\sigma_{\bar{X}}$	standard error of the mean (227)
$\sigma_{\bar{X}-\bar{Y}}$	standard error of the difference between two means (275)
μ, μ_X	mean of a population (57)
$\mu_{\bar{X}}$	mean of the sampling distribution of means (227)
ρ_{XY}	population Pearsonian correlation coefficient (132)
χ^2	chi-square (380)

English Letter Symbols

A.D.	average deviation (77)
A.O.	arbitrary origin (61)
a	Y intercept of a line (175)
b	slope of a line (175)
C	a constant (56)
C	confidence coefficient (250)

421

C_j	jth centile (31)
D	differences between paired scores (283)
$\overline{D}$	mean difference between paired scores (283)
df	degrees of freedom (296, 297)
F	variance ratio (363)
f	frequency (28)
f_e	expected frequency (380)
f_o	obtained frequency (380)
H_A	alternative hypothesis (241)
H_0	null hypothesis (241)
i	class interval width (27)
K	a constant (56)
k	coefficient of alienation (198)
k	number of subgroups in analysis of variance (359)
Mdn	median (57)
Mo	mode (57)
MS	mean square, or variance estimate (360n)
N	number of cases in a population (28)
n	number of cases in a sample (28)
n_i	number of cases in the ith subgroup (359)
P_{cell}	probability of a case falling in a cell (392)
Pr	probability (233)
Q	semiinterquartile range (76)
Q_j	jth quartile point (76)
r, r_{XY}	sample Pearsonian correlation coefficient (132)
r^2	coefficient of determination (203)
S, S_X	standard deviation of a sample (78)
S^2, S_X^2	variance of a sample (78)
S_c	standard deviation of a combined distribution (89)
$S_{Y'}^2$	variance of predicted scores (201)
S_{YX}	standard error of estimate (177)
S_{YX}^2	variance of obtained scores about their predicted scores (201)
s, s_X	estimate of a population standard deviation (240)
s^2, s_X^2	unbiased estimate of a population variance (265)
s_A^2	among-groups variance estimate (358)
s_C^2	column variance estimate (370, 371)
$s_{\overline{D}}$	estimate of the standard error of the mean of difference scores (283)
s_p^2	pooled estimate of the population variance (303)
s_R^2	row variance estimate (370, 371)

$s_{R \times C}{}^2$	row by column interaction variance estimate (370, 371)
$s_W{}^2$	within-groups variance estimate (358)
$s_{WC}{}^2$	within-cells variance estimate (370, 371)
$s_{\overline{X}}$	estimate of the standard error of the mean (240)
$s_{\overline{X}-\overline{Y}}$	estimate of the standard error of the difference between two means (276)
SS	sum of squares (360)
T	T score (114)
t	Student's t statistic (295)
t_p	t beyond which a given proportion of values fall (311)
X	raw scores (56)
X_j	jth raw score (56)
$\overline{X}$	mean of a sample (57)
$\overline{X}_c$	mean of a combined distribution (68)
$\overline{X}_W$	weighted mean (127)
$\overline{\overline{X}}$	mean of all scores, or grand mean (359)
x	deviation score (77)
$|x|$	absolute deviation (77)
x'	coded score (60)
Y	raw scores (56)
Y_j	jth raw score (56)
$\overline{Y}$	mean of a sample (57)
Y'	predicted raw score (166)
y	deviation score (77)
y'	predicted deviation score (172)
z	z score, or standard score (103)
z_p	z score beyond which a given proportion of values fall (249)
z'_Y	predicted z score (173)
Z'	Fisher's logarithmic transformation of ρ (323)
z'	Fisher's logarithmic transformation of r (321)

Statistical Tables

Contents

TABLE A Squares and Square Roots.[a] (Use of this table is described in Appendix A. See Sections A.11 and A.12.)

N	N^2	$\sqrt{N}$	$\sqrt{10N}$	N	N^2	$\sqrt{N}$	$\sqrt{10N}$
1.00	1.0000	1.00000	3.16228	1.50	2.2500	1.22474	3.87298
1.01	1.0201	1.00499	3.17805	1.51	2.2801	1.22882	3.88587
1.02	1.0404	1.00995	3.19374	1.52	2.3104	1.23288	3.89872
1.03	1.0609	1.01489	3.20936	1.53	2.3409	1.23693	3.91152
1.04	1.0816	1.01980	3.22490	1.54	2.3716	1.24097	3.92428
1.05	1.1025	1.02470	3.24037	1.55	2.4025	1.24499	3.93700
1.06	1.1236	1.02956	3.25576	1.56	2.4336	1.24900	3.94968
1.07	1.1449	1.03441	3.27109	1.57	2.4649	1.25300	3.96232
1.08	1.1664	1.03923	3.28634	1.58	2.4964	1.25698	3.97492
1.09	1.1881	1.04403	3.30151	1.59	2.5281	1.26095	3.98748
1.10	1.2100	1.04881	3.31662	1.60	2.5600	1.26491	4.00000
1.11	1.2321	1.05357	3.33167	1.61	2.5921	1.26886	4.01248
1.12	1.2544	1.05830	3.34664	1.62	2.6244	1.27279	4.02492
1.13	1.2769	1.06301	3.36155	1.63	2.6569	1.27671	4.03733
1.14	1.2996	1.06771	3.37639	1.64	2.6896	1.28062	4.04969
1.15	1.3225	1.07238	3.39116	1.65	2.7225	1.28452	4.06202
1.16	1.3456	1.07703	3.40588	1.66	2.7556	1.28841	4.07431
1.17	1.3689	1.08167	3.42053	1.67	2.7889	1.29228	4.08656
1.18	1.3924	1.08628	3.43511	1.68	2.8224	1.29615	4.09878
1.19	1.4161	1.09087	3.44964	1.69	2.8561	1.30000	4.11096
1.20	1.4400	1.09545	3.46410	1.70	2.8900	1.30384	4.12311
1.21	1.4641	1.10000	3.47851	1.71	2.9241	1.30767	4.13521
1.22	1.4884	1.10454	3.49285	1.72	2.9584	1.31149	4.14729
1.23	1.5129	1.10905	3.50714	1.73	2.9929	1.31529	4.15933
1.24	1.5376	1.11355	3.52136	1.74	3.0276	1.31909	4.17133
1.25	1.5625	1.11803	3.53553	1.75	3.0625	1.32288	4.18330
1.26	1.5876	1.12250	3.54965	1.76	3.0976	1.32665	4.19524
1.27	1.6129	1.12694	3.56371	1.77	3.1329	1.33041	4.20714
1.28	1.6384	1.13137	3.57771	1.78	3.1684	1.33417	4.21900
1.29	1.6641	1.13578	3.59166	1.79	3.2041	1.33791	4.23084
1.30	1.6900	1.14018	3.60555	1.80	3.2400	1.34164	4.24264
1.31	1.7161	1.14455	3.61939	1.81	3.2761	1.34536	4.25441
1.32	1.7424	1.14891	3.63318	1.82	3.3124	1.34907	4.26615
1.33	1.7689	1.15326	3.64692	1.83	3.3489	1.35277	4.27785
1.34	1.7956	1.15758	3.66060	1.84	3.3856	1.35647	4.28952
1.35	1.8225	1.16190	3.67423	1.85	3.4225	1.36015	4.30116
1.36	1.8496	1.16619	3.68782	1.86	3.4596	1.36382	4.31277
1.37	1.8769	1.17047	3.70135	1.87	3.4969	1.36748	4.32435
1.38	1.9044	1.17473	3.71484	1.88	3.5344	1.37113	4.33590
1.39	1.9321	1.17898	3.72827	1.89	3.5721	1.37477	4.34741
1.40	1.9600	1.18322	3.74166	1.90	3.6100	1.37840	4.35890
1.41	1.9881	1.18743	3.75500	1.91	3.6481	1.38203	4.37035
1.42	2.0164	1.19164	3.76829	1.92	3.6864	1.38564	4.38178
1.43	2.0449	1.19583	3.78153	1.93	3.7249	1.38924	4.39318
1.44	2.0736	1.20000	3.79473	1.94	3.7636	1.39284	4.40454
1.45	2.1025	1.20416	3.80789	1.95	3.8025	1.39642	4.41588
1.46	2.1316	1.20830	3.82099	1.96	3.8416	1.40000	4.42719
1.47	2.1609	1.21244	3.83406	1.97	3.8809	1.40357	4.43847
1.48	2.1904	1.21655	3.84708	1.98	3.9204	1.40712	4.44972
1.49	2.2201	1.22066	3.86005	1.99	3.9601	1.41067	4.46094
1.50	2.2500	1.22474	3.87298	2.00	4.0000	1.41421	4.47214
N	N^2	$\sqrt{N}$	$\sqrt{10N}$	N	N^2	$\sqrt{N}$	$\sqrt{10N}$

[a]From Table I of: P. Hoel, *Elementary Statistics*, 2nd ed., John Wiley & Sons, Inc., New York, 1966, with permission of the publisher.

TABLE A (*Continued*)

N	N²	$\sqrt{N}$	$\sqrt{10N}$		N	N²	$\sqrt{N}$	$\sqrt{10N}$
2.00	4.0000	1.41421	4.47214		2.50	6.2500	1.58114	5.00000
2.01	4.0401	1.41774	4.48330		2.51	6.3001	1.58430	5.00999
2.02	4.0804	1.42127	4.49444		2.52	6.3504	1.58745	5.01996
2.03	4.1209	1.42478	4.50555		2.53	6.4009	1.59060	5.02991
2.04	4.1616	1.42829	4.51664		2.54	6.4516	1.59374	5.03984
2.05	4.2025	1.43178	4.52769		2.55	6.5025	1.59687	5.04975
2.06	4.2436	1.43527	4.53872		2.56	6.5536	1.60000	5.05964
2.07	4.2849	1.43875	4.54973		2.57	6.6049	1.60312	5.06952
2.08	4.3264	1.44222	4.56070		2.58	6.6564	1.60624	5.07937
2.09	4.3681	1.44568	4.57165		2.59	6.7081	1.60935	5.08920
2.10	4.4100	1.44914	4.58258		2.60	6.7600	1.61245	5.09902
2.11	4.4521	1.45258	4.59347		2.61	6.8121	1.61555	5.10882
2.12	4.4944	1.45602	4.60435		2.62	6.8644	1.61864	5.11859
2.13	4.5369	1.45945	4.61519		2.63	6.9169	1.62173	5.12835
2.14	4.5796	1.46287	4.62601		2.64	6.9696	1.62481	5.13809
2.15	4.6225	1.46629	4.63681		2.65	7.0225	1.62788	5.14782
2.16	4.6656	1.46969	4.64758		2.66	7.0756	1.63095	5.15752
2.17	4.7089	1.47309	4.65833		2.67	7.1289	1.63401	5.16720
2.18	4.7524	1.47648	4.66905		2.68	7.1824	1.63707	5.17687
2.19	4.7961	1.47986	4.67974		2.69	7.2361	1.64012	5.18652
2.20	4.8400	1.48324	4.69042		2.70	7.2900	1.64317	5.19615
2.21	4.8841	1.48661	4.70106		2.71	7.3441	1.64621	5.20577
2.22	4.9284	1.48997	4.71169		2.72	7.3984	1.64924	5.21536
2.23	4.9729	1.49332	4.72229		2.73	7.4529	1.65227	5.22494
2.24	5.0176	1.49666	4.73286		2.74	7.5076	1.65529	5.23450
2.25	5.0625	1.50000	4.74342		2.75	7.5625	1.65831	5.24404
2.26	5.1076	1.50333	4.75395		2.76	7.6176	1.66132	5.25357
2.27	5.1529	1.50665	4.76445		2.77	7.6729	1.66433	5.26308
2.28	5.1984	1.50997	4.77493		2.78	7.7284	1.66733	5.27257
2.29	5.2441	1.51327	4.78539		2.79	7.7841	1.67033	5.28205
2.30	5.2900	1.51658	4.79583		2.80	7.8400	1.67332	5.29150
2.31	5.3361	1.51987	4.80625		2.81	7.8961	1.67631	5.30094
2.32	5.3824	1.52315	4.81664		2.82	7.9524	1.67929	5.31037
2.33	5.4289	1.52643	4.82701		2.83	8.0089	1.68226	5.31977
2.34	5.4756	1.52971	4.83735		2.84	8.0656	1.68523	5.32917
2.35	5.5225	1.53297	4.84768		2.85	8.1225	1.68819	5.33854
2.36	5.5696	1.53623	4.85798		2.86	8.1796	1.69115	5.34790
2.37	5.6169	1.53948	4.86826		2.87	8.2369	1.69411	5.35724
2.38	5.6644	1.54272	4.87852		2.88	8.2944	1.69706	5.36656
2.39	5.7121	1.54596	4.88876		2.89	8.3521	1.70000	5.37587
2.40	5.7600	1.54919	4.89898		2.90	8.4100	1.70294	5.38516
2.41	5.8081	1.55242	4.90918		2.91	8.4681	1.70587	5.39444
2.42	5.8564	1.55563	4.91935		2.92	8.5264	1.70880	5.40370
2.43	5.9049	1.55885	4.92950		2.93	8.5849	1.71172	5.41295
2.44	5.9536	1.56205	4.93964		2.94	8.6436	1.71464	5.42218
2.45	6.0025	1.56525	4.94975		2.95	8.7025	1.71756	5.43139
2.46	6.0516	1.56844	4.95984		2.96	8.7616	1.72047	5.44059
2.47	6.1009	1.57162	4.96991		2.97	8.8209	1.72337	5.44977
2.48	6.1504	1.57480	4.97996		2.98	8.8804	1.72627	5.45894
2.49	6.2001	1.57797	4.98999		2.99	8.9401	1.72916	5.46809
2.50	6.2500	1.58114	5.00000		3.00	9.0000	1.73205	5.47723
N	N²	$\sqrt{N}$	$\sqrt{10N}$		N	N²	$\sqrt{N}$	$\sqrt{10N}$

TABLE A (*Continued*)

N	N²	$\sqrt{N}$	$\sqrt{10N}$	N	N²	$\sqrt{N}$	$\sqrt{10N}$
3.00	9.0000	1.73205	5.47723	3.50	12.2500	1.87083	5.91608
3.01	9.0601	1.73494	5.48635	3.51	12.3201	1.87350	5.92453
3.02	9.1204	1.73781	5.49545	3.52	12.3904	1.87617	5.93296
3.03	9.1809	1.74069	5.50454	3.53	12.4609	1.87883	5.94138
3.04	9.2416	1.74356	5.51362	3.54	12.5316	1.88149	5.94979
3.05	9.3025	1.74642	5.52268	3.55	12.6025	1.88414	5.95819
3.06	9.3636	1.74929	5.53173	3.56	12.6736	1.88680	5.96657
3.07	9.4249	1.75214	5.54076	3.57	12.7449	1.88944	5.97495
3.08	9.4864	1.75499	5.54977	3.58	12.8164	1.89209	5.98331
3.09	9.5481	1.75784	5.55878	3.59	12.8881	1.89473	5.99166
3.10	9.6100	1.76068	5.56776	3.60	12.9600	1.89737	6.00000
3.11	9.6721	1.76352	5.57674	3.61	13.0321	1.90000	6.00833
3.12	9.7344	1.76635	5.58570	3.62	13.1044	1.90263	6.01664
3.13	9.7969	1.76918	5.59464	3.63	13.1769	1.90526	6.02495
3.14	9.8596	1.77200	5.60357	3.64	13.2496	1.90788	6.03324
3.15	9.9225	1.77482	5.61249	3.65	13.3225	1.91050	6.04152
3.16	9.9856	1.77764	5.62139	3.66	13.3956	1.91311	6.04979
3.17	10.0489	1.78045	5.63028	3.67	13.4689	1.91572	6.05805
3.18	10.1124	1.78326	5.63915	3.68	13.5424	1.91833	6.06630
3.19	10.1761	1.78606	5.64801	3.69	13.6161	1.92094	6.07454
3.20	10.2400	1.78885	5.65685	3.70	13.6900	1.92354	6.08276
3.21	10.3041	1.79165	5.66569	3.71	13.7641	1.92614	6.09098
3.22	10.3684	1.79444	5.67450	3.72	13.8384	1.92873	6.09918
3.23	10.4329	1.79722	5.68331	3.73	13.9129	1.93132	6.10737
3.24	10.4976	1.80000	5.69210	3.74	13.9876	1.93391	6.11555
3.25	10.5625	1.80278	5.70088	3.75	14.0625	1.93649	6.12372
3.26	10.6276	1.80555	5.70964	3.76	14.1376	1.93907	6.13188
3.27	10.6929	1.80831	5.71839	3.77	14.2129	1.94165	6.14003
3.28	10.7584	1.81108	5.72713	3.78	14.2884	1.94422	6.14817
3.29	10.8241	1.81384	5.73585	3.79	14.3641	1.94679	6.15630
3.30	10.8900	1.81659	5.74456	3.80	14.4400	1.94936	6.16441
3.31	10.9561	1.81934	5.75326	3.81	14.5161	1.95192	6.17252
3.32	11.0224	1.82209	5.76194	3.82	14.5924	1.95448	6.18061
3.33	11.0889	1.82483	5.77062	3.83	14.6689	1.95704	6.18870
3.34	11.1556	1.82757	5.77927	3.84	14.7456	1.95959	6.19677
3.35	11.2225	1.83030	5.78792	3.85	14.8225	1.96214	6.20484
3.36	11.2896	1.83303	5.79655	3.86	14.8996	1.96469	6.21289
3.37	11.3569	1.83576	5.80517	3.87	14.9769	1.96723	6.22093
3.38	11.4244	1.83848	5.81378	3.88	15.0544	1.96977	6.22896
3.39	11.4921	1.84120	5.82237	3.89	15.1321	1.97231	6.23699
3.40	11.5600	1.84391	5.83095	3.90	15.2100	1.97484	6.24500
3.41	11.6281	1.84662	5.83952	3.91	15.2881	1.97737	6.25300
3.42	11.6964	1.84932	5.84808	3.92	15.3664	1.97990	6.26099
3.43	11.7649	1.85203	5.85662	3.93	15.4449	1.98242	6.26897
3.44	11.8336	1.85472	5.86515	3.94	15.5236	1.98494	6.27694
3.45	11.9025	1.85742	5.87367	3.95	15.6025	1.98746	6.28490
3.46	11.9716	1.86011	5.88218	3.96	15.6816	1.98997	6.29285
3.47	12.0409	1.86279	5.89067	3.97	15.7609	1.99249	6.30079
3.48	12.1104	1.86548	5.89915	3.98	15.8404	1.99499	6.30872
3.49	12.1801	1.86815	5.90762	3.99	15.9201	1.99750	6.31664
3.50	12.2500	1.87083	5.91608	4.00	16.0000	2.00000	6.32456
N	N²	$\sqrt{N}$	$\sqrt{10N}$	N	N²	$\sqrt{N}$	$\sqrt{10N}$

TABLE A (*Continued*)

N	N²	√N	√10N	N	N²	√N	√10N
4.00	16.0000	2.00000	6.32456	4.50	20.2500	2.12132	6.70820
4.01	16.0801	2.00250	6.33246	4.51	20.3401	2.12368	6.71565
4.02	16.1604	2.00499	6.34035	4.52	20.4304	2.12603	6.72309
4.03	16.2409	2.00749	6.34823	4.53	20.5209	2.12838	6.73053
4.04	16.3216	2.00998	6.35610	4.54	20.6116	2.13073	6.73795
4.05	16.4025	2.01246	6.36396	4.55	20.7025	2.13307	6.74537
4.06	16.4836	2.01494	6.37181	4.56	20.7936	2.13542	6.75278
4.07	16.5649	2.01742	6.37966	4.57	20.8849	2.13776	6.76018
4.08	16.6464	2.01990	6.38749	4.58	20.9764	2.14009	6.76757
4.09	16.7281	2.02237	6.39531	4.59	21.0681	2.14243	6.77495
4.10	16.8100	2.02485	6.40312	4.60	21.1600	2.14476	6.78233
4.11	16.8921	2.02731	6.41093	4.61	21.2521	2.14709	6.78970
4.12	16.9744	2.02978	6.41872	4.62	21.3444	2.14942	6.79706
4.13	17.0569	2.03224	6.42651	4.63	21.4369	2.15174	6.80441
4.14	17.1396	2.03470	6.43428	4.64	21.5296	2.15407	6.81175
4.15	17.2225	2.03715	6.44205	4.65	21.6225	2.15639	6.81909
4.16	17.3056	2.03961	6.44981	4.66	21.7156	2.15870	6.82642
4.17	17.3889	2.04206	6.45755	4.67	21.8089	2.16102	6.83374
4.18	17.4724	2.04450	6.46529	4.68	21.9024	2.16333	6.84105
4.19	17.5561	2.04695	6.47302	4.69	21.9961	2.16564	6.84836
4.20	17.6400	2.04939	6.48074	4.70	22.0900	2.16795	6.85565
4.21	17.7241	2.05183	6.48845	4.71	22.1841	2.17025	6.86294
4.22	17.8084	2.05426	6.49615	4.72	22.2784	2.17256	6.87023
4.23	17.8929	2.05670	6.50384	4.73	22.3729	2.17486	6.87750
4.24	17.9776	2.05913	6.51153	4.74	22.4676	2.17715	6.88477
4.25	18.0625	2.06155	6.51920	4.75	22.5625	2.17945	6.89202
4.26	18.1476	2.06398	6.52687	4.76	22.6576	2.18174	6.89928
4.27	18.2329	2.06640	6.53452	4.77	22.7529	2.18403	6.90652
4.28	18.3184	2.06882	6.54217	4.78	22.8484	2.18632	6.91375
4.29	18.4041	2.07123	6.54981	4.79	22.9441	2.18861	6.92098
4.30	18.4900	2.07364	6.55744	4.80	23.0400	2.19089	6.92820
4.31	18.5761	2.07605	6.56506	4.81	23.1361	2.19317	6.93542
4.32	18.6624	2.07846	6.57267	4.82	23.2324	2.19545	6.94262
4.33	18.7489	2.08087	6.58027	4.83	23.3289	2.19773	6.94982
4.34	18.8356	2.08327	6.58787	4.84	23.4256	2.20000	6.95701
4.35	18.9225	2.08567	6.59545	4.85	23.5225	2.20227	6.96419
4.36	19.0096	2.08806	6.60303	4.86	23.6196	2.20454	6.97137
4.37	19.0969	2.09045	6.61060	4.87	23.7169	2.20681	6.97854
4.38	19.1844	2.09284	6.61816	4.88	23.8144	2.20907	6.98570
4.39	19.2721	2.09523	6.62571	4.89	23.9121	2.21133	6.99285
4.40	19.3600	2.09762	6.63325	4.90	24.0100	2.21359	7.00000
4.41	19.4481	2.10000	6.64078	4.91	24.1081	2.21585	7.00714
4.42	19.5364	2.10238	6.64831	4.92	24.2064	2.21811	7.01427
4.43	19.6249	2.10476	6.65582	4.93	24.3049	2.22036	7.02140
4.44	19.7136	2.10713	6.66333	4.94	24.4036	2.22261	7.02851
4.45	19.8025	2.10950	6.67083	4.95	24.5025	2.22486	7.03562
4.46	19.8916	2.11187	6.67832	4.96	24.6016	2.22711	7.04273
4.47	19.9809	2.11424	6.68581	4.97	24.7009	2.22935	7.04982
4.48	20.0704	2.11660	6.69328	4.98	24.8004	2.23159	7.05691
4.49	20.1601	2.11896	6.70075	4.99	24.9001	2.23383	7.06399
4.50	20.2500	2.12132	6.70820	5.00	25.0000	2.23607	7.07107
N	N²	√N	√10N	N	N²	√N	√10N

TABLE A (*Continued*)

N	N²	$\sqrt{N}$	$\sqrt{10N}$		N	N²	$\sqrt{N}$	$\sqrt{10N}$
5.00	25.0000	2.23607	7.07107		5.50	30.2500	2.34521	7.41620
5.01	25.1001	2.23830	7.07814		5.51	30.3601	2.34734	7.42294
5.02	25.2004	2.24054	7.08520		5.52	30.4704	2.34947	7.42967
5.03	25.3009	2.24277	7.09225		5.53	30.5809	2.35160	7.43640
5.04	25.4016	2.24499	7.09930		5.54	30.6916	2.35372	7.44312
5.05	25.5025	2.24722	7.10634		5.55	30.8025	2.35584	7.44983
5.06	25.6036	2.24944	7.11337		5.56	30.9136	2.35797	7.45654
5.07	25.7049	2.25167	7.12039		5.57	31.0249	2.36008	7.46324
5.08	25.8064	2.25389	7.12741		5.58	31.1364	2.36220	7.46994
5.09	25.9081	2.25610	7.13442		5.59	31.2481	2.36432	7.47663
5.10	26.0100	2.25832	7.14143		5.60	31.3600	2.36643	7.48331
5.11	26.1121	2.26053	7.14843		5.61	31.4721	2.36854	7.48999
5.12	26.2144	2.26274	7.15542		5.62	31.5844	2.37065	7.49667
5.13	26.3169	2.26495	7.16240		5.63	31.6969	2.37276	7.50333
5.14	26.4196	2.26716	7.16938		5.64	31.8096	2.37487	7.50999
5.15	26.5225	2.26936	7.17635		5.65	31.9225	2.37697	7.51665
5.16	26.6256	2.27156	7.18331		5.66	32.0356	2.37908	7.52330
5.17	26.7289	2.27376	7.19027		5.67	32.1489	2.38118	7.52994
5.18	26.8324	2.27596	7.19722		5.68	32.2624	2.38328	7.53658
5.19	26.9361	2.27816	7.20417		5.69	32.3761	2.38537	7.54321
5.20	27.0400	2.28035	7.21110		5.70	32.4900	2.38747	7.54983
5.21	27.1441	2.28254	7.21803		5.71	32.6041	2.38956	7.55645
5.22	27.2484	2.28473	7.22496		5.72	32.7184	2.39165	7.56307
5.23	27.3529	2.28692	7.23187		5.73	32.8329	2.39374	7.56968
5.24	27.4576	2.28910	7.23878		5.74	32.9476	2.39583	7.57628
5.25	27.5625	2.29129	7.24569		5.75	33.0625	2.39792	7.58288
5.26	27.6676	2.29347	7.25259		5.76	33.1776	2.40000	7.58947
5.27	27.7729	2.29565	7.25948		5.77	33.2929	2.40208	7.59605
5.28	27.8784	2.29783	7.26636		5.78	33.4084	2.40416	7.60263
5.29	27.9841	2.30000	7.27324		5.79	33.5241	2.40624	7.60920
5.30	28.0900	2.30217	7.28011		5.80	33.6400	2.40832	7.61577
5.31	28.1961	2.30434	7.28697		5.81	33.7561	2.41039	7.62234
5.32	28.3024	2.30651	7.29383		5.82	33.8724	2.41247	7.62889
5.33	28.4089	2.30868	7.30068		5.83	33.9889	2.41454	7.63544
5.34	28.5156	2.31084	7.30753		5.84	34.1056	2.41661	7.64199
5.35	28.6225	2.31301	7.31437		5.85	34.2225	2.41868	7.64853
5.36	28.7296	2.31517	7.32120		5.86	34.3396	2.42074	7.65506
5.37	28.8369	2.31733	7.32803		5.87	34.4569	2.42281	7.66159
5.38	28.9444	2.31948	7.33485		5.88	34.5744	2.42487	7.66812
5.39	29.0521	2.32164	7.34166		5.89	34.6921	2.42693	7.67463
5.40	29.1600	2.32379	7.34847		5.90	34.8100	2.42899	7.68115
5.41	29.2681	2.32594	7.35527		5.91	34.9281	2.43105	7.68765
5.42	29.3764	2.32809	7.36206		5.92	35.0464	2.43311	7.69415
5.43	29.4849	2.33024	7.36885		5.93	35.1649	2.43516	7.70065
5.44	29.5936	2.33238	7.37564		5.94	35.2836	2.43721	7.70714
5.45	29.7025	2.33452	7.38241		5.95	35.4025	2.43926	7.71362
5.46	29.8116	2.33666	7.38918		5.96	35.5216	2.44131	7.72010
5.47	29.9209	2.33880	7.39594		5.97	35.6409	2.44336	7.72658
5.48	30.0304	2.34094	7.40270		5.98	35.7604	2.44540	7.73305
5.49	30.1401	2.34307	7.40945		5.99	35.8801	2.44745	7.73951
5.50	30.2500	2.34521	7.41620		6.00	36.0000	2.44949	7.74597
N	N²	$\sqrt{N}$	$\sqrt{10N}$		N	N²	$\sqrt{N}$	$\sqrt{10N}$

TABLE A (*Continued*)

N	N²	$\sqrt{N}$	$\sqrt{10N}$	N	N²	$\sqrt{N}$	$\sqrt{10N}$
6.00	36.0000	2.44949	7.74597	6.50	42.2500	2.54951	8.06226
6.01	36.1201	2.45153	7.75242	6.51	42.3801	2.55147	8.06846
6.02	36.2404	2.45357	7.75887	6.52	42.5104	2.55343	8.07465
6.03	36.3609	2.45561	7.76531	6.53	42.6409	2.55539	8.08084
6.04	36.4816	2.45764	7.77174	6.54	42.7716	2.55734	8.08703
6.05	36.6025	2.45967	7.77817	6.55	42.9025	2.55930	8.09321
6.06	36.7236	2.46171	7.78460	6.56	43.0336	2.56125	8.09938
6.07	36.8449	2.46374	7.79102	6.57	43.1649	2.56320	8.10555
6.08	36.9664	2.46577	7.79744	6.58	43.2964	2.56515	8.11172
6.09	37.0881	2.46779	7.80385	6.59	43.4281	2.56710	8.11788
6.10	37.2100	2.46982	7.81025	6.60	43.5600	2.56905	8.12404
6.11	37.3321	2.47184	7.81665	6.61	43.6921	2.57099	8.13019
6.12	37.4544	2.47386	7.82304	6.62	43.8244	2.57294	8.13634
6.13	37.5769	2.47588	7.82943	6.63	43.9569	2.57488	8.14248
6.14	37.6996	2.47790	7.83582	6.64	44.0896	2.57682	8.14862
6.15	37.8225	2.47992	7.84219	6.65	44.2225	2.57876	8.15475
6.16	37.9456	2.48193	7.84857	6.66	44.3556	2.58070	8.16088
6.17	38.0689	2.48395	7.85493	6.67	44.4889	2.58263	8.16701
6.18	38.1924	2.48596	7.86130	6.68	44.6224	2.58457	8.17313
6.19	38.3161	2.48797	7.86766	6.69	44.7561	2.58650	8.17924
6.20	38.4400	2.48998	7.87401	6.70	44.8900	2.58844	8.18535
6.21	38.5641	2.49199	7.88036	6.71	45.0241	2.59037	8.19146
6.22	38.6884	2.49399	7.88670	6.72	45.1584	2.59230	8.19756
6.23	38.8129	2.49600	7.89303	6.73	45.2929	2.59422	8.20366
6.24	38.9376	2.49800	7.89937	6.74	45.4276	2.59615	8.20975
6.25	39.0625	2.50000	7.90569	6.75	45.5625	2.59808	8.21584
6.26	39.1876	2.50200	7.91202	6.76	45.6976	2.60000	8.22192
6.27	39.3129	2.50400	7.91833	6.77	45.8329	2.60192	8.22800
6.28	39.4384	2.50599	7.92465	6.78	45.9684	2.60384	8.23408
6.29	39.5641	2.50799	7.93095	6.79	46.1041	2.60576	8.24015
6.30	39.6900	2.50998	7.93725	6.80	46.2400	2.60768	8.24621
6.31	39.8161	2.51197	7.94355	6.81	46.3761	2.60960	8.25227
6.32	39.9424	2.51396	7.94984	6.82	46.5124	2.61151	8.25833
6.33	40.0689	2.51595	7.95613	6.83	46.6489	2.61343	8.26438
6.34	40.1956	2.51794	7.96241	6.84	46.7856	2.61534	8.27043
6.35	40.3225	2.51992	7.96869	6.85	46.9225	2.61725	8.27647
6.36	40.4496	2.52190	7.97496	6.86	47.0596	2.61916	8.28251
6.37	40.5769	2.52389	7.98123	6.87	47.1969	2.62107	8.28855
6.38	40.7044	2.52587	7.98749	6.88	47.3344	2.62298	8.29458
6.39	40.8321	2.52784	7.99375	6.89	47.4721	2.62488	8.30060
6.40	40.9600	2.52982	8.00000	6.90	47.6100	2.62679	8.30662
6.41	41.0881	2.53180	8.00625	6.91	47.7481	2.62869	8.31264
6.42	41.2164	2.53377	8.01249	6.92	47.8864	2.63059	8.31865
6.43	41.3449	2.53574	8.01873	6.93	48.0249	2.63249	8.32466
6.44	41.4736	2.53772	8.02496	6.94	48.1636	2.63439	8.33067
6.45	41.6025	2.53969	8.03119	6.95	48.3025	2.63629	8.33667
6.46	41.7316	2.54165	8.03741	6.96	48.4416	2.63818	8.34266
6.47	41.8609	2.54362	8.04363	6.97	48.5809	2.64008	8.34865
6.48	41.9904	2.54558	8.04984	6.98	48.7204	2.64197	8.35464
6.49	42.1201	2.54755	8.05605	6.99	48.8601	2.64386	8.36062
6.50	42.2500	2.54951	8.06226	7.00	49.0000	2.64575	8.36660
N	N²	$\sqrt{N}$	$\sqrt{10N}$	N	N²	$\sqrt{N}$	$\sqrt{10N}$

TABLE A (*Continued*)

N	N²	$\sqrt{N}$	$\sqrt{10N}$	N	N²	$\sqrt{N}$	$\sqrt{10N}$
7.00	49.0000	2.64575	8.36660	7.50	56.2500	2.73861	8.66025
7.01	49.1401	2.64764	8.37257	7.51	56.4001	2.74044	8.66603
7.02	49.2804	2.64953	8.37854	7.52	56.5504	2.74226	8.67179
7.03	49.4209	2.65141	8.38451	7.53	56.7009	2.74408	8.67756
7.04	49.5616	2.65330	8.39047	7.54	56.8516	2.74591	8.68332
7.05	49.7025	2.65518	8.39643	7.55	57.0025	2.74773	8.68907
7.06	49.8436	2.65707	8.40238	7.56	57.1536	2.74955	8.69483
7.07	49.9849	2.65895	8.40833	7.57	57.3049	2.75136	8.70057
7.08	50.1264	2.66083	8.41427	7.58	57.4564	2.75318	8.70632
7.09	50.2681	2.66271	8.42021	7.59	57.6081	2.75500	8.71206
7.10	50.4100	2.66458	8.42615	7.60	57.7600	2.75681	8.71780
7.11	50.5521	2.66646	8.43208	7.61	57.9121	2.75862	8.72353
7.12	50.6944	2.66833	8.43801	7.62	58.0644	2.76043	8.72926
7.13	50.8369	2.67021	8.44393	7.63	58.2169	2.76225	8.73499
7.14	50.9796	2.67208	8.44985	7.64	58.3696	2.76405	8.74071
7.15	51.1225	2.67395	8.45577	7.65	58.5225	2.76586	8.74643
7.16	51.2656	2.67582	8.46168	7.66	58.6756	2.76767	8.75214
7.17	51.4089	2.67769	8.46759	7.67	58.8289	2.76948	8.75785
7.18	51.5524	2.67955	8.47349	7.68	58.9824	2.77128	8.76356
7.19	51.6961	2.68142	8.47939	7.69	59.1361	2.77308	8.76926
7.20	51.8400	2.68328	8.48528	7.70	59.2900	2.77489	8.77496
7.21	51.9841	2.68514	8.49117	7.71	59.4441	2.77669	8.78066
7.22	52.1284	2.68701	8.49706	7.72	59.5984	2.77849	8.78635
7.23	52.2729	2.68887	8.50294	7.73	59.7529	2.78029	8.79204
7.24	52.4176	2.69072	8.50882	7.74	59.9076	2.78209	8.79773
7.25	52.5625	2.69258	8.51469	7.75	60.0625	2.78388	8.80341
7.26	52.7076	2.69444	8.52056	7.76	60.2176	2.78568	8.80909
7.27	52.8529	2.69629	8.52643	7.77	60.3729	2.78747	8.81476
7.28	52.9984	2.69815	8.53229	7.78	60.5284	2.78927	8.82043
7.29	53.1441	2.70000	8.53815	7.79	60.6841	2.79106	8.82610
7.30	53.2900	2.70185	8.54400	7.80	60.8400	2.79285	8.83176
7.31	53.4361	2.70370	8.54985	7.81	60.9961	2.79464	8.83742
7.32	53.5824	2.70555	8.55570	7.82	61.1524	2.79643	8.84308
7.33	53.7289	2.70740	8.56154	7.83	61.3089	2.79821	8.84873
7.34	53.8756	2.70924	8.56738	7.84	61.4656	2.80000	8.85438
7.35	54.0225	2.71109	8.57321	7.85	61.6225	2.80179	8.86002
7.36	54.1696	2.71293	8.57904	7.86	61.7796	2.80357	8.86566
7.37	54.3169	2.71477	8.58487	7.87	61.9369	2.80535	8.87130
7.38	54.4644	2.71662	8.59069	7.88	62.0944	2.80713	8.87694
7.39	54.6121	2.71846	8.59651	7.89	62.2521	2.80891	8.88257
7.40	54.7600	2.72029	8.60233	7.90	62.4100	2.81069	8.88819
7.41	54.9081	2.72213	8.60814	7.91	62.5681	2.81247	8.89382
7.42	55.0564	2.72397	8.61394	7.22	62.7264	2.81425	8.89944
7.43	55.2049	2.72580	8.61974	7.93	62.8849	2.81603	8.90505
7.44	55.3536	2.72764	8.62554	7.94	63.0436	2.81780	8.91067
7.45	55.5025	2.72947	8.63134	7.95	63.2025	2.81957	8.91628
7.46	55.6516	2.73130	8.63713	7.96	63.3616	2.82135	8.92188
7.47	55.8009	2.73313	8.64292	7.97	63.5209	2.82312	8.92749
7.48	55.9504	2.73496	8.64870	7.98	63.6804	2.82489	8.93308
7.49	56.1001	2.73679	8.65448	7.99	63.8401	2.82666	8.93868
7.50	56.2500	2.73861	8.66025	8.00	64.0000	2.82843	8.94427
N	N²	$\sqrt{N}$	$\sqrt{10N}$	N	N²	$\sqrt{N}$	$\sqrt{10N}$

TABLE A (*Continued*)

N	N²	$\sqrt{N}$	$\sqrt{10N}$		N	N²	$\sqrt{N}$	$\sqrt{10N}$
8.00	64.0000	2.82843	8.94427		8.50	72.2500	2.91548	9.21954
8.01	64.1601	2.83019	8.94986		8.51	72.4201	2.91719	9.22497
8.02	64.3204	2.83196	8.95545		8.52	72.5904	2.91890	9.23038
8.03	64.4809	2.83373	8.96103		8.53	72.7609	2.92062	9.23580
8.04	64.6416	2.83549	8.96660		8.54	72.9316	2.92233	9.24121
8.05	64.8025	2.83725	8.97218		8.55	73.1025	2.92404	9.24662
8.06	64.9636	2.83901	8.97775		8.56	73.2736	2.92575	9.25203
8.07	65.1249	2.84077	8.98332		8.57	73.4449	2.92746	9.25743
8.08	65.2864	2.84253	8.98888		8.58	73.6164	2.92916	9.26283
8.09	65.4481	2.84429	8.99444		8.59	73.7881	2.93087	9.26823
8.10	65.6100	2.84605	9.00000		8.60	73.9600	2.93258	9.27362
8.11	65.7721	2.84781	9.00555		8.61	74.1321	2.93428	9.27901
8.12	65.9344	2.84956	9.01110		8.62	74.3044	2.93598	9.28440
8.13	66.0969	2.85132	9.01665		8.63	74.4769	2.93769	9.28978
8.14	66.2596	2.85307	9.02219		8.64	74.6496	2.93939	9.29516
8.15	66.4225	2.85482	9.02774		8.65	74.8225	2.94109	9.30054
8.16	66.5856	2.85657	9.03327		8.66	74.9956	2.94279	9.30591
8.17	66.7489	2.85832	9.03881		8.67	75.1689	2.94449	9.31128
8.18	66.9124	2.86007	9.04434		8.68	75.3424	2.94618	9.31665
8.19	67.0761	2.86182	9.04986		8.69	75.5161	2.94788	9.32202
8.20	67.2400	2.86356	9.05539		8.70	75.6900	2.94958	9.32738
8.21	67.4041	2.86531	9.06091		8.71	75.8641	2.95127	9.33274
8.22	67.5684	2.86705	9.06642		8.72	76.0384	2.95296	9.33809
8.23	67.7329	2.86880	9.07193		8.73	76.2129	2.95466	9.34345
8.24	67.8976	2.87054	9.07744		8.74	76.3876	2.95635	9.34880
8.25	68.0625	2.87228	9.08295		8.75	76.5625	2.95804	9.35414
8.26	68.2276	2.87402	9.08845		8.76	76.7376	2.95973	9.35949
8.27	68.3929	2.87576	9.09395		8.77	76.9129	2.96142	9.36483
8.28	68.5584	2.87750	9.09945		8.78	77.0884	2.96311	9.37017
8.29	68.7241	2.87924	9.10494		8.79	77.2641	2.96479	9.37550
8.30	68.8900	2.88097	9.11043		8.80	77.4400	2.96648	9.38083
8.31	69.0561	2.88271	9.11592		8.81	77.6161	2.96816	9.38616
8.32	69.2224	2.88444	9.12140		8.82	77.7924	2.96985	9.39149
8.33	69.3889	2.88617	9.12688		8.83	77.9689	2.97153	9.39681
8.34	69.5556	2.88791	9.13236		8.84	78.1456	2.97321	9.40213
8.35	69.7225	2.88964	9.13783		8.85	78.3225	2.97489	9.40744
8.36	69.8896	2.89137	9.14330		8.86	78.4996	2.97658	9.41276
8.37	70.0569	2.89310	9.14877		8.87	78.6769	2.97825	9.41807
8.38	70.2244	2.89482	9.15423		8.88	78.8544	2.97993	9.42338
8.39	70.3921	2.89655	9.15969		8.89	79.0321	2.98161	9.42868
8.40	70.5600	2.89828	9.16515		8.90	79.2100	2.98329	9.43398
8.41	70.7281	2.90000	9.17061		8.91	79.3881	2.98496	9.43928
8.42	70.8964	2.90172	9.17606		8.92	79.5664	2.98664	9.44458
8.43	71.0649	2.90345	9.18150		8.33	79.7449	2.98831	9.44987
8.44	71.2336	2.90517	9.18695		8.94	79.9236	2.98998	9.45516
8.45	71.4025	2.90689	9.19239		8.95	80.1025	2.99166	9.46044
8.46	71.5716	2.90861	9.19783		8.96	80.2816	2.99333	9.46573
8.47	71.7409	2.91033	9.20326		8.97	80.4609	2.99500	9.47101
8.48	71.9104	2.91204	9.20869		8.98	80.6404	2.99666	9.47629
8.49	72.0801	2.91376	9.21412		8.99	80.8201	2.99833	9.48156
8.50	72.2500	2.91548	9.21954		9.00	81.0000	3.00000	9.48683
N	N²	$\sqrt{N}$	$\sqrt{10N}$		N	N²	$\sqrt{N}$	$\sqrt{10N}$

TABLE A (*Continued*)

N	N²	√N	√10N	N	N²	√N	√10N
9.00	81.0000	3.00000	9.48683	9.50	90.2500	3.08221	9.74679
9.01	81.1801	3.00167	9.49210	9.51	90.4401	3.08383	9.75192
9.02	81.3604	3.00333	9.49737	9.52	90.6304	3.08545	9.75705
9.03	81.5409	3.00500	9.50263	9.53	90.8209	3.08707	9.76217
9.04	81.7216	3.00666	9.50789	9.54	91.0116	3.08869	9.76729
9.05	81.9025	3.00832	9.51315	9.55	91.2025	3.09031	9.77241
9.06	82.0836	3.00998	9.51840	9.56	91.3936	3.09192	9.77753
9.07	82.2649	3.01164	9.52365	9.57	91.5849	3.09354	9.78264
9.08	82.4464	3.01330	9.52890	9.58	91.7764	3.09516	9.78775
9.09	82.6281	3.01496	9.53415	9.59	91.9681	3.09677	9.79285
9.10	82.8100	3.01662	9.53939	9.60	92.1600	3.09839	9.79796
9.11	82.9921	3.01828	9.54463	9.61	92.3521	3.10000	9.80306
9.12	83.1744	3.01993	9.54987	9.62	92.5444	3.10161	9.80816
9.13	83.3569	3.02159	9.55510	9.63	92.7369	3.10322	9.81326
9.14	83.5396	3.02324	9.56033	9.64	92.9296	3.10483	9.81835
9.15	83.7225	3.02490	9.56556	9.65	93.1225	3.10644	9.82344
9.16	83.9056	3.02655	9.57079	9.66	93.3156	3.10805	9.82853
9.17	84.0889	3.02820	9.57601	9.67	93.5089	3.10966	9.83362
9.18	84.2724	3.02985	9.58123	9.68	93.7024	3.11127	9.83870
9.19	84.4561	3.03150	9.58645	9.69	93.8961	3.11288	9.84378
9.20	84.6400	3.03315	9.59166	9.70	94.0900	3.11448	9.84886
9.21	84.8241	3.03480	9.59687	9.71	94.2841	3.11609	9.85393
9.22	85.0084	3.03645	9.60208	9.72	94.4784	3.11769	9.85901
9.23	85.1929	3.03809	9.60729	9.73	94.6729	3.11929	9.86408
9.24	85.3776	3.03974	9.61249	9.74	94.8676	3.12090	9.86914
9.25	85.5625	3.04138	9.61769	9.75	95.0625	3.12250	9.87421
9.26	85.7476	3.04302	9.62289	9.76	95.2576	3.12410	9.87927
9.27	85.9329	3.04467	9.62808	9.77	95.4529	3.12570	9.88433
9.28	86.1184	3.04631	9.63328	9.78	95.6484	3.12730	9.88939
9.29	86.3041	3.04795	9.63846	9.79	95.8441	3.12890	9.89444
9.30	86.4900	3.04959	9.64365	9.80	96.0400	3.13050	9.89949
9.31	86.6761	3.05123	9.64883	9.81	96.2361	3.13209	9.90454
9.32	86.8624	3.05287	9.65401	9.82	96.4324	3.13369	9.90959
9.33	87.0489	3.05450	9.65919	9.83	96.6289	3.13528	9.91464
9.34	87.2356	3.05614	9.66437	9.84	96.8256	3.13688	9.91968
9.35	87.4225	3.05778	9.66954	9.85	97.0225	3.13847	9.92472
9.36	87.6096	3.05941	9.67471	9.86	97.2196	3.14006	9.92975
9.37	87.7969	3.06105	9.67988	9.87	97.4169	3.14166	9.93479
9.38	87.9844	3.06268	9.68504	9.88	97.6144	3.14325	9.93982
9.39	88.1721	3.06431	9.69020	9.89	97.8121	3.14484	9.94485
9.40	88.3600	3.06594	9.69536	9.90	98.0100	3.14643	9.94987
9.41	88.5481	3.06757	9.70052	9.91	98.2081	3.14802	9.95490
9.42	88.7364	3.06920	9.70567	9.92	98.4064	3.14960	9.95992
9.43	88.9249	3.07083	9.71082	9.93	98.6049	3.15119	9.96494
9.44	89.1136	3.07246	9.71597	9.94	98.8036	3.15278	9.96995
9.45	89.3025	3.07409	9.72111	9.95	99.0025	3.15436	9.97497
9.46	89.4916	3.07571	9.72625	9.96	99.2016	3.15595	9.97998
9.47	89.6809	3.07734	9.73139	9.97	99.4009	3.15753	9.98499
9.48	89.8704	3.07896	9.73653	9.98	99.6004	3.15911	9.98999
9.49	90.0601	3.08058	9.74166	9.99	99.8001	3.16070	9.99500
9.50	90.2500	3.08221	9.74679	10.00	100.0000	3.16228	10.00000
N	N²	√N	√10N	N	N²	√N	√10N

TABLE B Areas under the Normal Curve Corresponding to Given Values of z.[a]

Column 2 gives the proportion of the area under the entire curve which is between the mean ($z = 0$) and the positive value of z. Areas for negative values of z are the same as for positive values, since the curve is symmetrical.

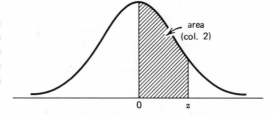

Column 3 gives the proportion of the area under the entire curve which falls beyond the stated positive value of z. Areas for negative values of z are the same, since the curve is symmetrical.

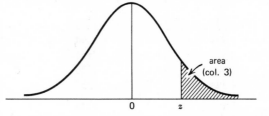

z	Area between mean and z	Area beyond z	z	Area between mean and z	Area beyond z
1	2	3	1	2	3
0.00	.0000	.5000	0.15	.0596	.4404
0.01	.0040	.4960	0.16	.0636	.4364
0.02	.0080	.4920	0.17	.0675	.4325
0.03	.0120	.4880	0.18	.0714	.4286
0.04	.0160	.4840	0.19	.0753	.4247
0.05	.0199	.4801	0.20	.0793	.4207
0.06	.0239	.4761	0.21	.0832	.4168
0.07	.0279	.4721	0.22	.0871	.4129
0.08	.0319	.4681	0.23	.0910	.4090
0.09	.0359	.4641	0.24	.0948	.4052
0.10	.0398	.4602	0.25	.0987	.4013
0.11	.0438	.4562	0.26	.1026	.3974
0.12	.0478	.4522	0.27	.1064	.3936
0.13	.0517	.4483	0.28	.1103	.3897
0.14	.0557	.4443	0.29	.1141	.3859

[a]From Appendix 2 of: R. Clarke, A. Coladarci, and J. Caffrey, *Statistical Reasoning and Procedures*, Charles E. Merrill Books, Inc., Columbus, Ohio, 1965, with permission of the publisher.

TABLE B (*Continued*)

z	Area between mean and z	Area beyond z	z	Area between mean and z	Area beyond z
1	2	3	1	2	3
0.30	.1179	.3821	0.65	.2422	.2578
0.31	.1217	.3783	0.66	.2454	.2546
0.32	.1255	.3745	0.67	.2486	.2514
0.33	.1293	.3707	0.68	.2517	.2483
0.34	.1331	.3669	0.69	.2549	.2451
0.35	.1368	.3632	0.70	.2580	.2420
0.36	.1406	.3594	0.71	.2611	.2389
0.37	.1443	.3557	0.72	.2642	.2358
0.38	.1480	.3520	0.73	.2673	.2327
0.39	.1517	.3483	0.74	.2704	.2296
0.40	.1554	.3446	0.75	.2734	.2266
0.41	.1591	.3409	0.76	.2764	.2236
0.42	.1628	.3372	0.77	.2794	.2206
0.43	.1664	.3336	0.78	.2823	.2177
0.44	.1700	.3300	0.79	.2852	.2148
0.45	.1736	.3264	0.80	.2881	.2119
0.46	.1772	.3228	0.81	.2910	.2090
0.47	.1808	.3192	0.82	.2939	.2061
0.48	.1844	.3156	0.83	.2967	.2033
0.49	.1879	.3121	0.84	.2995	.2005
0.50	.1915	.3085	0.85	.3023	.1977
0.51	.1950	.3050	0.86	.3051	.1949
0.52	.1985	.3015	0.87	.3078	.1922
0.53	.2019	.2981	0.88	.3106	.1894
0.54	.2054	.2946	0.89	.3133	.1867
0.55	.2088	.2912	0.90	.3159	.1841
0.56	.2123	.2877	0.91	.3186	.1814
0.57	.2157	.2843	0.92	.3212	.1788
0.58	.2190	.2810	0.93	.3238	.1762
0.59	.2224	.2776	0.94	.3264	.1736
0.60	.2257	.2743	0.95	.3289	.1711
0.61	.2291	.2709	0.96	.3315	.1685
0.62	.2324	.2676	0.97	.3340	.1660
0.63	.2357	.2643	0.98	.3365	.1635
0.64	.2389	.2611	0.99	.3389	.1611

TABLE B (*Continued*)

z	Area between mean and z	Area beyond z	z	Area between mean and z	Area beyond z
1	2	3	1	2	3
1.00	.3413	.1587	1.35	.4115	.0885
1.01	.3438	.1562	1.36	.4131	.0869
1.02	.3461	.1539	1.37	.4147	.0853
1.03	.3485	.1515	1.38	.4162	.0838
1.04	.3508	.1492	1.39	.4177	.0823
1.05	.3531	.1469	1.40	.4192	.0808
1.06	.3554	.1446	1.41	.4207	.0793
1.07	.3577	.1423	1.42	.4222	.0778
1.08	.3599	.1401	1.43	.4236	.0764
1.09	.3621	.1379	1.44	.4251	.0749
1.10	.3643	.1357	1.45	.4265	.0735
1.11	.3665	.1335	1.46	.4279	.0721
1.12	.3686	.1314	1.47	.4292	.0708
1.13	.3708	.1292	1.48	.4306	.0694
1.14	.3729	.1271	1.49	.4319	.0681
1.15	.3749	.1251	1.50	.4332	.0668
1.16	.3770	.1230	1.51	.4345	.0655
1.17	.3790	.1210	1.52	.4357	.0643
1.18	.3810	.1190	1.53	.4370	.0630
1.19	.3830	.1170	1.54	.4382	.0618
1.20	.3849	.1151	1.55	.4394	.0606
1.21	.3869	.1131	1.56	.4406	.0594
1.22	.3888	.1112	1.57	.4418	.0582
1.23	.3907	.1093	1.58	.4429	.0571
1.24	.3925	.1075	1.59	.4441	.0559
1.25	.3944	.1056	1.60	.4452	.0548
1.26	.3962	.1038	1.61	.4463	.0537
1.27	.3980	.1020	1.62	.4474	.0526
1.28	.3997	.1003	1.63	.4484	.0516
1.29	.4015	.0985	1.64	.4495	.0505
1.30	.4032	.0968	1.65	.4505	.0495
1.31	.4049	.0951	1.66	.4515	.0485
1.32	.4066	.0934	1.67	.4525	.0475
1.33	.4082	.0918	1.68	.4535	.0465
1.34	.4099	.0901	1.69	.4545	.0455

TABLE B (*Continued*)

z	Area between mean and z	Area beyond z	z	Area between mean and z	Area beyond z
1	2	3	1	2	3
1.70	.4554	.0446	2.05	.4798	.0202
1.71	.4564	.0436	2.06	.4803	.0197
1.72	.4573	.0427	2.07	.4808	.0192
1.73	.4582	.0418	2.08	.4812	.0188
1.74	.4591	.0409	2.09	.4817	.0183
1.75	.4599	.0401	2.10	.4821	.0179
1.76	.4608	.0392	2.11	.4826	.0174
1.77	.4616	.0384	2.12	.4830	.0170
1.78	.4625	.0375	2.13	.4834	.0166
1.79	.4633	.0367	2.14	.4838	.0162
1.80	.4641	.0359	2.15	.4842	.0158
1.81	.4649	.0351	2.16	.4846	.0154
1.82	.4656	.0344	2.17	.4850	.0150
1.83	.4664	.0336	2.18	.4854	.0146
1.84	.4671	.0329	2.19	.4857	.0143
1.85	.4678	.0322	2.20	.4861	.0139
1.86	.4686	.0314	2.21	.4864	.0136
1.87	.4693	.0307	2.22	.4868	.0132
1.88	.4699	.0301	2.23	.4871	.0129
1.89	.4706	.0294	2.24	.4875	.0125
1.90	.4713	.0287	2.25	.4878	.0122
1.91	.4719	.0281	2.26	.4881	.0119
1.92	.4726	.0274	2.27	.4884	.0116
1.93	.4732	.0268	2.28	.4887	.0113
1.94	.4738	.0262	2.29	.4890	.0110
1.95	.4744	.0256	2.30	.4893	.0107
1.96	.4750	.0250	2.31	.4896	.0104
1.97	.4756	.0244	2.32	.4898	.0102
1.98	.4761	.0239	2.33	.4901	.0099
1.99	.4767	.0233	2.34	.4904	.0096
2.00	.4772	.0228	2.35	.4906	.0094
2.01	.4778	.0222	2.36	.4909	.0091
2.02	.4783	.0217	2.37	.4911	.0089
2.03	.4788	.0212	2.38	.4913	.0087
2.04	.4793	.0207	2.39	.4916	.0084

TABLE B (*Continued*)

z	Area between mean and z	Area beyond z	z	Area between mean and z	Area beyond z
1	2	3	1	2	3
2.40	.4918	.0082	2.75	.4970	.0030
2.41	.4920	.0080	2.76	.4971	.0029
2.42	.4922	.0078	2.77	.4972	.0028
2.43	.4925	.0075	2.78	.4973	.0027
2.44	.4927	.0073	2.79	.4974	.0026
2.45	.4929	.0071	2.80	.4974	.0026
2.46	.4931	.0069	2.81	.4975	.0025
2.47	.4932	.0068	2.82	.4976	.0024
2.48	.4934	.0066	2.83	.4977	.0023
2.49	.4936	.0064	2.84	.4977	.0023
2.50	.4938	.0062	2.85	.4978	.0022
2.51	.4940	.0060	2.86	.4979	.0021
2.52	.4941	.0059	2.87	.4979	.0021
2.53	.4943	.0057	2.88	.4980	.0020
2.54	.4945	.0055	2.89	.4981	.0019
2.55	.4946	.0054	2.90	.4981	.0019
2.56	.4948	.0052	2.91	.4982	.0018
2.57	.4949	.0051	2.92	.4982	.0018
2.58	.4951	.0049	2.93	.4983	.0017
2.59	.4952	.0048	2.94	.4984	.0016
2.60	.4953	.0047	2.95	.4984	.0016
2.61	.4955	.0045	2.96	.4985	.0015
2.62	.4956	.0044	2.97	.4985	.0015
2.63	.4957	.0043	2.98	.4986	.0014
2.64	.4959	.0041	2.99	.4986	.0014
2.65	.4960	.0040	3.00	.4987	.0013
2.66	.4961	.0039	3.01	.4987	.0013
2.67	.4962	.0038	3.02	.4987	.0013
2.68	.4963	.0037	3.03	.4988	.0012
2.69	.4964	.0036	3.04	.4988	.0012
2.70	.4965	.0035	3.05	.4989	.0011
2.71	.4966	.0034	3.06	.4989	.0011
2.72	.4967	.0033	3.07	.4989	.0011
2.73	.4968	.0032	3.08	.4990	.0010
2.74	.4969	.0031	3.09	.4990	.0010

TABLE B (*Continued*)

z	Area between mean and z	Area beyond z	z	Area between mean and z	Area beyond z
1	2	3	1	2	3
3.10	.4990	.0010	3.20	.4993	.0007
3.11	.4991	.0009	3.21	.4993	.0007
3.12	.4991	.0009	3.22	.4994	.0006
3.13	.4991	.0009	3.23	.4994	.0006
3.14	.4992	.0008	3.24	.4994	.0006
3.15	.4992	.0008	3.30	.4995	.0005
3.16	.4992	.0008	3.40	.4997	.0003
3.17	.4992	.0008	3.50	.4998	.0002
3.18	.4993	.0007	3.60	.4998	.0002
3.19	.4993	.0007	3.70	.4999	.0001

The larger area 1	z 2	The smaller area 3		The larger area 1	z 2	The smaller area 3
.500	.0000	.500		.635	.3451	.365
.505	.0125	.495		.640	.3585	.360
.510	.0251	.490		.645	.3719	.355
.515	.0376	.485		.650	.3853	.350
.520	.0502	.480		.655	.3989	.345
.525	.0627	.475		.660	.4125	.340
.530	.0753	.470		.665	.4261	.335
.535	.0878	.465		.670	.4399	.330
.540	.1004	.460		.675	.4538	.325
.545	.1130	.455		.680	.4677	.320
.550	.1257	.450		.685	.4817	.315
.555	.1383	.445		.690	.4959	.310
.560	.1510	.440		.695	.5101	.305
.565	.1637	.435		.700	.5244	.300
.570	.1764	.430		.705	.5388	.295
.575	.1891	.425		.710	.5534	.290
.580	.2019	.420		.715	.5681	.285
.585	.2147	.415		.720	.5828	.280
.590	.2275	.410		.725	.5978	.275
.595	.2404	.405		.730	.6128	.270
.600	.2533	.400		.735	.6280	.265
.605	.2663	.395		.740	.6433	.260
.610	.2793	.390		.745	.6588	.255
.615	.2924	.385		.750	.6745	.250
.620	.3055	.380		.755	.6903	.245
.625	.3186	.375		.760	.7063	.240
.630	.3319	.370		.765	.7225	.235
				.770	.7388	.230

Table Continued on Following Page

TABLE C (*Continued*)

The larger area 1	z 2	The smaller area 3		The larger area 1	z 2	The smaller area 3
.775	.7554	.225		.900	1.2816	.100
.780	.7722	.220		.905	1.3106	.095
.785	.7892	.215		.910	1.3408	.090
.790	.8064	.210		.915	1.3722	.085
.795	.8239	.205		.920	1.4051	.080
.800	.8416	.200		.925	1.4395	.075
.805	.8596	.195		.930	1.4757	.070
.810	.8779	.190		.935	1.5141	.065
.815	.8965	.185		.940	1.5548	.060
.820	.9154	.180		.945	1.5982	.055
.825	.9346	.175		.950	1.6449	.050
.830	.9542	.170		.955	1.6954	.045
.835	.9741	.165		.960	1.7507	.040
.840	.9945	.160		.965	1.8119	.035
.845	1.0152	.155		.970	1.8808	.030
.850	1.0364	.150		.975	1.9600	.025
.855	1.0581	.145		.980	2.0537	.020
.860	1.0803	.140		.985	2.1701	.015
.865	1.1031	.135		.990	2.3263	.010
.870	1.1264	.130		.995	2.5758	.005
.875	1.1503	.125		.996	2.6521	.004
.880	1.1750	.120		.997	2.7478	.003
.885	1.2004	.115		.998	2.8782	.002
.890	1.2265	.110		.999	3.0902	.001
.895	1.2536	.105		.9995	3.2905	.0005

[a]Modified from: *Fundamental Statistics in Psychology and Education* by J. P. Guilford, Copyright © 1965, Mc-Graw-Hill Book Co., Inc. Used by permission of McGraw-Hill Book Company.

TABLE D Student's t Distribution.[a]

The first column identifies the specific t distribution according to its number of degrees of freedom. Other columns give the proportion of the area under the entire curve which falls beyond the tabled positive value of t. Areas for negative values of t are the same, since the curve is symmetrical.

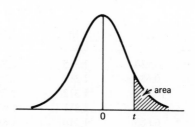

		Area in one tail				
df	.25	.10	.05	.025	.01	.005
1	1.000	3.078	6.314	12.706	31.821	63.657
2	0.816	1.886	2.920	4.303	6.965	9.925
3	0.765	1.638	2.353	3.182	4.541	5.841
4	0.741	1.533	2.132	2.776	3.747	4.604
5	0.727	1.476	2.015	2.571	3.365	4.032
6	0.718	1.440	1.943	2.447	3.143	3.707
7	0.711	1.415	1.895	2.365	2.998	3.500
8	0.706	1.397	1.860	2.306	2.896	3.355
9	0.703	1.383	1.833	2.262	2.821	3.250
10	0.700	1.372	1.812	2.228	2.764	3.169
11	0.697	1.363	1.796	2.201	2.718	3.106
12	0.696	1.356	1.782	2.179	2.681	3.054
13	0.694	1.350	1.771	2.160	2.650	3.012
14	0.692	1.345	1.761	2.145	2.624	2.977
15	0.691	1.341	1.753	2.132	2.602	2.947
16	0.690	1.337	1.746	2.120	2.584	2.921
17	0.689	1.333	1.740	2.110	2.567	2.898
18	0.688	1.330	1.734	2.101	2.552	2.878
19	0.688	1.328	1.729	2.093	2.540	2.861
20	0.687	1.325	1.725	2.086	2.528	2.845
21	0.686	1.323	1.721	2.080	2.518	2.831
22	0.686	1.321	1.717	2.074	2.508	2.819
23	0.685	1.320	1.714	2.069	2.500	2.807
24	0.685	1.318	1.711	2.064	2.492	2.797
25	0.684	1.316	1.708	2.060	2.485	2.787

[a]Modified from Section 2.1, *Handbook of Statistical Tables* by Donald B. Owen, Copyright © 1962, Addison-Wesley, Reading, Mass. Courtesy of U.S. Atomic Energy Commission.

Table Continued on Following Page

TABLE D (*Continued*)

df	.25	.10	.05	.025	.01	.005
			Area in one tail			
26	0.684	1.315	1.706	2.056	2.479	2.779
27	0.684	1.314	1.703	2.052	2.473	2.771
28	0.683	1.312	1.701	2.048	2.467	2.763
29	0.683	1.311	1.699	2.045	2.462	2.756
30	0.683	1.310	1.697	2.042	2.457	2.750
31	0.682	1.310	1.696	2.040	2.453	2.744
32	0.682	1.309	1.694	2.037	2.449	2.738
33	0.682	1.308	1.692	2.034	2.445	2.733
34	0.682	1.307	1.691	2.032	2.441	2.728
35	0.682	1.306	1.690	2.030	2.438	2.724
36	0.681	1.306	1.688	2.028	2.434	2.720
37	0.681	1.305	1.687	2.026	2.431	2.715
38	0.681	1.304	1.686	2.024	2.429	2.712
39	0.681	1.304	1.685	2.023	2.426	2.708
40	0.681	1.303	1.684	2.021	2.423	2.704
45	0.680	1.301	1.679	2.014	2.412	2.690
50	0.679	1.299	1.676	2.009	2.403	2.678
55	0.679	1.297	1.673	2.004	2.396	2.668
60	0.679	1.296	1.671	2.000	2.390	2.660
70	0.678	1.294	1.667	1.994	2.381	2.648
80	0.678	1.292	1.664	1.990	2.374	2.639
90	0.677	1.291	1.662	1.987	2.368	2.632
100	0.677	1.290	1.660	1.984	2.364	2.626
120	0.676	1.289	1.658	1.980	2.358	2.617
150	0.676	1.287	1.655	1.976	2.352	2.609
200	0.676	1.286	1.652	1.972	2.345	2.601
300	0.675	1.284	1.650	1.968	2.339	2.592
400	0.675	1.284	1.649	1.966	2.336	2.588
500	0.675	1.283	1.648	1.965	2.334	2.586
1000	0.675	1.282	1.646	1.962	2.330	2.581
∞	0.674	1.282	1.645	1.960	2.326	2.576

TABLE E Values of the Correlation Coefficient Required for Different Levels of Significance when H_0: $\rho = 0$.[a]

	Levels of significance for a one-tailed test			
	.05	.025	.01	.005
	Levels of significance for a two-tailed test			
df	.10	**.05**	.02	**.01**
1	.988	.997	.9995	.9999
2	.900	.950	.980	.990
3	.805	.878	.934	.959
4	.729	.811	.882	.917
5	.669	.754	.833	.874
6	.622	.707	.789	.834
7	.582	.666	.750	.798
8	.549	.632	.716	.765
9	.521	.602	.685	.735
10	.497	.576	.658	.708
11	.476	.553	.634	.684
12	.458	.532	.612	.661
13	.441	.514	.592	.641
14	.426	.497	.574	.623
15	.412	.482	.558	.606
16	.400	.468	.542	.590
17	.389	.456	.528	.575
18	.378	.444	.516	.561
19	.369	.433	.503	.549
20	.360	.423	.492	.537
21	.352	.413	.482	.526
22	.344	.404	.472	.515
23	.337	.396	.462	.505
24	.330	.388	.453	.496
25	.323	.381	.445	.487
26	.317	.374	.437	.479
27	.311	.367	.430	.471
28	.306	.361	.423	.463
29	.301	.355	.416	.456
30	.296	.349	.409	.449
32	.287	.339	.397	.436
34	.279	.329	.386	.424

[a]Table E is taken from Table V.A of Fisher: *Statistical Methods for Research Workers*, published by Oliver & Boyd Limited, Edinburgh, and by permission of the author and publishers. Supplementary values were calculated at San Jose State College by K. Fernandes.

Table Continued on Following Page

TABLE E (*Continued*)

	Levels of significance for a one-tailed test			
	.05	.025	.01	.005
	Levels of significance for a two-tailed test			
df	.10	**.05**	.02	**.01**
36	.271	.320	.376	.413
38	.264	.312	.367	.403
40	.257	.304	.358	.393
42	.251	.297	.350	.384
44	.246	.291	.342	.376
46	.240	.285	.335	.368
48	.235	.279	.328	.361
50	.231	.273	.322	.354
55	.220	.261	.307	.339
60	.211	.250	.295	.325
65	.203	.240	.284	.313
70	.195	.232	.274	.302
75	.189	.224	.265	.292
80	.183	.217	.256	.283
85	.178	.211	.249	.275
90	.173	.205	.242	.267
95	.168	.200	.236	.260
100	.164	.195	.230	.254
120	.150	.178	.210	.232
150	.134	.159	.189	.208
200	.116	.138	.164	.181
300	.095	.113	.134	.148
400	.082	.098	.116	.128
500	.073	.088	.104	.115
1000	.052	.062	.073	.081

TABLE F Values of Fisher's z' for Values of r.[a]

r	z'	r	z'	r	z'	r	z'	r	z'
.000	.000	.200	.203	.400	.424	.600	.693	.800	1.099
.005	.005	.205	.208	.405	.430	.605	.701	.805	1.113
.010	.010	.210	.213	.410	.436	.610	.709	.810	1.127
.015	.015	.215	.218	.415	.442	.615	.717	.815	1.142
.020	.020	.220	.224	.420	.448	.620	.725	.820	1.157
.025	.025	.225	.229	.425	.454	.625	.733	.825	1.172
.030	.030	.230	.234	.430	.460	.630	.741	.830	1.188
.035	.035	.235	.239	.435	.466	.635	.750	.835	1.204
.040	.040	.240	.245	.440	.472	.640	.758	.840	1.221
.045	.045	.245	.250	.445	.478	.645	.767	.845	1.238
.050	.050	.250	.255	.450	.485	.650	.775	.850	1.256
.055	.055	.255	.261	.455	.491	.655	.784	.855	1.274
.060	.060	.260	.266	.460	.497	.660	.793	.860	1.293
.065	.065	.265	.271	.465	.504	.665	.802	.865	1.313
.070	.070	.270	.277	.470	.510	.670	.811	.870	1.333
.075	.075	.275	.282	.475	.517	.675	.820	.875	1.354
.080	.080	.280	.288	.480	.523	.680	.829	.880	1.376
.085	.085	.285	.293	.485	.530	.685	.838	.885	1.398
.090	.090	.290	.299	.490	.536	.690	.848	.890	1.422
.095	.095	.295	.304	.495	.543	.695	.858	.895	1.447
.100	.100	.300	.310	.500	.549	.700	.867	.900	1.472
.105	.105	.305	.315	.505	.556	.705	.877	.905	1.499
.110	.110	.310	.321	.510	.563	.710	.887	.910	1.528
.115	.116	.315	.326	.515	.570	.715	.897	.915	1.557
.120	.121	.320	.332	.520	.576	.720	.908	.920	1.589
.125	.126	.325	.337	.525	.583	.725	.918	.925	1.623
.130	.131	.330	.343	.530	.590	.730	.929	.930	1.658
.135	.136	.335	.348	.535	.597	.735	.940	.935	1.697
.140	.141	.340	.354	.540	.604	.740	.950	.940	1.738
.145	.146	.345	.360	.545	.611	.745	.962	.945	1.783
.150	.151	.350	.365	.550	.618	.750	.973	.950	1.832
.155	.156	.355	.371	.555	.626	.755	.984	.955	1.886
.160	.161	.360	.377	.560	.633	.760	.996	.960	1.946
.165	.167	.365	.383	.565	.640	.765	1.008	.965	2.014
.170	.172	.370	.388	.570	.648	.770	1.020	.970	2.092
.175	.177	.375	.394	.575	.655	.775	1.033	.975	2.185
.180	.182	.380	.400	.580	.662	.780	1.045	.980	2.298
.185	.187	.385	.406	.585	.670	.785	1.058	.985	2.443
.190	.192	.390	.412	.590	.678	.790	1.071	.990	2.647
.195	.198	.395	.418	.595	.685	.795	1.085	.995	2.994

[a]From *Statistical Methods*, Second Edition, by Allen L. Edwards. Copyright © 1954, 1967 by Allen L. Edwards. Reprinted by permission of Holt, Rinehart and Winston, Inc.

TABLE G The χ^2 Distribution.[a]

The first column identifies the specific χ^2 distribution according to its number of degrees of freedom. Other columns give the proportion of the area under the entire curve which falls above the tabled value of χ^2.

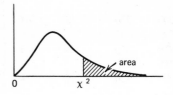

					Area in the upper tail					
df	.995	.99	.975	.95	.90	.10	**.05**	.025	**.01**	.005
1	.000039	.00016	.00098	.0039	.016	2.71	3.84	5.02	6.63	7.88
2	.010	.020	.051	.10	.21	4.61	5.99	7.38	9.21	10.60
3	.072	.11	.22	.35	.58	6.25	7.81	9.35	11.34	12.84
4	.21	.30	.48	.71	1.06	7.78	9.49	11.14	13.28	14.86
5	.41	.55	.83	1.15	1.61	9.24	11.07	12.83	15.09	16.75
6	.68	.87	1.24	1.64	2.20	10.64	12.59	14.45	16.81	18.55
7	.99	1.24	1.69	2.17	2.83	12.02	14.07	16.01	18.48	20.28
8	1.34	1.65	2.18	2.73	3.49	13.36	15.51	17.53	20.09	21.96
9	1.73	2.09	2.70	3.33	4.17	14.68	16.92	19.02	21.67	23.59
10	2.16	2.56	3.25	3.94	4.87	15.99	18.31	20.48	23.21	25.19
11	2.60	3.05	3.82	4.57	5.58	17.28	19.68	21.92	24.72	26.76
12	3.07	3.57	4.40	5.23	6.30	18.55	21.03	23.34	26.22	28.30
13	3.57	4.11	5.01	5.89	7.04	19.81	22.36	24.74	27.69	29.82
14	4.07	4.66	5.63	6.57	7.79	21.06	23.68	26.12	29.14	31.32
15	4.60	5.23	6.26	7.26	8.55	22.31	25.00	27.49	30.58	32.80
16	5.14	5.81	6.91	7.96	9.31	23.54	26.30	28.85	32.00	34.27
17	5.70	6.41	7.56	8.67	10.09	24.77	27.59	30.19	33.41	35.72
18	6.26	7.01	8.23	9.39	10.86	25.99	28.87	31.53	34.81	37.16
19	6.84	7.63	8.91	10.12	11.65	27.20	30.14	32.85	36.19	38.58
20	7.43	8.26	9.59	10.85	12.44	28.41	31.41	34.17	37.57	40.00
21	8.03	8.90	10.28	11.59	13.24	29.62	32.67	35.48	38.93	41.40
22	8.64	9.54	10.98	12.34	14.04	30.81	33.92	36.78	40.29	42.80
23	9.26	10.20	11.69	13.09	14.85	32.01	35.17	38.08	41.64	44.18
24	9.89	10.86	12.40	13.85	15.66	33.20	36.42	39.36	42.98	45.56
25	10.52	11.52	13.12	14.61	16.47	34.38	37.65	40.65	44.31	46.93
26	11.16	12.20	13.84	15.38	17.29	35.56	38.89	41.92	45.64	48.29
27	11.81	12.88	14.57	16.15	18.11	36.74	40.11	43.19	46.96	49.64
28	12.46	13.56	15.31	16.93	18.94	37.92	41.34	44.46	48.28	50.99
29	13.12	14.26	16.05	17.71	19.77	39.09	42.56	45.72	49.59	52.34
30	13.79	14.95	16.79	18.49	20.60	40.26	43.77	46.98	50.89	53.67
40	20.71	22.16	24.43	26.51	29.05	51.81	55.76	59.34	63.69	66.77
50	27.99	29.71	32.36	34.76	37.69	63.17	67.50	71.42	76.15	79.49
60	35.53	37.48	40.48	43.19	46.46	74.40	79.08	83.30	88.38	91.95
70	43.28	45.44	48.76	51.74	55.33	85.53	90.53	95.02	100.42	104.22
80	51.17	53.54	57.15	60.39	64.28	96.58	101.88	106.63	112.33	116.32
90	59.20	61.75	65.65	69.13	73.29	107.56	113.14	118.14	124.12	128.30
100	67.33	70.06	74.22	77.93	82.36	118.50	124.34	129.56	135.81	140.17
120	83.85	86.92	91.58	95.70	100.62	140.23	146.57	152.21	158.95	163.64

[a]Modified from Table 8: E. Pearson, and H. Hartley, *Biometrika Tables for Statisticians*, Vol. 1, 3rd ed., University Press, Cambridge, 1966, with permission of the Biometrika Trustees.

Note: When $df > 30$, the critical value of χ^2 may be found by the following approximate formula: $\chi^2 = df\left[1 - (2/9df) + z\sqrt{2/9df}\,\right]^3$, where z is the normal deviate above which lies the same proportionate area in the normal curve. For example, to find the value of χ^2 which divides the upper 1% of the distribution from the remainder when $df = 30$, we calculate: $\chi^2 = 30(1 - .00741 + 2.3263 \sqrt{.0074074})^3 = 50.91$ which compares closely with the tabled value of 50.89.

TABLE H The F Distribution.[a] Values of F Corresponding to 5% (Roman Type) and 1% (Boldface Type) of the Area in the Upper Tail

The specific F distribution must be identified by the number of degrees of freedom characterizing the numerator and the denominator of F.

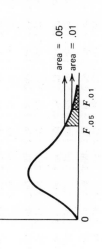

area = .05
area = .01

$F_{.05}$ $F_{.01}$

Degrees of Freedom: Numerator

Denominator	1	2	3	4	5	6	7	8	9	10	11	12	14	16	20	24	30	40	50	75	100	200	500	∞
1	161 **4,052**	200 **4,999**	216 **5,403**	225 **5,625**	230 **5,764**	234 **5,859**	237 **5,928**	239 **5,981**	241 **6,022**	242 **6,056**	243 **6,082**	244 **6,106**	245 **6,142**	246 **6,169**	248 **6,208**	249 **6,234**	250 **6,258**	251 **6,286**	252 **6,302**	253 **6,323**	253 **6,334**	254 **6,352**	254 **6,361**	254 **6,366**
2	18.51 **98.49**	19.00 **99.00**	19.16 **99.17**	19.25 **99.25**	19.30 **99.30**	19.33 **99.33**	19.36 **99.34**	19.37 **99.36**	19.38 **99.38**	19.39 **99.40**	19.40 **99.41**	19.41 **99.42**	19.42 **99.43**	19.43 **99.44**	19.44 **99.45**	19.45 **99.46**	19.46 **99.47**	19.47 **99.48**	19.47 **99.48**	19.48 **99.49**	19.49 **99.49**	19.49 **99.49**	19.50 **99.50**	19.50 **99.50**
3	10.13 **34.12**	9.55 **30.82**	9.28 **29.46**	9.12 **28.71**	9.01 **28.24**	8.94 **27.91**	8.88 **27.67**	8.84 **27.49**	8.81 **27.34**	8.78 **27.23**	8.76 **27.13**	8.74 **27.05**	8.71 **26.92**	8.69 **26.83**	8.66 **26.69**	8.64 **26.60**	8.62 **26.50**	8.60 **26.41**	8.58 **26.35**	8.57 **26.27**	8.56 **26.23**	8.54 **26.18**	8.54 **26.14**	8.53 **26.12**
4	7.71 **21.20**	6.94 **18.00**	6.59 **16.69**	6.39 **15.98**	6.26 **15.52**	6.16 **15.21**	6.09 **14.98**	6.04 **14.80**	6.00 **14.66**	5.96 **14.54**	5.93 **14.45**	5.91 **14.37**	5.87 **14.24**	5.84 **14.15**	5.80 **14.02**	5.77 **13.93**	5.74 **13.83**	5.71 **13.74**	5.70 **13.69**	5.68 **13.61**	5.66 **13.57**	5.65 **13.52**	5.64 **13.48**	5.63 **13.46**
5	6.61 **16.26**	5.79 **13.27**	5.41 **12.06**	5.19 **11.39**	5.05 **10.97**	4.95 **10.67**	4.88 **10.45**	4.82 **10.27**	4.78 **10.15**	4.74 **10.05**	4.70 **9.96**	4.68 **9.89**	4.64 **9.77**	4.60 **9.68**	4.56 **9.55**	4.53 **9.47**	4.50 **9.38**	4.46 **9.29**	4.44 **9.24**	4.42 **9.17**	4.40 **9.13**	4.38 **9.07**	4.37 **9.04**	4.36 **9.02**
6	5.99 **13.74**	5.14 **10.92**	4.76 **9.78**	4.53 **9.15**	4.39 **8.75**	4.28 **8.47**	4.21 **8.26**	4.15 **8.10**	4.10 **7.98**	4.06 **7.87**	4.03 **7.79**	4.00 **7.72**	3.96 **7.60**	3.92 **7.52**	3.87 **7.39**	3.84 **7.31**	3.81 **7.23**	3.77 **7.14**	3.75 **7.09**	3.72 **7.02**	3.71 **6.99**	3.69 **6.94**	3.68 **6.90**	3.67 **6.88**
7	5.59 **12.25**	4.74 **9.55**	4.35 **8.45**	4.12 **7.85**	3.97 **7.46**	3.87 **7.19**	3.79 **7.00**	3.73 **6.84**	3.68 **6.71**	3.63 **6.62**	3.60 **6.54**	3.57 **6.47**	3.52 **6.35**	3.49 **6.27**	3.44 **6.15**	3.41 **6.07**	3.38 **5.98**	3.34 **5.90**	3.32 **5.85**	3.29 **5.78**	3.28 **5.75**	3.25 **5.70**	3.24 **5.67**	3.23 **5.65**
8	5.32 **11.26**	4.46 **8.65**	4.07 **7.59**	3.84 **7.01**	3.69 **6.63**	3.58 **6.37**	3.50 **6.19**	3.44 **6.03**	3.39 **5.91**	3.34 **5.82**	3.31 **5.74**	3.28 **5.67**	3.23 **5.56**	3.20 **5.48**	3.15 **5.36**	3.12 **5.28**	3.08 **5.20**	3.05 **5.11**	3.03 **5.06**	3.00 **5.00**	2.98 **4.96**	2.96 **4.91**	2.94 **4.88**	2.93 **4.86**

[a]Reproduced by permission from *Statistical Methods*, 5th ed., by George W. Snedecor, Copyright © 1956 by The Iowa State University Press.

Table Continued on Following Page

TABLE H (Continued)

Degrees of Freedom: Numerator

Degrees of Freedom: Denominator	1	2	3	4	5	6	7	8	9	10	11	12	14	16	20	24	30	40	50	75	100	200	500	∞
9	5.12 / 10.56	4.26 / 8.02	3.86 / 6.99	3.63 / 6.42	3.48 / 6.06	3.37 / 5.80	3.29 / 5.62	3.23 / 5.47	3.18 / 5.35	3.13 / 5.26	3.10 / 5.18	3.07 / 5.11	3.02 / 5.00	2.98 / 4.92	2.93 / 4.80	2.90 / 4.73	2.86 / 4.64	2.82 / 4.56	2.80 / 4.51	2.77 / 4.45	2.76 / 4.41	2.73 / 4.36	2.72 / 4.33	2.71 / 4.31
10	4.96 / 10.04	4.10 / 7.56	3.71 / 6.55	3.48 / 5.99	3.33 / 5.64	3.22 / 5.39	3.14 / 5.21	3.07 / 5.06	3.02 / 4.95	2.97 / 4.85	2.94 / 4.78	2.91 / 4.71	2.86 / 4.60	2.82 / 4.52	2.77 / 4.41	2.74 / 4.33	2.70 / 4.25	2.67 / 4.17	2.64 / 4.12	2.61 / 4.05	2.59 / 4.01	2.56 / 3.96	2.55 / 3.93	2.54 / 3.91
11	4.84 / 9.65	3.98 / 7.20	3.59 / 6.22	3.36 / 5.67	3.20 / 5.32	3.09 / 5.07	3.01 / 4.88	2.95 / 4.74	2.90 / 4.63	2.86 / 4.54	2.82 / 4.46	2.79 / 4.40	2.74 / 4.29	2.70 / 4.21	2.65 / 4.10	2.61 / 4.02	2.57 / 3.94	2.53 / 3.86	2.50 / 3.80	2.47 / 3.74	2.45 / 3.70	2.42 / 3.66	2.41 / 3.62	2.40 / 3.60
12	4.75 / 9.33	3.88 / 6.93	3.49 / 5.95	3.26 / 5.41	3.11 / 5.06	3.00 / 4.82	2.92 / 4.65	2.85 / 4.50	2.80 / 4.39	2.76 / 4.30	2.72 / 4.22	2.69 / 4.16	2.64 / 4.05	2.60 / 3.98	2.54 / 3.86	2.50 / 3.78	2.46 / 3.70	2.42 / 3.61	2.40 / 3.56	2.36 / 3.49	2.35 / 3.46	2.32 / 3.41	2.31 / 3.38	2.30 / 3.36
13	4.67 / 9.07	3.80 / 6.70	3.41 / 5.74	3.18 / 5.20	3.02 / 4.86	2.92 / 4.62	2.84 / 4.44	2.77 / 4.30	2.72 / 4.19	2.67 / 4.10	2.63 / 4.02	2.60 / 3.96	2.55 / 3.85	2.51 / 3.78	2.46 / 3.67	2.42 / 3.59	2.38 / 3.51	2.34 / 3.42	2.32 / 3.37	2.28 / 3.30	2.26 / 3.27	2.24 / 3.21	2.22 / 3.18	2.21 / 3.16
14	4.60 / 8.86	3.74 / 6.51	3.34 / 5.56	3.11 / 5.03	2.96 / 4.69	2.85 / 4.46	2.77 / 4.28	2.70 / 4.14	2.65 / 4.03	2.60 / 3.94	2.56 / 3.86	2.53 / 3.80	2.48 / 3.70	2.44 / 3.62	2.39 / 3.51	2.35 / 3.43	2.31 / 3.34	2.27 / 3.26	2.24 / 3.21	2.21 / 3.14	2.19 / 3.11	2.16 / 3.06	2.14 / 3.02	2.13 / 3.00
15	4.54 / 8.68	3.68 / 6.36	3.29 / 5.42	3.06 / 4.89	2.90 / 4.56	2.79 / 4.32	2.70 / 4.14	2.64 / 4.00	2.59 / 3.89	2.55 / 3.80	2.51 / 3.73	2.48 / 3.67	2.43 / 3.56	2.39 / 3.48	2.33 / 3.36	2.29 / 3.29	2.25 / 3.20	2.21 / 3.12	2.18 / 3.07	2.15 / 3.00	2.12 / 2.97	2.10 / 2.92	2.08 / 2.89	2.07 / 2.87
16	4.49 / 8.53	3.63 / 6.23	3.24 / 5.29	3.01 / 4.77	2.85 / 4.44	2.74 / 4.20	2.66 / 4.03	2.59 / 3.89	2.54 / 3.78	2.49 / 3.69	2.45 / 3.61	2.42 / 3.55	2.37 / 3.45	2.33 / 3.37	2.28 / 3.25	2.24 / 3.18	2.20 / 3.10	2.16 / 3.01	2.13 / 2.96	2.09 / 2.89	2.07 / 2.86	2.04 / 2.80	2.02 / 2.77	2.01 / 2.75
17	4.45 / 8.40	3.59 / 6.11	3.20 / 5.18	2.96 / 4.67	2.81 / 4.34	2.70 / 4.10	2.62 / 3.93	2.55 / 3.79	2.50 / 3.68	2.45 / 3.59	2.41 / 3.52	2.38 / 3.45	2.33 / 3.35	2.29 / 3.27	2.23 / 3.16	2.19 / 3.08	2.15 / 3.00	2.11 / 2.92	2.08 / 2.86	2.04 / 2.79	2.02 / 2.76	1.99 / 2.70	1.97 / 2.67	1.96 / 2.65
18	4.41 / 8.28	3.55 / 6.01	3.16 / 5.09	2.93 / 4.58	2.77 / 4.25	2.66 / 4.01	2.58 / 3.85	2.51 / 3.71	2.46 / 3.60	2.41 / 3.51	2.37 / 3.44	2.34 / 3.37	2.29 / 3.27	2.25 / 3.19	2.19 / 3.07	2.15 / 3.00	2.11 / 2.91	2.07 / 2.83	2.04 / 2.78	2.00 / 2.71	1.98 / 2.68	1.95 / 2.62	1.93 / 2.59	1.92 / 2.57
19	4.38 / 8.18	3.52 / 5.93	3.13 / 5.01	2.90 / 4.50	2.74 / 4.17	2.63 / 3.94	2.55 / 3.77	2.48 / 3.63	2.43 / 3.52	2.38 / 3.43	2.34 / 3.36	2.31 / 3.30	2.26 / 3.19	2.21 / 3.12	2.15 / 3.00	2.11 / 2.92	2.07 / 2.84	2.02 / 2.76	2.00 / 2.70	1.96 / 2.63	1.94 / 2.60	1.91 / 2.54	1.90 / 2.51	1.88 / 2.49
20	4.35 / 8.10	3.49 / 5.85	3.10 / 4.94	2.87 / 4.43	2.71 / 4.10	2.60 / 3.87	2.52 / 3.71	2.45 / 3.56	2.40 / 3.45	2.35 / 3.37	2.31 / 3.30	2.28 / 3.23	2.23 / 3.13	2.18 / 3.05	2.12 / 2.94	2.08 / 2.86	2.04 / 2.77	1.99 / 2.69	1.96 / 2.63	1.92 / 2.56	1.90 / 2.53	1.87 / 2.47	1.85 / 2.44	1.84 / 2.42
21	4.32 / 8.02	3.47 / 5.78	3.07 / 4.87	2.84 / 4.37	2.68 / 4.04	2.57 / 3.81	2.49 / 3.65	2.42 / 3.51	2.37 / 3.40	2.32 / 3.31	2.28 / 3.24	2.25 / 3.17	2.20 / 3.07	2.15 / 2.99	2.09 / 2.88	2.05 / 2.80	2.00 / 2.72	1.96 / 2.63	1.93 / 2.58	1.89 / 2.51	1.87 / 2.47	1.84 / 2.42	1.82 / 2.38	1.81 / 2.36

TABLE H (Continued)

Degrees of Freedom: Numerator

Degrees of Freedom: Denominator	1	2	3	4	5	6	7	8	9	10	11	12	14	16	20	24	30	40	50	75	100	200	500	∞
22	4.30 7.94	3.44 5.72	3.05 4.82	2.82 4.31	2.66 3.99	2.55 3.76	2.47 3.59	2.40 3.45	2.35 3.35	2.30 3.26	2.26 3.18	2.23 3.12	2.18 3.02	2.13 2.94	2.07 2.83	2.03 2.75	1.98 2.67	1.93 2.58	1.91 2.53	1.87 2.46	1.84 2.42	1.81 2.37	1.80 2.33	1.78 2.31
23	4.28 7.88	3.42 5.66	3.03 4.76	2.80 4.26	2.64 3.94	2.53 3.71	2.45 3.54	2.38 3.41	2.32 3.30	2.28 3.21	2.24 3.14	2.20 3.07	2.14 2.97	2.10 2.89	2.04 2.78	2.00 2.70	1.96 2.62	1.91 2.53	1.88 2.48	1.84 2.41	1.82 2.37	1.79 2.32	1.77 2.28	1.76 2.26
24	4.26 7.82	3.40 5.61	3.01 4.72	2.78 4.22	2.62 3.90	2.51 3.67	2.43 3.50	2.36 3.36	2.30 3.25	2.26 3.17	2.22 3.09	2.18 3.03	2.13 2.93	2.09 2.85	2.02 2.74	1.98 2.66	1.94 2.58	1.89 2.49	1.86 2.44	1.82 2.36	1.80 2.33	1.76 2.27	1.74 2.23	1.73 2.21
25	4.24 7.77	3.38 5.57	2.99 4.68	2.76 4.18	2.60 3.86	2.49 3.63	2.41 3.46	2.34 3.32	2.28 3.21	2.24 3.13	2.20 3.05	2.16 2.99	2.11 2.89	2.06 2.81	2.00 2.70	1.96 2.62	1.92 2.54	1.87 2.45	1.84 2.40	1.80 2.32	1.77 2.29	1.74 2.23	1.72 2.19	1.71 2.17
26	4.22 7.72	3.37 5.53	2.98 4.64	2.74 4.14	2.59 3.82	2.47 3.59	2.39 3.42	2.32 3.29	2.27 3.17	2.22 3.09	2.18 3.02	2.15 2.96	2.10 2.86	2.05 2.77	1.99 2.66	1.95 2.58	1.90 2.50	1.85 2.41	1.82 2.36	1.78 2.28	1.76 2.25	1.72 2.19	1.70 2.15	1.69 2.13
27	4.21 7.68	3.35 5.49	2.96 4.60	2.73 4.11	2.57 3.79	2.46 3.56	2.37 3.39	2.30 3.26	2.25 3.14	2.20 3.06	2.16 2.98	2.13 2.93	2.08 2.83	2.03 2.74	1.97 2.63	1.93 2.55	1.88 2.47	1.84 2.38	1.80 2.33	1.76 2.25	1.74 2.21	1.71 2.16	1.68 2.12	1.67 2.10
28	4.20 7.64	3.34 5.45	2.95 4.57	2.71 4.07	2.56 3.76	2.44 3.53	2.36 3.36	2.29 3.23	2.24 3.11	2.19 3.03	2.15 2.95	2.12 2.90	2.06 2.80	2.02 2.71	1.96 2.60	1.91 2.52	1.87 2.44	1.81 2.35	1.78 2.30	1.75 2.22	1.72 2.18	1.69 2.13	1.67 2.09	1.65 2.06
29	4.18 7.60	3.33 5.42	2.93 4.54	2.70 4.04	2.54 3.73	2.43 3.50	2.35 3.33	2.28 3.20	2.22 3.08	2.18 3.00	2.14 2.92	2.10 2.87	2.05 2.77	2.00 2.68	1.94 2.57	1.90 2.49	1.85 2.41	1.80 2.32	1.77 2.27	1.73 2.19	1.71 2.15	1.68 2.10	1.65 2.06	1.64 2.03
30	4.17 7.56	3.32 5.39	2.92 4.51	2.69 4.02	2.53 3.70	2.42 3.47	2.34 3.30	2.27 3.17	2.21 3.06	2.16 2.98	2.12 2.90	2.09 2.84	2.04 2.74	1.99 2.66	1.93 2.55	1.89 2.47	1.84 2.38	1.79 2.29	1.76 2.24	1.72 2.16	1.69 2.13	1.66 2.07	1.64 2.03	1.62 2.01
32	4.15 7.50	3.30 5.34	2.90 4.46	2.67 3.97	2.51 3.66	2.40 3.42	2.32 3.25	2.25 3.12	2.19 3.01	2.14 2.94	2.10 2.86	2.07 2.80	2.02 2.70	1.97 2.62	1.91 2.51	1.86 2.42	1.82 2.34	1.76 2.25	1.74 2.20	1.69 2.12	1.67 2.08	1.64 2.02	1.61 1.98	1.59 1.96
34	4.13 7.44	3.28 5.29	2.88 4.42	2.65 3.93	2.49 3.61	2.38 3.38	2.30 3.21	2.23 3.08	2.17 2.97	2.12 2.89	2.08 2.82	2.05 2.76	2.00 2.66	1.95 2.58	1.89 2.47	1.84 2.38	1.80 2.30	1.74 2.21	1.71 2.15	1.67 2.08	1.64 2.04	1.61 1.98	1.59 1.94	1.57 1.91
36	4.11 7.39	3.26 5.25	2.86 4.38	2.63 3.89	2.48 3.58	2.36 3.35	2.28 3.18	2.21 3.04	2.15 2.94	2.10 2.86	2.06 2.78	2.03 2.72	1.98 2.62	1.93 2.54	1.87 2.43	1.82 2.35	1.78 2.26	1.72 2.17	1.69 2.12	1.65 2.04	1.62 2.00	1.59 1.94	1.56 1.90	1.55 1.87
38	4.10 7.35	3.25 5.21	2.85 4.34	2.62 3.86	2.46 3.54	2.35 3.32	2.26 3.15	2.19 3.02	2.14 2.94	2.09 2.82	2.05 2.75	2.02 2.69	1.96 2.59	1.92 2.51	1.85 2.40	1.80 2.32	1.76 2.22	1.71 2.14	1.67 2.08	1.63 2.00	1.60 1.97	1.57 1.90	1.54 1.86	1.53 1.84

Table Continued on Following Page

TABLE H (Continued)

	Degrees of Freedom: Numerator																							
Degrees of Freedom: Denominator	1	2	3	4	5	6	7	8	9	10	11	12	14	16	20	24	30	40	50	75	100	200	500	∞
40	4.08 / 7.31	3.23 / 5.18	2.84 / 4.31	2.61 / 3.83	2.45 / 3.51	2.34 / 3.29	2.25 / 3.12	2.18 / 2.99	2.12 / 2.88	2.07 / 2.80	2.04 / 2.73	2.00 / 2.66	1.95 / 2.56	1.90 / 2.49	1.84 / 2.37	1.79 / 2.29	1.74 / 2.20	1.69 / 2.11	1.66 / 2.05	1.61 / 1.97	1.59 / 1.94	1.55 / 1.88	1.53 / 1.84	1.51 / 1.81
42	4.07 / 7.27	3.22 / 5.15	2.83 / 4.29	2.59 / 3.80	2.44 / 3.49	2.32 / 3.26	2.24 / 3.10	2.17 / 2.96	2.11 / 2.86	2.06 / 2.77	2.02 / 2.70	1.99 / 2.64	1.94 / 2.54	1.89 / 2.46	1.82 / 2.35	1.78 / 2.26	1.73 / 2.17	1.68 / 2.08	1.64 / 2.02	1.60 / 1.94	1.57 / 1.91	1.54 / 1.85	1.51 / 1.80	1.49 / 1.78
44	4.06 / 7.24	3.21 / 5.12	2.82 / 4.26	2.58 / 3.78	2.43 / 3.46	2.31 / 3.24	2.23 / 3.07	2.16 / 2.94	2.10 / 2.84	2.05 / 2.75	2.01 / 2.68	1.98 / 2.62	1.92 / 2.52	1.88 / 2.44	1.81 / 2.32	1.76 / 2.24	1.72 / 2.15	1.66 / 2.06	1.63 / 2.00	1.58 / 1.92	1.56 / 1.88	1.52 / 1.82	1.50 / 1.78	1.48 / 1.75
46	4.05 / 7.21	3.20 / 5.10	2.81 / 4.24	2.57 / 3.76	2.42 / 3.44	2.30 / 3.22	2.22 / 3.05	2.14 / 2.92	2.09 / 2.82	2.04 / 2.73	2.00 / 2.66	1.97 / 2.60	1.91 / 2.50	1.87 / 2.42	1.80 / 2.30	1.75 / 2.22	1.71 / 2.13	1.65 / 2.04	1.62 / 1.98	1.57 / 1.90	1.54 / 1.86	1.51 / 1.80	1.48 / 1.76	1.46 / 1.72
48	4.04 / 7.19	3.19 / 5.08	2.80 / 4.22	2.56 / 3.74	2.41 / 3.42	2.30 / 3.20	2.21 / 3.04	2.14 / 2.90	2.08 / 2.80	2.03 / 2.71	1.99 / 2.64	1.96 / 2.58	1.90 / 2.48	1.86 / 2.40	1.79 / 2.28	1.74 / 2.20	1.70 / 2.11	1.64 / 2.02	1.61 / 1.96	1.56 / 1.88	1.53 / 1.84	1.50 / 1.78	1.47 / 1.73	1.45 / 1.70
50	4.03 / 7.17	3.18 / 5.06	2.79 / 4.20	2.56 / 3.72	2.40 / 3.41	2.29 / 3.18	2.20 / 3.02	2.13 / 2.88	2.07 / 2.78	2.02 / 2.70	1.98 / 2.62	1.95 / 2.56	1.90 / 2.46	1.85 / 2.39	1.78 / 2.26	1.74 / 2.18	1.69 / 2.10	1.63 / 2.00	1.60 / 1.94	1.55 / 1.86	1.52 / 1.82	1.48 / 1.76	1.46 / 1.71	1.44 / 1.68
55	4.02 / 7.12	3.17 / 5.01	2.78 / 4.16	2.54 / 3.68	2.38 / 3.37	2.27 / 3.15	2.18 / 2.98	2.11 / 2.85	2.05 / 2.75	2.00 / 2.66	1.97 / 2.59	1.93 / 2.53	1.88 / 2.43	1.83 / 2.35	1.76 / 2.23	1.72 / 2.15	1.67 / 2.06	1.61 / 1.96	1.58 / 1.90	1.52 / 1.82	1.50 / 1.78	1.46 / 1.71	1.43 / 1.66	1.41 / 1.64
60	4.00 / 7.08	3.15 / 4.98	2.76 / 4.13	2.52 / 3.65	2.37 / 3.34	2.25 / 3.12	2.17 / 2.95	2.10 / 2.82	2.04 / 2.72	1.99 / 2.63	1.95 / 2.56	1.92 / 2.50	1.86 / 2.40	1.81 / 2.32	1.75 / 2.20	1.70 / 2.12	1.65 / 2.03	1.59 / 1.93	1.56 / 1.87	1.50 / 1.79	1.48 / 1.74	1.44 / 1.68	1.41 / 1.63	1.39 / 1.60
65	3.99 / 7.04	3.14 / 4.95	2.75 / 4.10	2.51 / 3.62	2.36 / 3.31	2.24 / 3.09	2.15 / 2.93	2.08 / 2.79	2.02 / 2.70	1.98 / 2.61	1.94 / 2.54	1.90 / 2.47	1.85 / 2.37	1.80 / 2.30	1.73 / 2.18	1.68 / 2.09	1.63 / 2.00	1.57 / 1.90	1.54 / 1.84	1.49 / 1.76	1.46 / 1.71	1.42 / 1.64	1.39 / 1.60	1.37 / 1.56
70	3.98 / 7.01	3.13 / 4.92	2.74 / 4.08	2.50 / 3.60	2.35 / 3.29	2.23 / 3.07	2.14 / 2.91	2.07 / 2.77	2.01 / 2.67	1.97 / 2.59	1.93 / 2.51	1.89 / 2.45	1.84 / 2.35	1.79 / 2.28	1.72 / 2.15	1.67 / 2.07	1.62 / 1.98	1.56 / 1.88	1.53 / 1.82	1.47 / 1.74	1.45 / 1.69	1.40 / 1.62	1.37 / 1.56	1.35 / 1.53
80	3.96 / 6.96	3.11 / 4.88	2.72 / 4.04	2.48 / 3.56	2.33 / 3.25	2.21 / 3.04	2.12 / 2.87	2.05 / 2.74	1.99 / 2.64	1.95 / 2.55	1.91 / 2.48	1.88 / 2.41	1.82 / 2.32	1.77 / 2.24	1.70 / 2.11	1.65 / 2.03	1.60 / 1.94	1.54 / 1.84	1.51 / 1.78	1.45 / 1.70	1.42 / 1.65	1.38 / 1.57	1.35 / 1.52	1.32 / 1.49
100	3.94 / 6.90	3.09 / 4.82	2.70 / 3.98	2.46 / 3.51	2.30 / 3.20	2.19 / 2.99	2.10 / 2.82	2.03 / 2.69	1.97 / 2.59	1.92 / 2.51	1.88 / 2.43	1.85 / 2.36	1.79 / 2.26	1.75 / 2.19	1.68 / 2.06	1.63 / 1.98	1.57 / 1.89	1.51 / 1.79	1.48 / 1.73	1.42 / 1.64	1.39 / 1.59	1.34 / 1.51	1.30 / 1.46	1.28 / 1.43
125	3.92 / 6.84	3.07 / 4.78	2.68 / 3.94	2.44 / 3.47	2.29 / 3.17	2.17 / 2.95	2.08 / 2.79	2.01 / 2.65	1.95 / 2.56	1.90 / 2.47	1.86 / 2.40	1.83 / 2.33	1.77 / 2.23	1.72 / 2.15	1.65 / 2.03	1.60 / 1.94	1.55 / 1.85	1.49 / 1.75	1.45 / 1.68	1.39 / 1.59	1.36 / 1.54	1.31 / 1.46	1.27 / 1.40	1.25 / 1.37

TABLE H (*Continued*)

Degrees of Freedom: Numerator

Degrees of Freedom: Denominator	1	2	3	4	5	6	7	8	9	10	11	12	14	16	20	24	30	40	50	75	100	200	500	∞
150	3.91 **6.81**	3.06 **4.75**	2.67 **3.91**	2.43 **3.44**	2.27 **3.14**	2.16 **2.92**	2.07 **2.76**	2.00 **2.62**	1.94 **2.53**	1.89 **2.44**	1.85 **2.37**	1.82 **2.30**	1.76 **2.20**	1.71 **2.12**	1.64 **2.00**	1.59 **1.91**	1.54 **1.83**	1.47 **1.72**	1.44 **1.66**	1.37 **1.56**	1.34 **1.51**	1.29 **1.43**	1.25 **1.37**	1.22 **1.33**
200	3.89 **6.76**	3.04 **4.71**	2.65 **3.88**	2.41 **3.41**	2.26 **3.11**	2.14 **2.90**	2.05 **2.73**	1.98 **2.60**	1.92 **2.50**	1.87 **2.41**	1.83 **2.34**	1.80 **2.28**	1.74 **2.17**	1.69 **2.09**	1.62 **1.97**	1.57 **1.88**	1.52 **1.79**	1.45 **1.69**	1.42 **1.62**	1.35 **1.53**	1.32 **1.48**	1.26 **1.39**	1.22 **1.33**	1.19 **1.28**
400	3.86 **6.70**	3.02 **4.66**	2.62 **3.83**	2.39 **3.36**	2.23 **3.06**	2.12 **2.85**	2.03 **2.69**	1.96 **2.55**	1.90 **2.46**	1.85 **2.37**	1.81 **2.29**	1.78 **2.23**	1.72 **2.12**	1.67 **2.04**	1.60 **1.92**	1.54 **1.84**	1.49 **1.74**	1.42 **1.64**	1.38 **1.57**	1.32 **1.47**	1.28 **1.42**	1.22 **1.32**	1.16 **1.24**	1.13 **1.19**
1000	3.85 **6.66**	3.00 **4.62**	2.61 **3.80**	2.38 **3.34**	2.22 **3.04**	2.10 **2.82**	2.02 **2.66**	1.95 **2.53**	1.89 **2.43**	1.84 **2.34**	1.80 **2.26**	1.76 **2.20**	1.70 **2.09**	1.65 **2.01**	1.58 **1.89**	1.53 **1.81**	1.47 **1.71**	1.41 **1.61**	1.36 **1.54**	1.30 **1.44**	1.26 **1.38**	1.19 **1.28**	1.13 **1.19**	1.08 **1.11**
∞	3.84 **6.64**	2.99 **4.60**	2.60 **3.78**	2.37 **3.32**	2.21 **3.02**	2.09 **2.80**	2.01 **2.64**	1.94 **2.51**	1.88 **2.41**	1.83 **2.32**	1.79 **2.24**	1.75 **2.18**	1.69 **2.07**	1.64 **1.99**	1.57 **1.87**	1.52 **1.79**	1.46 **1.69**	1.40 **1.59**	1.35 **1.52**	1.28 **1.41**	1.24 **1.36**	1.17 **1.25**	1.11 **1.15**	1.00 **1.00**

TABLE I Random Digits.[a]

11339	19233	50911	14209	39594	68368	97742	36252	27671	55091
96971	19968	31709	40197	16313	80020	01588	21654	50328	04577
07779	47712	33846	84716	49870	59670	46946	71716	50623	38681
71675	95993	08790	13241	71260	16558	83316	68482	10294	45137
32804	72742	16237	72550	10570	31470	92612	94917	48822	79794
14835	56263	53062	71543	67632	30337	28739	17582	40924	32434
15544	14327	07580	48813	30161	10746	96470	60680	63507	14435
92230	41243	90765	08867	08038	05038	10908	00633	21740	55450
33564	93563	10770	10595	71323	84243	09402	62877	49762	56151
84461	55618	40570	72906	30794	49144	65239	21788	38288	29180
91645	42451	83776	99246	45548	02457	74804	49536	89815	74285
78305	63797	26995	23146	56071	97081	22376	09819	56855	97424
97888	55122	65545	02904	40042	70653	24483	31258	96475	77668
67286	09001	09718	67231	54033	24185	52097	78713	95910	84400
53610	59459	89945	72102	66595	02198	26968	88467	46939	52318
52965	76189	68892	64541	02225	09603	59304	38179	75920	80486
25336	39735	25594	50557	96257	59700	27715	42432	27652	88151
73078	44371	77616	49296	55882	71507	30168	31876	28283	53424
31797	52244	38354	47800	48454	43304	14256	74281	82279	28882
47772	22798	36910	39986	34033	39868	24009	97123	59151	27583
54153	70832	37575	31898	39212	63993	05419	77565	73150	98537
93745	99871	37129	55032	94444	17884	27082	23502	06136	89476
81676	51330	58828	74199	87214	13727	80539	95037	73536	16862
79788	02193	33250	05865	53018	62394	56997	41534	01953	13763
92112	61235	68760	61201	02189	09424	24156	10368	26527	89107
87542	28171	45150	75523	66790	63963	13903	68498	02981	25219
37535	48342	48943	07719	20407	33748	93650	39356	01011	22099
95957	96668	69380	49091	90182	13205	71802	35482	27973	46814
34642	85350	53361	63940	79546	89956	96836	81313	80712	73572
50413	31008	09231	46516	61672	79954	01291	72278	55658	84893
53312	73768	59931	55182	43761	59424	79775	17772	41552	45236
16302	64092	76045	28958	21182	30050	96256	85737	86962	27067
96357	98654	01909	58799	87374	53184	87233	55275	59572	56476
38529	89095	89538	15600	33687	86353	61917	63876	52367	79032
45939	05014	06099	76041	57638	55342	41269	96173	94872	35605
02300	23739	68485	98567	77035	91533	62500	31548	09511	80252
59750	14131	24973	05962	83215	25950	43867	75213	21500	17758
21285	53607	82657	22053	29996	04729	48917	72091	57336	18476
93703	60164	19090	63030	88931	84439	94747	77982	61932	21928
15576	76654	19775	77518	43259	82790	08193	63007	68824	75315
12752	33321	69796	03625	37328	75200	77262	99004	96705	15540
89038	53455	93322	25069	88186	45026	31020	52540	10838	72490
62411	56968	08379	40159	27419	12024	99694	68668	73039	87682
45853	68103	38927	77105	65241	70387	01634	59665	30512	66161
84558	24272	84355	00116	68344	92805	52618	51584	75964	53021
45272	58388	69131	61075	80192	45959	76992	19210	27126	45525
68015	99001	11832	39832	80462	70468	89929	55695	77524	20675
13263	92240	89559	66545	06433	38634	36645	22350	81169	97417
66309	31466	97705	46996	69059	33771	95004	89037	38054	80853
56348	05291	38713	82303	26293	61319	45285	75784	50043	44438

[a]From pp. 99 and 100 of: The Rand Corporation. *A Million Random Digits with 100,000 Normal Deviates*, The Free Press, Glencoe, Ill., 1955, with permission of the Rand Corporation.

TABLE I (*Continued*)

93108	77033	68325	10160	38667	62441	87023	94372	06164	30700
28271	08589	83279	48838	60935	70541	53814	95588	05832	80235
21841	35545	11148	34775	17308	88034	97765	35959	52843	44895
22025	79554	19698	25255	50283	94037	57463	92925	12042	91414
09210	20779	02994	02258	86978	85092	54052	18354	20914	28460
90552	71129	03621	20517	16908	06668	29916	51537	93658	29525
01130	06995	20258	10351	99248	51660	38861	49668	74742	47181
22604	56719	21784	68788	38358	59827	19270	99287	81193	43366
06690	01800	34272	65497	94891	14537	91358	21587	95765	72605
59809	69982	71809	64984	48709	43991	24987	69246	86400	29559
56475	02726	58511	95405	70293	84971	06676	44075	32338	31980
02730	34870	83209	03138	07715	31557	55242	61308	26507	06186
74482	33990	13509	92588	10462	76546	46097	01825	20153	36271
19793	22487	94238	81054	95488	23617	15539	94335	73822	93481
19020	27856	60526	24144	98021	60564	46373	86928	52135	74919
69565	60635	65709	77887	42766	86698	14004	94577	27936	47220
69274	23208	61035	84263	15034	28717	76146	22021	23779	98562
83658	14204	09445	41081	49630	34215	89806	40930	97194	21747
78612	51102	66826	40430	54072	62164	68977	95583	11765	81072
14980	74158	78216	38985	60838	82836	42777	85321	90463	11813
63172	28010	29405	91554	75195	51183	65805	87525	35952	83204
71167	37984	52737	06869	38122	95322	41356	19391	96787	64410
78530	56410	19195	34434	83712	50397	80920	15464	81350	18673
98324	03774	07573	67864	06497	20758	83454	22756	83959	96347
55793	30055	08373	32652	02654	75980	02095	87545	88815	80086
05674	34471	61967	91266	38814	44728	32455	17057	08339	93997
15643	22245	07592	22078	73628	60902	41561	54608	41023	98345
66750	19609	70358	03622	64898	82220	69304	46235	97332	64539
42320	74314	50222	82339	51564	42885	50482	98501	02245	88990
73752	73818	15470	04914	24936	65514	56633	72030	30856	85183
97546	02188	46373	21486	28221	08155	23486	66134	88799	49496
32569	52162	38444	42004	78011	16909	94194	79732	47114	23919
36048	93973	82596	28739	86985	58144	65007	08786	14826	04896
40455	36702	38965	56042	80023	28169	04174	65533	52718	55255
33597	47071	55618	51796	71027	46690	08002	45066	02870	60012
22828	96380	35883	15910	17211	42358	14056	55438	98148	35384
00631	95925	19324	31497	88118	06283	84596	72091	53987	01477
75722	36478	07634	63114	27164	15467	03983	09141	60562	65725
80577	01771	61510	17099	28731	41426	18853	41523	14914	76661
10524	20900	65463	83680	05005	11611	64426	59065	06758	02892
93815	69446	75253	51915	97839	75427	90685	60352	96288	34248
81867	97119	93446	20862	46591	97677	42704	13718	44975	67145
64649	07689	16711	12169	15238	74106	60655	56289	74166	78561
55768	09210	52439	33355	57884	36791	00853	49969	74814	09270
38080	49460	48137	61589	42742	92035	21766	19435	92579	27683
22360	16332	05343	34613	24013	98831	17157	44089	07366	66196
40521	09057	00239	51284	71556	22605	41293	54854	39736	05113
19292	69862	59951	49644	53486	28244	20714	56030	39292	45166
79504	40078	06838	05509	68581	39400	85615	52314	83202	40313
64138	27983	84048	42631	58658	62243	82572	45211	37060	15017

Table 1 (Continued)

Index